Pete
& Tii

MW00718687

Land Use Regulation

A Legal Analysis &
Practical Application
of Land Use Law

SECOND EDITION

Section of Real Property, Probate and Trust Law
American Bar Association

Defending Liberty
Pursuing Justice

Cover design by Jim Colao

The materials contained herein represent the opinions of the authors and editors and should not be construed to be the action of either the American Bar Association or the Section of Real Property, Probate and Trust Law unless adopted pursuant to the bylaws of the Association.

Nothing contained in this book is to be considered as the rendering of legal advice for specific cases, and readers are responsible for obtaining such advice from their own legal counsel. This book and any forms and agreements herein are intended for educational and informational purposes only.

Library of Congress Cataloging-in-Publication Data

Salsich, Peter W.
    Land use regulation / by Peter W. Salsich, Jr., Timothy J. Tryniecki.—2nd ed.
        p. cm.
Includes bibliographical references and index.
    ISBN 1-59031-228-7
    1. Land use—Law and legislation—United States. 2. Zoning law—United States. I. Tryniecki, Timothy J. II. Title.

KF5698.S243 2003
346.7304′5—dc21

                                        2003012798

An earlier edition of this book was published in 1991 by Shepard's/McGraw-Hill, Inc., entitled *Land Use Regulation: Planning, Zoning, Subdivision Regulation and Environmental Control.*

Discounts are available for books ordered in bulk. Special consideration is given to state bars, CLE programs, and other bar-related organizations. Inquire at Book Publishing, ABA Publishing, American Bar Association, 750 North Lake Shore Drive, Chicago, Illinois 60611.

www.ababooks.org

CONTENTS

ABOUT THE AUTHORS

Professor Peter W. Salsich, Jr., is McDonnell Professor of Justice in American Society at Saint Louis University School of Law. He holds a joint appointment in the Department of Public Policy Studies. He is a Fellow of the American College of Real Estate Lawyers, a former editor of the *ABA Journal of Affordable Housing and Community Development Law*, a former chair of the ABA Commission on Homelessness and Poverty, and a former member of the Council of the ABA Section of Real Property, Probate and Trust Law. He is a member of the American Planning Association, Association of American Law Schools, Missouri Bar, and the Bar Association of Metropolitan St. Louis.

Professor Salsich was the first chair of the Missouri Housing Development Commission and chaired the Board of Directors of Legal Services of Eastern Missouri, Inc., and the Ecumenical Housing Production Corporation of St. Louis. He is author of *Missouri Landlord-Tenant Relationship*, and is a co-author of *Property Law, State and Local Government in a Federal System*, and *State and Local Taxation and Finance in a Nutshell*. He is the author of chapters in a casebook on housing law and a treatise on state and local government financing. He has published numerous articles and has been an active participant in CLE programs at the local, state, and national levels. He teaches property, land use, real estate transactions, state and local government, and housing.

Professor Salsich received his J.D. from Saint Louis University and his A.B. from Notre Dame.

Timothy J. Tryniecki is chair of the Real Estate Practice Group of Armstrong Teasdale LLP in St. Louis, Missouri, and practices in the development, acquisition, disposition and leasing of real estate and zoning and condemnation law. He is a Fellow of the American College of Real Estate Lawyers. He has spoken at real estate seminars and is a member of the Real Estate and Local Government sections of the American Bar Association and the Property Law sections of the Missouri Bar. He co-authored the first edition of this work and the annual supplements to *Land Use Regulation*, formerly published by Shepard's/McGraw-Hill, Inc. He recently authored "Cellular Tower Siting Jurisprudence Under the Telecommunications Act of 1996—The First Five Years," published in the Summer 2002 Edition of the *Real Property, Probate and Trust*

Journal. He is author of the 2003 annual supplement to *Missouri Real Estate Practice*, Second Edition, published by West Group and working on the third edition of that treatise. He is listed in Best Lawyers in America.

Mr. Tryniecki graduated with honors from the University of Missouri in 1978 and received his law degree *cum laude* from Saint Louis University School of Law in 1981.

PREFACE

The vigorous pace of development in the law of land use regulation has continued unabated since the publication of the first edition of this work in 1998. The U.S. Supreme Court has occupied much of the headlines, continuing to make constitutional law with respect to the perhaps intractable problem of regulatory takings and the proper balance between land use regulation and property rights. We have noted an even greater level of activity, however, in other areas of land use law, notably at the state level. We estimate conservatively in excess of 1,100 reported cases deciding significant land use issues at the state court level, continuing at a rate of nearly 300 cases per year. State legislatures, in virtually all parts of the country, also continue to make new land use legal policy. According to the *Land Use Law and Zoning Digest*, approximately 100 state statutes pertaining to land use issues were enacted in the year 2001.

The activity has been greatest in the areas of regulatory takings, adult uses, nonconforming uses, telecommunications tower siting, vested rights, urban sprawl and growth management, environmental regulation, agricultural uses, intergovernmental conflicts, religious uses, and federal land use law and civil rights remedies.

We have not attempted to analyze the legal and societal underpinnings of the continued volume and pace of new cases and statutes, but we attempt, occasionally, to acknowledge certain obvious phenomena, such as a growing disposition of municipalities to act as private business organizations, with economic interests, in the areas of redevelopment and intergovernmental conflicts, the continued growth and sophistication of nonprofit and lay groups with respect to land use and environmental issues, urban sprawl, and the problems of the central cities and mature suburbs in reclaiming blighted properties and encouraging economic activity.

The second edition, like the first, strives to provide a general outline for the practicing attorney and municipal official, albeit of a complex and dynamic area of the law, but with all deference to our counterparts in the legal profession who have continued to provide more comprehensive treatises on the subject. We set out again to inform the text with academic and practical experience, in roughly equal parts, which we hope will be of some benefit to both practicing attorneys, as a resource, and nonlawyer municipal officials and students, as a handbook of sorts.

If we have been able to educate the bar and the public in some small way to further inform the vital debate about land use, we are gratified. As always, the opinions and statements provided in this work are our own, and we accept sole responsibility for the content, but invite any comment or insight the reader may have.

Peter W. Salsich, Jr.
Timothy J. Tryniecki

ACKNOWLEDGMENTS

Tim Tryniecki would like to acknowledge the patience and indulgence of his wife, Lisa, and their four children in the pursuit of this project.

The work would also not have been possible without the invaluable help of his assistant, Susan Swierkos, and his partners and associates at Armstrong Teasdale LLP in St. Louis, Missouri, including, particularly his associate, Mary Wynne. He would also like to thank his associates, Roger Walker and Danette Silva, who provided research and comments in the environmental and religious use areas, respectively.

Finally, Mr. Tryniecki is grateful for the continued support and insights of his partners and mentors, Donald U. Beimdiek and Theodore H. Hellmuth, senior real estate lawyers in the St. Louis area, and his co-author and professor, Peter W. Salsich, Jr., who originally invited his participation in this work.

Professor Salsich sends a particular note of appreciation to a friend and mentor, Daniel R. Mandelker, Howard A. Stamper Professor of Law, Washington University, for this encouragement and generous sharing of insights from his vast storehouse of knowledge about the American land use regulatory system.

Valuable research assistance was provided by a number of students at Saint Louis University, including Kevin Etzkorn, Dana Miller, and Brian Nolan.

Special thanks go to Patricia Cervenka and the library staff at Saint Louis University Law Library, along with Dean Jeffrey Lewis of Saint Louis University School of Law.

The manuscript would never have been finished were it not for the efforts of Lori Owens and Kay Graeff at Saint Louis University, who provided crucial secretarial support.

CHAPTER 1

Municipal Power to
Regulate Land Use

Forms of Land Use Regulation

Public regulation of the use and development of land comes in a variety of forms that generally focus on four aspects of land use:

1. the type of use, such as agricultural, commercial, industrial, or residential;
2. the density of use, manifested in concerns over the height, width, bulk, or environmental impact of the physical structures on the land;
3. the aesthetic impact of the use, which may include the design and placement of structures on the land; and
4. the effect of the use of the land on the cultural and social values of the community, illustrated by community conflicts over adult entertainment, housing for service-dependent groups such as low-income families and developmentally disabled persons, and whether the term *family* should be defined in land use regulations to include persons who are not related by blood or marriage.

The basic forms of modern land use regulation were established in the 1920s when the Supreme Court approved the concept of comprehensive zoning. Under comprehensive zoning, land in cities and counties is divided into zones or districts, and uniform regulations for land use, building height and area, as well as building setbacks, are imposed within those districts.[1] Earlier, the Court had approved of land use regulations prohibiting specific uses from particular areas when those uses were deemed to be harmful to people and land in the immediate vicinity.[2]

Zoning as a concept was tied to the notion of comprehensive planning. In theory, communities were supposed to prepare a comprehensive plan that was to be the basis for land use regulation. Zoning was to be the device for implementing that plan. In practice, many communities dispensed with the formal planning process, at least in written form, and went straight to a zoning ordinance. The courts acceded to this approach by concluding that adoption of a formal plan was not a condition precedent to a valid zoning scheme so long as the zoning ordinance itself contained evidence that the community had engaged in a rational process of deliberation about the future of the community.[3]

The comprehensive zoning approach tended to impose a grid pattern on development, partly because of the uniformity-of-treatment-within-districts requirement, which was based on the premise that homogeneity of use was desirable and that different types of land use should be segregated from one another. Comprehensive zoning was prospective in nature and thus was best suited for the regulation of new uses of previously undeveloped land. When comprehensive zoning was imposed on the developed areas of major cities, an extensive nonconforming use component had to be added in response to the reality of heterogeneous, market-focused development that already was in place in the cities.[4]

In the 1950s, a new generation of regulatory forms, popularized by the term *wait-and-see regulations,* took shape.[5] Flexibility was the goal. From the basic planned unit development (PUD) concept, in which the unit of regulation was shifted from an individual lot under traditional zoning to a relatively large parcel of land, evolved such devices as special district zoning, floating zones, overlay zones, floor area ratio, density transfer, and finally transfer of development rights (TDR). These new forms of zoning discarded the restrictive and passive approach of traditional zoning in favor of an active approach that used zoning "as an incentive to further growth and development of the community rather than as a restraint."[6]

A parallel development in land use regulation was the growth of subdivision regulations. These regulations began as devices for easing the process of subdividing land for development and grew through stages into a system for ensuring that public facilities such as streets, roads, sewers, and parks would be in place for the growth that was occurring. In some cases the regulations placed the costs of those public facilities on the persons responsible for the new development.[7]

The 1980s brought still another refinement to the basic land use scheme with the perfection of the exaction as a form of land use regulation. Exactions come essentially in two forms: required dedications of land or property interests in land and required payment of money through impact fees, in lieu fees, linkage fees, and the like. The purpose of exactions is to impose some or all of the public costs associated with a particular use of land on the persons who are putting the land to use.[8] Local governments also regulate land use through the authority granted by state urban redevelopment laws. Land use regulation pursuant to these statutes is not limited to the use of zoning authority.[9]

From the late 1980s through the 1990s, the power to use the exaction as a form of regulation was curtailed somewhat by judicial decisions restricting the situations in which an exaction may be considered a fair exercise of the police power. The Supreme Court has established essential nexus and "rough proportionality" standards that require municipalities to show by "individualized determinations" that the impact on the public of a proposed use and the impact of an exaction on the landowner proposing the use are related.[10]

In 1995, the American Planning Association embarked on a major effort, the Growing Smart[sm] project, to persuade states and local governments to modernize their land use planning and development laws. Major themes of Growing Smart[sm] include linking development regulations more effectively to formal planning, encouraging more cooperative approaches through regional and neighborhood collaborative planning, and responding to the siting difficulties encountered by *locally undesired land uses* (LULUs) such as adult businesses, group homes, landfills, and multifamily housing. The effort culminated in the *Growing Smart Legislative Guidebook*, a two-volume set of model planning and zoning statutes.[11] In advocating reform of land use planning and regulation statutes, the authors of the *Guidebook* identified four main reasons why, in their view, the 1920s legislation that formed the basis of state and local enabling legislation was no longer effective: "(1) the growth of a more significant intergovernmental dimension for planning, . . . (2) a marked shift in society's view of land, . . . (3) a more active citizenry, . . . (4) a more challenging legal environment."[12] Specific Growing Smart[sm] legislative recommendations will be discussed in the appropriate chapters of this book.

The Police Power

The authority to regulate the use and development of land is derived from the police power of the state.[13] The *police power* is the term given to the general governmental power to protect the health, safety, morals, and general welfare of the citizenry. Perhaps the most articulate description of the police-power concept is contained in the opinion of Justice Douglas upholding an urban renewal plan for the District of Columbia:

> We deal, in other words, with what traditionally has been known as the police power. An attempt to define its reach or trace its outer limits is fruitless, for each case must turn on its own facts. The definition is essentially the product of legislative determinations addressed to the purposes of government, purposes neither abstractly nor historically capable of complete definition. . . . Public safety, public health, morality, peace and quiet, law and order—these are some of the more conspicuous examples of the traditional application of the police power to municipal affairs. Yet they merely illustrate the scope of the power and do not delimit it. . . .
>
> The concept of the public welfare is broad and inclusive. The values it represents are spiritual as well as physical, aesthetic as well as monetary. It is within the power of the legislature to determine that the community should be beautiful as well as healthy, spacious as well as clean, well-balanced as well as carefully patrolled.[14]

While the power to protect the citizenry is extremely broad, specific provisions of the Fifth and Fourteenth Amendments to the Constitution—prohibiting the taking of private property for public use without just compensation,[15] proscribing the deprivation of life, liberty, or property without due process,[16] and guaranteeing all persons the equal protection of the laws—[17] place important limits on governmental use of the police power. The Supreme Court in 1894 provided a classic statement on the limitations of the police power:

> [I]t must appear, first, that the interests of the public . . . require [governmental] interference; and, second, that the means are reasonably necessary for the accomplishment of the purpose, and not unduly oppressive upon individuals.[18]

Land use regulation then, as an exercise of the police power, may be imposed only (1) for valid public purposes, (2) through means reasonably tailored to those purposes, and (3) in a manner that does not impose excessive costs on individuals. Courts traditionally have deferred to the legislature on the reasonableness of a particular form of land use regulation, refusing to second-guess the legislature if the question is "fairly debatable."[19]

The Supreme Court set the tone for a deferential approach in 1926 in *Village of Euclid v. Ambler Realty Co.*:

> The ordinance, now under review, and all similar laws and regulations, must find their justification in some aspect of the police power, asserted for the public welfare. The line which in this field separates the legitimate from the illegitimate assumption of power is not capable of precise delimitation. It varies with circumstances and conditions. A regulatory zoning ordinance, which would be clearly valid as applied to the great cities, might be clearly invalid as applied to rural communities. In solving doubts, the maxim "sic utere tuo ut alienum non laedas," which lies at the foundation of so much of the common law of nuisances, ordinarily will furnish a fairly helpful clue. . . . A nuisance may be merely a right thing in the wrong place, like a pig in the parlor instead of the barnyard. If the validity of the legislative classification for zoning purposes be fairly debatable, the legislative judgement must be allowed to control.[20]

A question is said to be fairly debatable when "its determination involved testimony from which a reasonable [person] could come to different conclusions." A decision is fairly debatable if it is "supported by substantial evidence on the record taken as a whole."[21]

The Supreme Court's willingness to set aside a zoning ordinance as it was applied to a particular tract of land in *Nectow v. City of Cambridge*,[22] only two years after *Euclid* was decided, suggested that the Court was prepared to supervise the application of local land use regulations. For the next 46 years, however, the Court refused to review land use regulatory decisions except for the 1962 case of *Goldblatt v. Town of Hempstead,* in which it sustained an ordinance prohibiting excavations for sand and gravel below the water table.[23] The ordinance had been enacted under general police powers rather than zoning powers.

In 1974, the Supreme Court returned to local land use regulation controversies in *Belle Terre v. Boraas.*[24] Over a strong dissent that presaged one of the continuing controversies in local land use decisions, the Court upheld a definition of "family" that effectively prevented a landowner from renting a single-family house to six unrelated college students. Focusing on the property rights aspect of the case, the Court held that the village's regulation was a reasonable exercise of its police power. Justice Marshall, in dissent, saw the regulation as an example of exclusionary zoning that unconstitutionally deprived college students of their personal freedom to associate with whom they chose.[25]

Four years later, in *Penn Central Transportation Co. v. New York City*,[26] the Court upheld New York City's landmarks preservation ordinance against a challenge that it amounted to an unconstitutional taking of property. In doing so, the Court articulated a three-factor test for making ad hoc fact-specific decisions regarding regulatory takings challenges. Courts were directed to consider (1) the character of the government action being challenged, (2) the economic impact of the challenged action on the landowner, in particular, and (3) "the extent to which the regulation has interfered with distinct investment-backed expectations."[27]

In the years following *Penn Central*, the Supreme Court has considered local land use issues on a regular basis, but has struggled to articulate clear rules for determining when land use regulations become takings. The Court established an alternative two-part test under which public land use regulations must (1) substantially advance legitimate state interests, and (2) not deny economically viable use of land.[28] It also concluded that compensation is the appropriate remedy when a regulation affects a taking,[29] and held that regulations imposing stricter standards on uses geared to particular classes of people, such as the developmentally disabled, may not be based on irrational fear of such people.[30] Landowners seeking to challenge in federal court the application of land use regulations to their property must meet a strict ripeness test by establishing that they have (1) obtained a final decision from local authorities, and (2) exhausted their remedies under state law.[31] The Court also has held that compensation must be paid when regulations deprive landowners of the power to exclude or deny them all economically viable use of their property.[32] Regulations requiring landowners to contribute property interests to the public as conditions for development approval must bear an essential nexus to the desired planning goal that is in "rough proportionality" to the expected impact of the proposed use.[33] Landowners may challenge land use restrictions even though the restrictions were in effect when they acquired their property,[34] but moratoria on land development are not subject to a per se takings test. Instead they must be analyzed under the *Penn Central* three-factor test.[35] These cases are discussed in chapter 3, *infra*.

Delegation by the State

The police power belongs to state governments, but all states have delegated the power to impose land use regulations to cities and counties.[36] Hawaii, though, has retained zoning power over most of its land.[37] This delegation has been accomplished in two ways: (1) general delegation of police power through constitutional or legislative authority to enact home rule charters;[38]

and (2) broad enabling statutes authorizing zoning, subdivision regulations, and other forms of land use control.[39] The Standard State Zoning Enabling Act, first published in mimeographed form in 1922, adopted the concept of local control over land use regulation.[40] Most first-generation state zoning statutes were based on this act, although building zone laws had been in existence in the United States since the turn of the 20th century, and comprehensive zoning had begun in New York City in 1916.[41] One year before the Supreme Court's approval of comprehensive zoning in *Village of Euclid v. Ambler Realty Co.*,[42] records maintained by the U.S. Department of Commerce indicated that 35 states and the District of Columbia authorized zoning, and 221 municipalities containing approximately 40 percent of the urban population had adopted the zoning technique.[43]

The stamp of approval given to comprehensive zoning by the Supreme Court removed most of the constitutional questions concerning the validity of the comprehensive zoning concept. The Supreme Court failed, however, to articulate a coherent national law regarding the extent to which the police power can be used to regulate land use through zoning. As a result, the state courts were thrust into the role of overseers of a complex, inefficient, and highly emotional legislative-administrative system that can trap the inexperienced and frustrate the experienced person.[44]

For the most part, courts have not questioned the propensity of local governments to zone in response to their perception of problems in their communities, even though zoning decisions may show little or no regard for the effects of those decisions on people and land outside their boundaries. Social issues, however, such as the lack of affordable housing in reasonable proximity to jobs, increasingly have caused state courts to remind local governments that the delegated land use regulatory power is a state power that must be exercised in such a way as to foster the general welfare of the citizens of the state, and not just those residing within the local government's environs.[45]

The Supreme Court's renewed interest in reviewing zoning or land use legislation has resolved several issues, such as payment of compensation for regulatory takings,[46] and compensatory per se takings resulting from governmentally sanctioned permanent physical occupations[47] and from regulations that deny landowners all economically viable use of their land.[48] The Court's continued reliance on ad hoc fact-based application of analytical factors, however, has prompted state and federal lawmakers to propose, and in some cases to enact, legislation that defines the point at which a particular exercise of the police power goes too far.[49] Prompted in part by the takings controversy, a group of land use experts has drafted new model laws to assist states and municipalities seeking to update outmoded statutes.[50]

Unlawful delegation of the power to zone may invalidate a zoning ordinance enacted pursuant to such delegation. In *County of Fairfax v. Fleet Industrial Park Limited Partnership*, the Virginia court struck down a zoning ordinance on the grounds that the state statute authorizing creation of a highway transportation improvement district unlawfully required unanimous consent of affected landowners before the enactment of a zoning change within the district.[51] State zoning laws commonly require a higher level of legislative approval in the municipality to enact a zoning ordinance in the event of a certain level of protests by adjacent landowners.[52] Under the nondelegation analysis of *Fairfax*, such statutes could be argued to impermissibly grant private landowners excessive control over zoning legislation, although *Fairfax* is distinguishable in that the statute created a veritable veto/consent power in the private landowners.

A corollary to the delegation issue is the question of local authority to adopt legislation by initiative and referendum. For example, in *La Ray Realty v. Town Counsel of Cumberland*,[53] the Rhode Island court struck down a local zoning ordinance adopted by initiative and referendum, where the process did not include a public hearing as required by state enabling legislation,[54] essentially holding that the municipal referendum authority was superseded by the state notice and hearing requirements. Thus, while the police power to zone and regulate subdivision of land may be delegated by the state, such delegation is not absolute and must be exercised in accordance with the statutory conditions on the delegation.

Challenges to Local Land Use Decisions

Challenges to a particular land use regulation as an invalid exercise of the police power generally are brought in one of two ways: (1) a direct challenge to the ordinance in its entirety on the grounds that "the existence and maintenance of the ordinance, in effect, constitutes a present invasion of . . . property rights and a threat to continue it," in violation of the Fifth and Fourteenth Amendments of the U.S. Constitution;[55] or (2) a challenge that the ordinance as applied in a particular manner to a particular tract of land is an arbitrary exercise of the police power because it does not bear a substantial relation to the public health, safety, morals, or general welfare, or it operates to confiscate private property.[56]

Because most state constitutions contain similar provisions regarding due process, equal protection, and taking of property, challenges may be brought either under the federal Constitution or applicable state constitutions. An alternative method of obtaining federal jurisdiction has been to allege that the land use regulation in question amounts to a deprivation of property in violation of the federal civil rights statutes.[57]

Landowners understandably may be concerned about the cost and delays associated with an "as-applied" challenge to a land use regulation. Appropriate groundwork must be laid by applying for the requisite planning permission or permit, having the application rejected, and then appealing the rejection through the applicable administrative machinery. The process may take months or even years and can produce an almost irresistible temptation to mount a facial challenge to the regulation instead. The Supreme Court's extreme reluctance to reach the merits of a dispute before the case is ripe for decision,[58] however, coupled with the tradition of judicial deference to legislative determination of the reasons for and the means to accomplish land use regulation, suggest that counsel should weigh very carefully the costs associated with the "as-applied" challenge against the significant probability that facial challenges to land use regulations will fail.[59]

Presumption of Legislative Validity

Because the states have chosen to delegate the police power to engage in land use regulation to local governments through enabling legislation,[60] the courts have treated the decision to engage in land use regulation, and for the most part the decisions implementing specific land use regulatory techniques, as legislative in character.[61] For that reason, courts generally have exercised restraint in reviewing land use regulatory decisions by applying the presumption-of-legislative-validity principle.[62]

When the presumption of legislative validity is coupled with the courts' recognition that "(t)he line which in this field separates the legitimate from the illegitimate assumption of power is not capable of precise delimitation,"[63] the result is the well-known *fairly debatable* rule.[64]

The judicial deference that flows from these concepts has been reaffirmed on numerous occasions by the Supreme Court, with the strongest statements coming at approximately 30-year intervals:

> Subject to specific constitutional limitations, when the legislature has spoken, the public interest has been declared in terms well-nigh conclusive. . . .

> The role of the judiciary in determining whether . . . [the police] power is being exercised for a public purpose is an extremely narrow one.[65]

In 1984, citing the 1954 *Berman v. Parker* opinion quoted above, Justice O'Connor concluded that

> the [constitutional requirement] is satisfied if the . . . [state] Legislature rationally could have believed that the [Act] would promote its objective. . . .

> Judicial deference is required because, in our system of government, legislatures are better able to assess what public purposes should be advanced by an exercise of the taking power.[66]

Some state courts do not apply the presumption of legislative validity to local land use regulatory decisions that appear to be legislative in character because they are made by the local legislative body, but that are quasi-judicial or administrative in nature because they either resolve a conflict over proper use of a particular tract of land or implement a land use regulatory policy by, for example, granting or refusing to grant a special-use permit.[67]

Proper Governmental Interest

One of the fundamental limitations on public regulation of land use is that the regulation must foster a proper governmental interest, or public purpose. The starting point for determining whether a land use regulation serves a proper public purpose is the legislation itself. As noted previously, courts in general, and the Supreme Court in particular, have been extremely reluctant to second-guess the legislature on this point. The Supreme Court's attitude may be summed up in the following statement:

> The public use clause is thus "coterminous with the scope of a sovereign's police powers." . . . Courts will not substitute their judgment for the legislature's judgment as to what constitutes a public use "unless the use be palpably without reasonable foundation."[68]

Since at least the 1880s, the Supreme Court has considered land use regulation cases and their relationship to the police power.[69] During that time, land use regulation has moved back and forth on a continuum from an emphasis on preventing harm[70] to a desire to confer a benefit on the public.[71] Courts generally have accepted that movement, at least as long as the regulation in question is rationally related to legitimate state interests.[72]

The fact that the judiciary is willing to defer generally to legislative determinations of public purpose does not mean that the courts will serve solely as a rubber stamp for any legislative pronouncement on the matter. Land use regulations that serve essentially private interests will not be sustained,[73] nor will those that seek to avoid some municipal obligation.

For example, while courts have had little difficulty in concluding that the common legislative goal of discouraging "premature and unnecessary conversion of open-space land to urban uses" is a legitimate public purpose,[74] courts have repeatedly struck down zoning regulations enacted "for the sole purpose of depressing the value of property that the municipality seeks to acquire through condemnation."[75] The New Jersey Supreme Court applied an objective test involving a consideration of the terms of an ordinance, its operation and effect, and the context in which it was enacted to conclude that the purpose of a downzoning ordinance was invalid while at the same time declining to second-guess the motives of the persons who enacted it.[76]

Reasonable Means

In addition to serving a proper governmental interest, a land use regulation must have a reasonable connection to the particular governmental interest being advanced.[77] The requirement that a municipality choose a reasonable means for accomplishing its regulatory purpose has been stated in a number of ways: the regulation must bear a rational relation to the health and safety of the community,[78] it must be reasonably necessary to the effectuation of a substantial public purpose,[79] the means of regulation must not be irrational,[80] the regulation must substantially advance legitimate state interests,[81] and it must be in rough proportionality to the impact of the regulated use on the public.[82]

As with the proper governmental-interest standard, the traditional judicial attitude toward the reasonable-means requirement has been one of great deference to legislative pronouncements on the subject. The strongest expression of judicial deference with respect to the means chosen to accomplish land use regulation is found in the words of Justice Douglas in *Berman v. Parker*:

> Once the object is within the authority of Congress, the means by which it will be attained is also for Congress to determine.
>
> . . .
>
> Once the question of the public purpose has been decided, the amount and character of land to be taken for the project and the need for a particular tract to complete the integrated plan rests in the discretion of the legislative branch.[83]

The traditional attitude of judicial deference stems from a desire not to second-guess the wisdom of a particular legislative program or technique.[84] If, however, a regulation is applied to a parcel of land, such as a small tract on the boundary between zoning districts, in such a way as to deny the owner reasonable use of that tract, courts have been willing to evaluate the purpose of the regulation and the means chosen and strike the regulation (means) if it is not persuaded that the regulation will affirmatively promote the purpose.[85]

The Court has moved away from its traditional deference for certain types of land use regulations. In *City of Cleburne v. Cleburne Living Center,* the Court struck down a regulation that required the owners of group homes for the developmentally disabled to obtain special permits to operate in multifamily districts, even though other types of institutions and multifamily housing were not required to obtain the special permits.[86] After declining to impose a higher standard of judicial scrutiny than the rational basis standard because the mentally retarded did not constitute a class requiring special protection, the Court nevertheless examined closely the means chosen (special-permit requirement) to effectuate land use regulation of group homes and concluded that it was not rationally related to a permissible public purpose, but instead "appears . . . to rest on an irrational prejudice against the mentally retarded."[87]

In *Nollan v. California Coastal Commission,* the Court invalidated a requirement of the California Coastal Commission that landowners dedicate an easement of lateral access along their beachfront property to preserve a public right of access to the beach guaranteed by the California constitution as a condition to receipt of a permit to demolish and replace a beachfront cottage.[88] In so doing, the Court concluded that the regulation "utterly fails to further the end advanced as the justification (for the regulation)."[89] Justice Scalia, writing for the majority, argued that when regulations are challenged as amounting to takings of property in violation of the Fifth Amendment,[90] the standard is not one of total deference to legislative pronouncements but rather one of scrutinizing whether the means chosen constitute a

> *substantial* advancing of a legitimate State interest. We are inclined to be particularly careful about the adjective where the actual conveyance of property is made a condition to the lifting of a land use restriction, since in that context there is heightened risk that the purpose is avoidance of the compensation requirement, rather than the stated police power objective.[91]

In *Dolan v. City of Tigard*, the Court created another hurdle for municipalities attempting to exact a benefit from the landowner in exchange for allowing a desired use.[92] In *Dolan*, the zoning board required a dedication of 10 percent of the owner's parcel in exchange for the right to expand an existing store and to pave a gravel parking lot. Dolan objected, claiming that the board was essentially "taking" her property without compensation. The Supreme Court agreed with her. Though the Court noted that the required exactions arguably could be said to have an "essential nexus" to the public purpose of preventing overcrowding, the exactions were still unconstitutional because in the Court's view, they were not "roughly proportional" to the impact of the proposed use on the purported public interest.[93] In *City of Monterey v. Del Monte Dunes*, the Court confined the *Dolan* rough-proportionality rule to exactions: a particular type of land use regulation "conditioning approval of development on the dedication of property to public use."[94]

Impact on Individuals

An important element in any analysis of the validity of a land use regulation is an evaluation of the impact of the regulation on individual landowners and other interested parties. Evaluation of the impact of land use regulations on particular landowners is important because of the restrictions imposed by the Fifth and Fourteenth Amendments on the power of government to interfere with the lives of individuals. In the classic words of Justice Holmes,

> a strong public desire to improve the public condition is not enough to warrant achieving the desire by a shorter cut than the constitutional way of paying for the change.[95]

One of the essential underpinnings of the American system of government is that individuals will not be asked to shoulder more than a reasonable share of the cost of public goods. In the context of property law, this means that the impact of land use regulations must not deprive landowners of all reasonable use of their property without payment of compensation.[96] Two questions are raised when the impact of a land use regulation is assessed: What actual economic use can be made of the land? What property rights does the landowner actually have?

When landowners enjoy "an average reciprocity of advantages"[97] as a result of a land use regulation, such as an increase in personal safety or a more healthy environment, the fact that the land use regulation causes a decrease in the market value of the property will not, by itself, have such an impact as to lead to the conclusion that the police power cannot be exercised in the manner proposed or that, if it is to be exercised in such manner, compensation must be paid.[98] The key question is whether, despite a substantial diminution in value, any economically viable use remains, based on the owner's reasonable expectations.[99]

Likewise, if a landowner does not have a property right to act in a certain manner, such as using his or her land in a way that causes harm to his or her neighbors, or to make full use of adjoining navigable waterways, a regulation that prevents such use is not proscribed by the Constitution, even though the impact on the landowner may be so great as to deprive him or her of all use of the property.[100]

When evaluating the impact of land use regulation on individual landowners, courts will also consider the character of the government action. Thus, if the government action constitutes a direct physical invasion or a direct interference with the power to transfer the property interest in question, the courts are likely to conclude that the regulation amounts to a taking of property requiring payment of compensation, even though the effect on the value or use of the property may be slight.[101]

Conversely, when the regulation in question does not amount to a physical occupation nor an interference with the power to transfer property, the determination of whether the regulation permits any reasonable economic use to be made of the land will be based on the impact of the regulation on the entire property interest held by the landowner, rather than on any segment or "strand of the property bundle," even though the impact on a particular segment or strand may be great.[102] Challenges to land use regulations as regulatory takings are not limited to persons who owned affected property when the challenged regulation was enacted, but may also be brought by landowners who acquired the affected property after the regulations were adopted.[103]

The Land Use Triangle[104]

Although land use litigation is often framed as a contest between a landowner[105] and a land use regulator, scholars and practitioners have recognized a third party in most land use conflicts.[106] An owner's proposed use of a particular tract often has an impact on two different groups of people. Adjacent landowners and residents experience the physical and aesthetic impacts of the size, shape, and density of the specific land use. A larger group of people, including residents and nonresidents of the governmental entity in which the land is located, may also experience a direct or indirect financial impact in the form of increased or decreased taxes. The degree of the impact on taxes depends on whether the particular land development increases the need for public services without a corresponding increase in the tax base, or whether the project increases the tax base without a corresponding increase in the demand for public services.[107] It is also possible for this larger group to experience variations in choice of housing or employment, depending on the nature of the particular development.[108] These groups will also experience the environmental effects of the development.

These groups and the owner/developer may expect the governmental entity responsible for regulating land use to represent their best interests when making land use regulatory decisions. When subgroups emerge either to support or oppose a land development project, the land use regulator may find itself caught in the middle of a struggle between competing values. The resulting relationship resembles a triangle with the owner/developer on one side, the neighbors on another, and the community-at-large on the third.[109]

All three groups are locked into this relationship because of the external effects of a land development project, which varies with the nature and size of the development.[110]

As with other relationships in which competing and common interests exist, owner/developers, neighbors, and the community-at-large need to support one another for land use relationships to succeed. Although land does not depreciate in the sense that a building does, it is a finite resource that can be wasted by unnecessary or harmful development. When poorly executed development plans waste land, it may be lost for the current generation because of the enormous cost and difficulty of reclaiming such land. Although landowners and developers make the decisions that produce land waste, they are also members of the community-at-large. As such, they too will benefit from land use regulations that effectively prevent land waste, and thus the community should urge developers to support such regulations.[111]

Likewise, land use regulators need property users and developers. With the exception of land set aside in public parks and wilderness areas, legislators generally aim their regulations at balancing desirable and undesirable uses of privately owned land to benefit society. If regulations are so onerous that they discourage even desirable development, they do not benefit the community. Thus the reaction of developers to land regulation provides important feedback to legislators concerning the utility of their regulations.

The availability of compensation as a remedy in taking cases is a significant addition to land use law. The compensation remedy supports those traditional arguments that accepted no difference in principle between "taking by dispossession and taking by excessive regulation."[112] In addition, compensation can serve as a necessary check on government and as a means of retaining (or perhaps restoring) the confidence of the people in their governments.[113] Finally, compensation can be viewed as the price for public willingness to accept the "innovative," "flexible," and "comprehensive" land use regulations that today's legislators believe are necessary.[114]

The American system of property law, with its emphasis on private ownership of land, has two basic goals: to maximize and protect individual freedoms and to effectively utilize land. To achieve these goals, the chief actors in the American property law system—landowners, developers, users, neighbors, and regulators—must respect one another's interests. Additionally, state and local governments must provide the community with appropriate vehicles for asserting these competing interests. Ideally, these interests should exist in equilibrium. If one is perceived to have an unfair advantage, the cooperation necessary for the system's functioning breaks down.[115]

Practitioner Perspectives

The Supreme Court has resolved some but not all of the constitutional questions raised by modern land use regulations. It is now clear that compensation is an available remedy when the application of a land use regulation violates the constitutional proscription against taking of private property.[116] No set formula to determine what constitutes a regulatory taking has been established, nor is one likely to be established.[117] In analyzing the effect of a particular regulation, the general rule remains that the entire parcel is the correct denominator, rather than a mere portion of the land, a segment of the property bundle, or a period of time.[118] Each case should be meticulously examined on its own facts, and the setting for the regulatory application should be given proper consideration.[119]

Even though a regulation or restriction may unquestionably provide widespread public benefit, the government may still have to compensate a property owner if the "beneficial" law has too severe an effect on his or her interest.[120] To do so, landowners must establish loss of all economic viability, rather than loss of the best economic use, in order to establish a compensable regulatory taking.[121] The application of a particular type of land use regulation to a specific parcel or area must be based on carefully drawn land use plans that identify specific governmental objectives and indicate that the land use techniques chosen have a rational connection to the objectives of the plans.[122] Although the fairly debatable rule has not been abolished, courts have been instructed to pay closer attention to the "nexus" between ends and means of land use regulations.[123]

Local governments seeking to require dedications of land to public use as conditions for approval of particular development proposals must establish that not only does an "essential nexus" exist between the proposed regulation and the perceived public benefit, but also a "rough proportionality" exists between any infringement on an owner's rights and the public benefit derived from such an infringement.[124]

Recognition of the compensation remedy has raised the stakes for land use disputes. Although the Court has recently taken a renewed interest in protecting the rights of property owners, it has by no means eliminated the greatest obstacles a landowner faces when trying to obtain compensation. Owners must still show a denial of all economically viable use. The Court still demonstrates a willingness to approve most land use regulatory techniques, especially where environmental issues are concerned. The complex nature of modern land use regulation requires practitioners to pay particular attention to the impact of local land use regulations on contract negotiations, relationships with neighboring landowners and residents, and effective resolution of disputes.

An important issue facing practitioners in contract negotiations for developable land is the allocation of risk regarding land use regulation. Absent an acquisition of a "vested right" in a particular zoning classification, landowners assume the risk that land use regulations may change.[125] The seller may not be too concerned about this possibility, but the developer-buyer should and usually will be quite concerned. Obtaining a "final decision" from local officials regarding the regulatory posture that will be assumed with respect to a particular project can be a difficult, frustrating, and time-consuming process, but one that is necessary in any constitutional challenge to an adverse decision.[126] The risk of adverse land use regulations must be considered at the contract negotiations stage because virtually any proposed change in the use of a tract will require regulatory review of some type.

This problem can be handled in several ways:

1. Seller obtains necessary zoning classifications and gives warranties surviving settlement respecting zoning classifications, permitted densities, availability of utilities, moratoria and growth caps, and environmental quality.

2. Buyer's duty to perform under the purchase contract is made conditional upon satisfactory determination of the feasibility of the proposed development, including an analysis of the applicable land use regulations. The length of time for performance of the feasibility study is an important item for negotiation, with the seller seeking an early determination that the sale will be completed and the buyer seeking to maximize the time before he or she is required to make the decision whether to move forward with the purchase. The more complicated the project, the greater the need for adequate time to evaluate project feasibility. The feasibility study period, however, can be a disguise for an inexpensive option that takes property off the market and effectively places it in the developer's inventory until the right time for development.

3. Buyer purchases an option for a price usually approximating the rental value of the land for the term of the option (for example, 90 days, 180 days, one year) and proceeds through the land use regulatory process. The decision of whether to exercise the option is made after the buyer obtains necessary land use classifications and permits or when the buyer is in a position to evaluate his or her prospects of obtaining such permits.

Relationships with neighbors and resolution of disputes are discussed in later chapters.[127]

Notes

1. Village of Euclid v. Ambler Realty Co., 272 U.S. 365 (1926); Gorieb v. Fox, 274 U.S. 603 (1927). Traditional forms of land use regulation are limited to actual uses on the land. Virtual uses, such as Internet transmission of video images from a residence, have been held to be outside the purview of a local zoning regulation. Voyeur Dorm, L.C. v. City of Tampa, 265 F.3d 1232 (11th Cir. 2001).

2. Hadacheck v. Sebastian, 239 U.S. 394 (1915) (prohibition of brickmaking in the city of Los Angeles); Reinman v. Little Rock, 237 U.S. 171 (1915) (prohibition of livery stables in certain areas of the city).

3. *See, e.g.,* Town of Bedford v. Village of Mt. Kisco, 33 N.Y.S.2d 178, 189, 306 N.E.2d 155, 160, 351 N.Y.S.2d 129, 138 (1973); Mott's Realty Corp. v. Town Plan & Zoning Comm'n, 152 Conn. 535, 539, 209 A.2d 179, 181 (1965); Ward v. Montgomery Township, 28 N.J. 529, 147 A.2d 248 (1959). *See generally* Charles M. Haar, *In Accordance with a Comprehensive Plan,* 68 Harv. L. Rev. 1154 (1955).

4. *See, e.g.,* State *ex. rel.* Manhein v. Harrison, 164 La. 564, 114 So. 159 (1927) (upholding Shreveport ordinance containing nonconforming use regulations); City of Aurora v. Burns, 319 Ill. 84, 149 N.E. 784 (1925) (upholding Illinois zoning-enabling act containing nonconforming use regulations); Building Inspector v. Stoklosa, 250 Mass. 52, 145 N.E. 262

(1924); *In re* Opinion of the Justices, 23 Mass. 597, 127 N.E. 525 (1920) (upholding Massachusetts zoning-enabling act and Middlesex ordinance containing nonconforming use regulations). *See generally* chapter 4.

5. *See* chapter 4, *infra*.

6. Asian Ams. for Equality v. Koch, 72 N.Y.2d 121, 129, 527 N.E.2d 265, 269, 531 N.Y.S.2d 782, 786 (1988) (upholding use of special district-incentive zoning in Chinatown area of New York City).

7. *See* chapter 8, *infra*.

8. *Id.*

9. In KLN Assocs. v. Metro Dev. & Hous. Agency, 797 S.W.2d 898, 902 (Tenn. Ct. App. 1990), the Tennessee Court approved the regulation of land use pursuant to a public housing authority's urban renewal plan. This authority was supported by the power the statutes granted to the municipality to redevelop blighted areas and undertake urban renewal projects.

10. Nollan v. California Coastal Comm'n, 483 U.S. 825 (1987); Dolan v. City of Tigard, 512 U.S. 374 (1994); City of Monterey v. Del Monte Dunes, 526 U.S. 687 (1999). *See* chapter 3.

11. AMERICAN PLANNING ASSOCIATION, GROWING SMART℠ LEGISLATIVE GUIDEBOOK: MODEL STATUES FOR PLANNING AND THE MANAGEMENT OF CHANGE (Stuart Meck ed. 2002).

12. *Id.* at xxix.

13. Nollan v. California Coastal Comm'n, 483 U.S. 825, 843 (1987) (Brennan, J., dissenting) (citing Agins v. Tiburon, 447 U.S. 255 (1980) (scenic zoning); Penn Cen. Transp. Co. v. New York City, 438 U.S. 104 (1978) (landmark preservation); Gorieb v. Fox, 274 U.S. 603 (1927) (building line setbacks); Village of Euclid v. Ambler Realty Co., 272 U.S. 365, 387 (1926) (comprehensive zoning).

14. Berman v. Parker, 348 U.S. 26, 32–33 (1954).

15. U.S. CONST. amend. V, ch. 4, made applicable to the states by the due process clause of the Fourteenth Amendment. B&QRR v. Chicago, 166 U.S. 226 (1897).

16. U.S. CONST. amend. V, ch. 3; *id.* amend. XIV, §1.

17. U.S. CONST. amend. XIV, §1.

18. Lawton v. Steele, 152 U.S. 133, 137 (1894) (quoted in Nollan v. California Coastal Comm'n, 483 U.S. 825, 843–44 n.1 (1987)) (Brennan, J., dissenting).

19. *See, e.g.,* Nollan v. California Coastal Comm'n, 483 U.S. 825, 844 n.1 (1987) (Brennan, J., dissenting) (citing Goldblatt v. Town of Hempstead, 369 U.S. 590, 594–95 (1962); Sproles v. Binford, 286 U.S. 374, 388 (1932). *See also* Village of Euclid v. Ambler Reality Co., 272 U.S. 365 (1926); Stone v. City of Wilton, 331 N.W.2d 398, 403 (Iowa 1983); Ranch 57 v. City of Yuma, 152 Ariz. 218, 731 P.2d 113, 119 (Ariz. Ct. App. 1987)).

20. 272 U.S. 365, 387–88 (1926) (citing Radice v. New York, 264 U.S. 292, 294 (1924)).

21. Howard County v. Dorsey, 45 Md. App. 692, 416 A.2d 23, 28 (1980); *rev'd on other grounds,* 292 Howard County v. Dorsey, 292 Md. 351, 438 A.2d 1339 (1982).

22. 277 U.S. 183 (1928).

23. 369 U.S. 590 (1962).

24. 416 U.S. 1 (1974).

25. 416 U.S. at 16 (Marshall, J., dissenting).

26. 438 U.S. 104 (1978).

27. *Penn Central,* 438 U.S. at 124.

28. Agins v. Tiburon, 447 U.S. 255, 260 (1980), *applied in* Keystone Bituminous Coal Ass'n v. DeBenedictis, 480 U.S. 470 (1987).

29. First English Evangelical Lutheran Church v. County of Los Angeles, 482 U.S. 304 (1987).

30. City of Cleburne v. Cleburne Living Ctr., 473 U.S. 432 (1985).

31. MacDonald, Sommer & Frates v. Yolo County, 477 U.S. 340 (1986); Williamson County Reg'l Planning Comm'n v. Hamilton Bank, 473 U.S. 172 (1985).

32. Lucas v. South Carolina Coastal Council, 505 U.S. 1003 (1992) (economically viable use); Loretto v. Manhattan CATV. Corp., 458 U.S. 419 (1982) (power to exclude).

33. City of Monterey v. Del Monte Dunes, 526 U.S. 687 (1999); Dolan v. City of Tigard, 512 U.S. 374 (1994); Nollan v. California Coastal Comm'n, 483 U.S. 825 (1987).

34. Palazzolo v. Rhode Island, 533 U.S. 606, 121 S. Ct. 2448 (2001).

35. Tahoe-Sierra Pres. Council v. Tahoe Reg'l Planning Agency, 535 U.S. 302, 122 S. Ct. 1465 (2002).

36. ALA. CODE §§ 11-52-1 *et seq.* (Michie 1994 & Supp. 2001); ALASKA STAT. ANN. §§ 29.40.010 *et. seq.* (Michie 2000 & Supp. 2001); ARIZ. REV. STAT. §§ 9-461 *et seq.* (West 1996 & Supp. 2001); ARK. STAT. ANN. §§ 14-56-201 *et seq.* (Michie 1998 & Supp. 2001); CAL. GOV'T CODE §§ 65100 *et seq.* (West 1997 & Supp. 2002); COLO. REV. STAT. §§ 24-65.1-101 *et seq.* (2001 & Supp. 2001); CONN. GEN. STAT. ANN. §§ 8-1 *et seq.* (West 2001 & Supp. 2002); DEL. CODE ANN. tit. 22 §§ 301 *et seq.* (Michie 1997 & Supp. 2000); D.C. CODE ANN. §§ 5-401 *et seq.* (Michie 1994 & Supp. 2001); FLA. STAT. ANN. §§ 163.3161 *et seq.* (West 2000 & Supp. 2002); GA. CODE ANN. §§ 36-66-1 *et seq.* (Michie 2000 & Supp. 2002); IDAHO CODE §§ 67-6501 *et seq.* (Michie 2001 & Supp. 2002); 65 ILL. COMP. STAT. §§ 5/11-13-1 *et seq.* (2000 & Supp. 2002); IND. STAT. ANN. §§ 36-7-4-100 *et seq.* (2000 & Supp. 2002); IOWA CODE ANN. §§ 414.1 *et seq.* (West 1999 & Supp. 2002); KAN. STAT. ANN. §§ 12-701 *et seq.* (West 2001); KY. REV. STAT. ANN. §§ 100.111 *et seq.* (Michie 1993 & Supp. 2001); LA. REV. STAT. ANN. §§ 33-4721 *et seq.* (West 1988 & Supp. 2002); ME. REV. STAT. ANN. tit.30-A §§ 4352 *et seq.* (West 1996 & Supp. 2001); MD. ANN. CODE tit. 66B, §§ 1.00 *et seq.* (Michie 1998 & Supp. 2001); MASS. ANN. LAWS ch. 40-A, §§ 1 *et seq.* (Law Co-op 1993 & Supp. 2002); MICH. STAT. ANN. §§ 5.2931 *et seq.* (Callaghan 1990 & Supp. 2002); MINN. STAT. ANN. §§ 462.351 to 462.375 *et. seq.* (West 2001 & Supp. 2002); MISS. CODE ANN. §§ 17-1-1 *et seq.* (1995 & Supp. 2001); MO. ANN. STAT. §§ 89.010 *et seq.* (2001); MONT. CODE ANN. §§ 76-1-101 *et seq.* (2001); NEB. REV. STAT. §§ 19-901 *et seq.* (1997 & Supp. 2000); NEV. REV. STAT. ANN. §§ 278.010 *et seq.* (Michie 2001); N.H. REV. STAT. ANN. §§ 672:1 *et seq.* (Michie 1996 & Supp. 2001); N.J. STAT. ANN. §§ 40:55-D1 *et seq.* (West 1991 & Supp. 2002); N.M. STAT. ANN. §§ 3-21-1 (Michie 1999 & Supp. 2002); N.Y. GEN. MUN. LAW §§ 234 –239A *et seq.* (McKinney 1999 & Supp. 2002); N.C. GEN. STAT. §§ 153A-340 *et seq.* (2001); N.D. CENT. CODE §§ 40-47-01 *et seq.* (1983 & Supp. 2001); OHIO REV. CODE tit.7, §§ 713.01 *et seq.* (1994 & Supp. 2002); OKLA. STAT. ANN. tit. 11, §§ 43-101 *et seq.* (West 1994 & Supp. 2002); OR. REV. STAT. §§ 227.010 *et seq.* (2001); PA. STAT. ANN. tit.53, §§ 10601 *et seq.* (1997 & Supp. 2002); R.I. GEN. LAWS §§ 45-24-27 *et seq.* (1999 & Supp. 2001); S.C. CODE ANN. §§ 5-23-10 *et seq.* (Michie Law Co-op 1977 & Supp. 2001); S.D. CODIFIED LAWS ANN. §§ 11-4-1 *et seq.* (1995 & Supp. 2002); TENN. CODE ANN. §§ 13-7-101 *et seq.* (1999 & Supp. 2001); TEX. LOC. GOV'T CODE ANN. §§ 211.001 *et seq.* (Vernon 1999 & Supp. 2002); UTAH CODE ANN. §§ 10-9-101 *et seq.* (1999 & Supp. 2001); VT. STAT. ANN. tit.24, §§ 4301 *et seq.* (1992 & Supp. 2001); VA. CODE ANN. §§ 15.2-2280 *et seq.* (Michie 1997 & Supp. 2002); WASH. REV. CODE ANN. §§ 36.70.010 *et seq.* (West 2000 & Supp. 2002); W. VA. CODE §§ 8-24-39 *et seq.* (Michie 1998 & Supp. 2001); WIS. STAT. ANN. §§ 62.23 *et seq.* (West 2000 & Supp. 2001); WYO. STAT. §§ 15-1-601 *et seq.* (Michie 2001 & Supp. 2002); 37. HAW. REV. STAT. §§ 205-1 *et seq.* (2001 & Supp. 2001).

38. *See, e.g.,* Brougher v. Bd. of Pub. Works, 205 Cal. 426, 271 P. 487, 493 (1928) (deriving San Francisco zoning power from home rule charter).

39. City of Cleburne v. Cleburne Living Ctr., 473 U.S. 432, 436 (1985) (local ordinance required special use permit for group home).

40. Standard State Zoning Enabling Act (U.S. Dept. of Commerce rev. ed. 1926). *See generally* ALI, A MODEL LAND DEVELOPMENT CODE (Tent. Draft No. 1, xvii 1968).

41. 1914 N.Y. Laws; 1916 N.Y. Laws 497, *cited in* E. Bassett, F. Williams, A. Bettman & R. Whitten, MODEL LAWS FOR PLANNING CITIES, COUNTIES AND STATES 10 n.7 (1935), *upheld in* Lincoln Trust Co. v. Williams Bldg. Corps., 229 N.Y. 313, 128 N.E. 209 (1920). *See also*

Welch v. Swasey, 214 U.S. 91 (1909) (upholding building height restrictions in Boston); *Ex parte* Quong Wo, 161 Cal. 220, 118 P. 714 (1911) (upholding prohibition of public laundries from residential districts in Los Angeles).

42. 272 U.S. 365 (1926).

43. Miller v. Bd. of Pub. Works, 195 Cal. 477, 234 P. 381, 384 (1925) (reviewing history of zoning and upholding a California zoning enabling statute enacted in 1917).

44. Sir Desmond Heap, former president of the Law Society in England, marveled at the difference between the land use regulating systems of the two countries in his Foreword to R. Babcock & C. Siemon, *The Zoning Game Revisited* (1985).

45. *See, e.g.*, Southern Burlington County NAACP v. Township of Mount Laurel, 67 N.J. 151, 336 A.2d 713, 727–28, *appeal dismissed & cert. denied*, 423 U.S. 808 (1975), *discussed in* chapter 9.

46. *See* discussion of *First English*, *Lucas*, and *Dolan* in chapter 3.

47. Loretto v. TelePrompTer Manhattan CATV Corp., 458 U.S. 419 (1982).

48. *See generally Lucas, supra* n. 32, in which the Court held that an ordinance enacted subsequent to the owner's purchase that disallowed the construction of any habitable structures on the property was a taking. *See Dolan, supra* n. 10, where the required dedication of a part of the owner's property in exchange for a permit to allow a new use was also considered a taking by the Court.

49. *See, e.g.*, Bert J. Harris, Jr., *Private Property Rights Protection Act*, FLA. STAT. ANN. § 70.001 (West 1990), *discussed in* Sylvia Lazos Vargas, *Florida's Property Rights Act: A Political Quick Fix Results in a Mixed Bag of Tricks*, 23 FLA. ST. U. L. REV. 315 (1995); and Ellen Avery, Comment, *The Terminology of Florida's New Property Rights Law: Will It Allow Equity to Prevail or Government to Be "Taken" to the Cleaners?* 11 J. LAND USE & ENV'TL L. 181 (1995). *See also* V.A.M.S. § 536.017 (1994) (September 1, 1997, sunset provisions removed, HB 88 (6/12/97)); Texas Private Real Property Rights Preservation Act of 1995, TEX. GOV'T CODE ANN. §§ 2007.001 *et seq.* (Vernon 2000 & Supp. 2002).

50. Growing Smart[sm] Directorate. The Directorate was formed to draft model legislation for states in all areas of land use planning. *See* American Planning Association, GROWING SMART[SM] LEGISLATIVE GUIDEBOOK: MODEL STATUTES FOR PLANNING AND THE MANAGEMENT OF CHANGE, (Stuart Meck ed.) PHASE I (1996), PHASE II (2002).

51. 242 Va. 426, 410 S.E.2d 669 (1991).

52. *See* chapters 4 and 5, *infra*.

53. 603 A.2d 311 (R.I. 1992).

54. *See* chapter 4, *infra*.

55. Village of Euclid v. Ambler Realty Co., 272 U.S. 365, 386 (1926). *See also* Pennell v. City of San Jose, 485 U.S. 1 (1988) (facial challenge to rent control ordinance as a taking rejected as premature); Keystone Bituminous Coal Ass'n v. DeBenedictis, 480 U.S. 470 (1987); First English Evangelical Lutheran Church v. County of Los Angeles, 482 U.S. 304 (1987).

56. Nectow v. City of Cambridge, 277 U.S. 183, 188 (1928). *See also* Nollan v. California Coastal Comm'n, 483 U.S. 825, 852 (1987).

57. 42 U.S.C. § 1983 (2002). *See, e.g.*, Tahoe-Sierra Pres. Council, Inc. v. Tahoe Reg'l Planning Agency, 535 U.S. 302, 122 S. Ct. 1465 (2002).

58. *See, e.g.*, MacDonald, Sommer & Frates v. Yolo County, 477 U.S. 340, 349 (1986); Williamson County Reg'l Planning Comm'n v. Hamilton Bank, 473 U.S. 172, 199–200 (1985) ("the effect [of] the Commission's application of the zoning ordinance . . . on the value of respondent's property . . . cannot be measured until a final decision is made as to how the regulations will be applied to [the developer's] property"); Hodel v. Virginia Surface Mining & Reclamation Ass'n, 452 U.S. 264, 297 (1981) ("[t]here is no indication in the record that

appellees have availed themselves of the opportunities provided by the Act to obtain administrative relief by requesting . . . a variance"); Agins v. City of Tiburon, 447 U.S. 255, 260 (1980) (because the owners "have not submitted a plan for development of their property as the ordinances permit, there is as yet no concrete controversy regarding the application of the specific zoning provisions"). *See also* Palazzolo v. Rhode Island, 533 U.S. 606, 630 (2001) (challenge to wetlands restriction was ripe for review); Suitum v. Tahoe Reg'l Planning Agency, 520 U.S. 725, 738–40 (1997) (denial of permission to construct house on lot was "final" decision even though location of receiving site for permissible transfer of development rights was not yet established).

59. In Tahoe-Sierra Pres. Council, Inc. v. Tahoe Reg'l Planning Agency, 535 U.S. 302, 122 S. Ct. 1465 (2002), the Supreme Court concluded that landowners who brought a facial challenge to a 32-month moratorium had not established that the moratorium was a compensable taking. The Court declined to adopt a per se rule, opting instead for review of moratoria under the three-factor *Penn Central* test.

60. *See, e.g.,* Standard State Zoning Enabling Act, § 1 (U.S. Dept. of Commerce rev. ed. 1926); N.Y. Town Law § 261 (McKinney 1987 & Supp. 2002); Cal. Gov't Code § 65800 (West 1997 & Supp. 2002); Tex. Gov't Code Ann. § 231.011 (Vernon 1999 & Supp. 2002); Pa. Stat. Ann. tit. 16, § 2026 (Purdon 1956 & Supp. 1991) (county zoning).

61. *See* chapter 6, *infra*.

62. *See, e.g.,* Nollan v. California Coastal Comm'n, 483 U.S. 825, 843 n.1 (1987) (Brennan, J., dissenting, citing Goldblatt v. Town of Hempstead, 369 U.S. 590, 594–95 (1962); Sproles v. Binford, 286 U.S. 374, 388 (1932)). *See also* Village of Euclid v. Ambler Realty Co., 272 U.S. 365 (1926); Stone v. City of Wilton, 331 N.W.2d 398, 403 (Iowa 1983); Ranch 57 v. City of Yuma, 152 Ariz. 218, 731 P.2d 113, 119 (Ariz. Ct. App. 1987).

63. Village of Euclid v. Ambler Realty Co., 272 U.S. 365, 387 (1926).

64. *Id.* at 388, citing Radice v. New York, 264 U.S. 292, 294 (1924).

65. Berman v. Parker, 348 U.S. 26, 32 (1954) (Douglas, J.).

66. Hawaii Hous. Auth. v. Midkiff, 467 U.S. 229, 242 (1984) (quoting Western & Southern Life Ins. Co. v. State Bd. of Equalization, 451 U.S. 648, 671–72 (1981)). *See also* Nelson v. City of Selma, 881 F.2d 836, 839 (9th Cir. 1989) (*fairly debatable* rule applied to uphold denial of rezoning after neighborhood opposition surfaced); Cheyenne Airport Bd. v. Rogers, 707 P.2d 717, 727 (Wyo. 1985) (facial challenges to economic and social legislation upheld if "debatable reasonableness" established); Stone v. City of Wilton, 331 N.W.2d 398, 405 (Iowa 1983) (*fairly debatable* rule applied to downzoning); Allright Mo., Inc. v. Civic Plaza Redev. Corp., 538 S.W.2d 320, 324 (Mo.), *cert. denied,* 429 U.S. 941 (1976) (*fairly debatable* rule applied to blighted areas); City of Del Mar v. City of San Diego, 133 Cal. App. 3d 401, 183 Cal. Rptr. 898, 903 (1982) (*fairly debatable* rule applied to legislative findings regarding regional effect of zoning ordinance).

67. The leading case is Fasano v. Bd. of County Comm'rs, 264 Or. 574, 507 P.2d 23 (1973), *overruled in part,* Neuberger v. City of Portland, 288 Or. 585, 607 P.2d 722 (1980) (decision by legislative body to anchor a floating zone permitting mobile home parks was administrative rather than legislative in character). *Contra,* Arnel Dev. Co. v. City of Costa Mesa, 28 Cal. 3d 511, 169 Cal. Rptr. 904, 620 P.2d 565 (1980) (generic classifications applied: zoning decisions, legislative; variances and subdivision map approvals, adjudicative). *See* chapter 6.

68. Hawaii Hous. Auth. v. Midkiff, 467 U.S. 229, 241 (1984) (quoting United States v. Gettysburg Elec. Ry., 160 U.S. 668, 680 (1896)).

69. Mugler v. Kansas, 123 U.S. 623 (1887).

70. "[A]ll property in this country is held under the implied obligation that the owner's use of it shall not be injurious to the community." *Id.* at 665.

71. "[The police power] is ample to lay out zones where family values and the blessings of quiet seclusion and clear air make the area a sanctuary for people." Village of Belle Terre v. Boraas, 416 U.S. 1, 9 (1974).

72. Hawaii Hous. Auth. v. Midkiff, 467 U.S. 229, 241 (1984). *See also* Steinbergh v. City of Cambridge, 413 Mass. 736, 604 N.E.2d 1269 (1992), *cert. denied*, 508 U.S. 909 (1993), where a subsection of a municipal rent-control ordinance, restricting the sale of individual condominium units by an owner owning more than one unit in the same building, was held not a compensable taking by the Supreme Judicial Court of Massachusetts. The plaintiff-owner of multiple condo units in a single building challenged the provision as a temporary regulatory taking because it denied the owner the right to sell individual units unless the Cambridge Rent Control Board granted a removal permit or the tenant had an exemption certificate. The Supreme Judicial Court of Massachusetts upheld the provision because it substantially advanced the Cambridge Rent Control Law by reducing illegal occupation of rent-controlled units by individuals buying such units.

73. *See, e.g.,* Pennsylvania Coal Co. v. Mahon, 260 U.S. 393, 413 (1922) (striking down a statute regulating the mining of coal because, among other reasons, it affected "a single private house" and "ordinary private affairs."). *See also* Keystone Bituminous Coal Ass'n. v. DeBenedictis, 480 U.S. 470, 487 (1987) (distinguishing the "private benefit" statute in *Pennsylvania Coal* from the public purposes of the statute in question). These cases are discussed in chapter 3.

74. *See, e.g.,* Agins v. Tiburon, 447 U.S. 255, 261 (1980).

75. Riggs v. Long Beach Township, 109 N.J. 601, 538 A.2d 808, 813 (1988). *See also* Sanderson v. Willmar, 282 Minn. 1, 162 N.W.2d 494, 497 (1968); Long v. City of Highland Park, 329 Mich. 146, 45 N.W.2d 10, 13 (1950); State v. Gurda, 209 Wis. 63, 243 N.W. 317 (1932); City of Miami v. Silver, 257 So. 2d 563, 569 (Fla. Dist. Ct. App. 1972).

76. Riggs v. Long Beach Township, 109 N.J. 601, 538 A.2d 808, 813–14 (1988) (invalidating downzoning of waterfront property because purpose was to depress fair-market value prior to condemnation).

77. Nollan v. California Coastal Comm'n, 483 U.S. 825, 861 (1987); Agins v. Tiburon, 447 U.S. 255 (1980); Penn Cent. Transp. Co. v. New York City, 438 U.S. 104, 148 (1978); Village of Euclid v. Ambler Realty Co., 272 U.S. 365, 392 (1926).

78. Village of Euclid v. Ambler Realty Co., 272 U.S. 365, 391 (1926).

79. Penn Cent. Transp. Co. v. New York City, 438 U.S. 104, 127 (1978).

80. Hawaii Hous. Auth. v. Midkiff, 467 U.S. 229, 243 (1984).

81. Nollan v. California Coastal Comm'n, 483 U.S. 825, 834 (1987) (quoting Agins v. Tiburon, 447 U.S. 225, 260 (1980)).

82. Dolan v. City of Tigard, 512 U.S. 374, 398 (1994).

83. 348 U.S. 26, 33, 35–36 (1954).

84. Hawaii Hous. Auth. v. Midkiff, 467 U.S. 229, 243 (1984) ("[e]mpirical debates about the wisdom of takings . . . are not to be carried out in the federal courts.").

85. *See, e.g.,* Nectow v. City of Cambridge, 277 U.S. 183, 188 (1928); Arverne Bay Constr. Co. v. Thatcher, 15 N.E.2d 587, 592 (N.Y. 1938).

86. 473 U.S. 432, 450 (1985).

87. *Id.* at 450. For a discussion of the case, *see* Gerald Korngold, *Single Family Use Covenants; For Achieving a Balance Between Traditional Family Life and Individual Autonomy,* 22 U.C. Davis L. Rev. 951, 983 (1989); Martha Minow, *When Difference Has Its Home: Group Homes for the Mentally Retarded, Equal Protection and Legal Treatment of Difference,* 22 Harv. CR-CL L. Rev. 111 (1987); Peter W. Salsich, Jr., *Group Homes, Shelters and Congregate Housing: Deinstitutionalization and the NIMBY Syndrome,* 21 Real Prop., Prob. & Tr. J. 413, 419–21 (1986).

88. 483 U.S. 825, 841–42 (1987).

89. *Id.* at 837.

90. *See* chapter 3, *infra*.

91. Nollan v. California Coastal Comm'n, 483 U.S. 825, 841 n.3 (1987).

92. Dolan v. City of Tigard, 512 U.S. 374 (1994).

93. 512 U.S. at 391–95.

94. 526 U.S. 687, 702 (1999).

95. Pennsylvania Coal Co. v. Mahon, 260 U.S. 393, 416 (1922).

96. First English Evangelical Lutheran Church v. County of Los Angeles, 482 U.S. 304 (1987).

97. Pennsylvania Coal Co. v. Mahon, 260 U.S. 393, 415 (1922).

98. Penn Cent. Transp. Co. v. New York City, 438 U.S. 104, 131 (1978) (citing Village of Euclid v. Ambler Realty Co., 272 U.S. 365 (1926) (75 percent diminution in value caused by zoning law); Hadacheck v. Sebastian, 239 U.S. 394 (1915) (87.5 percent diminution in value)).

99. Lucas v. South Carolina Coastal Council, 505 U.S. 1003, 1019 (1992) (where land was purchased with an interest to build a residence and subsequent regulations disallowed such use, the mere right to other, unprofitable uses did not render the property economically viable under the new regulation). *See* Woodbury Place Partners v. City of Woodbury, 492 N.W.2d 258, 261 (Minn. Ct. App. 1992), *cert. denied*, 508 U.S. 960 (1993). One month after a developer submitted a site proposal adjacent to an interstate highway, the city council imposed a two-year moratorium on consideration of any development proposals for property adjacent to the highway. Despite the developer's challenge, the static period was held not a compensable taking because "Woodbury property's economic viability was delayed, rather than destroyed . . . economic viability exists at the moratorium's end." *See also* Jafay v. Bd. of County Comm'rs, 848 P.2d 892 (Colo.), *reh'g denied*, 1993 Colo. LEXIS 389 (1993) (en banc), where the Colorado Supreme Court held that determination of whether downzoning of property constitutes a taking depends on whether the owner is left with reasonable use of the property. Summary judgment was held inappropriate because reasonable individuals can disagree on what constitutes reasonable use of the property. In *Iowa Coal Mining Co. v. Bd. of Supervisors*, 494 N.W.2d 664 (Iowa 1992), *cert. denied*, 508 U.S. 940 (1993), a county's refusal to rezone a mining company's property to permit its proposed landfill operation was held not a compensable taking even though such refusal effectively prevented the mining company's venture.

100. Keystone Bituminous Coal Ass'n v. DeBenedictis, 480 U.S. 470, 489–90 (1987); Mugler v. Kansas, 123 U.S. 623, 665 (1887) ("All property in this country is held under the implied obligation that the owner's use of it shall not be injurious to the community."); United States v. Cherokee Nation, 480 U.S. 700, 704–08 (1987) (regulation of navigable waters does not constitute a taking of property from riparian owners who use the stream bed because the property rights of such owners are subject to the "dominant servitude" of the government).

101. Hodel v. Irving, 481 U.S. 704, 714–17 (1987) (statute requiring small, unproductive land interests owned by individual American Indians to escheat to the owners' tribe rather than descend by intestacy or devise constituted a taking of property without just compensation); Loretto v. TelePrompTer Manhattan CATV Corp., 458 U.S. 419, 435–38 (1982) (statute requiring landlord to permit wires for cable television to be attached to outside of building constituted a taking because of permanent physical occupation).

102. Tahoe-Sierra Pres. Council v. Tahoe Reg'l Planning Agency, 535 U.S. at 332, 122 S. Ct. 1465, 1484 (2002) ("logically, a fee simple estate cannot be rendered valueless by a temporary prohibition on economic use, because the property will recover value as soon as the

prohibition is lifted"); Keystone Bituminous Coal Ass'n v. DeBenedictis, 480 U.S. 470 (1987); Penn Cent. Transp. Co. v. New York City, 438 U.S. 104, 130–31 (1978).

103. Palazzolo v. Rhode Island, 533 U.S. 606, 628 (2001).

104. An earlier version of this section appeared in Peter W. Salsich, Jr., *Keystone Bituminous Coal, First English and Nollan: A Framework for Accommodation?* 34 J. URB. & CONTEMP. L. 173, 187–90 (1988). Reprinted with permission.

105. The landowner may be the developer or a user of neighboring land who objects to the proposed use by the developer.

106. *See generally* DANIEL R. MANDELKER & ROGER A. CUNNINGHAM, PLANNING AND CONTROL OF LAND DEVELOPMENT 130–34 (1979); Peter W. Salsich, Jr., *Displacement and Urban Reinvestment: A Mount Laurel Perspective*, 53 U. CINN. L. REV. 333, 367 (1984).

107. This phenomenon is referred to as the "tax ratables" of a land development. The ratables are said to be positive if tax revenues generated by the project outweigh the cost of requiring public services and negative if the reverse is true. *See* ADVISORY COMMISSION ON INTERGOVERNMENTAL RELATIONS, FISCAL BALANCE IN THE FEDERAL SYSTEM I, 93–101, 265–66 (Oct. 1967), *reprinted in* DANIEL R. MANDELKER, MANAGING OUR URBAN ENVIRONMENT 44–47 (2d ed. 1971).

108. Perhaps the most dramatic example of this effect is the public controversy over exclusionary zoning. *See, e.g.,* Southern Burlington County NAACP v. Township of Mount Laurel, 92 N.J. 158, 456 A.2d 390 (1983) (upheld municipal requirement that land use regulations provide realistic opportunities for low- and moderate-income housing); Southern Burlington County NAACP v. Township of Mount Laurel, 67 N.J. 151, 336 A.2d 713 (1975), *appeal dismissed and cert. denied*, 423 U.S. 808 (1975) (a municipality may not use land use regulations to make it physically and economically impossible to provide low- and moderate-income housing); Blitz v. Town of New Castle, 94 A.D.2d 92, 463 N.Y.S.2d 832 (App. Div. 1983) (ordinance allowing multifamily housing construction providing a properly balanced and well-ordered community plan adequately considering regional needs presumptively valid); Robert E. Kurzius, Inc. v. Incorporated Village of Upper Bronxville, 51 N.Y.2d 338, 414 N.E.2d 680 (1980), *cert. denied*, 450 U.S. 1042 (1981) (upheld minimum lot requirements of five acres as valid exercise of village's police power, and bearing a substantial relation to the health, safety, and welfare of the community); *Appeal of Elocin, Inc.*, 501 Pa. 348, 461 A.2d 771 (1983) (residential zoning district upheld since municipality had provided for a reasonable share of multifamily dwellings); Surrick v. Zoning Hearing Bd. of Upper Providence Township, 476 Pa. 182, 382 A.2d 105 (1977) (court used fair-share test and determined that residential ordinance requiring one-acre minimum lot sizes unconstitutionally excluded multifamily dwellings); Township of Williston v. Chesterdale Farms, Inc., 462 Pa. 445, 341 A.2d 466 (1975) (ordinance providing for apartment construction in only 80 of 11,589 acres held unconstitutional); *Appeal of Girsh*, 437 Pa. 237, 263 A.2d 395 (1970) (zoning scheme's failure to provide for apartments unconstitutional, even though apartments were not explicitly prohibited by ordinance); National Land & Investment Co. v. Kohn, 419 Pa. 504, 215 A.2d 597 (1965) (four-acre-minimum-lot requirement held unconstitutional as impermissible means to create a greenbelt).

See generally Peter W. Salsich, Jr., *Displacement and Urban Reinvestment: A Mount Laurel Perspective*, 53 U. CINN. L. REV. 333, 361–70 (1984); McDougall, *The Judicial Struggle Against Exclusionary Zoning: The New Jersey Paradigm*, 14 HARV. C.R.-C.L. L. REV. 625 (1979); AFTER MOUNT LAUREL: THE NEW SUBURBAN ZONING (J. Rose & R. Rothman, eds., 1977). Exclusionary zoning is discussed in chapter 9.

109. While the triangle is a useful symbol of typical land use relationships, it is not totally accurate because the owner/developer will also be a member of the community-at-large and may, under certain circumstances, be a member of the neighborhood. For exam-

ple, when a resident-owner of adjacent property develops a vacant lot, he or she covers all three sides of the land use triangle.

110. Although size is an important indication of the likely external effects of land development, it is certainly not the only one. Some of the most emotional land use conflicts in recent years have involved buildings of relatively small size. City of Edmonds v. Oxford House, 514 U.S. 725, 115 S. Ct. 1776 (1995); *See, e.g.,* City of Cleburne v. Cleburne Living Ctr., 473 U.S. 432 (1985) (group homes for the mentally retarded); Village of Belle Terre v. Boraas, 416 U.S. 1 (1984) (unmarried college students sharing single-family residence).

111. Of course, the regulation must be effective in preventing land waste. For an eloquent warning against uncritical reliance on preservation techniques such as transfer of development rights (TDR), *see* David Richards, *Downtown Growth Control Through Development Rights Transfer,* 21 Real Prop., Prob. & Tr. J. 435, 474–83 (1986).

In addition, the argument might be made that landowners would benefit more from an open market in land if they use their land wisely and do not waste it because their better-used land would presumably be scarcer and thus more valuable. Even so, effective land use regulations that prevent land waste will increase the overall value of the total available land in the community and thus benefit the owners of that land.

112. *See, e.g.,* San Diego Gas & Elec. Co. v. City of San Diego, 450 U.S. 621, 638 (Brennan, J., dissenting).

113. *See generally* Robert Freilich, *Solving the "Taking" Equation: Making the Whole Equal Sum of the Parts,* 15 Urb. Law. 447, 479–83 (1983) (approving damages rather than compensation for tortious interferences with property rights).

114. *See, e.g.,* Lucas v. South Carolina Coastal Council, 505 U.S. 1003 (1992); First English Evangelical Lutheran Church of Glendale v. Los Angeles County, 482 U.S. 304, 340 (1987) (Stevens, J., dissenting); Nollan v. California Coastal Comm'n, 483 U.S. 825, 862 (1987) (Brennan, J., dissenting).

115. Morton P. Fisher, Jr., of Baltimore, Maryland, former Chair of the ABA Section of Real Property, Probate and Trust Law, forcefully stated the case for cooperation at a conference of real estate lawyers: "Every lawyer representing a developer has a silent client— the city. You must take time to understand it. A city has been described as an oversized marshmallow. You can knead it, punch it, roll it, shake it; but if you heat it up, it becomes very sticky." Address by Morton P. Fisher, Jr., American College of Real Estate Lawyers, *Land: Its Use, Abuse, Non-Use and Re-Use,* Baltimore, Maryland (Oct. 20, 1986).

116. Lucas v. South Carolina Coastal Council, 505 U.S. 1003 (1992); First English Evangelical Lutheran Church v. County of Los Angeles, 482 U.S. 304 (1987).

117. Tahoe-Sierra Pres. Council, Inc. v. Tahoe Reg'l Planning Agency, 535 U.S. at 327, 339, 122 S. Ct. 1465, 1481, 1489 (2002); Dolan v. City of Tigard, 512 U.S. 374 (1994); Keystone Bituminous Coal Ass'n v. DeBenedictis, 480 U.S. 470, 485 (1987); Penn Central Transp. Co. v. City of New York, 438 U.S. 104, 124 (1978); Pennsylvania Coal Co. v. Mahon, 260 U.S. 393 (1922). *See generally* Peter W. Salsich, Jr., *Life After the Takings Trilogy—A Hierarchy of Property Interests?* 19 Stetson L. Rev. 795 (1990); W. Falik & A. Shimko, *The Takings Nexus: The Supreme Court Forges a New Direction in Land-Use Jurisprudence,* 23 Real Prop., Prob. & Tr. J. 1 (1988); Daniel R.. Mandelker, *Investment-Backed Expectations: Is There a Taking?* 31 Wash. U. J. Urb. & Contemp. L. 3 (1987).

118. Tahoe-Sierra Pres. Council, Inc. v. Tahoe Reg'l Planning Agency, 535 U.S. at 327, 122 S. Ct. 1465, 1481 (2002).

119. Doubt about whether the Court will apply its "property-as-a-whole" standard to all future controversies arises from the narrowness of the decision in *Keystone* (5-4), reiterating that standard and the Court's willingness to depart from that standard when considering regulations that affect the power to exclude or the power to transfer rather than the

right to use property. *See, e.g.,* Presault v. Interstate Commerce Comm'n, 494 U.S 1, 928 (1990) (O'Connor, J., concurring) (power to exclude); Hodel v. Irving, 481 U.S. 704 (1987) (power to transfer); Loretto v. TelePrompTer Manhattan CATV Corp., 458 U.S. 419 (1982) (power to exclude); Kaiser Aetna v. United States, 444 U.S. 164 (1979) (power to exclude). *See generally* Peter W. Salsich, Jr., *Life After the Takings Trilogy—A Hierarchy of Property Interests?* 19 STETSON L. REV. 795 (1990). Justice Steven's strong opinion emphasizing the "parcel-as-a-whole" approach and the 6-3 majority he gained for that position in *Tahoe-Sierra Preservation Council*, 535 U.S. at 327, 122 S. Ct. 1465, 1481 (2002) appears to put the question to rest, at least for the time being.

120. Lucas v. South Carolina Coastal Council, 505 U.S. 1003 (1992); Keystone Bituminous Coal Ass'n v. DeBenedictis, 480 U.S. 470 (1987), First English Evangelical Lutheran Church v. County of Los Angeles, 482 U.S. 304 (1987).

121. *Lucas*, 505 U.S. 1003, 1019.

122. Dolan v. City of Tigard, 512 U.S. 374 (1994); Nollan v. California Coastal Comm'n, 483 U.S. 825 (1987).

123. *Nollan*, 483 U.S. 825, 838–39, 841 (1987).

124. City of Monterey v. Del Monte Dunes at Monterey, Ltd., 526 U.S. 687 (1999); *Dolan*, 512 U.S. 1003 (1994).

125. *See* vested rights discussion in chapter 8.

126. *See* the ripeness discussion in chapter 3.

127. *See* chapters 6, 8, and 10.

CHAPTER 2

Land Use Planning

Planning as an Essential Prerequisite to Exercise of the Police Power

Exercise of the police power is restricted in two basic ways: (1) a proper public purpose must exist, and (2) reasonable means must be employed for accomplishing the public purpose.[1] Identification of a proper public purpose and a reasonable means for accomplishing that purpose requires resorting to a decision-making process in which goals are identified, alternatives are evaluated, and policy decisions are made—in short, creating a planning process.[2]

Land use planning as a process is broader in concept than particular land use regulation techniques such as zoning[3] or subdivision regulation.[4] It is "an exercise of the State's inherent authority, of the very essence of an ordered and civilized society" to guide the physical, social, and economic development of the community in order to fulfill common goals and to protect common values.[5] Land use planning is designed to "provide an orderly method of land use regulation" so that such regulation will "be based on considerations which affect the whole community."[6] When formalized, land use planning results in a document called a "comprehensive plan" or "master plan," which makes "predictions of needs and resources for an estimated future period, . . . proposes goals for orderly growth and development, . . . [and] suggests methods for implementation and achievement of those goals."[7]

The Supreme Court has reemphasized the necessity of planning as a prerequisite to exercise of the police power with its requirement that an "essential nexus" exist between particular land use regulatory techniques and the articulated concerns the regulations are designed to address.[8] Establishing the required connection between ends and means is the essence of planning.

Although communities must engage in a planning process before they exercise the police power to regulate use and development of land, the majority of courts have concluded that the planning process does not have to be formal or separate from the regulatory process unless state law so requires.[9] In jurisdictions that do not have statutory requirements that formal plans be developed, the courts have interpreted the traditional statutory requirement that zoning be "in accordance with a comprehensive plan" as simply requiring that officials exercising the zoning power have a "generalized conception" of how the power shall be used, which may be "exhibited in the (comprehensive) zoning ordinance itself," rather than in a separate written plan.[10]

The New York Court of Appeals, in striking down a zoning amendment reclassifying a small parcel of land in a suburban community from business to residential, construed the statutory requirement that zoning conform to a "comprehensive plan" as follows:

> The thought behind the requirement is that consideration must be given to the needs of the community as a whole. . . . [T]he comprehensive plan is the essence of zoning. Without it, there can be no rational allocation of land use. It is the insurance that the public welfare is being served and that zoning does not become nothing more than just a Gallup poll.
>
> Moreover, the "comprehensive plan" protects the landowner from arbitrary restrictions on the use of his property which can result from the pressures which outraged voters can bring to bear on public officials. . . .
>
> Exactly what constitutes a "comprehensive plan" has never been made clear. . . . No New York case has defined the term "comprehensive plan." Nor have our courts equated the term with any particular document. We have found the "comprehensive plan" by examining all relevant evidence.[11]

In a 1975 survey of judicial attitudes regarding the relationship of planning to zoning, three general categories of decisions were noted:[12]

1. The *unitary view,* adopted by the majority of courts, which holds that zoning is a self-contained activity. A comprehensive zoning ordinance is the equivalent of a comprehensive plan.[13]

2. The *planning factor* doctrine, which reflects "an increasing judicial predisposition to grant legal status" to adopted master plans. If a planning document has been adopted, zoning decisions will be examined "in light of the standards and policies set out in the planning document."[14]

3. The *planning mandate* theory, accepted by a growing minority of jurisdictions, which recognizes the "conceptual invalidity" of the unitary view. In jurisdictions where "separately adopted" plans are required by statute,[15] zoning decisions must be consistent with the adopted plan.[16] In a 1989 survey, one of the authors of the 1975 survey noted that courts continued to be split concerning the weight to be given to comprehensive land use plans, but that an increasing number of states were enacting legislation requiring local plans to be adopted as conditions precedent to exercise of the zoning power and requiring zoning decisions to be consistent with the adopted plans.[17] In another survey in 2000, one of the authors observed that fewer cases were reported from the first category and an increasingly larger number came from the second and third categories.[18]

Planning-Enabling Legislation

The majority of states do not require local governments to engage in formal land use planning, although an increasing number of states are doing so.[19] The traditional approach consists of enabling legislation authorizing but not requiring local land use planning.[20] In these states, cities that do not adopt formal land use plans can satisfy the planning prerequisite to zoning by enacting comprehensive rather than piecemeal zoning ordinances.[21]

Planning-enabling statutes were influenced by the model Standard City Planning Enabling Act promulgated by the U.S. Department of Commerce,[22] although not to the extent that the Standard State Zoning Enabling Act[23] influenced zoning statutes. In addition to municipal planning, the Planning Enabling Act covered the related topics of subdivision control,[24] official maps,[25] and regional planning.[26] The drafters of the Planning Enabling Act stated that "sooner or later every State will need legislation covering all of these four general subjects," but they made the four parts severable because of the recognition that states might not be ready for all four activities at the same time.[27]

The Planning Enabling Act, like its zoning counterpart, was permissive rather than mandatory. For the most part, states that enacted planning-enabling legislation prior to the 1960s accepted the recommendations regarding municipal planning and subdivision regulation but ignored the recommended regional planning component. The official map portion received a mixed reception.[28]

The traditional form of urban planning based on the Planning Enabling Act has been noted for its concentration on location and intensity of particular uses of land and the type, design, and location of physical structures. Planners were said to have four basic objectives: (1) "maximize economic efficiency" by matching needs for and location of physical facilities, (2) "maximize desired relationships" between different activities and structures, (3) "allocate land to desired activities," and (4) provide a "pleasing" urban design.[29]

Critics of the traditional planning emphasis on physical development have argued that planning should pay more attention to economic and social forces within a community, particularly when physical development is contemplated. One study critical of the traditional approach of the Planning Enabling Act concluded that physical development plans for Denver and Washington had been based on

> five biases of planners, probably not shared by the community at large . . .
>
> (1) that scattered development is inherently evil; (2) that open space should be preserved; (3) that a city should have a strong, high density core; (4) that the journey to work should be reduced; and (5) that central urban residential locations are preferable to suburbs of single-family homes.[30]

Greater recognition is given to economic and social concerns in more recent planning statutes. For example, major revisions to the Pennsylvania Municipalities

Planning Code enacted in 1988 retain the permissive feature of municipal planning, but require municipal comprehensive plans to include elements respecting housing needs of present and prospective residents and a statement of "the interrelationships among the various plan components, which may include an estimate of the environmental, energy conservation, fiscal, economic development, and social consequences on the municipality."[31]

As noted earlier, the general permissive tone of the enabling acts led courts to conclude that zoning ordinances enacted by local legislative bodies did not have to conform to zoning plans adopted by local planning commissions as long as the zoning ordinances themselves were rational and the required absolute majority vote was obtained. A statement by an appellate court in Michigan is typical of this view:

> [T]here is no requirement in [the statute] that the "plan" be written or be anything beyond "a generalized conception by the members of the board as to how the districts in the township shall be . . . used." This "generalized conception" is exhibited in the zoning ordinance itself, since the document zones districts, prescribes variances, land uses, etc., for the entire township, and thus plans the township's future development.[32]

In a 1988 case, the Court of Appeals of New York upheld a New York City zoning amendment establishing the Special Manhattan Bridge District in Chinatown with the observation that "[a] well-considered plan need not be contained in a single document; indeed, it need not be written at all. . . . An amendment which has been carefully studied, prepared, and considered meets the general requirement for a well-considered plan and satisfies the statutory requirement."[33]

The American Planning Association's (APA) *Growing Smart[sm] Legislative Guidebook* offers four alternatives for state planning legislation: (1) planning as an advisory activity; (2) planning as an activity to be encouraged through the use of incentives, such as authorizing enactment of development impact fees and other supplemental powers; (3) planning as a mandatory activity that must produce an adopted comprehensive plan satisfying statutory criteria before zoning and other regulatory powers can be exercised; and (4) planning as a mandated activity, to be vertically and horizontally integrated so that regional and local plans are consistent with state plans, and neighboring local plans do not conflict with one another. APA researchers noted that "states were increasingly shaping their statutes to address problems that were unique to their circumstances" and accordingly developed recommended legislation "along a continuum that takes into account the degree of planning required and graduated levels of state or regional intervention." The alternatives offered are designed to enable states "to strike a balance between local self-determination and increasing state and regional involvement . . . and to make choices knowing some of the likely long-run consequences and trade-offs of each decision."[34]

State-Mandated Local Planning

A growing number of states, particularly the more populous ones such as California and Florida, are requiring local governments to engage in formal land use planning. The mandatory-planning requirement takes two forms. Some states require local governments to establish local planning agencies and adopt local comprehensive plans.[35] Other states require planning as a condition precedent to the exercise of zoning or other land use regulatory powers. These states, while retaining the permissive feature of the Planning Enabling Act, have added mandatory-planning components.[36]

For example, Nebraska amended its zoning-enabling statute in 1967 to permit zoning "only after the municipal legislative body has established a planning commission, received from its planning commission a recommended comprehensive development plan . . . , adopted such comprehensive development plan, and received the specific recommendation of the planning commission on the adoption or amendment of zoning regulations."[37] New Jersey does not permit zoning ordinances to be adopted until "after the planning board has adopted the land use plan element and the housing plan element of a master plan, and all of the provisions of [the] zoning ordinance[s] . . . shall either be substantially consistent with the land use plan element and the housing plan element of the master plan or designed to effectuate such plan elements," although by written resolution containing reasons, an absolute majority of the governing body can enact a zoning ordinance that is inconsistent with or not designed to effectuate the land use or housing plan elements.[38]

Although the adoption of a comprehensive plan is optional in Pennsylvania,[39] the zoning-enabling statute provides that zoning ordinances "should reflect the policy goals of the municipality as listed in a statement of community development objectives, . . . [which] may be supplied by reference to the community comprehensive plan . . . or may be the statement of community development objectives provided in a statement of legislative findings . . . describing the purposes and intent of the zoning ordinance."[40]

States that require local planning also tend to prescribe the topics that local plans must address in greater detail than traditional planning statutes modeled after the Planning Enabling Act. California requires local governments to adopt a "general plan" that sets forth "objectives, principles, standards, and plan proposals."[41] The statute requires the following nine topics to be included as separate elements of the plan: land use, traffic circulation, housing, natural resources conservation, open space, seismic safety, noise, scenic highways, and public safety. In addition, "the general plan may include any other elements or address any other subjects which, in the judgment of the legislative body, relate to the physical development of the county or city."[42]

The Florida mandatory local planning statute is similarly detailed regarding required elements of local plans. A local comprehensive plan must establish "principles, guidelines, and standards for the orderly and balanced future economic, social, physical, environmental and fiscal development of the area."[43] The statute lists nine required elements and ten optional elements, two of which—mass transit and port and aviation facilities—are required for the plans of local government units with populations in excess of 50,000.

Major emphasis is placed on capital-improvements planning and/or coordination of planning efforts, both within the several elements of a particular plan and among adjacent local governments within a region.[44] The statute requires "a specific policy statement indicating the relationship of the proposed development of the area to the comprehensive plans of adjacent municipalities, the county, adjacent counties, or the region and to the state comprehensive plan."[45]

The most significant innovation of the Florida planning statute is the "concurrency" requirement, which mandates that local governments have available those public facilities and services that are identified by the capital improvements element of their plans as necessary for development, or that local governments condition their approval of development proposals on the availability of necessary public facilities and services. Local governments have one year after submission of their required comprehensive plans to implement the concurrency requirement. After that date, local governments may not approve development proposals that would have the effect of reducing the level of public services from the level specified in the comprehensive plan.[46]

Florida communities must submit their proposed comprehensive plans or proposed amendments to existing plans to the Florida Department of Community Affairs, the state land-planning agency.[47] The department reviews submissions to determine whether proposed elements comply with the statutory requirements; whether local plans are internally consistent, as well as consistent with the state comprehensive plan and applicable regional policy plans; and whether local plans provide for adequate implementation, evaluation, and coordination of developmental activities with appropriate local, regional, and state governmental entities.[48] Local plans are "consistent" with state and regional plans if they are not in conflict with such plans or if they "take action in the direction of realizing goals or policies" of such plans.[49]

The Florida Supreme Court has held that amendments to comprehensive land use plans are entitled to judicial deference under the fairly debatable standard because they are legislative policy decisions rather than administrative decisions. As such, they should be approved if "reasonable persons could differ" concerning their validity.[50] A Florida court also has concluded that county officials' interpretation of their county's comprehensive plan is protected by sovereign immunity as a governmental function.[51]

The Oregon land use program features a Land Conservation and Development Commission (LCDC) that promulgates statewide standards for local planning and zoning.[52] LCDC has adopted 19 statewide planning goals and implementing guidelines, including the concept of "urban growth boundaries" and policies encouraging zoning for low-cost housing.[53] Oregon communities must prepare and adopt comprehensive plans in compliance with the statewide planning goals, and their zoning ordinances implementing the comprehensive plans likewise must comply with the statewide planning goals.[54] Local comprehensive plans must address each applicable statewide planning goal and give them equal weight.[55] Plans must be submitted to LCDC, which must review them for compliance with the goals and notify the counties of compliance.[56] Exercise of local zoning powers is "subordinate" to LCDC's statewide land use planning goals, and LCDC's regulations are consistent with the state's zoning-enabling statutes so long as they "do not allow *more* uses than the statutes."[57] A feature of the Oregon program is the Land Use Board of Appeals (LUBA), a state agency charged with the responsibility to hear appeals from local land use decisions and resolve conflicts between local land use regulations and state planning goals.[58]

By contrast, the Missouri planning-enabling statute provides only that a permissive city plan "show the commission's recommendations for the physical development and uses of land," including "general location, character and extent" of streets and other public facilities, public utilities, and terminals, along with acceptance, widening, abandonment, or changes in use of such facilities, and the "general character, extent and layout of the replanning of blighted districts and slum areas."[59]

States that require local governments to engage in comprehensive planning generally do not prescribe a particular form of planning entity. For example, California law creates a planning agency in each city and county and authorizes the local legislative body to assign the functions of the planning agency to a planning department; one or more planning commissions, administrative bodies, or hearing officers; the legislative body itself; or any combination of the above.[60] Florida permits local governments to exercise similar flexibility in determining how the planning function is to be implemented, including delegation of the planning function to a countywide planning entity or a council of local government officials representing all of the governing bodies in the county or planning area.[61]

As discussed in chapter 6, two important issues regarding judicial review of zoning decisions are the degree to which zoning decisions must be consistent with planning decisions and the extent to which the judiciary should defer to local legislatures in deciding that question.[62] In mandatory-planning states, the comprehensive plan should be recognized for what it is: a statement of policy rather than advice on what policy choices exist.[63] Zoning decisions should function, then, as means of implementing the plan,[64] and the judiciary should approach contested cases as administrative matters rather than as legislative matters. The standard of review would be less deferential, with the determination of whether a particular zoning decision is consistent with the applicable comprehensive plan being based on whether the decision is "supported by substantial evidence in the whole record,"[65] rather than whether the decision regarding consistency is "debatable."[66]

The difference in the two approaches is illustrated by the majority and concurring opinions in *Riggs v. Township of Long Beach,* a 1988 decision of the Supreme Court of New Jersey.[67] In *Riggs,* the township downzoned a parcel of land in a residential area that reduced the ability of the landowners to subdivide their tract of land from four lots to two lots but retained their ability to improve the property for residential use. The township argued that it was merely correcting a mistake to properly reflect a planning decision "to retain one of the last remaining open spaces on Long Beach Boulevard." Voters had previously approved a referendum to acquire "public open-space" property, and the township planning board adopted a master plan designating as public open space a five-block area including the Riggs property. Negotiations for the acquisition of the Riggs property had collapsed and an application to subdivide the property into four lots had been denied before the downzoning was enacted.

In overturning the downzoning decision, the Supreme Court of New Jersey focused on the requirement that a zoning ordinance must have a valid purpose, rather than the statutory requirement that a zoning ordinance be "substantially consistent" with adopted land use and housing plans. Concluding that the evidence established that the legislative purpose was to reduce the value of the property and thus lessen a pending condemnation award, the court invalidated the downzoning as an "abuse of the zoning power." In doing so, the court crossed the admittedly fuzzy line between legislative motive (normally not reviewable because of the subjective considerations involved) and legislative purpose (ordinarily reviewable but limited to an evaluation of the "objective facts surrounding the adoption of the ordinance").[68]

A lengthy concurring opinion took the majority to task for not concentrating on the statutory requirements of the recently enacted New Jersey Municipal Land Use Law. Rather than "walk the fuzzy line between motive and purpose to reach this result," the concurring justice argued that the court should have invalidated the downzoning because it "fails to comply with the standards requiring conformity with comprehensive planning" as required by the new statute. [69]

> It is . . . clear that the focus of the Municipal Land Use Law is on the enhanced role of planning and that it strengthens the planning process itself. The statutory enumeration of the factors to be considered in formulating a master plan, and the statutory directive that the master plan itself include an evaluation of proposed ordinances in light of these factors . . . serve the end of heightening the role of planning as a condition of proper zoning. It follows that the requirement that a zoning ordinance be substantially consistent with the master plan should be strictly enforced.[70]

Full application of the administrative review concept to zoning decisions in mandatory-planning states may require the establishment of state-level administrative review processes, such as the Oregon LUBA[71] and the New Jersey Council on Affordable Housing.[72] One of the principal reasons for creating LUBA was "to simplify the task of courts reviewing land use decisions, thereby speeding the process of judicial review."[73] LUBA has "exclusive jurisdiction" to review local land use decisions subject to certain statutory limitations.[74] The Council on Affordable Housing has authority to establish housing needs of low- and moderate-income persons in the state and determine whether municipalities are meeting their fair share of such needs by removing artificial barriers to such housing in local land use laws.[75]

Absent such statutory delegation of authority for administrative review of local land use decisions, courts have had continuing difficulty overcoming the apparent separation-of-powers problem posed by close judicial scrutiny of "legislative" zoning decisions, even in mandatory-planning states.[76] Some courts have construed mandatory-planning statutes as adding a second test of consistency that legislative decisions must meet. Under this approach, zoning regulations "must not only be nonarbitrary in the sense that they must be ascribable to some rational pursuit of the public welfare ('a comprehensive plan') but they must be consistent with or in accordance with the particular scheme portrayed in the adopted comprehensive plan."[77]

A Delaware court equated the "consistency-with-an-adopted-plan" question to a question of fact, to be reviewed based on the record before the local legislative body. Distinguishing "appropriate deference" to legislative fact findings from "blind acceptance" of such findings, the court struck down the rezoning of a 1.5-acre tract from medium-density residential to general commercial development as inconsistent with the "fundamental thrust" of the plan's "vision of appropriate commercial land development." The court noted that while the plan advocated discouraging commercial strip development along highways, the rezoning "can only be understood to constitute the approval of" such development.[78]

In affirming the court's decision, the Delaware Supreme Court expressed concern at "the disturbing trend which this case illustrates."

> We recognize that land use regulation is a legislative function and is exercised in an atmosphere of informality which sometimes attends the representative process. But important considerations of public policy and private property are at stake in land use regulation, and the rezoning process itself resembles a judicial determination. County Council does not have a free hand to grant rezoning upon request. It must conform with standards established by the General Assembly . . . and due process considerations. At a minimum, such proceedings require adequate notice to all concerned; a full opportunity to be heard by any person potentially aggrieved by the outcome; a decision which reflects the reasons underlying the result and, most importantly, an adherence to the statutory or decisional standards then controlling. Only when the administrative process affords these fundamental protections will the result receive judicial deference.[79]

The Supreme Court of Nevada, applying the Nevada statute requiring zoning to be in accordance with an adopted master plan,[80] stated that a master plan is a "standard that commands deference and a presumption of applicability [but is not] a legislative straightjacket from which no leave can be taken."[81] Applying that standard, the Nevada court affirmed a district court's grant of a writ of mandamus overturning denial of a rezoning request. Evidence established that the rezoning request to a higher density complied with the county's approved master plan. The number of area residents in favor of and against the proposed project was about equal, and surrounding properties were zoned and developed both at higher and lower densities. Under those circumstances, the court held that the county board of commissioners failed to give deference to the approved county master plan and in so doing abused its discretion.[82]

The Supreme Court of Idaho, construing the state's Local Land Use Planning Act,[83] held that while a local comprehensive plan is a "precondition to the validity of zoning ordinances,"[84] a comprehensive plan "is intended merely as a guideline whose primary use is in guiding zoning decisions." Denying a subdivision application that complied with the zoning ordinance solely because of noncompliance with the comprehensive plan "elevates the plan to the level of legally controlling zoning law" and is erroneous, the Court concluded.[85]

Because local legislative bodies are not required to conduct trial-type hearings in the exercise of their legislative function,[86] the record is not likely to be as extensive as might be expected in a quasi-judicial proceeding. For example, Florida courts have agreed that more than the traditional legislative deference standard should be applied in reviewing zoning decisions for consistency with mandated local plans but have disagreed on whether to use the intermediate "review-of-factual-findings" approach[87] or the "strict-judicial-scrutiny" approach.[88]

Planning as a Process

Although a written comprehensive plan that has been formally adopted by the local legislative body may be "a constitution for all future development within the city,"[89] land use planning is more accurately understood as a process of rational thought that proceeds from an analysis of a community's needs, resources, and values to the articulation of specific goals, objectives, and policies. Land use planning does not start and stop with the enactment of a comprehensive plan or a comprehensive zoning ordinance. It is a continuous process that shapes community policies as the aspirations and circumstances of its citizens change. The phenomenon of change, coupled with the reality that "there is never a plan to which everyone agrees,"[90] necessitates continuous rather than static activity.

The modern view that land use planning should "serve as a guide for public and private actions and decisions"[91] is a reflection of the belief that land use planning is a continual process. The land use plans of a community, whether reflected in formal, written comprehensive plans or embodied in a comprehensive zoning ordinance, are "continually subject to modification in the light of actual land use development."[92] The growing use of professionally obtained statistical data, studies, surveys, projections, and so forth,[93] as well as judicial rejection of plans that consist of nothing more than "a sheaf of uncoordinated documents stuffed into an unlabelled carton,"[94] emphasize the technical and professional aspects of the land use planning process. The essence of a successful planning effort is integration of the technical and professional aspects with the political processes of the community in a manner that enables necessary modifications to policy decisions suggested by changes in the community environment and implemented in a rational, rather than an arbitrary or whimsical, manner.

The requirement that basic public-policy decisions regarding land use regulation be made by elected officials or by popular vote creates a system that is "political by design."[95] The reluctance of courts to take on political questions may help explain the traditional hands-off judicial attitude with respect to legislative zoning matters. To the extent that more attention is placed on comprehensive land use planning, the courts may become less deferential to local zoning decisions because the political debate, at least in theory, would shift from zoning to planning.[96] Whether that will happen is problematic because of the institutionalization of zoning as "a legal concept" rather than "just a tool of planning," although that legal concept is "subject to test in the courtroom."[97]

Extraterritorial Planning

States generally permit local governments to engage in limited extraterritorial planning, particularly when no other governmental jurisdiction is engaging in land use planning of the affected area. Some states, such as Missouri, permit extraterritorial land use planning and regulation for a specified limited area of unincorporated land so long as the county in which the land is located has not created a county planning commission that has adopted an official master plan for the unincorporated area of the county.[98]

Other states, such as California and New York, do not place a specific distance limit for extraterritorial planning but permit local governments to include in their planning process extraterritorial lands that in the planning agency's judgment should be included.[99] Florida authorizes municipalities to engage in extraterritorial planning, as well as procedures for joint action by municipality and county in preparing, adopting, and implementing a comprehensive plan for the unincorporated area.[100]

Planning Commissions and Boards

States traditionally have provided that local land use planning is to be carried out by an independent public commission, a majority of whose members are private citizens.[101] The Standard City Planning Enabling Act, drafted in 1928 under the auspices of the U.S. Commerce Department,[102] took this approach and had enormous influence on the development of state planning-enabling legislation.[103] The theory behind such "citizen" planning is that a representative group of private citizens will be able to articulate effectively the aspirations and values of the residents of the community so that the plans that are developed for the community will in truth "best promote the general welfare."[104]

The Growing Smart[sm] project includes three alternative approaches to the organization of local planning commissions, with the first alternative having two versions:

    1A. All members would be appointed citizens, with no constituency representatives *or*

    1B. all members would be appointed citizens and constituencies would be represented;

  or

    2. Commissions would contain both appointed members and elected officials;

  or

    3. Commissions would include appointed members, administrative officials, and elected officials.[105]

Creation, appointment, and qualifications of planning commission members are prescribed by statute, with states generally fixing maximum and minimum limits on the size of the commission and providing that the majority of members shall not hold other public office in the locality.[106] Removal of planning commissioners is governed by statute. The Supreme Court of Vermont has held that a statute authorizing the local legislative body to remove commissioners "at any time" authorizes removing them at will.[107]

Planning commissions are public bodies. Their proceedings are public,[108] as are the records of those proceedings, but persons interested in videotaping planning commission meetings do not have a First Amendment right to do so.[109] Applicable "sunshine" laws requiring that meetings be open to the public must be complied with in order to take valid action,[110] although courts have been willing to permit private "gatherings of less than a majority . . . where decisions are not made and official actions are not taken," as well as "activities of a governmental body's individual members to secure information to be reported and acted upon at an open meeting."[111]

The primary function of a local planning commission is to give advice to the governing body concerning the development of the community. Advice is rendered in two basic ways: (1) by the adoption of formal plans that serve as "recommendations for the physical development and uses of land,"[112] and (2) by reviewing requests for modifications to existing land use regulations through the enactment of amendments to the zoning ordinance.[113]

Although a few states permit planning and zoning commissions to function in a legislative capacity by enacting zoning regulations,[114] most states do not give planning commissions authority to enact or modify land use regulations because such decisions establish public policy and are the prerogative of local legislative bodies.[115] Planning commissions, however, may be delegated the power to administer portions of a land use regulatory scheme, such as making decisions concerning the issuance of special-use permits, allocation of predetermined overall densities in cluster developments, and implementation of the legislative policy of a floating zone, provided that the delegation "is accompanied by standards sufficient to limit and direct the exercise of discretion on the part of the agency or official to whom the power is delegated."[116] Planning commissions may also be delegated the responsibility for approving subdivision plats,[117] site plans,[118] and building permits.[119] Challenges to proposed developments for which subdivision plat approval has not yet been sought or obtained have been dismissed as premature.[120]

Maintaining the distinction between rendering advice to the legislative body, impermissible exercise of the legislative function, and permissible exercise of an administrative function can be a complex undertaking for a planning commission. In Montgomery County, Maryland, an occurrence with the use of transferable development rights (TDRs) is a case in point.[121] The county adopted an agricultural lands preservation plan and corresponding amendments to its zoning code to restrict development of agricultural lands.[122] The plan permitted the owners of lands burdened by the downzoning to transfer the development rights to certain other properties in the county, which would be eligible for greater than normal intensity of development. The implementation phase of the plan, in which specific tracts of land were considered for inclusion in the TDR receiving zone, thereby becoming eligible for increases in density, was to be accomplished through the planning process by amendments to the master plan, but there was no provision for any changes to be made to the zoning map or text to reflect amendments to the master plan. Because the Court of Appeals of Maryland considered the decisions regarding designation of particular tracts of land as TDR receiving areas and granting such tracts particular density bonuses to be legislative decisions rather than planning recommendations, the court invalidated that portion of the agricultural lands preservation program. The court also concluded that the planning board was not engaging in permissible administrative implementation of an established legislative policy because there were no standards contained in the ordinance for determining which tracts should be placed in the TDR receiving zone or what TDR density should be assigned to tracts so designated.[123]

Professional Planning Department

Preparation of formal land use plans, reports, and studies generally is carried out in one of two ways: (1) by planning experts and consultants hired by the planning commission with funds appropriated for that purpose by the local legislative body,[124] or (2) by a full-time planning department that is an integral part of the local government structure.[125] The size and complexity of the local government generally will influence which approach a particular locality will adopt.

Many communities utilize a blend of citizens and professionals. In such instances, a planning department with a full-time professional staff prepares draft plans, conducts studies, and reviews applications for development permits and modifications to existing land use plans or regulations. A planning commission, the majority of whose members are private citizens serving without compensation, makes the actual decisions to approve or reject proposed plans or modifications. While the commission may or may not hire the professional staff,[126] the modern practice is for the professional staff to be part of a line agency within local government whose director makes staff hiring decisions in accordance with applicable local government personnel policies.[127]

States that have revised their planning statutes to require formal planning as a prerequisite to exercise of the land use regulatory power generally give local governments wide latitude to determine how the planning function is to be accomplished. For example, California and Florida require local governments to designate a "local planning agency" to carry out the mandatory land use planning function, but permit the localities to designate the local legislative body, a planning department, one or more local planning commissions, or a combination of entities as the local planning agency.[128]

Advisory versus Policy-Making Functions

Local land use planning traditionally has been viewed as a process for giving professional advice to local government policy-makers. Land use policy is made through legislative adoption of a land use regulation such as a comprehensive zoning ordinance.[129] Under this view of planning, adoption of a formal plan by the planning commission or planning department is one step by which the advisory process is formalized. Advice also is transmitted through the common requirement that the planning commission give its recommendation regarding any proposed changes in existing zoning and other land use regulations.[130]

Formal adoption of a comprehensive plan by the local legislative body can have important policy-making implications, however, even in a state that does not require adoption of formal plans as a prerequisite to exercise of the regulatory power. In an often-quoted opinion rendered prior to the enactment of mandatory-planning legislation, a California District Court of Appeals concluded that adoption of a general plan by the city council was subject to referendum under California law because the decision to adopt the plan was legislative in character.[131]

> It is apparent that the plan is, in short, a constitution for all future development within the city. . . . If the general plan is anything at all, it is a meaningful enactment and definitely affects the community and, among other things, changes land market values.[132]

Mandatory-planning statutes retain the distinction between the advisory and the policy-making functions. Both the California and Florida mandatory-planning statutes, for example, require local planning agencies to prepare comprehensive plans and make recommendations to local legislative bodies, but require that the plans be adopted by the legislative bodies.[133]

Creation of the Comprehensive Plan

When the land use planning process is formalized in a document separate from the comprehensive zoning ordinance, the document generally is described as a comprehensive, general, or master plan.[134] Comprehensive plans usually emphasize the physical development of the community,[135] although a broader approach to planning that integrates economic, social, physical, environmental, and fiscal development has been recognized.[136]

Comprehensive plans contain statements of development policies, maps or charts displaying existing and projected growth patterns of the community, and a series of textual statements commonly called "elements." The number of separate elements will vary, but mandatory-planning statutes usually require a land use element that describes general characteristics of the land and recommends appropriate distribution of various types of land use; a circulation element that describes traffic circulation patterns as well as existing and proposed major thoroughfares and transportation routes; a conservation element that discusses utilization and conservation of natural resources such as air, water, timber, and so forth; a recreation and open-space element that describes public parks and recreation policies; and a housing element designed to focus on the residential needs of all income levels in the community.[137]

Other elements that may be included, depending on the perceived needs in the particular state, are a noise element to discuss noise problems in the community;[138] a safety element to consider matters of public safety such as earthquakes, flooding, and fires;[139] and a coastal-management element focusing on the overall quality of the environment in coastal areas.[140] Comprehensive plans also are supposed to provide for coordination of the several elements of the plan and for coordination between the land use planning process and the capital-improvements planning and budgeting process.[141]

The Growing Smart[sm] project follows these general patterns, but adds to the required elements an issues-and-opportunities element; a telecommunications element; several elements with opt-out provisions, including economic-development, critical-and-sensitive-areas, and natural-hazards elements; and a program of implementation. Optional elements include agriculture, forest and scenic preservation, human services, community design, and historic preservation. Also recommended are provisions for adopting subplans, such as neighborhood plans, transit-oriented development plans, and redevelopment-area plans.[142]

Adoption of the Comprehensive Plan

Mandatory-planning statutes go to great lengths to prescribe an adoption procedure for local comprehensive plans that provides opportunities for public participation in the planning process and for review of the proposed plans by other governmental entities that would be affected by the plan. For example, California requires the planning agency to provide, during the preparation or amendment of the general plan, "opportunities for the involvement of citizens, public agencies, public utility companies, and civic, education, and other community groups, through public hearings and any other means . . . appropriate."[143] If a planning commission is authorized to make formal recommendations regarding preparation or amendment of a general plan, the planning commission must hold at least one public hearing before approving a recommendation.[144] The recommendation of the planning commission must be in writing, and if the recommendation is for approval, an affirmative vote of not less than a majority of the total membership of the commission is required.[145] In addition to the hearing required to be held by the planning commission, the legislative body must hold at least one public hearing prior to adopting or amending a general plan.[146]

In addition to the public-hearing requirements, the California statute requires the planning agency to refer a proposed general plan or amendment to the local-area formation commission (boundary commission) and to any adjacent local governments, areawide planning agencies, and federal agencies that "may be significantly affected" by the proposed plan or amendment, as determined by the planning agency. Each entity receiving a referral has 45 days to comment unless the planning agency specifies a longer period. The statute provides that the referral section is directory rather than mandatory, and failure to make an appropriate referral does not affect the validity of a decision to adopt a plan or an amendment.[147]

The California statute requires the legislative body to adopt or amend a general plan by resolution, with an affirmative vote of not less than a majority of the total membership of the legislative body. The legislative body may approve, modify, or disapprove the recommendations of the planning commission, if one exists in the community, but substantial modifications not previously considered by the commission must be returned to the commission for its recommendation. Failure of the commission to report within 45 calendar days of the reference, or within the time specified by the legislative body, is deemed to constitute a recommendation for approval.[148]

The Florida statute has similar requirements for public participation in the planning process. The local governing body is required to hold two public hearings, one prior to the submission of the proposed plan or amendment to the Florida Department of Community Affairs (the state land agency) for written comment and the other one prior to approval of the plan by the local governing body.[149] Immediately following the first hearing, the local governing body must submit ten copies of the proposed plan or amendment to the state land-planning agency for written comment. The state land-planning agency is required to distribute copies of the proposed plan or amendment within five working days of receipt to appropriate state agencies and regional and county planning agencies. Governmental agencies have 30 days to provide written comments to the state land-planning agency, and that agency has an additional 30 days to submit written comments to the local government that submitted the proposed plan or amendment.[150] Review by county and regional planning agencies is limited to the relationship of the proposed plan or amendment to county comprehensive plan elements and regional policy plans.[151]

Following receipt of the written comments from the state land-planning agency, the local government has 120 days to adopt or adopt with changes the proposed plan or amendment. As noted previously, a second public hearing must be held prior to formal adoption of the plan or amendment. The adopted plan must then be resubmitted to the state land-planning agency, which has 45 days to review the plan and determine whether it is consistent with the statutory requirements and thus in compliance with the statute. The determination of compliance may be based only on the agency's written comments prior to adoption and any changes that may have been made by the local government. In addition, the agency may not declare a plan to be not in compliance with the statute if it has not participated in the second public hearing after having been requested to do so by the local government. During the compliance-review period, the agency is required to issue a notice of intent to find that the plan or amendment is in compliance or not in compliance. If the agency issues a notice of intent to find compliance, any affected person may contest the proposed action by filing a petition within 21 days after publication of the notice. A hearing on the petition will be conducted by a state administrative law judge within the affected local jurisdiction. The determination of compliance will be upheld if it is fairly debatable.[152]

If the agency issues a notice of intent to find noncompliance, a hearing is held by a state administrative law judge in the affected jurisdiction. The local government's determination that the plan or amendment is in compliance is presumed to be correct and will be upheld unless it is shown by a preponderance of evidence that the plan is not in compliance. Local government determinations of internal consistency of plan elements will be upheld if the determinations are fairly debatable.[153] If the state administration commission concludes that a local plan is not in compliance with the statute, it is required to specify remedial actions to bring the plan into compliance and may order state agencies not to provide funds to increase the capacity of roads, bridges, or water and sewer systems within the boundaries of the local government, as well as denying the local government eligibility for various federal grants administered by the state.[154]

Adoption procedures are similar, but not quite as detailed, in states where comprehensive planning is permissive rather than mandatory. For example, Missouri permits local governments to adopt comprehensive plans, in whole or in part, by resolution following a public hearing. Adoption of the plan requires a majority vote of the full membership of the commission. The resolution must refer expressly to the maps, descriptive matter, and other matters "intended by the commission to form the whole or part of the plan." The adopted plan must be signed by the secretary of the commission, given a file number, and be filed in the office of the commission. A copy of the plan must be certified to the city clerk and legislative body, and a copy must be recorded in the county land records.[155] Nevada requires a two-thirds vote of the planning commission to adopt a master plan and forward it to the local governing body, which may adopt it by a simple majority.[156]

Requirements of planning-enabling statutes must be met, and failure to do so is grounds for invalidating zoning ordinances that are based on plans that have not been properly enacted.[157] A Missouri appellate court struck down a zoning ordinance in which the plan was embodied in the zoning map. The ordinance was recorded, but the zoning map was not. A statement in the ordinance purporting to incorporate the map into the ordinance by reference was held to be insufficient compliance with the recordation requirement of the planning- and zoning-enabling legislation.[158]

Administration of the Comprehensive Plan

Mandatory-planning states assign specific administrative functions to the planning agency following adoption of a comprehensive plan. For example, California requires local planning agencies to make recommendations regarding "reasonable and practical means for implementing the general plan or element of the general plan so that it will serve as an effective guide," and to submit an annual report to the legislative body on the status and implementation of the plan.[159] A coordinated program of proposed public works must be submitted annually to the planning agency in order to review whether the program conforms to the adopted general plan.[160] No property may be acquired or disposed of by the local government, or public buildings constructed, without the planning agency first rendering a report as to whether the proposed action conforms to the general plan.[161]

The Florida statute describes the planning program as "a continuous and ongoing process."[162] The local planning agency is required to submit periodic reports on the comprehensive plan, at least once every five years or upon request of the governing body. Reports must assess and evaluate the success or failure of the plan and discuss the following points: major problems of development, condition of each element of the plan, status of major plan objectives, and the extent to which unanticipated and unforeseen problems and opportunities have occurred. The report is to include recommendations for changes to the plan. The governing body is required to adopt or adopt with changes the report within 90 days of submission. Amendments to the plan based on the recommendations of the report may be adopted simultaneously with the adoption of the report or may be considered within one year after the report is adopted. The report, along with any amendments to the plan, must be transmitted to the state land-planning agency 90 days prior to the scheduled adoption date.[163]

Legal Effect of the Comprehensive Plan

Formal adoption of a comprehensive plan by a local legislative body has important legal consequences. In states where planning is permissive, adoption of a plan has been likened to a "constitution for all future development."[164] Zoning ordinances[165] and subdivision regulations[166] will be tested for their consistency with the plan. Failure of a municipality to comply with procedural requirements following adoption of the plan, such as filing a copy in the county land records, can invalidate a subsequently enacted comprehensive zoning ordinance.[167] Construction of streets, public utilities, and other public facilities must be approved by the planning agency for consistency with the plan, although the legislative body can overrule a planning agency's disapproval by a supermajority vote.[168]

In states that require a comprehensive plan to be adopted as a prerequisite to exercise of land use regulatory powers, adoption of the plan is a condition precedent to enactment of a valid zoning ordinance.[169] Likewise, existing zoning ordinances that are not consistent with a plan or an amendment to a plan must be brought into compliance by appropriate amendment.[170]

The Florida mandatory-planning statute provides that after a comprehensive plan, element, or portion of a plan is adopted, all land development regulations, development agreements, and authorized development must be consistent with the adopted plan. Consistency is determined by compatibility of permitted "land uses, densities or intensities, and other aspects of development" with the objectives, policies, land uses, and densities and intensities of the comprehensive plan, and compliance with other criteria enumerated in the plan.[171] Amendments to comprehensive plans in Florida are legislative in character, entitled to deference under the "fairly debatable" standard of review.[172] Interpretation of a comprehensive plan and refusal to issue a development permit as a result of that interpretation has been held to be protected by sovereign immunity as a governmental function.[173]

The New Jersey statute, which does not mandate local planning but makes adoption of the land use and housing plan elements of a master plan a condition precedent to the exercise of the zoning power,[174] requires zoning ordinances to be "substantially consistent" with the land use and housing-plan elements or "designed to effectuate" those elements. The statute does, however, permit enactment of zoning ordinances that are inconsistent or not designed to effectuate the plan elements but only by an affirmative vote of a majority of the full authorized membership of the governing body. The reasons for so acting must be specified in a resolution and recorded in the minutes of the meeting at which the decision was made.[175] In construing this provision, a New Jersey court held invalid the rezoning from commercial to residential use of a three-acre strip of land on a median between the northbound and southbound lanes of a state highway. The land use element of the master plan suggested that the median strip be placed in an office-use category, and the record indicated that the township planning board recommended that the strip be rezoned from commercial to office use. The township, however, rezoned the property to residential use apparently because, as the township's expert witness testified, "no one could propose another use which would be safe." The court rejected the rezoning as inconsistent with the land use element of the plan. The court refused to accept handwritten notes attached to the minutes of the meeting at which the rezoning decision was made, as well as a letter written four months later by a professional planner retained by the township as compliance with the statutory requirement that specific reasons for adopting inconsistent ordinance provisions be given. The court concluded that "[i]t is not sufficient to say, as did the trial judge, that the governing body would simply adopt the same zone scheme accompanied by a statement of reasons. Although that may be the eventual result, we cannot assume that will invariably occur."[176]

Comprehensive Zoning Ordinance as Comprehensive Plan

As noted earlier, the majority of states do not require local governments to engage in land use planning.[177] All states, however, require zoning to be "in accordance with a comprehensive plan." In states where local planning is permissive rather than mandatory, the courts have had little trouble reconciling the permissive-planning statute with the zoning mandate by finding the comprehensive plan to be contained in the zoning ordinance if the zoning ordinance is comprehensive in scope and establishes "an orderly method of land use regulation for the community."[178]

Zoning ordinances that embody the comprehensive plan must be comprehensive in scope: applying to the entire community; providing restrictions for the use of property in each district or zone; establishing procedures for nonconforming uses, conditional uses, amendments, and variances; and establishing an appellate process for review of decisions affecting individual parcels of land.[179]

The Official Map

Some communities use an additional land use planning and regulatory technique called the official map.[180] Official maps are maps of the community on which are located existing and proposed public buildings, facilities, streets, sewers, and so forth.[181] Official maps usually are prepared by the local planning agency. When approved by ordinance of the legislative body, official maps become land use regulations because building permits, subdivision approvals, and other development permissions that are not consistent with the map may not be obtained.[182] Official maps serve as records of streets and alleys that have been accepted for public maintenance. When rights-of-way for streets and alleys are accepted by formal act of the local governing body, the rights-of-way are drawn on the official map. Rights-of-way that are abandoned are taken off the map. The official map then becomes evidence of the acceptance of the right-of-way.[183]

Although official maps may be a useful means of identifying land for future public facilities, restrictions on the use of mapped land must permit the owner to make reasonable economic use of private property that is mapped, or compensation must be paid to the owner for mapped private property that cannot be used by its owner because of its designation as the site of a proposed public facility.[184]

Distinguishing the Planning Map, the Zoning Map, and the Official Map

In the course of their work, local land use planning agencies prepare numerous types of maps. Three types should be distinguished because of their different legal consequences:

1. *Planning maps* are prepared by the planning agency as part of their formal planning work. Statutes permitting or requiring preparation and adoption of local comprehensive plans require the plans to include appropriate maps so that existing and proposed land use activities can be identified. These maps, like the plans of which they are a part, serve as guides to local policy-makers and the public. Planning maps do not have separate regulatory force except for the requirement that land use decisions be consistent with the comprehensive plan.[185]
2. *Zoning maps* are prepared by the planning agency to illustrate the basic legislative decision of zoning: the territorial division of the land in the community into districts for the purpose of imposing comprehensive land use regulations. Zoning maps are approved by the legislative body as part of the comprehensive zoning ordinance and as such carry the force of law. They serve as the public "picture" of the land use policies of the community.[186]
3. *Official maps* are prepared by the planning agency to identify the location of existing and proposed public buildings and facilities. When approved by ordinance of the legislative body, they have regulatory force in that private land use activities incompatible with the official map are prohibited.[187]

State and Regional Planning: Growth Management

A number of states, particularly those that have experienced extensive growth or that have significant amounts of environmentally sensitive land, have established state and regional land use planning programs.[188] For the most part, these programs have been advisory in nature, although an increasing number are being given regulatory authority. This trend is particularly true for areas defined as environmentally sensitive, such as the Pinelands area in New Jersey.[189]

Oregon has perhaps the best-known state planning program that attempts to integrate local, regional, and state planning efforts. A state agency, the Land Conservation and Development Commission (LCDC), is charged with the responsibility of adopting state land use goals and guidelines. Under the Oregon scheme, the legislature enacted "broad policies" to guide LCDC, such as a directive to "consider various 'areas and activities' in preparing and adopting the goals and guidelines including among others, estuarine areas, wetlands, beaches and dunes, flood plains and areas of geologic hazard, unique wildlife habitats, and agriculture land."[190] Local land use plans are required to be in compliance with the adopted goals.[191] Additional state regulations may be imposed for designated "areas of critical state concern.[192] Counties, acting alone or in concert as regional planning authorities, are responsible for coordinating local planning activities "to assure an integrated comprehensive plan for the entire area." County plans are supposed to apply the "*statewide* land use planning goals," giving each goal equal weight. LCDC reviews the plans for compliance. If a conflict arises between LCDC's regulations and a county plan authorizing activities "otherwise permissible under [the] statute in furtherance of the state's land use goals," the LCDC regulations prevail.[193] A separate state administrative agency, the Land Use Board of Appeals (LUBA), hears appeals from local land use decisions that are challenged as being outside the "range of discretion" permitted by the applicable comprehensive plan and implementing ordinances.[194]

A significant increase in population during the 1980s, particularly in the Puget Sound area, led the Washington state legislature to enact a Growth Management Act (GMA) in 1990 and to amend it on a regular basis during the 1990s.[195] Growth pressures driving the legislation included the familiar litany of "traffic congestion, school overcrowding, urban sprawl, and loss of rural lands." [196] To meet these concerns, and to guide counties subject to the GMA[197] in the preparation and adoption of newly required comprehensive plans, the legislature articulated 13 planning goals, including encouragement of development "in urban areas where adequate public facilities and services exist or can be provided in an efficient manner" and discouraging sprawl by reducing the "inappropriate conversion of undeveloped land into sprawling, low-density development."[198] In order to meet the urban growth and sprawl-reduction goals, counties are required to establish "urban growth areas" where growth will be encouraged and "outside of which growth can occur only if it is not urban in nature."[199] Growth management hearing boards and enforcement mechanisms were added in 1991 and 1995, including authorization for the governor to impose economic sanctions against noncomplying local governments and to permit hearing boards to invalidate county plans or regulations that "substantially interfere with the fulfillment of the goals of the Act."[200] In a lengthy opinion that triggered a strong dissent, the Supreme Court of Washington concluded that the remedial powers of growth-management hearing boards were prospective in scope and did not include power to invalidate zoning regulations that had been adopted before the enactment of the GMA.[201] Two years later, the Washington court upheld an appeals board's conclusion that local zoning amendments authorizing conversion of agricultural land to athletic fields impermissibly conflicted with the GMA's requirement to conserve agricultural lands.[202]

Florida and New Jersey have extensive state and regional planning statutes. Florida enacted and periodically amends a legislative state plan that really is a statement of goals intended to be "direction-setting."[203] Florida also identifies "areas of critical state concern" and "developments of regional impact." Such designations trigger additional state and regional land use review of proposed development.[204] The New Jersey state planning act includes a provision for "cross-acceptance." An advisory State Development and Redevelopment Plan serves as the basis for the cross-acceptance concept. A preliminary plan is circulated to local planning officials who compare it with local master plans and engage in cross-acceptance. The objectives of cross-acceptance are to identify areas of agreement and disagreement, and to identify areas "requiring modification by parties to the cross-acceptance" so that "compatibility between local, county and state plans" may be attained. An interim plan is then prepared and is subjected to an assessment study leading to the adoption of a final plan.[205]

Consistency requirements, particularly in mandatory-planning states,[206] may also be applicable to adopted regional and state plans. For example, Florida law requires a proposed "development of regional impact," defined as a development that, "because of its character, magnitude, or location, would have a substantial effect upon the health, safety, or welfare of citizens of more than one county," to undergo "development-of-regional-impact review" and approval by a regional planning agency before receiving local approval. A complex review process, which may include application for a "binding letter of interpretation" from the state planning agency concerning the applicability of the review process to the development in question, and negotiation of a "preliminary development agreement" with the state planning agency to permit a limited amount of development to take place prior to issuance of a final development order, is mandated by the statute.[207] If the proposed development is located in an "area of critical state concern," additional review for compliance with established "principles for guiding development" takes place.[208]

Vermont's Act 250, one of the earliest growth-management statutes,[209] requires a developer of large projects—defined as commercial or industrial projects over ten acres, and residential developments exceeding ten units if each unit is on less than ten acres of land, and projects above 2,500 feet in elevation—to obtain development permits from district environmental commissions. A comprehensive list of environmental and fiscal factors must be considered by the commission. Decisions of the commission may be appealed to a state agency, the Environmental Board.[210] Board decisions are reviewable by the Vermont Supreme Court.[211] The board, and the state supreme court on appeal, may override a town's implementation of its own plan, but "only when the local construction of the town plan is plainly erroneous." While the Vermont court "must give deference to the determination of the Board, . . . the Board in turn must give deference to the determination of local bodies in applying the plan."[212]

Other states that have enacted growth-management statutes include Georgia[213] and Maryland.[214] The smart growth movement has influenced a significant number of state governors to issue growth-management executive orders and state legislatures to enact growth-management legislation. One study of the movement concluded that "the amount of executive and legislative interest in the topic of land use reform at the dawn of a new century is an indication that reliance on the planning and zoning enabling act modeled on 1920s model legislation . . . will not survive in the new century." [215]

Federal laws are having an increasing influence on state and regional planning programs. For example, the Intermodal Surface Transportation Efficiency Act of 1991 (ISTEA) and its successor, the Transportation Equity Act for the Twenty-first Century (TEA-21),[216] require recipients of federal highway and mass-transit funds to establish metropolitan transportation-planning programs for urban areas (50,000 or more in population) and to develop three-year transportation-improvement programs with a priority list of projects and a financial plan for implementation.[217] States must also establish a continuous state transportation-planning process.[218]

Neighborhood Collaborative Planning[219]

One of the identifiable forces shaping the effort to redefine American cities at the beginning of the new millennium is the neighborhood collaborative-planning movement. The interest in neighborhood collaborative planning stems in part from a quarter-century of federal governmental efforts to decentralize domestic social programs, beginning with the Community Development Block Grant program[220] and continuing through the current Empowerment Zone,[221] HOPE VI,[222] and Temporary Aid to Needy Families (TANF)[223] programs. It is also driven by the natural desire of persons everywhere to take control of the environment in which they live. In addition, neighborhood collaborative planning is a factor in efforts to articulate a legal alternative to the city/suburb dichotomy that would include rather than exclude persons who are "different."[224] The effort at redefining urban life to respond to its alienating features has for the most part been a centralized movement led by public and private leadership. This approach tends to devise programs based on political principles and fiscal priorities of the decision-makers. Neighborhood collaborative planning attempts to balance this approach with a decentralized, participatory process designed to encourage decision-making based on a broader community perspective.[225]

Neighborhood planning raises several issues: (1) whether and to what extent neighboring residents have legitimate interests in decisions affecting the use and development of private property, (2) the credentials of groups purporting to represent such community interests, (3) the ability of nongovernmental organizations to implement plans developed for a particular neighborhood, (4) the appropriate accountability for use of public funds by nongovernmental organizations, and (5) the extent to which nongovernmental organizations should be delegated traditional governmental functions.

Nongovernmental, neighborhood-based organizations do not fit neatly into traditional patterns of collaboration because of their informality of organization and uneven track record. Some state and local governments, drawing on the experiences of successful neighborhood-planning and -development organizations, have established standards for defining jurisdictions and delegating functions to neighborhood organizations.

Atlanta

The Atlanta City Code directs the department of budget and planning to designate Neighborhood Planning Units (NPUs) defined as "geographic areas composed of one (1) or more contiguous neighborhoods" that are based on criteria established by the department and approved by the city council. NPUs may comprise as many or as few neighborhoods as practicable and may cross council district boundaries. In designating NPUs, the department must consider existing citizens' organizations' boundaries and must establish a process for neighborhood boundary change. A neighborhood planning committee is established within each NPU with authority to "recommend an action, a policy or a comprehensive plan . . . on any matter affecting the livability of the neighborhood." Voting membership is open to all residents over age 18 and all organizations owning property or having a place of business or profession within the NPU.[226]

Connecticut

Connecticut authorizes municipalities to establish, by resolution of their legislative bodies, neighborhood revitalization zones in which neighborhood groups may develop a "collaborative process for federal, state and local governments to revitalize neighborhoods." Neighborboods eligible for this process must be ones in which "there is a significant number of deteriorated property and property that has been foreclosed, is abandoned, blighted or is substandard or poses a hazard to public safety." Cities adopting such resolutions facilitate the neighborhood-planning process by making available pertinent information, modifying municipal procedures, and establishing a process for determining neighborhood-revitalization-zone boundaries.[227]

Following the passage of a neighborhood-revitalization planning resolution, a neighborhood-revitalization planning committee is organized to develop both a short- and long-term plan for the neighborhood. Membership must "reflect the composition of the neighborhood," with residents making up a majority of the committee. A municipal official may be appointed as a voting member by the mayor or chief executive official. The plan must be designed to promote the following legislatively articulated goals: "self-reliance in the neighborhood and home ownership, property management, sustainable economic development, effective relations between landlords and tenants, coordinated and comprehensive delivery of services to the neighborhood and creative leveraging of financial resources and . . . neighborhood capacity for self-empowerment."[228]

Los Angeles

On June 6, 1999, voters in Los Angeles approved a new city charter.[229] Article IX of the new charter established an Office of Neighborhood Empowerment, with responsibilities to plan and assist in the creation of a "citywide system of neighborhood councils."[230] A system for determining neighborhood council boundaries is to be included in the regulations. Neighborhood boundaries are to be maintained "to the maximum extent feasible" and community-planning district boundaries may be considered "where appropriate."[231] All areas of the city are to be given "an equal opportunity to form neighborhood councils."[232]

Neighborhood councils have the right to give advice to city officials concerning "local matters" under procedures to be established by the regulations and to present an annual list of budget priorities to the mayor and council.[233] Local matters "include decisions that may potentially impact a neighborhood or area residents," as defined by the regulations.[234] The city council may grant "decision-making authority" by ordinance to neighborhood councils for specified local matters.[235]

Neighborhood councils seeking recognition from the city must submit a plan and bylaws providing "at a minimum:" (1) officership is open to all residents, workers, and property owners of the neighborhood (stakeholders), (2) assurance that officers "will reflect the diverse interests" of the neighborhood, (3) a system for regular communication with stakeholders, (4) a system for financial accountability of its funds, and (5) guarantees that all meetings will be open and that all stakeholders will be permitted to "participate in the conduct of business, deliberation and decision-making."[236] Evaluation of the charter provision, the regulations, and the "efficacy of the system of neighborhood councils" must be conducted within five years after implementation of the plan. In the meantime, the "powers, duties or functions" of the Office of Neighborhood Empowerment may not be transferred to other agencies.[237]

Minnesota

Minnesota statutes authorize first-class cities (Minneapolis and St. Paul) to establish neighborhood-revitalization programs (NRPs) and expend funds generated by tax-incremental financing for those programs.[238] Neighborhood-planning workshops organized by city officials are responsible for preparing neighborhood action plans. These workshops must be conducted in such a way that available resources, information, and technical assistance are presented to interested persons in the neighborhood.

NRP cities must establish a policy board made up of representatives of governmental agencies within the city, such as the city council, county board, school board, citywide library and park board, the mayor or his or her designate, and representatives from the city's house of representatives and state senate delegations. The policy board may also include representatives of citywide community organizations, neighborhood organizations, business owners, labor, and neighborhood residents, when invited by the governmental members of the policy board.

The policy board is delegated the authority to enter into contracts and expend funds, and it is authorized to enter into agreements with governmental agencies and with nongovernmental organizations represented on the policy board for services required to implement the NRP plan. Plans prepared by neighborhood planning workshops are submitted to the policy board, which has jurisdiction to review, modify, and approve. The policy board forwards its recommendations for final action to the governing bodies of the governments represented on the policy board. Final approval is given by the governing bodies that have programmatic jurisdiction over specific aspects of the plan.

Neighborhood Improvement Districts

An alternative approach to neighborhood planning is the creation of special districts that are legal entities with jurisdiction to develop and carry out plans for a defined area of a city. Such districts would be designed to enable residents in a large city to identify with local government at a meaningful level. The popular business improvement district could form a model for neighborhood improvement districts.

A number of states have authorized a variety of special districts to carry out projects designed to benefit local businesses and encourage economic development. For example, Illinois constitutional provisions and statutes authorize the creation of Special Service Areas within a municipality or county in which special governmental services are provided in addition to those services provided generally throughout the municipality or county, with the cost of the special services to be paid from revenues collected from taxes levied or imposed on property within that area.[239]

Missouri constitution and statutory provisions authorize cities and counties to create Neighborhood Improvement Districts and incur indebtedness and issue general obligation bonds to pay for all or part of the cost of public improvements within such districts.[240]

New York authorizes municipalities to adopt local laws creating Business Improvement Districts based on the creation of a district plan. District plans must include a map of the district; a description of the boundaries of the proposed district, along with present and proposed uses of land; cost estimates for proposed improvements; proposed sources of financing; an estimated implementation schedule, as well as proposed rules and regulations applicable to the district; a list of properties to be benefited; and a statement of the method by which the expenses of a district will be imposed upon benefited properties, in proportion to the benefits received by such properties, to defray the cost of implementation of the plan.[241]

Implementing Agreements

Agreements among governmental units to implement regional plans and monitor the results of those plans offer a possible model for neighborhood planning. Oregon statutes require counties and cities to enter into cooperative agreements with each special district that provides an urban service within an urban growth boundary. Agreements must describe the responsibilities of the respective governments for comprehensive planning, periodic review of land use regulations, and provision of urban services.[242]

An implementing agreement should describe (1) how the municipality will involve the neighborhood association or other participating nongovernmental organization in all phases of planning, including plan preparation, plan amendments, periodic review, and amendments to land use regulations; (2) the specific responsibilities of the neighborhood association in both the planning and implementation phases, including whether the neighborhood association will be responsible for writing all or a portion of the plan, and whether the neighborhood association will be expected to carry out all or a portion of the plan; (3) the relationship of neighborhood plans to citywide comprehensive plans; and (4) whether the neighborhood association will have a decision-making role in both the planning and implementation phases or whether its role will be advisory.[243] The implementing agreement also should establish rights and responsibilities with respect to expenditure of public funds, retention of staff and advisors, reporting requirements, and coordination with other interested parties.

Practitioner Perspectives

The important weight now given to land use planning in most jurisdictions suggests that the prudent practitioner should begin an analysis of a particular land use matter with the comprehensive plan for the applicable jurisdiction. If a separate document does not exist, the comprehensive zoning ordinance should be reviewed for its articulation of the community's planning goals. Planning decisions and their articulation in planning documents form an essential part of the land use regulatory process. They provide the rationale for exercise of the police power through land use regulation, as well as the link between the goals of the community (public purpose) and the means (regulatory techniques) chosen to achieve those goals.

The plan should be examined for consistency, both internally (the document itself) and externally (its implementation through specific land use regulatory decisions). Consistency means compatibility, so questions to be asked include whether the land use decision being sought or being questioned is compatible with the planning goals of the community, whether it furthers those goals, and whether it meets specific criteria that may be required before the particular decision can be made.[244] As noted earlier in this chapter, courts and legislatures are requiring local governments to take seriously their comprehensive plans when they make land use regulatory decisions.[245]

Because an extremely small percentage of land use decisions end up in court, an important question for the practitioner is, Whom do I really have to persuade to accomplish my client's objective?[246] That person may well be a planner on the staff of the local government planning office. An experienced land use practitioner in Oregon offers the following generalizations about planners:

> First, planners often have a peculiar perspective on law and lawyers. The planner is not likely to have any significant legal training, though

they might have taken a class called "Planning Law" in college. Planners often think they know more law than they really do. At the same time, planners also recognize the law (and lawyers) limit their official and professional discretion. The idea of the law having the "final say" is sometimes taken as a professional put-down—a relegation of planning to an inferior professional position to law. And lawyers make more money. Hence, consciously or otherwise, planners often resent statutes and ordinances and attorneys as somewhat negative forces that constrain them officially and professionally.

Second, planners are typically busy, hard-pressed, yelled-at, underappreciated.

Third, planners recognize that the policy and procedural framework within which they operate is not perfect. As a result, they are often a bit insecure about how they must make decisions. As a further result, they are always looking for a good reason, on a common-sense basis, why what they do or are being asked to do is a good thing to do.

Fourth, while planners recognize the policies they administer sometimes require them to say no, their basic training is to be facilitators—to make things happen, to resolve issues, to move things from square one to square two.

Fifth, because they are on the firing line so much, a planner is frequently someone who has a very low toleration of being publicly embarrassed.

Sixth, the planner is someone with considerable influence—with colleagues in the municipal planning office, with the planning commission or zoning board (or whatever it is called in your jurisdiction), and with the elected governing body, who in some instances may hear appeals of your matter. The planner is also someone who usually has periodic dealings and credibility with local media. The planner may even know the paper's editorial writers, or TV news reporters.[247]

The advice most often given by experienced practitioners is to deal with planners on a common-sense, rather than an adversarial, level. Although planners should know that the lawyer is a master of the relevant legal doctrine, it is better that the planner learn this by reputation rather than by lecture. The most important point is to persuade the planner that the project or objective being discussed is a good one, that it is in the best interests of the community, and that there is a genuine interest in identifying any problems that may be posed by the project or objective so that they may be resolved to the extent possible.

Because planners are busy professionals, practitioners can help move the review process along by sitting down with the planner and explaining the proposal in detail, explaining exactly what is being proposed, what land use policies apply to the proposal, and how they apply. As with other areas of practice, such as litigation and administrative proceedings, practitioners commonly prepare suggested reports, findings, orders, and the like. This is an important step in the process and should not be overlooked. A written submission, in the local format for staff reports, can be an extremely effective method of conveying desired information and professional evaluation to the planner responsible for preparing recommendations to the decision-making authority. There is nothing improper about lawyers who are proposing or opposing land use activities submitting draft recommendations to planning staff as long as the document is part of the public record and no effort is made to undermine the objectivity of the planning analysis by promises of favors, nondisclosure of material facts, or misrepresentation of facts or law.

Other important steps to take prior to the application stage of the land use process are identification of potential supporters and opponents, along with interested members of the media, and arranging discussions between the client and responsible members of community groups likely to be affected by the proposal: neighboring land owners, civic organizations, environmental groups, and the like. Frank discussions concerning strengths and weaknesses and a willingness to consider reasonable modifications to a proposal can have an extremely positive effect on the climate in which the proposal is evaluated. Because the land use process is political in both a good sense (policy choices are made) and a bad sense (fears and prejudices may be voiced), the temper of that climate will help define the public image of the proposal.[248]

The ability to appreciate the "other person's point of view" is an important ingredient in a successful neighborhood collaborative-planning effort. By its very nature, collaborative planning should involve all elements of the community in the planning process. The essence of this new version of grassroots planning is to be less confrontational and more collaborative. An appreciation for, and ability to include, all points of view is critical for success of the effort. Neighborhood collaborative planning must be inclusive if it is going to produce meaningful change in the way decisions are made. A system that confines the appointment or voting process to property owners, as statutory business or neighborhood improvement districts often do, is not inclusive because it leaves out renters and nonresident workers. An approach in which the city funds a group of staffers whose job is to organize neighborhood councils also fails to be inclusive. Perhaps the best solution is a system that encourages neighborhood residents to organize themselves, requires inclusivity of all interest groups, and offers funding and administrative support to enable the councils to choose their own staffs. [249]

Notes

1. Nollan v. California Coastal Comm'n, 483 U.S. 825 (1987); Lawton v. Steele, 152 U.S. 133, 137 (1894).

2. *See, e.g.,* FLA. STAT. § 163.3191(1) (2000) ("The planning program shall be a continuous and ongoing process."). The seminal work on the relationship of planning to zoning is Charles M. Haar, *In Accordance with a Comprehensive Plan,* 68 HARV. L. REV. 1154 (1955).

3. *See* chapters 4 and 5.

4. *See* chapter 8.

5. O'Loane v. O'Rourke, 42 Cal. Rptr. 283, 286 (1965) (quoting Angermeier v. Borough of Sea Girt, 142 A.2d 624, 629–30 (N.J. 1958)).

6. Bell v. City of Elkhorn, 364 N.W.2d 144, 148 (Wis. 1985).

7. West Montgomery County Citizens Ass'n v. Maryland-National Capital Park and Planning Comm'n, 522 A.2d 1328, 1334 (Md. 1987) (quoting Bd. of County Comm'rs v. Stephens, 408 A.2d 1017, 1019 (Md. 1979)).

8. Nollan v. California Coastal Comm'n, 483 U.S. 825, 836–37 (1987); *see also* Stoney-Brook Dev. Corp. v. Town of Fremont, 474 A.2d 561, 563 (N.H. 1984) (quoting Patenaude v. Town of Meredith, 392 A.2d 582, 585 (N.H. 1978) ("Comprehensive planning with a solid scientific, statistical basis is the key element in land use regulation in New Hampshire").

9. *See, e.g.*, Bell v. City of Elkhorn, *supra* n. 6, at 158; Columbia Oldsmobile, Inc. v. City of Montgomery, 564 N.E.2d. 455, 460 (Ohio 1990), *cert. denied*, 501 U.S. 1231, 111 S. Ct. 2854 (1991); State *ex rel.* Chiavola v. Village of Oakwood, 886 S.W.2d 74 (Mo. Ct. App. 1994), *cert. denied*, 514 U.S. 1078, 115 S. Ct. 1724 (1995).

10. Bell v. City of Elkhorn, *supra* n. 6, at 147 (quoting Lanphear v. Antwerp Township, 214 N.W.2d. 66 (Mich. 1973)). Connecticut has amended its state enabling legislation to provide expressly that local zoning regulations may not be enacted without a comprehensive plan as a separate document. Connecticut Public Act 92-50, approved May 25, 1992, CONN. GEN. STAT. ANN. § 8-2, n.39 (West 2001). Previously, Connecticut courts had held that the zoning ordinance itself could satisfy the requirement of the enabling statute that zoning regulations be made "in accordance with a comprehensive plan." *See also* Wolf v. City of Ely, 493 N.W.2d 846, 849 (Iowa 1992) (holding that while Iowa would remain in the majority of mandatory plan states that hold that "a plan external to the zoning ordinance is not required," there was no evidence on the record before it of any rational land use planning).

11. Udell v. Haas, 235 N.E.2d 897, 900–02 (N.Y. 1968). The New York state legislature subsequently has defined municipal comprehensive plans. *See, e.g.*, N.Y. GEN. CITY LAW § 28-a(3)(a) (McKinney 1995).

12. Edward J. Sullivan and Lawrence L. Kressel, *Twenty Years After—Renewed Significance of the Comprehensive Plan Requirement,* 9 URB. L. ANN. 33, 41 (1975).

13. Cited as best representing the unitary view is Kozesnik v. Township of Montgomery, 131 A.2d 1, 8 (N.J. 1957), holding that planning "may readily be revealed in the end product—here the zoning ordinance—and no more is required by the statute." Sullivan & Kressel, *supra* n. 12, at 42–44. New Jersey has since joined the mandatory-planning states. N.J. STAT. ANN. § 40:55D–62(a), *discussed in* Edward J. Sullivan and Thomas G. Pelham, *Report of the Comprehensive Planning and Growth Management Subcommittee,* 27 URB. LAW. 781, 793–97 (1995). *See also* State *ex. rel.* Chiavola v. Village of Oakwood, 886 S.W.2d 74, 79–82 (Mo. Ct. App. 1994), *cert. denied,* 514 U.S. 1078 (1995), *discussed in* Sullivan and Pelham, *supra*, at 791–93, reviewing decisions from Connecticut, Idaho, New Jersey, and New York in holding that the validity of a comprehensive zoning ordinance does not depend on the existence of a separate comprehensive plan.

14. The planning-factor theory is said to be best illustrated by *Udell v. Haas,* 235 N.E.2d 897 (N.Y. 1968), in which the court invalidated a downzoning enacted to frustrate a proposed commercial use. Sullivan & Kressel, *supra* n. 12, at 45–47. "Planning-factor" states include Alaska and Iowa. Sullivan & Pelham, *supra*, n. 13, at 782–84, 790–91. Rhode Island and South Carolina have moved by statutes from "planning-factor" to "plan" states. R.I. GEN. LAWS § 45-24-29(b)(2) (1999); S.C. CODE ANN. § 6-29-310 to -1200 (Law. Co-op. Supp. 1994). Sullivan and Pelham, *supra*, at 798–800.

15. *See* pp. 27–33.

16. Fasano v. Bd. of County Comm'rs, 507 P.2d 23 (Or. 1973), ushered in the planning mandate era with its rejection of a decision to anchor a floating zone because the decision was inconsistent with the adopted master plan. Sullivan & Kressel, *supra* n. 12, at 49–52. Other "plan states" include California, Florida, New Jersey, Rhode Island, South Carolina, and Washington. Sullivan & Pelham, *supra* n. 13, at 784–91, 793–97, 798–800.

17. Edward J. Sullivan, *The Comprehensive Plan: Two Steps Forward and One Step Back,* in Richard J. Roddewig, *Recent Developments in Land Use, Planning and Zoning,* 21 URB. LAW. 769, 834–40 (1989).

18. Edward J. Sullivan, *The Evolving Role of the Comprehensive Plan*, 32 Urb. Law. 813, 814 (2000).

19. *See* pp. 27–33.

20. *See, e.g.*, N.Y. Gen. Mun. La., § 234 (McKinney 2000); Mo. Rev. Stat. § 89.310 (1998); Pa. Stat. Ann. tit. 53, § 10201 (West 1997); Wis. Stat. Ann. §§ 62.23(1), (2) (West 2001).

21. Bell v. City of Elkhorn, 364 N.W.2d 144, 147 (Wis. 1985), (citing D. Mandelker, Land Use Law, § 3.14, at 57 (1982), and explanatory note to § 3 of the Standard State Zoning Enabling Act commenting that the requirement that zoning be in accordance with a comprehensive plan "will prevent haphazard or piecemeal zoning. No zoning should be done without such a comprehensive study." ALI, A Model Land Development Code (Tentative Draft No. 1, app. A, 215 (1968)).

22. Standard City Planning Enabling Act, U.S. Dep't of Commerce 1928, *reproduced as* ALI, A Model Land Development Code, app. B (Tentative Draft No. 1, 1968).

23. Standard State Zoning Enabling Act, U.S. Dep't of Commerce (1922).

24. Discussed in chapter 8.

25. Discussed on pp. 43–44.

26. Discussed on pp. 44–47.

27. Standard City Planning Enabling Act, General Statement (U.S. Dep't of Commerce, 1928), *reproduced as* ALI, A Model Land Development Code, app. B, at 222 (Tentative Draft No. 1, 1968).

28. *See, e.g.*, Mo. Rev. Stat. §§ 89.300–.490 (Vernon 1998 & Supp. 2002).

29. ALI, A Model Land Development Code, Proposed Official Draft commentary on art. 3, at 127–28 (1975).

30. *Id.* at 129, *citing* William Wheaton, *Operations Research for Metropolitan Planning*, 25 J. Am. Inst. Planners 250 (1963).

31. Pa. Stat. Ann. tit. 53, § 10301 (West 1997). Dr. Wheaton had argued in his 1963 study for greater attention to the economic and social consequences that might flow from a particular development pattern. Wheaton, *supra* n. 30.

32. Lanphear v. Antwerp Township, 214 N.W.2d 66, 70 (Mich. 1973) (*quoted with approval in* Bell v. City of Elkhorn, 364 N.W.2d 144, 147–48 (Wis. 1985)); *see also* Columbia Oldsmobile, Inc. v. City of Montgomery, 564 N.E.2d 455, 460 (Ohio 1990), *cert. denied*, 501 U.S. 1231, 111 S. Ct. 2854 (1991) (permissive planning legislation does not require a formal adoption of comprehensive plan as a condition to the exercise of the zoning power).

33. Asian-Americans for Equality v. Koch, 527 N.E.2d 265, 270–71 (N.Y. 1988).

34. American Planning Association, Growing Smart[SM] Legislative Guidebook xii–xiv (Stuart Meck ed., 2002). The model statutes and continuum are discussed in detail in chapter 2 of the Guidebook.

35. *See, e.g.*, Alaska Stat. § 29.40.010(a) (Michie 2001); Cal. Gov't Code §§ 65100, 65103 (West 2001); Fla. Stat. Ann. § 163.3167 (West 2001); Idaho Code § 67-6503 (Michie 2001) Me. Rev. Stat. Ann. tit. 30-A, §§ 4323, 4324 (West 2001); Or. Rev. Stat. § 197.175 (2001); Wash. Rev. Code Ann. §§ 36.70A.040, 36.70A.070 (West 2002).

36. Or. Rev. Stat. § 197.225 (2001).

37. Neb. Rev. Stat. § 19-901(2) (2001); Village of McGrew v. Steidley, 305 N.W.2d 627 (Neb. 1981) (comprehensive zoning ordinance invalidated for failure of village to adopt a comprehensive development plan prior to enactment of the ordinance).

38. N.J. Stat. Ann. § 40:55D-62 (West 2002).

39. 53 Pa. Con. Stat. Ann. §§ 10209.1, 10302. *Cf. In re* deBotton, 474 A.2d. 706, 712, n. †7 (Pa. Commw. Ct. 1984); Forks Township Bd. of Supervisors v. George Calantoni & Sons, 297 A.2d 164, 166–67 (Pa. Commw. Ct. 1972) ("The comprehensive plan is a general guideline to the legislative body of the municipality for its consideration of the municipality's program

of land utilization and the needs and desires of the community. . . . [A] comprehensive plan is abstract and recommendatory; whereas the zoning ordinance is specific and regulatory.").

40. 53 PA. CON. STAT. ANN. § 10606. The Pennsylvania legislature apparently backed away from its earlier mandatory language ("shall contain a statement") in favor of the more exhortatory "should" after courts refused to invalidate zoning ordinances for failure to include the requisite statement of community development objectives. McClimans v. Bd. of Supervisors, 529 A.2d. 562 (Pa. Commw. Ct. 1987); *In re* deBotton, 474 A.2d. 706, 712 (Pa. Commw. Ct. 1984) ("For this Court to invalidate the ordinance merely because it does not contain a cross-reference to the Township's Land Use Plan would be to raise form over substance"). *See generally* David W. Sweet & Lee P. Symons, *Pennsylvania's New Municipalities Planning Code: Policy, Politics and Impact Fees*, 94 DICK. L. REV. 61, 72 (1989).

41. CAL. GOV'T CODE § 65302 (West 1997).

42. CAL. GOV'T CODE § 65303 (West 1997).

43. FLA. STAT. ANN. § 163.3177(1) (West 2000).

44. *Id.* §§ 163.3177 (2)–(7).

45. *Id.* § 163.3177 (4)(a).

46. *Id.* § 163.3202(2)(g). *See generally* Thomas G. Pelham, *Adequate Public Facilities Requirements: Reflections on Florida's Concurrency System for Managing Growth*, 19 FLA. ST. U. L. REV. 973 (1992).

47. FLA. STAT. ANN. § 163.3167 (2)(b) (West 2000).

48. *Id.* § 163.3177 (9).

49. *Id.* § 163.3177 (10)(a).

50. Martin County v. Yusem, 690 So. 2d 1288, 1295 (Fla. 1997), *quoted in* Martin County v. Section 28 Partnership, 772 So. 2d 616, 619 (Fla. App. 2000). *See gen. infra.* chapter 4. *See also* Minnaugh v. Broward County, 783 So. 2d 1054, 1055 (Fla. 2001) (decisions about small-scale development amendments under § 163.3187(1)(c) are legislative in nature and subject to the fairly debatable standard of review).

51. Paedae v. Escambia County, 709 So. 2d 575 (Fla. App. 1998).

52. OR. REV. STAT. § 197.225 (2001).

53. OR. ADMIN. R. 660–15–000 11 (2002).

54. OR. REV. STAT. §§ 197.175(2); 215.050 (2001).

55. *Id.* § 197.340(1).

56. *Id.* §§ 197.250, 197.251(1).

57. Lane County v. Land Conservation and Development Comm'n, 942 P.2d 278 (Or. 1997). *See also*, Jackson County Citizens' League v. Jackson County, 15 P.3d 42, 49 (Or. Ct. App. 2000) (construing *Lane County* and holding that while the LCDC may limit permissible uses under zoning-enabling statutes, until it does so, statutory permitted uses remain in effect).

58. OR. REV. STAT. §§ 197.805–860. *See* Mary J. Deits and Martin B. Vidgoff, *There's Something About LUBA (Land Use Board of Appeals)*, 36 WILLIAMETTE L. REV. 431 (2000); Edward J. Sullivan, *Reviewing the Reviewer: The Impact of the Land Use Board of Appeals on the Oregon Land Use Program, 1979-1999*, 36 WILLIAMETTE L. REV. 441 (2000).

59. MO. REV. STAT. § 89.340 (1998).

60. CAL. GOV'T CODE § 65100 (West 1997).

61. FLA. STAT. ANN. § 163.3174 (West 2000).

62. *See infra* chapter 6.

63. *See, e.g.* Martin County v. Yusem, 690 So. 2d 1288 (Fla. 1997) (amendments to comprehensive plans are legislative decisions subject to the fairly debatable standard of review); Section 28 Partnership, Ltd. v. Martin County, 642 So. 2d 609 (Fla. Dist. Ct. App. 1994), *rev. denied*, 654 So. 2d 920 (Fla. 1995) (county's decision not to amend its comprehensive plan was legislative rather than quasi-judicial). Judicial review of planning and zoning decisions is discussed in chapter 6.

64. *See, e.g.,* FLA. STAT. ANN. § 163.3202 (West 2000) (requiring the adoption of local land development regulations "to implement the adopted comprehensive plan"); Asian-Americans for Equality v. Koch, 527 N.E.2d 265, 270 (N.Y. 1988) ("function of land regulation is to implement a plan for the future development of the community"—New York is a "planning-factor" rather than a "planning-mandate" state); Fasano v. Bd. of County Comm'rs, 507 P.2d 23 (Or. 1973).

65. *See, e.g.,* Younger v. City of Portland, 752 P.2d 262, 269 (Or. 1988).

66. *See, e.g.,* Riggs v. Long Beach Township, 538 A.2d 808, 812 (N.J. 1988) (invalidating a downzoning because of an improper purpose related to the planned acquisition of the site for open-space purposes).

67. 538 A.2d 808 (N.J. 1988).

68. *Id.* at 813–14.

69. N.J. STAT. ANN. §§ 40:55D-1 *et seq.* (West 2001).

70. *Riggs,* 538 A.2d. at 817 (Handler, J., concurring).

71. OR. REV. STAT. §§ 197.805–860 (2001).

72. N.J. STAT. ANN. §§ 52:27D–301 *et seq.* (West 2001).

73. Younger v. City of Portland, 752 P.2d 262, 269 (Or. 1988). *See generally* Sullivan, *The Comprehensive Plan: Two Steps Forward and One Step Back, reprinted in* Roddewig, *Recent Developments in Land Use, Planning and Zoning,* 21 URB. LAW. 769, 834–40 (1989).

74. OR. REV. STAT. § 197.825 (2001).

75. N.J. STAT. ANN. § 52:27D–307 (West 2001). The constitutionality of the New Jersey Fair Housing Act establishing the council was upheld in *Hills Dev. Co. v. Bernards Township,* 510 A.2d 621 (N.J. 1986). *See* chapter 9 *infra.*

76. *See, e.g.,* Haines v. City of Phoenix, 727 P.2d 339 (Ariz. Ct. App. 1986), *discussed in* Edward J. Sullivan, *The Comprehensive Plan as Law, in* Linda Bozung, *Land Use, Planning and Zoning in 1987: A National Survey,* 19 URB. LAW. 899, 972–74 (1987) (rejecting quasi-judicial characterization of zoning in line of cases from *Fasano v. Board of County Comm'rs,* 507 P.2d 23 (Or. 1973) and adopting a qualified rational basis standard of review in which the test is whether "from the evidence before it the city council could have determined that the rezoning was in basic harmony with the general plan"). *See also* LaBonta v. City of Waterville, 528 A.2d 1262 (Me. 1987); Green v. County Council, 508 A.2d 882 (Del. Ch. 1986), *aff'd,* 516 A.2d. 480 (Del. 1986).

77. Green v. County Council, *supra,* n. 76, at 890; Southwest Ranches Homeowners Ass'n v. Broward County, 502 So. 2d. 931, 936 (Fla. Dist. Ct. App. 1987).

78. Green v. County Council, *supra,* n. 76, at 891.

79. County Council v. Green, 516 A.2d. 480, 481 (Del. 1986).

80. NEV. REV. STAT. § 278.250 (2001).

81. Enterprise Citizens v. Clark Co. Comm'rs, 918 P. 2d 305 (Nev. 1996).

82. County of Clark v. Doumani, 952 P.2d 13 (Nev. 1998).

83. IDAHO CODE §§ 67-6501 *et seq.*

84. Sprenger, Grubb & Assocs. v. City of Hailey, 986 P.2d 343, 345 (Idaho 1999).

85. Urrutia v. Blaine County, 2 P.3d 738, 743–44 (Idaho 2000).

86. *See* chapter 4.

87. Southwest Ranches Homeowners Ass'n v. Broward County, *supra,* n. 77, at 936 (stricter scrutiny than "fairly debatable" standard applied to decisions permitting more-intensive uses than contemplated by plan, but legislative scheme calls for more flexibility than permitted under strict adherence to plan standard).

88. Machado v. Musgrove, 519 So. 2d. 629 (Fla. Dist. Ct. App. 1987) (applying strict judicial scrutiny, trial court rejection of rezoning affirmed because proposed use was inconsistent with neighborhood study element of comprehensive plan); City of Cape Canaveral v. Mosher, 467 So. 2d. 468 (Fla. Dist. Ct. App. 1985). *See generally* Edward J. Sullivan, *The*

State of the Comprehensive Land-Use Plan in 1987, reprinted in Linda Bozung, *Recent Developments in Environmental Preservation and the Rights of Property Owners,* 20 URB. LAW. 969, 971–75 (1988).

89. O'Loane v. O'Rourke, 42 Cal. Rptr. 283, 288 (Cal. Ct. App. 1965).

90. Peter Abeles, *Planning and Zoning,* in CHARLES M. HAAR AND JEROLD S. KAYDEN, ZONING AND THE AMERICAN DREAM 126 (1989). The author, president of a planning consultant firm in New York City, noted that disputes over land use planning alternatives "have given rise to a group of planners whose professional task is to counter the master plans." *Id.*

91. Quinn v. Town of Dodgeville, 354 N.W.2d. 747, 753 (Wis. 1984), *aff'd,* 364 N.W.2d 149 (Wis. 1985) (quoting WIS. STAT. ANN. § 59.97 (3)(d)). The early focus of planning on end-state master plans was criticized severely in the 1960s and 1970s as based on an unrealistic assumption that a community "has a clear vision of an end state for itself and that little, if anything, can happen to mar that vision." Jan Z. Krasnowiecki, *The Basic System of Land Use Control, reprinted in* NORMAN MARCUS AND MARILYN W. GROVES, THE NEW ZONING 4 (1970). *See also* ALI, A MODEL LAND DEVELOPMENT CODE (Proposed Official Draft 132, 1975) ("In the view of many planners, . . . few [master] plans have had a demonstrable impact on development").

92. West Montgomery County Citizens Ass'n v. Maryland-National Capital Park & Planning Comm'n, 522 A.2d 1328, 1334 (Md. 1987) (quoting Montgomery County v. Woodward & Lothrop, 376 A.2d. 483 (Md. 1977), *cert. denied,* 434 U.S. 1067 (1978)).

93. *See, e.g.,* Russ Bldg. Partnership v. City & County of San Francisco, 234 Cal. Rptr. 1, 6 (Cal. Ct. App. 1987), *aff'd in part & rev'd in part on other grounds,* 750 P.2d 324 (Cal.), *appeal dismissed,* 488 U.S. 881 (1988) (upholding transit impact-fee ordinance and noting the city's use of consultants, numerous studies, and public hearings to determine the reasonable costs of increased transit services necessitated by downtown development).

94. Camp v. Mendocino County Bd. of Supervisors, 176 Cal. Rptr. 620, 630, n.8 (1981) (noncompliance of land use, housing, and noise elements with statutory requirements invalidated comprehensive plan).

95. Wheaton, *Zoning and Land Use Planning: An Economic Perspective,* in C. HAAR AND J. KAYDEN, ZONING AND THE AMERICAN DREAM 324 (1989).

96. Of course, the problem of judicial deference to a legislatively adopted plan would then surface. *See, e.g.,* Selby Realty Co. v. City of San Buenaventura, 109 Cal. Rptr. 799 (1973) (adoption of a master plan is a legislative act for which declaratory relief is not available "to probe the merits of the plan absent allegation of a defect in the proceedings leading to its enactment") .

97. Abeles, *Planning and Zoning,* in C. HAAR AND J. KAYDEN, ZONING AND THE AMERICAN DREAM 126 (1989). *See generally* chapter 4, *infra.*

98. Mo. REV. STAT. § 89.144 (West 1998) (two miles).

99. CAL. GOV'T CODE § 65300 (West 1997 & Supp. 2002); N.Y. GEN. MUN. LAW § 237 (McKinney 1999).

100. FLA. STAT. ANN. § 163.3171 (West 2000). For a discussion of the issues that arise when one governmental body with zoning jurisdiction attempts to regulate property owned by another governmental or quasi-governmental body, *see* pp. 139–141 and 278, *infra.*

101. *See, e.g.,* MO. REV. STAT. § 89.320 (West 2001); N.Y. GEN. MUN. LAW § 234 (McKinney 1999).

102. Standard City Planning Enabling Act (U.S. Dep't. of Commerce 1928), *reproduced as* ALI, A MODEL LAND DEVELOPMENT CODE, app. B (Tentative Draft No. 1, 1968).

103. ALI, A MODEL LAND DEVELOPMENT CODE (Proposed Official Draft 1975).

104. Mo. REV. STAT. § 89.350 (2001).

105. AMERICAN PLANNING ASSOCIATION, GROWING SMART^{SM} LEGISLATIVE GUIDEBOOK §§ 7-32 to 7-38 (Stuart Meck ed., 2002).

106. *See, e.g.,* MO. REV. STAT. § 89.320 (2002); N.Y. GEN. MUN. LAW § 234 (McKinney 1999); N.J. STAT. ANN. § 40:55D-23 (West 2002); PA. STAT. ANN. tit. 53, § 10205 (West 1997).

107. Brennan v. Town of Colchester, 730 A.2d 601, 603 (Vt. 1999).

108. Allan-Deane Corp. v. Township of Bedminister, 379 A.2d 265, 267, *cert. denied,* 377 A.2d 676 (N.J. 1977) (local planning boards are subject to state Open Public Meetings Act).

109. *See, e.g.,* MO. REV. STAT. § 89.330 (2001); 53 PA. CONS. STAT. ANN. § 10209(1)(10) (West 1997); Whiteland Woods, L.P. v. Township of West Whiteland, 193 F.3d 177, 183–84 (3d Cir. 1999). State statutes, though, may require videotaping to be permitted. *Id.* at 178.

110. *See, e.g.,* Polillo v. Deane, 379 A.2d 211, 214–16 (N.J. 1977) (discussing history and purpose of "sunshine" laws).

111. Telegraph Herald, Inc. v. City of Dubuque, 297 N.W.2d 529, 533–34 (Iowa 1980) (reviewing cases). *See also* Adler v. City Council of Culver City, 7 Cal. Rptr. 805 (Cal. Ct. App. 1960) (dinner hosted by developer who later applied for variance and attended by eight of nine members of planning commission was not a meeting within purview of open meetings law).

112. MO. REV. STAT. § 89.340 (2001). *See also* West Montgomery County Citizens Ass'n v. Maryland-National Capital Park & Planning Comm'n, 522 A.2d 1328, 1337 (Md. 1987).

113. *See* chapter 5, *infra.*

114. *See, e.g.,* CONN. GEN. STAT. § 8-2 (West 2001); Dram Assoc. v. Planning & Zoning Comm'n, 574 A.2d 1317, 1319 (Conn. App. Ct. 1990) (planning and zoning commission has broad discretion when acting in its legislative capacity).

115. *See, e.g.,* CAL. GOV'T CODE §§ 65850 *et seq.* (West 1997); FLA. STAT. ANN. § 163.3202 (West 1999); MD. CODE ANN. art. 66B, § 4.02 (2002); MO. REV. STAT. § 89.020 (1998); N.J. STAT. ANN. § 40:55D-62 (West 2002); N.Y. GEN. CITY LAW §§ 20.24–25 (McKinney 1999).

116. West Montgomery County Citizens Ass'n. v. Maryland-National Capital Park & Planning Comm'n, 522 A.2d 1328, 1336 (Md. 1987) (discussing examples of acceptable "carefully limited and directed delegations of zoning authority"). *See generally* chapter 5, *infra.*

117. *See, e.g.,* ARK. STAT. ANN. § 14-56-417 (Michie 2001); Richardson v. City of Little Rock Planning Comm'n., 747 S.W.2d 116 (Ark. 1988) (planning commission exceeded authority by denying approval of preliminary plat on considerations other than minimum standards of subdivision ordinance); TENN. CODE ANN. § 13-4-302 (2001); West Meade Homeowners Ass'n v. WPMC, Inc., 788 S.W.2d 365, 367 (Tenn. Ct. App. 1989) (suit to enjoin subdivision of land held premature because planning commission had not approved nor even considered an application for approval of a subdivision plat). *See generally* chapter 8, *infra.*

118. *See, e.g.,* N.J. STAT. ANN. § 40:55D-37 (West 2002). *See generally* chapter 8, *infra.*

119. *See, e.g.,* Guinnane v. San Francisco Planning Comm'n, 257 Cal. Rptr. 742, 747, *cert. denied,* 493 U.S. 936, 110 S. Ct. 329 (1989) (planning commission authorized by charter to exercise independent discretionary review of building permit application).

120. West Meade Homeowners Ass'n v. WPMC, Inc., 788 S.W.2d 365 (Tenn. Ct. App. 1989).

121. The transferable development rights concept is discussed in chapter 4, *infra.*

122. Agricultural lands preservation programs are discussed in chapter 10, *infra.*

123. *West Montgomery County Citizens Ass'n, supra* n. 116.

124. *See, e.g.,* MO. REV. STAT. § 89.330 (1998); N.Y. GEN. MUN. LAW § 235 (McKinney 2002).

125. *See, e.g.,* CAL. GOV'T CODE § 65100 (West 1997); FLA. STAT. ANN. § 163.3174 (West 2001).

126. *See, e.g.,* MD. CODE ANN. art. 66B, § 3.04 (2001) (Commission may appoint "employees necessary for its work").

127. *See, e.g.,* St. Louis County Charter, §§ 4.030, 4.240–.260 (1979) (planning commission exists within department of planning; director of department manages department and appoints employees under the merit system in accordance with provisions of charter and applicable ordinances). *See generally* ALI, A MODEL LAND DEVELOPMENT CODE, 35 (Tentative Draft No. 1, 1968) (60 percent of 427 cities surveyed in 1963 hired professional staff through executive department rather than independent commission); *Id.* (Proposed Official Draft 144–46, 1975) (reviewing criticism, as well as use, of independent planning commission and concluding that local governments should retain option of choosing the preferable approach).

128. CAL. GOV'T CODE § 65100 (West 1997); FLA. STAT. ANN. § 163.3174 (West 2001).

129. Bell v. City of Elkhorn, 364 N.W.2d 144, 148 (Wis. 1985); *West Montgomery County Citizens Ass'n, supra* n. 116, at 1337.

130. *See* chapter 5 *infra* (review by planning agency).

131. O'Loane v. O'Rourke, 42 Cal. Rptr. 283, 288–89 (Cal. Dist. Ct. App. 1965).

132. *Id.* at 288.

133. CAL. GOV'T CODE § 65300 (West 1997), FLA. STAT. ANN. §§ 163.3167, .3174 (West 2001).

134. *See, e.g.,* CAL. GOV'T CODE § 65300 (West 1997) ("comprehensive, long-term general plan"); FLA. STAT. ANN. § 163.3167 (West 2001) ("comprehensive plan"); MD. CODE ANN. art. 28, § 7-108 2001 (master plan); MO. REV. STAT. § 89.340 (1998) ("city plan"); NEB. REV. STAT. § 19-903 (2001) ("comprehensive development plan"); N.Y. GEN. MUN. LAW § 236 (McKinney 2002); WIS. STAT. ANN. § 62.23 (West 2001) ("master plan").

135. *See, e.g.,* CAL. GOV'T CODE §§ 65300, 65302 (West 1997); MO. REV. STAT. §89.340 (1998).

136. *See, e.g.,* FLA. STAT. ANN. § 163.3177 (1) (West 2000); N.J. STAT. ANN. § 40:55D-28 (West 2002).

137. CAL. GOV'T CODE § 65302 (West 1997); FLA. STAT. ANN. § 163.3177 (West 2000).

138. CAL. GOV'T CODE § 65302 (f) (West 1997).

139. *Id.* §65302 (g).

140. FLA. STAT. ANN. § 163.3177 (g) (West 2000).

141. *See, e.g., id.* §§ 163.3177 (2)–(3).

142. AMERICAN PLANNING ASSOCIATION, GROWING SMART℠ LEGISLATIVE GUIDEBOOK §§ 7-70 to 7-195 (Stuart Meck ed., 2002).

143. CAL. GOV'T CODE § 65351 (West 1997).

144. *Id.* § 65351.

145. *Id.* § 65354.

146. *Id.* § 65355. When a planning agency that is separate from the local legislative body makes a recommendation to the legislative body regarding a proposed amendment to an approved general plan, interested parties may file a written request for a hearing before the legislative body within five days of the planning agency's action. *Id.* § 65355.5.

147. *Id.* § 65352.

148. *Id.* § 65356.

149. FLA. STAT. ANN. § 163.3184 (15) (West 2000).

150. *Id.* §§ 163.3184 (3), (4), and (6).

151. *Id.* § 163.3184 (5).

152. *Id.* §§ 163.3184 (7)–(9).

153. *Id.* § 163.3184 (10).

154. *Id.* § 163.3184 (11).

155. MO. REV. STAT. § 89.360 (1998).

156. NEV. REV. STAT. §§ 278.210, 278.220, *construed in* Falcke v. County of Douglas, 3 P.3d 661, 664 (Nev. 2000).

157. *See, e.g.,* Pop Realty Corp. v. Springfield Bd. of Adjustment, 423 A.2d 688, 695 (N.J. Super. Ct. Law Div. 1980) (enabling legislation requirement that report be received from zoning commission, planning board, or planning commission before enactment of zoning ordinance is mandatory).

158. State *ex rel.* Casey's Gen. Stores, Inc. v. City of Louisiana, 734 S.W.2d 890, 895–96 (Mo. Ct. App. 1987).

159. CAL. GOV'T CODE § 65400 (West 1997).

160. *Id.* § 65401.

161. *Id.* § 65402.

162. FLA. STAT. ANN. § 163.3191 (1) (West 2000).

163. *Id.* § 163.3191.

164. O'Loane v. O'Rourke, 42 Cal. Rptr. 283, 288 (Cal. Dist. Ct. App. 1965).

165. *See* chapter 4 *infra. See also* NEV. REV. STAT. § 278.250 (2001); County of Clark v. Doumani, 952 P.2d 13, 17–18 (Nev. 1998) (district court determination that town board abused its discretion by failing to give deference to the master plan when it denied a rezoning request for an allowable density in compliance with the master plan upheld).

166. Coffey v. Maryland-National Capital Park & Planning Comm'n, 441 A.2d. 1041, 1044 (Md. 1982); Camp v. Mendocino County Bd. of Supervisors, 176 Cal. Rptr. 620, 636 (1981). *But see* Urrutia v. Blaine County, 2 P.3d 738, 744 (Idaho 2000) (denial of subdivision application solely because of noncompliance with comprehensive plan overturned). *See generally* chapter 8, *infra.*

167. *See, e.g.,* State *ex rel.* Casey's General Stores, Inc. v. City of Louisiana, 734 S.W.2d. 890 (Mo. Ct. App. 1987).

168. *See, e.g.,* MO. REV. STAT. § 89.380 (1998).

169. Enterprise Partners v. County of Perkins, 619 N.W. 2d 464, 467 (Neb. 2000); Love v. Bd. of County Comm'rs, 671 P.2d 471 (Idaho 1983); Fasano v. Bd. of County Comm'rs, 507 P.2d 23 (Or. 1973).

170. *See, e.g.,* Land Waste Mgmt. v. Contra Costa County Bd. of Supervisors, 271 Cal. Rptr. 909, 914 (Cal. Ct. App. 1990).

171. FLA. STAT. ANN. §§ 163.3194, 163.323 (West 2000).

172. Martin County v. Yusem, 690 So. 2d 1288 (Fla. 1997); Martin County v. Section 28 Partnership, 772 So. 2d 616, 621 (Fla. Dist. Ct. App. 2000) (county's decision not to amend plan upheld). *See also* Minnaugh v. Broward County, 783 So. 2d 1054, 1055 (Fla. 2001) (decisions about small-scale development amendments under Section 163.3187(1)(c) are legislative in nature and are subject to the fairly debatable standard of review).

173. Paedae v. Escambia County, 709 So. 2d 575, 578 (Fla. Dist. Ct. App. 1998).

174. N.J. STAT. ANN. § 40:55D-62 (West 2002); Baptist Home Borough of Riverton, 492 A.2d 1100, 1104–05 (1984) (municipality not required to adopt zoning ordinance, but may do so only with the participation of a planning board).

175. N.J. STAT. ANN. § 40:55D–62.a (West 2002).

176. Route 15 Assocs. v. Jefferson Township, 455 A.2d 518, 521 (N.J. Super. Ct. App. Div. 1982).

177. *See* pp. 27–32.

178. *See, e.g.,* Bell v. City of Elkhorn, 364 N.W.2d 144, 158 (Wis. 1985).

179. *Id.* For an example of a generalized and substantive attack on a municipal zoning ordinance, *see* East Marlborough Township v. Jensen, 590 A.2d 1321 (Pa. Commw. 1991), in which a mall developer unsuccessfully attacked a town's zoning ordinance on the grounds that it did not set aside a fair share of property for rental housing, multihousing units, and commercial development. The court held that the comprehensive zoning ordinance need not call for a "fair share" of any specific and discrete use such as a shopping

center. *Id.* at 1322. The court applied a three-part analysis to determine the "fair share" issue: (1) whether the community in question is a logical area for development and population growth; (2) the present level of development within the particular community; and (3) whether the challenged zoning scheme was exclusionary or whether there was any other evidence of a primary purpose to zone out the natural growth of population. *Id.* at 1323. The court held that these standards in no way required equal shares of both residential and commercial development.

180. *See, e.g.,* Headley v. City of Rochester, 5 N.E.2d 198 (N.Y. 1936) (upholding official map statute as serving valid public purpose).

181. *See, e.g.,* West Meade Homeowners Ass'n v. WPMC, Inc., 788 S.W.2d 365, 366–67 (Tenn. Ct. App. 1989) (right-of-way drawn on official map is evidence that right-of-way has been accepted by municipality).

182. *See, e.g.,* Zale Constr. Co. v. Hoffman, 494 N.E.2d 830, 836 (Ill. App. Ct. 1986) ("final approval for a subdivision plat is conditioned on compliance with such official map of comprehensive plan.").

183. West Meade Homeowners Ass'n v. WPMC, 788 S.W.2d 365 (Tenn. Ct. App. 1989).

184. *See, e.g.,* Howard County v. JJM, Inc., 482 A.2d 908 (Md. 1984); Ventures in Property I v. City of Wichita, 594 P.2d 671 (Kan. 1979); Miller v. City of Beaver Falls, 82 A.2d 34 (Pa. 1951).

185. *See* pp. 35–42.

186. *See* chapter 4, *infra.*

187. *See* pp. 43–44.

188. *See, e.g.,* Cal. Gov't Code §§ 65060 *et seq.* (West 1997); Fla. Stat. Ann. §§ 186.501 *et seq.* (West 2000) (regional planning), 187.101 *et seq.* (state comprehensive plan), 380.032 (state land-planning agency), 380.05 (areas of critical state concern), 380.06 (developments of regional impact); N.J. Stat. Ann. §§ 40:55D-84 (West 1991 & Supp. 2002) (regional planning boards), 52:18A-196 *et seq.* (state planning); 52:27D-301 *et seq.* (regional fair share housing plans); Or. Rev. Stat. §§ 197.030 (1995) (state Land Conservation and Development Commission), 197.025 (regional coordination of planning activities), 197.225 (statewide planning goals); 53 Pa. Cons. Stat. Ann. §§ 2341 *et seq.* (West 1997) (regional planning).

189. N.J. Stat. Ann. §§ 13:18A-8 *et seq.* (West 1991 & Supp. 1997).

190. Lane County v. Land Conservation and Dev. Comm'n, 942 P.2d 278, 285 (Or. 1997), quoting Or. Rev. Stat. § 197.230.

191. Or. Rev. Stat. § 197.225 (2001).

192. *Id.* § 197.405.

193. Lane County v. Land Conservation and Dev. Comm'n, 942 P.2d 278, 285–86 (Or. 1997) (LCDC did not exceed its authority in adopting additional restrictions on "high-value farmland" (emphasis in original).

194. Or. Rev. Stat. §§ 197.030, 197.175, 197.190, 197.225, 197.805–.860 (1995).

195. Wash. Rev. Code Ann. §§ 36.70A.010 *et seq.* (West 1991).

196. Skagit Surveyors and Engineers, L.L.C. v. Friends of Skagit County, 958 P. 2d 962, 964 (Wash. 1998), citing Richard L. Settle & Charles G. Gavigan, *The Growth Management Revolution in Washington: Past, Present, and Future,* 16 U. Puget Sound L. Rev. 867, 880 (1993); Jeffrey M. Eustis, *Between Scylla and Charybdis: Growth Management Act Implementation That Avoids Takings and Substantive Due Process Limitations,* 16 U. Puget Sound L. Rev. 1181, 1185 (1993).

197. Wash. Rev. Code Ann. § 36.70A.040 requires urban and urbanizing counties to adopt comprehensive land use plans and implementing development regulations. Other counties may choose to plan under § 36.70A.040. *See* Moore v. Whitman County, 18 P.3d 566, 568–69 (Wa. 2001) (statute needs no judicial "interpretation").

198. Skagit Surveyors, *supra*, n. 196, at 964–65, quoting Wash. Rev. Code Ann. §§ 36.70A.020 (West 1991) (legislative goals), 36.70A.040 (mandatory planning), 36.70A.070 (required elements of county plans include (1) land use, (2) housing, (3) capital facilities, (4) utilities, (5) rural areas, and (6) transportation).

199. *Id.* at 965, quoting Wash. Rev. Code Ann. § 36.70A-110(1).

200. Wash Rev. Code Ann. §§ 36.70A.300(2) (now .302) (invalidation), 36.70A.330(3) (economic sanctions).

201. *Skagit Surveyers, supra* n. 196. *See also* Association of Rural Residents v. Kitsap County, 4 P.3d 115, 118–19 (Wash. 2000) (county's interim urban growth area was not in effect when developer submitted completed application, thus preexisting zoning ordinance governed).

202. King County v. Central Puget Sound Growth Mgm't Hearings Bd., 14 P.3d 133, 141–43 (Wash. 2000).

203. Fla. Stat. Ann. §§ 187.101 *et seq.* (West 2000).

204. *Id.* §§ 380.05, 380.06.

205. N.J. Stat. Ann. §§ 52:18A-202, -202.1 (West 2001).

206. *See* pp. 28–34, *supra*.

207. Fla. Stat. Ann. § 380.06 (West 2000).

208. *Id.* § 380.05.

209. An Act to Create an Environmental Board and District Environmental Commissions, 1969 Vt. Acts & Resolves 250, Vt. Stat. Ann. tit. 10, §§ 6001–6108 (1997 & Supp. 2001).

210. *Id.* at § 6086.

211. *Id.* at § 6089(4)(b).

212. *In re* Kisiel, 772 A.2d 135, 143 (Vt. 2000). *See also In re* Wal-Mart Stores, Inc., 702 A.2d 397, 404 (Vt. 1997) (upholding Board's denial of development permits in small town.) Commentators have criticized Act 250 as ineffective in managing growth in Vermont because of its "reactive" nature and the lack of a statewide plan for development. *See* Justin Shoemake, Note, *The Smalling of America?: Growth Management Statutes and the Dormant Commerce Clause*, 48 Duke L. J. 891, 904 (1999), citing J. Barry Cullingworth, The Political Culture of Planning: American Land Use Planning in Comparative Perspective 139 (1993); Jessica E. Jay, Note, *The "Malling" of Vermont: Can the "Growth Center" Designation Save the Traditional Village from Suburban Sprawl?*, 21 Vt. L. Rev. 929, 950 (1997), and discussing potential application of the Commerce Clause to Wal-Mart–type cases.

213. Ga. Code Ann. § 50-8-1 (2000). *See* John M. Degrove, The New Frontier for Land Policy: Planning and Growth Management in the States 99–106 (1992); David L. Callies, *The Quiet Revolution Revisited: A Quarter Century of Progress,* 26 Urb. Law. 197, 205–06 (1994).

214. 1992 Md. Laws 437. *See* Patricia E. Salkin, *Statewide Comprehensive Planning, the Next Wave* (chapter 13), in Buchsbaum & Smith, *supra* at 248–49.

215. Patricia E. Salkin, *The Smart Grown Agenda: A Snapshot of State Activity at the Turn of the Century*, 21 St. Louis U. Pub. L. Rev. 271, 272 (2002).

216. 23 U.S.C. § 101 *et seq.* (2000).

217. 23 U.S.C. § 134.

218. 23 U.S.C. § 135. *See, e.g.,* Haw. Rev. Stat. § 279E-1 (1995); Ky. Rev. Stat. Ann. § 100.187 (Banks-Baldwin 2001); Md. Code Ann. art. 66B, § 3.05 (2002); Minn. Stat. § 462.352 (2001); N.H. Rev. Stat. Ann. § 228:99 (2001); N.Y. Transp. § 15-a (Consol. 2002).

219. An earlier version appeared in Peter W. Salsich, Jr., *Grassroots Consensus Building and Collaborative Planning,* 3 Wash U. J.L. & Pol'y 709, 710–12, 717–21 (2000). Reprinted with permission.

220. 42 U.S.C.A. § 5301 *et seq.* (1995).

221. Omnibus Budget Reconciliation Act of 1993, Pub. L. No. 103-66, § 13301.

222. 42 U.S.C. § 1437 (1995).

223. Personal Responsibility and Work Opportunity Reconciliation Act of 1996, Pub. L. No. 104-193, 110 Stat. 2105 (1996) (adding Block Grants for Temporary Assistance for Needy Families, §§ 101–115, *striking* §§ 401–417, 419, 1108).

224. Gerald E. Frug, City-Making: Building Communities without Building Walls (1999). Frug proposes redefining cities as "situated subjects" within a region or as "postmodern subjects" in which legal boundaries would give way to collaborations by people with similar interests throughout a region. In the situated subject model, new regional legislatures would be created that would promote interlocal collaboration in land use decisions and delivery of public services. Neighborhoods would be important in this model because representatives from the neighborhoods would serve on the regional legislatures. *Id.* at 73–91. In the "postmodern subject" models, neighborhoods identified by place would be deemphasized in place of coalitions of people uniting around common problems. In both models, "[d]ecentralization would be designed to foster public freedom and community building rather than mimic state or national power on the local level." *Id.* at 111.

The Congress of the New Urbanism (CNU), an organization "committed to addressing the social and economic implications of design decisions" states in its charter that: "The neighborhood, the district, and the corridor are the essential elements of development and redevelopment in the metropolis. They form identifiable areas that encourage citizens to take responsibility for their maintenance and evolution." Congress of the New Urbanism Charter of the New Urbanism (Michael Leccese & Kathleen McCormick, eds.) 1, 73 (2000). CNU places the neighborhood, the district, and the corridor in the "middle scale" between the region, "the largest scale," and the block, the street, and the building, "the smallest scale" of its Charter. *Id.* at 13, 71, 121. Neighborhood collaborative planning will be an essential ingredient in implementation of CNU's vision for the middle scale.

But not all observers are optimistic about the potential for meaningful change in the "sprawling" nature of most major metropolitan areas. *See, e.g.,* William W. Buzbee, *Urban Sprawl, Federalism, and the Problem of Institutional Complexity,* 68 Fordham L. Rev. 57, (1999) (containing an exhaustive review of the economic, political, and social forces influencing urban sprawl and concluding that "[s]ustained and effective anti-sprawl measures, however, have been and are likely to remain a rarity").

225. Wendelyn A. Martz, Neighborhood-Based Planning, Advisory Service Report No. 455 (APA 1995).

226. Atlanta City Code §§ 6-3011 to 6-3019.

227. Conn. Gen. Stat. Ann. § 7-600 (1999).

228. *Id.* §§ 7-601(a), (b); §§ 7-605, 7-606.

229. Draft Unified Los Angeles City Charter, art. IX § 903(b), (c) (1999) (copy on file with author).

230. *Id.* at § 903(d).

231. *Id.* at § 903(e), (f).

232. *Id.* at § 904.

233. Draft Unified Los Angeles City Charter at § 908.

234. *Id.* at § 906.

235. *Id.* at § 907.

236. *Id.* at § 905.

237. *Id.* at § 910, 911.

238. Minn. Stat. § 469.1831 (2001).

239. Ill. Const. art. 7, §§ 6–7; 35 Ill. Comp. Stat. 200/27 (2001).

240. Mo. Const. art. 3, § 38(c); Mo. Rev. Stat., §§ 67.453–67.475 (1998).

241. N.Y. Gen. Mun. L. § 980(p) (McKinney 1999).

242. Or. Rev. Stat. §§ 195.020 *et seq.*, 195.060 *et seq.*

243. Or. Rev. Stat. § 195.020 (2001).

244. *See, e.g.,* Fla. Stat. Ann. § 163.3194(3)(a) (West 2000) (land development regulations are consistent with comprehensive plans if "land uses, densities or intensities, and other aspects of development permitted . . . are compatible with and further the objectives, policies, land uses, and densities and intensities in the comprehensive plan and if it meets all other criteria enumerated by the local government").

245. *See* notes 164–176 and accompanying text.

246. The text accompanying this endnote is adapted from a presentation by Henry R. Richmond, former Executive Director, 1000 Friends of Oregon, at a satellite program sponsored by the Continuing Legal Education Satellite Network, Inc., October 4, 1988. Reprinted with permission.

247. *Id.*

248. Mr. Richmond also advocates addressing policy issues with the media concerning pending land use matters, cautioning that care must be taken to avoid arguing the truth or falsity of any factual issues that may arise in connection with the matter. *Id.*

249. Salsich, *supra* n. 219, at 739.

CHAPTER 3

Constitutional Restrictions
on Land Use Regulation

The Fifth Amendment

Two clauses of the Fifth Amendment have special relevance for land use regulation: (1) the prohibition against deprivation of property without due process of law and (2) the prohibition against taking of private property for public use without payment of just compensation.[1] The due process clause of the Fourteenth Amendment makes these provisions applicable to state and local governments.[2] The Supreme Court has concluded that the Fifth Amendment's property-protection provisions were "designed to bar Government from forcing some people alone to bear public burdens which, in all fairness and justice, should be borne by the public as a whole."[3]

The two property clauses of the Fifth Amendment establish specific constitutional limitations on police power. The due process clause limits the exercise of police power through regulation, which is the traditional manner in which the zoning technique is implemented,[4] to activities that seek to advance "legitimate state interests"[5] through reasonable means that are "not unduly oppressive upon individuals."[6] The takings clause limits the exercise of police power through the exercise of eminent domain by prohibiting the sovereign from acquiring private property except for a proper public purpose[7] and by requiring the payment of just compensation to the owner of property so taken.[8] Ever since Justice Holmes's 1922 admonition that "while property may be regulated to a certain extent, if regulation goes too far, it will be recognized as a taking,"[9] controversy has swirled around the application of the taking clause to land use regulation cases, primarily with respect to the appropriate way to determine when a land use regulation goes "too far."[10]

Compensatory Takings

Proponents of the due process clause as the appropriate method of analysis for cases involving "excessive regulation" argued that the proper remedy was a declaration of invalidity and injunction against enforcement of the invalid regulation, rather than payment of compensation under the rubric of "inverse condemnation" for the property interest that was taken by the offending regulation.[11] For more than 60 years, the Court declined to settle the remedy question until ruling in the 1987 case of *First English Evangelical Lutheran Church v. County of Los Angeles* that the constitutional right to compensation for a taking of private property is self-executing and applicable to situations in which the "government's activities have . . . worked a taking of all use of property."[12] In that decision, however, the Court did not rule that a compensable taking had occurred but remanded for consideration of that question. The Court also left open the question of what constitutes a taking "in the case of normal delays in obtaining building permits, changes in zoning ordinances, variances and the like. . . ."[13] Fifteen years later, in *Tahoe-Sierra Preservation Council, Inc. v. Tahoe Regional Planning Agency,*[14] the Court refused to establish a bright-line rule regarding delays caused by development moratoria, concluding that such concerns are best handled by a multifactor analytical approach articulated in *Penn Central Transportation Company v. New York City.*[15]

The increasing sophistication of land use regulatory techniques, particularly environmental protection devices first developed in the 1960s,[16] has triggered a decades-long search for bright-line rules to discern when exercise of the regulatory-oriented police power crosses over the line and becomes a compensable taking. Aside from the traditional exercise of the power of eminent domain, the Supreme Court has articulated such bright-line rules in only two regulatory contexts: permanent physical occupation and denial of all economically viable use. In permanent physical occupation cases, which are discussed in the next section, a compensable per se taking will be found if physical occupation, however minimal, is permanent[17] and without the acquiescence of the landowner.[18] Regulatory deprivation of all economically viable use of property, discussed as follows, will be a per se taking even though the regulation serves a valid public purpose, as long as the proposed activity would not be prohibited by state nuisance or property law.

Permanent Physical Occupation as a Per Se Taking

In physical occupation cases, "the government physically intrudes upon private property either directly or by authorizing others to do so."[19] Such physical invasion is virtually a per se taking. Thus, in *Loretto v. TelePrompTer Manhattan CATV Corp,*[20] a New York law that required a landlord to allow a cable TV company to string cable on the property for a nominal payment of $1 constituted a taking for which just compensation was due.[21] In its holding, described as "very narrow," the Supreme Court explained that physical occupation cases differ from nonpossessory regulatory cases when the element of "required acquiescence" in the occupation is present.[22]

[P]roperty law has long protected an owner's expectation that he will be relatively undisturbed at least in the possession of his property. To require, as well, that the owner permit another to exercise complete dominion literally adds insult to injury. . . . Furthermore, such an occupation is qualitatively more severe than a regulation of the *use* of property, even a regulation that imposes affirmative duties on the owner, since the owner may have no control over the timing, extent, or nature of the invasion.[23]

In a case construing a federal statute authorizing the Federal Communications Commission (FCC), in the absence of state regulation, to regulate leases between public utility landlords and cable TV operators permitting cable operators to attach their cables to utility poles, the Court held that the statute permitting the FCC to regulate the rates charged for pole attachments did not constitute a per se taking under *Loretto* because there was no "required acquiescence" in occupation. The occupation was by "invitation" of the landlord. The difference between the FCC-approved rent of $1.79 and the landlord-demanded rent of $7.15 per pole was merely the result of permissible regulation of the "economic relations of landlords and tenants," the Court concluded.[24]

Cases in which the government takes property rights from owners and gives them to others also fall into this category. For example, in *Hall v. City of Santa Barbara,* the Ninth Circuit overruled a lower court's dismissal of a challenge to an ordinance that required mobile-home operators to offer their tenants leases of unlimited duration.[25] Although the court remanded, not deciding the taking issue, it analyzed the plaintiff's claim as one for taking by physical occupation. The court reasoned that because the ordinance transferred the right to occupy property in perpetuity to tenants, and because the tenants could transfer this right without the landlord's approval, "appellants' claims would amount to the type of interference with the property owner's rights the Court described so eloquently in *Loretto*."[26] The Ninth Circuit refused to accept the city's argument that rent control is "conclusively constitutional," distinguishing other cases in which rent-control ordinances had been upheld because the Santa Barbara ordinance contained a unique provision allowing tenants to transfer their rights to possession at reduced rental rates on the open market:[27]

> This is not a minor difference; it is crucial. . . . The Santa Barbara ordinance . . . changes the fundamental relationship between the parties. . . . On the one hand, the landlord loses forever a fundamental aspect of fee simple ownership: the right to control who will occupy his property and on what terms. On the other hand, the tenant gets an interest that he can liquidate and take with him when he leaves the property, or even the City of Santa Barbara. . . . [L]andlords are left with the right to collect reduced rent while tenants have practically all other rights in the property they occupy. As we read the Supreme Court pronouncements, this oversteps the boundaries of mere regulation and shades into permanent occupation of the property for which compensation is due.[28]

In *Yee v. City of Escondido,* the Supreme Court upheld a mobile-home rent-control ordinance against a takings challenge.[29] The Court held that the ordinance did not authorize an "unwanted physical occupation" of the landowners' property and thus did not amount to a per se taking under *Loretto v. TelePrompTer Manhattan CATV Corp.*[30] The Court also held that due process and regulatory takings claims were not properly before it. The Supreme Court of Washington, however, interpreting the state constitution, concluded that a statutory grant to qualified mobile-home tenants of a right of first refusal to purchase a mobile-home park was a compensatory taking. Rather than order compensation to be paid, the court invalidated the statute because it also transgressed an "absolute prohibition" in the state constitution against taking property for a private use.[31]

Where an owner's power to exclude others from his or her property is deprived by government action, a taking may occur. This issue can arise in a variety of contexts: where political demonstrators are granted access by the courts into shopping centers over the owner's objections,[32] or where the government asserts a navigational servitude, a scenic easement,[33] or a servitude to commit a nuisance.[34] Aircraft overflights may trigger compensation for physical encroachment of privately owned airspace below navigable limits, but only if the overflights "directly, immediately, and substantially interfere with the land's use and enjoyment."[35]

The New York Court of Appeals found a per se compensable taking in a New York City ordinance prohibiting the demolition of single-room-occupancy buildings (SROs) and requiring SRO owners to restore their units to habitable levels and offer them at controlled rents. Over a strong dissent that objected to the court's acceptance of a facial challenge to the ordinance, the majority held that the requirement that owners of SROs rehabilitate and rent out each available unit at controlled rents amounted to a taking of the right to possess and the power to exclude others by virtue of the ordinance's command that such owners get into or remain in the residential landlord-tenant business. Although the court accepted the argument that the state's police power as delegated to the city could be used to require SRO owners to put their property to "public use," the court held that the owners would have to be compensated for such taking of property.[36]

The Supreme Judicial Court of Maine held that a state statute granting a public easement for "recreation" on privately owned intertidal land was an unconstitutional taking in violation of both the United States and the Maine Constitutions. The common law received by Maine when it became a state after separating from Massachusetts includes an ordinance enacted in 1647 by the Massachusetts Bay Colony granting intertidal landowners title to the land between the high- and low-tide water marks in fee, subject to a public easement for "fishing, fowling, and navigation." In reviewing the history of the colonial ordinance, the court concluded that the scope of the public easement did not include modern recreational activities such as bathing, sunbathing, and walking. Therefore, the challenged statute was not simply a reasonable interpretation of state common law, but rather an unconstitutional attempt to take a comprehensive public recreational easement without payment of compensation.[37]

Occasionally, courts are confronted with taking challenges to requirements that regulated businesses continue in operation. The general rule is that
a person "cannot be compelled to carry on even a branch of business at a loss,
much less the whole business."[38] This rule has been construed narrowly, and
courts have refused to recognize per se takings when persons are denied the
right to cease business operations in a "pervasively regulated industry,"
where the regulations include a requirement to obtain permission from a regulatory agency prior to terminating service to the public.[39]

Applying the regulated industry exception, the Court of Appeals of New
York found no taking from the application of a state regulation prohibiting a
nursing home from closing its doors until reasonable alternative arrangements could be made for the continued care of the patients. Over the objections of the owners that the order to remain open had the effect of a physical
occupation of the property, the court concluded that closing the nursing home
after only four days' notice threatened an "imminent injury to the public," and
action by the state to prevent that harm from occurring was not a taking of
property. Conferral of "an exclusive franchise upon an individual incidental
to providing a public good" does not require the state to submit to the "uncon-
trolled discretion of the individual to instantaneously create a public emergency," the court stated.[40]

A failure to compensate after physical occupation by the government can
be justified only by emergency conditions. For example, in *National Board of
Young Men's Christian Association v. United States,* government troops occupied
two buildings owned by the plaintiff in the Atlantic section of the Canal Zone
at its boundary with Panama.[41] A riot resulted in which the plaintiff's buildings were damaged. The Supreme Court held that the Fifth Amendment did
not require compensation to be paid in this case, reasoning that the troops'
occupation did not deprive the plaintiffs of use of their building because the
ongoing riot prevented any use.[42] Also, fairness did not require that the plaintiff's loss "be borne by the public as a whole" because the troops had entered
the building primarily to defend it for the plaintiffs.[43]

The Supreme Court in *United States v. Central Eureka Mining Company*[44]
described the policy base of the "war exception" to the taking clause. "War,
particularly in modern times, demands the strict regulation of nearly all
resources. It makes demands which otherwise would be insufferable. But
wartime economic restrictions, temporary in character, are insignificant when
compared to the widespread uncompensated loss of time and freedom of
action which war traditionally demands."[45]

Deprivation of All Reasonable Use as a Per Se Taking

In *Lucas v. South Carolina Coastal Council,*[46] the Supreme Court adopted a new
per se taking rule requiring compensation for the deprivation of "all economically beneficial uses," even though the regulation may substantially advance
legitimate state interests.[47] In *Lucas,* David H. Lucas paid $975,000 for two res-
idential lots on the Isle of Palms. Thereafter, South Carolina enacted its Beachfront Management Act, barring him from erecting any habitable structures on

the property. The state trial court found that his parcels were rendered valueless by the act. The Supreme Court recounted its regulatory takings jurisprudence, stating again that this area of the law defies clear and objective formulas for decision making, except in cases of direct physical takings or nonphysical takings that clearly deprive the owner of all economic use of land.[48]

Given the uncontested assumption in the record that Lucas's land was rendered valueless by the legislation, the case seemed to fall squarely within the rule articulated in *Agins v. City of Tiburon*,[49] denying all reasonable economic use constitutes a taking; however, the Court, through Justice Scalia, went on to take note of the "unexceptional" recognition that a regulation consistent with the state's power to abate nuisances would not constitute a taking, even if it eliminated the property's only economically productive use because, essentially, the use would not have been allowed "under relevant property and nuisance principles."[50]

The Court ultimately remanded the case to the state court for a determination under state law as to whether the ills sought to be avoided by the Beachfront Management Act would have been illegal under the common law of private or public nuisance, recognizing that it was unlikely this would be the case.[51] Anticipating the obvious criticism of its decision, the Court stressed that proof that the harm would have been a nuisance at any rate would have to consist of more than mere self-serving recitals in the preamble to the state legislation.

The *Lucas* decision was the subject of a flood of scholarly and media attention, running the spectrum from hailing the case as a landmark in land use jurisprudence to dismissing it as a narrow holding limited solely to a rather unusual state court factual record.[52] The Court's holding that a regulation that deprives the owner of "all economically viable use" of his or her property must be justified under "background principles of state common law," namely nuisance law, to avoid a takings conclusion may be seen as quite limited. Few regulators will be unable to produce some credible evidence of economically viable use. Because the Supreme Court's opinion in *Lucas* does not rely on the extent of diminution in value, but rather the amount of value remaining, namely nothing, resourceful regulator's counsel will marshall evidence that any piece of property, no matter how extensively regulated, has market value, if nothing else as a buffer or park. Whether value as a buffer qualifies as "economic viability" is unclear. Seen in this light, however, the *Lucas* decision may scarcely increase the scant leverage that regulated landowners have in attacking land use restrictions.

In *Palazzolo v. Rhode Island*,[53] the Supreme Court refused to find a taking resulting from a state's refusal to permit development on wetlands because an upland portion of the landowner's property had substantial economic value. One year later, in *Tahoe-Sierra Preservation Council, Inc. v. Tahoe Regional Planning Agency*, the Court refused to apply the *Lucas* rule to a 32-month moratorium because that would violate "the parcel as a whole" standard. The Court emphasized that the parcel-as-a-whole standard has a temporal as well as a physical dimension.[54]

The Court has stressed that proper focus in a taking inquiry is on the still-permitted uses, not the prohibited uses,[55] and has traditionally upheld land use regulations that resulted in severe, but not total, economic loss to landowners.[56] Many other cases demonstrate the rule that regulations that result in only minimal losses will not constitute a taking.[57] Thus, in a case illustrating what is perhaps the point of greatest controversy concerning the permissible reach of land use regulations, denial of the best economic use of land during the time an invalid regulation was in effect was held to be an insufficient basis for compensation by the Third Circuit because other reasonable uses were available.[58]

When a property owner can establish, however, that the regulation prevents all reasonable economic uses of land, the *Agins/Lucas* per se taking rule may be invoked.[59] Thus, in *Rippley v. City of Lincoln,* the Supreme Court of Nebraska concluded that a taking was effected by a local regulation that zoned privately owned land for "public" use, thereby making it impossible for the owner to make private economic use of the property.[60]

Because the property owner has no right to commit a nuisance, regulations that deprive a landowner of a use that amounts to a nuisance do not constitute a taking.[61] In such cases a "harm/benefit" test may be used to evaluate a regulation.[62] If the regulation prevents a harm, the use of police power generally has been upheld despite the impact on land use;[63] if the regulation extracts a public benefit, however, such as a scenic easement, courts have held that a taking is effected.[64] Of course, one person's "prevention of harm" may be another person's "conferral of benefit." The Florida Supreme Court required compensation to be paid for the state-ordered destruction of thousands of healthy citrus plants and trees that had been purchased from a nursery where a form of citrus canker had been detected. The compensation order was based on the court's conclusion that destruction of the healthy trees may have served a valid public purpose and it also "benefitted the entire citrus industry and, in turn, Florida's economy, thereby conferring a public benefit rather than preventing a public harm."[65] The dissent "totally disagree[d]," characterizing the state's "entire course of action as one designed to prevent a public harm."[66] The case highlights the limitations of the "harm/benefit" test. The same result could have been reached simply by determining whether the destruction of the trees constituted a loss of property.[67]

Successful recovery of compensation for a regulatory taking involving deprivation of use requires that a clear distinction be drawn between regulations that affect the value or exploitation potential of land from those that actually prevent the owner from making reasonable economic use of the land. Although it may be possible to obtain an injunction against the application of an overly oppressive regulation,[68] compensation for a taking will not be granted unless loss of all reasonable use is pleaded and proved.

For example, the Third Circuit denied compensatory relief to a landowner, a portion of whose property had been downzoned from industrial to agricultural as a result of community opposition to the early stages of an industrial development project. The landowner successfully challenged the downzoning in state court as an illegal spot zoning. Although the rezoned property was alleged to have dropped in value from $495,600 to $52,000 as a result of the downzoning, the Third Circuit concluded that no compensable taking had occurred because the "substantial" value retained gave evidence of "residual economically feasible uses." The court drew a distinction between denial of the *best* use and denial of *all* economically viable use, noting that the second count of the amended complaint alleged that the challenged ordinances "were designed to prevent [the landowner] from 'exercising *an* economically viable use,' not *all* economically viable uses, of its property." The court also noted that the landowner "[did] not allege that alternative forms of industrial development or other profitable uses were foreclosed by the rezoning . . . [nor] that the value of its entire tract dropped significantly as a result of the rezoning."[69]

The Ninth Circuit held that a compensable taking claim was stated by allegations that a moratorium on new water hookups enacted by a public utility district denied landowners all reasonable economic use of their land because county land use regulations required water hookups to be secured before building permits would be issued.[70]

Downzonings and revocations of permits that blocked continued development of previously approved projects have been held to cause compensable takings when the effect of the reversal of prior approval is the denial of reasonable economic use of property.[71] The Supreme Court of Georgia held that the addition of conditions and modificiations to a "planned development" zoning classification caused a compensable taking. The Court concluded that the conditions and modifications made it impossible for a developer to build cluster homes on property whose location made both commercial and detached single-family development unfeasible.[72] The Supreme Court of Florida concluded that closure of an apartment building for one year following two incidents of cocaine sales on the premises was a compensatory taking but that closure of a motel for six months because of drug- and prostitution-related nuisance activity was not.[73] The Supreme Court of Wisconsin, over a strong dissent by Chief Justice Shirley Abrahamson, has ruled that a valid claim for a temporary regulatory taking under the Wisconsin Constitution was stated by allegations that denial of a special exception permit to build an access driveway so that permissible residential development could take place amounted to a legally imposed restriction on all reasonable economic use for the time the denial was in effect.[74]

Zoning of land for public uses, such as schools and government buildings, has been held a compensable taking,[75] as has the zoning of land "solely for the conservation of open space."[76] Rezoning to block expansion of a mobile-home park by changing the zoning classification[77] and imposition of large minimum lot-size requirements that precluded development of a mobile-home park have been held to be compensable takings.[78] Regrading a road that blocked a landowner's access to the road was held to be a taking, even though alternative access routes were available.[79] A state statute extending the public trust portion of coastal shorelands was a compensatory taking of beachfront owners' property, the Supreme Court of New Hampshire held.[80]

What constitutes a "reasonable use" may depend on the existing use of the property. In *Esposito v. South Carolina Coastal Council*,[81] the court noted that courts will look to the existing use of a property to determine if interference with the owner's expectations has occurred. Thus, even though it was undisputed that the owner's property *value* had been diminished substantially by the South Carolina Beachfront Management Act, the court held that no taking occurred when the owner's present *use* had not been affected. *Lucas v. South Carolina Coastal Council* makes it clear that a regulation that deprives a property of all economically viable use may yet be upheld where the economically viable use would have violated state nuisance law.[82]

Multifactor Analysis of Regulatory Effects

Most land use regulatory conflicts do not rise to the level of either per se taking category. Instead, they involve differences of opinion about appropriate use of land and the impact public regulation of use may have on land value.[83] Justice Holmes's admonition that "while property may be regulated to a certain extent, if regulation goes too far, it will be recognized as a taking"[84] originated the Court's self-styled regulatory takings jurisprudence.[85] The Supreme Court has been frank to admit its inability to develop any "set formula," stressing that the question requires ad hoc determinations involving the balancing of public and private interests.[86] The Court has pursued the question on an almost annual basis since 1974, following a half-century in which it took a laissez-faire attitude about local land use regulation.[87]

Three-Factor Test. In 1978, the Court identified three factors that it considered relevant in deciding regulatory takings cases: (1) the character of the government action in question, for example, whether it constituted physical occupation or merely economic regulation; (2) the economic impact of the regulation on the landowner; and (3) "the extent to which the regulation has interfered with distinct investment-backed expectations."[88] Applying those factors, the Court upheld the application of New York City's Landmarks Preservation Law to prevent the owners of Grand Central Terminal from constructing a multistory office building above the terminal. The Court refused to divide the property into discrete segments (e.g., airspace, surface, and below ground) or to consider the impact of the landmark's regulation on the use of the air rights, holding that the proper focus is on "rights in the parcel as a whole."[89] Noting that the government action was not invasive, did not interfere with existing uses of the property, and was in pursuit of a proper public purpose, the Court concluded that no taking had occurred.[90]

Two-Factor Test. An alternative, two-factor test first articulated in 1980,[91] and applied in *Keystone Bituminous Coal Association v. DeBenedictis*, concludes that a land use regulation crosses the takings line if it "does not substantially advance legitimate state interests, . . . or denies an owner economically viable use of his land."[92] In *Keystone Bituminous*, the Court held that a state statute regulating the mining of coal and requiring that 50 percent of the coal located under certain structures be left in place in order to prevent subsidence of land did not constitute a taking because it was enacted for a substantial public purpose and did not deprive the property owner of all use of the property.[93]

The tests are applied through ad hoc judicial inquiries in which the precise facts are critical to the outcome of the cases. That being so, landowners have a better chance of prevailing under these multifactor tests by bringing as-applied challenges, although, as noted later in this chapter, substantial procedural barriers tend to push objectors toward facial challenges instead.[94] The recognition in *Lucas* that regulatory deprivation of all economically viable use of property can be a per se compensable taking[95] spurred a decade-long effort to expand the coverage of the *Lucas* rule at the expense of the *Penn Central* ad hoc analytical approach.[96]

But in 2002, a six-justice majority refused to apply the *Lucas* per se rule to a 32-month moratorium imposed on residential development along the shores of Lake Tahoe. Instead, the Court, in *Tahoe-Sierra Preservation Council, Inc. v. Tahoe Regional Planning Agency,* affirmed the Ninth Circuit's conclusion that the *Penn Central* multifactor analysis standard "was the appropriate framework for analysis."[97] In refusing to establish a categorical rule, the Court asserted that both its takings precedents and the "fairness and justice" principle underlying the Takings Clause required rejection of a categorical rule.[98]

What Is Property for "Taking" Purposes?[99]

Rights in the Parcel as a Whole: The Aggregate Theory

The Fifth Amendment's prohibitions against deprivation of property without due process and against taking private property for public use without payment of just compensation reflect the founding fathers' determination to limit the regulatory powers of government with respect to private property. As noted previously, regulations that deprive a property owner of all reasonable use of the property constitute takings of property for which compensation must be paid. Implementation of this rule requires, among other things, a working definition of property.

The Supreme Court's decision in *Penn Central Transportation Co. v. New York City,* upholding the application of New York City's landmarks preservation law to Grand Central Station, was based in part on the majority's conclusion that:

> "[t]aking" jurisprudence does not divide a single parcel into discrete segments and attempt to determine whether rights in a particular segment have been entirely abrogated. . . . [T]his Court focuses rather both on the character of the action and on the nature and extent of the interference with rights in the parcel as a whole.[100]

Applying the parcel-as-a-whole or aggregate theory of property, the Court in *Penn Central* held that air rights above Grand Central Station did not constitute a discrete segment of property such that a regulation denying the owner use of that segment would constitute a compensatory taking. Because the owner could still use the entire parcel of property and could realize an economic return on that use, a regulation that denied the owner use of the air-space above the station was not viewed as a taking of property.[101] In a later case, the aggregate theory was used by the Court in upholding a federal regulation prohibiting the sale of parts of protected birds, but allowing the possession, transportation, donation, or devise of the birds.[102]

The aggregate theory survived its most important test in *Keystone Bituminous Coal Association v. DeBenedictis*.[103] Although a Pennsylvania statute required owners of the rights to 27 million tons of coal to leave the coal in the ground as part of an effort to prevent subsidence of the land above the coal and thus effectively took from the owners the use of the coal in place (underground) and the support estate (the right to leave coal in place or remove it, along with the earth under the surface), the Court concluded that the statute did not amount to a taking of property because the coal in place and the support estate were not separate segments of property, but merely "part of the entire bundle of rights" of the owner of the surface or of the coal.[104]

While noting that "we have at times expressed discomfort with the logic of this rule," the Court applied the parcel-as-a-whole rule in *Palazzolo v. Rhode Island*.[105] Despite ruling that a subsequent purchaser could bring a compensatory takings challenge against an earlier-enacted land use restriction, the Court agreed with the Rhode Island Supreme Court's conclusion that no categorical taking had occurred because the uplands portion of the petitioner's land had a $200,000 value.[106] One year later, in *Tahoe-Sierra Preservation Council, Inc. v. Tahoe Regional Planning Agency*,[107] the Court applied the parcel-as-a-whole rule to a temporary development moratorium, concluding that temporal segmentation is no less problematic than physical segmentation.[108]

> An interest in real property is defined by the metes and bounds that describe its geographic dimensions and the term of years that describes the temporal aspect of the owner's interest. . . . Both dimensions must be considered if the interest is to be viewed in its entirety. Hence, a permanent deprivation of the owner's use of the entire area is a taking of "the parcel as a whole," whereas a temporary restriction that merely causes a dimunition in value is not. Logically, a fee simple estate cannot be rendered valueless by a temporary prohibition on economic use, because the property will recover value as soon as the prohibition is lifted.[109]

Petitioners had made a facial challenge to successive moratoria totaling 32 months. Because petitioners had not briefed or argued the *Penn Central* analytical factors, however, the Court did not consider the impact of the moratorium on petitioners.[110]

In the context of regulatory takings, the definition of the parcel as a whole has interesting permutations. In one unreported decision, the landowner had serially subdivided and developed its 43-acre tract over a period of years so that what remained was a two-acre tract consisting almost entirely of wetlands.[111] The zoning authority refused permission to develop the two-acre tract, based on its wetlands regulations. Clearly, if the property subject to the takings analysis was indeed only the two-acre tract, the property owner had been denied all economically viable use of that tract. The trial court disagreed with the property owner, however, finding the relevant whole parcel to be the original 43-acre tract. The Supreme Court of Virginia found no error and refused a petition for appeal.[112] The property owner's petition for *certiorari* was denied by the U.S. Supreme Court.[113]

The actual unit of property that is the subject of takings analysis is critical under the per se takings rule of *Lucas v. South Carolina Coastal Council*.[114] Justice Scalia raised the segment theory question in a well-known footnote in *Lucas v. South Carolina Coastal Council*.

> When, for example, a regulation requires a developer to leave 90 percent of a rural tract in its natural state, it is unclear whether we would analyze the situation as one in which the owner has been deprived of all economically beneficial use of the burdened portion of the tract, or as one in which the owner has suffered a mere diminution in value of the tract as a whole. The answer to this difficult question may lie in how the owner's reasonable expectations have been shaped by the State's law of property – *i.e.*, whether and to what degree the State's law has accorded legal recognition and protection to the particular interest in land with respect to which the takings claimant alleges a diminution in (or elimination of) value.[115]

The smaller the unit of property at issue, the greater the likelihood that "all economically viable use" has been denied. Property owners may be tempted to subdivide property to the smallest parcel permitted by existing zoning and subdivision ordinances in order to argue deprivation of all economically viable use regarding a given parcel. This strategy may work both ways, however, because it may legitimize a regulation applied to the remaining property, limiting the landowner's damages and thereby his leverage in attacking the regulation.[116]

In *Loveladies Harbor, Inc. v. United States*[117] and *Florida Rock Industries, Inc. v. United States*,[118] the Court of Appeals for the Federal Circuit addressed the so-called denominator problem of the deprivation-of-use test: What property is the measure of the economic value affected by the regulation?[119] In *Loveladies*, the court concluded that a 12.5-acre tract subject to wetlands regulations was the relevant property for a takings analysis, rather than a 51-acre tract of which it was a part or the 250-acre tract originally purchased by the landowner, by applying what it called "a flexible approach designed to account for factual nuances," rather than a bright-line standard under which the denominator is the parcel for which the owner seeks a permit.[120] In *Florida Rock*, the court remanded for a third time a permit-denial case for a valid determination of "after imposition" value of land in order to determine whether a "partial loss of economic use of the property has crossed the line from a noncompensable 'mere diminution' to a compensable 'partial taking.'"[121] In an important footnote, the court suggested that the different strands of the property bundle should be analyzed separately for a regulatory taking just as is done for a physical taking.[122]

The *Florida Rock* court's suggestion was rejected by the Tenth Circuit in favor of the "more traditional analysis" of *Penn Central*[123] that the "relevant denominator must be derived from the entire bundle of rights associated with the parcel of land."[124] The Supreme Court of Colorado, reviewing U.S. Supreme Court opinions, concluded that the "appropriate 'denominator' for determining the economic impact of a regulation is the contiguous parcel of property owned by the landowner, not merely the segment most severely affected."[125] Applying *Keystone*, the court also concluded that "property rights as an aggregate" must be considered in takings inquiries, rather than only one segment, such as mineral rights.[126]

Specific Strands of the Bundle (Segment Theory)

Chief Justice Rehnquist dissented vigorously from the decisions in *Penn Central* and *Keystone* because he believed that the regulations at issue in those cases destroyed the property rights in a column of air (*Penn Central*) and a column of dirt (*Keystone*). Under applicable state law, the airspace above the Grand Central Station and the lands underneath the surface in Pennsylvania had substantial economic value separate and distinct from the value of the surface property and were capable of severance from the ownership of the surface. Justice Rehnquist argued that they should be treated as separate segments of property when evaluating the effect of government regulation of their use and enjoyment.[127] Two other justices joined him in *Penn Central*,[128] and he picked up a fourth vote in *Keystone*.[129]

Citing the celebrated case of *United States v. Causby*,[130] where the Court held that repeated overflights by military aircraft constituted a compensatory taking of a navigation easement, Chief Justice Rehnquist, in *Keystone*, distinguished the ability to divide or segment the physical characteristics of property from the metaphorical concept of a bundle of sticks. In his view, the physical size of an item of property is not merely "one strand in the bundle" but rather constitutes the tangible description of the property res to which the metaphorical bundle attaches.[131] If the res is capable of being divided—either by division of the surface space into separate parts or by severance of the column of air or column of dirt from the surface land—separate property bundles attach to each identifiable property segment.[132]

Because the 27 million tons of coal required to be left in the ground by the Pennsylvania statute constituted an identifiable property interest to Justice Rehnquist, he concluded that the regulatory action prohibiting the owner from removing the coal destroyed completely "any interest in a segment of property," rather than only "one strand of the bundle," as effectively as if the government had taken possession of the land or mined the coal.[133] As a result of the government action, the property owner could make no use of its property interest in the coal.[134]

Although Chief Justice Rehnquist was unable to muster a majority for his view in *Keystone*, the Court has been willing to consider segments of property for takings analysis in several other contexts. In addition to *Causby*, in *Kaiser Aetna v. United States*, the Court found an unconstitutional taking of property when a federal regulation required the owner of a freshwater pond to grant a navigation servitude of public access.[135] The Court also found a taking occurred, in *Loretto v. TelePrompTer Manhattan CATV Corp,* when state regulations required a landlord to permit cable TV lines to be attached to apartment buildings so that tenants could obtain cable TV service.[136] Segmentation of property played a role in these two physical invasion cases because (1) the pond was part of a larger tract of land,[137] and (2) the cable TV lines were being attached to very small portions of the landowner's buildings.[138]

Another interesting aspect of *Causby, Kaiser Aetna,* and *Loretto* is the Court's apparent willingness to evaluate the effect of a regulation on particular strands of the property bundle. In all three cases, the property interest that was taken was the power to exclude others from the owner's land—the government in *Causby,* the public in *Kaiser Aetna,* and cable TV lines in *Loretto.* Justice Marshall, writing for the majority in *Loretto,* concluded that the invasion of the owner's property directly extinguished too many property interests, including the power to exclude, "which has traditionally been considered one of the most treasured strands in an owner's bundle of property rights."[139]

In *Penn Central,* the Court acknowledged its willingness to consider the effect of government regulation on discrete property interests, but rather than attempting to label the property strands it was willing to consider separately, the Court described this process as an evaluation of the character of the governmental action. The Court noted that governmental acts of physical appropriation or physical invasion were more likely to be found to be takings than were regulations "adjusting the benefits and burdens of economic life to promote the common good."[140]

Returning to the theme of discrete property interests in another 1987 case, *Hodel v. Irving,*[141] the Court found that a 1983 statute, whose primary purpose was "to facilitate consolidation of tribal lands and reduce the number of small fractional interests in individually allotted lands,"[142] established several methods by which undivided interests in Indian lands might be consolidated.[143] These methods included a stipulation that upon the death of a person holding a small fractional share of land, the decedent's interest would escheat to the decedent's tribe, regardless of whether the decedent sought to transfer it by devise to selected persons or to heirs by intestate succession.[144] In an opinion written by Justice O'Connor, the Court struck down the escheat provision as a taking of an important ownership interest: the power to transfer property to one's heirs.[145]

Justice O'Connor noted that the statute did not impose any restrictions on the owners' use and enjoyment of the land during their lifetimes, nor did it limit the power to transfer inter vivos. There was little in the way of "investment-backed expectations" because the highly fractionated ownership patterns generally made such investment difficult. In addition, there was a degree of an "average reciprocity of advantage,"[146] in that consolidation of Indian lands in a tribe would benefit all members of that tribe.[147]

These considerations were outweighed, however, by the fact that the regulation destroyed the right to transfer property to one's heirs. Quoting *Kaiser Aetna v. United States,*[148] that the right to exclude others is one of the most essential sticks in the bundle commonly characterized as property rights, Justice O'Connor compared the right to transfer property to one's heirs with the power to exclude others and concluded that a statute that abolishes both descent and devise of particular property interests "goes too far."[149]

> In one form or another, the right to pass on property—to one's family in particular—has been part of the Anglo-American legal system since feudal times. . . . The fact that it may be possible for the owners of these interests to effectively control disposition upon death through complex *inter vivos* transactions such as revocable trusts, is simply not an adequate substitute for the rights taken given the nature of the property.[150]

Justice O'Connor emphasized the fundamental aspect of the "right to exclude" in her concurring opinion in *Presault v. Interstate Commerce Commission*.[151] In that case, the Court held that a takings challenge to the federally supported rails-to-trails program was premature. To encourage development of hiking trails and preserve established railroad rights-of-way, Congress authorized the Interstate Commerce Commission (ICC) to postpone the vesting of reversionary interests in railroad rights-of-way originally acquired as easements.[152] The Court held that the program was a valid exercise of Congressional authority under the Commerce Clause and that holders of reversionary interests who objected to ICC postponement action could not bring a constitutional takings challenge without first seeking compensation from the United States. The Court noted that the Tucker Act[153] granted jurisdiction to the U.S. Claims Court to hear claims against the federal government "founded on the Constitution" and concluded that claims of reversionary interest holders fall into that category.[154]

In concurring with the Court's decision, Justice O'Connor emphasized that a taking could be found under state property law (the basis for taking analysis) if the ICC denied holders of reversionary interests the opportunity to exercise their right to exclude when the reversionary interests vested as a result of the abandonment of railroad rights-of-way easements. Although the ICC may have the power to postpone enjoyment of reversionary interests, Justice O'Connor noted, exercise of that power may trigger the requirement of just compensation.[155]

Under state condemnation law governing garden-variety physical takings, the taking of a portion of the owner's property is compensable to the extent of the difference in the value of the property before and after the taking.[156] The very definition of the "property" subject to such measurement may have great economic significance: The larger the parcel that is deemed to be the relevant whole, the greater the owner's claim of severance damages.

Character of the Government Action

The "character of the government action" prong of the *Penn Central* three-factor analytical approach requires courts to analyze the relationship between the articulated public-purpose goal and the regulatory means chosen to achieve that goal. Although courts will not second-guess a legislative articulation of a public purpose nor the wisdom of the means chosen to achieve it,[157] they will examine the relationship between the ends and the means, particularly when local governments extract concessions from landowners in return for development approval. For "generally applicable" land use laws, a deferential standard of review is applied.[158]

In *Nollan v. California Coastal Commission,* the Court struck down a condition attached to a coastal development permit that required the landowner to record a deed restriction granting an easement permitting the public to cross a portion of their beachfront property.[159] Justice Scalia, writing for the majority, focused on the public-purpose aspects of the regulation. In an action reminiscent of the Court's approach in *City of Cleburne v. Cleburne Living Center,*[160] Justice Scalia refused to give a deferential reading to the California Coastal Commission's stated purpose for its regulation, which was to counter the effects of construction of the proposed new house. According to the Commission, the house, along with other area development, would cumulatively "burden the public's ability to traverse to and along the shorefront" because the house would further a trend toward blocking the view of the ocean and add to the development of "a wall" of residential structures "that would prevent the public 'psychologically . . . from realizing a stretch of coastline exists nearby that they have every right to visit,' . . . and would also increase private use of the shorefront."[161]

> We view the Fifth Amendment's property clause to be more than a pleading requirement, and compliance with it to be more than an exercise in cleverness and imagination. As indicated earlier, our cases describe the condition for abridgement of property rights through the police power as a *"substantial* advanc[ing]" of a legitimate State interest. We are inclined to be particularly careful about the adjective where the actual conveyance of property is made a condition to the lifting of a land use restriction, since in that context there is heightened risk that the purpose is avoidance of the compensation requirement, rather than the stated police power objective.[162]

Imposing a standard of review that Justice Brennan in dissent characterized as requiring "a degree of exactitude that is inconsistent with our standard for reviewing the rationality of a state's exercise of its police power,"[163] Justice Scalia concluded that the Commission's requirements for an easement of lateral access across the Nollans' beach property lacked the "essential nexus" to the Commission's stated purposes of reducing the visual and psychological barriers to public use of the beach, and thus was "not a valid regulation of land use but 'an out-and-out plan of extortion.'"[164]

Justice Brennan, in dissent, disagreed sharply with Justice Scalia's insistence on closely examining the means-end relationship of the Commission's action and purpose. Justice Brennan argued that the Commission's regulation was a "reasonable effort to respond to intensified development along the California coast."[165] Arguing that the private property owners could make no claim that the regulation disrupted their reasonable expectations, Justice Brennan stated that the Court's decision gave a windfall to the landowners.[166] Clearly, Justice Brennan believed that a reasonable relationship existed between the Commission's action and the burdens that the regulation placed on the public right of access.[167]

In *Dolan v. City of Tigard,* the Supreme Court invalidated city-imposed conditions attached to an expansion permit that required the landowner to dedicate 10 percent of the land in a floodplain for a greenway and to permit a pedestrian/bicycle pathway to cross the land.[168] In applying and extending the *Nollan*[169] nexus doctrine, the Court emphasized that the conditions required the landowner to give up "her ability to exclude others." The Court held that the city could not extract such a condition without making an "individualized determination" that the required dedication is related both in nature and extent to the impact of the proposed development.[170]

Economic Impact: Impairment of Use

Government action that results in an impairment of an owner's use of his or her property does not result in a taking for which compensation is due, if reasonable use of the property remains after the impairment. The Court in *Palazzolo* emphasized that the *Lucas* per se rule and the *Penn Central* multifactor test establish a two-level process for judicial analysis of regulatory takings claims. The per se inquiry is undertaken first. If a compensatory taking is found, compensation is awarded. If a per se taking is not found, but the regulation does restrict land use and development, a second inquiry should be made using the *Penn Central* multifactor test.[171] Courts applying *Palazzolo* generally have concluded that the ad hoc analysis should be "broad and inclusive,"[172] although the Supreme Court of Colorado construed the *Palazzolo* standard narrowly in concluding that "the level of interference must be very high for the per se prong to be applicable. . . . [W]e note that the likely purpose of the fact specific test is to provide an avenue of redress for a landowner whose property retains value that is slightly greater than de minimis."[173]

Despite the publicity given to the Supreme Court's decision in *First English,*[174] that compensation must be paid when local land use regulations deny landowners all reasonable use of their land, the Court in *First English* did not decide whether a taking actually occurred in that case.[175] After concluding that the Constitution requires that compensation be paid to landowners when local land use regulations effect a taking of property, the Supreme Court remanded the case for a consideration of the taking issue. Upon remand, the California Court of Appeals held that the challenged regulation—a temporary moratorium on building construction or reconstruction that prohibited a church camp from rebuilding structures that had been swept away in a flood—did not amount to a taking because the temporary moratorium served a lawful public purpose and permitted other uses to be made of the camp, such as cooking meals, playing games, giving lessons, and pitching tents. The Supreme Court denied review.[176]

In discussing the taking issue, the California court stated:

> On balance, the public benefits this regulation confers far exceed the private costs it imposes on the individual property owner [especially after factoring in the public benefits this property owner shares]. . . .
>
> This case presents a dramatic illustration of the principle of "reciprocity of advantage." *First English* enjoys the safety benefits accompanying the prohibition of construction on the other properties along the

riverbed in return for the "reciprocal" safety benefits that flow to the other landowners because *First English* is subject to a similar ban.[177]

Examples of cases in which a regulation was held not to constitute a taking under this standard include:

- a ten-month interim moratorium on development in a newly designated gaming district, during which a proposed sale of an historic building fell through because an application for a special use-permit had been suspended[178]
- a noise ordinance variance granted to a racetrack adjoining the plaintiff's property[179]
- a rezoning of an adjacent property to permit a sanitary landfill[180]
- a government setback that trapped floodwaters on the plaintiff's land for longer than the water normally would have been trapped[181]
- a requirement that a permit be obtained before discharging fill material into wetlands[182]
- the creation of a city sewer assessment district that had been sought in part by the landowner, which, because the land continued to be zoned agricultural, rendered valueless/useless the sewer built on the landowner's property[183]

Courts also have held that use-impairing regulations did not effect compensable takings in the following situations:

- a New York City ordinance requiring property owners to remove or encapsulate any asbestos that would be disturbed by planned renovation or demolition of buildings[184]
- application of a county ordinance in Idaho requiring a 100-foot setback to a lot that was only 105 feet deep, where a conditional-use permit and variance to move an existing two-story residence to the lot had been denied for valid reasons and the owner had not sought a variance to use the property in other ways[185]
- denial of a variance to permit land on the residential side of a boundary between a residential district and a commercial district to be used for commercial purposes[186]
- imposition of higher fees for building permits and other construction-related costs by an Illinois municipality following a court-ordered rezoning to allow a townhouse development[187]
- a county ordinance in Washington state prohibiting new construction in wetlands, which prohibited development of a portion of a larger tract of land[188]
- application of the New York City Landmarks Law to prevent a church from replacing a church-owned auxiliary building with an office tower because, while the law may have "frozen" existing uses, it did not deny reasonable use of the property[189]
- prohibition of the construction of any pipelines within 100 feet of the center line of a state highway without the state's permission and

required removal at the owner's expense of any lines installed without the requisite permission[190]

- a downzoning from residential to preservation and park use that blocked plans for a residential subdivision but permitted development of a private golf course that was "economically viable . . . [but] not as profitable" as the proposed resort[191]

- designation of the majority of a tract of land as wetland and an environmental area under Michigan shoreland and wetlands protection statutes, and the subsequent denial of a state permit to construct a drainage ditch as the first step in a proposed residential development project[192]

- refusal to recognize a prohibited use as a valid nonconforming use in the absence of evidence that the property actually had been used in its nonconforming configuration prior to the effective date of the zoning ordinance[193]

- denial of a building permit, even though unlawful, when other uses could be made of the property[194]

Other regulations upheld against takings challenges include:

- enforcement of an ordinance prohibiting commercial vehicular access to an alley that was within 20 feet of abutting residential districts when access was permitted to the landowner's property from a main thoroughfare[195]

- a prohibition of surface coal mining on a small portion of a large tract in order to protect an "archaeologically significant" area[196]

- a refusal to rezone land zoned agricultural to permit operation of a rock quarry[197]

- a moratorium and permanent ban on time-share developments in residential areas[198]

- denial of a landfill permit[199]

- a settlement agreement requiring off-site mitigation of erosion control[200]

- an ordinance prohibiting rebuilding of destroyed structures seaward of a baseline[201]

- the designation of a building as historic without the owner's consent[202]
- enforcement of state standards for manufactured homes[203]
- revocation of a rental dwelling license[204]
- a prohibition of billboards in residential areas[205]
- a ban on the use of tents for full-time residential use on lots zoned for single-family dwellings[206]
- a denial of setback variances from statutory wetlands regulations in effect at the time the owner acquired the property[207]
- refusal to rezone from residential to residential lakeside[208]
- denial of a variance to permit permanent residence on a lot restricted to seasonal use[209]
- entrance on land by federal officials to install wells for monitoring groundwater migration from adjacent properties[210]

- denial of a Clean Water Act permit to dredge and fill 9 acres of a lake for a 62-acre residential subdivision with waterfront lots and a small marina[211]
- requirement that owners of private property completely surrounded by public National Forest System lands obtain special-use permits for any use of National Forest System lands exceeding uses by the general public[212]
- suspension and subsequent revocation of a mining permit covering 91 percent of coal a petitioner expected to mine[213]
- application of an ordinance increasing minimum lot size from 1.5 acres to 6 acres during the period before it was invalidated as arbitrary and unreasonable[214]
- change in zoning from residential to solely recreational use of land, which had been used as a private golf course for more than 70 years[215]

Delays in obtaining permits have been frequent, although generally unsuccessful, subjects for compensable takings claims. The Ninth Circuit held that a three-year delay in obtaining a building permit for a commercial building because of litigation over a conditional variance requiring approximately 10 percent of the subject property to be deeded to the city for a proposed street widening did not constitute a compensable taking. Although the California courts invalidated the condition, the landowner did not allege that he was deprived of substantially all reasonable use of his property because he did not discuss in his complaint the effect, if any, that the conditional variance had on a carpet contracting business he was conducting on the subject property. Although the California courts had determined that the conditional variance had "invaded" the landowner's property rights, the Ninth Circuit concluded that "this was not an 'invasion' of sufficient magnitude to have denied [the landowner] the 'justice and fairness' guaranteed by the fifth and fourteenth amendments."[216]

Other cases involving delays in which courts have denied takings claims include:

- delays resulting from successful legal challenges to downzoning ordinances and other land use regulatory decisions[217]
- a seven-year moratorium on sewer connection permits because of an overloaded sewage plant that had fallen out of compliance with federal and state regulations[218]
- a seven-month delay in processing a subdivision application because of the failure to include a certificate of water availability with the subdivision application in violation of county rules for processing such applications, even though the certificate was unavailable because of a moratorium on the issuance of such certificates imposed by the local water district[219]
- an 18-month moratorium on land development imposed by the New Jersey Council on Affordable Housing to preserve scarce land resources deemed essential to fulfillment of a township's "fair share" of regional affordable housing needs[220]

- a seven-year delay in seeking condemnation of property under an urban redevelopment plan while continuing to refuse applications for more intensive uses because viable economic uses continued to be permitted and the city had made no official announcement of intent to condemn or had not taken any other action to move from the "planning stage" to the "acquiring stage" of a proposed public waterfront park and open-space area[221]
- an 11-year delay, and subsequent cancellation, of a proposed highway project traversing land being prepared for commercial development[222]

A claim by property owners that the rezoning of lots across the street from residential to commercial devalued their property to such an extent that a compensable taking occurred was denied by the Supreme Court of Arkansas because the objectors' current use of their property for residential purposes was not taken by the rezoning decision.[223] The Supreme Court of New Jersey refused a landowner's temporary taking claim for damages during the time an ordinance that quadrupled minimum residential lot size was in effect before its as-applied invalidation because the owner had not established loss of all economically beneficial use as a result of the invalid ordinance.[224]

Interference with Investment-Backed Expectations

Penn Central's multifactor analytical approach to as-applied takings cases places special emphasis on landowner expectations triggered by investment.[225] Adapted from a famous 1967 article by Professor Frank Michelman of Harvard,[226] the investment-backed expectations prong has been troublesome to courts and commentators.[227] The legal status of the landowner's title is a critical element in the application of the expectations factor. The Supreme Court has struggled to articulate an answer to the "difficult question [of] what role the temporal relationship between regulatory enactment and title acquisition plays in the proper *Penn Central* analysis."[228] The timing of a regulation's enactment is relevant but not conclusive. Thus a person who takes title with notice of a regulation is not, by that reason alone, barred from asserting an investment-backed expectation about use of the property.[229] Justice O'Connor, concurring in *Palazzolo*, stressed that investment-backed expectations were "not talismanic" under *Penn Central*. She identified several important, but not conclusive, considerations, including (1) the "state of regulatory affairs at the time of acquisition" and (2) the "nature and extent of permitted development" compared with the development "sought by the claimant."[230] She also stressed that acquisition by purchase was not a requirement for compensation eligibility. "We also have never held that a takings claim is defeated simply on account of the lack of a personal financial investment by a post enactment acquirer of property, such as donee, heir, or devisee."[231]

In a case decided eight days after *Palazzolo*, the Supreme Court of New Hampshire held that denial of a permit for a 34-unit cluster subdivision because the proposed subdivision did not connect to a town- or state-maintained road in violation of a local ordinance was not a compensatory taking. The court concluded that the 100-foot frontage requirement served an important safety feature of ensuring that emergency vehicles can reach homes in cluster developments. The town's application of the ordinance gave "due regard, under all the facts and circumstances, to [the owner's] property rights" because of the ordinance's public health and safety emphasis and because the landowner knew of the frontage requirement when he purchased the property.[232] Although knowledge by the landowner of a regulation's existence is an important aspect of the investment-backed expectations analysis, knowledge alone cannot be a basis for denying a variance, the Maryland Court of Appeals has concluded. Citing *Palazzolo* and reviewing cases from other jurisdictions, the court held that "a purchase with knowledge" of a land use restriction does not by itself constitute a "self-created hardship" that would make the landowner ineligible for a use variance.[233]

The Federal Circuit Court of Appeals, in denying a rehearing of a case in which it found no taking prior to *Palazzolo*, emphasized the importance of the investment-backed expectation factor in regulatory takings cases, particularly those involving highly regulated industries such as coal mining. "The likelihood of regulatory restraint is especially high with regard to possible adverse environmental effects . . . which have long been regarded as proper subjects for the exercise of the state's police power," the court noted.[234] In a similar vein, the Federal Circuit denied a takings claim in 1999 involving wetlands in the Florida Keys because the property owner "lacked a reasonable, investment-backed expectation that he would obtain regulatory approval needed to develop the property at issue."[235] The court stressed the landowner's awareness of the "regulatory climate" at the time he acquired the property and his seven-year delay in seeking regulatory approval. The court also stressed that the *Lucas* categorical taking rule did not eliminate the requirement that a landowner have a reasonable, investment-backed expectation of developing the land, noting that Mr. Lucas had met that criterion.[236]

Development Moratoria

A common planning device is the development moratorium, in which local governments prohibit new development for a temporary period while new land use plans are prepared. The moratorium is designed to give local planning officials faced with significant change and growth pressures some breathing room while they consider how best to manage the change/growth their community is experiencing. Moratoria can become extremely controversial because, while they permit landowners to continue existing uses of land, the temporary halt to new development may severely impact landowners who have expended funds on development plans but have not yet received development permits or who have anticipated selling their property at substantial profit because of its development potential. The duration of moratoria obviously is an important factor in any assessment of their validity. Most moratoria last for several months, although moratoria of more than a year have been imposed. Some states have enacted legislation authorizing moratoria for up to two years in length.[237]

Moratoria survived a direct takings challenge in *Tahoe-Sierra Preservation Council, Inc. v. Tahoe Regional Planning Agency*, as the Supreme Court refused to declare the imposition of development moratoria totaling 32 months to be a categorical compensatory taking. Instead, the Court remanded the case for analysis under the *Penn Central* three-factor test, with special emphasis on the investment-backed expectations prong.[238]

Exactions

Governments often impose conditions, called *exactions*,[239] on the issuance of development permits to individual property owners. The *Nollan/Dolan*[240] rule requires conditions attached to development permits to meet a two-part test of (1) an "essential nexus" (relationship) between the permit condition and the public impact of the proposed development, and (2) a "rough proportionality" between the magnitude of the burden exacted by the condition and the likely effects of the proposed development.[241] The rough proportionality standard must be met by an "individualized determination" that the exaction is related "both in nature and extent" to the impact of the proposed development.[242] The *Nollan/Dolan* rule was formulated in two cases involving requirements that landowners dedicate permanent easements to the public as conditions for approval of development permits and imposes a heightened judicial scrutiny on such conditions.[243] In both cases, the Supreme Court invalidated the conditions because of failure by the government entities involved to establish the required relationship between the problems encountered and the conditions imposed. In *City of Monterey v. Del Monte Dunes, Inc.*,[244] the Court confined the *Nollan/Dolan* rule to exactions of property interests in land, declining to extend *Nollan/Dolan* to landowners' challenges "based not on exactions but on denial of development."[245]

Curtis v. Town of South Thomaston[246] is an example of a state court's application of the *Nollan/Dolan* rule. A town ordinance required a subdivision developer to construct a fire pond if no adequate water supply existed and to convey an access easement to allow the town to pump water out of the pond to fight fires. The Supreme Judicial Court of Maine first found an essential nexus "between the Town's interest in public safety and the permit condition." It then made a factual finding "that a more than sufficient proportionality exists between the fire protection demands created by the subdivision plan and the easement requirement designed to meet these demands."[247]

In *Ehrlich v. City of Culver City*,[248] the Supreme Court of California extended the reach of *Nollan/Dolan* to individualized monetary exactions imposed as a condition to issuance of a development permit, but declined to apply the rule and its heightened scrutiny to a "generally applicable development fee or assessment." The court saw no logical difference between a requirement that a landowner convey a property interest or pay a monetary amount, when either is imposed on individuals under the government's monopoly power over development permits.[249] The court held that the city had met its burden of establishing a nexus between a rezoning and the imposition of a fee to mitigate the loss of land available for private recreational use, but remanded the case because the city's evidence concerning the amount of the fee ($280,000) was insufficient under the rough proportionality standard.[250] However, the court declined to apply the *Nollan/Dolan* rule to "generally applicable development fees or assessments."[251]

A concurring opinion stressed that "the taking of money is different, under the Fifth Amendment, from the taking of real or personal property." Monetary exactions such as taxes, special assessments, and user fees receive substantial judicial deference, and development fees that are "categorically applied to a general class—to all developments or to certain types of development" have and should continue to receive similar judicial deference.[252] The California Court applied the *Ehrlich* distinction between individualized monetary exactions and generalized development fees in *San Remo Hotel L.P. v. City and County of San Francisco*[253] to uphold a local housing replacement fee. Applying a "more deferential type of review" rather than the *Nollan/Dolan/Ehrlich* "heightened takings scrutiny," the court concluded that the housing replacement fees assessed "[bore] a reasonable relationship to loss of housing."[254] Courts in Arizona,[255] Colorado,[256] Kansas,[257] and Maryland[258] have reached similar conclusions with respect to fees established by the legislature affecting entire areas of a city, distinguishing them from the *Dolan*-type adjudicative decision to impose a fee affecting only an individual parcel.[259] The Supreme Court of Ohio, on the other hand, has concluded that the *Nollan/Dolan* "dual rational-nexus" test should be applied to impact fees as well as land dedications because it "balances both the interest of local governments and real estate developers without unnecessary restrictions."[260]

The Due Process Clause

The second major constitutional limitation on public land use regulation is expressed in the due process clauses of the Fifth and Fourteenth Amendments, which prohibit the deprivation of property "without due process of law."[261] Similar clauses exist in state constitutions.[262] The due process guaranty is designed to prevent abuses of police power and requires that the exercise of police power be "reasonably necessary for the accomplishment of the [public] purpose, and not unduly oppressive upon individuals."[263] Due process questions usually are categorized as raising either substantive due process or procedural due process issues, with substantive relating to the reasonableness of the particular regulation and procedural relating to the process by which the regulation was imposed.

Substantive Due Process

Substantive due process is an examination of the reasonableness of a particular exercise of police power. Courts apply a three-part test of (1) proper public purpose and (2) reasonable means to accomplish that purpose that (3) are not unduly oppressive on individuals.[264] Although the public-purpose prong is rarely the basis for a successful challenge to a land use regulation, the Supreme Court of Illinois reminded local governments in an eminent domain context that the public-purpose requirement is meaningful.[265] Substantive due process has been described as "the idea that depriving a person of life, liberty, or property can violate the due process clause . . . even if there are no procedural irregularities" and as a "tenacious but embattled concept."[266]

The explosion of regulatory takings litigation has brought on its coattails a minor explosion of substantive due process litigation. In many of the regulatory takings cases, property owners also allege violations of substantive due process.[267] It is axiomatic that a substantive due process claimant must allege and prove a protected property interest.[268] The entitlement analysis applied by the Second Circuit in *RRI Realty Corporation v. Incorporated Village of South-hampton* may overlap analytically the "bundle of rights" analysis discussed earlier in the takings section. Clearly, if the license, permit, or other property interest is found significant enough to be an "entitlement" under substantive due process analysis, it may very well be a protectable property interest under a takings analysis. The two approaches, however, may be distinguishable in that an arguably minor property interest such as a license or permit may not be sufficient to constitute a compensable property interest, but may be deemed to have been "arbitrarily and unreasonably denied" as a matter of substantive due process.[269] But federal courts will resist "[d]ressing a takings claim in the raiment of a due process violation" in order to avoid the exhaustion of state remedies requirements discussed below.[270]

In making substantive due process reviews, courts generally apply a standard of deference to the legislative body and often go to great lengths to state their unwillingness to second-guess the wisdom of a particular legislative decision. The guiding principle for federal substantive due process analysis has been stated by the Supreme Court as whether the state "could rationally have decided" that a particular action might achieve a legitimate governmental objective.[271] This principle has been applied in a "hands-off" manner by the federal courts,[272] although the appropriateness of continuing judicial deference to local legislative decisions has been questioned by the Supreme Court in a takings case:

> [O]ur cases describe the condition for abridgement of property rights through the police power as a "substantial advanc[ing]" of a legitimate State interest. We are inclined to be particularly careful about the adjective where the actual conveyance of property is made a condition to the lifting of a land use restriction, since in that context there is a heightened risk that the purpose is avoidance of the compensation requirement, rather than the stated police power objective.[273]

In the Court's next opportunity to consider the appropriate extent of judicial scrutiny of local police power regulations, the Court backed away from a stricter standard of review and applied the traditional standard of deference in holding that a rent-control ordinance did not "on its face" violate the due process clause, and that consideration of whether the ordinance amounted to a taking of property was premature because the ordinance had not yet been applied.[274]

Although both federal and state courts approach the substantive due process review with an attitude of deference to the legislative body, the federal courts traditionally have been less willing than have state courts to overturn a local land use regulation on due process grounds. An example of the difference of approach between state and federal courts occurred in litigation concerning a Pennsylvania township's downzoning of a tract of land from industrial to agricultural. The Commonwealth Court of Pennsylvania invalidated the downzoning after imposing the burden of justifying the downzoning on the township and finding that the township "has failed to show any substantial relationship between the rezoning . . . and the public health, safety, morals, or welfare."[275]

In a later federal action in which the landowner sought damages for loss of use of the property prior to the state court's invalidation of the rezoning, the Third Circuit affirmed a denial of the damages claim for failure to allege a deprivation of substantive due process. In discussing what the court characterized as a "far more active scrutiny . . . than would be appropriate in federal substantive due process analysis" on the part of the state court and the "very limited . . . review" available to the federal courts, the Court of Appeals noted that, instead of requiring the township to justify its decision as the state court had, the federal courts "must look . . . to whether, given the facts alleged . . . , the township could have had a legitimate reason for its decision. When we examine that pleading, . . . we find nothing to suggest that the Township's (action) . . . was anything other than a land use planning decision about which reasonable minds might differ."[276] The Fourth Circuit applies a three-part test: (1) plaintiff was deprived of a property interest (2) by the state (3) through action that "falls so far beyond the outer limits of legitimate governmental action that no due process can cure the deficiency."[277] The Fifth Circuit has concluded that failure of a local government to follow state-mandated procedures contained in its own ordinance was not per se irrational.[278] In upholding an ordinance limiting the number of pigs a landowner may keep on his property, the Sixth Circuit concluded that the approach of "limiting the number of swine, of any size, was a rational means of controlling odor," the public goal of the ordinance.[279] The Seventh Circuit has summed up the federal courts' approach to substantive due process questions: "Of course if a zoning decision is based on considerations that violate specific constitutional guarantees [such as First Amendment protection of religion or speech], it is invalid; but in all other cases the decision can be said to deny substantive due process only if it is irrational."[280]

Strict scrutiny is employed in the federal courts only if the legislation impinges on a fundamental right.[281] Courts rarely find that public regulations infringe on fundamental rights, as evidenced by the decision of the Fifth Circuit to uphold a local regulation prohibiting the transfer of waterfront property that was not properly supported to prevent the banks from caving in because "(t)he right freely to alienate real property is not a 'fundamental right' that calls for the application of strict scrutiny."[282]

State courts, on the other hand, may employ a stricter standard of review by denying the presumption of legislative validity if the regulatory decision is deemed to be administrative or quasi-judicial in nature rather than legislative.[283] The Supreme Court of Rhode Island, for example, concluded that landowners had established a prima facie substantive due process case under

42 U.S.C. Section 1983 through evidence that a local building official had unilaterally adjudged the landowners to be zoning violators, and as a result had refused to issue them a building permit.[284] The Supreme Court of Washington held that a landowner may bring a Section 1983 claim for violation of substantive due process rights because of a city council–mandated delay of two months in the issuance of a previously authorized grading permit. The fact that the permit later was issued does not prevent the landowner from seeking relief, the court concluded.[285]

Inquiries into the motives of administrative decision may be proper in substantive due process actions, but only when the decision being challenged is alleged to be based on "considerations personal to either the applicant (e.g., race or gender discrimination) or personal to one or more members of the agency (e.g., bribery or political retaliation)," the Supreme Court of Indiana concluded after reviewing reported decisions.[286]

A substantive due process inquiry will often focus on the legitimacy of the end for which the legislation was enacted. Thus zoning to preserve historical landmarks has been declared by the Supreme Court to be a valid end.[287] Zoning for aesthetic purposes has been considered legitimate,[288] as has zoning to preserve property value and slow growth[289] in order to preserve the environment.[290] In addition, a Tennessee court has declared that the integration of mentally and physically handicapped people into society is a valid purpose of zoning.[291]

Procedural Due Process

A challenge to land use regulations based on an alleged violation of procedural due process normally involves an argument that particular land use legislation was enacted or applied without reasonable notice to the landowner and opportunity to be heard.[292] Procedural due process claims are said to be based on "expectation[s] that the system is fair and has provided an adequate forum for the aggrieved to air [their] grievance[s]."[293] As with substantive due process claims, the crucial first step in a procedural due process case is the determination whether the complainant has a "cognizable property interest."[294] The right to procedural due process, however, does not attach unless the plaintiff has a property interest in the thing taken away.[295]

Procedural due process and substantive due process are closely related. In the words of the Seventh Circuit:

> As often, the line between "procedure" and "substance" is hazy in the setting of the regulation of land uses. The denial of the plaintiffs' site plan without a full statement of reasons is what gives the denial such arbitrary cast as it may have, and thus lends color to the claim of irrationality, which is the substantive due process claim; but the failure to give reasons is also the cornerstone of the procedural due process claim.[296]

As is the case for substantive due process questions, courts generally take a deferential attitude toward the local legislative body when procedural due process issues are raised. Procedures established by the legislative body that may be imperfect, but that "provide a suitable form of predeprivation hearing coupled with the availability of meaningful judicial review" are not likely to be overturned by a federal court.[297] The First Circuit has held that a developer is not entitled to a predeprivation administrative hearing before an agency that has refused to process construction drawings and a construction permit application when postdeprivation administrative and judicial review procedures permit the developer to present its allegations of administrative error and misconduct before appropriate reviewing bodies.[298] More drastic steps, such as stop-work orders and vacation of previously approved plats without a predeprivation hearing, have been held violative of procedural due process.[299]

Notice requirements do not have to meet rigid standards of precision as long as the notice is "reasonably calculated to impart useful and pertinent information under the circumstances then obtaining," a requirement that can be met by notice that is "timely, informative, and accurate."[300] A statute permitting revocation of a site plan before providing notice to the landowner provided that interested parties are given notice and an opportunity to request a hearing after the revocation passed due process muster, the Supreme Court of New Hampshire concluded.[301]

When a hearing is required, it must be conducted fairly. In *Shelton v. City of College Station,* the court held that a hearing was not unfair merely because a government official involved in a hearing belonged to a church that opposed the plaintiff's request.[302] A full-scale, judicial hearing—which would provide for cross-examination of witnesses—is not required because of the characterization of zoning decisions as legislative or quasi-legislative.[303]

In *Pelkey v. City of Presque Isle,* however, the Supreme Court of Maine held that a developer was denied the minimum standards of due process in the denial of a special-exception permit that would allow him to construct additional apartments on his property.[304] One of the members of the board that made the challenged decision had been a vocal opponent of the project at the public hearing and had been appointed to the board after the hearing. In addition, three of the five members present at the hearing had been replaced by the time the decision was made. In addition to the requirements of notice and an opportunity to be heard, "procedural due process also assumes that Board findings will be made only by those members who have heard the evidence and assessed the credibility of the various witnesses," the court stated.[305] The Supreme Court of Idaho held that city council members' receipt of ex parte telephone calls from unidentified citizens prior to a public hearing violated procedural due process. The subsequent public hearing did not cure the violation because, under Idaho law, the city council must base its decision on the record produced at its own appeal proceeding, and the ex parte calls were outside that record.[306]

The failure of an agency to follow its own regulations is not a per se denial of procedural due process.[307]

The Equal Protection Clause

A third constitutional limitation on local land use regulation is the Equal Protection Clause, which provides that no state shall deny any person within its jurisdiction the equal protection of the laws. In the context of land use legislation, this means that landowners who are similarly situated must be similarly treated.[308]

The standard used to test the validity of legislation under the Equal Protection Clause is similar to the rational relation test of substantive due process: The legislation must bear a rational relation to a permissive state objective.[309] The Supreme Court, in *City of Cleburne v. Cleburne Living Center*, applied the rational-basis standard to invalidate denial of a special-use permit for a group home because of "irrational" fear and prejudice against the class of people to occupy the residence.[310] A standard of strict scrutiny, however, is employed if the legislation creates a suspect classification and thereby discriminates on a basis such as race or gender.[311] Strict scrutiny is also employed when a fundamental right is lost as a result of the legislation.[312]

Allegations of irrational classifications may be based on the language of a regulation or statute itself[313] or on the administration of a facially neutral regulation or statute.[314] Because "the Fourteenth Amendment's guarantee of equal protection is based on federal, rather than state, standards of equality,"[315] the mere allegation that a local government violated state law by failing to enforce a zoning ordinance against a neighboring landowner will not support a federal equal protection claim unless there is also alleged: "1) a classification of similarly situated persons caused by intentional or purposeful discrimination on the part of the statute's administrators; and 2) . . . that the State's failure to enforce its law constituted a denial of a right, privilege, or immunity secured by the federal constitution."[316] Selective use of regulatory powers can trigger equal protection claims, even by a single plaintiff,[317] but improper motivation on the part of government officials must be alleged and proved.[318]

Courts applying the rational-basis standard have upheld the following:

- denials of special permits for day-care centers and other establishments that exceed a reasonable maximum number of occupants in order to limit noise and congestion[319]
- denial of a sign permit variance[320]
- delay in granting a building permit until after the contract to purchase the building had expired[321]
- refusal to renew a conditional alcoholic beverage license because of application of distance requirements that were not imposed on establishments in a riverfront development district[322]
- denial of plat approval unless the developer agreed to pave a portion of a city street or pay a pro rata share of the city's cost of paving[323]

In *Christian Gospel Church v. San Francisco*, denial of a conditional-use permit to allow a church to hold services in a residence within a district zoned residential was upheld.[324] The court found that there was no equal protection violation because the city's purpose (preserving the welfare and character of its neighborhoods) was rationally related to its decision not to issue the permit.

Ripeness

Although a landowner's constitutional challenge of a zoning ordinance may have merit, a court will decide the case only when the merits of the case are ready for review, or *ripe*.[325] As first discussed by the Supreme Court in *Agins v. City of Tiburon*, as-applied regulatory takings claims require a "concrete controversy regarding the application of the specific zoning provisions."[326] Depending on the type of claim that is brought, different standards for evaluating ripeness exist. Traditionally, four species of zoning challenges are recognized: compensable taking, substantive due process, procedural due process, and equal protection.[327]

Compensable Taking. A landowner or developer may claim that the state has "taken" his or her property through the enforcement of a zoning ordinance without compensation in violation of the Just Compensation Clause of the Fifth Amendment. The landowner or developer seeks monetary damages as a remedy. The damages consist of compensation for the value of the property rights taken for the duration of the taking. For the claim to be ripe, some governmental act must have taken place that forms the basis of the takings claim.[328] The plaintiff must overcome two hurdles that comprise the final decision rule. The plaintiff must demonstrate that (1) the regulatory body has made a final decision regarding how the property can be developed, and (2) the landowner has sought and been denied compensation under available state procedures.[329]

The landowner must demonstrate that the zoning board has made a final decision regarding the application of the regulation to his or her property. To do this, the plaintiff must show that the municipality denied the landowner specific use. This involves a two-step process: (1) the landowner or developer must request rezoning or other necessary land use permission that is denied and then (2) apply for a variance of the use of the property.[330] In some cases this means that a developer must also submit a plan for development of the property.[331] If a variance is granted, then there has not been a taking. Without a final decision on the matter, a court cannot determine whether a regulation has gone too far unless the court can measure how far the regulation will extend.[332]

What constitutes a final regulatory decision was examined by the Supreme Court in *Suitum v. Tahoe Regional Planning Agency.*[333] In *Suitum*, the Court held that a landowner's taking claim was ripe even though she had not attempted to sell the transferable development rights (TDRs) granted her by the planning agency when it declared her property to be ineligible for development.[334] The Court reversed decisions by the District Court and the Ninth Circuit that a final decision had not been made because of the lack of action on the TDRs. Justice Souter, writing for the Court, reviewed the ripeness precedents and concluded that a final decision had been made concerning the petitioner's land because the regulatory agency had no discretion to permit any increase in land use intensity. Action on the petitioner's TDRs was not necessary for ripeness because the regulatory agency had identified the particular TDRs to which she was entitled. The only remaining decision was whether a potential buyer may lawfully use the TDRs. "But whether a particular sale of TDRs may be completed is quite different from whether TDRs are saleable; so long as the particular buyer is not the only person who can lawfully buy, the rights would not be rendered unsaleable even if the agency were to make a discretionary decision to kill a particular sale."[335] Because the petitioner was "definitively barred from taking any affirmative step to develop her land," her claim, which raised a question about the value of the TDRs, was ripe for adjudication, the Court concluded.[336]

The Court returned to this question in *Palazzolo v. Rhode Island*.[337] Efforts were made in the 1960s and the 1980s to develop waterfront property designated by Rhode Island as coastal wetlands. Planning permission was denied because the petitioner sought to fill 11 acres of salt marshes to accommodate cars, boat trailers, and picnic facilities, something that required a showing, under regulations promulgated by the Rhode Island Coastal Resources Management Council, of "a compelling public purpose which provides benefits to the public as a whole as opposed to individual or private interests."[338] Palazzolo filed an inverse condemnation suit, denial of which was upheld by the Rhode Island Supreme Court on several grounds, including ripeness.

In reversing the not-ripe determination, the Supreme Court distinguished cases involving questions whether an agency's "full discretion" had been exercised.

> Under our ripeness rules a takings claim based on a law or regulation which is alleged to go too far in burdening property depends upon the landowner's first having followed reasonable steps to allow regulatory agencies to exercise their full discretion in considering development plans for the property, including the opportunity to grant any variances or waivers allowed by law. . . . The rulings of the Council interpreting the regulations at issue, and the briefs, arguments, and candid statements by counsel for both sides, leave no doubt on this point: On the wetlands there can be no fill for any ordinary land use. . . . And with no fill there can be no structures and no development on the wetlands. Further permit applications were not necessary to establish this point.[339]

The Court also concluded that its ripeness rules did not require Mr. Palazzolo to seek permission to develop the uplands portion of his property, nor the 74-lot subdivision that would have been built on the filled land.[340]

In addition to obtaining a final regulatory decision, the plaintiff must also utilize state procedures for obtaining compensation for the taking. "[I]f a State provides an adequate procedure for seeking just compensation, the property owner cannot claim a violation of the Just Compensation clause until it has used the procedure and been denied just compensation."[341] For example, the Supreme Court of Wisconsin held that, while denial of a special-exception permit application gave rise to a temporary taking claim, the plaintiffs' federal due process and takings claims were not ripe because a temporary regulatory takings claim was available under the Wisconsin constitution, but the plaintiffs had not pursued the state claim.[342] The state remedy must be pursued even though the availability of compensation for inverse condemnation may be uncertain because state courts may not yet have faced the particular claim at issue.[343]

The Ninth Circuit applied the final decision rule to an inverse condemnation proceeding in *Daniel v. County of Santa Barbara*.[344] In 1974 and 1977, previous owners of beachfront property had executed and recorded 25-year

"Firm Continuing Offers to Dedicate" (FCOTD) a five-foot easement across the property for bicycle and pedestrian traffic. These FCOTDs had been attached as conditions to subdivision and building permits issued by the California Coastal Commission. No appeal beyond the Coastal Commission was made. In 1988, shortly after the *First English*[345] and *Nollan*[346] decisions were announced, the Coastal Commission demanded and received a 25-year "Irrevocable Offer to Dedicate" (IOTD) from the then-current landowner, who registered no challenge or appeal. The current owners purchased the property in 1997. In 1998 the county adopted a resolution accepting the 1987 IOTD. Although the *Palazzolo* rule permits a successor-in-interest to challenge a previously enacted regulation as a compensatory taking,[347] the failure of the predecessors to challenge the exactions in a timely manner acted as a bar to the current owner because the statute of limitations had expired, the Ninth Circuit ruled.[348] The Court also noted that if an option to acquire an easement is a taking, it becomes so at the time the option is acquired. Therefore, the current owners acquired the property subject to the option and suffered no compensable taking.[349] Finally, the court noted that the plaintiffs sought the wrong remedy: an injunction against exercise of the option. The proper remedy was damages, the court held, but plaintiffs had not sought that remedy.[350]

Substantive Due Process. The landowner or developer may utilize a claim of a denial of substantive due process. In a substantive due process claim, a plaintiff would argue that the ordinance is arbitrary and capricious because it does not bear a substantial relation to the protection of public health, safety, morals, or general welfare. Unlike the takings claim, in which the plaintiff must prove that he or she has suffered a taking, as evidenced by the final decision by the city, a substantive due process claim need only establish that there has been arbitrary and capricious conduct by the zoning board. The plaintiff must still establish that a final decision has been made, but need not show that he or she has applied for compensation through the state procedures when seeking invalidation of an ordinance.[351] The plaintiff's denial of due process occurred the moment the arbitrary zoning decision was made,[352] unlike a taking, in which the violation occurs only when the ordinance is applied to a parcel of property. A final decision is necessary only to determine how the regulation will be applied to the property. The standard, therefore, is lower than in a taking claim.

The plaintiff need not have applied for variance if the substantive due process claim is a *facial* challenge.[353] If the challenge to the constitutionality of the ordinance, however, is that it denies substantive due process *as applied*, then the plaintiff must demonstrate that he or she has satisfied the final decision rule.[354] In *Eide v. Sarasota County*, an as-applied challenge to the constitutionality of an amendment to a statutorily mandated land use plan that required a developer to obtain a rezoning before he could make commercial use of his land was rejected as not ripe because the developer had not demonstrated that the plan restrictions had been applied to his property.[355] The developer had applied for the required rezoning, but no decision had been made because the developer never completed a traffic impact analysis, which was required as part of the rezoning application. There was no basis on which to consider the as-applied challenge because the lack of a decision by the county on the zoning request meant that the challenged plan provision had not yet actually been applied to the developer's property, the court concluded.[356]

Procedural Due Process. The final decision rule must be satisfied in order for a procedural due process claim to be ripe for adjudication.[357] There can be no violation of procedural due process until the claimant has availed him or herself of the procedures available. He or she has not suffered an injury until he or she has applied for rezoning and a variance, and the requests are denied. In this sense, a claim of a violation of procedural due process is subject to the same ripeness requirements as a taking claim, depending on the circumstances of the case.[358] In some circumstances, the ripeness requirement for a procedural due process claim is not as strict as for a taking claim. In *Harris v. County of Riverside,* the plaintiff brought both a taking claim and a procedural due process claim, which was independent of the taking claim. The plaintiff claimed that the city's requirement that he pay a nonreturnable fee to apply to regain the commercial use of his land violated his procedural due process rights. Because this claim was independent of the taking claim, the court found that the plaintiff did not need a final determination before he could go forward with his procedural due process claim. Furthermore, the plaintiff asserted that he was entitled to individual service of process of the pending zoning change, rather than mere notice by publication. The court found that the plaintiff had been denied procedural due process on both claims.[359]

The ripeness doctrine may require not only full exploitation of state remedies, such as variance proceedings, but also the pursuit of a "less ambitious" plan of development.[360] A set of circumstances that may not be ripe for one constitutional claim may indeed be ripe for another.[361] In *Nasierowski Brothers Investment Company v. City of Sterling Heights,* the violation of a property owner's procedural due process rights was held to be ripe for judicial review when a zoning change was enacted without adequate notice, even though the property owner did not seek a variance from the zoning, where there was evidence of immediate injury to the landowner upon enactment of the unfavorable zoning.[362] This case also makes it clear that the ripeness threshold is reached earlier in procedural due process cases than in takings cases.[363]

Equal Protection. Equal protection claims arising out of land use decisions have not been required to meet the special ripeness rules of *Williamson County,* so long as they are not "just a single takings claim with different disguises."[364] The Seventh Circuit has allowed a landowner to maintain an equal protection claim based on allegations that local officials required the landowner to convey a buffer strip to one of the officials in return for village approval of the landowner's final plat.[365]

Remedies for Unconstitutional Land Use Regulation

The intersection of two constitutional doctrines—regulatory takings and substantive due process—in modern land use law has provoked controversy about the appropriate remedy for overzealous land regulation from the inception of comprehensive zoning. With the Supreme Court's decision in *First English* that compensation is constitutionally required when a land use regulation effects a taking,[366] efforts to articulate separate analytical tests for compensable takings and noncompensable due process violations assume new significance, although the two doctrines have been characterized as "analytically identical."[367]

Landowners victimized by public regulations that cross the boundary line from permissible to unconstitutional exercise of police power traditionally have been limited to the equitable remedies of declaratory judgment, injunction, and mandamus.[368] The California Supreme Court expressed the traditional viewpoint as follows: "In combination, the need for preserving a degree of freedom in the land-use planning function, and the inhibiting financial force which inheres in the inverse condemnation remedy, persuade us that on balance mandamus or declaratory relief rather than inverse condemnation is the appropriate relief under the circumstances."[369]

The alternative approach of awarding compensation through the eminent domain process was first suggested, but not implemented, by Justice Holmes in *Pennsylvania Coal v. Mahon,* when he noted that when diminution in value as a result of public regulation "reaches a certain magnitude, in most if not in all cases there must be an exercise of eminent domain and compensation to sustain the act."[370] Although the Constitutional origin of the right to compensation for takings of property was recognized as early as 1933,[371] the availability of compensation through inverse condemnation actions for regulatory actions that amount to taking of property was not recognized by the Supreme Court until 1987.[372]

The *First English* Case

First English involved a challenge to an interim ordinance enacted by Los Angeles County prohibiting construction or reconstruction of buildings located in the floodplain of Mill Creek following a disastrous flood that had destroyed a campground owned and operated by the First English Evangelical Lutheran Church.[373]

After dispensing with a series of procedural questions that had stalled the Court on four previous occasions[374] by concluding that the lower courts' summary dismissal of a damages claim for regulatory deprivation of all use of a campground "isolates the remedial question for our consideration,"[375] the Court held that the California courts' conclusion that the only remedy for excessive regulation was nonmonetary relief through declaratory judgment or mandamus declarations of invalidity[376] was "inconsistent with the requirements" of the Fifth Amendment.[377] Although the Court did not decide whether the ordinance in question actually amounted to a regulatory taking by denying all reasonable use of the property, nor whether a compensable taking could be avoided by characterizing the ordinance as a safety regulation within the "nuisance exception" discussed in *Keystone,* the Court clearly established compensation as a remedy for regulatory takings.[378]

Noting that it is well established that a government can decide to continue to impose a regulation that affects a taking by electing to pay compensation for the taking that occurs by the continuance, the Chief Justice reasoned that cases that required the government to pay compensation for temporary takings, such as wartime appropriations of property or condemnation of leasehold interests, "reflect the fact that 'temporary' takings which, as here, deny a landowner all use of his property, are not different in kind from permanent takings, for which the Constitution clearly requires compensation."[379]

The Court distinguished prior decisions holding that mere diminution in value as a result of preliminary action by the government prior to the actual taking is not compensable, stating that these cases simply reaffirmed the rule that valuation for compensation purposes is determined as of the date of taking, and did not stand for the proposition that temporary regulatory takings prior to a declaration of invalidity could not be compensable.[380]

The Court declined to require that a government that had engaged in a regulatory taking must exercise the power of eminent domain at the behest of the property owner, a suggestion advanced by the Solicitor General. "We merely hold that where the government's activities have already worked a taking of all use of property, no subsequent action by the government can relieve it of the duty to provide compensation for the period during which the taking was effective."[381]

In an important limitation on the reach of the decision, the Court stated that it was not dealing "with the quite different questions that would arise in the case of normal delays in obtaining building permits, changes in zoning ordinances, variances, and the like which are not before us."[382]

Temporary Takings

The compensation remedy is available for temporary as well as permanent takings[383] and should be in an amount that is "a full and perfect equivalent for the property taken."[384] The property should be valued at the time of the taking, which will be the time when a government activity has the effect of depriving a landowner of "all use of property" rather than the time when a court ultimately determines that the challenged activity is invalid because it effects a taking.[385]

In a temporary taking situation, where the landowner is prohibited from using his or her land temporarily, the measure of damages will not be the entire cost of the fair-market value of the land, but only a fraction of the whole. Courts have awarded damages that measure the value of the use of the property during the temporary period that the land is taken.[386] In *Wheeler v. City of Pleasant Grove*, the developers and purchasers of an apartment complex sued the city after it withdrew their building permit.[387] The Eleventh Circuit found a temporary taking in the city's confiscation of their right to build the apartment complex. Although the fair-market value of the land remained steady, the fair-market value of the right to develop this property changed over that time. Appellants were found entitled to be compensated for the fluctuation in value of the right to develop the property.[388] The Supreme Judicial Court of

Massachusetts held that a Massachusetts statute exempting landowners from real estate taxes for property taken by eminent domain applied to temporary regulatory takings, entitling a landowner who suffered a temporary regulatory taking to a refund for real estate taxes paid during the time of the temporary taking.[389]

In *Yuba Natural Resources, Inc. v. United States,* the government asserted an interest in Yuba's land, which was being used to mine gold and other minerals.[390] The court declared a temporary taking by the government of Yuba's mineral rights. The court awarded damages for the amount that the landowner would have received as rent and minimum royalties during that time. The court declared, however, that the landowner was not entitled to recover the drop in fair-market value of the minerals during that period.[391]

In *State v. Doyle,* landowners who owned property near an airport brought suit for inverse condemnation because of a substantial increase in noise from aircraft as a result of runway expansion.[392] The court awarded damages for the loss of the market value that was attributed to the noise level. The court also noted that a landowner could also make a claim for loss of appreciation of the property that could have been realized at the time of the taking.[393] A dedication requirement attached to a rezoning approval that meets the *Nollan* nexus test but fails the *Dolan* rough proportionality test is a taking, the Eighth Circuit Court of Appeals concluded; however, the landowner's remedy is not necessarily an order to rezone the property because the city may have a legitimate interest in declining to rezone. The landowner can seek compensation but must prove that the refusal to rezone without the dedication requirement cost the landowner damages, such as by the loss of an enforceable contract to sell the property. Despite not citing Section 1983 in the complaint or argument, the landowner who prevailed on the taking claim can obtain attorney fees as a vindication of the legislative policy to encourage meritorious civil rights claims, but only a partial award because he did not prevail on the rezoning or damages claim, the court concluded.[394]

42 U.S.C. Section 1983

The private remedy for deprivation of constitutional rights found in 42 U.S.C. Section 1983 added a new dimension to land use litigation, especially so since the 1987 takings trilogy. Section 1983 provides as follows:

> Every person who, under color of any statute, ordinance, regulation, custom, or usage, of any State or Territory or the District of Columbia, subjects, or causes to be subjected, any citizen of the United States or other person within the jurisdiction thereof to the deprivation of any rights, privileges, or immunities secured by the Constitution and laws, shall be liable to the party injured in that action at law, suit in equity, or other proper proceeding for redress.[395]

Section 1983 claims are cognizable under the concurrent jurisdiction of state courts.[396] The plaintiff must show both deprivation of a federal constitutional or statutory right and that the defendant acted under color of state law.[397] The 1983 remedy is made more attractive by the recoverability of attorneys' fees under 42 U.S.C. Section 1988.[398]

The Supreme Court, in *City of Monterey v. Del Monte Dunes*,[399] held that landowners filing Section 1983 takings and due process claims can obtain jury trials. The Court concluded that Section 1983 actions seeking legal relief are actions at law within the meaning of the Seventh Amendment's guarantee of a jury trial. Distinguishing eminent domain cases in which the government "concedes the landowner's right to receive just compensation," the Court held that "[w]hen the government takes property without initiating condemnation proceedings, it 'shifts to the landowner the burden to discover the encroachment and to take affirmative action to recover just compensation.'"[400] In holding that issues of liability in a regulatory taking claim are properly submitted to a jury, the Court held that "the issue whether a landowner has been deprived of all economically viable use of his property is a predominantly factual question."[401] The Court distinguished Section 1983 cases from "ordinary inverse condemnation" cases, the jury's role in which it did not address. It did "not attempt a precise demarcation of the respective provinces of judge and jury in determining whether a zoning decision substantially advances legitimate governmental interests." The Court noted that in Section 1983 actions, "the disputed questions were whether the government had denied a constitutional right in acting outside the bounds of its authority and, if so, the extent of any resulting damages. These were questions for the jury."[402]

The Ninth Circuit distinguished *Del Monte Dunes* in holding that a landowner's spot-zoning allegation[403] is not entitled to a jury trial. In doing so, the court acknowledged that it had "some difficulty parsing the distinctions laid out by the Supreme Court concerning when a jury trial is required." Noting that *Del Monte Dunes* did not address the issue of unreasonable application of general regulations (spot zoning) and did not consider traditional summary judgment standards, the Ninth Circuit concluded that the spot-zoning allegation was a due process claim rather than a takings claim that was properly within the province of the district court.[404]

At first blush, it would seem that virtually every constitutional right discussed in this chapter would invoke a remedy under Section 1983. As a practical matter, however, the Section 1983 cause of action may be more difficult to bring to fruition, possibly because it usually includes an attack on—and claim for money damages against—public servants. Thus the cases in which constitutional violations have occurred seem more numerous than cases in which those violations were redressed by Section 1983 verdicts. Presumably, practitioners recognize the reluctance by courts and juries to redress anything but the most grievous violations by payment of damages out of the public treasury.

In addition, legislative public officials, but not the governmental entity itself, enjoy absolute immunity for conduct in furtherance of legislative functions, although in some courts such immunity may not extend to local legislators.[405] The Section 1983 cause of action may include private parties as defendants only where there is evidence of a conspiracy among the private parties and the governmental entity.[406]

The Section 1983 remedy is available regardless of the availability of any state tort remedy.[407] A cause of action under Section 1983 for a temporary taking caused by an invalid zoning ordinance accrues for purposes of the statute of limitations at the time the ordinance is declared invalid, and such declaration is subject to no further appeal.[408] However, a Section 1983 cause of action for alleged takings resulting from enactment of an ordinance restricting off-site billboards accrues when the ordinance is enacted. The applicable statute of limitations will be borrowed from state law.[409]

In the context of regulatory takings, a prerequisite to a Section 1983 cause of action is the denial of just compensation under state condemnation law.[410] In *GM Engineers and Associates v. West Bloomfield Township*,[411] the court dismissed a Section 1983 complaint in which the plaintiff did not allege that Michigan's inverse condemnation procedures were inadequate.

The First Amendment

Land use regulations directed at activities associated with speech or religion are subject to greater judicial scrutiny because of the special protection afforded such activities by the First Amendment. The First Circuit, reviewing recent Supreme Court opinions, noted that the Court has applied a "triage" rule:[412] (1) all communication in a public forum may not be banned,[413] (2) content-based restrictions may be acceptable "only if they are justified by compelling state interests,"[414] and (3) content-neutral restrictions are acceptable if they are reasonable "time, place and manner" regulations. They are upheld provided they are "narrowly tailored to serve a significant governmental interest, and allow for reasonable alternative channels of communication."[415] In the context of land use planning, First Amendment issues often arise when a city attempts to regulate adult entertainment, signs, and the location or operation of churches.

Adult Entertainment

Adult theaters can be regulated constitutionally if the regulation is aimed not at suppressing the content of the speech but rather at limiting the secondary effects of adult entertainment on the surrounding community.[416] Such regulations are reviewed under standards applicable to content-neutral time, place, and manner regulations, and have been upheld when shown to be serving a substantial government interest and permitting reasonable alternative avenues of communication.[417] The leading case is *City of Renton v. Playtime Theaters, Inc.*,[418] which further defined the standards set forth in another important case, *Young v. American Mini Theaters, Inc.*[419] In *City of Renton*, plaintiffs challenged a statute that prohibited adult theaters from locating within 1,000 feet of a residential zone, church, park, or school. In upholding the statute, the court found that the statute was not an attempt to suppress adult entertainment entirely, but was merely an attempt to regulate the time, place, and manner of the adult entertainment.[420] Furthermore, the statute was valid because it was designed to preserve the quality of life (substantial government interest) and did not make it impossible for the theaters to locate within the city limits (alternative avenues of communication).[421] Significantly, the court held that a city, in proving the presence of a government interest, can rely on the studies and experiences of other cities.[422] Applying *Renton*, the Supreme Court held that the city of Los Angeles could rely on a study of adult businesses by its own police department in prohibiting more than one adult business in the same building.[423] In reaching its decision, the Court disagreed sharply on what value to place on specific studies. A plurality, Justices O'Connor, Scalia, and Thomas and Chief Justice Rehnquist, agreed that Los Angeles acted reasonably in assuming that, because its study showed that a high concentration of adult business establishments are associated with high crime rates, high concentrations of adult business operations in one locale would produce a similar high crime rate.[424] Justice Kennedy concurred in the judgment but disagreed with the plurality's rationale because he feared a "subtle expansion" of *Renton*.[425] Justices Souter, Stevens, Ginsburg, and Breyer dissented, believing that the Los Angeles study did not provide sufficient evidence to warrant changing from a policy of dispersal of adult establishments to a policy of "dividing them in two," particularly because of "how close to a content basis adult business zoning can get."[426]

Live entertainment, including nonobscene nude dancing, has received First Amendment protection as a form of expression.[427] The Supreme Court has concluded that ordinances banning public nudity may be applied to restrict nude dancing if they satisfy a four-factor test for evaluating restrictions on symbolic speech.[428] The regulation must be (1) "within the constitutional power of the government" to enact, (2) further an "important or substantial government interest" (3) "unrelated to the suppression of free expression," and (4) must be "no greater than is essential to the furtherance of the government interest."[429] A common form of regulation has been through licensing,[430] but such ordinances have been struck down when no time limit has been set for necessary inspections to occur and no avenue for prompt judicial review of license denials has been established.[431] Ordinances have also been struck down when no discernible standards have been articulated to guide the exercise of discretion in granting licenses,[432] when information demanded from applicants "serves no legitimate governmental purpose"[433] or lacks a "substantial relation" to a governmental purpose.[434]

Ordinances regulating the hours of operation of nude entertainment establishments, minimum age of patrons, and distance from houses, churches, or schools have been upheld as permissible neutral-time, -place, and -manner regulations when the standards established are reasonable.[435] Likewise, courts have accepted reasonable restrictions on signage, painting, and viewing booth configurations,[436] as well as requirements for buffer zones between patrons and performers and unobstructed views by inspecting law enforcement personnel.[437] Ordinances banning totally nude dancing have been upheld because laws prohibiting public indecency further important governmental interests despite "incidental burdens on some protected speech."[438]

Adult businesses are entitled to a reasonable opportunity to locate within the zoning jurisdiction. In *Woodall v. City of El Paso*, the Fifth Circuit struck down an El Paso zoning ordinance restricting adult businesses to locations at which, for physical or legal reasons, it would have been impossible to operate.[439] The record showed that the ordinance restricted adult business sites to approximately 1,433 of El Paso's 158,000 acres, and that the available land constituted industrial warehouse areas, drainage areas, areas with hostile restrictive covenants, airport land, and undeveloped desert areas.[440]

Not all alternate locations for adult businesses must be economically desirable in order to survive a First Amendment claim, however. In *Lakeland Lounge v. City of Jackson*,[441] the Fifth Circuit rather dismissively held that the adult business ordinance need not concern itself with the economic viability of the permitted industrial sites, quoting the Supreme Court's pronouncement in *Renton*[442] that "the inquiry for First Amendment purposes is not concerned with economic impact."[443] The court also quoted its own decision in *SDJ, Inc. v. City of Houston*[444] in stating that "alternative sites need not be commercially viable."[445]

The Supreme Court of New Jersey, after reviewing federal and state decisional law, concluded that the constitutionality of a state statute restricting the availability of sites for adult businesses, unless otherwise permitted by local ordinance, "need not be determined solely by reference to the boundaries of the municipality in which the business challenging the restriction seeks to locate." A three-step analytical process is required: (1) determine the "market area relevant to the [proposed] site, [which] should include areas located in other municipalities 'within reasonable proximity'" to the site in question; (2) determine the "relative availability of sites within that market," and (3) determine whether the "extent of the availability of alternative channels of communication, in relation to the size of the relevant market, is adequate." The court placed the burden of proof with respect to the adequacy of alternative avenues of communication on the township that enforced the law, in this case by denying a certificate of occupancy.[446]

In *Topanga Press, Inc. v. Los Angeles*,[447] the Ninth Circuit upheld a preliminary injunction prohibiting enforcement of an adult entertainment business zoning ordinance. The Ninth Circuit further held that a site for relocation may be considered part of the relevant real estate market when the following criteria are met: (1) there is a genuine possibility that the site will be available; (2) the site is within reasonable access of the general public; and (3) the site is supported with appropriate infrastructure (i.e., lighting, sidewalks, and roads). Additionally, a site that hosts a nonspecific commercial enterprise may be part of the real estate market, and commercially zoned relocation sites are part of the market. The Eleventh Circuit, in *David Vincent, Inc. v. Broward County*, canvassed the circuits and concluded that determination whether particular sites are reasonable locations for adult businesses can be resolved "with the aid of a few general rules."

> First, the economic feasibility of relocating to a site is not a First Amendment concern. Second, the fact that some development is required before a site can accommodate an adult business does not mean that the land is, *per se*, unavailable for First Amendment purposes. The ideal lot is often not to be found. Examples of impediments to the relocation of an adult business that may not be of a constitutional magnitude include having to

build a new facility instead of moving into an existing building; having to clean up waste or landscape a site; bearing the costs of generally applicable lighting, parking, or green space requirements; making due with less space than one desired; or having to purchase a larger lot than one needs. Third, the First Amendment is not concerned with restraints that are not imposed by the government itself or the physical characteristics of the sites designated for adult use by the zoning ordinance. It is of no import under *Renton* that the real estate market may be tight and sites currently unavailable for sale or lease, or that property owners may be reluctant to sell to an adult venue.[448]

Applying these rules, the court upheld a zoning ordinance establishing distance regulations for adult businesses and requiring nonconforming adult businesses to move to conforming sites within five years.[449]

Political and Commercial Speech

Statutes that regulate political or commercial speech are reviewed under standards similar to those explained previously. Local governments may regulate signs if the regulations advance significant government interests, are not content-based, and allow other reasonable methods of communication. For example, in *Georgia Outdoor Advertising v. City of Waynesville*,[450] a city's prohibition against virtually all off-premise advertising (i.e., billboards) was upheld because it furthered goals of aesthetics and safety, applied to all commercial signs, and allowed businesses to advertise on their own property.[451] In *American Legion Post 7 v. City of Durham*, the Fourth Circuit upheld a city ordinance regulating the display of flags. Flags are a protected means of communication, the court held, but an ordinance regulating the size of flags and the height at which they could be flown was an acceptable time, place, and manner regulation.[452] The Eleventh Circuit, in *Horton v. City of St. Augustine*, upheld an ordinance prohibiting street performances in a four-block area of a historic district as a valid time, place, and manner regulation.[453] But the Ninth Circuit concluded that an ordinance prohibiting sales and solicitations, except by news vendors and nonprofit organizations, along the Venice Beach, California boardwalk was unconstitutionally broad. Although the City of Los Angeles had articulated "significant state interests" in protecting public safety and convenience, it adopted an ordinance that was "overly inclusive because it prohibits not only purely commercial interests, but also protected expressive activities." The court was not persuaded that the "distinction between expressive activities" of nonprofits and other persons was reasonable or narrowly tailored.[454]

A city cannot totally suppress political speech. In *Matthews v. Town of Needham*, a statute that barred political signs on residential property was held unconstitutional because it effectively barred political speech.[455] A "floating" buffer zone requiring demonstrators to stay at least 15 feet from people and vehicles coming and going from abortion clinics was invalidated, whereas "fixed" buffer zones and doorways, driveways, and driveway entrances of such clinics were upheld in *Schenck v. Pro-Choice Network of Western New York*.[456] In reaching its decision, the Court reaffirmed its 1994 decision that content-neutral injunctions "must burden no more speech than necessary to serve a significant governmental interest."[457]

Municipalities may not require door-to-door canvassers to register and receive permits before contacting residents, the Supreme Court held in *Watchtower Bible and Tract Society v. Village of Stratton*.[458] In a facial challenge to the prior-approval requirement, the Court held that the Village's legitimate concerns about preventing fraud and crime and protecting privacy were outweighed by the significant impact the ordinance had on protected speech, particularly because the ordinance was not tailored effectively to the Village's interest. "It is offensive . . . that in the context of everyday public discourse a citizen must first inform the government of her desire to speak to her neighbors and then obtain a permit to do so," the Court asserted.[459] In *Pennsylvania Alliance For Jobs and Energy v. Council of the Borough of Munhall*, four ordinances from different cities restricting door-to-door canvassing to daylight hours and, in the case of two of the ordinances, to Saturday mornings, were held to be constitutional.[460] The court held that the ordinances were imposed without reference to the content of the speech, served the significant government interests of privacy and crime prevention, and left open ample alternative channels for communication.[461]

In *Plain Dealer Publishing Company v. City of Lakewood*,[462] the Sixth Circuit held that a city could constitutionally ban newsracks from the city streets where the regulation was content-neutral, served the government purposes of aesthetics, traffic safety, and so forth, and left open other means of distributing newspapers. The Supreme Court affirmed other parts of the *Plain Dealer* decision without addressing the constitutionality of this particular provision of the ordinance, thereby letting the Sixth Circuit's ruling stand.[463] This issue might arise in the land use context where, for example, a zoning regulation prohibits newsracks in residential areas.

Shopping Centers and Free Speech

The issue in shopping-center free-speech cases is whether an owner of a shopping center can prohibit certain people—who wish to demonstrate, collect signatures, or picket inside the shopping center—from entering. The Supreme Court has held that although there is no federal right of access to a private shopping center for the purpose of expressive activity,[464] states are free to construe their own constitutions in a way more expansive than the minimum federal constitutional level, thereby granting a right to enter private shopping centers that are open to the public to those who wish to exercise their state constitutional right of free speech.[465]

The First Amendment may also be implicated by a claim that a land use regulation was enacted in retaliation for political expression.[466]

Free Exercise of Religion Clause

Constitutional challenges to land use regulation as violative of the Free Exercise of Religion Clause have produced controversial results. One category of challenges involves cases in which a local law restricts activities of a church on a basis other than religion. In 1963 the Supreme Court articulated a balancing test under which a government regulation that substantially burdened a religious practice had to be justified by a compelling state interest.[467] In *Employment Division v. Smith,* however, the Supreme Court declined to subject "neutral laws of general applicability" to the compelling-interest standard.[468] Congress responded to the Court's decision by enacting the Religious Freedom Restoration Act of 1993 (RFRA), which restored the compelling-interest standard for general laws.[469]

The RFRA was invalidated by the Court in *City of Boerne v. Flores,* which held that the Act went beyond Congress's power to enforce the Fourteenth Amendment and encroached on the Court's power to interpret the Constitution.[470]

> Regardless of the state of the legislative record, RFRA cannot be considered remedial, preventive legislation, if those terms are to have any meaning. RFRA is so out of proportion to a supposed remedial or preventive object that it cannot be understood as responsive to, or designed to prevent, unconstitutional behavior. It appears, instead, to attempt a substantive change in constitutional protection. . . . This is a considerable congressional intrusion into the States' traditional prerogatives and general authority to regulate for the health and welfare of their citizens.[471]

In a strong dissent, Justice O'Connor repeated her opinion that *Smith* was wrongly decided and urged the Court to reconsider that holding.

> [T]he Free Exercise Clause is properly understood as an affirmative guarantee of the right to participate in religious activities without impermissible governmental interference, even where a believer's conduct is in tension with a law of general application. Certainly, it is in no way anomalous to accord heightened protection to a right identified in the text of the First Amendment.[472]

Congress responded to *City of Boerne* by enacting the Religious Land Use and Institutionalized Persons Act of 2000 (RLUIPA),[473] which is discussed in chapter 7 of this book. RLUIPA survived its first constitutional hurdle in *Freedom Baptist Church of Delaware County v. Township of Middletown.* In that case, a federal district court in Pennsylvania held that RLUIPA was a permissible exercise of Congress's broad powers under the Commerce Clause and Section 5 of the Fourteenth Amendment.[474] Although "zoning is traditionally a local matter," the court concluded that Congress has "broad authority to regulate economic activity even when it is primarily intrastate in nature." The court also held that RLUIPA was a codification of the individual assessments jurisprudence in Free Exercise cases originating in *Sherbert v. Verner,*[475] for which Congress had authority under Section 5 of the Fourteenth Amendment.[476]

Prior to RFRA and *Boerne,* lower courts had reached different results concerning the applicability of local land use restrictions to church buildings. In *St. Bartholomew's Church v. City of New York,*[477] New York's Landmark Preservation

Law required that an owner of a recognized landmark had to apply to the city before alerting the building. The directors of St. Bartholomew's Church wanted to replace its landmarked community house with a higher tower building to increase their revenue. The city declined the request, and the church challenged that the ordinance burdened the free exercise of religion and was therefore unconstitutional. The court upheld the ordinance as a valid neutral law, reasoning that "we understand Supreme Court decisions to indicate that neutral regulations that diminish the income of a religious organization do not implicate the free exercise clause."[478] The court noted that the test for determining a violation of the Free Exercise Clause was whether the "claimant has been denied the ability to practice his religion or coerced in the nature of those practices."[479]

The Supreme Court of Washington, however, struck down a landmarks ordinance as applied to a church as an unconstitutional restraint of religion. The ordinance placed specific controls on alterations to the church's exterior. The court defined the crux of the problem as whether the court should prefer the free exercise of religion over the police power of the state. The court noted that "although First Amendment rights are not absolute, 'freedom of religion [is] in a preferred position.'"[480] The test the court utilized in determining whether there had been a First Amendment violation was that the petitioner must show:

1. "the coercive effect of the enactment as it operates against him in the practice of his religion."[481]
2. If established, then the court analyzes the legislation under strict scrutiny to determine whether
   (a) a compelling state interest is present, and whether
   (b) the least restrictive means are used to achieve the goal.[482]

Applying the test, the court found that the ordinance could not be justified as a compelling governmental interest and struck it down as unconstitutional when applied to religious organizations.[483]

A New Jersey court held that denying a variance to a church for the construction of a radio antenna and tower on its property was a violation of the First Amendment because it interfered with a proposed religious use (i.e., the broadcast of liturgies).[484]

Denial of a conditional-use permit for the establishment of a church in a residential district was held not to violate the Free Exercise Clause because the denial did not burden religion. In reaching this decision, the Ninth Circuit used a three-part test examining:

1. the magnitude of the statute's impact on the exercise of the religious belief;
2. the existence of a compelling state interest justifying the imposed burden on the exercise of the religious belief; and
3. the extent to which recognition of an exemption from the statute would impede the objectives sought to be advanced by the state.[485]

The Supreme Court of Virginia in *Tran v. Gwinn* upheld a requirement that churches and other places of worship obtain a special-use permit before locating in residential zones. Canvassing reported cases, the Court concluded that the special-use permit requirement imposed only a "minimal and incidental burden" on the free exercise of religion and met the neutrality and general applicability standards of *Smith*.[486] But the Court vacated an injunction issued by the trial court as overly broad and too vague.[487] In *Elsaesser v. Hamilton Board of Zoning Appeals,* an Ohio court upheld a 30-foot setback requirement as applied to the erection of crosses on the property owner's front yard, affirming the Board of Zoning Appeals' finding that the cross constituted a "structure."[488]

In *State v. Cameron,* the Supreme Court of New Jersey held that a zoning ordinance prohibiting "churches and similar places of worship" from residential zones could not be applied to prohibit a minister from temporarily using his home to hold weekly, one-hour religious services because "it cannot . . . be determined with sufficient certainty what kinds of religious practices were intended to be governed by the ordinance."[489]

The Sixth Circuit, in a case of first impression, held that a city's decision to develop rather than close a previously dedicated roadway between two lots owned by a church was not a violation of the Free Exercise or Establishment clauses. Noting that the Free Exercise Clause "does not entitle a religious organization to special benefits," the Court found no evidence that the city engaged in religious discrimination by the decision to develop the roadway. The Establishment Clause allegation was dismissed for the same reason.[490]

Establishment of Religion Clause

The Establishment Clause of the First Amendment, made applicable to the states by the Fourteenth Amendment, prohibits laws "respecting an establishment of religion."[491] The clause requires government to be neutral toward religion, which, in some instances, requires accommodation of religion.[492] In *Lemon v. Kurtzman,* the Supreme Court articulated a three-prong test of (1) secular purpose, (2) neutral effect, and (3) no excessive governmental entanglement with religion for evaluating governmental actions affecting religion.[493] Applying the *Lemon* test, the Fourth Circuit upheld a Montgomery County zoning ordinance that exempted parochial schools from obtaining a special exception before constructing improvements on land in a residential zone that is owned by a religious organization. The Court concluded, after reviewing case law, that it "plow[ed] no new ground" in holding that the exemption from the special-exception requirement was a permissible accommodation of religion.[494]

In *First Assembly of God v. City of Alexandria,* conditions to the issuance of a special-use permit that included building a fence were held not to be a violation of the Establishment Clause because the conditions had a purely secular purpose, the promotion of health, safety, and welfare. Nor did the conditions violate the plaintiff's right to free speech because the conditions were not an attempt to regulate the plaintiff's conduct.[495]

Other Constitutional Issues

The Fourth Amendment

The Supreme Court has held that a mobile-home tenant's right to privacy under the Fourth Amendment may be violated by forcible eviction by the landlord with the aid of local sheriff's deputies.[496] Although the case does not involve a land use regulation but rather an eviction of a tenant, it may signal an extension of protection from property seizures to protection of privacy in one's own property.

In *Butcher v. City of Detroit,* a Michigan court held that an ordinance that required one- or two-family residential dwellings to be inspected before they were sold did not violate the Fourth Amendment prohibition of unreasonable searches.[497] The court reasoned that the ordinance restricted the search to published guidelines and had no connection to criminal investigations.[498] Although some ordinances require a search warrant to be obtained if an owner refuses to consent to an inspection, the challenged ordinance differs because the inspection is a condition of a legal sale. Because the owner can choose not to sell the house and thereby avoid the inspection, "the right to require a warrant . . . becomes rather meaningless."[499]

The Seventh Amendment

In actions by the government seeking civil penalties and injunctive relief under the Clean Water Act, the Seventh Amendment guarantees a jury trial to assess liability but not to determine the amount of the penalty.[500]

One Person–One Vote Requirement

In *Quinn v. Town of Dodgeville,* a town board's action of vetoing a rezone was challenged as being in violation of the one person–one vote requirement of the Fourteenth Amendment.[501] The court disagreed, however, because the town could veto only those zoning changes within the town boundaries.

The Commerce Clause

In *Norfolk Southern Corporation v. Oberly,* the Delaware Coastal Zone Act was upheld against a dormant commerce clause challenge.[502] The Act prohibits all heavy industry in the coastal zone not in operation as of June 28, 1971.

In evaluating environmental statutes that impose incidental burdens on interstate commerce against commerce clause challenges, the Third Circuit applied the balancing test of *Pike v. Bruce Church.*[503] The test is as follows: "If a statute regulates 'evenhandedly' and imposes only incidental burdens on interstate commerce, the courts must nevertheless strike it down if 'the burden imposed on such commerce is clearly excessive in relation to the putative local benefits.'"[504]

Using this test, the court found that the Delaware Coastal Zone Act did not violate the dormant commerce clause because the local benefits of the act outweighed any burden on interstate commerce.

In *Cranberry Hill Corporation v. Shaffer*, a New York law was invalidated because it violated the commerce clause.[505] The law required those who market out-of-state lots for lease or sale within New York to file with the state and to pay a filing fee. Because most intrastate developers were exempt from these requirements, the court held that the law was invalid because it discriminated against interstate commerce. In *Fort Gratiot Sanitary Landfill v. Michigan Department of Natural Resources*, the Supreme Court held that a Michigan statute permitting counties to refuse out-of-state waste violated the commerce clause as discriminatory.[506]

Takings Clauses in State Constitutions

All state constitutions have takings clauses, many of which include damage to property as well as taking of property.[507] For example, the California Constitution provides that "[p]rivate property may be taken or damaged for public use only when just compensation . . . has first been paid."[508] California courts have held that this clause gives landowners "broader protection" than does the Fifth Amendment of the federal constitution.[509] The definition of "damage" does not encompass mere diminution in value,[510] however, and rezoning of plaintiff's property from commercial to single-family residential, although it decreased the value of the plaintiff's property, was held not to be a taking under the California constitution.[511] The Supreme Court of Colorado has interpreted a similar damage clause in the Colorado constitution as providing "broader rights" than the federal provision, but has limited the damage clause to "situations in which the damage is caused by governmental activity in areas adjacent to the landowner's land.[512]

Aside from special coverage that may be occasioned by the damage provision, state courts tend to apply federal case law interchangeably with state case law in resolving takings cases.[513] For example, in *Animas Valley Sand and Gravel, Inc. v. Board of County Commissioners*, the Supreme Court of Colorado used *Palazzolo*'s two-step analysis—(1) a per se taking inquiry, and (2) if no per se taking, a *Penn Central* fact-specific multifactor review—and concluded that the economic impact of adoption of a county land use plan must be determined by reference to "the contiguous parcel of property owned by the landowner, not merely the segment most severely affected." [514]

The New Hampshire constitution has been interpreted as prohibiting "any taking of private property by whatever means without compensation."[515] In *Dugas v. Town of Conway*, Dugas successfully challenged the denial of a permit for a nonconforming use.[516] The court held that the denial was a taking of property without just compensation. "A past use . . . [creates] vested rights to a similar future use, so that a town may not unreasonably require the discontinuance of a nonconforming use."[517] In another New Hampshire case, the court ruled that a taking had occurred under the state's constitution when a portion of plaintiff's property was included in a conservation zone.[518] The Supreme Court of Washington, examining "six nonexclusive neutral criteria," noted that "private use" is defined more literally under the state takings

clause than under the Fifth Amendment and that "public use" has been interpreted more restrictively in Washington. Applying the broader protection of
private property under the state constitution, the court invalidated a statute
giving tenants of mobile-home parks a right of first refusal before the owner
can sell the park as an unconstitutional taking of private property for private
use. Whether the owner eventually receives compensation is irrelevant, the
court held, because the Washington state constitution's prohibition against
taking private property for private use was absolute.[519]

Some states recognized a remedy for a temporary taking before the
Supreme Court endorsement in *First English*.[520] In *Rippley v. City of Lincoln*,[521]
the court held that when an ordinance amounts to a taking, a city must either
(1) pay compensation or (2) rescind the challenged ordinance and compensate
for the temporary taking.[522]

Due Process Clauses in State Constitutions

State due process clauses are often interpreted as imposing more stringent
standards than the federal constitution.[523] In *Charter Township of Delta v. Dinolfo*,
an ordinance was questioned that limited the number of unrelated persons living in a single-family dwelling to two.[524] The city had attempted to enforce the
ordinance against members of a religious group who lived together in the
same homes. Although the ordinance did not violate the due process clause of
the federal constitution,[525] the ordinance was in violation of a similar state
clause because it was not rationally related to valid ends, such as preservation
of family values.[526]

In *Board of County Commissioners of the County of Boulder v. Thompson*, a
statute that excluded "junk yards" from agricultural zones was not in violation of the due process clauses of either the federal or Colorado constitutions.[527] The Court held that the exclusion was neither so "illogical, arbitrary
and unreasonable as to be constitutionally void,"[528] nor too vague to be
enforced.[529]

Practitioner Perspectives

A lawyer faced with a constitutional issue in a zoning faces several important
hurdles.[530] First and foremost is the question of whether a final decision has
occurred that will make the constitutional challenge ripe for adjudication. Resolution of that question requires a careful analysis of state and local land use
law, including any local procedures that may be a necessary part of an appeals
process. Because appeals cost money and time, landowners may wish to
bypass such procedures in the hopes of getting a quick decision on the case's
merits. One of the important lessons of the ripeness cases, however, is the
necessity for completing local appeals procedures unless there is clear evidence that such an approach is futile.

Once ripeness is established, the landowner faces the formidable task of
establishing that the challenged regulation prohibits all reasonable economic
use, or that the government has failed to make an "individualized determina-

tion" of the necessity for the regulation and thereby has exceeded the rough proportionality standard of *Nollan/Dolan*, or that the *Penn Central* multifactor analysis leads to a takings conclusion. The temptation to bring a facial challenge can be almost overwhelming because of the time and money involved in an as-applied challenge. Reported cases indicate that landowners lose far more often than they win in such instances. When landowners win, however, the budgetary impact on the government can be substantial as a result of *First English*.

The Supreme Court's approval of a 32-month moratorium in *Tahoe-Sierra* reinforces the notion that delay is an inevitable part of the land use planning and regulatory process. The case also reemphasizes the importance of seeking ways to accommodate the legitimate interests of both landowners and local governments. The 6-3 split indicates that the Court remains divided on the proper approach to the difficult problem of determining when a land use regulation crosses the line and becomes a compensable taking. Advocates of a categorical rule lost ground because only three members of the Court were willing to apply that approach to development moratoria. The ad hoc, multifactor analytical approach of *Penn Central* gained new life from Justice Stevens's strong endorsement, his refusal to apply the categorical approach of possessory takings law to governmental regulations that do not amount to physical appropriations, and his endorsement of the parcel-as-a-whole approach that was first articulated by Justice Brennan in *Penn Central*.

In emphasizing the effect a broad per se rule could have on governmental efforts to implement comprehensive planning goals through diverse land use regulations, Justice Stevens endorsed the communitarian principles that land is a natural resource to be used and enjoyed by present and future generations, and that individual property rights are naturally limited by the fact that human beings are social persons who belong to communities. Decisions regarding the use of privately owned land are subject to reasonable regulations imposed by the government on behalf of the community.

For 80 years, the Court has wrestled with Justice Holmes's admonition that regulation that goes "too far" is a taking.[531] Land use regulations have become increasingly sophisticated as growth pressures have reduced the amount of developable land and costs of public infrastructure have escalated. Property owners have pushed repeatedly, in the courts and more recently the legislatures, for a set of categorical rules that would define compensable regulatory takings. Justice Scalia moved the Court in the categorical rule direction with his opinions in *Nollan* and *Lucas*. Justice Stevens in *Tahoe-Sierra* has brought the Court back to Justice Brennan's multifactor analysis applied to an entire parcel of property on a case-by-case basis.

From a landowner's perspective, a major problem with the *Penn Central* multifactor approach is the emphasis it places on the impact of individual application. To establish such impact, and corresponding ripeness for judicial review, landowners must work their way through the local land use process. This requirement can add considerable time and corresponding expense to the development process, as well as uncertainty regarding the ultimate acceptance of the development proposal. Thus landowners prefer categorical rules that reduce the expense and uncertainty of development. Such rules often are sought, as in *Tahoe-Sierra*, through a facial challenge. The weakness in that strategy was demonstrated in *Tahoe-Sierra*. The regulation was clothed with a presumption of validity, and no evidence was produced concerning any particular deleterious impact, leaving the landowners with an almost insurmountable burden of persuasion.

Local governments, on the other hand, face increasing pressure from their constituents to provide costly infrastructure and services, protect the environment, and keep taxes to a minimum. To develop and implement effective plans responding to local concerns and desires, local governments must use flexible techniques that allow them to encourage creative and responsive development while restricting excessive and insensitive development. Accomplishing those goals becomes difficult if not impossible if compensation becomes a "normal" price local governments must pay to accomplish public goals.

The *Penn Central* analytical process, reinvigorated by Justice Stevens in *Tahoe-Sierra*, provides a framework for balancing the interests of landowners and local governments. *First English, Nollan/Dolan,* and *Lucas* provide compensatory protection to landowners who suffer loss of possessory rights (e.g., occupation, exclusion, permanent loss of use) through regulation. *Penn Central/ Tahoe-Sierra* provide a process for measuring the effect of regulations restricting use but not possession, and for determining whether a regulation "goes too far." Lest local governments think they now are free from court supervision, Justice Stevens's lengthy review of "fairness and justice" concerns is a reminder that local governments have a serious responsibility to review their regulatory decision-making processes and to make sure that land use regulations not only foster articulated public goals but also permit private landowners to use their property in some reasonable economic manner.

Practioners and planners speaking at an American Planning Association–sponsored audio conference on *Tahoe-Sierra* stressed the importance of establishing policies before regulations are enacted. Moratoria can be useful tools for the policy-making phase, but ordinances imposing moratoria should include fact-based and clearly articulated reasons why such a move is necessary. Objectives should be clear, strategies should be realistic, and sufficient resources and time should be allocated to permit meaningful citizen participation in the planning and policy making during the moratorium. Failure to do so can lead to successful as-applied takings challenges of moratoria.[532] The American Bar Association's (ABA) Section on State and Local Government Law has published an excellent collection of essays on constitutional issues in land use regulation: *Taking Sides on Takings Issues,* by Thomas E. Roberts, editor (2000).

A possible alternative to Justice Stevens's feared "litigation explosion"[533] would be to establish a mechanism to identify potential regulatory takings as early as possible. The purposes of the mechanism[534] would be to allow aggrieved landowners to raise regulatory taking challenges sooner rather than later and to give the regulatory body a vehicle for responding to and resolving any resulting disputes.

Early-review systems are available in several other land use control contexts. For example, the Pennsylvania eminent domain statute provides a landowner whose property is subject to eminent domain proceedings with an early hearing from the local board. Under the statute, local boards can award just compensation on the ground that the delay in prosecuting the eminent domain action itself amounts to a taking.[535] Additionally, the Supreme Court's reluctance to review the merits of taking cases until the aggrieved landowner has exhausted all local and state appeal procedures[536] highlights the importance of statutory provisions that authorize landowners to bring inverse condemnation actions when an excessive delay occurs in the prosecution of an eminent domain action.[537]

The concern over delay is equally important in the land use regulation context. Developers have a relatively brief window of opportunity for particular projects.[538] Instability of interest rates, costs of construction, and the expense of maintaining non–income-producing land can increase the cost of a project beyond the developer's financial ability.[539]

Regulatory takings raise an additional question that is inapplicable in the eminent domain context: Does delay caused by the regulatory process effect a taking in a situation in which the government has no plans to acquire a property interest? In the eminent domain setting, the government decides to acquire a property interest. The landowner's concern with the delay aspect of a regulatory procedure is whether the government will pay just compensation if market values drop during the time required to complete the regulation process.[540] Resolution of this regulatory taking question requires sophisticated analysis of the relationship between regulatory delay, reasonable expectations of landowners, including investment-backed expectations, and the possible uses for the land during the delay period. This analysis may be carried out in the local regulatory process as well as in the courthouse.

Landmark preservation programs use an administrative review process to evaluate the economic impact of the regulation of property owners.[541] For example, the Seattle Landmarks Preservation Ordinance requires the administering board to seek an agreement with the owner of a designated landmark on an appropriate range of "controls and incentives" to preserve property.[542] If the parties are unable to reach an agreement within a designated time, the board prepares recommended controls and incentives and forwards them to a hearing examiner, who conducts a public hearing on the matter.[543] Following the hearing, the hearing examiner may submit recommendations to the Seattle City Council, which has authority to enact ordinances establishing specific controls and economic incentives with respect to designated landmarks.[544]

An important limitation on the Seattle landmarks regulatory process is that no regulation may deprive landowners of "a reasonable economic return."[545] In determining the reasonable return on a site, the ordinance limits consideration to five factors:

1. The market value of the site before and after the imposition of controls or incentives

2. The owner's yearly net return on the site for the previous five years
3. Estimates of future net returns on the site, with and without the controls or incentives in question
4. The net return and the rate of return necessary to attract capital for investment on the site after the imposition of controls, if available, or on a comparable site with comparable controls
5. The net return and rate of return realized on comparable sites with comparable controls[546]

Another area in which local governments employ early-warning administrative review procedures is rent control. The rent-control ordinance upheld by the Supreme Court in *Pennell v. City of San Jose*[547] established an advisory commission on rents and rental disputes and a hearing officer to mediate rental increase disputes.[548] The San Jose ordinance allows rent increases of up to 8 percent per year.[549] Unless a tenant has appealed to the hearing officer, increases in excess of 8 percent may go into effect automatically after landlords have given notice of the increase to the affected tenants. Tenants who wish to appeal must file a timely petition for a hearing.[550] The hearing officer is to conduct a hearing and determine within ten days whether, in light of all the evidence presented, the proposed rent increase is reasonable.[551]

If the hearing officer determines that any part of the proposed increase is unreasonable, a 30-day mediation process commences in which the landlord and tenants seek an appropriate rental increase. If the parties fail to reach an agreement, the hearing officer determines and grants a reasonable increase.[552] Each party has seven days to appeal the hearing officer's decision to an arbitrator. The arbitrator conducts a hearing and reviews the report of the hearing officer and any additional documentation the parties supply within ten days after the hearing. Within 17 days of the appeal hearing, the arbitrator makes a final determination of the allowable rental increase, supported by written findings of fact.[553] The entire process is set up to permit landlords a fair and reasonable return on the value of their property while protecting tenants from arbitrary, capricious, or unreasonable rent increases.[554]

An early-warning administrative review process would give landowners an opportunity to voice their concerns about the effects land use regulations may have on their property rights.[555] The early-review process would alert the responsible authorities before the particular regulation actually effects a taking. Early review would also encourage affected parties to identify and accommodate common interests through compromise following negotiation or mediation. Finally, early review would give the municipality a greater role in framing the issues for judicial review because the aggrieved party would base his or her appeal on the record developed at the local arbitration hearing.

Rather than creating another layer of review that might contribute to the existing delays, state and local governments could incorporate the early-review process into the basic land use regulatory system.

Effective use of an early-review system, along with regulations carefully tailored to specific land use policies, would enable municipalities to continue to plan and regulate land in comprehensive, flexible, and innovative ways.

Keystone established that a challenged regulation must deprive the owner of all economic use of his or her land, not just the economic use of a "string of the property bundle." *First English* recognized that compensation is a property remedy when a *Keystone* taking occurs. Although *Nollan* and *Dolan* impose a stricter standard of review and a means-end relationship, the Court also approved a wide range of regulatory techniques in which the regulators can establish the requisite means-end relationship. As a result, landowners have access to the compensation remedy but continue to have an extremely difficult time proving a taking. Cities that fear the compensation remedy can prevent a taking by implementing an early review system.

Other approaches that governments may consider include statutory limitations on the amount of compensation that landowners may recover, the granting of immunity to planning and regulatory officials for decisions made in their official capacities, shortened statutes of limitations for compensation claims, and the use of mediation techniques to settle disputes before the compensation issue arises.[556]

First Amendment issues, particularly with respect to adult businesses, have triggered intense controversies in municipalities across the country. The ABA Section of State and Local Government Law has published a useful review of land use issues relating to the First Amendment: *Protecting Free Speech and Land Use Law* (2001). Scott Bergthold, a Scottsdale, Arizona attorney who drafted an amicus brief for the American Planning Association in *City of Los Angeles v. Alameda Books, Inc.*,[557] published *How to Avoid the Top Ten Pitfalls of Adult Business Regulation* in the May and July 2002 issues of *Land Use Law & Zoning Digest*.[558]

Notes

1. U.S. CONST. amend. V.
2. Chicago B.&Q. Co. R.R. v. Chicago, 166 U.S. 226 (1897).
3. Armstrong v. United States, 364 U.S. 40, 49 (1960).
4. *See, e.g.,* Village of Euclid v. Ambler Realty Co., 272 U.S. 365 (1926).
5. Nollan v. California Coastal Comm'n, 483 U.S. 825, 834 (1987).
6. Lawton v. Steele, 152 U.S. 133, 137 (1894), *quoted in* Nollan v. California Coastal Comm'n, 483 U.S. 825, 845 (1987) (Brennan, J., dissenting).
7. Hawaii Hous. Auth. v. Midkiff, 467 U.S. 229 (1984).
8. For a discussion of the elements of just compensation, see Almota Farmers Elevator & Warehouse Co. v. United States, 409 U.S. 470 (1973); United States v. Fuller, 409 U.S. 488 (1973).
9. Pennsylvania Coal Co. v. Mahon, 260 U.S. 393, 415 (1922).
10. Justice O'Connor, in her concurring opinion in Palazzolo v. Rhode Island, 533 U.S. 606, 630 (2001), warned: "The temptation to adopt what amount to *per se* rules in either direction must be resisted. The Takings Clause requires careful examination and weighing of all the relevant circumstances in this context." *Id.* at 636.
11. First English Evangelical Lutheran Church v. County of Los Angeles, 482 U.S. 304, 339 (1987) (Stevens, J., dissenting).
12. *Id.* at 321.
13. *Id.*

14. Tahoe-Sierra Pres. Council, Inc. v. Tahoe Reg'l Planning Agency, 535 U.S. 302, 122 S. Ct. 1465 (2002).

15. 438 U.S. 104, 124 (1978).

16. *See* chapter 10 *infra.*

17. Loretto v. TelePrompTer Manhattan CATV Corp., 458 U.S. 419 (1982).

18. Yee v. City of Escondido, 503 U.S. 519 (1992) (mobile-home rent-control ordinance not a taking because it did not authorize "unwanted physical occupation").

19. Hall v. City of Santa Barbara, 833 F.2d 1270, 1275 (9th Cir. 1986), *cert. denied,* 485 U.S. 940 (1988) (abrogated by *Yee,* n. 18, on other grounds).

20. 458 U.S. 419 (1982).

21. *See also* United States v. General Motors Corp., 323 U.S. 373 (1945) (Government did not take title or occupy warehouse but did effect taking when it deprived General Motors of all or most of interest in the subject matter by ousting General Motors from warehouse leased during World War II).

22. *Loretto,* 458 U.S. 419, 441 (1982), *discussed in* FCC v. Florida Power Corp., 480 U.S. 245, 252 (1987) (statute authorizing FCC to review rents charged by public utility landlords who have voluntarily entered into leases with cable company tenants renting space on utility poles did not effect a per se taking).

23. *Loretto,* 458 U.S. at 436.

24. FCC v. Florida Power Corp., 480 U.S. 245, 252–53 (1987).

25. Hall v. City of Santa Barbara, 833 F.2d 1270 (9th Cir. 1986), *cert. denied,* 485 U.S. 940 (1988). *But see* Yee v. City of Escondido, 503 U.S. 519 (1992).

26. *Hall,* 833 F.2d at 1276.

27. *Id.* at 1278, n. 19 and n. 20 (citing Block v. Hirsh, 256 U.S. 135 (1921)); Woods v. Cloyd W. Miller Co., 333 U.S. 138 (1948); Fisher v. City of Berkeley, 471 U.S. 1124 (1985); Fresh Pond Shopping Ctr., Inc. v. Callahan, 464 U.S. 875 (1983); Troy Ltd. v. Renna, 727 F.2d 287 (3d Cir. 1984). *But see* Hall v. City of Santa Barbara, 833 F.2d 1270 (9th Cir. 1986).

28. Hall v. City of Santa Barbara, 833 F.2d at 1279–80. *Accord,* Pinewood Estates v. Barnegat Township Leveling Bd., 898 F.2d 347 (3d Cir. 1990) (mobile-home park rent-control ordinance granting tenants permanent, transferable right to occupy mobile-home pads effected taking of property).

29. 503 U.S. 519 (1992).

30. 458 U.S. 419 (1982). The Court had refused to hear an earlier rent-control case, Pennell v. City of San Jose, 485 U.S. 1 (1988), because disputed provisions requiring rent-control administrators to consider tenants' ability to pay as one setting allowable rents had not yet been implemented.

31. Manufactured Hous. Cmtys. v. State, 13 P.3d 183, 193, 196 (Wash. 2000).

32. *See, e.g.,* Pruneyard Shopping Ctr. v. Robins, 447 U.S. 74, 79 (1980) (provision in state constitution allowing persons to collect signatures in privately owned shopping center is a reasonable use of police power through a restriction on private property and is not an unconstitutional taking of property rights because it does not unreasonably impair the value or use of the property as a shopping center). *See also* the discussion of shopping centers and free speech, p. 108 *supra.*

33. Kaiser Aetna v. United States, 444 U.S. 164 (1979) (navigation servitude); City of Austin v. Teague, 570 S.W.2d 389, 394 (Tex. 1978) (scenic easement).

34. United States v. Causby, 328 U.S. 256 (1946). *See also* Griggs v. Allegheny County, 369 U.S. 84 (1962) (a local government that owns and operates an airport with a runway ending 3250 feet from appellant's house, thus allowing low-altitude flights over the house and causing damage to the house and making it unbearable for dwelling, has "taken" the property "for public use" and must compensate the property owner).

35. City of Austin v. Travis County Landfill, 73 S.W.3d 234, 240 (Tex. 2002), applying United States v. Causby, 328 U.S. 256, 266 (1946) and Griggs v. Allegheny County, 369 U.S. 84, 87 (1962); Claassen v. City and County of Denver, 30 P.3d 710, 712–14 (Colo. Ct. App 2000), *cert. denied* (Colo. 2001).

36. Seawall Assocs. v. City of New York, 542 N.E.2d 1059, 1065–71 (N.Y.), *cert. denied*, 493 U.S. 976 (1989).

37. Bell v. Town of Wells, 557 A.2d 168, 172–73, 176–79 (Me. 1989).

38. Birnbaum v. State, 541 N.E.2d 23, 27 (N.Y. 1989), *cert. denied*, 494 U.S. 1078 (1990) (quoting Brooks-Scanlon Co. v. Railroad Comm'n, 251 U.S. 396, 399 (1920)).

39. *Birnbaum,* 541 N.E.2d at 27 (citing National Wildlife Fed. v. Interstate Commerce Comm'n, 850 F.2d 694 (D.C. Cir. 1988); Gibbons v. United States, 660 F.2d 1227 (7th Cir. 1981); Lehigh & New England v. Interstate Commerce Comm'n, 540 F.2d 71 (3d Cir. 1976).

40. *Birnbaum,* 541 N.E.2d at 28.

41. 395 U.S. 85 (1969). *See also* United States v. Caltex, Inc. (Philippines), 344 U.S. 149 (1952) (wartime destruction of private property by the government did not entitle owner to compensation under the Fifth Amendment).

42. *Nat'l Board of YMCA,* 395 U.S. at 93.

43. *Id.* at 92.

44. 357 U.S. 155 (1985).

45. *Id.* at 168.

46. 505 U.S. 1003 (1992).

47. *Id.* at 1018.

48. *Id.* at 1015.

49. 447 U.S. 255 (1980).

50. *Lucas,* 505 U.S. at 1030.

51. *Id.* at 1032.

52. *See, e.g.,* Robert H. Freilich, *Time, Space and Value* in *Inverse Condemnation: A Unified Theory for Partial Takings Analysis,* 24 U. Haw. L. Rev. 589 (2002); Glenn P. Sugameli, *Lucas v. South Carolina Coastal Council: The Categorical & Other "Exceptions" to Liability for Fifth Amendment Takings of Private Property Far Outweigh the "Rule,"* 29 Envtl. L. 939 (1999). Douglas Kmiec, *Inserting the Last Remaining Pieces into the Takings Puzzle,* 38 Wm. & Mary L. Rev. 995 (1997) and *At Last, The Supreme Court Solves the Takings Puzzle,* 19 Harv. J. L. & Pub. Pol'y 147 (1995) (*Lucas,* along with *Nollan* and *Dolan,* anchor takings law where it belongs—in the common law); Daniel R. Mandelker, *Of Mice and Missiles: A True Account of Lucas v. South Carolina Coastal Council,* 8 J. Land Use & Envtl. L. 285 (1993). *See also* John R. Nolon, *Footprints in the Shifting Sands of the Isle of Palms: A Practical Analysis of Regulatory Takings Cases,* 8 J. Land Use & Envtl. L. 1 (1992). For helpful reviews of the *Lucas* takings analysis, containing useful suggestions for practitioners, *see* James J. Brown, *Takings: Who Says It Needs to Be So Confusing?,* 22 Stetson L. Rev. 379 (1993), and Richard A. Lazarus, *Putting the Correct "Spin" on Lucas,* 45 Stanford L. Rev. 1411 (1993).

On remand from the U.S. Supreme Court, the South Carolina Supreme Court in *Lucas* ruled unanimously that Mr. Lucas had suffered a temporary taking by the enforcement of the state's Beachfront Management Act, and that the land use sought to be regulated by the act was not a nuisance under state law. 424 S.E.2d 484 (S.C. 1992). The case was settled by the state purchasing the property for about $1 million. The state reportedly sold the land and recouped most of its investment.

53. 533 U.S. 606, 121 S. Ct. 2448, 2464 (2001).

54. 535 U.S. 302, 332, 122 S. Ct. 1465, 1484 (2002).

55. Penn Cent. Transp. Co. v. New York City, 438 U.S. 104 (1978) (application of New York City's landmarks preservation law to Grand Central Terminal building held not a taking.).

56. *See, e.g.,* Village of Euclid v. Ambler Realty Co., 272 U.S. 365 (1926) (75 percent reduction in value); Hadacheck v. Sebastian, 239 U.S. 394 (1915) (value reduced from $800,000 to $60,000).

57. *See, e.g.,* Hodel v. Virginia Surface Mining & Reclamation Ass'n, 452 U.S. 264 (1981); Furey v. City of Sacramento, 780 F.2d 1448 (9th Cir. 1986) (taking only if regulation results in total loss of all economic uses); National Western Life Ins. Co. v. Commodore Cove Improvement Dist., 678 F.2d 24 (5th Cir. 1982); Braunagel v. City of Devel's Lake, 629 N.W. 2d 567, 573 (N.D. 2001) (landowner failed to demonstrate that refusal to annex agricultural land and rezone it for multifamily use deprived him of all or substantially all use of his land).

58. Pace Res., Inc. v. Shrewsbury Township, 808 F.2d 1023 (3d Cir. 1987), *cert. denied,* 482 U.S. 906 (1987) (landowner who successfully challenged rezone of portion of land from industrial to agricultural not entitled to compensation for loss of property during time the rezone was being challenged because reasonable economic uses of property still existed while property was zoned agricultural).

59. Agins v. City of Tiburon, 447 U.S. 255 (1980); Lucas v. S. Carolina Coastal Council, 505 U.S. 1003 (1992).

60. 330 N.W.2d 505 (Neb. 1983).

61. *See, e.g.,* Hadacheck v. Sebastian, 239 U.S. 394 (1915) (brickyard regarded by the court as a nuisance); Balent v. City of Wilkes-Barre, 492 A.2d 1196 (Pa. Commw. Ct. 1985) (no taking where city tore down a building that had become dangerous to the public).

62. Cheyenne Airport Bd. v. Rogers, 707 P.2d 717, 731 (Wyo. 1985), *appeal dismissed,* 476 U.S. 1110 (1985).

63. *See, e.g.,* First English Evangelical Lutheran Church v. County of Los Angeles, 210 Cal. App. 3d 1353, 258 Cal. Rptr. 893, 904 (1989), *cert. denied,* 493 U.S. 1056 (1990) (*First English II*), *citing* Miller v. Schoene, 276 U.S. 272 (1928) (upholding requirement that property owners cut down diseased red cedar trees to protect neighboring apple orchards).

64. *See, e.g.,* City of Austin v. Teague, 570 S.W.2d 389, 394 (Tex. 1978), concluding that denial of an application for a permit to channel and enclose a creek crossing the landowners' property amounted to the taking of a scenic easement "at no cost which . . . singled out plaintiffs to bear all of the cost for the community benefit without distributing any cost among the members of the community." For a discussion of the harm/benefit test, *see* Joseph Sax, *Takings and the Police Power,* 74 YALE L. J. 36 (1964).

65. Department of Agriculture and Consumer Services v. Mid-Florida Growers, Inc., 521 So. 2d 101, 103 (Fla. 1988), *cert. denied,* 490 U.S. 1020 (1989) *See also* Florida Rock Indus. v. United States, 18 F.3d 1560 (Fed. Cir. 1994) (denial of permit for limestone mining because of possible contamination of aquifer insufficient basis for application of nuisance exception to takings clause).

66. *Mid-Florida Growers,* 521 So. 2d at 105 (McDonald, C.J., dissenting).

67. *See, e.g.,* Lamar Adver., Inc. v. City of Albany, 389 S.E.2d 216 (Ga. 1990) (ordinance requiring removal of nonconforming signs without payment of just and adequate compensation invalidated as taking of private property). *See also* City of Fort Collins v. Root Outdoor Adver., Inc., 788 P.2d 149 (Colo. 1990) (five-year amortization period for uncompensated removal of signs does not satisfy just-compensation requirement of controlling federal statute regulating outdoor advertising signs). The Supreme Court has rejected the harm/benefit test as "simply the progenitor of our more contemporary statements" regarding regulations that advance legitimate state interests. Lucas v. S. Carolina Coastal Comm'n, 505 U.S. 1003, 1023 (1992).

68. *See* discussion of due process issues, notes 261 to 307 and accompanying text *infra.*

69. Pace Res., Inc. v. Shrewsbury Township, 808 F.2d 1023, 1031 (3d Cir. 1987), *cert. denied,* 482 U.S. 906 (1987). *See also* Bensch v. Metro. Dade County, 541 So. 2d 1329 (Fla. Ct.

App. 1989) (failure to allege deprivation of *all* beneficial uses of property precluded consideration of constitutional taking claim).

70. Lockary v. Kayfetz, 917 F.2d 1150, 1154 (9th Cir. 1990).

71. *See, e.g.*, AA Profiles, Inc. v. City of Ft. Lauderdale, 850 F.2d 1483 (11th Cir. 1988), *cert. denied*, 490 U.S. 1020 (1989) (revocation of permits for wood-chipping business and subsequent downzoning effected a compensable taking of property interest in completed project); Wheeler v. City of Pleasant Grove, 664 F.2d 99 (5th Cir. Unit B. Dec. 1981), *cert. denied*, 456 U.S. 973 (1982) (*Wheeler I*); Wheeler v. City of Pleasant Grove, 746 F.2d 1437 (11th Cir. 1984) (*Wheeler II*) (withdrawal of permit for construction of apartment complex and subsequent downzoning in response to public opposition to apartment development was arbitrary and capricious, requiring compensation to be paid for the temporary taking that ensued).

72. Henry County v. Tim Jones Props., 539 S.E.2d 167, 169 (Ga. 2000).

73. Keshbro, Inc. v. City of Miami, 801 So.2d 864, 867, 876–77 (Fla. 2001).

74. Eberle v. Dane County Bd. of Adjustment, 595 N.W.2d 730, 739–40 (Wis. 1999).

75. Rippley v. City of Lincoln, 330 N.W.2d 505 (Neb. 1983).

76. Corrigan v. City of Scottsdale, 720 P.2d 513, 514 (Ariz. 1986), *cert. denied*, 479 U.S. 986 (1986); Burrows v. City of Keene, 432 A.2d 15 (N.H. 1981).

77. Poirier v. Grand Blanc Township, 423 N.W.2d 351 (Mich. App. Ct. 1988), *leave denied*, 431 Mich. 913 (1988).

78. Guy v. Brandon Township, 450 N.W.2d 279 (Mich. App. Ct. 1989).

79. State *ex rel.* OTR v. City of Columbus, 667 N.E.2d 8, 13 (Ohio 1996).

80. Purdie v. Attorney Gen., 732 A.2d 442, 446–47 (N.H. 1999).

81. 939 F.2d 165, 170 (4th Cir. 1991), *cert. denied*, 505 U.S. 1219 (1992). *See also* Glisson v. Alachua County, 558 So. 2d 1030, 1037 (Fla. Dist. Ct. App. 1990) (holding that a zoning regulation permitting "most existing uses of the property" and providing for variances did not deny property owners of all economically viable uses).

82. 505 U.S. 1003 (1992).

83. Although landowners emphasize loss in value because of inability to develop land in a particular manner, supporters of public regulation emphasize the enhancement in value that property owners receive from sound comprehensive planning and effective land use regulation. Justice Holmes's "average reciprocity of advantage" characterization of comprehensive zoning makes this point, Pennsylvania Coal v. Mahon, 260 U.S. 393, 415 (1922), as does the theory of "givings." *See, e.g.*, Abraham Bell & Gideon Parchomovsky, *Givings*, 111 Yale L. J. 547 (2001); C. Ford Runge et al., Government Actions Affecting Land and Property Values: An Empirical Review of Takings And Givings (Lincoln Institute of Land Policy, Working Paper No. WP96CR1, 1996).

84. *Pennsylvania Coal*, 260 U.S. at 415.

85. Tahoe-Sierra Pres. Council, Inc. v. Tahoe Reg'l Planning Agency, 535 U.S. at 325–26, 122 S. Ct. 1465, 1480 (2002), quoting Lucas v. South Carolina Coastal Council, 505 U.S. 1003, 1014 (1992).

86. Penn Cent. Transp. Co. v. New York City, 438 U.S. 104, 124 (1978), *reh'g denied*, 439 U.S. 883 (1978).

87. Village of Belle Terre v. Boraas, 416 U.S. 1 (1974), was the first local zoning case the Supreme Court decided since the 1920s.

88. *Penn Central*, 438 U.S. at 124.

89. *Id.* at 130–31.

90. *Id.* at 138.

91. Agins v. City of Tiburon, 447 U.S. 225, 260 (1980).

92. 480 U.S. 470 (1987).

93. 480 U.S. at 495.

94. *See* endnotes 325 to 365 and accompanying text.

95. Lucas v. South Carolina Coastal Council, 505 U.S. 1003 (1992); Williams v. City of Central, 907 P.2d 701, 705–06 (Colo. Ct. App. 1995), *cert. denied* (Dec. 4, 1995).

96. Daniel Hulsebosch has characterized this effort as a debate between Justice Scalia, who advocates "hard rules and static background principles," and Justices O'Connor and Breyer, who "are groping toward a *customary* conception of property rights." (Emphasis added.) Daniel J. Hulsebosch, *The Tools of Law and the Rules of Law: Teaching Regulatory Takings After Palazzolo*, 46 St. Louis U.L.J. 713, 729 (2002).

97. 535 U.S. at 319, 122 S. Ct. 1465, 1477.

98. *Id.* at 1478.

99. An earlier version of this section appeared in Peter W. Salsich, Jr., *Life After the Takings Trilogy—A Hierarchy of Property Interests?*, 19 Stetson L. Rev. 795, 799–804 (1990). Reprinted with permission.

100. 438 U.S. 104, 130–31 (1978).

101. *Id.*

102. Andrus v. Allard, 444 U.S. 51, 65–66 (1979) ("[W]here an owner possesses a full 'bundle' of property rights, the destruction of one 'strand' of the bundle is not a taking, because the aggregate must be viewed in its entirety.").

103. 480 U.S. 470 (1987).

104. *Id.* at 500.

105. 533 U.S. 606, 121 S. Ct. 2448, 2465 (2001).

106. *Id.* at 2464–65.

107. 535 U.S. 302, 122 S. Ct. 1465 (2002).

108. *Id.* at 1483.

109. *Id.* at 1484.

110. *Id.* at 1477, 1489

111. Tull v. Commonwealth of Virginia and Bd. of Supervisors of Accomack County, Chancery No. 88-CH-128, Circuit Court of Accomack County, Virginia, declined to follow by *Koram v. State Dep't of Env. Protection*, 308 N.J. Super. 225, 705 A.2d 1221 (N.J. Super Ct. App. Div. 1998).

112. Record No. 911891, March 5, 1992.

113. 61 U.S.L.W. 3226 (1992).

114. 505 U.S. 1003, 1016 n. 7, *remanded*, 424 S.E.2d 484 (S.C. 1992). *See p.* 71.

115. *Lucas*, 505 U.S. at 1016, n. 7. *See also* Animas Valley and Gravel, Inc. v. Bd. of County Comm'rs of the County of LaPlata, 38 P.3d 59, 68, n. 9 (Colo. 2001) (commenting that Justice Scalia's footnote "may leave the door open to rights severance if the right at issue is fundamental," but noting that "[p]recisely which rights may fit this exception is not before us in the current case").

116. *See also* Bevan v. Brandon Township, 475 N.W.2d 37 (Mich. 1991), *cert. denied*, 502 U.S. 1060 (1992).

117. 28 F.3d 1171 (Fed. Cir. 1994).

118. 18 F.3d 1560 (Fed. Cir. 1994), *cert. denied*, 513 U.S. 1109 (1995).

119. *Loveladies Harbor*, 28 F.3d at 1180.

120. *Id.* at 1181.

121. *Florida Rock*, 18 F.3d at 1570 ("mere diminution" refers to "shared economic impacts" in which the landowner has received some compensating benefit).

122. *Id.* at 1572, n. 32.

123. Penn Central Transp. Co. v. New York City, 438 U.S. 104, 130–31.

124. Clajon Prod. Corp. v. Petera, 70 F.3d 1566, 1577 (10th Cir. 1995) (Wyoming Game and Fish Commission regulation limiting the number of available hunting licenses does not deprive landowners of all economically beneficial use of their property).

125. Animas Valley Sand & Gravel, Inc. v. Bd. County Comm'rs of the County of LaPlata, 38 P.3d 59, 68 (Colo. 2001), *reh'g denied*, 2002 Colo. LEXIS 3 (Jan. 14, 2002).

126. *Id.*

127. Keystone Bituminous Coal Ass'n v. DeBenedictis, 480 U.S. 470, 517 (1987) (Rehnquist, C.J., dissenting).

128. Penn. Cent. Transp. Co. v. New York City, 438 U.S. 104, 138 (1978) (Rehnquist, J., dissenting).

129. *Keystone,* 480 U.S. at 506 (Rehnquist, C.J., dissenting).

130. 328 U.S. 256, 261 (1946) (noise and glare from aircraft lights caused landowner's chickens to go berserk, resulting in virtual destruction of his chicken farming business).

131. Keystone, 480 U.S. at 516–18 (Rehnquist, C.J., dissenting).

132. *Id.* at 519–20.

133. *Id.* at 516–17.

134. *Id.* at 517–18.

135. 444 U.S. 164 (1979).

136. 458 U.S. 419 (1982).

137. *Kaiser Aetna,* 444 U.S. at 167.

138. *Loretto,* 458 U.S. at 438.

139. *Id.* at 435.

140. 438 U.S. 104, 124 (1978).

141. 481 U.S. 704 (1987).

142. 25 U.S.C. §§ 2201–10 (1983), *discussed in* Comment, *Escheat of Indian Land as a Fifth Amendment Taking in* Hodel v. Irving: *A New Approach to Inheritance,* 43 U. Miami L. Rev. 739, 743 (1989).

143. Hodel v. Irving, 481 U.S. at 709.

144. *Id.*

145. *Id.* at 718.

146. Pennsylvania Coal Co. v. Mahon, 260 U.S. 393, 415 (1922).

147. Hodel v. Irving, 481 U.S. at 715.

148. 444 U.S. 164, 176 (1979).

149. Hodel v. Irving, 481 U.S. at 718 (quoting *Pennsylvania Coal,* 260 U.S. at 415 (per Holmes, J.)).

150. *Id.* at 716.

151. 494 U.S. 1, 24 (1990).

152. National Trails System Act Amend. of 1983, Pub. L. No. 98-11, 97 Stat. 42, to the National Trails System Act, Pub. L. 90-543, 82 Stat. 919, codified, as amended 16 U.S.C. § 1241 *et seq.* (1988). Section 8(d) of the amended act provides that interim trail use "shall not be treated . . . as an abandonment" of railroad rights-of-way easements, thus postponing the vesting of reversionary interests that may be triggered by application of state law to abandonment of easements. *Presault,* 494 U.S. at 8.

153. 28 U.S.C. § 149(a)(1) (1994). *Presault,* 494 U.S. at 11.

154. *Presault,* 494 U.S. at 11–12.

155. *Id.* at 23–24.

156. *See, e.g.,* Missouri Approved Jury Instructions, § 9.02.

157. *Cf.* Hawaii Hous. Auth. v. Midkiff, 467 U.S. 229, 241 (1984) ("[T]he Court has made it clear that it will not substitute its judgment for a legislature's judgment as to what constitutes a public use 'unless the use be palpably without reasonable foundation,'" quoting United States v. Gettysburg Elec. Co., 160 U.S. 668, 680 (1896)).

158. *See, e.g.,* San Remo Hotel v. City and County of San Francisco, 41 P.3d 87, 107 (Cal. 2002) (housing replacment fee upheld as having a "reasonable relationship to loss of housing").

159. 483 U.S. 825 (1987).

160. 473 U.S. 432 (1985).

161. *Nollan,* 483 U.S. at 828–29.

162. *Id*. at 841.

163. *Id*. at 842–43.

164. *Nollan*, 483 U.S. at 837. *But see* Thrasher v. Barrick, 986 F.2d 1246 (8th Cir. 1993), *reh'g denied en banc* (8th Cir. 1993) (conveyance of access easement as condition to providing water service to person requesting service not a taking).

165. *Id*. at 842. Justice Brennan noted:

> State agencies . . . require considerable flexibility in responding to private desires for development in a way that guarantees the preservation of public access to the coast. They should be encouraged to regulate development in the context of the overall balance of competing uses of the shoreline. The Court today does precisely the opposite, overruling an eminently reasonable exercise of an expert state agency's judgment, substituting its own narrow view of how this balance should be struck. Its reasoning is hardly suited to the complex reality of natural resource protection in the twentieth century.

166. *Id*. at 842.

167. *Id*. at 853.

168. 512 U.S. 374 (1994).

169. Nollan v. California Coastal Comm'n, 483 U.S. 825 (1987).

170. Dolan v. City of Tigard, 512 U.S. 374, 391 (1994).

171. Palazzolo v. Rhode Island, 121 S. Ct. 2448, 2457–58 (2001).

172. Animas Valley Sand and Gravel, Inc. v. Bd. of County Comm'rs of the County of LaPlata, 38 P.3d 59, 72–73 (Colo. 2001) (Kourlis, J., concurring, discussing R&Y, Inc. v. Municipality of Anchorage, 34 P.3d 289 (Alaska 2001) (landowner failed to meet his burden under expansive, four-factor test)); Cwynar v. City and County of San Francisco, 90 Cal. App. 4th 637, 109 Cal. Rptr. 2d 233 (2001), *rev. denied*, 2001 Cal. LEXIS 6617 (Cal. Sept. 26, 2001) (plaintiffs alleged sufficient facts under a 13-step test to survive a demurrer).

173. *Animas Valley*, 38 P.3d at 65.

174. 482 U.S. 304 (1987).

175. That opinions can be misread was demonstrated in *Lake Forest Chateau, Inc. v. City of Lake Forest*, 549 N.E.2d 336, 340 (Ill. 1989), in which the Supreme Court of Illinois stated that "[t]he United States Supreme Court held that [the ordinance in *First English*] deprived the landowner of all use of its property, and the Court required that the county compensate the landowner." *See also* Moore v. City of Costa Mesa, 886 F.2d 260, 263 (9th Cir. 1989), *cert. denied*, 496 U.S. 906 (1990), in which the Ninth Circuit stated that "[t]he Court [in *First English*] decided that compensation must be paid for the time the interim ordinance was in effect because it denied *all* use of property," and Jack v. City of Olathe, 781 P.2d 1069, 1076 (Kan. 1989) (distinguishing *First English* because the Los Angeles ordinance "precluded any further use of the property").

The Court in *First English* did not decide that the ordinance denied all use to the landowner; it merely assumed that to be so because the case came to the Court in the procedural posture of an appeal from the granting of a motion to strike an inverse condemnation claim from the complaint. Allegations of facts are taken as true for the purpose of deciding such motions. "We accordingly have no occasion to decide whether the ordinance at issue actually denied appellant all use of its property." 482 U.S. at 313. First English Evangelical Lutheran Church v. County of Los Angeles, 210 Cal. App. 3d 1353, 258 Cal. Rptr. 893, 902 (1989), *cert. denied*, 493 U.S. 1056 (1990).

176. First English Evangelical Lutheran Church v. County of Los Angeles, 210 Cal. App. 3d 1353, 258 Cal. Rptr. 893, 902 (1989), *cert. denied*, 493 U.S. 1056 (1990).

177. *Id*. at 905.

178. Williams v. City of Central, 907 P.2d 701, 704 (Colo. Ct. App. 1995) (ten-month delay not extraordinary).

179. Citizen's Ass'n v. Int'l Raceways, Inc., 833 F.2d 760, 762–63 (9th Cir. 1987) (racing was not constant and occurred only six months a year).

180. Taylor-Chalmers, Inc. v. Bd. of Comm'rs, 474 N.E.2d 531, 536 (Ind. Ct. App. 1985) (rezone of adjoining property to permit sanitary landfill not a taking where all reasonable uses of plaintiff's property were permitted).

181. Danforth v. United States, 308 U.S. 271, 287 (1939). *See also* Ballam v. United States, 806 F.2d 1017, 1022 (Fed. Cir. 1986) (no taking where erosion caused by artificial government waterway did damage of $664 to land worth $65,000).

182. United States v. Riverside Bayview Homes, 474 U.S. 121, 138–39 (1985).

183. Furey v. City of Sacramento, 780 F.2d 1448, 1457 (9th Cir. 1986).

184. Kaufman v. City of New York, 891 F.2d 446, 447 (2d Cir. 1989), *cert. denied*, 495 U.S. 957 (1990).

185. Daley v. Blaine County, 701 P.2d 234, 239 (Idaho 1985).

186. Buskey v. Town of Hanover, 577 A.2d 406, 411 (N.H. 1990). *See also* DiMillio v. Zoning Bd. of Review of South Kingston, 574 A.2d 754, 756–57 (R.I. 1990) (denial of variance from merger provision of zoning ordinance to permit construction on vacant nonconforming lot not a taking because vacant lot can be used to enlarge existing nonconforming use on adjacent lot).

187. Lake Forest Chateau, Inc. v. City of Lake Forest, 549 N.E.2d 336 (Ill. 1990).

188. Presbytery of Seattle v. King County, 787 P.2d 907, 915 (Wash. 1990), *cert. denied*, 498 U.S. 911 (1990), *overruling* Allingham v. Seattle, 749 P.2d 160 (Wash. 1988). As was the case in *First English,* the court did not decide the merits of the taking issue in this case because of the plaintiff's failure to exhaust administrative remedies, but held that the effect of the challenged regulation on the entire parcel of land, rather than on a portion of it, must be considered.

189. St. Bartholomew's Church v. City of New York, 914 F.2d 348 (2d Cir. 1990), *cert. denied*, 499 U.S. 905 (1991) (*applying* Penn Central Transp. Co. v. New York City, 438 U.S. 104 (1978), *reh'g denied*, 439 U.S. 883 (1978)).

190. Grand Forks-Traill Water Users, Inc. v. Hjelle, 413 N.W.2d 344 (N.D. 1987) (reasonable restriction on use of underground land rather than permanent physical occupation).

191. Kaiser Dev. Co. v. City & County of Honolulu, 913 F.2d 573, 575 (9th Cir. 1990) (cause of action for "inequitable precondemnation activities" alleges a regulatory taking).

192. Bond v. Dep't of Natural Res., 454 N.W.2d 395, 399 (Mich. Ct. App. 1989) (wetland/environmental area designations, "absence of any clearly established standards . . . [to] guide development," and denial of drainage ditch permit do not deprive landowner of all economically viable uses when landowner has not applied for other development projects that might be approved).

193. *In re* Coleman Highlands, 777 S.W.2d 621 (Mo. Ct. App. 1989) (construing relationship of comprehensive zoning ordinance and successive 20-year "zoning with compensation" ordinances). *See also* Bd. of Zoning Appeals v. Leisz, 702 N.E. 2d 1026, 1031 (Ind. 1998) (forfeiture of nonconforming use through nonregistration not a taking).

194. Bello v. Walker, 840 F.2d 1124, 1131 (3d Cir. 1988), *cert. denied*, 488 U.S. 851 (1988). *See also* City of Virginia Beach v. Virginia Land Inv. Ass'n No. 1, 389 S.E.2d 312, 316 (Va. 1990) (invalid piecemeal downzoning did not deprive owner of all economically viable uses of property).

195. Atlanta Bd. of Zoning Adjustment v. Midtown North, Ltd., 360 S.E.2d 569, 571 (Ga. 1987). *See also* Town Council v. Parker, 726 N.E. 2d 1217, 1227 (Ind. 2000) (no compensable taking resulted when town placed chain across property bordering landowner's

property, refused to issue improvement permits, and asked landowner to share costs of extending additional utilities); Merritt v. State, 742 P.2d 397, 402 (Idaho 1986) (limitation on access by removal of two of five access points to corner lot not a taking).

196. Dep't of Natural Res. v. Indiana Coal Council, Inc., 542 N.E.2d 1000, 1007 (Ind. 1989), *cert. denied,* 493 U.S. 1078 (1990). *See also* McClimans v. Bd. of Supervisors, 529 A.2d 562, 570 (Pa. Commw. Ct. 1987) (regulation of strip mining by zoning ordinance not a taking unless landowners establish that "they are conclusively prevented by the terms of the ordinance from extracting coal"). *See also* St. Louis County v. Kienzle, 844 S.W.2d 118, 123 (Mo. Ct. App. 1992), where an ordinance limiting homeowner's home office employment roster solely to those family members residing on the premises was upheld, preventing the homeowner's operation of a home business to that extent. The homeowner's employment of nonresident nieces was held not to be a customary or incidental use of the premises for residential purposes. Although the owners intentionally included the office for their business when they built the home, the court of appeals held that application of the zoning ordinance limiting home office employees to related residents of the home did not give rise to private detriment or any diminution in their property value.

197. Cottonwood Farms v. Bd. of County Comm'rs, 763 P.2d 551, 557–58 (Colo. 1988) (en banc). *See also* Jack v. City of Olathe, 781 P.2d 1069 (Kan. 1989) (refusal to rezone single-family property to permit expansion of adjoining apartment complex, although invalid as unreasonable, held not a compensable taking because reasonable economic uses remained). *See also* Iowa Coal Mining Co. v. Bd. of Supervisors, 494 N.W.2d 664, 671–72 (Iowa 1993), *cert. denied,* 508 U.S. 940 (1993) (county's refusal to rezone mining company's property to permit its proposed landfill operation held not a compensable taking when such refusal effectively prevented mining company's venture); Woodbury Place Partners v. City of Woodbury, 492 N.W.2d 258, 261 (Minn. Ct. App. 1992), *cert. denied,* 508 U.S. 960 (1993) (two-year moratorium on consideration of any development proposals for property adjacent to the highway enacted one month after submission of site proposal upheld because the economic viability of the proposal "was delayed rather than destroyed"); and Jafay v. Bd. of County Comm'rs, 848 P.2d 892, 900 (Colo. 1993) (summary judgment is inappropriate for as-applied taking case because reasonable individuals can disagree on what constitutes reasonable use of the property).

198. Jackson Court Condominiums v. City of New Orleans, 874 F.2d 1070, 1083–84 (5th Cir. 1989).

199. B.H. Kettlewell Excavating, Inc. v. Michigan Dep't of Natural Res., 931 F.2d 413 (6th Cir. 1991), *rev'd as violative of commerce clause,* 502 U.S. 353 (1992). *See also* Barrett v. Poinsett County, 811 S.W.2d 324 (Ark. 1991).

200. Leroy Land Dev. v. Tahoe Reg'l Planning Agency, 939 F.2d 696, 699 (9th Cir. 1991).

201. Esposito v. South Carolina Coastal Council, 939 F.2d 165, 171 (4th Cir. 1991), *cert. denied,* 505 U.S. 1219 (1992).

202. United Artists' Theater Circuit, Inc. v. City of Philadelphia, 635 A.2d 612, 620 (Pa. 1993). *See also* Webster v. Town of Candia, 778 A.2d 402, 410 (N.H. 2001) (refusal to permit landowners to remove trees alongside designated scenic road not a taking); BSW Dev. Group v. City of Dayton, 699 N.E.2d 1271, 1276–77 (Ohio 1998) (denial of permit to demolish building on National Register of Historic Places not a taking), *cert. denied,* 526 U.S. 1067 (1999).

203. Texas Manuf. Hous. Ass'n, Inc., v. City of Nederland, 101 F.3d 1095 (5th Cir. 1996).

204. Zeman v. City of Minneapolis, 552 N.W.2d 548, 554–55 (Minn. 1996). *See also* Worsley Companies, Inc. v. Town of Mount Pleasant, 528 S.E.2d 657, 660–61 (S.C. 2000) (refusal to issue water and sewer permit to lessee in absence of easement from property owners not a taking).

205. Outdoor Graphics, Inc. v. Burlington, Iowa, 103 F.3d 690, 695 (8th Cir. 1996).

206. County of Contra Costa v. Humore, Inc., 45 Cal. App. 4th 1335 (1996), *cert. denied,* 117 S. Ct. 1336 (1997).

207. Gazza v. N.Y. State Dep't of Envtl. Conservation, 679 N.E.2d 1035 (N.Y. 1997). *See also* Kim v. City of New York, 681 N.E.2d 312 (N.Y. 1997); Basile v. Tower of Southhampton, 678 N.E.2d 489 (N.Y. 1997); and Anello v. Zoning Bd. of Appeals, 678 N.E.2d 870 (N.Y. 1997) (all rejecting takings claims).

208. Gwinnett County v. Davis, 492 S.E.2d 523 (Ga. 1997).

209. Shadan v. Town of Skowhegan, 700 A.2d 245, 249–50 (Me. 1997).

210. Hendler v. United States, 175 F.3d 1374, 1385–86 (Fed. Cir. 1999).

211. Forest Props., Inc. v. United States 177 F.3d 1360, 1366–67 (Fed. Cir. 1999) *cert. denied,* 528 U.S. 951 (1999) (distinguishing Loveladies Harbor, Inc. v. United States, 28 F.3d 1171 (Fed. Cir. 1994). *See also* R&Y, Inc. v. Municipality of Anchorage, 34 P.3d 289, 294–96 (Alaska 2001) (development restriction in a 20-foot-wide setback band beginning 80 feet from lake shoreline not a compensable taking); R.W. Docks & Slips v. State Dep't of Natural Res., 628 N.W.2d 781, 790–91 (Wis. 2001) (denial of final dredging permit to protect a small emergent weedbed on the shore of Lake Superior neither a categorical nor an ad hoc regulatory taking; Sea Cabins of the Ocean IV Homeowners' Ass'n, Inc. v. City of North Myrtle Beach, 548 S.E.2d 595, 604–05 (S.C. 2001) (denial of application, subsequently reversed, to build a pier not a temporary taking); McQueen v. S. Carolina Coastal Council, 530 S.E.2d 628, 634–35 (S.C. 2000) (denial of permits to build bulkheads on filled lots not a taking).

212. Adams v. United States, 255 F.3d 787, 794–95 (9th Cir. 2001).

213. Rith Energy, Inc. v. United States, 270 F.3d 1347, 1350–51 (Fed. Cir. 2001).

214. Pheasant Bridge Corp. v. Township of Warren, 777 A.2d 334, 343–46 (N.J. 2001), *cert. denied,* 122 S. Ct. 1959 (2002).

215. Bonnie Briar Syndicate, Inc. v. Town of Mamaroneck, 721 N.E.2d 971 (N.Y. 1999), *cert. denied,* 529 U.S. 1094 (2000).

216. Moore v. City of Costa Mesa, 886 F.2d 260, 264 (9th Cir. 1989), *cert. denied,* 496 U.S. 906 (1990). *See also* Bellow v. Walker, 840 F.2d 1124 (3d Cir. 1988), *cert. denied,* 488 U.S. 868 (1988) (delays in issuing building permit not a compensable taking absent extraordinary circumstances).

217. Pheasant Bridge Corp. v. Township of Warren, 777 A.2d 334, 343–46 (N.J. 2001 *cert. denied,* 122 S. Ct. 1959 (2002) (no compensable taking from temporary application of ordinance increasing minimum lot requirement from 1.5 acres to 6 acres and subsequently ruled invalid as arbitrary and unreasonable); Sea Cabins on the Ocean IV Homeowners Ass'n v. City of North Myrtle Beach, 548 S.E.2d 595, 605 (S.C. 2001) (no taking where city denied pier application based on its zoning ordinance; Miller & Son Paving, Inc. v. Plumstead Township, 717 A.2d 483, 486 (Pa. 1998), *cert. denied,* 525 U.S. 1121 (1999) (economically beneficial use remained unaffected by unvalidated regulation); Chioffi v. City of Winooski, 676 A.2d 786, 790 (Vt. 1996) (regulatory delay from denial of variance later judicially ordered to be granted not a taking); Smith v. Town of Wolfeboro, 615 A.2d 1252, 1258 (N.H. 1992) (inherent delay "in process of obtaining subdivision approval . . . is one of the incidents of ownership" and not a taking); Cornish Town v. Koller, 817 P.2d 305, 308 (Utah 1991) (no temporary taking because continued farming practices were permitted); City of Virginia Beach v. Virginia Land Inv. Ass'n, 389 S.E.2d 312, 316 (Va. 1990) (no temporary taking because all use of land not prohibited). *But see contra.* Eberle v. Dane County Bd. of Adjustment, 595 N.W.2d 730, 739–740 (Wis. 1999) (denial of special-exception permit, overturned judicially, supports temporary regulatory taking claims under state constitution).

218. Estate of Scott v. Victoria County, 778 S.W.2d 585, 592 (Tex. Ct. App. 1989) (mere expectancy of sewer service, in the absence of a contract, is not a vested right, and temporary loss of such service is not a taking).

219. County of Nassau v. Eagle Chase Assocs., 144 Misc.2d 641, 643, 544 N.Y.S.2d 904 (N.Y. Sup. Ct. 1989) ("normal delay" rather than "temporary taking").

220. Tocco v. Council on Affordable Hous., 576 A.2d 328, 330–31 (N.J. Super. Ct. App. Div. 1990) (imposition for reasonable time of moratorium on land development of several tracts for environmental and other public-interest reasons does not constitute temporary taking), *distinguishing* Lomarch Corp. v. Mayor of Englewood, 237 A.2d 881, 884 (N.J. 1968) (one-year development moratorium applied to single piece of property while city considered it for park constituted temporary taking).

221. Terminals Equip. Co. v. City & County of San Francisco, 221 Cal. App. 3d 234, 247, 270 Cal. Rptr. 329 (1990).

222. Standard Indus., Inc. v. Dep't of Transp., 454 N.W.2d 417, 419 (Mich. Ct. App. 1990) ("promulgation and publication of plans alone do not constitute a taking, even though resultant publicity hinders a property's sale"). *See also* Westgate Ltd. v. State, 843 S.W.2d 448, 458 (Tex. 1992), where the Texas Supreme Court reversed an award for inverse condemnation, holding that the diminished marketability of the owner's property, resulting from a government announcement of plans to condemn property, did not constitute a direct restriction on the owner's use of the property.

223. Cline v. City of Clarksville, 746 S.W.2d 56, 57 (Ark. 1988).

224. Pheasant Bridge Corp. v. Warren, N.J., 777 A.2d 334 (N.J. 2001), *cert. denied*, 122 S. Ct. 1959 (2002).

225. Penn Central Transp. Co. v. City of New York, 438 U.S. 104, 124 (1978) ("the economic impact . . . and, *particularly*, the extent to which the regulation has interfered with *distinct investment-backed expectations*") (emphasis added).

226. Frank I. Michelman, *Property, Utility and Fairness: Comments on the Ethical Foundations of "Just Compensation" Law*, 80 HARV. L. REV. 1165 (1967), *noted in* Steven J. Eagle, *The Rise and Rise of "Investment-Backed Expectations,"* 32 URB. LAW. 437, 438–40 (2000) (arguing that Professor Michelman's notion of property rights was utilitarian, "instrumental . . . [of] no instrinsic meaning" and differed "substantially from that of the Founders").

227. *See, e.g.* Steven J. Eagle, *supra* n. 226 (reviewing cases and commentary); Daniel R. Mandelker, *Investment-Backed Expectations in Taking Law*, 27 URB. LAW. 215 (1995); Richard A. Epstein, *Lucas v. South Carolina Coastal Council: A Tangled Web of Expectations*, 45 STANFORD L. REV. 1369 (1993).

228. Palazzolo v. Rhode Island, 533 U.S. 606, 121 S. Ct. 2448, 2465 (2001) (O'Connor, J., concurring).

229. *Palazzolo*, 121 S. Ct. at 2464. *See also* O'Connor, J., concurring: "our decision today . . . simply restores balance to [the *Penn Central*] inquiry. Courts properly consider the effect of existing regulations under the rubric of investment-backed expectations in determining whether a compensable taking has occurred," 121 S. Ct. at 2467.

230. 121 S. Ct. at 2466–67.

231. *Id.* at 2467, citing Hodel v. Irving, 481 U.S. 704, 714–718 (1987).

232. Sanderson v. Town of Candia, 787 A.2d 167, 169 (N.H. 2001).

233. Richard Roeser Prof'l Builder, Inc. v. Anne Arundel County, Md., 793 A.2d 545, 551, 553 (Md. 2002).

234. Rith Energy, Inc. v. United States, 270 F.3d 1347, 1351 (Fed. Cir. 2001).

235. Good v. United States, 189 F.3d 1355, 1363 (Fed. Cir. 1999), *cert. denied,* 529 U.S. 1053 (2000).

236. *Id.* at 1361–62. In a subsequent decision, a panel of the Federal Circuit attempted to separate categorical from noncategorical takings cases, concluding that investment-backed expectations are not relevant to categorical takings. This in turn triggered a sharp dissent. Palm Beach Isles Assocs. v. United States, 231 F.3d 1354, 1363–64, 1370 (Fed. Cir.

2000). *See also* McQueen v. S. Carolina Coastal Council, 530 S.E.2d 628, 633–35 (S.C. 2000) (applying *Good* principle and concluding that "prolonged neglect of the property and failure to seek developmental permits in the face of ever more stringent regulations demonstrate a distinct lack of investment-backed expectations").

237. Justice Stevens surveyed the states in footnote 37 of his *Tahoe-Sierra* opinion:
Several states already have statutes authorizing interim zoning ordinances with specific time limits. See CAL. GOVT. CODE ANN. § 65858 (West Supp. 2002) (authorizing interim ordinance of up to two years; COLO. REV. STAT. § 30-28-121 (2001) (six months); KY. REV. STAT. ANN. § 100.201 (2001) (one year); MICH. COMP. LAWS ANN. § 125.215 (2001) (three years); MINN. STAT. § 394.34 (2000) (two years); N.H. REV. STAT. § 674:23 (2001) (one year); ORE. REV. STAT. ANN § 197.520 (1997) (10 months); S.D. CODIFIED LAWS §11-2-10 (2001) (two years); UTAH CODE ANN. § 17-27-404 (1995) (18 months); WASH. REV. CODE § 35.63.200 (2001); WIS. STAT. § 62.23(7)(d) (2001) (two years).
122 S. Ct. at 1489.

238. 122 S. Ct. 1465, 1489 (2002).

239. *See* chapter 8 *infra*.

240. Nollan v. California Coastal Comm'n, 483 U.S. 825 (1987); Dolan v. City of Tigard, 512 U.S. 374 (1994).

241. Ehrlich v. City of Culver City, 911 P.2d 429, 433 (Cal. 1996) (summarizing *Nollan/Dolan* test).

242. *Dolan*, 512 U.S. at 391.

243. *Nollan*—lateral access easement across beach area; *Dolan*—easement for bike trail across real property.

244. 526 U.S. 687, 119 S. Ct. 1624 (1999).

245. 119 S. Ct. at 1635

246. 708 A.2d 657 (Me. 1998).

247. *Id.* at 660.

248. 911 P.2d 429, 447 (Cal. 1996).

249. *Id.* at 444.

250. *Id.* at 448–50.

251. *Id.* at 447, 450 (requirement to provide either art or a cash equivalent is a reasonable aesthetic regulation similar to building setbacks, parking and lighting conditions, landscaping requirements, and other design conditions).

252. *Id.* at 454–55.

253. 41 P.3d 87 (Cal. 2002).

254. *Id.* at 103–07.

255. Homebuilders Ass'n of Central Arizona v. City of Scottsdale, 902 P.2d 1347, 1354 (Ariz. Ct. App. 1995), *cert. denied*, 117 S. Ct 2512 (1997).

256. Krupp v. Breckenridge Sanitation Dist., 19 P.3d 687, 698 (Colo. 2001).

257. McCarthy v. City of Lewood, 894 P.2d 836, 845 (Kan. 1995).

258. Waters v. Montgomery County, 650 A.2d 712, 724 (Md. 1994).

259. See *Homebuilders*, 902 P.2d at 1351. *See also* Nancy Stroud & Susan Trevarthen, *Defensible Exactions after* Nollan v. California Coastal Commission *and* Dolan v. City of Tigard, 25 STETSON L. REV. 719 (1996); EXACTIONS, IMPACT FEES & DEDICATIONS: SHAPING LAND-USE DEVELOPMENT AND FUNDING INFRASTRUCTURE IN THE DOLAN ERA, Robert H. Freilich & David W. Bushek, eds. (1995).

260. Home Builders Ass'n v. City of Beavercreek, 729 N.E.2d 349, 356 (Ohio 2000).

261. U.S. CONST. amends. V and XIV.

262. *See, e.g.*, COLO. CONST. art. II, § 25; Sellon v. Manitou Springs, 745 P.2d 229, 232 (Colo. 1987).

263. Lawton v. Steele, 152 U.S. 133, 137 (1894).

264. *See, e.g.,* Lisa's Party City, Inc. v. Town of Henrietta, 185 F.3d 12, 17 (2d Cir. 1999) ("federal courts should not become zoning boards of appeal," quoting Zahra v. Town of Southold, 48 F.3d 674, 679–80 (2d Cir. 1995); Pace Res. Inc. v. Shrewsbury Township, 808 F.2d 1023, 1034 (3d Cir. 1987), *cert. denied,* 482 U.S. 906 (1987); Kaiser Dev. Co. v. City & County of Honolulu, 649 F. Supp. 926, 943 (D. Hawaii 1986), *citing* Williamson v. Lee Optical, 348 U.S. 483, 487–88 (1955), *aff'd* 898 F.2d 112 (9th Cir. 1990), *op. amended & superseded by* Kaiser Dev. Co. v. City and County of Honolulu, 913 F.2d 573 (9th Cir. 1990). *See* Upper Deerfield Township v. Seabrook Hous. Corp., 604 A.2d 972, 976 (N.J. Super. Ct. 1992), in which an ordinance requiring certificates of occupancy was invalidated because its application to all sales of improved property reached "beyond the legitimate police power concerns of the municipality and [became] confiscatory." The occupancy requirement as applied to Seabrook's purchase of a vacant, boarded-up structure "[did] not reasonably and rationally achieve the public need," the court held. *See also* Nollan v. California Coastal Comm'n, 483 U.S. 825, 842 (1987) (Brennan, J., dissenting); Lawton v. Steele, 152 U.S. 133, 137 (1894).

265. Southwestern Illinois Dev. Auth. v. Nat'l City Envtl. LLC, 768 N.E.2d 1, 25 (Ill. 2002) (taking of land for reconveyance to private entity for expanded parking violated public-use clause).

266. Coniston Corp. v. Village of Hoffman Estates, 844 F.2d 461, 465 (7th Cir. 1988).

267. *See, e.g.,* Esposito v. South Carolina Coastal Council, 939 F.2d 165, 171 (4th Cir. 1991), *cert. denied,* 505 U.S. 1219 (1992) (South Carolina Beachfront Management Act neither taking nor a violation of substantive due process because act is substantially related to state's legitimate interest in protecting its beaches); PFZ Props., Inc. v. Rodriguez, 928 F.2d 28, 31–32 (1st Cir. 1991), *cert. granted,* 502 U.S. 956 (1992), *cert. dismissed as improvidently granted,* 503 U.S. 257 (1992) (no due process in refusal to issue construction permit; not a taking case); Kaiser Dev. Co. v. Honolulu, 898 F.2d 112 (9th Cir. 1990) (beachfront zoning regulations substantially tied to legitimate state interest and thus not violative of substantive due process), *op. amended & superseded by* Kaiser Dev. Co. v. City & County of Honolulu, 913 F.2d 573 (9th Cir. 1990); Johnson v. Sunray Services, 816 S.W.2d 582, 587 (Ark. 1991) (ordinance establishing two-mile buffer zone between landfill and service water not violative of substantive due process; not a taking case); Cash Inn of Dade, Inc. v. Metro. Dade County, 938 F.2d 1239, 1241 (11th Cir. 1991) (ordinance limiting hours of operation of pawn shops to 7 a.m. to 5 p.m. rationally related to governmental interest of limiting the sale of stolen goods); Schroeder v. City of Chicago, 927, 961 F.2d 957 (7th Cir. 1991) (in which Judge Posner, writing for the court, took a limited view of the viability and helpfulness of the substantive due process concept in a case involving a regulatory takings claim in a context other than land use, namely, receipt of disability benefits. The court held that the applicant's state remedies for review of benefits denial were more than adequate and affirmed the dismissal of the applicant's complaint for failure to state a claim); Chesterfield Dev. Corp. v. City of Chesterfield, 963 F.2d 1102, 1105 (8th Cir. 1992) (federal court will not review state zoning under guise of substantive due process, even in the case of bad faith by municipal officials); RRI Realty Corp. v. Incorporated Village of Southhampton, 870 F.2d 911, 912 (2d Cir. 1989) (no protectable interest in building permit under due process clause, reversing jury verdict of $2.7 million, and discussing the "entitlement" analysis in land use regulation cases applied by the Second Circuit); Sintra, Inc. v. City of Seattle, 829 P.2d 765, 777 (Wash. 1992) (en banc) (housing ordinance requiring replacement of low-income housing or payment into fund violates due process), *cert. denied,* 506 U.S. 1028 (1992); St. Lucas Ass'n v. City of Chicago, 571 N.E.2d 865, 875 (Ill. App. Ct. 1991) (denial of rezoning request from residential to commercial held unconstitutional, where surrounding property was commercial); Lutheran Daycare v. Snohomish County, 829 P.2d 746, 762–63 (Wash. 1992),

cert. denied, 506 U.S. 1079 (1993) (property owner's substantive due process rights violated by county council's arbitrary and capricious denial of conditional-use permit).

268. *See, e.g.,* Bryan v. City of Madison, 213 F.3d 267, 274–75 (5th Cir. 2000) (while a contract to purchase creates an interest in land, it does not by itself give purchaser a right to develop the land and thus cannot support a substantive due process claim based on delay in obtaining a building permit); Blumenthal Inv. Trust v. City of West Des Moines, 636 N.W.2d 255, 265–66 (Iowa 2001) (landowner may have property right in receiving land plat when it complies with state subdivision statute but "it is clearly not a fundamental right"); Thorp v. Town of Lebanon, 612 N.W.2d 59, 75–76 (Wis. 2000) (landowner does not have a property interest in town's compliance with statutory procedures for enacting a zoning ordinance); Mission Springs, Inc. v. City of Spokane, 954 P.2d 250, 257 (Wash. 1998) ("procedural rights respecting permit issuance create property rights when they impose significant substantive restrictions on decision making").

269. *RRI Realty Corp.,* 870 F.2d at 917, 918.

270. Deniz v. Municipality of Guaynabo, 285 F.3d 142, 149 (1st Cir. 2002).

271. Minnesota v. Clover Leaf Creamery Co., 449 U.S. 456, 466 (1981).

272. *See, e.g.,* Pace Res., Inc. v. Shrewsbury Township, 808 F.2d 1023, 1034 (3d Cir. 1987); Shelton v. City of College Station, 780 F.2d 475, 482–83 (5th Cir. 1986) (en banc), *cert. denied,* 477 U.S. 905, *reh'g den.* 479 U.S. 822 (1986).

273. *Nollan,* 483 U.S. at 841.

274. Pennell v. City of San Jose, 485 U.S. 1, 9–14 (1988).

275. Pace Res., Inc. v. Shrewsbury Township Planning Comm'n, 492 A.2d 818 (Pa. Commw. Ct. 1985).

276. Pace Res., Inc. v. Shrewsbury Township, 808 F.2d 1023, 1034–35 (3d Cir. 1987), *cert. denied,* 482 U.S. 906 (1987). Many cases in federal courts have sustained the validity of particular land use legislation against constitutional challenges based on substantive due process. *See, e.g.,* First Assembly of God v. City of Alexandria, 739 F.2d 942, 944 (4th Cir. 1984), *cert. denied,* 469 U.S. 1019 (1984) (conditions to issuance of special-use permit that included building a fence are valid because the conditions are rationally related to the preservation of important municipal objectives such as traffic safety and fire prevention); Kaplan v. Clear Lake City Water Auth., 794 F.2d 1059, 1066 (5th Cir. 1986); National Western Life Ins. Co. v. Commodore Cove Improvement Dist., 678 F.2d 24, 29 (5th Cir. 1982) (challenge to a water control and improvement regulation that prohibited the transfer of any lot that lacked a bulkhead); Coniston Corp. v. Village of Hoffman Estates, 844 F.2d 461, 466–67 (7th Cir. 1988) (rejection of site plan did not amount to deprivation of plaintiff's right to substantive due process); Burrell v. City of Kankakee, 815 F.2d 1127, 1131 (7th Cir. 1987); Kaiser Dev. Co. v. City and County of Honolulu, 649 F. Supp. 926, 949 (D. Hawaii 1986), *aff'd,* 898 F.2d 112 (9th Cir. 1990) (challenge to general zoning ordinance), *op. amended & superseded by* Kaiser Dev. Co. v. City and County of Honolulu, 913 F.2d 573 (9th Cir. 1990).

277. Southern Blasting Serv., Inc. v. Wilkes County, 288 F.3d 584, 594 (4th Cir. 2002), quoting Sylvia Dev. Corp. v. Calvert County, 48 F.3d 810, 827 (4th Cir. 1995) (ordinances regulating use and storage of explosives upheld); Tri-County Paving, Inc. v. Ashe County, 281 F.3d 430, 440–41 (4th Cir. 2002) (allegations that County violated state law in enacting moratorium do not meet requirements of the third prong of the substantive due process test).

278. Smith v. City of Picayune, 795 F.2d 482, 488 (5th Cir. 1986).

279. Richardson v. Township of Brady, 218 F.3d 508, 513–15 (6th Cir. 2000) (denying both facial and as-applied challenges).

280. Coniston Corp. v. Village of Hoffman Estates, 844 F.2d 461, 467 (7th Cir. 1988). *See also* LC&S, Inc. v. Warren County Area Plan Comm'n, 244 F.3d 601, 605 (7th Cir. 2001) (tavern operator has "no right, vested or otherwise, to freeze zoning laws as of the date he obtains his [liquor] license").

281. *See, e.g.*, City of Cleburne v. Cleburne Living Ctr., 473 U.S. 432, 440 (1985); Village of Arlington Heights v. Metro. Hous. Dev. Corp., 429 U.S. 252, 259 (1977).

282. National Western Life Ins. Co. v. Commodore Cove Improvement Dist., 678 F.2d 24, 26 (5th Cir. 1982).

283. *See, e.g.*, Woodland Hills Conservation Ass'n v. City of Jackson, 443 So. 2d 1173, 1180 (Miss. 1983); Fasano v. Bd. of City Comm'rs, 507 P.2d 23, 26 (Or. 1973). *Contra*, Quinn v. Town of Dodgeville, 364 N.W.2d 149 (Wis. 1985). Judicial review of zoning decisions is discussed in chapter 6.

284. Pitocco v. Harrington, 707 A.2d 692, 697 (R.I. 1998).

285. Mission Springs, Inc. v. City of Spokane, 954 P.2d 250, 261 (Wash. 1998). *But see* Harper v. Summit County, 26 P.3d 193, 199–200 (Utah 2001) (incorrect administrative interpretation of development code "is not the basis for a due process claim"); Kennedy v. Town of Sunapee, 784 A.2d 685, 689–90 (N.H. 2001) (public benefit of public sewer system outweighed any harm to property owner from requirement to connect to sewer system and lack of any procedure for obtaining waiver).

286. Equicor Dev., Inc. v. Westfield-Washington Township Plan Comm'n, 758 N.E.2d 34, 38 (Ind. 2001) (alleged hostility to cluster housing insufficient basis for motive review).

287. Penn Central Transp. Co. v. New York City, 438 U.S. 104, 137–38 (1978); *reh'g denied*, 439 U.S. 883 (1978).

288. *See, e.g.*, Georgia Outdoor Adver. v. City of Waynesville, 833 F.2d 43, 46–47 (4th Cir. 1987) (challenge to billboard ordinance that almost completely banned off-premise outdoor advertising); Temple Baptist Church, Inc. v. City of Albuquerque, 646 P.2d 565, 574 (N.M. 1982) (constitutionality of sign ordinance upheld, but contrary authority noted); Sun Oil Co. of Pennsylvania v. City of Upper Arlington, 379 N.E.2d 266, 269 (Ohio Ct. App. 1977).

289. *See, e.g.*, Horizon Concepts v. City of Balch Springs, 789 F.2d 1165, 1168 (5th Cir. 1986) (zoning ordinance classifying modular houses and mobile homes as special uses and requiring special-use permits for each modular house built upheld).

290. Kaiser Dev. Co. v. City and County of Honolulu, 649 F. Supp. 926 (D. Haw. 1986), *aff"d* 898 F.2d 112 (9th Cir. 1990).

291. Nicholas v. Tullahoma Open Door, Inc., 640 S.W.2d 13, 18 (Tenn. Ct. App. 1982).

292. In *Ridenour v. Jessamine County Fiscal Court*, 842 S.W.2d 532, 535 (Ky. Ct. App. 1992), the court held that, while a property owner who had a full hearing at the planning and zoning commission level has no right to notice of a fiscal court's consideration of the owner's proposal, the owner's procedural due process rights were violated when the fiscal court met in closed meeting in violation of the State Open Meeting Law, especially where the fiscal court considered off-record evidence.

293. Weinberg v. Whatcom County, 241 F.3d 746, 752 (9th Cir. 2001).

294. *Id.* at 753.

295. *Id.* at 753 (under Washington law, landowner had protected property interest in "validly approved" permits and short plats); Richard v. Township of Brady, 218 F.2d 508, 517 (6th Cir. 2000) (landowner "can have no legitimate claim of entitlement to a discretionary decision"); Zenco Dev. Corp. v. City of Overland, 843 F.2d 1117 (8th Cir. 1988) (under Missouri law, no property interest in renewal of municipal liquor license). *See also*, State Bank of Omaha v. Means, 746 S.W.2d 269, 272 (Tex. Ct. App. 1988) (a mortgage is a substantial property interest that is entitled to the constitutional protection of due process, citing Mennonite Bd. of Missions v. Adams, 462 U.S. 791 (1983)). If the subject property interest is held not to be an "entitlement" under state law, procedural due process is not implicated. *See* Gardner v. Baltimore Mayor & City Council, 969 F.2d 63, 69 (4th Cir. 1992) (developer had no "claim of entitlement" to public works agreement that was prerequisite

to issuance of building permit); Midnight Sessions, Ltd. v. City of Philadelphia, 945 F.2d 667, 679 (3d Cir. 1991) (dance hall license denial not subject to claim of violation of procedural due process), *on remand,* 1992 WL 97275 (ED. Pa. 1992). It has been held that existing zoning may be the subject of a property interest sufficient to constitute a basis for procedural due process claim. In Nasierowski Bros. Inv. Co. v. City of Sterling Heights, 949 F.2d 890 (6th Cir. 1991), a developer had expended substantial sums in reliance on current city zoning, which was changed in executive session to prohibit the intended development. The public notice of the proposed change was inconsistent with the change actually enacted. Based on the notice, the landowner did not attend the public hearing and did not oppose the unfavorable change of zoning.

296. Coniston Corp. v. Village of Hoffman Estates, 844 F.2d 461, 468 (7th Cir. 1988). *See also* Ramsbottom Co. v. Bass/Zebulon Roads Neighborhood Ass'n, 546 S.E.2d 778, 780–81 (Ga. 2001) (nearby residents objecting to rezoning approval for church suffered no due process violation from city's failure to give notice of a vacancy on the planning and zoning commission.).

297. Chongris v. Bd. of Appeals of Town of Andover, 811 F.2d 36, 40 (1st Cir. 1987), *cert. denied,* 483 U.S. 1021 (1989) (notice sufficient where one applicant for a building permit received notice of hearing by mail, notice was printed in a newspaper on two occasions, and the petition underlying an appeal was filed in the clerk's office and available for the public to see for two months before the hearing). *See also* Tri-County Paving, Inc. v. Ashe County, 281 F.3d 430, 437 (4th Cir. 2002) ("conducting open community meetings and giving affected parties the opportunity to speak on behalf of their project is constitutionally sufficient"); Brady v. City of Mason, 250 F.3d 432, 437 (6th Cir. 2001) (opportunity to give public comment on special-use permit application together with availability of state court review was sufficient due process for property owners who were objecting to issuance of special-use permit); Blumenthal Investment Trusts v. City of West Des Moines, 636 N.W.2d 255, 264 (Iowa 2001); Thorp v. Town of Lebanon, 612 N.W.2d 59, 77 (Wis. 2000) (availability of certioran is adequate postdeprivation remedy satisfying procedural due process requirement).

298. PFZ Props., Inc. v. Rodriguez, 928 F.2d 28, 31 (1st Cir. 1991), *cert. granted,* 502 U.S. 956 (1992), *cert. dismissed as improvidently granted,* 503 U.S. 257 (1992).

299. Weinberg v. Whatcom County, 241 F.3d 746, 754 (9th Cir. 2001).

300. Chongris v. Bd. of Appeals of Town of Andover, 811 F.2d 36, 41 (1st Cir.), *cert. denied,* 483 U.S. 1021 (1987). *See also* Minton v. Fiscal Court of Jefferson County, 850 S.W.2d 52 (Ky. Ct. App. 1992), in which published legal notices, signs communicating a proposed zoning change and scheduled public hearing, and notice delivered to some (but not all) "applicable property owners," was held sufficient notice for rezoning. Although notice requirements regarding hearings for zoning amendments are mandatory and jurisdictional, the court held that failure to comply with the procedural requirements may be "excusable or curable . . . when there has been actual notice and no material prejudice." *Minton,* 850 S.W.2d at 54. The court acknowledged that property owners other than those protected by statutory notice requirements may be adversely impacted by zone changes; however, because the opportunity to participate in the public hearing was advertised through publication and posting of a schedule, "the parties received actual notice of the hearing, participated in the hearing or suffered no prejudice thereby." *Id.* at 55.

The state appellate court, limited in its review of the Planning Commission's actions, held that the commission acted within its statutory powers. Because the appellants were not denied procedural due process, the appellate court was not authorized to conduct a de novo review.

301. Brewster v. Town of Amherst, 742 A.2d 121, 126–27 (N.H. 1999).

302. 780 F.2d 475 (5th Cir.), *cert. denied,* 479 U.S. 822 (1986).

303. *Chongris,* 811 F.2d at 41.

304. 577 A.2d 341 (Me. 1990).

305. *Id.* at 343 (citing Mutton Hill Estates, Inc. v. Town of Oakland, 468 A.2d 989, 992 (Me. 1983).

306. Idaho Historic Pres. Council, Inc. v. City Council, 8 P.3d 646, 649–50 (Idaho 2000).

307. Smith v. City of Picayune, 795 F.2d 482 (5th Cir. 1986).

308. PFZ Props., Inc. v. Rodriguez, 928 F.2d 28, 31 (1st Cir. 1991), *cert. granted,* 502 U.S. 956 (1992), *cert. dismissed as improvidently granted,* 503 U.S. 257 (1992) (refusal to process construction drawings did not rise to requisite level of "invidious classification" or "egregious procedural irregularities or abuse of power" necessary to support equal protection claim); Muckway v. Craft, 789 F.2d 517, 519 (7th Cir. 1986).

309. Pennell v. City of San Jose, 485 U.S. 1, 14 (1988); Thorp v. Town of Lebanon, 612 N.W.2d 59, 72 n. 11 (Wis. 2000) ("ordinarily there is no discernible difference in intent between the Equal Protection and Due Process Clauses under the Wisconsin Constitution and the United States Constitution").

In Nat'l Western Life Ins. Co. v. Commodore Cove Improvement Dist., 678 F.2d 24, 29 n. 20 (5th Cir. 1982), the standard was stated as follows:

> The constitutional safeguard is offended only if the classification rests on ground wholly irrelevant to the achievement of the State's objective. State legislatures are presumed to have acted within their constitutional power despite the fact that, in practice, their laws result in some inequality. A statutory discrimination will not be set aside if any state of facts reasonably may be conceived to justify it (quoting McGowan v. Maryland, 366 U.S. 420, 425–26 (1961)).

Applying the standard, the court concluded that a law that distinguished between landowners who transferred title and those who did not was not in violation of the equal protection clause.

See also First Assembly of God v. City of Alexandria, 739 F.2d 942 (4th Cir.), *cert. denied,* 469 U.S. 1019 (1984) (revocation of special-use permit not unconstitutional when church failed to comply with conditions); Carolan v. City of Kansas City, Missouri, 813 F.2d 178 (8th Cir. 1987) (stricter enforcement of building code against plaintiff not a violation of due process because the action was a rational response to the Regency skywalk disaster); Second Baptist Church v. Little Rock Historic Dist. Comm'n, 732 S.W.2d 483 (Ark. 1987) (denial of application of church to construct a parking lot in a historic district was reasonable where it wishes to build on a "fragile boundary" of the historic zone, whereas other applicants did not); Butcher v. City of Detroit, 401 N.W.2d 260 (Mich. Ct. App. 1986), *cert. denied,* 482 U.S. 905 (1987) (classification in city ordinance requiring inspection for one- and two-family dwellings at point of sale were rationally related to legitimate government interests and thus were not a violation of equal protection); State *ex rel.* Graham v. San Juan County, 686 P.2d 1073 (Wash. 1984) (county board could rationally conclude that a home built by the owner-resident for his or her personal use warranted less governmental regulation than a commercially built structure).

The failure to follow procedures provided for by state law is not a per se denial of the right to equal protection. Smith v. City of Picayune, 795 F.2d 482 (5th Cir. 1986); Muckway v. Craft, 789 F.2d 517, 523 (7th Cir. 1986).

310. 473 U.S. 432, 452–55 (1985).

311. In cases where racial discrimination is alleged, plaintiffs must show a racially discriminatory intent or purpose, not merely a discriminatory impact, before the courts will employ strict scrutiny. Village of Arlington Heights v. Metropolitan Hous. Dev. Corp., 429 U.S. 252, 265 (1976). In *Arlington Heights,* the Court listed sources of evidence that can be

used to prove discriminatory intent. These included (1) a pattern of legislation that has a discriminatory impact, (2) a sequence of events leading to a decision from which a discriminatory intent may be inferred, and (3) legislative and administrative history. *Id.* at 266–68.

312. *See generally* Carolan v. City of Kansas City, Missouri, 813 F.2d 178, 182 (8th Cir. 1987).

313. *See, e.g.,* Nat'l Western Life Ins. Co. v. Commodore Cove Improvement Dist., 678 F.2d 24 (5th Cir. 1982) (regulation that distinguished between landowners who transferred title and those who did not was not a violation of equal protection).

314. *See, e.g.,* Thorp v. Town of Lebanon, 612 N.W.2d 59, 73–74 (Wis. 2000) ("[t]he pleadings indicate that the Town may have engaged in wholesale rezoning efforts, without examining the particular suitability of the land to its zoned usage").

315. Muckway v. Craft, 789 F.2d 517 (7th Cir. 1986) (property owners unsuccessfully challenged county's action of failing to enforce a zoning ordinance against a nearby junkyard).

316. *Id.* at 523.

317. Village of Willowbrook v. Olech, 528 U.S. 562, 120 S. Ct. 1073 (2000).

318. Tri-County Paving, Inc. v. Ashe County, 281 F.3d 430, 439–40 (4th Cir. 2002); Bryan v. City of Madison, 213 F.3d 267, 277 (5th Cir. 2000), *cert. denied,* 531 U.S. 1145 (2001).

319. Howard v. City of Garland, 917 F.2d 898 (5th Cir. 1990).

320. Lisa's Party City, Inc. v. Town of Henrietta, 185 F.3d 12, 16–17 (2d Cir. 1999).

321. Bryan v. City of Madison, 213 F.3d 267, 276–77 (5th Cir. 2000), *cert. denied,* 531 U.S. 1145 (2001).

322. Consol. Gov't of Columbus v. Barwick, 549 S.E.2d 73, 75 (Ga. 2001).

323. Blumenthal Inv. Trusts v. City of West Des Moines, 636 N.W.2d 255, 268–69 (Iowa 2001).

324. 896 F.2d 1221, 1225 (9th Cir. 1990) (*citing* Rinaldi v. Yeager, 384 U.S. 305, 308–09 (1966)).

325. Standing and abstension issues are discussed in chapter 6 *infra.*

326. 447 U.S. 255, 260 (1980).

327. Eide v. Sarasota County, 908 F.2d 716, 720 (11th Cir. 1990), opinion withdrawn, substituted by 908 F.2d 716 (11th Cir. 1991), *cert. denied,* 498 U.S. 1120 (1991).

328. Spanish Cove Sanitation, Inc. v. Louisville-Jefferson County Metro Sewer Dist., 72 S.W.3d 918, 921 (Ky. 2002); Williamson County Reg'l Planning Comm'n v. Hamilton Bank, 473 U.S. 172 (1985); East-Bibb Twiggs Neighborhood Ass'n v. Macon Bibb Planning and Zoning Comm'n, 896 F.2d 1264 (11th Cir. 1989); Sinaloa Lake Owners Ass'n v. City of Simi Valley, 864 F.2d 1475 (9th Cir. 1989).

329. Palazzolo v. Rhode Island, 533 U.S. 606, 618–621, 121 S. Ct. 2448, 2458–59 (2001).

330. Eide v. Sarasota County, 908 F.2d 716 (11th Cir. 1990), *cert. denied,* 498 U.S. 1120 (1991) (must apply for a variance even when there is no apparent chance of prevailing); Tahoe-Sierra Pres. Council, Inc. v. Tahoe Reg'l Planning Agency, 911 F.2d 1331 (9th Cir. 1990) (in just compensation and due process takings claim, plaintiff must seek a final decision and apply for variances before the court will consider the claim ripe for review); Coniston Corp. v. Village of Hoffman Estates, 844 F.2d 461 (7th Cir. 1988); Lerman v. City of Portland, 675 F. Supp. 11 (D. Me. 1987), *cert. denied,* 493 U.S. 894 (1989).

331. Agins v. City of Tiburon, 447 U.S. 255 (1980); Kinzli v. City of Santa Cruz, 818 F.2d 1449, 1454 (9th Cir. 1987) (claim for taking is not ripe until there is a final decision: "1) a rejected development plan, and 2) a denial of a variance.") (citing Hamilton Bank, 473 U.S. at 187–89).

332. Williamson County Reg'l Planning Comm'n v. Hamilton Bank, 473 U.S. 172 (1985).

333. 520 U.S. 725 (1997).

334. Transferable development rights (TDRs) are discussed in chapter 4. While the *Suitum* decision was unanimous, Justice Scalia, joined by Justices O'Connor and Thomas, filed a lengthy concurring opinion in which he disagreed strongly with the notion that one's ability to sell TDRs may be relevant to the question of whether the "final decision" requirement has been met. TDRs "have nothing to do with the use or development of the land to which they are (by regulatory decree) 'attached'," he stated. 117 S. Ct. at 1671. The relevant final decision was the decision to deny permission to build a house on the lot in question. *Id.* at 1673.

335. 117 S. Ct. at 1668.

336. 117 S. Ct. at 1670.

337. 533 U.S. 606, 121 S. Ct. 2448 (2001).

338. 533 U.S. at 615, 121 S. Ct. at 2456, quoting Rhode Island Coastal Resources Management Program (CRMP) § 130A(1).

339. 533 U.S. at 620–21, 121 S. Ct. at 2459.

340. 533 U.S. at 624, 121 S. Ct. at 2461.

341. *Williamson County,* 473 U.S. at 195; Suitum v. Tahoe Reg'l Planning Agency, 520 U.S. 725, 734 (1997); Forseth v. Village of Sussex, 199 F.3d 363, 372–73 (7th Cir. 2000) (substantive due process and takings claims were not ripe for failure "to utilize . . . state law remedies").

342. Eberle v. Dane County Bd. of Adjustment, 595 N.W. 2d 730, 739–740 (Wis. 1999).

343. Deniz v. Municipality of Guaynabo, 285 F.3d 142, 147 (1st Cir. 2002).

344. 288 F.3d 375 (9th Cir. 2002).

345. 482 U.S. 304 (1987).

346. 483 U.S. 825 (1987).

347. 121 S. Ct. 2448, 2462–64 (2001).

348. 288 F.3d 375, 381 (9th Cir. 2002).

349. *Id.* at 383.

350. *See also* Estate of Himelstein v. City of Fort Wayne, 898 F.2d 573 (7th Cir. 1990) (takings claim not ripe until state inverse condemnation claim is pursued).

A landowner may go directly to federal court to challenge the application of a land use ordinance as a taking, but bears the burden of proving that state inverse condemnation remedies are inadequate. Broughton Lumber Co. v. Columbia River Gorge Comm'n, 975 F.2d 616 (9th Cir.), *cert. denied,* 510 U.S. 813 (1993) (burden not met, claim not ripe).

Despite the ripeness requirement of *Williamson,* parties continue to attempt to redress constitutional claims directly in federal court, perhaps assuming that the Section 1983 cause of action, created by federal statute, must be redressed in a federal forum. *See* Thomas E. Roberts, *Facial Takings Claims Under Agins-Nectow: A Procedural Loose End,* 24 U. HAW. L. REV. 623 (2002). Another effect of the ripeness requirement is to effectively close the door against federal court claims subsequent to exhaustion of state court remedies because of the application by the federal courts of the doctrine of res judicata regarding state court judgments. Greenbriar, Ltd. v. City of Alabaster, 881 F.2d 1570 (11th Cir. 1989), *reh'g denied,* 893 F.2d 346 (11th Cir. 1989); Thomas E. Roberts, *Fifth Amendment Taking Claims in Federal Court: The State Compensation Requirement and Principles of Res Judicata,* 24 URB. LAW. 479 (1992).

351. *Daniel,* 288 F.3d at 385.

352. Greenbriar, Ltd., 881 F.2d at 1574; Mission Springs, Inc. v. City of Spokane, 954 P.2d 250, 258 (Wash. 1998).

353. Smithfield Concerned Citizens for Fair Zoning v. Town of Smithfield, 907 F.2d 239, 242 (1st Cir. 1990), quoting Village of Euclid v. Ambler Realty Co., 272 U.S. 365, 386 (1926).

354. Fry v. City of Hayward, 701 F. Supp. 179, 181 (N.D. Cal. 1988). *But see* Forseth v. Village of Sussex, 199 F.3d 363, 372–73 (7th Cir. 2000) (applying both prongs of ripeness rule

to substantive due process claim); Eberle v. Dane County Bd. of Adjustment, 595 N.W.2d 730, 744 (Wis. 1999) (same ripeness evaluation for due process and takings claims).

355. 908 F.2d 716 (11th Cir. 1990), *cert. denied*, 498 U.S. 1120 (1991).

356. *Id.* at 724.

357. Hoehne v. County of San Benito, 870 F.2d 529, 532 (9th Cir. 1989) (citing Herrington v. Sonoma County, 857 F.2d 567, 569 (9th Cir. 1988)).

358. Harris v. County of Riverside, 904 F.2d 497, 500 (9th Cir. 1990).

359. *Id.* at 500.

360. *See* Executive 100, Inc. v. Martin County, 922 F.2d 1536 (11th Cir. 1991), *cert. denied*, 502 U.S. 810. But there is a limit to the number of times a regulatory body may require revisions, as the Supreme Court noted in *Del Monte Dunes*, 526 U.S. 687, 698–99.

361. Executive 100, Inc., 922 F.2d at 1542 (taking claim not ripe, equal protection and due process claims held ripe). *See also* Bigelow v. Michigan Dep't of Natural Res., 970 F.2d 154 (6th Cir. 1992) (challenge to fishing rights plan not ripe for review in the absence of pursuit of state inverse condemnation claim); Macene v. MJW, Inc., 951 F.2d 700 (6th Cir. 1991) (exclusion of licensed site from state's solid waste management plan not ripe for review).

362. 949 F.2d 890 (6th Cir. 1991).

363. *Id.* at 893. *See also* Alaska Airlines, Inc. v. City of Long Beach, 951 F.2d 977, 986–87 (9th Cir. 1991) (due process challenge to noise abatement held ripe for review even though no flights had been cut off because the threat of such action was very real).

364. Hager v. City of West Peoria, 84 F.3d 865, 870 (7th Cir. 1996).

365. Forseth v. Village of Sussex, 199 F.3d 363, 371 (7th Cir. 2000) (applying rule that plaintiff must show "'governmental action wholly impossible to relate to legitimate governmental objectives,'" quoting Esmail v. Macrane, 53 F.3d 176, 180 (7th Cir. 1995)).

366. First English Evangelical Lutheran Church of Glendale v. County of Los Angeles, 482 U.S. 304 (1987).

367. Orion Corp. v. State, 747 P.2d 1062, 1076 (Wash. 1987), *cert. denied*, 486 U.S. 1022 (1988).

368. *See, e.g.*, Agins v. City of Tiburon, 598 P.2d 25 (Cal. 1979), *aff'd on other grounds*, 447 U.S. 255 (1980).

369. 598 P.2d at 31.

370. Pennsylvania Coal Co. v. Mahon, 260 U.S. 393, 413 (1922).

371. Jacobs v. United States, 290 U.S. 13, 16 (1933).

372. First English Evangelical Lutheran Church of Glendale v. County of Los Angeles, 482 U.S. 304 (1987).

373. *Id.*

374. MacDonald, Sommer & Frates v. Yolo County, 477 U.S. 340 (1986); Williamson County Reg'l Planning Comm'n v. Hamilton Bank, 473 U.S. 172 (1985); San Diego Gas & Elec. Co. v. City of San Diego, 450 U.S. 621 (1981); Agins v. Tiburon, 447 U.S. 255 (1980).

375. *First English*, 482 U.S. at 311.

376. *See, e.g.*, Agins v. Tiburon, 598 P.2d 25, 29–31 (Cal. 1979), *aff'd on other grounds*, 447 U.S. 255 (1980).

377. *First English,* 482 U.S. at 311.

378. *Id.* at 313. On remand, the California Court of Appeal held that the church had failed to state a cause of action for a compensable taking because the interim ordinance was a reasonable safety regulation that did not deny the church all use of its property. First English Evangelical Lutheran Church v. County of Los Angeles, 210 Cal. App. 3d 1353, 258 Cal. Rptr. 893 (1989), *cert. denied*, 493 U.S. 1056 (1990). *See* n. 176 and accompanying text.

379. *First English,* 482 at 318.

380. *Id.* at 320.

381. *Id.* at 321.

382. *Id.*

383. *Id.* at 318.

384. Monongahela Navigation Co. v. United States, 148 U.S. 312, 326 (1893).

385. *First English,* 482 U.S. at 320, n. 10 (citing Kirby Forest Indus. v. United States, 467 U.S. 1, 5 (1984) and distinguishing Williamson County Reg'l Planning Comm'n v. Hamilton Bank, 473 U.S. 172 (1985)).

386. Yuba Natural Res., Inc. v. United States, 904 F.2d 1577 (Fed. Cir. 1990).

387. 896 F.2d 1347 (11th Cir. 1990).

388. *Id.* at 1351–52.

389. Lopes v. City of Peabody, 718 N.E.2d 846, 852 (Mass. 1999).

390. 904 F.2d 1577, 1582 (Fed. Cir. 1990).

391. *Id.*

392. State v. Doyle, 735 P.2d 733 (Alaska 1987).

393. *Id.* at 737.

394. Goss v. City of Little Rock, 151 F.3d 861, 863–65 (8th Cir. 1998).

395. 42 U.S.C. § 1983 (2000).

396. Sintra v. City of Seattle, 829 P.2d 765, 770 (Wash. 1992) (en banc).

397. *Id.*

398. 42 U.S.C. § 1988(b) (2000).

399. 526 U.S. 687, 119 S. Ct. 1624 (1999).

400. *Id.* at 1640.

401. *Id.* at 1644.

402. *Id.* at 1644.

403. Spot zoning is discussed in chapter 5, *infra.*

404. Buckles v. King County, 191 F.3d 1127, 1141–42 (9th Cir. 1999).

405. *See* Brown v. Crawford County, 960 F.2d 1002, 1011 (11th Cir. 1992); Robinson v. City of Seattle, 830 P.2d 318, 335 (Wash. 1992) (en banc).

406. Bowman v. City of Franklin, 980 F.2d 1104 (7th Cir. 1992), *reh'g denied,* 1993 U.S. App. LEXIS 21 (7th Cir.), *cert. denied,* 508 U.S. 940 (1993).

407. Zinermon v. Burch, 494 U.S. 113 (1990). *But see* n. 411, *infra,* and accompanying text.

408. Corn v. City of Lauderdale Lakes, 904 F.2d 585 (11th Cir. 1990).

409. National Adver. Co. v. City of Raleigh, 947 F.2d 1158, 1161 (4th Cir. 1991).

410. Williamson County Reg'l Planning Comm'n v. Hamilton Bank, 473 U.S. 172 (1985), *on remand,* 779 F.2d 50 (6th Cir. 1985).

411. 922 F.2d 328 (6th Cir. 1990).

412. Knights of Columbus, Council #94 v. Town of Lexington, 272 F.3d 25, 31 (1st Cir. 2001). In *Knights of Columbus,* the First Circuit upheld a town's ban on unattended structures, including creche, on historic Battle Green as a reasonable time, place, and manner restriction. *See also* Watchtower Bible & Tract Soc'y of N.Y. v. Village of Stratton, 122 S. Ct. 2080 (2002) (ordinance prohibiting uninvited canvassers from going door to door without a permit invalidated).

413. *Knights of Columbus,* 272 F.2d at 31, citing Perry Educ. Ass'n v. Perry Local Educ. Ass'n, 460 U.S. 37, 46 (1983). *See also* Lewis v. Colorado Rockies Baseball Club, Ltd., 941 P.2d 266, 276–77 (Colo. 1997) (total ban on vending outside baseball stadium during games by anyone not holding baseball club's exclusive license invalidated); Horton v. City of Augustine, 272 F.3d 1318, 1333 (11th Cir. 2001) (prohibition of street performers in a four-block area closed to automobile traffic upheld); Vasquez v. Housing Authority of El Paso, 271 F.3d 198, 203 (5th Cir. 2001) (application of trespass after warning statute to bar campaigning on public housing property invalidated as "unreasonable restriction on residents' first amendment rights"). *See also* Graff v. City of Chicago, 986 F.2d 1055 (7th Cir. 1993), where

an ordinance regulating operation of a newsstand on the public forum of city streets was subject to a successful facial challenge. The Seventh Circuit held that the ordinance's vesting of the Commissioner of Public Works with the absolute authority to grant or deny permits, as well as the power of judicial review over permits he denies, fails to accord citizens the procedural safeguards necessary when a city seeks to license expressive activity.

414. *Knights of Columbus,* 272 F.2d at 31, citing Capitol Square Review & Advisory Bd. v. Pinette, 515 U.S. 753, 761 (1995) (requiring strict scrutiny).

415. *Knights of Columbus,* 272 F.2d at 31, quoting Globe Newspaper Co. v. Beacon Hill Architectural Comm'n, 100 F.3d 175, 186 (1st Cir. 1996).

416. City of Renton v. Playtime Theaters, Inc., 475 U.S. 41 (1986), *reh'g denied,* 475 U.S. 1132. *See also* Int'l Eateries of America v. Broward County, 941 F.2d 1157 (11th Cir. 1991) (ordinance proscribing a minimum distance between adult entertainment and residential or church uses upheld as in furtherance of the substantial governmental interest of "protecting quality of urban life" from the secondary effects of adult businesses, citing *City of Renton;* Stringfellow's of New York, Ltd. v. City of New York, 694 N.E.2d 407, 414–20 (N.Y. 1998) (applying *Renton* and New York law to uphold one-year moratorium on creation or enlargement of adult-use establishments as well as new adult-use zoning restrictions expected to require 80 percent of existing establishments to relocate).

417. *City of Renton,* 475 U.S. at 59.

418. 475 U.S. 41 (1986).

419. 427 U.S. 50 (1976).

420. *City of Renton,* 475 U.S. at 46–47.

421. *Id.* at 52–54. *See also* D.H.L. Assocs., Inc. v. O'Gorman, 199 F.3d 50, 59–61 (1st Cir. 1999), *cert. denied,* 529 U.S. 111 (2000) (applying *Renton* and upholding zoning ordinance restricting adult business to a particular zone); Restaurant Row Assocs. v. Horry County, 516 S.E.2d 442, 448 (S.C. 1999), *cert. denied,* 528 U.S. 1020.

422. *City of Renton* at 50; LLEH, Inc. v. Wichita County, Tex., 289 F.3d 358, 367 (5th Cir. 2002) (rural county may review urban studies in effort to prevent blight from spreading). A city must show some proof, however, that in regulating adult entertainment it "was actually attempting to address the problem of urban blight." Christy v. City of Ann Arbor, 824 F.2d 489 (6th Cir. 1987), *cert. denied,* 484 U.S. 1059 (1988). The city's burden of proof is "to show that more than a rational relationship exists between the ordinance" and the government interest. *Id.* at 493. *See* Wolff v. City of Monticello, 803 F. Supp. 1568 (D. Minn. 1992), where the district court invalidated an ordinance establishing zoning categories "adult use/accessory," covering businesses providing adult goods and services on a limited basis, and "adult use/principal" covering businesses primarily offering adult goods and services. The ordinance restricted these "adult uses" to specific parts of the city and prohibited both "internal and external advertising and signing of adult materials and products." *Id.* at 1570, 1571. Furthermore, resolutions 92-3 and 92-1, aimed at regulating the negative impact of adult uses by licensing adult businesses, established a yearly application process with respective annual fees of $250 and $1000 for "adult use/accessory" and "adult use/principal license"; such licenses were subject to city inspection officials' unqualified "right to enter, inspect, and search the premises of a licensee during business hours."

Operators of a video store that rented general-release and adult-only videos, where adult videos occupied only 10 percent of the floor space, challenged this regulation of adult-only enterprises. The district court held the ordinance unconstitutional because of a lack of evidence establishing that "adult use/accessory" businesses, as opposed to "adult use/principal" businesses, had a detrimental effect on communities. The city failed to show that all businesses providing adult material, regardless of the extent to which they deal in such material, have a detrimental effect on communities. Furthermore, the court concluded that the ordinance (1) lacked necessary specificity regarding the city council's discretion to grant or deny licenses, (2) failed to preserve the status quo during the licensing process, and (3) unconstitutionally restricted speech in the limitations it imposed on advertising.

An Akron, Ohio, ordinance banning live nude dancing was struck down as unconstitutionally overbroad because it made no distinction between erotic adult entertainment and other types of nudity. Triplett Grille, Inc. v. City of Akron, 816 F. Supp. 1249 (N.D. Ohio 1993).

423. City of Los Angeles v. Alameda Books, Inc., 122 S. Ct. 1728, 1738 (2002).

424. *Id.* at 1733–38.

425. *Id.* at 1739–43.

426. *Id.* at 1744–51.

427. City of Erie v. Pap's A.M., 529 U.S. 277, 120 S. Ct. 1382, 1391 (2000) (nude dancing is "expressive conduct . . . [but] it falls only within the outer ambit of First Amendment protection"); Barnes v. Glen Theatre, Inc., 501 U.S. 560, 565–66 (1991); Schad v. Mount Ephraim, 452 U.S. 61 (1981); City of Wichita v. Wallace, 788 P.2d 270, 276 (Kan. 1990) (ordinance requiring license to operate erotic dance studio but establishing no standards for exercise of discretion in granting license rejected as too vague).

428. *City of Erie*, 120 S. Ct. at 1394–95.

429. *Id.*, 1395–97, applying four-factor test of United States v. O'Brien, 391 U.S. 367, 377–82 (1968). See also Furfaro v. Seattle, 27 P.3d 1160, as amended by 36 P.3d 1005 (Wash. 2001) (nude dancing does not receive same level of First Amendment protection as do books and film, *rev'd. on other grounds*), *cert. denied*, 122 S. Ct. 2587 (2002).

430. *See, e.g.*, Baby Tam & Co. v. City of Las Vegas, 247 F.3d 1003 (9th Cir. 2001).

431. FW/PBS, Inc. v. City of Dallas, 493 U.S. 215 (1990).

432. City of Wichita v. Wallace, 788 P.2d 270 (Kan. 1990).

433. Pleasureland Museum, Inc. v. Beutter, 288 F.3d 988, 999–1000 (7th Cir. 2002).

434. Lady J. Lingerie, Inc. v. City of Jacksonville, 176 F.3d 1358, 1366–67 (11th Cir. 1999, *cert. denied*, 529 U.S. 1053 (2000).

435. *Id.* at 1364–66 (11th Cir. 1999), *cert. denied*, 529 U.S. 1053 (2000) (hours of operation and minimum size of establishment); 7250 Corp. v. Bd. of County Comm'rs for Adams County, 799 P.2d 917 (Colo. 1990).

436. Pleasureland Museum, Inc., 288 F.3d at 1001–04.

437. LLEH, Inc., 289 F.3d at 367–69 (5th Cir. 2002).

438. City of Erie v. Pap's A.M., 529 U.S. 277, 120 S. Ct. 1382, 1394 (2000); Barnes v. Glen Theatre, Inc., 501 U.S. 560, 565–66 (1991).

439. 950 F.2d 255 (5th Cir. 1992), *opinion withdrawn in part on reh'g*, 939 F.2d 1305 (5th Cir.).

440. *Id.* at 257–58.

441. 973 F.2d 1255 (5th Cir. 1992), *reh'g denied en banc*, 979 F.2d 211 (5th Cir.), *cert. denied*, 507 U.S. 1030 (1993).

442. 475 U.S. 41 (1986).

443. *Lakeland Lounge*, 973 F.2d at 1260.

444. 837 F.2d 1268 (5th Cir. 1988), *cert. denied*, 489 U.S. 1052 (1989).

445. *Lakeland Lounge*, 973 F.2d at 1260.

446. Township of Saddle Brook v. A.B. Family Ctr., Inc., 722 A.2d 530, 532–33, 537 (N.J. 1999).

447. 989 F.2d 1524 (9th Cir. 1993), *cert. denied*, 511 U.S. 1030 (1994). *See also* Lim v. City of Long Beach, 217 F.3d 1050, 1056 (9th Cir. 2000) (*Topanga Beach* requires property to have "a genuine possibility of [be]coming available for commercial use to be considered part of the relevant commercial market").

448. 200 F.3d 1325, 1334–35 (11th Cir. 2000).

449. *Id.* at 1336–37.

450. 833 F.2d 43 (4th Cir. 1987).

451. *See also* Naegele Outdoor Adver. v. City of Durham, 844 F.2d 172 (4th Cir. 1988) (ordinance prohibiting billboards within city valid); Lindsay v. City of San Antonio, 821 F.2d 1103 (5th Cir. 1987), *cert. denied*, 484 U.S. 1010 (1988) (ban on portable signs constitutionally valid).

452. 239 F.3d 601, 609–11 (4th Cir. 2001).

453. 272 F.3d 1318, 1333–34 (11th Cir. 2001).

454. Perry v. Los Angeles Police Dep't, 121 F.3d 1365, 1368–71 (9th Cir. 1997).

455. Matthews v. Town of Needham, 764 F.2d 58 (1st Cir. 1985).

456. 117 S. Ct. 855 (1997).

457. *Id.* at 864, applying Madsen v. Women's Health Ctr., Inc., 512 U.S. 753 (1994).

458. 122 S. Ct. 2080 (2002).

459. *Id.* at 2089. *See also* Vasquez v. Housing Authority of El Paso, 271 F.3d 198, 203–06 (5th Cir. 2001) (ban on door-to-door canvassing by nonresidents of public housing unreasonably restricts public housing residents' First Amendment rights); Statesboro Publ'g Co. v. City of Sylvania, 516 S.E.2d 296, 298–99 (Ga. 1999) (ordinance prohibiting distribution of free printed material in yards and driveways held violative of freedom of speech and press).

460. 743 F.2d 182 (3d Cir. 1984).

461. *Id.* at 185, 187 (3d Cir. 1984) (citing Heffron v. Int'l Soc'y for Krishna Consciousness, Inc., 452 U.S. 640, 648 (1981).

462. 794 F.2d 1139 (6th Cir. 1986).

463. City of Lakewood v. Plain Dealer Publ'g Co., 486 U.S. 750 (1988).

Justice Brennan, writing for the majority, stated that the Court of Appeals "decided that the absolute ban on residential newsrack placements was both constitutional and severable. Its decision in that respect is not challenged here." *Id.* at 755, n. 4. The dissent noted:

> The Court quite properly does *not* establish any constitutional right of newspaper publishers to place newsracks on municipal property. The Court expressly declines to 'pass' on the question of the constitutionality of an outright municipal ban on newsracks. Ante, at 2147, n.7. My approach to the specific question before us, which differs from that of the majority, requires me to consider this question; and, as discussed below, our precedents suggest that an outright ban on newsracks on city sidewalks would be constitutional, particularly where (as is true here) ample alternate means of 24-hour distribution of newspapers exist. In any event, the Court's ruling today cannot be read as any indication to the contrary: cities remain free after today's decision to enact such bans.

Id. at 773 (White, J., dissenting).

464. Pruneyard Shopping Ctr. v. Robins, 447 U.S. 74, 82–83 (1980).

465. For state cases upholding the right to enter private property for the purposes of expressive activity, *see* New Jersey Coalition Against War in the Middle East v. J. M. B. Realty Corp., 650 A.2d 757 (N.J. 1994) (leaflet distribution concerning social issues allowed but reasonable conditions may be imposed); Batchelder v. Allied Stores Int'l, Inc., 445 N.E.2d 590 (Mass. 1983) (plaintiff's right to seek signatures in connection with access to ballot in public election in a shopping mall, subject to reasonable restriction by the owner); Commonwealth v. Tate, 432 A.2d 1382 (Pa. 1981) (upholding students' right to distribute leaflets on private college campus during anticrime symposium open to the public); Alderwood Assocs. v. Washington Envt'l Council, 635 P.2d 108 (Wash. 1981) (upholding right to solicit for signatures in connection with an initiative inside a shopping mall), Robins v. Pruneyard Shopping Ctr., 592 P.2d 341 (Cal. 1979), *aff'd*, 447 U.S. 74 (1980) (solicitation of signatures for political campaign in shopping mall).

For contrary rulings, see Western Pennsylvania Socialist Workers 1982 Campaign v. Connecticut Gen. Life Ins. Co., 515 A.2d 1331 (Pa. 1986) (privately owned shopping center can ban all political solicitations); Woodland v. Michigan Citizens Lobby, 378 N.W.2d 337 (Mich. 1985) (owners may deny or restrict access to individuals seeking to exercise rights of free expression); Cologne v. Westfarms Assocs., 469 A.2d 1201 (Conn. 1984) (no constitutional right under Connecticut constitution to disseminate political views in shopping center).

466. *See* Nester Colon Medina & Sucesores, Inc. v. Custodio, 964 F.2d 32 (1st Cir. 1992) (plaintiff stated a cause of action for violation of First Amendment in claiming that residential site permit was denied because of plaintiff's political views).

467. Sherbert v. Verner, 374 U.S. 398 (1963).

468. 494 U.S. 872 (1990).

469. 42 U.S.C. §§ 2000bb *et seq.* (2000). (Pub. L. 103-141, § 2, Nov. 16, 1993, 107 Stat. 1488).

470. 117 S. Ct. 2157, 2162–64 (1997).

471. 117 S. Ct. at 2170–71.

472. 117 S. Ct. at 2185.

473. Pub. L. No. 106-274, 114 Stat. 803–07, codified at 42 U.S.C. §§ 2000cc–2000cc-5.

474. 204 F. Supp. 2d 856 (E.D. Pa. 2002).

475. 374 U.S. 398 (1963).

476. Freedom Baptist Church, 204 F. Supp. 2d at 862, n. 6. Doubts about RLUIPA's constitutionality are raised by Ada-Marie Walsh, *Religious Land Use and Institutionalized Persons Act of 2000: Unconstitutional and Unncessary*, 10 Wm. & Mary Bill Rts. J. 189 (2001).

477. 914 F.2d 348 (2d Cir. 1990), *cert. denied*, 499 U.S. 905 (1991).

478. *Id.* at 355.

479. *Id.*

480. First Covenant Church v. City of Seattle, 787 P.2d 1352, 1356 (Wash. 1990) (quoting Murdock v. Pennsylvania, 319 U.S. 105, 115 (1943)).

481. *Id.* at 1357, quoting School Dist. v. Schempp, 374 U.S. 203, 223 (1963).

482. *First Covenant*, 787 F.2d at 1357.

483. *Id.* at 1361. In another battle between police power and the First Amendment rights of a church, the church won. First Covenant Church of Seattle v. Seattle, 840 P.2d 174 (Wash. 1992) (state's interest in its Landmarks Preservation Ordinance was noncompelling and did not overcome church's interest in free exercise of religion, so that external alterations to church need not be justified by liturgical considerations).

484. Burlington Assembly of God v. Zoning Bd. of Adjustment, 570 A.2d 495, 497 (N.J. Super. Ct. 1989).

485. Christian Gospel Church, Inc. v. City and County of San Francisco, 896 F.2d 1221, 1224 (9th Cir.), *cert. denied*, 498 U.S. 999 (1990).

486. 554 S.E.2d 63, 66–68 (Va. 2001).

487. *Id.* at 69–70.

488. 573 N.E.2d 733 (Ohio Ct. App. 1990).

489. State v. Cameron, 498 A.2d 1217, 1225 (N.J. 1985).

490. Prater v. City of Burnside, Ky., 289 F.3d 417, 427–31 (6th Cir. 2002).

491. U.S. Const., amend. I.

492. Ehlers-Renzi v. Connelly School of the Holy Child, Inc., 224 F.3d 283, 287 (4th Cir. 2000), reviewing case law.

493. 403 U.S. 602, 612–13 (1971).

494. *Ehlers-Renzi*, 224 F.3d at 288–92.

495. First Assembly of God v. City of Alexandria, 739 F.2d 942 (4th Cir.), *cert. denied*, 469 U.S. 1019 (1984).

496. Soldal v. Cook County, 506 U.S. 56 (1992).

497. 401 N.W.2d 260 (Mich. Ct. App. 1986); 347 N.W.2d 702 (Mich. Ct. App. 1984).

498. 401 N.W.2d at 262.

499. *Id.* at 264.

500. Tull v. United States, 481 U.S. 412 (1987).

501. 354 N.W.2d 747 (Wis. Ct. App. 1984), *aff'd*, 364 N.W.2d 149 (Wis. 1985).

502. 822 F.2d 388 (3d Cir. 1987).

503. *Id.* at 405 (citing Pike v. Bruce Church, Inc., 397 U.S. 137 (1970)).

504. Pike v. Bruce Church, Inc., 397 U.S. 137 (1970).

505. 629 F. Supp. 628 (N.D.N.Y. 1986).

506. 504 U.S. 353 (1992).

507. *See, e.g.,* Ala. Const. art. I, § 23 (Eminent domain); Alaska Const. art I, § 18 (Eminent domain); Az. Const. art. 2 § 17 (Eminent domain; just compensation for private property taken; public use as judicial question); Ark. Const. art. 2, § 22 (Property rights: taking without just compensation prohibited); Cal. Const. art. I, § 19 (Eminent domain; just compensation; possession); Colo. Const. art. I, § 15 (Taking property for public use: compensation, how ascertained); Ct. Const. art. I, § 11 (Right of private property); Haw. Const. art. I, § 20; Idaho Const. art. I, § 14 (Right of eminent domain); Ill. Const. art. I, § 15 (Right of eminent domain); Iowa Const. art. I, § 18; Ky. Const. § 242; La. Const. art. I, § 4 (Right to property); Md. Const. art. 3, § 40 *et seq.* (Eminent domain); Mich. Const. art. 10, § 2 (Eminent domain; compensation); Mo. Const. art. I, § 26 (Compensation for property taken by eminent domain—condemnation juries—payment—railroad property); Neb. Const. art. I, § 21 (Private property compensated for); N.H. Const. pt. I, art. 12 (Protection and taxation reciprocal); N.J. Const. art. I, pt. 20 (Private property for public use); N.Y. Const. art. I, § 7; Or. Const. art. I, § 18; Va. Const. art. I, § 11.

508. Cal. Const., art. I, § 19.

509. HFH, Ltd. v. Superior Court of Los Angeles County, 542 P.2d 237, 244 (Cal. 1975), *cert. denied,* 425 U.S. 904 (1976) (citing Albers v. County of Los Angeles, 398 P.2d 129 (Cal. 1965); Reardon v. San Francisco, 6 P. 317 (Cal. 1885). *cf.* County of San Diego v. Miller, 532 P.2d 139 (Cal. 1975).

510. *HFH,* 542 P.2d at 244.

511. *Id.* at 244.

512. Animas Valley Sand and Gravel, Inc. v. Bd. of County Comm'rs, 38 P.3d 59, 63 (Colo. 2001).

513. *See, e.g. Animas Valley,* 38 P.3d at 64 ("we look to both Colorado and federal case law for guidance").

514. 38 P.3d at 65–68.

515. N.H. Const. pt. I, art. 12, as interpreted in Dugas v. Town of Conway, 480 A.2d 71, 75 (N.H. 1984) (quoting Burrows v. City of Keene, 432 A.2d 15 (N.H. 1981)).

516. 480 A.2d 71 (N.H. 1984).

517. *Id.* at 75 (quoting Loundsbury v. City of Keene, 453 A.2d 1278, 1280 (N.H. 1982)).

518. Burrows v. City of Keene, 432 A.2d 15 (N.H. 1981) (". . . [a]rbitrary and unreasonable restrictions which substantially deprive the owner of the 'economically viable use of his land' in order to benefit the public in some way constitute a taking within the meaning of our New Hampshire Constitution requiring the payment of just compensation." 432 A.2d at 20).

519. Mfr. Hous. Cmtys. of Washington v. State, 13 P.3d 183, 190–95 (Wash. 2000). The neutral criteria include (1) textual language of state provision, (2) differences in parallel texts of state and federal consitutions, (3) state constitutional and common law history, (4) preexisting state law, (5) differences in structure between state and federal constitutions, and (6) matters of particular state interest or local concern, 13 P.3d at 188–90.

520. First English Evangelical Lutheran Church v. County of Los Angeles, 482 U.S. 304 (1987).

521. 330 N.W.2d 505 (N.D. 1983).

522. *Id.* at 511, *relying on J. Brennan's dissent in* San Diego Gas & Elec. Co. v. San Diego, 450 U.S. 621 (1981).

523. In an influential article, former Justice William Brennan argued persuasively that state constitutions often offered greater protection of individual rights than did the federal constitution. William J. Brennan, Jr., *State Constitutions and the Protection of Individual Rights*, 90 Harv. L. Rev. 489 (1977).

524. 351 N.W.2d 831 (Mich. 1984).

525. *Id.* at 838, 843.

526. *Id.* at 843–44.

527. 493 P.2d 1358 (Colo. 1972) (property owner enjoined from storing old cars on land zoned agricultural, where "junk yard" was excluded from the definition of the agricultural zone).

528. *Id.* at 1361.

529. *Id.* "Junk yard" was defined as "[a] building, structure or parcel of land, or portion thereof, used for collecting, dismantling, storage or sale of waste paper, rags, scrap metal, or discarded materials; or for the collecting, dismantling, storage, salvaging, or demolition of vehicles, machinery or other materials." *Id.* at 1360.

530. An earlier version of parts of this section appeared in Peter W. Salsich, Jr., *Keystone Bituminous Coal, First English and Nollan: A Framework for Accommodation?*, 34 J. Urb. & Contemp. L. 173, 191–95, 200 (1988). Reprinted with permission.

531. Pennsylvania Coal Co. v. Mahon, 260 U.S. 393, 415 (1922).

532. *Defensible Moratoria: Lessons Learned from the U.S. Supreme Court's Tahoe-Sierra Opinion*, American Planning Ass'n Audio Tele-Conference, June 26, 2002.

533. First English Evangelical Church v. County of Los Angeles, 482 U.S. 304, 341 (1987) (Stevens, J., dissenting).

534. Such a mechanism could be created by state statute as a local administrative review board or established by local ordinance as a taking review process within the established land use regulation system.

535. 26 Pa. Cons. Stat. Ann., § 1-502(e) (West 1997).

536. *See, e.g.,* Williamson County Reg'l Planning Comm'n v. Hamilton Bank, 473 U.S. 172, 194–97 (1985); Pennell v. City of San Jose, 485 U.S. 1 (1988); Shelter Creek Dev. Corp. v. City of Oxnard, 838 F.2d 375 (9th Cir. 1988), *cert. denied,* 488 U.S. 851 (1988).

537. *See, e.g.,* Cal. Civ. Proc. Code § 1245.260 (West 1982); Cassettari v. County of Nevada, 824 F.2d 735, 738 (9th Cir. 1987).

538. Address by Assistant Professor Alan Weinberger, Saint Louis University School of Law (August 24, 1987).

539. First English Evangelical Church v. County of Los Angeles, 482 U.S. 304, 339 (1987) (Stevens, J., dissenting). Thus a developer's window of opportunity can rapidly close as a result of inordinate delays in the construction process, whether those delays are caused by acts of God or "improperly motivated, unfairly conducted, or unnecessarily protracted governmental decisionmaking." *Id. See also* Advisory Comm'n on Regulatory Barriers to Affordable Housing, *Not In My Back Yard: Removing Regulatory Barriers to Affordable Housing* (HUD, 1991) (concluding that excessive regulation can add substantially to costs and delays of development).

540. Condemnation blight cases raise this issue, and courts that accept the argument that governmental delay has artificially depressed property values usually backdate the assessment of just compensation to the date at which the delay became excessive. *See* Lange v. State, 547 P.2d 282 (Wash. 1976). *See generally* Peter W. Salsich, Jr., *Displacement and Urban Reinvestment: A Mount Laurel Perspective*, 53 U. Cinn. L. Rev. 333, 359 n. 115 (1984).

541. *See e.g.,* SEATTLE, WA. CODE § 25.12.010 (1977) (Landmarks Preservation Ordinance).

542. *Id.* at § 25.12.490 (1977). For a superb analysis of the use of negotiated agreements as a basis for land use regulation, *see* Judith W. Wegner, *Moving Toward the Bargaining Table: Contract Zoning, Development Agreements, and the Theoretical Foundations of Government Land Use Deals,* 65 N.C. L. REV. 957 (1987). *See also* David L. Callies & Julie A. Tappendorf, *Unconstitutional Land Development Conditions and the Development Agreement Solution: Bargaining for Public Facilities After Nollan and Dolan,* 51 CASE W. RES. L. REV. 663 (2001).

543. SEATTLE, WA., CODE §§ 25.12.520–25.12.560.

544. *Id.* at § 25.12.610.

545. *Id.* at § 25.12.580.

546. *Id.* at § 25.12.590.

547. 485 U.S. 1 (1988).

548. SAN JOSE, CA., MUN. CODE, § 17.23.290 (1979). *See:* http://www.ci.san-jose.ca.us/.

549. *Id.* at §§ 17.23.180–17.23.210.

550. *Id.* at §§ 17.23.250, 17.23.280.

551. SAN JOSE, CA., MUN. CODE § 17.23.410. Generally, the landlord has the burden of proving the reasonableness of a particular rent increase. In determining reasonableness, the hearing officer must consider several factors relating to costs of capital improvements, maintenances and operation, rehabilitation, debt service, rental condition of the premises, increases or decreases in services, and "the economic and financial hardship imposed on the . . . tenants." (The tenant hardship provision was the subject of the *Pennell* case.).

552. *Id.* at § 17.23.310.

553. *Id.* at § 17.23.360.

554. *Id.* at §§ 17.23.020 (fair return rent increase) and 17.23.440 (standards of reasonableness to be applied to rent increases.

555. In the context of land use regulation, the Supreme Court defines property to include the owner's right to make economically viable use of his land. Keystone Bituminous Coal Ass'n v. DeBenedictis, 480 U.S. 470, 485 (1987) (quoting Agins v. Tiburon, 447 U.S. 255, 260 (1980), and citing Penn Central Transp. Co. v. New York City, 438 U.S. 104, 124 (1978)).

556. For an excellent review of creative approaches to resolving land use conflicts, *see* G. Bingham, Resolving Environmental Disputes: A Decade of Experience (1986). *See also* Erin Ryan, *Zoning, Taking, and Dealing: The Problems and Promise of Bargaining in Land Use Planning Conflicts,* 7 HARV. NEGOT. L. REV. 337 (2002); Jonathan M. Davidson & Susan L. Trevarthen, *Land Use Mediation: Another Smart Growth Alternative,* 33 URB. LAW. 705 (2001); Rosemary O'Leary et al., *The State of the States in Environmental Dispute Resolution,* 14 OHIO ST. J. DISP. RESOL. 515 (1999). The Lincoln Institute of Land Policy has published papers on resolving land use conflicts, including Lawrence Susskind et al., *Mediating Land Use Disputes* (2002).

557. 122 S. Ct. 1728 (2002).

558. APA, *Land Use Law & Zoning Digest,* n. 54, nos. 5 & 7 (2002). *See also* Eric Damien Kelly and Connie B. Cooper, *Everything You Always Wanted to Know About Regulating Sex Businesses,* Planning Advisory Service Report no. 495/496 (2001).

CHAPTER 4

Zoning

Definition of Zoning

Zoning is "a recognized tool of community planning"[1] by which local governments divide land areas into districts "according to the present and potential use of the properties"[2] and regulate the "reconstruction, alteration, repair, or use of buildings, structures, or land" within those districts.[3] Comprehensive zoning is "regulation with forethought to a uniform plan or design"[4] that is applicable to all the land in the community. Although the term *zoning* has a generic meaning roughly inclusive of all forms of local land use regulation, the key elements of zoning, in the literal sense, that set it apart from other forms of land use regulation are the division of land into physical districts and the application of land use regulations that are "uniform for each class or kind of buildings throughout each district" but that may vary from district to district.[5]

Zoning is premised on the idea that certain uses are incompatible and should therefore be segregated. Most ordinances designed to achieve this end effect a system of "permissive zoning" in which the zoning ordinance identifies the permitted uses for each district. Any uses that are not expressly permitted are prohibited.[6] "[Zoning regulations] permit a municipality to apply constant and consistent pressure upon landowners to the end that land use will be guided by the community plan and the public interest."[7]

For example, the 1986 Zoning Code for the City of St. Louis, Missouri, divided the city into 12 zoning districts ("A" through "L"), creating a pyramidal pattern of regulation: each district incorporating the uses permitted in the preceding districts.[8] The "A" single-family dwelling district is the most restrictive, limiting use of property to single-family dwellings, two-family dwellings in areas bordering multifamily areas, certain home occupations, parks and playgrounds, accessory uses, temporary buildings during periods of construction, and authorized signs. Eleven types of "public" uses, such as churches, governmental buildings, hospitals, parking facilities, and schools, may be permitted through the special-use permit procedure discussed in chapter 5.[9] Buildings or premises in the "B" two-family dwelling district may be used only for "any use permitted in the 'A' single-family dwelling district," as well as two-family dwellings without territorial restriction, semi-detached two-family dwellings, or multiple-family dwellings for not more than four families in boundary areas, along with accessory buildings and temporary construction buildings.[10] The "C" multiple-family dwelling district permits all uses of the "B" district and adds additional permitted uses. The "D" multiple-family dwelling district permits all uses of the "C" district and adds additional permitted uses, and so on, up to the "K" unrestricted district, in which "buildings and premises may be used for any purposes whatsoever not in conflict with [nuisance regulations]," although no new residential structures may be constructed nor existing buildings converted to residential use.[11] Suburban communities that have experienced considerable growth have even more complex zoning district schemes. The 1982 comprehensive zoning ordinance for St. Louis County created 25 separate district classifications, including 11 residential-use districts ranging from single-family homes on one-acre tracts to multiple-family dwellings with minimum lot requirements of 500 square feet per unit.[12] Less-developed communities are likely to have fewer districts but generally follow the same pyramidal organization. For example, a 1986 zoning map for the predominantly rural Township of Bedminister in Somerset County, New Jersey, identified seven districts ranging from 3 percent Rural Residential to OR (Office Research).[13]

Within a zoning scheme, definitional issues may be substantial. The drafters of the Standard State Zoning Enabling Act did not include definitions of terms, believing them unnecessary because of what was felt to be common understanding of terms employed in the Act, as well as a "source of danger" because "[t]hey give to words a restricted meaning."[14] For example, the Maryland Court of Appeals concluded that the word *land* in the Maryland zoning enabling statute was not limited to the "dry, solid earth found within [the zoning authority's] borders," but included submerged lands, thus permitting a county to regulate waterfront development by limiting the extent to which riparian land owners could install piers, mooring piles, and floats,[15] so long as the land in question is privately owned rather than state-owned.[16] Some modern enabling acts now define the term *land*. In the New Jersey Municipal Land Use Law, for example, *land* is defined as "improvements and fixtures on, above or below the surface."[17]

A variety of techniques designed to maximize the flexibility of local land use regulation are subsumed under the zoning rubric. For example, application of Planned United Development (PUD) status to a specific parcel of land is considered an "act of rezoning."[18] Other zoning techniques include floating zones,[19] overlay zones,[20] special areas of regulation, such as historic districts,[21] performance zoning,[22] development impact analysis ("zoning with intensity"),[23] and incentive zoning.[24] Land use attorneys will recognize overlap and redundancy among zoning, as the act of creating use districts and permitting and prohibiting uses within those districts, and such land use regulatory devices or plan review processes.[25]

Although zoning generally is a form of regulation of land use, the concept also embraces specific forms of building or structure regulation, such as height, number of stories, size, and signage.[26] The zoning ordinance approved by the Supreme Court in *Euclid v. Ambler,* for example, defined six classes of use districts, three classes of height districts ("H-1" to "H-3"), and four classes of area districts ("A-1" to "A-4").[27] Today, height and size limitations are likely to be included within use district classifications.[28]

Zoning is an exercise of the police power, a legislative function that has been delegated by the states to local legislative bodies.[29] Judicial review of local zoning decisions is of course available, but it is highly deferential, as described in chapter 6.[30] Courts will decline to order a particular zoning amendment, in the sense of making land use policy, when devising remedies for unconstitutional or otherwise illegal zoning ordinances.[31]

Vested Rights

At the heart of the definition of zoning is the question of whether a particular designation may be retroactively revoked, thereby rendering an existing use illegal. As will be discussed later, retroactive zoning amendments, as applicable to existing uses, may create legal, but "nonconforming" uses.[32] A municipality may seek to "zone out" an existing, unwelcome use, for legitimate land use planning reasons or for less altruistic reasons, such as vindictiveness.

At some point, American courts began to hold that an existing zoning classification, especially one relied on by substantial economic investment, became a "vested right," and therefore protected by the Constitution from a retroactive zoning amendment otherwise rendering it illegal.[33] A *vested right* has been defined as "an expectation that is so far perfected that it cannot be taken away by legislation" and a "complete and unconditional demand or exemption that may be equated with a property interest."[34] In this vein, zoning may be viewed as a judicial or quasi-judicial judgment right or as a property right, rather than as a purely legislative pronouncement.

The vested rights doctrine applies in contexts other than zoning designations or amendments, including issuance of any development permit,[35] and in some cases may be implicated by mere oral assurances by zoning officials. The traditional common law view is that a permit is subject to the law at the time of issuance, not the time of application, thus exposing the applicant to risk of legislative changes occuring after, and sometimes in direct response to, the application.[36] In recent years, however, courts have begun to take a more liberal view.

States vary regarding the point at which a zoning designation becomes a vested right. The greater the investment, the greater likelihood that the right is vested and therefore partially protected. States' actions range from vesting the right upon immediate enactment of the rezoning to requiring an actual construction and use of improvements. Other states, by statute, provide bright-line determinations, such as vesting use rights for a period of years from submission of a development proposal.[37] In Virginia, the law of vested rights has been codified without a bright line. The Virginia statute provides that a development right vests upon (1) a significant affirmative governmental act permitting a use that would not otherwise have been allowed, (2) reliance by the landowner in good faith upon the government act, and (3) a substantial change in position or the incurring of a significant expense or obligation by the applicant in good faith.[38] A proposed model zoning-enabling statute includes two alternative treatments: a bright-line determination and an estoppel-based approach.[39]

The law of vested rights has evolved substantially and liberally in the 1980s and 1990s, at a pace roughly proportionate to its cousin, regulatory takings.[40] The two doctrines overlap at the point where the courts focus on the nature of the right forfeited by the developer when a city changes its position at a given point in the approval process. Unlike the law of regulatory takings, however, the law of vested rights first focuses on the nature and scope of the applicant's expenditures in reliance on a municipal position.[41] In all cases, the applicant will be helped by evidence of diligent pursuit of a final building permit and expenditure of significant sums in both soft and hard costs, together with good faith.[42]

Billboard installations are the focus of a disproportionate amount of vested rights litigation. In many jurisdictions, billboards are a politically current topic, subject to frequent changes in regulation at both local and state levels. As states consider statutes and constitutional amendments substantially limiting the location of billboards, the market value of existing sites spikes, and developers rush to file applications, if not erect billboards. Substantial economic rights may be affected by relatively near misses in effective dates. In one case, a court held that the sign company had no vested right to use a billboard erected without a permit when the application was submitted one day after a moratorium went into effect.[43]

The point at which a zoning designation or other development permit becomes vested has substantial implications in the development of real estate. Many developers, and even developers' counsel, believe that the battle is over upon approval of a rezoning, issuance of a permit, or other final legislative or administrative act after a protracted series of hearings. Equity and mortgage financing transactions are closed and acquisitions are completed in reliance on such approvals, but in many states, the approvals are subject to amendment, if not outright repeal, prior to completion of construction and the commencement of any use. This truism, taken literally, would stifle real estate financing and development, and many developers' and lenders' counsel seek estoppel letters from cities requesting that the cities certify the existing zoning and expressly acknowledge reliance by the developer or lender. Many cities resist the issuance of such letters, however, and even if issued, the certification letter may not establish a full-blown vested right.

The appropriate middle ground in analyzing retroactive zoning legislation or zoning legislation that does not expressly exempt existing uses is more fully discussed with respect to the amortization, or gradual invalidation of illegal existing uses, known as "nonconforming uses."[44] It has been held expressly, noting the obvious, that there is no analytical distinction, from a constitutional standpoint, between an ordinance that expressly operates retroactively and one that does not exempt present uses.[45]

Zoning as a Political Process

In the local regulatory regime, fundamental policy decisions are made by the local legislative body. Zoning is therefore an inherently political process. The political nature of modern zoning may be an outgrowth of a philosophy prevalent in the early part of the 20th century, which sought to solve social problems through technology applied by a "professional public bureaucracy" and to "excise municipal decisions from the influence of party politics" through such devices as nonpartisan local elections and the city manager form of government. For land use matters, professional bureaucrats were to utilize planning technology "to chart rationally the future growth of urban areas by allocating land uses to specific geographic sectors." Although the original goal was to remove land use decisions from partisan politics, the "shift in the basis of local decision making on land use matters from a partisan legislature to a planning bureaucracy created a tension that in many cases made zoning the most political of local functions."[46]

Seymour Toll, in his history of the American zoning movement, states that drafters of the first comprehensive zoning ordinance in the United States, the 1916 New York City zoning code, were influenced to a great degree by the success of planning and zoning in Germany.[47] Zoning, which was the heart of the German urban planning system, was first proposed for American cities at the First National Conference on City Planning in Washington, D.C., May 21–22, 1909, as part of a social reform effort aimed at eliminating the harmful byproducts of the urbanism of the Industrial Revolution.[48]

> The most important part of City Planning, as far as the future health of the city is concerned, is the districting of the city into zones or districts in which buildings may be a certain number of stories or feet in height and cover a specified proportion of the site, that is, the determining of the cubage or volume of the buildings.[49]

Speakers at the conference extolled the virtues of the German city and repeated the theme in other forums in succeeding years. A 1912 article in *Scribner's* set the tone of the times:

> The German city is the most finished as well as the most efficient political agency in the modern world because it is free, free to experiment, free to have dreams and to realize these dreams in its own way. This awakens the people. It inspires them to effort. It gives them a sense of affection for their city like that which they have for the fatherland.[50]

Toll notes that important differences in German and American attitudes about governing affected the way in which zoning was implemented in the two countries. In Toll's view, persons often sought local offices in American cities "expecting to take," whereas their German counterparts expected "to give." In addition, Americans tended to oversimplify whereas Germans tended to overcomplicate public office. At the turn of the 20th century, German local officials "were not only well trained, but in sharp contrast with American public officials, they were also well paid and well regarded socially."[51]

The 1916 zoning ordinance for New York City was enacted as a result of "the combined pressure of housing, taxation, and other social reformers in alliance with conservative business interests [who sought to preserve real estate values on Fifth Avenue from the encroaching garment district]."[52] What was sought by "municipal 'consultant-experts' operating as conduits between the political process and city managements"[53] was a "virtually self-administering" system for preventing the "harmful consequences" of locating "incompatible uses . . . near one another."[54]

The result was a prescriptive, static machine that is forced into constant change as local officials grapple with fluctuating market conditions, consumer interests, economic trends, and new concerns such as environmentalism. "The practical consequences of this gap between theory and practice are abundantly visible in any suburban newspaper. Zoning hearings and decisions fill columns of space. Inevitably, decisions are subject to enormous political pressure."[55] In practice, the political aspect of zoning dominates the legal aspect. The practitioner must manage the tension between the two. The political essence of the zoning process is the primary reason for judicial deference to zoning decisions as "legislative."[56]

The Power to Zone

The power to enact and enforce zoning ordinances is derived from the police power inherent in the state.[57] Local governments have no inherent power to zone or rezone property and can exercise that power only when it is delegated to local government bodies by the state legislature.[58] States typically delegate the zoning power through a statute called the "enabling act."[59] In a few states, however, local governments derive the power to zone not only from specific enabling acts but also from state constitutions[60] or general police power statutes.[61] One state has retained the zoning power at the state level.[62]

Delegation of zoning power is accomplished in two ways: (1) general delegation of police power through constitutional or legislative authority to enact home rule charters,[63] and (2) broad enabling statutes authorizing zoning, subdivision regulations, and other forms of land use control.[64] Delegation can be traced to the Standard State Zoning Enabling Act, first published in 1922,[65] which adopted the concept of local control over land use regulation. Most first-generation state zoning statutes were based on this act, although building zone laws had been in existence in the United States since the turn of the 20th century, and comprehensive zoning had begun in New York City in 1916.[66] One year before the Supreme Court's approval of comprehensive zoning in *Village of Euclid v. Ambler Realty Company*,[67] 35 states and the District of Columbia had authorized zoning, and 221 municipalities with approximately 40 percent of the country's urban population had adopted zoning measures.[68]

The typical enabling act delegates zoning power directly from the state to the legislative body of the local government, such as a city council or board of aldermen. In large cities, however, substantial land use regulatory power is further delegated by the city to administrative bodies, not all of which are contemplated expressly in the enabling act. Such authorities include redevelopment and historical preservation commissions and boards. This type of power, while not typically denominated as "zoning," is now nearly universally accepted.

The characterization of a governmental act as zoning may have important consequences, similar to those discussed in chapter 6 with respect to the issue of whether an act or measure is legislative or administrative. In one case, a separate sphere of power over land use was specifically acknowledged and upheld as against a developer's claim that an urban Housing Authority enacted an urban renewal plan that was inconsistent with the general zoning ordinance and that the zoning ordinance should prevail.[69] The court concluded that the urban renewal plan, even though it regulated land use, was not a "zoning ordinance" within the state statute.[70]

Typically, the delegated authority exercised by urban renewal and redevelopment bodies operates to narrow the land use permitted within the renewal area rather than widen it. The ultimate development authorization is the product of negotiation with a specific developer, typically reflected in a redevelopment plan, and is tailored to the developer's project. The benefit to the developer is not relaxed zoning regulation, but usually property tax abatement or some other financial incentive to redevelop.

Because the power purely to zone is a legislative function, the judiciary has no power of its own to zone, but may in extreme cases order rezoning to remedy a constitutional violation.[71]

The power to zone may be exercised only according to procedures mandated by the enabling act. Although it is often declared that failure to follow such procedures invalidates the purported act of zoning,[72] a multitude of cases have held procedural flaws to be harmless or otherwise not of such consequence that would invalidate the legislative outcome.

Occasionally, the city's power to zone clashes with that of a county or another city, as in the case of a city that owns property outside of its boundaries. In resolving such conflicts, courts have used a variety of tests, including the "governmental-proprietary," "superior sovereign," "eminent domain," "statutory guidance" (legislative intent), and "balancing of interests" tests.[73] In recent years, courts have favored the statutory guidance/legislative intent test[74] or the balancing of interests test[75] as more likely to focus attention on the "public interests implicated in a particular land use dispute."[76] Local zoning power may also be preempted to some extent by state regulatory agencies, notably environmental agencies, and regulators of regional or technical uses, such as airports.[77]

In some cases, the powers delegated to a state agency, public utility, or political district, such as a school district, may conflict with the local zoning power.[78] In the case of state agencies, one court has ruled that absent a specific legislative grant authorizing a state agency to override local zoning laws, a state agency is subject to the jurisdiction of the local zoning board.[79] Where a statute authorizes a state agency to override local zoning regulations, however, the agency is exempted from having to comply with a zoning regulation.[80] The Supreme Court of New Jersey held that a municipal ordinance prohibiting helicopter landing pads as accessory uses was not a bar to an agency's issuance of a state helicopter license, where the State's Aviation Act empowered the agency to license aeronautical activities and the agency paid "due attention to the lawful zoning expressions of local governments" in exercising that power.[81]

State Enabling Legislation

As already noted, state governments traditionally have delegated the power to zone to political subdivisions by enacting state enabling legislation.[82] Some states delegate the zoning power simultaneously to two local governments in the same area, such as counties and towns, and the requisite sharing of the zoning power has been upheld.[83]

Most state enabling acts include certain elements. First, the statute describes the purposes of zoning and the jurisdictional prerequisites for a city to use the zoning power.[84] The term *purpose* served two functions in the Standard State Zoning Enabling Act: (1) to define and limit local government powers under the police power ("promoting health, safety, morals, or the general welfare of the community"),[85] and (2) as "a direction from the legislative body as to the purposes in view in establishing a zoning ordinance and the manner in which the work of preparing such an ordinance shall be done . . . the 'atmosphere' under which zoning is to be done."[86]

> Such regulations shall be made in accordance with a comprehensive plan and designed to lessen congestion in the streets; to secure safety from fire, panic, and other dangers; to promote health and the general welfare; to provide adequate light and air; to avoid undue concentration of population; to facilitate the adequate provision of transportation, water, sewerage, schools, parks, and other public requirements. Such regulations shall be made with reasonable consideration, among other things, to the character of the district and its particular suitability for particular uses, and with a view to conserving the value of buildings and encouraging the most appropriate use of land throughout such municipality.[87]

Second, the enabling act prescribes procedures for local enactment of zoning ordinances.[88] Key requirements include a public hearing at which all persons, not just affected property owners, may be heard, preceded by adequate public notice and "ample time" for persons to study the proposals and "make their opposition manifest."[89] Typically, public hearings are held before an administrative, nonelected planning and zoning commission that must make a recommendation to the elected legislative body, which thereafter holds its own public hearing.

In keeping with the public-notice policy, enabling statutes may require that a zoning map be prepared as part of the zoning ordinance.[90] The Arkansas

Supreme Court held that a statutory zoning-map provision was mandatory and consequently invalidated a comprehensive zoning ordinance that contained only text and no map. The court was unimpressed with the city's argument that it was trying to save money and refused to accept a "working map" drawn up by a city planner some time after the ordinance was enacted. The court also held that statutory provisions concerning where the text and map are to be filed were directory rather than mandatory, concluding that filing a zoning text and map in a city's planning office, entrance to which was through the city clerk's office, was sufficient compliance with a statutory requirement that zoning ordinances and maps be filed in the city clerk's office.[91] The "existence of a map" is the essence of zoning, but the "place a map is filed" is not, the court reasoned.[92]

The enabling act may also require adoption of a comprehensive development plan.[93] The Supreme Court of Nebraska held that a comprehensive zoning ordinance that merely restated the purpose clauses of the state zoning-enabling statute could not be considered to be a comprehensive development plan and thus was invalid as a zoning ordinance.[94]

In some cases, the power to zone is delegated to a city by a means other than zoning-enabling legislation. The city of Philadelphia, for example, derives its power to govern itself and enact zoning regulations from the Pennsylvania home rule statute.[95] Because zoning was not one of the limitations the statute imposed on home rule powers, courts have upheld the city's exercise of zoning power under its home rule charter.[96]

State Statutory Restrictions on Local Zoning Powers

Although state zoning-enabling statutes are broad grants of zoning power to local governments,[97] states occasionally put specific limitations on exercise of the zoning power. For example, a Florida statute prohibits local governments from enacting ordinances that prohibit the "installation of solar collectors, clotheslines, or other energy devices based on renewable resources."[98] The statute includes a statement of legislative intent that the provision is designed to conserve resources and avoid regulations that have the "ultimate effect, however unintended, of driving the costs of owning and operating commercial or residential property beyond the capacity of private owners to maintain."[99]

Likewise, a Texas statute requires local governments, in the exercise of their zoning powers, to treat coin-operated amusement machines, such as video games, as having the same use as the principal use to which the property where the machines are located is devoted, although under the statute cities may restrict the operation of such machines within 300 feet of a church, school, or hospital.[100] On the basis of the statute, a Texas appellate court invalidated a zoning ordinance of a home rule city that applied the 300-feet restriction to all residentially zoned property.[101]

In one case,[102] the court struck down a floating "inebriate district," which required use permits for a pawn shop, as violative of Arizona's enabling statute, which required that "all zoning regulations shall be uniform for each class or kind of . . . use of land throughout each zone."

The enabling act may also expressly preempt certain local regulations or immunize certain uses or industries, such as farming or mining. One court invalidated a zoning ordinance that purported to prohibit oil and gas drilling in residential areas in contradiction of a state statute that prohibited local governments from requiring local permitting to drill or operate wells. The court affirmed the local government's right to regulate the use and operation of such wells consistent with its right to protect the health, safety, and welfare of its residents, but it held that the absolute prohibition was barred by the statute.[103] Generally, municipalities may adopt more restrictive regulations than found in the statute, but procedural requirements, such as protest votes, are usually required to be consistent with express requirements of the statute.[104]

Comprehensive Zoning Ordinances

Comprehensive zoning ordinances apply to the entire geographic area of a city or county and are enacted to implement public decisions about the appropriate use and development of land within the community.[105] Comprehensive zoning is not limited to the initial decision to zone a community but occurs whenever zoning decisions are made that affect the entire community.

Subsequent comprehensive ordinances often are called comprehensive rezoning ordinances. Comprehensive rezoning is said to be "the product of thorough, deliberate consideration of extant facts and circumstances" and is entitled to the same general presumption of legislative validity as is the original zoning ordinance.[106]

The essence of zoning is the regulation in the comprehensive ordinance of the land use in relation to other, usually adjacent, land. Land uses that are permitted in one district, therefore, may be prohibited in other districts. As long as the zoning ordinance treats property in a particular district the same as other similarly situated property in that district, the fact that a prohibited use may be permitted in another district does not per se invalidate a classification. Zoning ordinances are not invalid because they prohibit the most desirable or most convenient use of land, and courts generally will not interfere with a legislative judgment that "one use is more or less objectionable than another."[107]

Comprehensive zoning ordinances may reflect political philosophies, but must meet the requirements of state zoning-enabling legislation and state and federal constitutions. For example, comprehensive zoning ordinances must be objective and precise enough to permit reliance by owners and fair and uniform application by local officials.[108]

Enforcement officials have substantial legal power in interpreting zoning ordinances. The general rule is that a court will give great deference to the interpretation of an official regularly charged with enforcement,[109] but the official may not rewrite the ordinance or make a plainly irrational interpretation.[110] Enforcement officials have even greater leverage against applicants who cannot tolerate the delay, risk, or expense of litigation.

Cumulative Zoning

Most comprehensive zoning ordinances are cumulative in nature, meaning that, in the regulation of uses, the ordinance establishes a scheme of gradual reduction in exclusivity of use from a particular reference point—usually detached, single-family housing on large lots. The most exclusive use may be designated with a letter and the number 1 (e.g., "R–1" for single-family dwellings). Each succeeding district permits all uses from the preceding classification while adding uses. The R–2 district, for example, might permit both single-family dwellings and duplexes, while the R–3 district might permit single-family dwellings, duplexes, and apartment buildings. The process goes on, with varying degrees of complexity, until all of the uses the community is willing to permit have been designated and classified by district.[111]

Ordinances of this type typically also authorize "accessory uses," ones that are "customarily incident to the principal use," such as a private garage in a single-family residential use district.[112]

Noncumulative Zoning

The cumulative or pyramid form of zoning has given way in many communities to more rigid segregation of perceived incompatible uses, particularly in areas zoned commercial or industrial. Reasons include a desire to maximize the industrial or commercial potential of land so zoned, concern about possible nuisance-type disputes triggered by residents in industrial or commercial districts over such common industrial and commercial byproducts as noise, odor, smoke, and traffic, and the realization that cumulative zoning makes development harder to control.[113]

Challenges to noncumulative zoning generally have been unsuccessful. The Supreme Court of Illinois reviewed the reasons noted previously for segregating residences from commercial and industrial and concluded that, while noncumulative zoning is a "radical departure from our thinking and opinions in the past," it is within the state's police power. The court also found authority for municipal enactment of noncumulative zoning ordinances in the enabling statute's provisions authorizing the creation of zoning districts and the prohibition of uses "incompatible with the character of such districts." The court warned that "caution will have to be used" in applying the noncumulative zoning technique because of the potential for unreasonable discrimination based on the "present character" of a developed area, and deprivation of property without due process if there is "no reasonably immediate use" that can be made of land zoned commercial or industrial, as well as the possibility that a noncumulative district "may not be part of a comprehensive and consistent plan." The court, however, found no per se constitutional problem with noncumulative zoning.[114]

A California court upheld the creation of an exclusive industrial district with the comment:

> [I]t cannot be held that there is anything arbitrary or unreasonable *per se* in the plan of zoning to prevent the so-called "higher" uses from invading a "lower" use area. . . . In fact, the term "higher" as applied to residential uses, or to uses closer than others to domestic purposes, is not an accurate one; for, although the use of property for homes is "higher" in the sense that commercial and industrial uses exist for the purpose of serving family life, the better these secondary uses can accomplish their purpose, the better is the primary use of property served.[115]

Courts have invalidated noncumulative zoning districts when the classification does not permit reasonable use of land, such as industrial zoning of land far removed from existing manufacturing activities and not likely to be needed for industrial uses in the near future,[116] and when the challenged zoning classification is not compatible with the actual development and use of land in the district.[117]

Communities desiring to create noncumulative districts may be better off specifying that type of district in their zoning ordinances. For example, a Pennsylvania court refused to permit a township to forbid the construction of a planned residential development in a general business district. The court held that there was nothing in the ordinance clearly prohibiting residential uses from general business areas. If the township "does not desire the pyramiding of zoning, then it should not have worded its Zoning Ordinance" as it did, the court concluded.[118]

A Kentucky court overturned a zoning board of adjustment decision revoking the permit for a halfway house in an industrial-use district, holding that halfway houses were not specifically prohibited in industrial districts by the zoning ordinance, although the court was satisfied that halfway houses were not contemplated uses when the ordinance was enacted in 1967. Observing that "industrial zoning has always been the stepchild of a community's planning," the court concluded that halfway houses were not incompatible with the range of permitted uses as long as they complied with area, yard, and height requirements. The reasoning was that the industrial district sections of the ordinance made specific reference to the requirement that residential uses comply with such requirements, and the actions of the planning director and building inspector in approving the original permit application evidenced a municipal interpretation that halfway houses were permitted uses in the industrial districts.[119]

Relationship of the Zoning Ordinance to the Comprehensive Plan

Although communities must engage in a planning process before they exercise police power to regulate use and development of land, most courts have concluded that the planning process need not be formal or separate from the regulatory process unless state law so requires.[120] In jurisdictions that lack statutory requirements that formal plans be developed, the courts have interpreted the traditional statutory requirement that zoning be "in accordance with a comprehensive plan" as simply requiring that officials exercising the zoning power have a "generalized conception" of how the power shall be used, which may be "exhibited in the (comprehensive) zoning ordinance itself," rather than in a separate written plan.[121]

The New York Court of Appeals, in striking down a zoning amendment reclassifying a small parcel of land in a suburban community from business to residential, construed the statutory requirement that zoning conform to a comprehensive plan as follows:

The thought behind the requirement is that consideration must be given to the needs of the community as a whole. In exercising their zoning powers, the local authorities must act for the benefit of the community as a whole following a calm and deliberate consideration of the alternatives, and not because of the whims of either an articulate minority or even majority of the community. . . . [T]he comprehensive plan is the essence of zoning. Without it, there can be no rational allocation of land use. It is the insurance that the public welfare is being served and that zoning does not become nothing more than just a Gallup poll. Moreover, the "comprehensive plan" protects the landowner from arbitrary restrictions on the use of his property which can result from the pressures which outraged voters can bring to bear on public officials. . . . Exactly what constitutes a "comprehensive plan" has never been made clear. . . . No New York case has defined the term "comprehensive plan." Nor have our courts equated the term with any particular document. We have found the "comprehensive plan" by examining all relevant evidence. . . . [T]he "comprehensive plan" requires that the rezoning should not conflict with the fundamental land use policies and development plans for the community. These policies may be garnered from any available source, most especially the master plan of the community, if any has been adopted, the zoning law itself and the zoning map.[122]

A zoning action may be invalid, however, where no evidence in the record shows that it was enacted in consideration of the comprehensive plan, despite the zoning authority's argument that it enacted the rezoning in accordance with "a" comprehensive plan, the court holding that once a specific comprehensive plan is enacted and reduced to writing, there must be evidence that the rezoning was enacted in specific consideration of the provisions of the plan.[123]

As noted in chapter 2, surveys of judicial attitudes regarding the relationship of planning to zoning in 1975[124] and in 1989[125] identified three general approaches taken by courts: (1) zoning is a "self-contained" activity; (2) the adopted master plan has separate legal status that requires consideration; and (3) zoning decisions must be consistent with the statutorily mandated plan.

The nature of the relationship of the comprehensive zoning ordinance to the comprehensive plan is determined by the applicable enabling act. The Standard Zoning Enabling Act, for example, states that regulation of land use "shall be in accordance with a general plan," and most state zoning-enabling statutes use similar language.[126] There is no constitutional requirement that zoning be accomplished according to a comprehensive plan,[127] and courts have upheld land use regulations having the effect of zoning under general police power principles, even in the absence of a statutorily prescribed comprehensive plan.[128]

The exact meaning of a "general plan" has been interpreted differently. Many courts have taken the position that a separately written and adopted comprehensive plan is not a necessary condition to the exercise of the zoning power, as long as the zoning ordinance is comprehensive in the sense of being "geographically complete" and is worded with clarity.[129]

In general, the comprehensive zoning ordinance is not required to mirror the terms of the general plan. A zoning ordinance may place more restrictive use or density limitations on land than is required under the applicable comprehensive plan when there is a legitimate reason for so doing, such as in cases where land uses in transition areas are expected to increase in intensity under a comprehensive plan but the timing is not yet right for that increase.[130]

In states that treat comprehensive plans as advisory documents for the legislative body, a comprehensive zoning ordinance prevails over a comprehensive plan when the two conflict and "questions of a citizen's property rights are at issue."[131] When compliance with a comprehensive plan is mandatory, however, such as before approval can be given to subdivision plats in many states, the fact that a subdivision plat application conforms to a zoning ordinance does not overcome its failure to comply with the applicable plan.[132]

A master plan that has not been adopted according to prescribed procedures has no legal effect. Thus a rezoning request cannot be rejected on the sole ground that it does not conform with a master plan that has not yet been adopted by the community.[133]

Inconsistencies between comprehensive plans and zoning ordinances, and especially between comprehensive plans and individual land use approvals such as rezonings or special-use permits, are fertile territory for litigants. Cities are naturally much slower to revise master plans, which often require expensive and time-consuming outside planning consultants, than zoning ordinances. If the comprehensive plan truly has meaning independent of the comprehensive zoning ordinance, it should often differ from the ordinance in content, not just tone. One objector has even argued, unsuccessfully, of "repeal by implication" of a zoning ordinance by a later-enacted comprehensive plan.[134]

Review by the Planning Agency

The role of the planning agency, or planning commission, in the enactment or revision of a comprehensive zoning ordinance is dictated by the enabling act, which generally requires the planning agency to review a zoning proposal prior to its enactment.[135]

Traditionally, the role of the planning agency is considered to be merely advisory. Some enabling acts, however, require local legislative bodies to give special attention to recommendations of disapproval by planning bodies, generally by imposing a supermajority voting requirement to approve a zoning proposal over the objection of the planning body.[136]

In construing a supermajority voting requirement, the Supreme Court of Connecticut held that the requirement applied to the number of authorized board members (five) rather than to the number present when the vote was taken (four) and upheld a determination that a three-to-one vote in favor of a proposal was insufficient to overcome the disapproval of the planning commission.[137]

As noted earlier,[138] enabling statutes may delegate to planning agencies the power to perform adjudicatory or quasi-judicial duties, such as acting on applications for special permits, subdivision plats, and street extensions.[139] When a planning agency is acting quasi-judicially, courts have applied "stricter rules of fairness," such as voiding planning board decisions when a board member fails to act impartially.[140]

Public Notice and Hearing Requirements

Notice of a public hearing has been required to be "couch[ed] . . . in language which reasonably informs the average lay person of the nature of the proposed changes to the zoning regulations which presently control the use of his or her real estate."[141] Applying that standard, the Supreme Court of Rhode Island upheld the published notice of the public hearing concerning a comprehensive rezoning proposal. The notice was a six-page advertisement that included a map of the community sufficiently accurate to enable "a non-lawyer landowner using reasonable diligence" to determine how the proposal would affect the land in the community. Proposed zoning districts and their respective classifications were marked by bold black lines on the map. Streets were "clearly marked by easily discernible black lines," although individual street names were not provided.[142]

When two public hearings are held, one by the advisory planning commission and one by the legislative body making the rezoning decision, the planning commission's failure to follow statutory notice provisions may not cause a rezoning decision to be invalidated, as long as the legislative body complies with the notice rules for its public hearing.[143]

When construing statutory notice requirements, courts have looked to the substance of the notice policy and have refused to invalidate zoning decisions in which statutory notice requirements were not followed completely, but the complaining parties nevertheless had actual knowledge of the proceedings, appeared, and were heard.[144] When statutory notice requirements have not been met, however, and there is no evidence of substantial compliance, courts have not hesitated to invalidate zoning ordinances,[145] even when, in one case, the challenge to the notice provisions came as late as five years after enactment of the ordinance.[146]

The purpose of the requirement of the public hearing is to help ensure that the zoning process is fair and equitable. Although there is no federal constitutional due process requirement that a public hearing be held before a zoning decision is made,[147] state enabling acts universally require a hearing before enactment or amendment of a zoning ordinance.[148]

Various tests have been formulated to determine whether a public hearing meets the requirement of fairness, depending on the type of hearing. The Supreme Court of Washington stated that the "test of fairness" for hearings that are legislative in nature

> is whether a fair-minded person in attendance at all of the meetings on a given issue could, at the conclusion thereof, in good conscience say that everyone had been heard who, in all fairness, should have been heard and that the legislative body required by law to hold the hearings gave reasonable faith and credit to all matters presented, according to the weight and force they were in reason entitled to receive.[149]

Applying that test, the court invalidated a rezoning of a large tract of land when the planning commission first announced that the public hearing it had conducted had been concluded and then permitted proponents, but not opponents, to speak further at a subsequent executive session.[150]

In protracted matters, development proposals evolve over a series of meetings, and both city staff and applicant's attorneys must be careful of enacting legislation or approvals that are substantially different from the advertised request. In one case, rezoning for a restaurant use was invalidated on the basis of a notice that referred only to specialty retail shops.[151] More subtle notice issues arise, such as changes in legal descriptions (either expanding or contracting), over the weeks or months of hearings. Some municipalities include a warning in the notices that action may change from that advertised.

At legislative public hearings, formal rules of evidence and procedure generally do not apply. There is no right to cross-examination, for example. The Court of Appeals of Maryland distinguished comprehensive rezonings that are legislative in character from piecemeal rezonings that may be more adjudicative in nature and concluded that the focus in a comprehensive rezoning on a large number of properties "as they relate to [one another] and to the surrounding area" raises legislative policy issues that are not amenable to the adjudicative, fact-finding process that includes cross-examination of witnesses.[152] Other states do not distinguish between comprehensive and piecemeal rezonings and treat both as purely legislative, subject to no rules of evidence.

The "legislative" characterization supports substantial judicial deference to local procedures and even substantive defects. Legislative hearings will not be invalidated, for example, merely because comments by members of the legislative body during the hearing indicate that positions may already have been taken on the matter, so long as all persons who seek to address the hearing are given a reasonable opportunity to do so and the legislative body acts in a "deliberative" manner.[153]

When a zoning ordinance is invalidated because of defects in the conduct of the public hearing, such as a 90-minute gap in the tape recording of the proceedings, the fact that another hearing must be conducted and a new ordinance enacted is not grounds for a cause of action in negligence against the city for improper conduct of the hearing or for violation of the "appearance of fairness" requirement unless the violations can be shown to be the proximate cause of injury to the landowner.[154]

Some zoning statutes require a second hearing if, after the first hearing, substantial changes are made in the proposed ordinance. Failure to conduct the second hearing may invalidate the ordinance. In one case, a proposed Maryland ordinance provided that all existing airports were nonconforming uses that could not be enlarged or extended except by being granted conditional-use status by the board of appeals. After a hearing, the ordinance was changed to provide that all existing airports were designated conditional uses without the necessity of obtaining approval from the board of appeals. This "180-degree change of position" was held to be substantial enough to require a second hearing.[155]

The standard governing when a new hearing is required is usually found in the local zoning ordinance and based on the materiality of the proposed change. The issue is most common in connection with the inevitable changes in large commercial rezonings. Such rezonings are most often accomplished through the planned commercial district device.[156] Textual and development plat provisions evolve over months of give-and-take between the developer and the municipality, which may be representing a variety of constituencies. The proposed zoning change may be altered substantially from the content of the original public notice, which typically refers simply to the original zoning amendment application on file with the city. The practical need for closure of public debate often argues against conducting successive public hearings. In the tradition of judicial deference to zoning amendment decisions, the procedural decision of the elected officials will not likely be disturbed by the courts, the enabling statutes being silent on the issue. In practice, however, local elected officials usually err on the side of excessive public debate.

Judicial deference notwithstanding, local ordinances concerning public hearings must comply with mandatory state statutes. A California court invalidated those portions of a zoning ordinance enacted by an initiative that limited public hearings to cases involving the location of subdivisions or commercial manufacturing facilities to which opposition has been expressed. The decision was based on a conflict with state statutes requiring public hearings before the adoption or amendment of *any* zoning ordinance.[157]

Voting Requirements for Enactment

Some enabling acts provide voting requirements for enactment of zoning ordinances. More typically, however, the acts are silent and the local governing body is left with discretion to develop its own voting requirements.[158] The major exception is a provision found in most enabling statutes and ordinances that a supermajority is required to enact or amend a zoning regulation when a protest has been lodged in proper form by the requisite number of landowners within a stated perimeter of the subject property.[159]

Use of the Initiative to Enact a Comprehensive Zoning Ordinance

The initiative is the power of the electorate to enact new laws.[160] Ordinances that are legislative in character may be enacted by initiative, whereas ordinances dealing with administrative matters may not.[161]

The initiative permits voters to enact comprehensive zoning ordinances despite enabling act language delegating zoning power only to the local "legislative body."[162] In upholding the use of the initiative to zone and rezone, the Colorado Supreme Court reasoned that (1) decisions legislative in character are subject to initiative; and (2) zoning is legislative in character because it is an action that "relates to subjects of permanent or general character," as opposed to actions that are temporary in operation or effect.[163]

Some courts deny the use of initiative for zoning amendments by distinguishing legislative acts of zoning from administrative or quasi-judicial acts of zoning. A test of what types of zoning constitute legislative actions subject to initiative was proposed in *Allison v. Washington County*.[164] In *Allison*, the Oregon Court of Appeals drew a distinction between zoning that affected a large area made up of property owned by many persons, which the court held to be legislative in character, and quasi-judicial decisions that applied only to a specific interest such as rezonings, variances, or conditional-use permits. Use of the initiative in quasi-judicial actions would not be permitted, the court reasoned, because such use would violate the constitutional right to notice and hearing.[165]

Use of the initiative to rezone land may violate the due process rights of the affected landowner. For example, in *Andover Development Corporation v. City of New Smyrna Beach*,[166] the Florida Court of Appeals invalidated an ordinance enacted by initiative because the initiative was in effect a rezoning of the plaintiff's land and because the objective of the initiative was to overrule the fact-finding of the planning commission.

Other courts, led by the California Supreme Court, have refused to make a distinction between legislative rezonings subject to initiative and quasi-judicial rezonings not subject to initiative, concluding that the better approach is to draw the line between legislative and nonlegislative matters, at least for initiative purposes, at the point where the legislative body makes the decision. Thus all rezonings in California are legislative in character and subject to initiative, but special permits and variances are not.[167]

Prospective developers have successfully challenged the use of zoning by initiative as a means to block development. In one case, the Supreme Court of Hawaii concluded that "zoning by initiative," also known as "ballot-box zoning," was inconsistent with the legislative policy expressed in the zoning-enabling act.[168] At issue was a proposal to construct a planned residential development on a tract of land that had been zoned for residential purposes since 1954, but that was within the Shoreline Management Area governed by a separate statute that required the developer to obtain a special-use permit for a management area from the City and County of Honolulu.[169] The permit application triggered opposition from those who feared that the development would harm a nearby beach.

An initiative petition rezoning the property from residential to preservation was approved after the Supreme Court of Hawaii stayed a lower court's injunction against the election. The process of rezoning an area to a more restrictive classification is called *downzoning*. When the court examined the merits, however, it concluded that the initiative did not validly amend the development plan and zoning designation. The court did not reach the constitutional question of whether use of the initiative to rezone land violated the due process rights of the landowner but limited itself to construction of the zoning-enabling act. Agreeing with the reasoning of courts in New Jersey, Washington, and Nebraska on the use of referenda in zoning matters,[170] the court first declared that use of the initiative to make "piecemeal attacks" on zoning ordinances was inconsistent with the legislative emphasis on "comprehensive planning for reasoned and orderly land use development." The court also noted that the zoning-enabling statute in Hawaii was enacted before initiative became available at the state or local level.

The court distinguished cases approving the use of initiative and referenda in zoning matters from jurisdictions in California,[171] Colorado,[172] Florida,[173] Minnesota,[174] Ohio,[175] and Oklahoma[176] on the grounds that clear constitutional or statutory provisions permitting initiative and referenda in zoning matters were in existence when zoning-enabling acts in those states were enacted. The court concluded that while the zoning-enabling act may give local governments discretion in the manner in which local zoning regulations are promulgated, the "thrust" of the enabling act is "to assure that, however enacted, those ordinances comport with [the applicable] long-range general plan," and thus a charter provision authorizing the initiative must give way to the provisions of the enabling act.[177]

A strong dissent argued that the majority failed to give a reasoned and persuasive explanation for its decision to "divest the people . . . of a right granted under the City's charter," but rather succumbed to "fears . . . that the objectives of planning would be jeopardized if the people were given the opportunity to effect zoning changes through the [initiative] process." The dissent saw no real difference between zoning by initiative and zoning by referendum and stated that the majority's attempt to distinguish an earlier Hawaii case where the court had approved of the repeal of a zoning ordinance by referendum vote[178] was not persuasive. Finally, the dissent distinguished the cases cited by the majority on the grounds that in those states the zoning-enabling acts contained more procedural directions to local governments than did the Hawaii statute.[179] As noted by the dissent in *Kaiser Hawaii*, some states impose greater control of the procedural aspects of local zoning. For example, New Jersey's Municipal Land Use Law expressly prohibits zoning by initiative or referendum.[180]

In an important challenge to ballot-box zoning in California, a California appellate court upheld an initiative in the City of Walnut Creek that the court concluded was inconsistent with the city's existing general plan.[181] The initiative, designated Measure H, was approved by a narrow margin. It consisted of a declaration of policy that traffic levels exceeding 85 percent of street capacity "pose an immediate threat to the public health, safety, and welfare," and a moratorium on any real estate development that would cause commute-hour traffic to exceed the 85 percent level. Although California law[182] requires a city's land use regulations to be consistent with its general plan, the court upheld Measure H by construing it as an amendment to the general plan as well as a land use regulation.

In finding that Measure H was inconsistent with the existing general plan, the court distinguished "broad statements of developmental policy" from "narrowly defined polic[ies] and specific directive[s]," both of which may be in the same plan. Even though the initiative may have been consistent with "broad, conservation-oriented platitudes" in the policy portion of the plan, the court found a "direct inconsistency" with the circulation element of the plan, which included statements that traffic congestion "will continue to increase as new development occurs" and "drivers will have to adjust to an increased level of congestion."[183]

Drawing on "the duty of the courts to jealously guard [the initiative] right of the people," the court held that claims that Measure H was too detailed and specific to be considered a plan amendment and that it had not been denominated as a plan amendment did not prevent it from being so considered in order to overcome the problem of inconsistency and uphold the will of the electorate. Adoption of the initiative was a "clear expression of intent to turn away from the policy of tolerance and acceptance" of traffic congestion provided in the circulation element of the plan. Because initiatives "are seldom models of technical legal perfection," the court dismissed as inconsequential the initiative's failure to describe itself as a plan amendment.[184]

One federal court has held that the initiative may not be used with regard to fiscal matters simply because land use regulation is involved.[185] The initiative would have required certain sized commercial developments to perform rehabilitation or construction of low- or moderate-income housing or contribute to a trust fund for such purpose.

Use of the Referendum to Challenge Zoning Ordinances

The referendum is an election by which voters approve or reject an ordinance already adopted by the legislative body.[186] In *City of Eastlake v. Forest City Enterprises*,[187] the Supreme Court approved the use of the referendum in zoning matters. In *Eastlake*, the plaintiff challenged a city charter amendment requiring that any changes in land use be approved by a 55 percent vote in a referendum, arguing that the amendment was an unconstitutional delegation of legislative power to the people. The court disagreed, reasoning that because under federal constitutional principles all power derives from the people, the people can withhold power "to deal directly with matters which might otherwise be assigned to the legislature."[188] This sort of reservation of power is the basis of the referendum, which allows voters a species of veto authority over legislative enactments.

The court also stated that the referendum does not violate due process because a referendum that results in an arbitrary or capricious action is subject to challenge in state court.[189] The dissent argued that the charter amendment challenged by the plaintiff was unconstitutional as a violation of due process because the amendment "places a manifestly unreasonable obstacle in the path of every property owner seeking any zoning change," and because it "provides no standards or procedures for exempting particular parcels or claims from the referendum requirement."[190]

States differ, however, on the availability of zoning by referendum. One view holds that zoning statutes are specific, detailed, and by definition planning-oriented, and therefore are incompatible with the case-by-case nature of initiatives and referenda. This view prohibits zoning by referendum.[191]

In one case, use of referenda to repeal ordinances authorizing extension of sewer lines to two proposed subsidized housing developments did not constitute a violation of the Federal Fair Housing Act[192] because "the strong policy considerations underlying referenda" militate against congressional intent to apply the discriminatory-effects test to referenda unless "highly unusual circumstances," not found in the case before the court, are present.[193]

State courts have observed the same distinction between legislative and administrative matters as is the case for initiatives,[194] permitting referenda on zoning matters considered to be legislative in character and invalidating referenda on administrative matters.[195] The referendum may be used to challenge a resolution of condemnation passed by a City Council because such resolutions are essentially legislative in nature.[196]

Local ordinances typically include procedural requirements and limitations periods for referenda. Petitioners who did not secure the required number of signatures within the specified time after enactment of a rezoning amendment in Kansas City, Missouri, were prevented from submitting a supplemental list of petitioners because there was no provision for filing a supplemental list in the applicable Kansas City charter provisions.[197]

Nonconforming Uses

Nonconforming uses, often thought of as "grandfathered" uses, are uses lawfully in existence but that are prohibited or otherwise illegal by reason of a subsequent ordinance.[198] The nonconforming use is allowed to continue as a vested right of the owner. Thus the term *nonconforming* is misleading, inasmuch as the use is by definition legal. The drafters of the Standard State Zoning Enabling Act deliberately omitted any reference to nonconforming uses, while recognizing that the "almost universal practice is to make zoning ordinances nonretroactive," in order to preserve the possibility of local governments dealing retroactively "with some isolated case[s]" involving "local conditions of a peculiar character."[199]

Some state zoning-enabling acts specifically recognize nonconforming uses, either by expressly permitting them[200] or by prohibiting zoning ordinances from operating retroactively.[201] Failure to "properly 'grandfather' preexisting, nonconforming uses" as required by the state enabling statute prohibiting retroactive application of zoning regulations was held to be an unconstitutional taking of a vested property right when a town in New Hampshire adopted an ordinance regulating free-standing signs that included a proviso requiring extinguishment of nonconforming signs that had been discontinued for one year or damaged 100 percent.[202] Even in states that do not expressly regulate nonconforming uses, the common practice is to permit such uses, although most zoning ordinances include an amortization feature.[203]

Validation of nonconforming uses may be founded on an equitable estoppel theory that nonrecognition would be unfair to affected landowners who had invested money in reliance on conformity[204] or, as noted above, on a property law theory of vested right to continue a lawful use.[205]

In the early days of zoning, drafters of zoning ordinances were "very generally agreed that the destruction of an existing nonconforming use would be a dangerous innovation of doubtful constitutionality, and that a retroactive provision might jeopardize the entire ordinance."[206] Because zoning "looks to the future, not the past," and the common law of nuisance was available to require the removal of existing uses that were truly threatening to the community, courts took the position that requiring the removal without compensation of nonconforming uses that were not nuisances was an unreasonable exercise of police power because of its extraordinary impact on traditional private property rights.[207]

Not every preexisting use, however, will qualify as a permitted noncon-forming use. Sometimes, for example, the preexisting use is so intermittent or temporary that the use may be denied a landowner after the enactment of an ordinance without infringing on the landowner's constitutional rights. Thus a person who infrequently repaired trucks on his property prior to the time this use was prohibited by a zoning ordinance can be denied permission to con-tinue the activity as a nonconforming use.[208] The nonconforming use doctrine requires *actual and continuous* use, so that the doctrine does not protect an owner simply because he may have purchased property in reliance on exist-ing zoning.[209]

In an interesting case involving the convergence of procedural due process, taking, and vested rights issues, however, the Sixth Circuit held that a property owner had a protectable property interest in a zoning classification, even where it has not actually engaged in a "use" of the property.[210] In *Nasierowski*, the court held that the act of purchasing property in reliance on the prior zoning, in addition to expending sums in preparing site plans and in petitioning the city for a variance from the prior zoning, could constitute the reliance necessary to establish a property interest in the prior zoning. It is per-haps here that the constitutional analysis required by a procedural due process or taking claim would depart from the state common-law analysis required by the nonconforming use doctrine. It is doubtful that the landowner in *Nas-ierowski* would have had a valid nonconforming use or vested rights claim, even if he had purchased the property in reliance on the prior zoning, if there had been no procedural or substantive due process violations in the same case. *Nasierowski* does illustrate that any nonconforming use or vested rights case might also be analyzed as a possible constitutional violation, especially where the actual level of use was not sufficient as a matter of the state com-mon law of nonconforming uses. Stated another way, the property interest necessary for a constitutional violation may be construed more liberally than that necessary for a finding of nonconforming use at state common law. In one case, $5 million in damages was awarded to a developer when in response to political pressure a city rezoned the project during construction, the owner having acquired a vested property right in the existing zoning status and building permit.[211]

Until vested rights legislation,[212] however, there was generally no vested right in a particular zoning status, only in a particular *use* arising out of that status. It is use that may rise to a property interest protectable by the due process clause of the Fourteenth Amendment.[213]

Conflicts arise when a landowner's need to expand an operation, which might be accomplished without incident if the activity were a permitted use, clashes with the desire of the municipality that the nonconforming use even-tually cease. Resolution of these conflicts may turn on the characterization of activities as permissible intensification or impermissible expansion.[214] Ordi-nances typically expressly deal with the expansion of uses within buildings, or after casualties, such as fires, and struggle with definition and expansion of the favorable nonconforming status in large, mixed-use properties such as shopping centers. Thus cities may attempt to analyze and amortize separately, subuses within one multiuse property. Even under ordinances that specifically contemplate such fine-tuning, gradations remain, such as a retail stall that is part retail and part restaurant, for example, triggering different parking requirements.

Noting that the "objective of zoning . . . is 'to eliminate nonconforming uses,'" the Court of Appeals of South Carolina rejected the claim of an adult bookstore and video store operator that it had a vested right to expand its lawful nonconforming use on the first floor of a building to include the second floor.[215] Prior to the enactment of a zoning amendment prohibiting adult bookstores and similar establishments from locating within 1,000 feet of a residential district, dwelling, church, or park, or within one mile of a school, which made the operation in question a nonconforming use, the operator had begun to convert the upstairs living quarters into an expansion of its store. In denying the operator's claim that it had a right to nonconforming-use status for both floors, the court stressed that nonconforming-use status could be granted only for lawful uses in existence prior to the new regulation. The prior expansion activities were illegal under the previous regulations because they were carried out without building or occupancy permits, so there was no prior lawful nonconforming use on the second floor. In addition, there was no showing that the use of the first floor for commercial purposes manifested an intent to "preempt" use of the rest of the building for commercial uses, particularly in view of the fact that one of the two residential quarters upstairs had been occupied.[216]

"Expansion" of a nonconforming use is itself a conclusion. Nonconforming-use status on a portion of a large parcel does not necessarily attach to the entire parcel. This issue is very significant with respect to large parcels, mixed-use parcels, and certain kinds of uses, such as mining uses. In the context of mining uses, the extension of nonconforming-use status over an entire, yet unused parcel, is known as the "diminishing asset doctrine." The doctrine, adopted in some states, holds that

> the very nature of the excavating business contemplates the use of the land as a whole, not a use limited to a portion of the land already excavated. Such a diminishing-asset enterprise is "using" all of the land contained in a particular asset; as a practical matter, it must begin digging at one spot and continue from there to the boundary of its land.[217]

Under the general police power to protect the public health, safety, welfare, and/or morals, nonconforming-use status does not immunize a use from regulation of land use apart from zoning, such as a building code or environmental regulation. Such nonzoning regulations may be retroactive. For example, a city can require the owners of a nonconforming use such as a quarry to fence the quarry's boundaries for safety reasons[218] or require the owners of a nonconforming retail stand along a roadway to pave the gravel parking lot to control dust.[219] A requirement that trees be trimmed to conform to height restrictions around an airport has been upheld.[220] As long as a regulation does not deprive an owner of all economic benefit of the nonconforming use and does not change the character of a nonconforming use so drastically that those in the surrounding community would fail to recognize the use, an otherwise valid police power regulation can be applied to nonconforming uses.[221]

Even though ordinances regulating nonconforming uses typically do not permit expansion or resumption after voluntary discontinuance,[222] they usually permit reasonable repair and maintenance activities.[223] The line often is drawn at new construction involving structural alteration.[224] Some zoning ordinances allow a landowner to switch from one nonconforming use to another, as long as the uses are related. In one case, where the ordinance provided that the new nonconforming use must be in the same or a more restrictive classification, a Kentucky appeals court held that use as a gas station was in the same classification as the new use, a used-car dealership, and upheld the change in use.[225]

Courts have used a three-part test to determine whether a modification or alteration, as opposed to expansion, in a nonconforming use is permissible: "(1) Whether the [current] use reflects the 'nature and purpose' of the [prior] use, and (2) Whether there is a difference in the quality or character, as well as the degree, of use, and (3) Whether the current use is 'different in kind in its effect on the neighborhood.'"[226]

The question of nonconforming uses may be raised in connection with any change of zoning, including a change resulting from municipal annexation. Any annexation ordinance or resolution should specifically assess necessary changes in zoning and the extent of resultant nonconforming uses.[227]

Nonconforming-use status attaches to a structure, not its owner. It "[does] not have a life separate from the [building],"[228] and therefore generally is not affected by changes in ownership.[229] One court, however, has held that nonconforming-use status did not attach to a boat, where the owner did not own the river bottom beneath the boat.[230]

In addition to nonconforming *uses*, ordinances also treat nonconforming sites, or *lots*, with respect to area, setback, and parking requirements, for example.

Amortization of Nonconforming Uses

Even though a municipality may not prohibit nonconforming uses immediately upon inception of the nonconformity, most states allow municipalities to phase out nonconforming uses.[231] This process is known as *amortization*.

Supporters of amortization argue that the original assumption behind the acceptance of nonconforming uses that such uses would gradually disappear over a relatively short period was not borne out by experience, thus preventing attainment of established planning and zoning goals.[232] In approving an amortization ordinance with a 25-year deadline, the Supreme Court of Texas stated:

> There are strong policy arguments and a demonstratable public need for the fair and reasonable termination of nonconforming property uses which most often do not disappear but tend to thrive in monopolistic positions in the community. We are in accord with the principle that

municipal zoning ordinances requiring the termination of nonconforming uses under reasonable conditions are within the scope of municipal police power; and that property owners do not acquire a constitutionally protected vested right in property uses once commenced or in zoning classifications once made.[233]

The most common objections to amortization are that in allowing, then prohibiting, a use amortization effects a taking, and that amortization as applied to a particular use is unreasonable because the period for amortization is too short.

The taking argument is based on the notion that the "value of property lies in the right to use it," and that an existing lawful use of property "constitutes a 'vested property right' which is guaranteed to the landowner . . . until such time as it is voluntarily terminated or abandoned.[234] Courts that have upheld amortization ordinances have reasoned that there is little practical difference between a statute that prohibits future uses and one that requires a use to be discontinued after a reasonable time.[235]

The amortization period has been described as a grace period that puts the owner on notice that a certain period is allowed to achieve compliance, rather than a mechanism for granting compensation to an owner for the taking of a property interest.[236] The amortization period must be reasonable, which is determined by balancing the public gain and the individual loss as evidenced by the circumstances of a particular case.[237] Those circumstances include the nature and location of the nonconforming use, the character of the structure, the length of the amortization period, the percentage of the individual's total business affected by the amortization requirement, the effect of the amortization on depreciation and salvage values, the use of public streets (applicable to signs because of their public messages), and "the monopoly or advantage, if any, resulting from the fact that similar new structures are prohibited in the same area."[238]

Some early amortization ordinances had extremely long periods, such as a 25-year period adopted in 1940 by University Park, Texas, for commercial uses in residential areas,[239] but most modern ordinances have amortization periods ranging from one to five years.[240] Shorter periods have been upheld when the burden on existing businesses is not unreasonable, such as a three-month amortization period for pornographic theaters, where the theaters could continue to operate by showing more mainstream attractions.[241] However, the Ninth Circuit Court of Appeals refused to enforce a 60-day amortization period for adult bookstores because of its severe financial impact on a bookstore owner who had signed a five-year lease shortly before the ordinance was passed.[242]

In a critique of the amortization policy, the drafters of the American Law Institute's *Model Land Development Code* noted that local governments have been reluctant to exert strong pressure on nonconforming uses, particularly where the nonconforming use merely is different from the permitted uses, such as commercial uses in residential districts. This reluctance may stem, in part, from "a general public disbelief in the original underlying principle of comprehensive zoning—that cities should be divided into districts of homogeneous uses." Perhaps it is also felt that buyers acquire properties in the neighborhood with knowledge of the nonconformity and cannot be heard to complain about it, provided the nonconformity does not amount to common-law nuisance. Reviewing courts likewise are likely to view with suspicion efforts to eliminate nonconforming uses in areas where local governments have allowed numerous deviations from their regulations. Finally, the drafters criticize attempts to eliminate nonconforming uses through amortization in substantially undeveloped areas as "even more tenuous." Extensive use of "wait-and-see" techniques[243] to "hold" land until the proper time for development "makes the traditional concept of nonconforming use obsolete."[244] More recent amortization efforts, however, have focused on specific uses that tend to generate public controversy, such as adult entertainment facilities and off-site signs.

When the state zoning-enabling act contains no mention of amortization of nonconforming uses, most courts that have considered the question have read the power to prohibit into the power to regulate.[245] For example, the Supreme Court of Delaware held that the state's enabling statute, modeled after the Standard State Zoning Enabling Act, granted municipalities the power to amortize nonconforming uses even though this authority was not expressly set forth in the enabling legislation.[246] In reaching its conclusion, the court canvassed the cases and accepted the view of the majority that enabling act authorization to "regulate and restrict" land use "necessarily entails a possible prohibition of some kind," and that "regulation may take the character of prohibition . . . in proper cases."[247]

Amortization is also accomplished in the nonconforming-use provisions of local zoning ordinances by prohibition of material expansion, alteration, or enlargement of the use or of reconstruction or repair after a stated period of nonuse, often one year, whether nonuse is voluntary or by reason of damage or destruction. Even involuntary cessation of use may terminate nonconforming-use status.[248]

Height Regulations

Zoning ordinances usually impose height limitations for buildings. Height control preceded comprehensive zoning, first drawing attention nationally when San Diego enacted height regulations in 1912.[249] Drafters of the Standard State Zoning Enabling Act linked limitations on the number of stories of a building with height regulation in order to forestall any effort by courts to "construe [height] narrowly."[250]

The basic validity of height restrictions was upheld by the Supreme Court as part of its decision approving comprehensive zoning.[251] Height restrictions are imposed for several reasons, including regulation of overall development density through limitations on building size,[252] provision of open space, light, and air,[253] preservation of rural character,[254] and safety, such as from aircraft landing and taking off from airports.[255]

Density Controls

In addition to height restrictions, municipalities control the density of land use by regulating the manner in which populations and buildings are distributed, through such devices as minimum lot sizes,[256] setback requirements,[257] and ratios of permissible usable space to lot or floor areas.[258]

Density controls have traditionally been regarded as valid uses of police power: "A quiet place where yards are wide, people few, and motor vehicles restricted are legitimate guidelines in a land-use project addressed to family needs."[259] Controls must meet the standard of reasonableness, however, as measured by the rational-basis test.[260]

Applying that test, the Supreme Court of Connecticut invalidated a 1,300-square-foot minimum floor-area requirement for single-family homes.[261] In an exhaustive opinion, the court concluded that a minimum floor-area requirement that was not linked to the number of persons occupying the regulated structure had no rational relationship to protection of public health, and that the minimum bore no rational relationship to conservation of property values. The court rejected arguments that "more expensive single-family houses are more desirable and . . . more such houses generate more taxes from persons better able to pay more taxes with perhaps less demand upon municipal services." The trial court had not found that the proposed houses, which were designed for 1,026 square feet of floor space, would "decrease or destabilize" building values.[262]

The court stressed that possible beneficial effects are not the only items considered in evaluating the reasonableness of a regulation, but that possible harmful effects must also be considered. A minimum floor-area requirement that is higher than that required for health or safety reasons causes a substantial, but unnecessary increase in the cost of houses and a corresponding decrease in affordability, the court noted. The difference in cost between the proposed 1,026-square-foot house and required 1,300-square-foot house was estimated to be approximately $10,000, increasing the construction costs from $59,000 to approximately $70,000. This, plus the lack of evidence that the proposed modular houses would be "significantly undersized," cheap, or "aesthetically incompatible" with other houses in the neighborhood, as well as the lack of any link between the floor-area requirement and public health concerns, led the court to conclude that there was no rational basis for the requirement.[263]

In an important point with implications for local efforts to target the location of affordable housing, the court dismissed as irrelevant the municipality's stress on significant efforts it had made in other districts to encourage more construction of affordable housing by reducing minimum floor-area requirements and permitting multiple-family dwellings. The court noted that the Connecticut zoning-enabling act had been amended to require zoning regulations to "encourage the development of housing opportunities for all citizens of the municipality consistent with soil types, terrain and infrastructure capacity."[264] Emphasizing the requirement that housing opportunities be encouraged for "*all* citizens," not just "in some zones for some citizens," the court concluded that what was done in other districts was irrelevant to the challenged minimum floor-area requirement in the absence of any showing that the 1,300-square-foot requirement had any bearing on "soil types, terrain and infrastructure capacity" of the districts in which the 1,300-square-foot minimum was in place.[265]

A dissenting opinion characterized the majority's finding of no rational relationship between floor-area requirements and conservation of property values as "an exercise in appellate fact-finding upon a subject where . . . reasonable differences of opinion exist." Noting that the overall reduction in the cost of the proposed housing by elimination of the 1,300-square-foot requirement would be about 10 percent, from $109,000 to $99,000, the dissent doubted that such a reduction would have "any significant impact upon the affordability of housing." The "seriousness" of the problem of affordable housing should not be ignored, but a legislative rather than a judicial response is the only way an "adequate solution" can be found to "a social problem of this nature," the dissent concluded.[266]

Flexibility in the use of density controls is achieved by ordinances allowing "cluster zoning" or "density zoning." Under such schemes, a developer who has a large tract of land to develop can vary the density within the tract, making some areas more dense than is allowed under the provisions of the zoning laws, provided that the overall density is within the limits imposed on the rest of the community.[267] Such density variation within a large tract is also a common feature of the planned unit development (PUD) concept.[268]

Where restrictions other than density controls prevent a developer from building on parts of a tract under development, the question sometimes arises whether such restricted land can be included in the overall density measurement of the entire tract. The Court of Appeals of New York held that even though a developer could not build on 210 of his 450 acres because of the existence of a conservation easement, under a cluster zoning law the land burdened by the conservation easement could be counted in determining the number of units that could be constructed on the remaining 240 acres.[269]

Another density-control technique is the building-permit limitation. Courts are suspicious of building-permit caps or quotas, however. In one case, the Supreme Court of New Hampshire invalidated an ordinance that limited the number of building permits that could be issued yearly to 3 percent of the total existing dwellings because of a lack of evidence linking the 3 percent limit to a legitimate growth-management concern. "Growth controls are intended to regulate and control the timing of development, not the prevention of development," the court stated.[270]

Density is also controlled through the use of definitions. Perhaps the most meaningful and litigated definition is that of the word *family*, in the sense of one that may live in a single-family zone.[271] The Supreme Court has upheld—over a strong dissent that did not agree that a definition of family affected density of use—an ordinance that defined *family* to mean "one or more persons related by blood, adoption, or marriage, or not more than two persons."[272]

Density calculations also implicate subdivision ordinances, which may require subdivision plans to meet the density requirements of the master plan.

Courts have enforced the subdivision ordinance requirement of consistency with the master plan even though the subdivision plan meets the density requirements of the zoning ordinance.[273] When a development plan does meet the density requirements of the master plan, it cannot be rejected without good reasons.[274]

The Zoning Envelope

The multiplicity of controls on the size and placement of buildings, such as minimum lot sizes, building setback lines, height limitations, minimum square-footage provisions, and floor-area ratios establish a three-dimensional enclosure or "envelope" inside which buildings may be located.[275] Lack of flexibility in prescribing the outer boundaries of the envelope may restrict the range of building design choices. Increased use of more flexible controls such as floor area and open-space ratios rather than absolute minimums and maximums may broaden design choices without compromising bulk and density goals.

In addition to the perhaps unintended effect that the zoning envelope can have on design choice, the zoning envelope is the basis for the transfer-of-development-rights (TDR) concept often advocated as a compromise technique to accommodate conflicting development and preservationist interests.[276]

Innovative Land Use Controls

Dissatisfaction with the rigidity of the Euclidean zoning response to explosive development growth in the decades after World War II led local governments to search for regulatory alternatives that would preserve the basic concept of zoning but add flexibility to the process. In addition to flexibility in administration, many communities sought to achieve higher standards of quality, such as larger houses, more open space, and less density. In 1968, the National Commission on Urban Problems called attention to the changes taking place in land use regulation. Regulations became more detailed, as evidenced by a substantial increase in the number of separate districts for the same general use, such as residential use, added to many zoning ordinances, a shift from identifying prohibited uses to permitted uses in particular districts, and new ways of evaluating density standards by applying them to an entire development rather than individual lots.[277]

Following the growth decades of the 1950s and 1960s, concerns over growth management, environmental problems, and shortages of affordable housing caused local governments to engage even more aggressively in land use regulation. The performance standard concept was introduced in which land use regulation is achieved by measuring physical characteristics and functions of particular land uses against predetermined criteria and standards.[278] Cities offered development incentives such as density bonuses for affordable housing or development of urban-versus-suburban commercial projects. Zoning became a device to foster, as well as to restrain, particular types of growth and development.[279]

A New Hampshire statute enacted in 1983 and amended as new techniques became popular[280] lists the following "innovative" land use controls:

timing incentives, phased development,[281] intensity and use incentives, transfer of development rights,[282] planned unit development,[283] cluster development,[284] impact zoning,[285] performance standards,[286] flexible and discretionary zoning,[287] environmental characteristics zoning,[288] inclusionary zoning,[289] and accessory dwelling unit standards.[290] The statute permits local governments to adopt innovative land use controls in the normal way that zoning ordinances are adopted, but such controls must "contain within [them] the standards which guide the person or board which administers the ordinance."[291] Innovative land use controls may be administered by planning boards, zoning boards of adjustment, local legislative bodies, or other persons or designated bodies. If the planning commission is not the designated administrator, it must submit written comments concerning any proposals that must be considered by the administrator before a final decision is made. If the planning board's comments are not directly incorporated into the decision, the administrator must provide written findings and reasons for not incorporating those comments.[292]

One town in California has considered a ten-year plan that would create the modern-day equivalent of the company town, whereby approval for an office campus development would be conditioned upon the establishment of child-care facilities, a retail center, public and private parks, a hotel, and company-sponsored transit.[293] Because of an acute shortage of affordable housing in the area, the plan would require that the company construct housing at its own expense, presumably benefiting itself in the form of lower employee turnover as a result of decreased commuting time and lower salaries as a result of stabilization of housing prices.

The concept of co-housing has garnered some interest in the United States.[294] The co-housing movement, originating in Denmark, is a form of property ownership whereby privately owned households share common areas such as offices, cooking areas, and recreational areas. The concept begs the comparison to condominium communities, but presumably is closer to communal living than the modern condominium, entailing somewhat more intimate sharing of the property on a daily basis. One interesting benefit of the co-housing concept may be the ability to serve the needs of nontraditional, nonnuclear families such as single parents, the elderly, and career-oriented families.[295]

Planned Unit Development/Cluster Zoning

Perhaps the most popular regulatory device for encouraging flexibility is the planned unit development (PUD) or cluster development. Most large-scale shopping center projects are zoned "planned district" and have comprehensive, negotiated zoning ordinances specifically applicable to the given project, including everything from permitted uses, setbacks, height limitations, and sign regulations to procedures for future amendments. The PUD permits the developer of a minimum-size tract to mix uses within the tract and to deviate from generalized density requirements.

In a traditional Euclidean zoning ordinance, density standards described previously[296] create zoning envelopes that limit the number of residential units to the number of lots in a residential district, for example. A PUD or cluster-zone provision permits units to be clustered on a portion of the acreage, as long as the balance of the tract remains undeveloped and the density for the total number of permissible lots is not exceeded.[297] Clustering is accomplished by relaxing one or more of the zoning standards (e.g., lot size requirements or minimum setbacks) for a portion of the tract in return for retaining the balance of the tract in an undeveloped state.[298] Changes in permissible uses may not be made through the PUD process unless the comprehensive zoning ordinance permits mixed uses, but such zoning usually permits a variety of permitted uses (e.g., detached, semi-detached, attached, or multistory residential structures) to be included in a single residential PUD project.[299]

Like traditional zoning district designations, PUDs must meet reasonable standards of harmony with the surrounding area and must be consistent with adopted comprehensive plans. For example, a New York statute authorizing PUDs through cluster zoning permits the zoning modifications to be made "simultaneously with the approval of a plat or plats," and authorizes towns to require PUD developers to submit detailed applications including site development plans, as well as imposing conditions "necessary to assure preservation" of lands designated for park, open-space, or recreational use.[300]

As with other zoning decisions, when PUD applications are denied, written findings must be made to enable the developer to make corrections to the plan where feasible and to permit "meaningful" judicial review.[301] Approval may not be denied solely because of community displeasure with the proposed development,[302] but courts have been unwilling to overturn a denial as inappropriately influenced by vocal opposition unless the record presented, including the findings of the decision-maker, shows evidence that "citizen pressure influenced the . . . decision."[303]

Floating Zones

Floating zones are zoning districts in which certain types of uses are authorized, but that are assigned no fixed location in the community at the time of authorization.[304] Such uses are said to float above the community until anchored at a specific location. The anchoring process is achieved through a second zoning decision, typically treated as a rezoning,[305] in which the owner of a particular parcel applies for a rezoning in order to develop the land in the manner contemplated by the floating zone. If approved, the land is rezoned and the floating zone "comes to rest" at that site.

The first generally recognized use of the floating-zone technique was in 1947 in Tarrytown, New York.[306] The Court of Appeals of New York upheld the two-step process for creating and anchoring floating zones against a variety of challenges, concluding with the following observations:

> In sum, the 1947 amendment was merely the first step in a reasoned plan of rezoning, and specifically provided for further action on the part of the board. That action was taken by the passage of the 1948 ordinance which fixed the boundaries of the newly created zone and amended the zoning map accordingly. It is indisputable that the two amendments, read together as they must be, fully complied with the requirements of the Vil-

lage Law and accomplished a rezoning of village property in an unexceptionable manner.[307]

Although floating zones were invalidated in some early cases because of concern with lack of legislative authorization or potential for spot zoning,[308] courts generally have been receptive to floating zones. For example, the Missouri Court of Appeals canvassed the cases over a 30-year period and found those upholding floating zones to be persuasive:

> [Approval of floating zones] serves as a recognition that municipal legislative bodies need a certain flexibility in determining whether particular types of uses should be allowed within the environs of an area zoned for some other use where the newly allowed use can be made compatible with the existing uses.[309]

It is not unusual for cluster zoning to be implemented through the floating-zone technique.[310]

Flexible Zoning

Several communities have experimented with a variety of techniques designed to achieve greater flexibility than that available through cluster and floating zoning. These newer techniques generally are based on performance regulation rather than territorial regulation, although cities often implement the techniques through a territorial scheme.

Incentive Zoning

Incentive zoning attempts to persuade landowners to allocate land to desirable uses by offering economic incentives. As described by the Court of Appeals of New York, it is "based on the idea that zoning can be used as an incentive to further growth and development of the community rather than as a restraint."[311] The basic technique or incentive is the allowance of higher densities than permitted under general zoning rules in return for greater amenities in a project, rehabilitation of slums, or construction of public facilities or affordable housing. Under this approach, the developer earns a "density bonus."[312]

The key to successful use of incentive zoning, according to the Court of Appeals of New York, is to ensure that "[t]he bonus awarded for each amenity [is] carefully structured . . . to make the cost-benefit equation favorable enough to induce the developer to provide the desired uneconomic benefit to the city but sufficiently limited to avoid a windfall to it."[313]

Incentive zoning may be linked to particular areas through special district zoning in which the incentives are offered to landowners in the special district,[314] or it may be used to encourage a particular activity, such as the use of passive solar techniques in residential developments, throughout the community.[315]

Performance Zoning

Performance zoning systems base their regulation of land uses on the performance of the uses ("their actual physical characteristics and functions") when "measured against predetermined criteria and standards."[316] For example, the New Jersey Municipal Land Use Law authorizes municipalities to include in their zoning ordinances "reasonable standards of performance and standards for the provision of adequate physical improvements including, but not limited to, off-street parking and loading areas, marginal access roads, other circulation facilities, and water, sewerage, and drainage facilities."[317] The ordinance authorizes the city to require the developer to produce "performance guarantees" of up to 120 percent of the cost of installation of improvements and "maintenance guarantees" for up to two years and 15 percent of the cost of the improvements.[318]

Construing the performance standards provision, the Supreme Court of New Jersey upheld a zoning ordinance requiring every single-family residence to have a minimum of two off-street parking spaces, "one of which shall be in a garage." A landowner converted an attached garage into a recreation room and then sought a variance of the garage requirement in order to obtain a certificate of occupancy. In affirming the denial of the variance by the zoning board of adjustment, the court reversed lower court rulings that the parking garage requirement was unreasonable. The court found the garage requirement to be compatible with legitimate statutory goals to "promote the free flow of traffic [and avoid] congestion . . . [as well as] a desirable visual environment through creative development techniques and good civic design and arrangements."

Replying to the charge that the garage requirement had "no substantial relationship" to the municipality's goals, the court declared:

> Obviously, there will always be people for whom a garage will be a place to store bicycles, lawn mowers, or outboard motors. But in the nature of things many people will probably store their cars in their garage. This can have the good effect envisioned by the ordinance of having less cluttered streets. A car in every garage thus may not be an actuality, but it is certainly a realistic possibility. We find that the rational relationship between the means chosen to achieve the legitimate zoning purpose is "at least debatable," and therefore the ordinance is to be sustained.[319]

Otherwise-valid permits may be rescinded when performance standards are not met, and off-site factors may be considered in evaluating whether performance standards have been met.[320]

A study of performance zoning systems published by the Urban Land Institute in 1988 concluded that most communities that employ performance zoning use it in conjunction with the traditional prescriptive system. Although performance zoning has existed in some form since 1950, its growth has been "slow and uncertain." The study found that it has been used primarily to enable planning commissions and city councils to make more informed decisions by supplying "better project information and policy ratings" rather than for its theoretical premise of allowing such decisions to be delegated to administrators. Factors such as relative degree of controversy in proposed land use changes, confidence in the ability of administrators to reflect community attitudes, ability of zoning ordinances to give "close guidance" without extensive interpretation, and the interest of public officials in land use matters were found to be important considerations in determining the advisability of adopting a performance standard approach.[321]

Development Impact Analysis

A third form of flexible zoning, development impact analysis, focuses on a municipality's existing infrastructure. As described by an official in the Division of Development and Planning of Georgetown, Texas, development impact analysis requires all new development proposals to be evaluated on the basis of "both proposed use and projected impact" on existing infrastructure.[322] The idea is to measure the performance of a proposed use by its impact on public facilities so that new development will not overwhelm a community's resources. As originally proposed in Georgetown, Texas, development impact analysis was intended to replace traditional zoning, presumably because there would be no need for rigid prescription of uses based on territorial division if the infrastructure could absorb new development; however, because of fears that development impact analysis criteria "would not be strong enough to guarantee compatibility of adjacent uses," it was added "as another regulatory tool."[323]

The concurrency requirement of the Florida mandatory local planning statute discussed in chapter 2[324] requires local communities to engage in formal development impact analysis and prohibits them from approving development proposals that would result in effective reductions of public services from levels specified in adopted local comprehensive plans. It may be argued that such analysis is what local officials have always done, but the Florida scheme requires the locality to make a record, perhaps providing fodder for attack in the courts.

Neo-Traditional Planning and Zoning

Some have touted a "return to the good old days" of the American small town as an antidote to the rigidities and perceived weaknesses of modern suburban zoning. As described in *Planning,* the magazine of the American Planning Association, "neo-traditional" town planning emphasizes a return to a grid pattern of streets and a reorientation of communities away from "automobile orientation." Mixed uses are approved, even required, so that residents will be able to walk to neighborhood commercial areas. A model "traditional neighborhood development" ordinance has been promulgated by the Foundation for Traditional Neighborhoods to encourage the reintroduction of a small-town, walking-oriented philosophy to suburban America.[325]

Overlay Zones

Overlay zoning is a technique in which new, more restrictive zoning is "laid over" an existing zone or zones in order to further regulate or restrict certain permitted uses.[326] In a typical scheme, the Cincinnati Municipal Code authorized the city council to create environmental quality districts (EQDs) that overlay the existing zoning districts in cases where there is public concern that use under the existing regulations might damage the quality of the urban environment. An EQD was created that prevented development of a fast-food restaurant at a particular site. The Supreme Court of Ohio upheld the constitutionality of overlay zoning in this context as a reasonable exercise of police power to promote flexibility "in its attempt to preserve and protect the character of certain neighborhoods that the city deems important."[327]

The typical overlay district is not an independent zoning district but simply a layer that supplements the underlying zoning district regulations. Another example of an overlay district is the floodplain overlay district, which restricts the development of property in federally designated floodplains or floodways, whatever the underlying zoning.

The validity of overlay zoning is analyzed like any other zoning designation. The Supreme Court of Washington struck down an overlay zone regulating 14 designated greenbelt areas in the city of Seattle. The greenbelt areas were primarily linear bands of undeveloped, treed hillsides located in various zoning districts. The underlying districts regulated the types of permissible uses, while the greenbelt overlay required between 50 and 70 percent of the land to be preserved in an undeveloped state. The court invalidated the overlay ordinance as a taking because it deprived landowners of "all profitable use of a substantial portion of their land."[328] In a later case, not dealing with overlay zones, the court overruled that portion of its decision in which it found a taking because of the impact of the overlay regulations on a portion of property and reaffirmed the majority view that taking analysis must focus on the impact of regulations on an entire parcel.[329]

Historic Districts and Landmarks Preservation

A popular form of overlay zoning enables municipalities to enact ordinances to protect places deemed to be of historic interest.[330] Inspired by the National Historic Preservation Act of 1966,[331] which established a national program to assist state and local preservation efforts, a typical statute authorizes municipalities to create by ordinance a historic district commission that is to recommend to the city council a list of structures or sites of sufficient historical interest to be designated landmarks or historic districts. When an area is considered to have historic or cultural significance, either because of the number of individual buildings of importance or because of the role the area played in the municipality's development, a district is created in which more restrictive regulations are imposed to preserve the historic character of the area. After such designation by the city council, an owner must obtain a "certificate of appropriateness" before building, modifying, or destroying a structure in the district.[332]

The basic constitutional question is whether the preservation of historical aspects of a community is a valid end of police power. Although federal and state courts have overwhelmingly approved the principle,[333] application of historic or landmark district controls to particular property through downzoning is constrained by the same rules and presumptions as other exercises of the zoning power and seems especially the focus of attack, probably because subjective matters of taste often apply.[334] When designation of landmark status and subsequent downzoning deprives the property owner of all reasonable use, including the right to demolish the structure, or impermissibly interferes with First Amendment freedom of religion rights, courts have invalidated the action.[335]

When the creation of a historic district is thought to effect a taking, a municipality may grant transferable development rights (TDRs) to the owner as compensation, although in some states TDRs are not considered just compensation.[336]

The National Historic Preservation Act requires federal agencies to consider the effect of federally funded projects on "any district, site, building, structure, or object" that has historic significance.[337] An area or neighborhood may be eligible for protection if it is "included in or eligible for inclusion" in the National Register of Historic Places.[338]

Design Control and Aesthetics

In addition to use, location, and size, zoning ordinances regulate the design of buildings, particularly in residential districts. Design control has become increasingly popular as the courts have expressed greater willingness to accept aesthetics as a permissible goal of public regulation of land use.[339]

In a leading case, the Supreme Court of Missouri upheld the denial of a building permit for a single-family residence because the "unusual design" had not been approved by the city's architectural board. The controversial design was for a residence that had "a pyramid shape, with a flat top, and with triangular shaped windows or doors at one or more corners." Homes in the immediate vicinity were predominantly of Colonial, English Tudor, or French Provincial design. The court evaluated the "aesthetic factors" that the board was to review, described in the ordinance as "conformity with surrounding structures and . . . certain minimum architectural standards of appearance," as well as avoidance of "unsightly, grotesque and unsuitable structures," along with the "effect that the proposed residence would have upon the property values in the area." In approving the architectural board's action, the court stressed that the impact of aesthetic factors on property values was "directly related" to the general welfare of the community and was a reasonable basis for the exercise of the land use regulatory power.[340]

Architectural Board of Review

Design control and review typically is carried out by a local administrative body made up of architects and other design specialists as well as laypersons. The architectural review board reviews a project at the permit application stage, although design review sometimes takes place as part of the initial land use control process, particularly if land use review is triggered by an application for rezoning.

Architectural review boards have two primary functions: (1) to develop "appearance and architectural" standards and (2) to review specific proposals for compliance with those standards.[341]

Architectural review boards, like all administrative agencies, must apply legislatively detailed standards that are sufficiently clear to constrain the exercise of administrative discretion within the boundaries of the applicable policy. In addition to detail, standards must have sufficient coverage. In one case, the Sixth Circuit invalidated a Cleveland, Ohio, ordinance requiring architectural-board-of-review approval of the design of newsracks as giving the board "standardless discretion" because a newsrack is not a building. The only standard to guide the board was a requirement that the board regulate the construction or alteration of buildings according to "accepted and recognized architectural principles."[342]

Urban Design Performance Standards

Some communities have adopted performance standards for urban design. As described in *The Practice of Local Government Planning,* published by the International City Management Association, the City of Pittsburgh subjects all downtown development projects to a project review process that requires building designs to conform to performance standards written by the planning department specifically for the subject project. For example, a building design might be expected to "block as little sunlight as possible from public open spaces."[343]

Zoning with Compensation

Zoning with compensation has received court approval in at least two states[344] and may receive more public attention in view of the Supreme Court's mandate that compensation be paid for regulatory takings.[345] Unlike almost any other zoning scheme, zoning with compensation compensates landowners for the diminution in value caused by restrictive zoning. The process requires the creation of "restricted residence districts" under state legislative authorization and the acquisition by eminent domain of the "right to exercise the power [to prohibit uses other than those permitted in the restricted residence district.]"[346]

Zoning with compensation has been upheld as a "joint exercise of the power of eminent domain and the police power" in which the local government regulates land use "with extraordinary consideration for the property owners involved."[347] Scholars have dubbed it "Zoning by Special Assessment Financed Eminent Domain (ZSAFED)."[348]

Transferable Development Rights

The zoning envelope creates a three-dimensional block of permitted use that, if treated as property, can be transferred to other tracts of land. This concept is said to create transferable development rights (TDRs). With the use of TDRs, a municipality that restricts the use of property can anticipate objections that its regulation amounts to a taking by granting compensation in the form of the right to develop property elsewhere. One court has described this technique as "permitting the transfer of development rights from the burdened property to certain other properties in the political subdivision," giving value to the rights transferred by "permitting a greater than normal intensity of development of the transferee or 'receiving' property."[349] Development rights not used by the transferor can be sold to the transferee, compensating the transferor for the loss caused by the original restriction.

The Supreme Court has never ruled directly on the constitutional validity of TDRs, but in *Penn Central Transportation Company v. New York City*, the court did mention that TDRs should be considered in a taking analysis. "While these rights [TDRs] may well not have constituted 'just compensation' if a 'taking' had occurred, the rights nevertheless undoubtedly mitigate whatever financial burdens the lot has imposed on appellants and, for that reason, are to be taken into account in considering the impact of regulation."[350] Because the court held that New York City's Landmarks Preservation Law as applied to Grand Central Terminal was not a taking, the court did not have to rule directly on the validity of TDRs as compensation. Some state courts, however, have invalidated the use of TDRs as compensation.[351]

In *Suitum v. Tahoe Regional Planning Agency*, the Supreme Court discussed TDRs in the context of a ripeness question.[352] All nine justices agreed that a challenge to the Tahoe agency's decision that an undeveloped lot near Lake Tahoe was ineligible for development was a "final decision" and thus ripe for review.[353] Justice Souter writing for a six-justice majority considered the facts that the landowner was entitled to TDRs under the applicable regulation and that no discretionary decision was necessary before she could sell her TDRs as evidence that a "final decision" had been reached.[354]

Justice Scalia, writing a concurring opinion joined by Justices O'Connor and Thomas, objected strongly to the notion that TDRs should be considered "on the taking rather than the just compensation side of the equation." Because TDRs have nothing to do with the use of the property being regulated, they are not relevant to the taking question, he asserted:

> I do not mean to suggest that there is anything undesirable or devious about TDRs themselves. To the contrary, TDRs can serve a commendable purpose in mitigating the economic loss suffered by an individual whose property use is restricted, and property value diminished, but not so substantially as to produce a compensable taking. They may also form a proper part, or indeed the entirety, of the full compensation accorded a landowner when his property is taken. . . . I suggest only that the relevance of TDRs is limited to the compensation side of the takings analysis, and that taking them into account in determining whether a taking has occurred will render much of our regulatory takings jurisprudence a nullity.[355]

Conditional Zoning

Municipalities, developers, and affected neighbors compromise many land use controversies by adding conditions to approval of the particular project. In a leading case, the Court of Appeals of New York upheld a municipality's decision to condition an amendment to its zoning ordinance on the execution of a declaration of conveyance by the developer that provided in part that "no construction may occur on the property so rezoned without the consent of the municipality."[356] An application to enlarge and extend an existing structure on the premises was later denied. In upholding the condition against the charge that it was arbitrary and capricious, the court made the following comments about conditional zoning:

> Probably the principal objection to conditional rezoning is that it constitutes illegal spot zoning, thus violating the legislative mandate requiring that there be a comprehensive plan for, and that all conditions be uniformed within, a given zoning district. When courts have considered the issue, the assumptions have been made that conditional zoning benefits particular land owners rather than the community as a whole and that it undermines the foundation upon which comprehensive zoning depends, by destroying uniformity within used districts. Such unexamined assumptions are questionable. First, it is a downward change to a less restrictive zoning classification that benefits the property rezoned and not the opposite imposition of greater restrictions on land use. Indeed, imposing limiting conditions, while benefitting surrounding properties, normally adversely affects the premises on which the conditions are imposed. Second, zoning is not invalid per se, mainly because only a single parcel is involved or benefitted; the real test for spot zoning is whether the change is other than part of a well considered and comprehensive plan calculated to serve the general welfare of the community. Such a determination, in turn, depends on the reasonableness of the rezoning in relation to neighboring uses—an inquiry required regardless of whether the change in zone is conditional in form. Third, if it is initially proper to change a zoning classification without the imposition of restrictive conditions notwithstanding that such change may depart from uniformity, then no reason exists why accomplishing that change, subject to condition should automatically be classified as impermissible spot zoning. . . . Another fault commonly voiced in disapproval of conditional zoning is that it constitutes an illegal bargaining away of a local government's police power. . . . The imposition of conditions on property sought to be rezoned may not be classified as a prospective commitment on the part of the municipality to zone as requested if the conditions are met; nor would the municipality necessarily be precluded on this account from later reversing or altering its decision. . . . Conditional rezoning is a means of achieving some degree of flexibility in land use control by minimizing the potentially deleterious effect of a zoning change on neighboring properties; reasonably conceived conditions harmonize the landowners' need for rezoning with the public interest, and certainly fall within the spirit of the neighboring legislation.[357]

Development Agreements and Contract Zoning

Because of the uncertainty of the more flexible review processes described previously, developers often seek "developer agreements," authorized in several states, to set the "rules of the game" for the review process.[358] More significantly, however, the developer may want assurance on substantive zoning issues. The rise in incentive-based urban and suburban redevelopment has given way to the issue of "contract zoning"—a conclusion that the government has illegally bargained away its legislative obligation to independently engage in land use zoning and regulation. In virtually all urban and redevelopment projects, the developer and city enter into a development agreement or redevelopment agreement. The essence of such agreements, which are true legal agreements, is a promise by the city to provide economic incentives and often eminent domain rights to the developer in exchange for a promise by the developer to acquire and develop the property.

In most such agreements, subsequent land use approvals by the very entity that is a party to the agreement is assumed, but not necessarily contractual. Thus the agreement is entered into, but the developer may not legally bind the city to a promise to grant subseqent rezonings or subdivision approvals. The developer will always reserve such items as contingencies, however. Given the universal validity and use of development agreements, there is a new relevance to the issue of contract zoning, which involves the duality of the city's identity as both a private business party or even "partner" with the developer and as the government, with power and statutory obligation to regulate, independent of its contractual promises.

The states vary in their scrutiny of city commitments or promises to grant or "cooperate" in approvals. Thus, in one recent case, a Florida court held that an agreement by a county to "support and expeditiously process" a rezoning application was unenforceable.[359] The issue of contract zoning is related to the issue of the government's power to grant, or as detractors would say, "sell to the highest bidder" its condemnation rights, and the condemnation issue of what use is public, as discussed in chapter 3.[360]

Another species of the development agreement is specifically designed to protect the developer from changes in land use ordinances over the course of a long-term project and has been specifically validated as not amounting to contract zoning. Thus California has enacted legislation vesting rights by enforceable development agreements between city and developer, limiting the power of the city to apply new ordinances to pending developments.[361] Such agreements have survived contract zoning challenges, provided that the city has not "surrendered control of all of its land use authority," in a case in which the court affirmed an award of $727,500 in damages to an apartment developer when the city reduced the approved density from 140 to 55 units by amending the zoning after entering into a development agreement with the developer.[362] At least ten other states have enacted similar development agreement legislation.[363] Florida has also enacted development agreement legislation but takes a different view regarding the issue of contract zoning. In one case, a Florida court invalidated as contract zoning, a development agreement in which the city had agreed to "support and expeditiously process" a rezoning application, even though the statute expressly permits development agreements establishing vested rights.[364]

Development Moratoria

A moratorium is a temporary ban on development while new zoning regulations, which are usually more restrictive, are enacted. For example, in a small town without a zoning ordinance, sudden growth brought on by discovery of the town by developers would likely lead to haphazard development. Thus a moratorium restricting certain types of development can be enacted to give the town time to create zoning ordinances.

Moratoria are subject to the usual constitutional restrictions on use of the zoning power. In one case, a water authority imposed a moratorium on service until a new sewage plant was built. The Fifth Circuit held that because of a "capacity problem," a rational basis existed for the moratorium.[365] However, where a city limited growth by refusing within a year to issue building permits in excess of 3 percent of the city's existing structures, the ordinance was invalidated because the 3 percent limit was imposed arbitrarily.[366]

The land use practitioner may consider whether in many communities hostility to development or changing land use patterns rises to the level of a moratorium. In an interesting case involving the definition of *development moratorium* under a California statute, it was held that refusal of a public agency to negotiate for the sale of land to a developer constituted a development moratorium within the meaning of a statute authorizing the extension of a time during which development must proceed after receipt of approval.[367]

A moratorium may constitute a zoning ordinance for purposes of state law requiring adoption of a comprehensive plan before enactment of any zoning ordinance.[368]

Growth Management

In the 1990s, perhaps the most discussed topic in land use regulation was growth management, usually in the context of the problem of decaying urban cores, suburban sprawl, overdependence on the automobile, and nonsustainable development. Many older large cities find that their downtown cores have decayed at the expense of unrestricted growth on the suburban rims. As noted by one commentator:

> The problem arises when our growth-acclimated society is (or soon will be) forced to reconcile its notion of development with the fact that the world is changing, and *not* necessarily for the better. There are plenty of people in the world, Americans among them, who can already attest to the fact that their lives are not better than those of their parents, and they do not anticipate that their children's lives will be better than their own.[369]

Communities experiencing strong growth pressures have resorted to sophisticated combinations of land use regulatory techniques to prevent growth from running ahead of or overwhelming available public facilities and the local environment. Development moratoria,[370] performance and incentive zoning,[371] development impact analyses,[372] along with subdivision controls, exactions, and site plan reviews[373] are local, but often not regional methods of regulating the timing and intensity of permitted forms of land development.

At the start of the 1990s, the most closely watched growth-management technique was the Florida concurrency management program requiring development approvals to be conditioned upon a showing that adequate levels of public services and facilities are available.[374]

The Orange County, Florida, plan illustrates local responses to the concurrency requirements:

> Development orders or permits, including those for institutional uses, will be issued subject to the condition that facilities and services sufficient to maintain adopted level of service standards will be available concurrent with the impacts of development. . . . If services and facilities sufficient to maintain adopted level of service standards are not available concurrent with the impacts of development, the development will be phased such that the services and facilities will be available when the impacts of development occur or the development orders and permits will be denied. Implementation of this policy shall not limit or modify the rights of any person to complete any development that has been authorized as a development of regional impact pursuant to Chapter 380; or development that has been issued a final local development order and development has commenced and is continuing in good faith; or development that has vested rights as determined by applicable case law determining vested rights. . . .

> The latest point in the application process for the determination of concurrency is prior to the approval of an application for a development order or permit which contains a specific plan for development, including the densities and intensities of development. Developments may be approved in stages or phases so that facilities and services needed for each phase will be available in accordance with the standards of this policy. . . .

> Within the Urban Service Area, in addition to the normal County construction of public facilities, the County shall provide programs to make possible the provision of infrastructure by joint effort and investment between the public and private sectors.

> When reviewing applications for such development orders, the County shall perform a Concurrency Assessment to ensure that public facilities are available concurrent with the impacts of the proposed development. To conduct the assessment, the Concurrency Inventory shall be used as a base for the establishment of existing conditions. The capability of existing public facilities to service new development shall then be determined by using the adopted Level of Service Standards. Finally, a determination of concurrency shall be made. Such determination may include conditions of approval which are deemed necessary for concurrency to be ensured.

> Prior to the issuance of a development order for a proposed new development the following shall be identified:

> 1. The impacts created by the proposed development;

2. Whether the public facilities covered under the Concurrency Management System will be available concurrent with the impacts of new development at the adopted level;
3. The facility improvements or additions that are required to ensure the finding of concurrency; and,
4. The entity responsible for the design and installation of all required facility improvements or additions.

All development approvals shall have a time period specified in the development order or permit in which development must commence. The time period may involve two or more phases but the timing of each phase shall be specified in the development order or permit. If necessary, the development order or permit may prescribe a time schedule for the initiation of the various components of the development process such as, but not limited to, land clearing, filling, and foundation pouring.[375]

Growth-management initiatives have received a generally favorable reception from the courts,[376] subject to the constitutional limitations discussed in chapter 3.

The State of Washington strengthened its 1990 Growth Management Act by permitting the governor to cut off state funds to local governments that have not complied with the act. The statute also requires that local plans address urban growth, affordable housing, and joint city-county planning.[377] In 1996, the State authorized the establishment of a "bank" of industrial sites similar to Florida's concurrency approach, imposing criteria such as available infrastructure, mitigation of environmental impacts, and regulation of adjoining development.[378]

Consistent with the neo-traditional movement in planning and zoning discussed earlier, the World Watch Institute has advocated a change in the focus of zoning to "controlling the pattern, not the pace" of growth, by encouraging integration of homes with workplaces and amenities.[379] The report advocates greater regional cooperation and state laws to encourage and implement the same.

The Maine Growth Management Act of 1988 requires that every town and city in Maine prepare a comprehensive plan and provides matching grants to local governments. The state legislation met some local opposition and resentment, but for the most part, local participation was at least initially vigorous and productive.[380] Other states that have enacted state growth-management legislation include Florida, Georgia, New Jersey, Rhode Island, and Vermont.

Practitioner Perspectives

Communities and developers alike have found that rigid development schemes do not adjust easily to changes in market demands. As a result, both have sought to foster flexibility in the approval process and expansion of the forms of approval.

If anything is certain in the law of land use regulation, it is that a smorgasbord of devices have been created to resolve the competing land use interests of owner/developer, neighbor, local elected official, community, and society as a whole. The devices on the menu perhaps overlap more than not, and in some cases are simply restatements of each other, the smorgasbord becoming an analytical stew.[381]

The result for the land use advocate is a fertile environment for creative advocacy. He or she should encourage the selection of the most favorable device for the client in the sense of the standards applicable to the approval process at the local level and those applicable to judicial review, discussed in chapters 5 and 6.

Flexibility, of course, is a two-edged sword. Flexibility produces uncertainty, which makes it difficult for developers to plan financial and construction commitments. Flexibility can prove tempting to officials who are disposed to exercise power in inappropriate ways or to achieve inappropriate ends. In practice, communities experienced with development pressure are irreversibly committed to flexibility, especially in the planned commercial development context, usually resulting in a negotiated rezoning. The neo-traditionalist movement, however, may represent one reaction against perceived excessive flexibility and a move back toward more specific, perhaps less-politicized standards of development.

The factual findings required to determine whether a particular regulation effects a taking necessitate a sophisticated analysis of highly technical data. Much of the factual material is prospective in nature, such as market trends and cost projections. The compensation remedy requires municipalities to incorporate those determinations in their existing processes of developing and evaluating land use regulations. The takings cases discussed in chapter 3 illustrate that municipalities that retain the traditional, nonprofessional citizen format for land use regulation and engage in land use regulation without the technical capability to make taking and nexus determinations may endanger the public fisc.

An example of the use of technical experts and public hearings to establish a requisite nexus for an impact fee regulation is the San Francisco Transit Impact Development Fee Ordinance, upheld in *Russ Building Partnership v. City & County of San Francisco*.[382] By requiring developers of downtown commercial property to pay a transit fee of up to $5 per square foot of office space, the legislators intended to offset anticipated costs of getting new riders to and from the new buildings. In approving the ordinance, the court noted that the city performed numerous studies and held public hearings to determine the reasonable cost of the increased transit services.[383] With this in mind, the city hired consultants to project the long-term needs and costs of transit services.[384]

Planning is an "endeavor that requires a search for consensus."[385] The earlier in the process that the search begins in earnest, the less likelihood there is of destructive controversy. The remedy of compensation provides an incentive that should enhance that search, thereby encouraging consensus. One means of obtaining consensus is to communicate with the property owner whose land is threatened. For example, the Seattle Landmarks Preservations Ordinance[386] permits the owner of property designated as a landmark to initiate a consultation process with the Landmarks Preservation Board and staff. The parties meet with the purpose of reaching agreement on specific elements of a building to be preserved and the methods of preservation.[387] State and local governments might implement a similar process to trigger a "taking review" and search for accommodation that would help eliminate the taking issue.[388] In addition, this process could allow the government to confront the taking question and to compensate the owner through a zoning with compensation device.[389]

A built-in consultation process would encourage ex parte contacts. Therefore, care should be taken to ensure that the public interest is protected, possibly by requiring any agreements developed by such consultation to be subject to public review through a public hearing and a ratification vote by the decision-making body.[390] As a practical matter, in any significant development proposal, today's planning staff and elected officials will meet extensively with developers to understand and to whittle down proposals prior to public airing. This process may affect public confidence, but perhaps is the only way to process rezoning requests efficiently. Technical issues on major projects have simply become too numerous to handle with complete public input. The ultimate protection for the citizen may be the ballot box.

If anything is apparent from analysis of the basic zoning issues discussed in this chapter and in day-to-day land use practice before zoning officials, it is that modern zoning, in the general sense, is a negotiation, not simply an application and response. The applicant and the government often discuss and trade on numerous issues, including permitted uses, density, conditions, traffic-generation fees, development incentives, and all of the physical limitations included within the zoning envelope. The scope of matters open to negotiation is almost as broad as legislation generally, and as cities act more aggressively and fiscally like private players in the business world, is ever-expanding, including issues completely unrelated to land use.

Early prohibitions against contract zoning, seen as the bargaining away of police power, have given way to urban and suburban redevelopment incentives for which land uses are open to negotiation in consideration of a whole toolbox of ameliorations to be considered and offered by the applicant, in collaboration with zoning staff and elected officials. We have seen, however, that developers should not rely on promises or commitments to grant subsequent land use approvals, even in the context of development incentive agreements.[391] It has been suggested wisely that in any long-term project, the developer should retain a set of all city ordinances dated as of the date of approval to make the record regarding the baseline legislation.[392] At any rate, the negotiation view of modern zoning permits the practitioner to be creative and unconstrained by more traditional, mapping-oriented views of zoning. The legal structure of the negotiation process is considered next.

Notes

1. City of Brookside Village v. Comeau, 633 S.W.2d 790, 792 (Tex. 1982).
2. Devaney v. Bd. of Zoning Appeals of City of New Haven, 45 A.2d 828 (1946).
3. Standard State Zoning Enabling Act, § 2 (U.S. Dep't of Commerce, rev. ed. 1926), *reprinted as* Appendix A, A MODEL LAND DEVELOPMENT CODE, Tentative Draft No. 1 (American Law Institute 1968).

4. Smith v. Collison, 6 P.2d 277, 278 (Cal. App. 1931).

5. *See, e.g.,* Md. Code Ann. Art. 66B, § 4.02 (1997). The drafters of the Standard State Zoning Enabling Act, after which virtually all of the first-generation zoning-enabling statutes were patterned, stated that the possibility that regulations may differ from district to district was the "essence of zoning" and warned state legislatures that "without this express authority . . . to make different regulations in different districts zoning might be of doubtful validity." A Standard State Zoning Enabling Act, § 2, n. 20 (U.S. Dep't of Commerce, rev. ed. 1926), *reprinted as* Appendix A, A Model Land Development Code, Tentative Draft No. 1 (American Law Institute 1968).

6. St. Charles County v. McPeak, 730 S.W.2d 611 (Mo. Ct. App. 1987) (county validly prohibited truck repair in a district zoned residential, even though the truck repairs were infrequent, because truck repair was not a permitted use).

See also Gorieb v. Fox, 274 U.S. 603 (1927) (ordinance that divides city into residential and business districts and establishes setback requirements is constitutional). The constitutionality of banning certain uses from some districts but not from others was also considered in Reinman v. Little Rock, 237 U.S. 171, 177 (1915) ("[S]o long as the regulation in question is not shown to be clearly unreasonable or arbitrary, and operates uniformly upon all persons similarly situated in the particular district, the district itself not appearing to be arbitrarily selected, it cannot be judicially declared that there is a deprivation of property without due process of law, or a denial of the equal protection of the laws.") See pp. 71–75.

In practice, the zoning of land uses is hardly as rigid as indicated by the foregoing definition. *See* chapter 5.

7. Snake River Brewing Company v. Town of Jackson, 39 P.3d 397, 403 (Wyo. 2002), quoting 1, Kenneth H. Young, Anderson's American Law of Zoning, § 1.13 (4th ed. 1996).

8. St. Louis Rev. Code, Ord. 59979, § 26.12.010 (1986).

9. St. Louis Rev. Code, Ord. 59979, § 26.20.010 (1986).

10. St. Louis Rev. Code, Ord. 59979, § 26.24.010 (1986).

11. St. Louis Rev. Code, Ord. 59979, § 26.60.010 (1986). The 12th district, "L," governs the Jefferson Memorial area of the St. Louis riverfront where the Arch is located and permits uses authorized in the "I" Central Business District. St. Louis Rev. Code, Ord. 59979, §26.64.010 (1986).

12. St. Louis County Code, § 1003.030 (1982).

13. Bedminister Township Zoning Map, prepared by Richard Thomas Coppola, P.P., Bordentown Township, N.J. (September 10, 1986).

14. A Standard State Zoning Enabling Act, Explanatory Note No. 7 (U.S. Dep't of Commerce, rev. ed. 1926), *reprinted as* Appendix A, A Model Land Development Code, Tentative Draft No. 1 (American Law Institute 1968).

15. Harbor Island Marina, Inc. v. Bd. of County Comm'rs, 407 A.2d 738 (Md. Ct. Spec. App. 1979). *See also,* Wynn v. Margate City, 157 A. 565 (N.J. 1931) (word *land* in zoning ordinance included land under water).

16. People's Counsel for Baltimore County v. Maryland Marine Mfg. Co., 560 A.2d 32 (Md. 1989).

17. N.J. Rev. Stat., § 40:55D-4 (1997).

18. Lutz v. Longview, 520 P.2d 1374 (Wash. 1974); Johnson v. City of Mount Vernon, 679 P.2d 405 (Wash. Ct. App. 1984); Kenart & Assoc. v. Skagil County, 680 P.2d 439 (Wash. Ct. App. 1984) ("A request for approval of a planned unit development is treated as a request for a rezone").

19. *See* p. 179.

20. *See* pp. 182–83.

21. *See* pp. 183–84.

22. *See* pp. 180–82.

23. *See* p. 182.

24. *See* p. 180.

25. *See, e.g.,* City of Colorado Springs v. Securcare Self Storage, Inc., 10 P.3d 1244 (Colo. banc 2000) (rejecting claim that disapproval of development plan constituted rezoning).

26. *See, e.g.,* N.Y. Gen. City Law § 20.24 (West 1997); Md. Code Ann. Art. 66B, § 4.01 (1997).

27. 272 U.S. 365 (1926).

28. *See, e.g.,* St. Louis County Code, § 1003.111 (R–1 Residence District), par. 6 (height limitations for structures), par. 7 (lot area, yard, and density requirements); St. Louis Rev. Code § 26.20.050 (height regulations for "A" Single-Family Dwelling District), § 26.20.080 (minimum lot area for "A" Single-Family Dwelling District).

29. Nopro Co. v. Town of Cherry Hills Village, 504 P.2d 344 (Colo. 1972); Strandberg v. Kansas City, Mo., 415 S.W.2d 737, 742 (Mo. banc 1967); Roll v. City of Troy, 120 N.W.2d 804 (Mich. 1963).

30. *See generally* pp. 249–54.

31. Schwartz v. City of Flint, 395 N.W.2d 678 (Mich. 1986) (reviewing cases). In *Schwartz,* the court invalidated the "Zaagman procedures" by overruling Ed Zaagman, Inc. v. City of Kentwood, 277 N.W.2d 475 (Mich. 1979). The Zaagman procedures permitted a judge, following a finding that a particular zoning ordinance was unconstitutional, to grant interim relief to the plaintiff by implementing "the most equitable or 'midsatisfactory use' to be made of the plaintiff's parcel." *Id.* The Schwartz court held that this procedure—in effect a rezoning—was an improper usurpation by the judiciary of the legislative function, and was therefore unconstitutional on separation-of-powers grounds. "Zoning is a legislative function that cannot constitutionally be performed by a court, either directly or indirectly—in law or equity." *Id.*

Teed v. King Council, 677 P.2d 179, 185 (Wash. Ct. App. 1984), *quoting* Bishop v. Town of Houghton, 420 P.2d 368, 372 (1966) ("Courts simply do not possess the power to amend zoning ordinances or to rezone a zoned area, and they cannot and should not invade the legislative arena or intrude upon municipal zoning determinations, absent a clear showing of arbitrary, unreasonable, irrational or unlawful zoning action or inaction"). *See generally* pp. 154–56 and pp. 263–65.

32. See chapter 4, at p. 169.

33. People v. Miller, 106 N.E.2d 34 (N.Y. 1952).

34. First of America Trust Company v. Armstead, 664 N.E.2d 36 (Ill. 1996).

35. *See, e.g.,* Bd. of Zoning Appeals of Bland County v. Caselin Systems, Inc., *supra,* n. 39, holding that no governmental approval, defined as "an official response to a detailed request for a use of a particular property that would not otherwise be allowed under law" had occurred sufficient to vest a right in the applicant.

36. Avco Cmty. Dev. v. South Coast Reg'l Comm'n , 17 Cal.3d 785, 795 (Cal. 1976); Baby Tam v. Las Vegas, 247 F.3d 1003 (9th Cir. 2001).

37. *See, e.g.,* Texas Gov't Code Ann. § 481.141; Wash. Rev. Code §§ 19.27.095 and 58.17.033 (1996); Herr v. Pequea Township, 2000 U.S. Dist. Lexis 11057 (E.D. Pa.) (analyzing § 53 Pa. Stat. Ann. 10508(4)(I), prohibiting changes in regulations for five years after development proposal is submitted); Jim Sowell Construction Co., Inc. v. City of Coppell, 2000 WL 968782 (2000) (N.D. Tex. 2000); Noble Manor Co. v. Pierce County, 913 P.2d 417 (Wash. Ct. App. 1996). See also n. 212. For a general discussion of vested rights legislation, see 34 The Urban Lawyer 131 Winter 2002.

38. Virginia Code § 15.2-2307; see n. 37; see also McPherson v. City of Manhattan Beach, 93 Cal. Rptr. 2d 725 (Cal. 2000) (discussing California subdivision Map Act providing that subdivision rights vest upon the time of recording of the map).

39. Section 8-501, Vesting, Legislative Guidebook: Model Statutes for the Management of Change, 2002 edition, American Planning Association (Stuart Meck, FAICP, general editor).

40. *See* chapter 3.

41. Even this aspect of vested rights analysis is similar to regulatory takings analysis. *See* "investment-backed expectations," Penn Central Transp. Co. v. New York City, 438 U.S. 104 (1978), chapter 3, *supra,* at n. 225.

42. Bd. of Zoning Appeals of Bland County v. Caselin Systems, Inc., 501 S.E.2d 397 (Va. 1998) (landowner seeking to establish a vested property right to build medical waste incinerator must identify single official act and diligent pursuit of the authorized use, together with good-faith incurring of expense); Bd. of Supervisors of Fairfax County v. Cities Serv. Oil Co., 193 S.E.2d 1 (Va. 1972) (where landowner purchased property for $186,500 based on value as zoned with special-use permit authorizing service station plus additional sums in preparing and filing a site plan, court held that landowner's right vested on filing of the site plan, even though building permit had not been issued).

43. PNE AOA Media v. Jackson County, North Carolina, 554 S.E.2d 657, 664 (N.C. Ct. App. 2001); *see also* City of Roswell v. Outdoor Systems, Inc., 549 S.E.2d 90 (Ga. 2001) (billboard company unsuccessfully attempted to file several applications for building permits during temporary moratorium); Florida Outdoor Adver. v. City of Boynton Beach, 182 F. Supp. 2d 1201 (S.D. Fla. 2001) (billboard company held to have vested rights in sign permits where city ordinance held unconstitutional).

44. *See* p. 169.

45. *See,* Sullivan v. Zoning Bd. of Adjustment, 478 A.2d 912 (Pa. 1984).

46. D. PORTER, P. PHILLIPS & T. LASSAR, FLEXIBLE ZONING: HOW IT WORKS 5 (Urban Land Institute, 1988), *citing* W. FISCHEL, THE ECONOMICS OF ZONING LAWS: A PROPERTY RIGHTS APPROACH TO AMERICAN LAND USE CONTROLS 32 (1985).

47. S. TOLL, ZONED AMERICAN, pp. 123–140 (1969).

48. *Id.* at 124, 129.

49. *Id.* at 124, *quoting* B. MARSH, AN INTRODUCTION TO CITY PLANNING 5 (1909).

50. *Id.* at 130, *quoting* Howe, *In Defense of the American City,* SCRIBNER'S, pp. 485–86 (April, 1912).

51. *Id.* at 134.

52. Randle, *Professors, Reformers, Bureaucrats, and Cronies: The Players in* Euclid v. Ambler, *in* C. HAAR & J. KAYDEN, ZONING AND THE AMERICAN DREAM 37 (1989), *quoting* R. LUBOVE, THE PROGRESSIVES AND THE SLUMS: TENEMENT HOUSE REFORM IN NEW YORK CITY, 1890–1917, at 237 (1962).

53. Randle, *supra* n. 52, characterizing Edward M. Bassett and Robert H. Whitten, two of the leading champions of zoning.

54. D. PORTER, P. PHILLIPS & T. LASSAR, FLEXIBLE ZONING: HOW IT WORKS 5 (1988).

55. *Id.* at 8–9. A typical zoning code requires that written notice of an application for a conditional-use permit be sent to the alderman in whose ward the conditional use is proposed. *See, e.g.,* ST. LOUIS REV. CODE, § 26.80.010.3.B.

56. *See* chapter 6, p. 261 for a discussion of judicial deference.

57. Agins v. Tiburon, 447 U.S. 255 (1980); Penn Central Transp. Co. v. New York City, 438 U.S. 104 (1978); Village of Euclid v. Ambler Realty Co., 272 U.S. 365 (1926); Deutsch v. City of Ladue, 728 S.W.2d 239, 241 (Mo. Ct. App. 1987).

Indian tribes retain authority to zone land owned by Indians within reservation boundaries irrespective of state authority. In Tribes & Bands of Yakima Indian Nation v. Whiteside, 828 F.2d 529, 534 (9th Cir. 1987), the court said of the Yakima Indian Nation that "it is beyond question that land use is within the Tribe's legitimate sovereign authority over its land." A tribe may also zone non-Indian fee interests within the reservation boundaries, but this authority is divested when "its exercise is inconsistent with overriding federal interests." *Id.* at 533. *Aff'd in part, reversed in part,* Brendale v. Confederated Tribes and Bands of Yakima Indian Nation, 4292 U.S. 408 (1989).

58. Schwartz v. City of Flint, 395 N.W.2d 678, 685 (Mich. 1986); Forman v. Eagle Thrifty Drugs and Markets, Inc., 516 P.2d 1234 (Nev. 1974); West Montgomery County Citizens Ass'n v. Maryland-National Capital Park and Planning Comm'n, 522 A.2d 1328, 1334 (Md. Ct. App. 1987).

59. *See* Ch.1, n. 36 for citations to state zoning-enabling acts.

60. For examples of constitutional provisions that grant the zoning power to local governmental bodies, *see* Cal. Const. Art. XI, § 7; Ga. Const. Art. IX, § II, para. IV; La. Const. Art. VI, § 17; Mich. Const. Art. VII, § 22; N.Y. Const. Art. IX, § 2 (c)(ii)(10); *see generally* Rohan, Zoning and Land Use Controls, § 35.03[2].

61. City of Brookside Village v. Comeau, 633 S.W.2d 790, 793, n. 4 (Tex 1982); Commonwealth Dep't of Gen. Serv. v. Ogontz Area Neighbors Ass'n, 483 A.2d 448, 451 (Pa. 1984) (Philadelphia Home Rule Act).

62. Haw. Rev. Stat. § 205-1 *et seq.* (1985).

63. *See, e.g.,* Brougher v. Bd. of Public Works of San Francisco, 271 P. 487, 493 (Cal. 1928) (San Francisco zoning power derived from home rule charter).

64. *See* pp. 5–7.

65. Standard State Zoning Enabling Act (U.S. Dep't of Commerce, rev. ed. 1926). *See generally* American Law Institute, A Model Land Development Code, Tentative Draft No. 1, xvii (1968).

66. N.Y. Laws 1914, c. 470; N.Y. Laws 1916, c. 497, *cited in* E. Bassett, F. Williams, A. Bettman & R. Whitten, Model Laws for Planning Cities, Counties and States 10, n. 7 (1935), *upheld in* Lincoln Trust Co. v. Williams Bldg. Corps., 128 N.E. 209 (N.Y. 1920). *See also* Welch v. Swasey, 214 U.S. 91 (1909) (upholding building height restrictions in Boston); Ex Passtie Quona, 118 P. 714 (Cal. 1911) (upholding prohibition of public laundries from residential districts in Los Angeles).

67. 272 U.S. 365 (1926).

68. Miller v. Bd. of Public Works of Los Angeles, 234 P. 381, 384 (Cal. 1925) (reviewing history of zoning and upholding a California zoning enabling statute enacted in 1917).

69. KLN Assocs. v. Metro Dev. & Housing, 797 S.W.2d 898 (Tenn. Ct. App. 1990).

70. *Id.* at 903.

71. Schwartz v. City of Flint, 395 N.W.2d 678, 684, 692–93 (Mich. 1986) (court may not rezone to remedy invalid zoning ordinance, but may issue declaration that proposed use is reasonable and enjoin government from interfering with that use); Southern Burlington County NAACP v. Township of Mount Laurel, 456 A.2d 390, 452 (1983) (*Mount Laurel II*) (builder's remedy may be granted to successful *Mount Laurel* litigants). See chapter 6.

72. West Montgomery County Citizen's Ass'n v. Maryland-National Capital Park & Planning Comm'n, 522 A.2d 1328 (Md. 1987).

73. *See* pp. 303–04; City of Ames v. Story County, 392 N.W.2d 145, 147–49 (Iowa 1986).

74. Davidson County v. City of High Point, 354 S.E.2d 280 (N.C. Ct. App. 1987).

75. City of Ames v. Story County, 392 N.W.2d 145 (Iowa 1986); City of St. Louis v. City of Bridgeton, 705 S.W.2d 524 (Mo. 1986).

76. St. Louis v. Bridgeton, 705 S.W.2d at 529.

77. See chapter 10; *see also* Willow Creek Ranch, L.L.C. v. Town of Shelby, 611 N.W.2d 693, 698 (Wis. 2000). *See in re* Commercial Airfield, 752 A.2d 13 (Vt. 2000) (zoning of airport uses not preempted).

78. *See* Macon-Bibb County Planning and Zoning Comm'n v. Bibb County School Dist., 474 S.E.2d 70 (Ga. Ct. App. 1996) (holding school district constructing football stadium immune from zoning).

79. Commonwealth Dep't of Gen. Serv. v. Ogontz Area Neighbors Ass'n, 483 A.2d 448 (Pa. 1984).

80. London Grove Township v. Southeastern Chester County Refuse Auth., 517 A.2d 1002 (Pa. Commw. Ct. 1986) (Refuse authority was an instrumentality of Pennsylvania for purposes of a law that exempts instrumentalities of the Commonwealth from complying with zoning ordinances adopted by second-class townships).

81. Garden State Farms, Inc. v. Bay, 390 A.2d 1177, 1185 (1978).

82. *See* pp. 5–7.

83. Quinn v. Town of Dodgeville, 364 N.W.2d 149 (Wis. 1985) (statute granting towns veto power over county zoning ordinances upheld).

84. Nopro Co. v. Town of Cherry Hills Village, 504 P.2d 344 (Colo. 1972).

85. Standard State Zoning Enabling Act, § 1 (U.S. Dep't of Commerce, rev. ed. 1926), *reprinted as* Appendix A, A MODEL LAND DEVELOPMENT CODE, Tentative Draft No. 1 (American Law Institute 1968). *See* Section 1.2.

86. Standard State Zoning Enabling Act, § 3, n. 21 (stressing that the two purposes should be "clearly differentiated").

87. Standard State Zoning Enabling Act, § 3.

88. Bisson v. Town of Milford, 249 A.2d 688 (N.H. 1969).

89. Standard State Zoning Enabling Act, § 4, n. 29.

90. *See, e.g.,* ARK. CODE. ANN. § 14-56-416(a)(2).

91. The distinction between mandatory and directory statutes is based on the effect the provision has on "the essence of the thing to be done." *Id.*

92. Osborne v. City of Camden, 784 S.W.2d 596, 598 (Ark. 1990).

93. *See* pp. 28; 160–62.

94. Village of McGrew v. Steidley, 305 N.W.2d 627, 633–34 (Neb. 1981) (court refused to accept a corrected version of the village board minutes showing adoption of the plan prior to enactment of the zoning ordinance. The corrected minutes had been approved on the night before the trial of a challenge to the ordinance, over two years after the challenged ordinance was enacted. Thus the special meeting was merely a "valiant but futile effort to correct a deficiency" in the ordinance.)

95. PA. STAT. ANN. tit. 53, § 13101 *et seq.* (West 1996).

96. Commonwealth Dep't of Gen. Serv. v. Ogontz Area Neighbors Ass'n, 483 A.2d 448 (Pa. 1984).

97. Bd. of County of Boulder v. Thompson, 493 P.2d 1358, 1361 (Colo. 1972).

98. FLA. STAT. ANN. § 163.04 (West 1997).

99. *Id.*

100. TEX. REV. CIV. STAT. ANN. Art. 8814 (West 1995).

101. B & B Vending Co. v. City of Garland, 711 S.W.2d 132 (Tex. Ct. App. 1986).

102. Jachimek v. Superior Court of County of Maricopa, 819 P.2d 487, 489 (Ariz. 1991).

103. Newbury Township Bd. of Township Trustees v. Lomak Petroleum, Inc., 583 N.E.2d 302 (Ohio 1992).

104. *See* Bartlett v. Town of Stonington, 707 A.2d 389 (Me. 1998) (statute included provision that in event of conflict between statute and ordinance, more restrictive controlled).

105. Plaza Recreation Ctr. v. Sioux City, 111 N.W.2d 758, 765 (Iowa 1961).

106. Cardon Ins. v. Town of New Market, 466 A.2d 504 (Md. Ct. Spec. App. 1983), *aff'd,* 485 A.2d 678 (Md. 1984).

107. Bd. of County Comm'rs of County of Boulder v. Thompson, 493 P.2d 1358, 1361 (Colo. 1972) (exclusion of junkyard from agricultural district upheld).

108. *See, e.g.,* Harris v. Zoning Comm'n of Town of New Milford, 788 A.2d 1239 (Conn. 2002).

109. *See* Bd. of Zoning Appeals of City of Norfolk v. Kahhal, 499 S.E.2d 519, 521 (Va. 1998).

110. *See, e.g.,* State *ex rel.* Helujon v. Jefferson County, 964 S.W.2d 531 (Mo. App. 1998).

111. Village of Euclid v. Ambler Realty Co., 272 U.S. 365, 381 (1926). While the ordinance in Euclid had three separate types of districts—use districts, area districts, and height districts—most modern ordinances blend area and height restrictions into the use districts and employ overlay zones to add additional restrictions, such as environmental quality standards, across use district lines. See discussion following n. 8.

112. *See* p. 291; Village of Euclid v. Ambler Realty Co., 272 U.S. 365; Boulder County v. Thompson, 493 P.2d at 1361 (junkyard not an accessory use in agricultural district); St. Charles County v. McPeak, 730 S.W.2d 611, 613 (Mo. Ct. App. 1987) (commercial truck repair not an accessory use to a single-family dwelling).

113. INTERNATIONAL CITY MANAGEMENT ASSOCIATION, THE PRACTICE OF LOCAL GOVERNMENT PLANNING, 269–71 (F. So & J. Getzels, eds., 2d ed., 1988). *See, e.g.,* People *ex rel.* Skokie Town House Builders v. Village of Morton Grove, 157 N.E.2d 33, 36 (Ill. 1959) (exclusion of residences from commercial or industrial districts held within police power of state); ST. LOUIS COUNTY CODE, § 1003.151 (1982) (permitting 17 designated nonresidential uses in "M–1" Industrial District, along with 13 other nonresidential uses by special permit).

114. *Skokie Town House Builders,* 157 N.E.2d at 35–36. *See also* Kozesnik v. Township of Montgomery, 131 A.2d 1, 9 (N.J. 1957) (zoning-enabling statute does not require "higher" uses to be permitted in less-restricted districts); Roney v. Bd. of Supervisors of Contra Costa County, 292 P.2d 529 (reviewing cases and upholding exclusive industrial-use district).

115. Roney v. Bd. of Supervisors of Contra Costa County, 292 P.2d at 532.

116. Courthouts v. Town of Newington, 99 A.2d 112 (Conn. 1953).

117. Comer v. City of Dearborn, 70 N.W.2d 813, 816 (Mich. 1955) (prohibition of motel in industrial district held unreasonable because "neighborhood may not be regarded as an industrial one"); Katobimar Realty Co. v. Webster, 118 A.2d 824, 831 (N.J. 1955) (prohibition of shopping center from light industrial-use district invalid for failure to recognize compatibility of proposed use with permitted uses). One of the practices that triggered the celebrated *Mount Laurel* litigation was the zoning of large tracts of land for noncumulative industrial purposes when little or no industrial activity was taking place or appeared likely. Southern Burlington County NAACP v. Township of Mount Laurel, 336 A.2d 713, 719 (N.J. 1975), *appeal dismissed & cert. denied,* 423 U.S. 808 (1975) (*Mount Laurel I*) (4,100 acres zoned industrial but only 100 acres occupied by industrial uses).

118. Forks Township Bd. of Supervisors v. George Calantoni & Sons, Inc., 297 A.2d 164, 167 (Pa. 1972).

119. Transitions, Inc. v. Bd. of Zoning Adjustment of City of Ashland, 729 S.W.2d 459, 460–61 (Ky. Ct. App. 1987).

120. *See, e.g.,* Bell v. City of Elkhorn, 364 N.W.2d 144, 148 (Wis. 1985) (citing sources).

121. *Id.* at 147, quoting Lanphear v. Antwerp Township, 214 N.W.2d 66 (Mich. App. 1973).

122. Udell v. Haas, 235 N.E.2d 897, 900–902 (N.Y. 1968). The seminal article on the topic is Haar, *In Accordance With a Comprehensive Plan,* 68 HARV. L. REV. 1154 (1955).

123. Webb v. Giltner, 468 N.W.2d 838 (Iowa 1991). Where the state enabling statute does not expressly so require, however, a municipality may be permitted to enact a zoning ordinance without a comprehensive plan. *See* Columbia Oldsmobile, Inc. v. City of Montgomery, 564 N.E.2d 455 (Ohio 1992).

124. Sullivan & Kressel, *Twenty Years After—Renewed Significance of the Comprehensive Plan Requirement,* 9 URB. LAW. ANN. 33, 41 (1975). Cited as best representing the unitary view is *Kozesnik v. Montgomery Township,* 131 A.2d 1, 8 (N.J. 1957), holding that planning "may readily be revealed in the end product—here the zoning ordinance—and no more is required by the statute." *Id.* at 42–44. The planning factor theory is said to be best illustrated

by Udell v. Haas, 235 N.E.2d 897 (N.Y. 1968), in which the court invalidated a downzoning enacted to frustrate a proposed commercial use. *Id.* at 45–47.

125. Sullivan, *The Comprehensive Plan: Two Steps Forward and One Back,* in Richard J. Roddewig, *Recent Developments in Land Use, Planning and Zoning,* 21 URB. LAW. 769, 834–40 (1989).

126. *See, e.g.,* MD. CODE ANN. § 4.03; MO. REV. STAT. § 89.040. *See generally* chapter 2.

127. Quinn v. Town of Dodgeville, 354 N.W.2d 747 (Wis. Ct. App. 1984).

128. City of Brookside Village v. Comeau, 633 S.W.2d 790 (Tex. 1982) (ordinances regulating location of mobile-home parks held valid exercise of general police power, even though village had no comprehensive zoning plan).

129. *See* Forks Township Bd. of Supervisors v. George Calatoni & Sons, Inc., 297 A.2d 164 (1972). "A comprehensive plan does not control the ordinance, rather a comprehensive plan should be reflected in the zoning ordinance. The comprehensive plan is a general guideline of the legislative body of the municipality for its consideration of the municipality's program of land utilization." *Id.* at 166, 167.

130. Marracci v. City of Scappoose, 552 P.2d 552 (Or. 1976). In a case that followed *Marraci* and adopted its reasoning, the court held that a city was not required to grant a rezone of property to multifamily residential use even though the comprehensive plan anticipated such use in the future. Clinkscales v. City of Lake Oswego, 615 P.2d 1164 (Or. App. 1980).

131. *George Calatoni & Sons,* 297 A.2d at 167 ("comprehensive plan is abstract and recommendatory; . . . zoning ordinance is specific and regulatory").

132. *Coffey v. Maryland-National Capital Park,* 441 A.2d 1041 (Md. 1982) (affirming rejection of subdivision plat with density of 7.38 units per acre for failure to comply with master plan density restrictions of 2.7 to 3.5 units per acre, even though maximum permissible density under zoning ordinance was 8.0 to 11.9 units per acre); Shoptaugh v. Bd. of County Comm'rs of El Paso County, 543 P.2d 524, 527 (Colo. Ct. App. 1975), *cert. denied* ("subdivider must first meet the zoning regulations and then additionally must comply with the state and county subdivision regulations"); Popular Refreshments, Inc. v. Fuller's Milk Bar, Inc., 205 A.2d 445, 449 (1964), *cert. denied,* 209 A.2d 143 (1965) ("[p]lanning board consideration of a proposed land subdivision involves other factors in addition to the local zoning requirements"). *See generally* chapter 8.

133. Biske v. City of Troy, 166 N.W.2d 453 (Mich. 1969).

134. *In re* Approval of Request for Amendment to Frawley Planned Unit Development, 638 N.W.2d 552 (S.D. 2002).

135. *See, e.g.,* Wilgus v. City of Murfeesboro, 532 S.W.2d 50, 53 (Tenn. 1975) ("If a proposed zoning ordinance is amended so substantially that a new proposal is, in effect, created we think it clear that both the state statute and municipal code provision require it to be submitted to the planning commission for its consideration before the municipal legislative body may finally act upon it.").

136. *See, e.g.,* CONN. GEN. STAT. § 8-3a (1997) (two-thirds vote of all members of zoning commission required for approval of proposal rejected by planning commission). *See also* N.J. STAT. ANN. § 40:55D-26 (West 1997) (governing body may disapprove or change recommendation of planning board by majority of "its full authorized membership").

137. Hahn v. Zoning Commission of Town of Vernon, 293 A.2d 9 (Conn. 1972).

138. *See* chapter 2.

139. McClendon v. Shelby County, 484 So. 2d 459 (Ala. Civ. App. 1985), *cert. denied,* 479 U.S. 815 (1986) (refusal of planning commission to change previous decision approving extension of street to connect with neighboring subdivision upheld).

140. Winslow v. Town of Holderness Planning Bd., 480 A.2d 114 (N.H. 1984).

141. Golden Gate Corp. v. Town of Narragansett, 359 A.2d 321, 324 (R.I. 1976).

142. *Id.*

143. F. P. Plaza, Inc. v. Waite, 196 S.E.2d 141, 144 (Ga. 1973).

144. *See, e.g.,* White v. Henry, 285 S.W.2d 353, 359 (Tenn. 1955) (improper publication immaterial because of attendance at hearings). *See also* Conrad v. Lexington-Fayette Urban County Gov't, 659 S.W.2d 190 (Ky. 1983) (substantial compliance with notice requirements for sanitary sewer project by publication in paper with smaller circulation than required by statute when accompanied by widespread publicity and mailing of individual notices to affected property owners).

145. State *ex rel.* Casey's Gen. Stores, Inc. v. City of Louisiana, 734 S.W.2d 890, 895 (Mo. Ct. App. 1987) (hearings held within 6 and 14 days of notice in violation of statutory 15-day notice requirement).

146. Hartman v. Buckson, 467 A.2d 694, 698–99 (Del. Ch. 1983).

147. Eastlake v. Forest City Enterprises, Inc., 426 U.S. 668 (1976) (approving use of initiative and referendum in zoning matters over objections that affected landowners would be deprived of right to be heard and to have decision made by a qualified, impartial decision-maker).

148. *See, e.g.,* CAL. GOV'T CODE §§ 65853, 65854, 65856 (West 1996) (legislative body to hold hearing before approving zoning ordinance); KY. REV. STAT. ANN. § 100.207 (Michie 1997) (planning commission to hold hearing); MD. CODE ANN. Art. 668, § 4.04 (1997) (legislative body to provide for at least one public hearing); MO. REV. STAT. § 89.050 (1996) (legislative body to provide for at least one public hearing); N.J. STAT. ANN. § 40:55D-10 (West 1997) (hearing held by planning board or governing body).

149. Smith v. Skaget County, 453 P.2d 832, 847 (Wash. 1969).

150. *Id.* at 848.

151. City of Mobile v. Cardinal Woods Apartments, Ltd., 727 So. 2d 48 (Ala. 1999).

152. Montgomery County v. Woodward & Lothrop, 376 A.2d 483, 498 (Md. 1977).

153. Golden Gate Corp. v. Town of Narragansett, 359 A.2d at 326.

154. Alger v. City of Mukilteo, 730 P.2d 1333, 1336–37 (Wash. 1987) (remedy for violation of appearness of fairness doctrine is to void ordinance in question).

155. Von Lusch v. Bd. of County Comm'rs of Queen Anne's County, 302 A.2d 4, 10 (Md. Ct. Spec. App. 1973).

156. *See* pp. 178–79.

157. Patterson v. County of Tehama, 235 Cal. Rptr. 867, 895 (Cal. Ct. App. 1987); *vacated,* 235 Cal. Rptr. 867 (Cal. App. 1987).

158. *See, e.g.,* F.P. Plaza, Inc. v. Waite, 196 S.E.2d 141 (1973) (where local government is given authority to zone within its jurisdiction, it has almost unrestricted authority to provide for decision-making procedures).

159. *See, e.g.,* MO. REV. STAT. § 89.060 (1996) (three-fourths favorable vote of all members of legislative body required when protest signed and acknowledged by owners of at least 10 percent of land included in proposed change or within 185 feet of boundaries of proposed change); N.J. STAT. ANN. § 40:55D-63 (West 1997) (two-thirds favorable vote of all members of governing body required for signed protest from owners of at least 20 percent of land included in proposed change or within 200 feet of proposed boundaries).

160. Forman v. Eagle Thrifty Drugs and Markets, 516 P.2d 1234 (Nev. 1974).

161. Arnel Dev. Co. v. City of Costa Mesa, 620 P.2d 565 (Cal. 1980) (zoning by initiative approved); State *ex rel.* Hickman v. City Council, 690 S.W.2d 799 (Mo. Ct. App. 1985) (zoning is proper subject for initiative and referendum). *But see,* Camden Community Dev. Corp. v. Satton, 5 S.W.3d 439 (Ark. 1999) (rezoning held administrative and not subject to initiative).

162. Committee of Seven Thousand v. Superior Court, 754 P.2d 708 (Cal. 1988) (citing California planning and zoning cases).

163. Margolis v. District Court, 638 P.2d 297, 304 (Colo. 1981). A similar test was used in State *ex. rel.* Hickman v. City Council, 690 S.W.2d 799 (Mo. Ct. App. 1985).

164. 548 P.2d 188 (Ore. Ct. App. 1976). *See also* Fleming v. City of Tacoma, 502 P.2d 327, 331 (Wash. 1972).

165. *Id. See also* Forman v. Eagle Thrifty Drugs and Markets, 516 P.2d at 1236 (neither initiative nor referendum may be used to resolve dispute over rezoning of 3.5-acre parcel of land at intersection).

166. 328 So. 2d 231 (Fla. Ct. App. 1976).

167. Arnel Dev. Co. v. City of Costa Mesa, 620 P.2d 565 (Cal. 1980).

168. Kaiser Hawaii Kai Dev. Co. v. City and County of Honolulu, 777 P.2d 244 (Haw. 1989).

169. HAW. REV. STAT. ch. 205A.

170. *See* pp. 168–69.

171. Associated Home Builders v. City of Livermore, 557 P.2d 473 (Cal. 1976) (initiative).

172. Margolis v. District Court, 638 P.2d 297 (Colo. Ct. App. 1981) (initiative and referendum).

173. City of Coral Gables v. Carmichael, 256 So. 2d 404 (Fla. App. 1972), *cert. dismissed,* 268 So. 2d 1 (Fla. 1972) (referendum).

174. Denney v. City of Duluth, 202 N.W.2d 892 (Minn. 1972) (referendum).

175. City of Eastlake v. Forest City Enterprises, Inc., 426 U.S. 668 (1976) (referendum).

176. State *ex rel.* Hunziker v. Pulliam, 37 P.2d 417 (Okla. 1934).

177. Kaiser Hawaii Kai Dev. Co. v. City and County of Honolulu, 777 P.2d 244, 250 (Haw. 1989).

178. County of Kauai v. Pacific Standard Life Ins. Co., 653 P.2d 766 (Haw. 1982).

179. *Kaiser Hawaii Kai Dev. Co.,* 777 P.2d at 250.

180. N.J. STAT. ANN. § 40:55D-62.b (1997).

181. Lesher Communications, Inc. v. City of Walnut Creek, 262 Cal. Rptr. 337, 345 (Cal. App. 1989); *superseded,* 783 P.2d 184 (Cal. 1989); *reversed,* 802 P.2d 317 (Cal. 1990). California is a mandatory-planning state. Required elements of a comprehensive plan in mandatory-planning states are discussed in pp. 28–34.

182. CAL. GOV'T CODE § 65860 (West 1996).

183. See note 181.

184. *Id.*

185. Hessey v. District of Columbia Bd. of Elections and Ethics, 601 A.2d 3 (D.C. 1991).

186. Forman v. Eagle Thrifty Drugs and Markets, 516 P.2d 1234 (Nev. 1974).

187. City of Eastlake v. Forest City Enterprises, 426 U.S. 668 (1976).

188. *Id.* at 672.

189. *Id.* at 677.

190. *Id.* at 694.

191. *See, e.g.,* I'on, L.L.C. v. Town of Mt. Pleasant, 526 S.E.2d 716, 720 (S.C. 2000).

192. 42 U.S.C. § 3601 *et seq.* (1997); *see* page 102.

193. Arthur v. City of Toledo, 782 F.2d 565, 575 (6th Cir. 1986).

194. *See* pp. 165–68.

195. *See, e.g.,* County of Kauai v. Pacific Standard Life Ins. Co., 653 P.2d 766 (Haw. 1982) (referendum repealing zoning ordinance not barred by equitable estoppel unless final discretionary action to approve project has been taken prior to referendum vote); Margolis v. District Court, 638 P.2d 297 (Colo. 1981) (zoning and rezoning subject to initiative and referendum); Forman v. Eagle Thrifty Drugs and Markets, Inc., 516 P.2d 1234 (Nev. 1973) (comprehensive zoning subject to initiative and referendum, but changes in zoning classifica-

tions for particular areas not subject to initiative and referendum as administrative in character); Allison v. Washington County, 548 P.2d 188 (Or. Ct. App. 1976) (comprehensive zoning subject to initiative and referendum, but zoning changes affecting single pieces of property, variances, and conditional-use permits not subject to initiative and referendum as quasi-judicial in character); O'Loane v. O'Rourke, 42 Cal. Rptr. 283 (1965) (adoption of general plan subject to referendum).

196. Wang v. Patterson, 469 N.W.2d 577 (S.D. 1991). The court also stated that it would construe liberally the availability of the referendum on any given matter. *See also* Albright v. City of Portage, 470 N.W.2d 657 (Mich. Ct. App. 1991) (holding referendum available to challenge amendment to zoning ordinance).

197. Davis v. Brenneman, 701 S.W.2d 487 (Mo. Ct. App. 1985).

198. *See, e.g.,* N.J. Rev. Stat. § 40:55D-5 (West 1997), defining "nonconforming use" as "a use or activity which was unlawful prior to the adoption . . . of a zoning ordinance, but which fails to conform to the requirements of the zoning district in which it is located by reason of such adoption. . . ."

199. Explanatory Note 9, Standard State Zoning Enabling Act (U.S. Department of Commerce, revised edition 1926), *appearing as* Appendix A, A Model Land Development Code, Tentative Draft no. 1 (American Law Institute, 1968).

200. *See, e.g.,* N.J. Rev. Stat. § 40:55D-68 (West 1997).

201. *See, e.g.,* N.J. Rev. Stat. § 674:19 (West 1997).

202. Dugas v. Town of Conway, 480 A.2d 71, 76 (N.J. 1984).

203. *See* discussion following n. 230.

204. Alfred Bettman, one of the "fathers" of zoning, commented that "non-conforming uses are permitted to remain . . . and are departures from the ideal plan in the interest of fairness to existing structures." Bettman, *Constitutionality of Zoning*, 37 Harv. L. Rev. 834, 850 (1924). *See* Kolesar v. Zoning Hearing Bd. of Borough of Bell Acres, 543 A.2d 246, 248 (Pa. 1988), requiring good-faith reliance on an existing zoning status, use, or permit to the economic detriment of the property owner, thereby estopping the municipality from prohibiting the use.

205. *See, e.g.,* New London Land Use Ass'n v. New London Zoning Bd. of Adjustment, 543 A.2d 1385, 1387 (N.H. 1988) (nonconforming use is vested right recognized by state constitution and statutes). See discussion following n. 32.

206. Jones v. City of Los Angeles, 295, 14, 17 (Cal. 1930).

207. *Jones*, 295, at 17–19, *quoting* Chamberlain and Pierson, *Zoning Laws and Ordinances*, 10 A.B.A.J. 185 (1924).

208. St. Charles County v. McPeak, 730 S.W.2d 611, 613 (Mo. Ct. App. 1987). *See also* New London Land Use Ass'n v. New London Zoning Bd. of Adjustment, 543 A.2d 1385, 1387 (N.J. 1988) ("nonconforming use is a use in fact existing on the land at the time of adoption of the ordinance"). The "use" requirement of the nonconforming-use doctrine may be met by evidence of expenditures in preparing for development. *See* Nemmers v. City of DuBuque, 716 F.2d 1194 (8th Cir. 1983). In Lakeview Dev. Corp. v. South Lake Tahoe, 915 F.2d 1290 (9th Cir. 1990), *cert. denied*, 501 U.S. 1251 (1990), however, the Court held that the developer had no vested right in the second phase of a very large and time-consuming development, merely because of issuance of a special-use permit for the first phase, where 12 years separated the commencement of the first phase and the second phase.

209. In *Brady v. Town of Colchester*, 863 F.2d 205 (2d Cir. 1988), for example, the court denied summary judgment on the issue of nonconforming use, where an issue of material fact remained as to whether an existing two-story building had indeed been used commercially prior to the owners' acquisition of the property.

210. Nasierowski Bros. Inv. v. City of Sterling Heights, 949 F.2d 890 (6th Cir. 1991).

211. Town of Orangetown v. Magee, 643 N.Y.S.2d 21 (N.Y. App. Div. 1996).

212. See chaper 4, p. 151 for a general discussion of vested rights.

213. *Id.* at 211–12. *See,* however, the state of Washington's vested rights statutes, WASH. REV. CODE §§ 19.27.095 and 58.17.033 (1996), vesting development rights upon receipt of building permits or mere filing of subdivision applications, discussed in Noble Manor Co. v. Pierce County, 913 P.2d 417 (Wash. Ct. App. 1996). See discussion at p. 151, *supra.*

214. In New London Land Use Ass'n v. New London Zoning Bd. of Adjustment, 543 A.2d 1385 (N.H. 1988), the Supreme Court of New Hampshire drew a distinction between expansion that is "a natural activity, closely related to the manner in which a piece of property is used" when the ordinance was enacted (permissible), from expansion that is "substantial and . . . render[s] . . . property proportionally less adequate" (impermissible).

215. Condor, Inc. v. City of North Charleston, 380 S.E.2d 628 (S.C. Ct. App. 1989).

216. *Condor, Inc.* 380 S.E.3d at 629–30. *See also* McDowell v. Lafayette County Comm'n, 802 S.W.2d 162 (Mo. Ct. App. 1990) (mere planning and preparation for nonconforming use does not constitute establishment); Smith v. Copeland, 787 S.W.2d 420 (Tex. Ct. App. 1990) (temporary one-year permits that were not renewed did not constitute establishment of lawful nonconforming massage parlor).

217. City of University Place v. McGuire, 30 P.3d 453, 458 (Wash. banc 2001); *see also* Town of West Greenwich v. A. Cardi Realty Assocs., 786 A.2d 354 (R.I. 2001).

218. Miller & Son Paving, Inc v. Wrightstown Township, 401 A.2d 392 (1979).

219. Watanabe v. City of Phoenix, 683 P.2d 1177, 1180 (Ariz. Ct. App. 1984).

220. Cheyenne Airport Bd. v. Rogers, 707 P.2d 717 (Wyo. 1985).

221. *Id.*; *Watanabe,* 683 P.2d at 1180.

222. *See, e.g.,* Forsyth County v. Shelton, 329 S.E.2d 730 (N.C. Ct. App. 1985), *rev. denied,* 333 S.E.2d 485 (N.C. 1985) (commercial nonconforming use could not be reestablished after four-year voluntary discontinuance). *See also* Derby Refining Co. v. City of Chelsea, 555 N.E.2d 534, 538 (1990) (mere nonuse or sale does not, by itself, constitute abandonment terminating lawful nonconforming use).

223. *See, e.g.,* N.J. REV. STAT. § 40:55D-68 (nonconforming structure may be restored or replaced in the event of partial destruction).

224. *See, e.g.,* Weldon v. Zoning Bd. of City of Des Moines, 250 N.W.2d 396, 403 (Iowa 1977) (voluntary demolition of building resulted in extinguishment of nonconforming use).

225. Prewitt v. Johnson, 710 S.W.2d 238 (Ky. Ct. App. 1986).

226. Derby Refining Co., 555 N.E.2d at 539 (finding that operation of property as a liquid asphalt storage facility was permissible under the nonconforming use designation of a "petroleum storage facility"); *See also* New London Land Use Ass'n v. New London Zoning Bd. of Adjustment, 543 A.2d 1385 (N.H. 1988) (demolition of nonconforming 17-unit motel structure and replacement with new structure almost twice as large held impermissible expansion of nonconforming use), and Pappas v. Zoning Bd. of Adjustment of City of Philadelphia, 589 A.2d 675 (Pa. 1991) (holding that change of use from sandwich shop to full-service pizza restaurant constituted an expansion of nonconforming use, but not an abandonment thereof, thereby approving the expansion as part of the nonconforming use).

227. *See, e.g.,* Browning-Ferris Indus. of St. Louis, Inc. v. City of Maryland Heights, 747 F. Supp. 1340 (E.D. Mo. 1990) (holding that landfill operator had vested right in use of property in face of subsequent incorporation of city and city's refusal to issue permit).

228. *Weldon,* 250 N.W.2d at 403.

229. Bell v. Cloud, 764 S.W.2d 105, 109 (Mo. Ct. App. 1988) (change in ownership of sign did not destroy nonconforming use). *See also* New London Land Use Ass'n, 543 A.2d

1385, 1388 (N.H. 1988) (change from tenant occupancy to owner occupancy not impermissible extension of nonconforming use).

230. Young v. Planning Comm'n of County of Kawa'i, 974 P.2d 40 (Hawaii 1999).

231. *See, e.g.,* Colo. Rev., c. 45A, § 19, Ga. Code, § 69.835; Or. Comp. Laws, § 86-1210. For early discussions of the amortization question, *see* Note, *Elimination of Nonconforming Uses,* 35 Va. L. Rev. 348 (1949); Babcock, *The Illinois Supreme Court and Zoning: A Study in Uncertainty,* 15 U. Chi. L. Rev. 87 (1947); Note, *Amortization of Property Uses Not Conforming to Zoning Regulations,* U. Chi. L. Rev. 477 (1942).

232. Bd. of Supervisors of Cerro Gordo County v. Miller, 170 N.W.2d 358, 362 (Iowa 1969) (nonconforming uses are "inconsistent with . . . basic aim and ultimate purpose of zoning"); City of Los Angeles v. Gage, 274 P.2d 34, 40–41 (Cal. Ct. App. 1954). *See generally* Peterson & McCarthy, *Amortization of Legal Land Use Nonconformities as Regulatory Takings: An Uncertain Future,* 35 Wash. U. J. Urb. & Contemp. L. 37 (1989); Reynolds, *The Reasonableness of Amortization Periods for Nonconforming Uses—Balancing the Private Interest and the Public Welfare,* 34 Wash. U. J. Urb. & Contemp. L. 99 (1988); American Law Institute, Model Land Development Code 169–74 (1975); Mandelker, *Prolonging the Nonconforming Use: Judicial Restriction of the Power to Zone in Iowa,* 8 Drake L. Rev. 23 (1958); Norton, *Elimination of Incompatible Uses & Structures,* 20 Law & Contemp. Probs. 305 (1955).

233. City of University Park v. Benners, 485 S.W.2d 773, 778 (Tex. 1972) (citing Note, *Amortization of Property Uses Not Conforming to Zoning Regulations,* 9 U. Chi. L. Rev. 477, 479 (1942)).

234. Mayor and Council of New Castle v. Rollins Outdoor Adver., 475 A.2d 355, 357 (Del. Sup. Ct. 1984), reviewing the history of amortization and discussing decided cases.

235. *City of University Park,* 485 S.W.2d at 777; City of Los Angeles v. Gage, 274 P.2d 34, 44 (Cal. Ct. App. 1954).

236. Temple Baptist Church, Inc. v. City of Albuquerque, 646 P.2d 565, 572 (N.M. 1982).

237. *Id.*

238. Art Neon Co. v. City and County of Denver, 488 F.2d 118, 122 (10th Cir. 1973), *cert. denied,* 417 U.S. 932 (1974) (approving five-year amortization period for signs, but disapproving different periods of amortization for signs having different "replacement" costs).

239. *City of University Park,* 485 S.W.2d 773 (order to discontinue nonconforming commercial use in residential district upheld).

240. *See, e.g.,* Mayor and Council of New Castle v. Rollins Outdoor Adver., 475 A.2d 355 (Del. 1984) (approving three-year amortization period, but remanding for as-applied consideration to off-site signs); John Donnelly and Sons, Inc. v. Outdoor Adver. Bd., 339 N.E.2d 709 (Mass. 1975) (approving five-year amortization period for nonconforming off-site signs); City of Seattle v. Martin, 2d 541, 342 P.2d 602 (Wash. 1959) (upholding one-year amortization period for nonconforming uses "not in a building"); City of Los Angeles v. Gage, 274 P.2d 34 (Cal. Ct. App. 1954) (upholding five-year period for commercial uses in residential districts); State *ex rel.* Dema Realty Co. v. McDonald, 121 So. 613, *cert. denied,* 280 U.S. 556 (1929). *See generally* American Law Institute, A Model Land Development Code 170–72 (1975) (collecting cases).

241. Northend Cinema, Inc. v. City of Seattle, 585 P.2d 1153, 1159–60 (Wash. 1978).

242. Ebel v. City of Corona, 767 F.2d 635, 639 (9th Cir. 1985).

243. Drafters of the ALI Model Land Development Code credit the National Commission on Urban Problems with coining the term *wait and see* to describe a range of regulatory techniques designed to maximize the flexibility of local land use regulators by restricting land development until local authorities decide that a particular use is acceptable. American Law Institute, A Model Land Development Code 175 (1975), *citing* National Commission on Urban Problems, Building the American City 206 (1968).

244. American Law Institute, A MODEL LAND DEVELOPMENT CODE 174–77 (1975).

245. *See, e.g.*, Standard Oil Co. v. City of Tallahassee, 183 F.2d 410 (5th Cir.), *cert. denied*, 340 U.S. 892 (1950); Livingston Rock & Gravel Co. v. County of Los Angeles, 272 P.2d 4 (Cal. 1954); Grant v. Mayor and City of Baltimore, 129 A.2d 363 (Md. Ct. App. 1957).

246. Mayor and Council of New Castle v. Rollins Outdoor Adver., 475 A.2d 355 (Del. 1984).

247. *Id.* at 358.

248. *See* Badger v. Ferrisburgh, 712 A.2d 911 (Vt. 1998).

249. S. TOLL, ZONED AMERICAN 139 (1969).

250. Section 1, Standard State Zoning Enabling Act, n. 7 (U.S. Dep't of Commerce, rev. ed. 1926), *appearing as* Appendix A, A MODEL LAND DEVELOPMENT CODE 213, Tentative Draft no. 1 (ALI, 1968).

251. Village of Euclid v. Ambler Realty Co., 272 U.S. 359 (1926). *See also* Gorieb v. Fox, 274 U.S. 603, 608 (1927) ("We have recently held, . . . that comprehensive zoning laws and ordinances, prescribing, among other things, the height of buildings to be erected . . . are, in their general scope, valid under the federal Constitution"); Sisters of Bon Secours Hospital v. City of Grosse Pointe, 154 N.W.2d 644, 653 (Mich. 1967) ("concept of building height restrictions is virtually universally accepted as bearing a substantial relation to public health, safety, morals and welfare").

252. *See, e.g.*, Welsh v. Swasey, 214 U.S. 91, 105–6 (1909) (upholding validity of state statute limiting height of buildings in cities).

253. *See, e.g.*, Alexander v. Town of Hampstead, 525 A.2d 276 (N.H. 1987) (upholding 1.5-story limitation for houses in recreational-use district); State Dep't of Ecology v. Pacesetter Constr. Co., 571 P.2d 196, 201 (Wash. 1977) (upholding building height restriction in wetland areas adjoining lake and requiring height to be measured from average grade level in the natural state of land to protect view of lake).

254. Alexander v. Town of Hampstead, 525 A.2d 276, 279 (N.H. 1987) (1.5-story height limitation for residences); Town of Bay Harbor v. Driggs, 522 So. 2d 912, 915 (Fla. Ct. App. 1988) (substantial evidence that prohibition of multilevel parking garage would protect small-town character of community).

255. Roger v. City of Cheyenne, 747 P.2d 1137, 1139 (Wyo. 1987) (height limitation for trees in noninstrument airport landing approach upheld as reasonable regulation and not compensable taking of flight easement). *See also* Cheyenne Airport Bd. v. Rogers, 707 P.2d 717 (Wyo. 1985), *cert. denied*, 476 U.S. 1110 (1986).

256. *See, e.g.*, Friends of the Shawangunks, Inc. v. Knowlton, 476 N.E.2d 988 (N.Y. 1985) (one-acre minimum lot size required for residential unit); Negin v. Bd. of Building and Zoning Appeals of the City of Mentor, 433 N.E.2d 165 (Ohio 1982) (ordinance establishing minimum lot size for home construction invalidated as applied to particular lot).

257. Gorieb v. Fox, 274 U.S. 603, 608 (1927) (upholding building line setback requirement from street).

258. *See, e.g.*, Builders Serv. Corp. v. Planning & Zoning Comm'n of Town of East Hampton, 545 A.2d 530, 536 (Conn. 1988) (statutory authority to regulate size of buildings includes authority to establish minimum floor-area requirements).

259. Village of Belle Terre v. Boraas, 416 U.S. 1, 9 (1974).

260. *See, e.g.*, Builders Serv. Corp., 545 A.2d at 539 (1988) (rejecting argument that Supreme Court in Nollan v. California Coastal Comm'n, 483 U.S. 825 (1987), established a stricter standard of review for land use regulation cases).

261. Builders Serv. Corp. v. Planning & Zoning Comm'n of Town of East Hampton, 545 A.2d 530 (Conn. 1988).

262. *Id.* at 544.

263. *Id.* at 550.

264. Conn. Gen. Stat. § 8-2.225 (1997).

265. *Builders Serv. Corp.*, 545 A.2d at 548–50.

266. *Builders Serv. Corp.*, 545 A.2d at 551–53.

267. *See, e.g.,* N.Y. Town Law § 281 (McKinney 1997); Friends of the Shawangunks, Inc. v. Knowlton, 476 N.E.2d 988, 992 (N.Y. 1985) (cluster zoning involves "trade-off of increased density on the developed portion of the land in return for preserving undeveloped the remainder of the land").

268. *See, e.g.,* Lutz v. City of Longview, 520 P.2d 1374, 1376 (Wash. 1974) ("PUD achieves flexibility by permitting specific modifications of the customary zoning standards as applied to a particular parcel"); Johnson v. City of Mount Vernon, 679 P.2d 405, 408–409 (Wash. Ct. App. 1984) (PUD request is akin to a rezone and denial must be accompanied by written findings including reasons for denial). *See generally* pp. 178–79.

269. Friends of the Shawangunks, Inc. v. Knowlton, 476 N.E.2d 988 (N.Y. 1985).

270. Stoney-Brook Dev. v. Town of Fremont, 464 A.2d 561, 564 (N.H. 1984) (growth-rate limit chosen because it was growth rate of year of enactment held arbitrary as "taken out of a hat"). *See generally* pp. 189–191.

271. *See* pp. 284–88.

272. Village of Belle Terre v. Boraas, 416 U.S. 1, 2 (1974). *See generally* pp. 284–286.

273. Coffey v. Maryland-National Capital Park, 441 A.2d 1041 (Md. 1982). *See generally* chapter 8.

274. Kenert & Assocs. v. Skagit County, 680 P.2d 439 (Wash. Ct. App. 1984).

275. *See generally* D. Mandelker & R. Cunningham, Planning and Control of Land Development 324–29 (3d ed. 1990); International City Management Ass'n, The Practice of Local Government Planning 274–78 (F. So & J. Getzeb eds., 2d ed. 1988); J. Costonis, Space Adrift 28–34 (1974).

276. *See* p. 184.

277. National Commission on Urban Problems, Building the American City 205–08 (1968).

278. Urban Land Institute, Flexible Zoning 11 (1988).

279. *See, e.g.,* Asian Americans for Equality v. Koch, 527 N.E.2d 265, 269 (N.Y. 1988) (special district zoning granting density bonuses for mixed-income housing development on vacant land in inner-city neighborhood upheld).

280. N.H. Rev. Stat. Ann. § 674:21 (1995).

281. *See* chapter 8.

282. *See* p. 184.

283. *See* pp. 178–79.

284. *Id.*

285. *See* pp. 180–182.

286. *Id.*

287. *Id.*

288. *See* chapter 10.

289. *See* chapter 9.

290. *Id.*

291. N.H. Rev. Stat. § 674:21 (1995).

292. *Id.*

293. McCloud, *Tandem Plans a "Town" in Silicone Valley,* N.Y. Times, September 22, 1991.

294. Levinson, *Share and Share Alike,* Planning, July 1991.

295. *See also* pp. 284–88.

296. *See* pp. 175–77.

297. *See, e.g.,* Lutz v. City of Longview, 520 P.2d 1374, 1376 (1974) (imposition of PUD on specific parcel of land constitutes rezoning); Kenert & Assocs. v. Skagit County, 680 P.2d

439 (Wash. Ct. App. 1984) (denial of PUD proposal for 80 houses on a 79.5-acre tract, with 39 acres of clustered residential development, 30 acres of open space, and 10 acres of a gravel pit reversed and remanded for failure to make findings that provide reasonable guidance to developer and permit meaningful appellate review).

298. *See, e.g.,* N.Y. Town Law § 281 (McKinney 1997); Friends of Shawangunks, Inc. v. Knowlton, 476 N.E.2d 988, 992 (N.Y. 1985) (discussing with approval "trade-off" of increased density on developed portion in return for preserving undeveloped remainder of land).

299. N.Y. Town Law § 281 (McKinney 1997).

300. *Id.*

301. Johnson v. City of Mount Vernon, 679 P.2d 405 (Wash. Ct. App. 1984) (denial of PUD reversed where reasons for denial of permit inadequate to guide the developer in addressing the concerns of the county and to "permit meaningful judicial review").

302. *Kenart & Assocs,* 680 P.2d at 444.

303. West v. Mills, 380 S.E.2d 917, 921 (Va. 1989).

304. *See, e.g.,* Treme v. St. Louis County, 609 S.W.2d 706, 710 (Mo. Ct. App. 1980) (upholding planned commercial district as floating zone).

305. *Kenart & Assocs, supra; Treme, supra.*

306. Rodgers v. Village of Tarrytown, 96 N.E.2d 731 (N.Y. 1951) (upholding floating zone for garden apartments against spot zoning charges).

307. *Id.*

308. *See, e.g.,* Summerell v. Phillips, 282 So. 2d 450 (La. 1973); Eves v. Zoning Bd. of Adjustment of Lower Gwynedd Township, 164 A.2d 7 (Pa. 1960); Hartnett v. Austin, 93 So. 2d 86 (Fla. 1956).

309. Treme v. St. Louis County, 609 S.W.2d 706 (Mo. Ct. App. 1980) (upholding planned commercial district as floating zone, reviewing cases).

310. *See, e.g., id.*

311. Asian Americans for Equality v. Koch, 527 N.E.2d 265, 269 (N.Y. 1988).

312. *See, e.g.,* Southern Burlington County NAACP v. Township of Mount Laurel, 456 A.2d 390, 445–46 (1983) (*Mount Laurel II*) (citing Fox & Davis, *Density Bonus Zoning to Provide Low and Moderate Cost Housing,* 3 HASTINGS CONST. L. Q. 1015, 1060–62 (1977) and expressing concern that sole reliance on incentive zoning may prove insufficient to achieve affordable housing objective). *See* p. 394.

313. *Asian Americans for Equality,* 527 N.W. 2d 265.

314. *See, e.g., id.* at 269 (upholding creation of special district to encourage production of affordable housing and community facilities for persons who work in the garment, tourist, and related industries in the Chinatown area of New York City).

315. *See, e.g.,* CONN. GEN. STAT. § 8-2 (1997) (authorizing cluster development, higher development and performance standards for roads, sidewalks, and underground facilities to developers using passive solar-energy techniques).

316. D. PORTER, P. PHILLIPS & T. LASSAR, FLEXIBLE ZONING: HOW IT WORKS 11 (ULI, 1988).

317. N.J. STAT. ANN. § 40:55D-65.d (West 1997).

318. N.J. STAT. ANN. § 40:55D-53 (West 1997).

319. Zilinsky v. Zoning Bd. of Adjustment of Verona, 521 A.2d 841, 844 (N.J. 1987).

320. Terino v. Town of Hartford Zoning Bd. of Adjustment, 538 A.2d 160 (Vt. 1987).

321. D. PORTER, P. PHILLIPS & T. LASSAR, FLEXIBLE ZONING: HOW IT WORKS 14, 98 (ULI, 1988).

322. Kingma, *Zoning with Intensity,* PLANNING, vol. 56, no. 10, at p. 18 (APA, October, 1990).

323. *Id.*

324. FLA. STAT. ANN. § 163.3202 (2)(g) (West 1997). *See* pp. 28–34.

325. Knack, *Repent, Ye Sinners, Repent,* PLANNING, vol. 55, no. 8, at p. 4, 6–7 (APA, August, 1989).

326. *See, e.g.,* Franchise Developers, Inc. v. City of Cincinnati, 505 N.E.2d 966, 968 (Ohio 1987).

327. *Id.* at 971.

328. Allingham v. City of Seattle, 749 P.2d 160, 163, *modified,* 757 P.2d 533 (Wash. 1988).

329. Presbytery of Seattle v. King County, 787 P.2d 907, 915 (Wash. 1990).

330. *See, e.g.,* Second Baptist Church v. Little Rock Historic Dist. Comm'n, 732 S.W.2d 483, 485 (Ark. 1987).

331. 16 U.S.C.A. § 470 *et seq.* (1997).

332. See, e.g., ARK. CODE. ANN. § 14-172-201, *et seq.* (Michie 1995), *construed in* Second Baptist Church v. Little Rock Historic Dist. Comm'n, 732 S.W.2d 483 (Ark. 1987) (upholding denial of permit for construction of parking lot in historic district).

333. *See, e.g., id.* at 485.

334. A landmark preservation district was upheld against a claim that the designation was an attempt to preserve the theater industry as such. Shubert Organization, Inc. v. Landmarks Pres. Comm'n of the City of New York, 570 N.Y.S.2d 504 (Sup. Ct. 1991). In United Artists Theater Circuit, Inc. v. City of Philadelphia, 635 A.2d 612, 619 (Pa. 1993), the Pennsylvania Supreme Court held that designation of a building as historic is not a taking, even though the owner has not consented to such designation.

335. *See, e.g.,* Society of Jesus of New England v. Boston Landmarks Comm'n, 564 N.E.2d 571 (Mass. 1990) (landmark status for interior of church held violative of First Amendment rights of Jesuit owners); Harris Trust & Savings Bank v. Duggan, 435 N.E.2d 130 (Ill. App. Ct. 1982), *aff'd.,* 449 N.E.2d 69 (Ill. 1983).

336. *See* p. 185.

337. *See, e.g.,* Boyd v. Roland, 789 F.2d 347 (5th Cir. 1986) (although a developer building a nursing home with funds from HUD was required to consider the effect of development on the community, denial of injunction to stop development was affirmed where construction had already begun).

338. U.S.C.A. § 470f (1997), construed in Boyd v. Roland, 789 F.2d 347 (5th Cir. 1986), as making neighborhood surrounding a demolished retirement home eligible for inclusion in the National Register and thus subject to protection, although the court denied a preliminary injunction against construction of a new building assisted with federal funds because of the "progress of the project."

339. *See, e.g.,* Berman v. Parker, 348 U.S. 26, 33 (1954) ("The values . . . [public welfare] represents are spiritual as well as physical, aesthetic as well as monetary. . . .").

340. State *ex rel.* Stoyanoff v. Berkeley, 458 S.W.2d 305, 309–10 (Mo. 1970) (reviewing cases).

341. *See, e.g.,* Plain Dealer Publ'g Co. v. City of Lakewood, 794 F.2d 1139, 1146 (6th Cir. 1986), *aff'd in part and remanded on other grounds,* 486 U.S. 750 (1988) (invalidating standardless discretion over design of newsracks).

342. *Id.* at 1146.

343. Barnett, *Urban Design,* in THE PRACTICE OF LOCAL GOVERNMENT PLANNING, 175, 187 (F. So & J. Getzels eds., 2d ed. 1988).

344. *See, e.g.,* City of Kansas v. Kindle, 446 S.W.2d 807 (Mo. 1969); State v. Houghton, 176 N.W. 159 (Minn. 1920).

345. *See generally* chapter 3.

346. *See, e.g.,* MINN. STAT. ANN. §§ 462.12 to 462.17 (1996).

347. City of Kansas v. Kindle, 446 S.W.2d at 813.

348. D. HAGMAN & J. JUERGENSMEYER, URBAN PLANNING AND LAND DEVELOPMENT CONTROL LAW 347 (2d ed. 1986).

349. West Montgomery County Citizen's Ass'n v. Maryland-National Capital Park & Planning Comm'n, 522 A.2d 1328, 1330 (Md. 1987).

350. Penn Central Transp. Co. v. New York City, 438 U.S. 104, 137 (1978).

351. *See, e.g.,* Corrigan v. City of Scottsdale, 720 P.2d 513 (Ariz. 1987) (TDRs not just compensation under Arizona constitution, which requires compensation in money).

352. 117 S. Ct. 1659 (1997).

353. Ripeness is discussed on pp. 95–99.

354. 117 S. Ct. at 1667.

355. *Id.* at 1672.

356. Collard v. Incorporated Village of Flower Hill, 421 N.E.2d 818 (N.Y. 1981).

357. *Id.* at 821–822.

358. *See, e.g.,* Cal. Gov't Code §§ 65864–65869.5 (West 1996); Fla. Stat. Ann. § 163.220(1)–(4) (West 1997). *See generally* Wegner, *Moving Toward the Bargaining Table: Contract Zoning, Development Agreements, and the Theoretical Foundations of Government Land Use Deals,* 65 N.C. L. Rev. 958 (1987).

359. Morgran Company, Inc. v. Orange County, 818 So. 2d 640 (Fla. App. 2002).

360. See Southwestern Illinois Dev. Auth. v. Nat'l City Envtl., LLC, 768 N.E.2d 1 (Ill. 2002) *cert. denied,* 123 S. Ct. 88, Oct. 2002.

361. Cal. Gov't Code § 65865 *et. seq.* See Daniel J. Curtin, Jr., *Vested Rights—Property Development Agreements in an Era of Smart Growth Legislation,* 24 State & Local Law News, no. 1, Fall 2000, American Bar Association, Section of State and Local Government Law. See discussion of vested rights, this chapter, *supra.*

362. Stephens v. City of Vista, 994 F.2d 650 (9th Cir. 1993).

363. See Curtin, *Vested Rights—Property Development Agreements in an Era of Smart Growth Legislation,* supra, n. 361.

364. Morgran Company, Inc. v. Orange County, 818 So. 2d 640 (Fla. App. 2002), construing §§ 163.3220–.3243 Fla. Stat. Ann. (1999).

365. Kaplan v. Clear Lake City Water Auth., 794 F.2d 1059, 1064 (5th Cir 1986).

366. Stoney-Brook Dev. Corp. v. Town of Fremont, 474 A.2d 561 (N.H. 1984).

367. *In re* Eastport Assocs., 935 F.2d 1071 (9th Cir. 1991).

368. *See* Pro-Eco, Inc. v. Bd. of Comm'rs, 956 F.2d 635 (7th Cir. 1992).

369. Anna K. Schwab & David J. Brower, *Sustainable Development: Implementation at the Local Level,* Land Use Law, April 1997, pp. 3–7.

370. *See* p. 189.

371. *See* pp. 180–82.

372. *See* pp. 182.

373. *See* chapter 8.

374. *See* chapter 2. Fla. Stat. Ann. § 163.3202(2)(g) (West. Supp. 1991).

375. 6th Adoption Draft, 1990–2010 updated Orange County, Florida Comprehensive Policy Plan 37–46 (1991).

376. *See, e.g.,* Constr. Indus. Ass'n v. City of Petaluma, 522 F.2d 897 (9th Cir. 1975), *cert. denied,* 424 U.S. 934 (1976) (upholding use of annual residential building-permit quotas as part of a comprehensive growth management plan); Assoc. Home Builders v. City of Livermore, 555 P.2d 473, 135 (Cal. 1976) (upholding development moratorium until public services supply problems were solved); Golden v. Planning Bd., 285 N.E.2d 291 (N.Y. 1972), *appeal dismissed,* 409 U.S. 1003 (1972) (upholding phased development controls in conjunction with adopted capital improvements budget). *See generally* J. Dukeminier & J. Krier, Property 1250–52 (2d ed. 1988); Ellickson, *Suburban Growth Controls: An Economic and Legal Analysis,* 86 Yale L.J. 385 (1977).

377. *See* Wash. Rev. Code § 36.70A (1990 and Supp. 1996).

378. Wash. Laws, 1996 H.B. 2467.

379. *See* SHAPING CITIES: THE ENVIRONMENTAL AND HUMAN DIMENSIONS, World Watch Institute, 1991.

380. *See Downeasters Take On Growth Management,* PLANNING, August, 1991.

381. *See, e.g.,* Vidal v. Lisanti Foods, 679 A.2d 206 (N.J. Ct. App. 1996) (holding that a board of adjustment may not grant use variances to such an extent that it usurps the power of the local legislative body to enact zoning amendments).

382. 234 Cal. Rptr. 1 (Cal. Dist. Ct. App. 1987).

383. *Id.* at 6.

384. *Id.*

385. Professor Juliah H. Levi, Hastings College of Law, Statement at Annual Meeting Program of the *ABA Section of Urban, State and Local Government Law,* San Francisco, California (August 10, 1987).

386. SEATTLE, WA., CODE, § 25.12.010 (1977).

387. *Id.*

388. Legislation authorizing development agreements is one possible approach to accommodating the interests. *See generally* Wegner, *supra* n. 357, at 1008–27.

389. "Zoning with compensation" is not a new idea, but it has not been used very often because of the Supreme Court's acceptance of noncompensatory zoning in Village of Euclid v. Ambler Realty Co., 272 U.S. 365 (1926). When courts find both a proper public purpose and a substantial relationship to public health, safety, morals, or general welfare of the community, courts will approve government action as a "joint exercise of the power of eminent domain and the police power." City of Kansas City v. Kindle, 446 S.W.2d 807, 813 (Mo. 1969).

390. Professor Wegner discusses in considerable detail the problem of protecting the public interest in the context of contingent zoning and development agreements. *See* Wegner, *supra* n. 357, at 986–94, 1008–27.

391. See discussion re development agreements, Stephans v. City of Vista, 994 F.2d 650 (9th Cir. 1993) (upholding verdict of $727,500 against city, which had amended its zoning ordinance to reduce density to 55 units, after entering into development agreement to approve 140 apartment units).

392. Daniel J. Curtin, Jr., *Vested Rights—Property Development Agreements in an Era of Smart Growth Legislation,* 24 STATE AND LOCAL LAW NEWS, no. 1, Fall 2000, American Bar Association, Section of State and Local Government Law.

CHAPTER 5

The Local Land Use Approval Process

The Dynamics of Land Use Regulation

Enactment of the comprehensive zoning ordinance is, of course, only the beginning of the land use regulation process. Interpretation and amendment of zoning regulations is as dynamic as land use and development.

To enable local governments to cope with changes in demand for land use while preserving certain community values, zoning-enabling statutes have authorized three basic local regulatory devices: zoning amendments, special-use permits, and variances.[1] Some states permit other devices, such as transfer of development rights, floating zones, incentive and inclusionary zoning, planned unit development, performance zoning, and various types of "exactions," such as impact fees.[2]

Enforcement of Zoning Ordinances

Enabling statutes and local ordinances provide for the appointment of a qualified person, the zoning officer or administrator, to administer the comprehensive zoning ordinance.[3] The zoning administrator enforces the ordinance chiefly by granting or denying building permits.[4] The administrator has no discretion to permit activity that does not conform to the ordinance or to otherwise amend or waive the literal terms of the ordinance.[5] This action (or inaction) is the jurisdictional trigger to municipal-level discretionary and nondiscretionary action, usually through the planning commission, and onward to the elected body, the city council or board of aldermen. Largely because of budget constraints, local zoning ordinances vary widely in quality of draftsmanship, however, and in practice, zoning administrators and other city staff have significant power to interpret the inevitable ambiguities and fill in gaps in local zoning legislation. The substantial cost and risk of further appeals also vest the administrator with the power of a gatekeeper. This power often is exercised as a means of furthering the agenda of the constituency of the staff, usually the mayor or other city executive.

In addition to denying or granting building permits, statutes and ordinances authorize injunctive relief to stop zoning violations and imposition of fines following civil enforcement proceedings.[6] Statutes and common law principles also may give power to institute enforcement proceedings to landowners or tenants who can show that their "property or person will be substantially affected by the alleged violation."[7] The common law of most states also permits proof of zoning ordinance violations as evidence of nuisance.[8]

In a celebrated enforcement case, the Court of Appeals of New York upheld a decision by New York City to revoke an erroneously issued building permit after a building was constructed that was 12 stories higher than permitted by the applicable zoning district regulations. The developer argued to no avail that it was the city's mistake rather than the developer's that caused the problem. "Reasonable diligence by a good faith inquirer would have disclosed the true facts and the bureaucratic error. . . ."[9] In settling the case, the developer, the mayor, and a neighborhood group agreed that the top 12 stories of the building would be removed, but the developer would be allowed to construct another (conforming) structure nearby, and both structures would be allowed property tax abatement.[10] Despite the strong message in this case that zoning is very serious business, another court has held that injunctive relief is not always appropriate. In an Indiana Court of Appeals case, the court found that the trial court's order to remove several structures built on a farm in violation of a zoning ordinance was too severe[11] because the structures, while causing the change in zoning classification from agricultural to commercial, in fact would be used for agricultural purposes.[12]

In any enforcement proceeding, due process requires that notice of alleged violations be given to affected persons. The notice must be in writing and state the name of the owner of record, the location of the property charged, the specific violation or violations with a description of the requirements that have not been met, dates by which compliance steps must begin and be completed, the time for filing an appeal, and a statement of the penalties for noncompliance.[13] When affected landowners or tenants are given power to institute enforcement actions, their power usually is conditioned upon their giving the municipality sufficient advance notice (e.g., 30 days) to enable the municipality to seek enforcement through its own procedures.[14]

In one case it was held that failure to give the landowner proper notice of a claimed zoning violation did not prevent enforcement actions from being taken, including the issuance of an injunction ordering a building to be moved to remedy a setback violation. The court also held, however, that the negligent municipality would have to bear the cost of the move rather than the nonresident landowner, who was unaware of the zoning violation while construction was underway.[15]

Enforcement actions may be appealed to the local zoning board of adjustment in accordance with procedures established for such appeals.[16]

The Zoning Amendment

The zoning amendment or "rezoning" is the change in the local zoning district designation or substantive zoning ordinance provisions applicable to a parcel or parcels of property. It is the classic and perhaps most familiar forum for land use regulation and disputes, and permits the most fundamental (and discretionary) policy debate. The most important effect and the very purpose of the typical zoning amendment is change in permitted land uses.

Most jurisdictions hold that rezonings are purely legislative functions, and this is the most political and volatile of actions involving land development. Courts adopting the "legislative view" of zoning amendments have reasoned that a decision to amend or to refuse to amend a zoning ordinance is a decision concerning what the law regulating use of land should be and is thus "law making" rather than implementation or application of existing law.[17] Thus only local governing bodies with legislative authority, such as city councils or county commissions, are authorized to amend zoning ordinances.[18] Nonelected administrative agencies, such as zoning boards of adjustment or planning and zoning commissions, do not have legislative authority and thus are not competent to amend zoning ordinances, either expressly or by action that amounts to a zoning amendment.[19] Land use lawyers and officials know, however, that the line between law making, by overt rezoning, and law interpreting, by conditional-use permitting and grants of variances, is often not meaningful. Thus local officials and participating citizens exercise subjective, and often wide-ranging, discretion in "nondiscretionary" matters.

The amendment is also used to carry out a policy to encourage a use in advance of specific application by any landowner for amendment. In applying what is known as the "floating zone" device, the legislative body follows a two-stage process: (1) identification of the desired use (e.g., mobile homes, mixed-use developments, or shopping centers) that will be permitted if certain standards are met; and (2) identification of the location or "district" where the zone will be "anchored," and the use permitted. Both decisions are made by adoption of zoning amendments. The first decision clearly is legislative; the second decision is also considered legislative by most courts,[20] but a growing body of judicial opinion treats the second decision as administrative in character because it is seen as a decision to implement the previously established policy, rather than a decision concerning what the law should be.[21] For such administrative decisions, there should be no objection to delegation of that authority to a nonelected administrative body such as a local planning and zoning commission, provided the accepted standards for delegation of administrative authority are met, and several states have authorized such delegation.[22]

Standards for Amending the Zoning Ordinance

Because of the general statutory requirement, discussed in chapter 2, that the city engage in planning prior to regulating land use, zoning ordinances may not be amended unless consistent with long-range planning goals.[23] The primary reason for this rule is the concern that special favors not be granted to individual landowners, whether purposely or inadvertently, when the community attempts to manage change through the zoning amendment process.

The popular expression of the avoidance of special favors rule is the term *spot zoning*, although the term is a misnomer when used in this context. Spot zoning is the practice of singling out a relatively small tract of land, or spot, on the zoning map and applying a different set of restrictions to that tract than the immediately adjacent tracts.[24] The term implies lack of appropriate transition from the subject tract to surrounding tracts.

There is nothing necessarily inappropriate about a zoning district that is an island. The island land use may not be incompatible with or antagonistic to surrounding land use. Courts will balk, however, where a parcel is zoned without consideration of the community's values as expressed in its legislatively articulated[25] goals and objectives,[26] and as a result the "rezoned land is . . . treated unjustifiably different from similar surrounding land."[27] Because of a dreary history of local zoning scandals and "mistakes,"[28] the term *spot zoning* is often only a conclusion used to characterize any illegal zoning. In the end, the term is not analytically helpful. The term is still used as a standard, however, and one court has stated the elements for spot zoning to be (1) a use "significantly" different from the predominant neighborhood land uses; and (2) the amendment amounts to favoritism or "special" legislation benefiting only one property owner.[29] The size of a rezoned parcel (small) has also been held to be relevant.[30]

The basic issues raised by the zoning amendment are the same as that governing original zoning: whether the requested change will advance the public health, safety, and welfare, will adversely affect property values, or will otherwise be consistent with good land use planning. Some jurisidctions, however, at least superficially analyze changes differently, measuring the request against the status quo. These jurisdictions ask whether current existing land use regulations are responsive to legitimate, current community land use concerns and objectives. If existing regulations are responsive to such public considerations, then, theoretically, an amendment is not necessary. If regulations are not responsive to community concerns, then amendments are in order.[31] This approach ignores the basic policy-making power of the local legislative body, however, and is no more realistic than requiring certain circumstances to exist before allowing a state legislative body to change state law. The drafters of the Standard State Zoning Enabling Act assumed that regulations would have to be changed "as conditions change[d] or new conditions [arose]," but said little about how to determine when those factors were present.[32]

Under the change approach, the standard has been stated rigidly as requiring proof that the prior zoning was based on "error or mistake"[33] and elsewhere as whether the character of the area covered by the regulations in question has so changed as to "necessitate" a change in the regulations.[34]

Application of the change or mistake rule requires a close analysis of the original zoning decisions and the planning process that led to those decisions, as well as the community setting in which the current rezoning proposal is brought. The Maryland Court of Special Appeals has identified two ways in which a zoning decision can be erroneous and thus subject to modification:

(1) at the time of the comprehensive zoning the Council failed to take into account then existing facts, or projects or trends which were reasonably foreseeable of fruition in the future, so that the Council's action was premised initially on a misapprehension, . . . [or]

(2) events occurring subsequent to the comprehensive zoning have proven that the Council's initial premises were incorrect.[35]

Applying these standards, the Maryland court concluded that a decision to zone a tract for residential uses in an effort to increase the residential density surrounding a neighborhood school that residents sought to prevent from closing was erroneous. The reasons were that the property was not part of the actual neighborhood served by the school, the property was unsuited for residential development, and the character of the surrounding parcels made it unlikely that residential development would occur in the vicinity.[36]

The change or mistake rule, advocated as a means of ensuring stability for homeowners who "invest a substantial portion of their entire lifetime earnings, relying upon a zoning ordinance,"[37] was not a part of the Standard State Enabling Act. Drafters believed that the necessary stability could be obtained by the requirement that amendments be approved by a three-fourths vote of all the members of the local legislative body when appropriate protests were filed by neighbors.[38]

Most courts have moved away from the rigidity of the change or mistake rule to a more flexible rule that tests the validity of a zoning amendment against "considerations which affect the whole community"[39] such as "the use (of land) which is most beneficial to the comprehensive plan."[40] As a practical matter, most rezonings are won or lost on the merits of the proposed use rather than the existing use. Applying the more flexible standard, the Wisconsin Supreme Court approved residential-to-commercial rezoning of two parcels of land on one corner of an intersection, where the other three corners were already zoned and being used for commercial purposes.[41] The Pennsylvania Supreme Court similarly accepted the rezoning of four acres of land containing five separate lots on two busy thoroughfares with commercial uses existing directly across one of the roads.[42]

Of course, as the standards for permitting zoning amendments become more flexible, the possibilities for abuse increase. Some courts have dealt with this problem by characterizing zoning amendments that change the permissible use of a specific piece of property, rather than establish general policies, as exercises of administrative or judicial rather than legislative authority. Zoning decisions that fit the administrative or judicial mold are subject to a more stringent standard of judicial review, in which the party proposing the change has the burden of proving that the change is consistent with the planning goals of the community.[43]

As noted earlier,[44] a traditional legislative response to the potential for abuse inherent in spot zoning is the requirement that a supermajority of the legislative body approve the proposed amendment when a specified percentage of the landowners living in proximity to the parcel in question file a formal protest against the proposed rezoning.[45]

Similarly, some states require zoning amendments to be ratified by the voters by referendum.[46] Because referendum ordinarily is not available to review administrative or judicial decisions, however, zoning amendments generally must be characterized as legislative in order for the referendum process to apply.[47] Some states, such as New Jersey, have prohibited the use of initiative or referendum for adopting or amending zoning ordinances.[48]

What constitutes a zoning amendment is sometimes arguable, particularly when flexible techniques requiring multiple stages of review are involved, such as planned unit developments and floating zones. In *McCarty v. City of Kansas City*,[49] the Missouri Court of Appeals concluded that a change in a development plan that was required to be approved before building permits could be issued under a planned business center zoning district constituted a change in zoning, even though the original zoning district designation did not change, because the modified plan called for a "substantial change" in permitted use from automobile parking/open space to automobile sales and repair facility. The court adopted the reasoning of a California court:

> [T]he zoning characteristics of the district consist not only in the classification of the district . . . but in the components of the general plan accompanying the application for the creation of the district and any subsequent amendments to the plan that may properly be adopted. Accordingly, any substantial change or alteration in the actual physical characteristics of the district and its configuration amount to a rezoning of the district.[50]

In the case of amending a planned district, by definition a flexibility device, the zoning administrator must decide whether the change is minor and may be handled administratively or significant, requiring public hearing and legislative action. The zoning authority may avoid public and political input into planned district changes by adopting in the initial creation of the planned district specific provisions that allocate administrative decision-making power with respect to future issues, such as signage or landscaping. Most general planned district procedural ordinances set forth basic standards requiring legislative, or public, amendment in the event of significant changes. The determination of significance, however, is made by the zoning administrator.

Zoning amendments are subject to the same constitutional standards as the initial zoning ordinance. Amendments must be enacted for a proper public purpose, have a rational nexus between the goals of the legislation and the means chosen to achieve those goals, permit the landowner to make a reasonable economic use of the regulated parcel, and be enacted through proper procedures designed to give adequate notice and an opportunity to be heard to interested parties.[51] Although the fact that a zoning amendment may cause financial hardship to a landowner is a factor to be considered in deliberation over a zoning amendment, it is not conclusive.[52]

The Preapplication Conference

Many communities, particularly those with professional planning staffs, recommend a preapplication conference between landowners contemplating development and the planning staff.[53] The preapplication conference serves several purposes and may result in substantial savings of time and money for landowners by weeding out projects that have little merit and identifying desirable or necessary modifications to projects with merit. The municipality benefits by removing clutter from public meetings.[54]

Preapplication conferences with planning staff members are routine and do not conflict with the open meetings policy of state and local "sunshine" laws,[55] as long as they do not involve two or more members of the planning commission or legislative body. One-on-one discussions are not meetings unless the public official has decision-making authority,[56] which members of the planning staff typically do not have. In addition, open meetings laws generally have not been applied to meetings of advisory groups that do not have decision-making authority.[57] In any event, the practitioner should take care to avoid informal contacts with more than one member of the decision-making body because those contacts may well be held to be subject to the open meetings standards.[58] Municipal staff should scrupulously avoid assurances, especially those that could establish reliance or even a vested right.[59]

The Application for Amendment

The zoning amendment process usually is initiated by the property owner by filing an application for a change in zoning designation, although it may also be initiated by a resolution of intention from the planning body or legislative body of the community.[60] Unless initiated within the jurisdiction itself, the application must be filed by someone having a legal interest in the property or an authorized representative, and in some jurisdictions must be verified.[61] The primary purpose of the written application is to present basic information concerning the land in question, thus ordinances typically require the application to contain "such data and information so as to assure the fullest practicable presentation of facts,"[62] although in practice the application is usually perfunctory and includes little substantive information or allegations. It often is neither read nor discussed in the approval process. It is, at most, a disclosure document.

The applicant is often required to indicate information such as the applicant's name, interest in the property, owner of record, current zoning designation, desired zoning designation, legal description of the property by metes and bounds, a survey by a registered engineer or land surveyor showing the dimensions (bearings and distances) of the property, north point, scale, and location map, acreage to the nearest tenth of an inch, and the current uses of the property. In some jurisdictions the applicant must attest to the fact that no arrangements have been made to pay any commission, gratuity, or consideration to public officials with respect to the application, and that he or she will comply with all requirements of the jurisdiction or is unable to comply.[63]

Petitions seeking a change in zoning for which development plans must be reviewed and approved, such as planned unit development designations and floating zone anchorings, must include considerable information concerning the proposed use of the property. Such submittals, which require professional services, can be expensive. For example, St. Louis County, Missouri, requires such applicants to file a preliminary development plan and other information that includes the following:

1. proposed uses and structures
2. existing and proposed contours at intervals of five feet or less referred to Mean Sea Level datum
3. location of all existing tree masses and isolated trees having a trunk diameter of six inches or more
4. two-section profiles through the site showing preliminary building form, existing grade, and final grade
5. proposed ingress and egress to the site
6. a preliminary plan for the provision of sanitation and drainage facilities
7. a sketch plan, if the petition seeks Planned Environment Unit (PEU) designation, drawn to a scale of 100 feet or less to the inch and including north point, scale, and location map
8. a statement documenting the historic, architectural, cultural, archeological, or aesthetic significance of the property, if the petition seeks Landmarks and Preservation Area (LPA) designation[64]

In order to avoid delays in the public hearing schedule, the applicant should meet with staff prior to assembling the application package. Such meetings will enhance the credibility of the application and the public presentation of the proposal.

Review by the Planning Commission

Although the legal power of the planning commission is typically only advisory to the legislative body, in practice the commission is often much more powerful. The commission, typically apolitical, can delay a project, impose costly or fatal conditions, or foment, intentionally or not, public opposition. Theoretically more expert in real estate development than the elected officials at the next level, the commission also often serves as a convenient scapegoat for such officials. Although enabling statutes based on the original model act typically do not require proposed zoning amendments to be referred to a planning or zoning commission,[65] modern enabling statutes and local zoning ordinances commonly require such referral for "study and investigation" and a written report by the planning body.[66] It is not uncommon for the enabling statute or ordinance to impose a deadline (e.g., 45 days) for receipt of written recommendations from the planning agency and to provide that if recommendations are not received within that time, the proposed amendment is deemed approved or introduced in the form of a proposed ordinance and may be acted on by the legislative body without the planning agency's formal report.[67]

The planning agency review process may include a considerable amount of give and take between the landowner proposing an amendment and the

planning agency. Some modern ordinances contemplate and encourage negotiation with express provisions for resubmittal of revised petitions to the planning agency that incorporate agency comments and recommendations prior
to transmittal of the formal report to the legislative body.[68] At this stage in the
process, negotiating skills and flexibility produce more favorable results than
do adversarial skills. The staff, planning commission, and, to some extent, the
legislative body have considerable leverage over the applicant primarily in
the form of lack of tolerance for delay in the project and expense of litigation
and secondarily of deferential standards of judicial review if the application is
litigated.

Although a favorable recommendation from the planning agency does
not guarantee legislative approval of a proposed zoning amendment, the
requirement that zoning decisions be based on a rational planning process,
including the necessity for establishing a nexus between ends and means,[69]
imposes a clear responsibility on the legislative body to consider seriously the
findings and recommendations of the planning agency. Zoning statutes
require a supermajority vote for enactment of a zoning amendment or special-
procedure ordinance contrary to a planning agency recommendation,[70]
although a given statute may not define "contrary." A contrary planning and
zoning commission recommendation may also be used as evidence against the
zoning authority.[71]

The Public Hearing Before the Planning Commission

Statutes and ordinances usually require planning agencies to conduct public
hearings as part of the process of review for zoning amendment petitions.[72] In
many cases, the result is two hearings: one before the planning agency and
one before the legislative body. That practice, however, is not universal.[73]
Ordinances may require the public hearing to be set within a prescribed time,
such as 90 days, from the date of the filing of a petition for rezoning.[74]

Public notice requirements, like many features in the zoning process, are
set forth redundantly in both the enabling statute and the local ordinance.
Notice often must be given in more than one form, including mailing or deliv-
ering notice to the owner of the affected property, the project applicant, and
the property owners within a specified distance from the property, publication
in a newspaper of general circulation in the community, and posting of signs
on the premises in question announcing the proposed rezoning and the date
of the public hearing.[75] Copies of the hearing notice may also be required to
be sent to public agencies affected by the proposal, such as highway departments, parks and recreation agencies, public works departments, and water
and sewer districts. Public agencies of the jurisdiction before which the zoning amendment is pending may be required to submit any comments to both
the planning agency and the petitioner within a specified number of days
prior to the hearing.[76]

Defects in notice, such as failure to provide personal notice, as well as constructive notice, may not be jurisdictional or fatal, at least when there is proof
both of actual notice at the hearing of the complaining party or counsel in person
and of failure to object to inadequate notice.[77] When a rezoning is accomplished

by the adoption of a general comprehensive development plan, there may be no constitutional right to personal notice of the proposed rezoning.[78]

The public hearing before the planning agency need not be a formal, record proceeding as long as all interested persons are given a reasonable opportunity to receive information and express their views regarding the proposal.[79] The format is legislative, not adjudicative, and the rules of evidence do not apply. Because judicial review is not based on the record but is typically de novo, the record, if any, is informal—but certainly any statements may later be significant as admissions of a party. Some states do require public hearings to be conducted according to specified procedures. For example, California requires zoning agencies to formulate and publish procedural rules for the conduct of public hearings. A record must be made and preserved when a matter is contested, with copies available at cost. Planning staff reports must be made public prior to or at the beginning of the hearing and must be made part of the public record.[80]

Perhaps in the interest of consistency and due process, some states have mandated more formal hearings, with provisions for issuing subpoenas, taking testimony under oath, and permitting cross-examination at the discretion of the presiding officer, who may impose reasonable limitations on speaking time and number of speakers.[81] Several states authorize the hearing to be conducted by appointed hearing officers.[82] As already noted, technical rules of evidence are not applicable, but irrelevant, immaterial, or unduly repetitious evidence may be excluded.[83]

Planning Commission Report to the Legislative Body

The amendment procedures within comprehensive zoning ordinances commonly require, consistent with the enabling statute, a written report of the planning agency to the legislative body, commenting on the proposed rezoning.[84] The purpose of the report is to give the legislative body an objective and often more technical or professional analysis of the proposal under submission, as well as to inform it of the impact of the rezoning. The report also organizes and distills the issues, often deflecting a certain amount of debate away from the legislative docket. The planning commission is created as an administrative body of nonelected citizens with experience in real estate development, whereas elected legislative officials may have no particular expertise.

In some communities, the planning agency report is a basis for negotiations between the petitioner and the community to resolve differences concerning specific aspects of the petitioner's proposed use of the land in question. The ordinances may even require the planning agency to submit its findings and recommendations to the petitioner before they are transmitted to the city's legislative body. The petitioner is given an opportunity to consider the recommendations of the planning agency and may incorporate those recommendations into an amended petition, which is then resubmitted to the planning agency.[85] In this process, the landowner has an opportunity to respond to the planning agency's evaluation before the agency takes final action and submits its recommendations to the legislative body. The opportunity to respond to the planning agency at this stage of the process can be particularly important in jurisdictions that require a supermajority vote by the legislative body to override a recommendation of the planning agency.[86]

The Legislative Public Hearing

As is the case for all municipal ordinances, a public hearing must be held prior to a vote on a zoning amendment.[87] The hearing is a legislative, rather than judicial, proceeding, and the formalities of the judicial process need not be observed. Because of the tension between the legislative and adjudicatory functions previously noted,[88] however, several states require the legislative body to make findings of fact and conclusions of law. The Maryland statute is illustrative:

> Where the purpose and effect of the proposed amendment is to change the zoning classification, the local legislative body shall make findings of fact in each specific case including, but not limited to, the following matters: population change, availability of public facilities, present and future transportation patterns, compatibility with existing and proposed development for the area, the recommendation of the planning commission, and the relationship of such proposed amendment to the jurisdiction's plan.[89]

The Washington Supreme Court, concluding that rezoning ordinances are adjudicatory rather than legislative in character, has imposed on local legislative bodies the requirement that a record of the proceedings be kept and that written "findings of fact be made and conclusions or reasons based thereon be given for the action taken."[90] The written findings and conclusions are necessary, in the court's view, for two reasons: (1) to give guidance to the developer who may wish to respond to the objections of the legislative body by modifying the rezoning proposal or preparing another application, and (2) to facilitate appellate review of the legislative body's decision.[91] Failure to enter such findings and conclusions has been held to constitute arbitrary or capricious action, rendering the subsequent decision regarding the rezoning proposal invalid.[92]

The Supreme Court of Delaware similarly has reasoned that local legislative bodies must establish records or give reasons for their rezoning decisions because courts would have no basis for reviewing a zoning decision without such record or reasons. Because the zoning power is delegated by the state to local governments subject to certain standards, such as consistency with a comprehensive plan, exercise of that power is subject to judicial review to determine compliance with the statutory standards. Such review, the court concluded, requires evidence of the reasons for the action.[93]

A California statute underscores the importance of the public hearing and the making of a record by limiting the issues that may be raised in a legal attack on a rezoning decision to issues raised at the public hearing or in written correspondence delivered to the agency conducting the hearing prior to or at the hearing. A new issue may be raised, however, if the court finds that either the issues could not have been raised at the hearing through reasonable diligence or the issue was not permitted to be raised at the hearing by the agency conducting the hearing.[94]

In many states, however, review of purely legislative zoning decisions is by plenary de novo action, and judicial review is not based on the underlying record but on evidence offered at a trial in the reviewing court.[95]

As a legislative process, zoning matters are a work in progress, and new issues or concerns often arise "off record," either in the nonpublic portion of city council meetings or between meetings via nonpublic lobbying efforts. Although such uncertainty is unavoidable, the advocate must monitor the process by staying in contact with city staff. The applicant may be denied due process when not given the opportunity to respond to concerns that are raised in private or at least after the public portion of the meeting.[96]

Voting Requirements for Enactment

Legislative land use regulations are subject to the entire body of municipal procedural law, usually including Robert's Rules of Order, applicable to other forms of local regulation. This body of law includes voting requirements, abstentions,[97] requirements for a quorum, conflicts of interest,[98] and recordkeeping.

Enactment of a rezoning ordinance usually requires a simple majority vote. Many jurisdictions, however, require a supermajority, typically a three-fourths or two-thirds vote, if the voting body receives a written protest by a specified number of landowners (e.g., 10 percent) living within a measured area of land subject to the proposal (e.g., 185 feet from the boundary of the rezoned parcel).[99]

According extra weight to the opinions of adjacent landowners, especially without any requirement of a basis for opposition, may be carried too far, however. In one case, a Virginia statute required a local board of supervisors to obtain the consent of all affected property owners to zoning changes within a certain transportation improvement district. The consent requirement was struck down as an unlawful delegation of legislative power to private individuals.[100]

In practice, compliance with notice requirements is critical because an opposing party, even if given actual notice and in attendance at the hearing, may argue that the protest/supermajority feature may have been triggered if parties who did not receive notice had appeared and protested. In addition, the opposing party may have argued that the outcome could have been affected by more public debate. When failure of notice is deliberate, attorneys' fees may be awarded to the prevailing landowners and against the applicant.[101] Exercise of the right to protest is not evidence of a conspiracy to deprive a landowner of constitutional rights.[102]

The Zoning Amendment Ordinance

A change in zoning regulations is accomplished by passage of an ordinance by the local legislative body. Standards applicable to enactment of municipal ordinances generally are applicable to zoning amendment ordinances, with the additional limitation that zoning ordinances generally may not be formally introduced until the planning agency has submitted its report, if one is required, or the deadline for submitting the report has passed.[103]

As noted previously, although there is no general requirement that municipal legislation be supported by findings of fact, an increasing number of states are requiring such findings as part of the ordinance or otherwise, because of the "resemblance" that legislative rezonings have to judicial determinations.[104]

Special-Use Permits

The second major method of land use regulation is the special-use permit, sometimes called a special-exception or a conditional-use permit ("C.U.P."). The classic zoning ordinance identifies two classes of authorized uses: "permitted" and "conditional" uses. Conditional uses are allowed only by conditional-use permit. The conditional use is best viewed as a probationary use and legal only upon meeting certain extra standards. It is usually subject to conditions set forth in a specific written special-use or conditional-use permit granted after a quasi-judicial public hearing.[105]

The basic standards governing whether to allow the particular use, as well as the power to place some limits on the use not imposed on other, permitted uses, are codified in the special-use permit section of the comprehensive zoning ordinance. Most courts, therefore, consider the decision of whether to issue a special-use permit, which usually is made by an administrative agency such as a zoning board of adjustment[106] or a planning agency,[107] to be "an administrative decision quasi-judicial in nature."[108] The Iowa Supreme Court has characterized the role of the special permit–issuing agency as follows:

> As the arbiter and dispenser of these permits, the Zoning Board serves in an ancillary role of implementing the city's land use policy and allocating land use to accomplish changes without intervention of a formal amendment of a zoning ordinance.[109]

Special-use permits differ from zoning amendments, which are legislatively granted changes in the range of permitted uses within a particular zoning district, and variances, which are administratively granted waivers of prohibitions on uses or objective standards such as height, area, or setback limitations. The special-use permit process is not applicable unless the proposed use is expressly authorized as a special or conditional use in the applicable zoning district section of the comprehensive zoning ordinance. Special-use permits thus are legislatively authorized but administratively issued.

The special-use permit device, while adding some flexibility to the zoning laws, also allows a municipality to regulate more closely particular types of more controversial or problematic uses, such as automobile service stations, drive-through fast-food restaurants, convenience stores, trash disposal sites, and taverns. Special uses may provide desirable services for residents but because of traffic, hours of operation, noise, or other unpleasant side effects, "may or may not be in accord with the general purpose and intent of the municipality's land policy and the surrounding environment."[110]

An administrative agency such as the zoning board of adjustment or the planning agency is often the authority responsible for issuing special-use permits, although in some cases the city council may serve this function, particularly when the permit process is combined with more sophisticated techniques of flexibility, such as the planned unit development (PUD) device.[111]

Application for Special-Use Permit

The application for a special-use permit is similar to the application for a zoning amendment, except that it typically calls for more detail. Because the special-use permit is by definition a fine-tuning of the regulatory process, the regulating agency needs more information concerning the proposed use and the surrounding property than in the case of a pure zoning amendment. Application forms are prescribed by the administering agency, and copies generally must be submitted simultaneously to the administering agency and the planning agency. Ordinances may also require that written notification of the filing of an application for a special-use permit be sent to the elected representative of the district in which the land subject to the permit application is located.[112]

The application is filed with the administrative agency that has been delegated the power to issue such permits and is referred to the planning agency for its review and analysis if the planning agency is not the issuing agency.

Standards for Grant or Denial of Special-Use Permit

A typical comprehensive zoning ordinance sets up a set of standards albeit in general, subjective terms, for the grant of special-use permits. Following is one set of special or conditional-use standards:

> **Standards.** No special use shall be granted by the Zoning Board of Appeals unless the special use:
>
> (1) (a) Is necessary for the public convenience at that location; (b) Is so designed, located and proposed to be operated that the public health, safety and welfare will be protected; and
>
> (2) Will not cause substantial injury to the value of other property in the neighborhood in which it is to be located; and
>
> (3) It is within the provisions of "Special Uses" as set forth in the applicable sections in Articles 7, 8, 9 and 10 or pursuant to Section 6.5-4(4); and
>
> (4) Such special use shall conform to the applicable regulations of the district in which it is to be located; and
>
> (5) In a Planned Manufacturing District, Special Uses shall conform to all applicable regulations and standards as set forth in Title 17, and in addition shall also conform to the supplemental use regulations as set forth in 16-8-080-4(a-e).
>
> The standards set forth in this section shall not apply to adult uses.[113]

The Supreme Court of Iowa upheld an ordinance that required special uses to "be harmonious with and in accordance with the general principles and proposals of the Land Use Policy Plan." The ordinance also required, among other things, that the proposed use not change the "essential character" of the area, that the use improve nearby property, that existing public facilities be adequate, and that the use "be consistent with the intent and purpose of the zoning district in which it is proposed to locate such use." In sustaining the ordinance against a challenge that it was unconstitutionally vague, the court stated:

> While the ordinance does rely on general standards, these guidelines are designed to allow the Board to make findings and determinations that are appropriate to the peculiar circumstances presented by each special use application. . . . [Z]oning standards need not be so detailed as to eliminate entirely any element of discretion from the Board's decision.[114]

In this vein, it is not unusual to encounter a special use standard which requires "compliance with this comprehensive zoning ordinance."

Standards must be "specific enough to be uniformly applied so as to instruct an applicant as to his burden of proof and to provide an adequate framework for review,"[115] but may not be based on "irrational prejudice" against special categories such as mentally retarded persons.[116]

An ordinance requiring a finding of public necessity for the grant of a conditional-use permit was upheld against a landowner's claim that the requirement invalidly required showing of "absolute public need," the court interpreting the requirement to mean that the public interest and welfare must be weighed against the individual interest adversely affected by issuance of the permit.[117]

Delegation of Decision-Making Authority to Administrative Agency

The specific standards for granting a special-use permit must also be sufficiently definite to avoid charges of unlawful delegation of legislative authority, while at the same time flexible enough to provide sufficient discretion to the administering agency so that changes in land use can be accomplished without effectively amending the zoning code.[118]

Although conditional-use permits are typically considered and approved by the local legislative body (acting administratively), where that authority is delegated to a nonelected body, the issue of unlawful delegation arises. Where the special-use permitting process is simply the application of stated standards to specific requests, delegation to an agency of the authority to do so has been approved by the courts. Provided the delegation is accompanied by standards that are sufficiently definite to enable the agency to "make findings and determinations that are appropriate to the peculiar circumstances presented by each special use application," courts are unlikely to invalidate the delegation.[119] Under this test, standards containing language such as "harmonious" and "hazardous or disturbing to existing or future uses" have been upheld.[120]

When a zoning board of adjustment considers an application for a special-use permit, it is exercising original rather than appellate jurisdiction and does not have to make the "hardship" or "difficulties" findings required of variances.[121]

The Special-Use Permit Public Hearing

Like the other major regulatory devices—rezoning and the variance—the special-use permit may not be granted without a public hearing upon prior notice.[122] Because of the administrative/adjudicatory nature of the permit process, the agency must take care in the conduct of the hearing and the presentation of evidence. Appeals from agency decisions generally are governed by the state administrative procedure statute and are based on the record established before the agency, with the hearing being the focal point for the development of the record. In an increasing number of jurisdictions, full- or part-time hearing examiners are appointed and delegated the responsibility to conduct public hearings for various aspects of the land use regulatory process, including applications for special-use permits.[123]

If substantial changes in the scope of the proposed permit occur after a hearing, the proposed action may have to be readvertised and a new hearing conducted. For example, the Maryland Court of Appeals concluded that a change in a proposed zoning amendment shifting airport use from a proposed category of nonconforming use—subject to stringent restrictions on expansion as well as an amortization provision—to a proposed category of conditional use—under which existing airports would be grandfathered and not be subject to the amortization requirement—was such a substantial change that a second public hearing focusing on the conditional-use proposal was required before valid action could be taken on the proposal.[124]

Issuance of the Special-Use Permit

As already noted on page 226, "Standard for Grant or Denial of Special-Use Permits," ordinances providing for the issuance of special-use permits generally proscribe required elements. Following are typical jurisdictional standards:

1. The use will not be detrimental to public health, safety, morals, or general welfare.
2. The use will not cause serious injury to neighboring property use or values.
3. The use will enhance the specific location.
4. The use will be compatible with surrounding use and will not have a negative impact on adjacent uses or community facilities.
5. The use will be compatible with the plan for the area in question and will comply with all applicable zoning standards and regulations.[125]

Most notably, the issuing agency may, and by definition is, expected to impose "conditions reasonably necessary to meet such standards."[126] A provision authorizing the imposition of conditions is designed to permit only such conditions as are necessary to ensure compliance with the jurisdictional standards, and does not authorize the imposition of a requirement that a supermajority approve the grant when neighbors protest the proposed action.[127]

Special-use permit standards are jurisdiction limiting. Theoretically, administrative discretion may not go beyond determining compliance with the stated standards. Once a determination is made that a proposed use complies with the applicable standards, the administering agency is obligated to issue a special-use permit, regardless of the feelings of neighboring residents who oppose the issuance of the permit.[128] For the advocate, this distinction between the special-use permit and the rezoning is critical. The permit process, in theory, is not a political referendum on the right to the use per se, but an examination of reasonable conditions on the use, which is by definition permitted in the subject district. Thus the advocate must not let the conditions destroy the use.

In practice, however, the public regards the permit process often as broadly as the rezoning. As is evident from the previous example, the permit standards are broad and subjective. A creative or ambitious agency member may assert free range approaching the power of a legislator. In turn, the process often becomes as political as a legislative rezoning, even though judicial review is substantially less deferential and based on the administrative record. In such cases, counsel for the agency will be most challenged in protecting the process from degenerating into a purely political referendum.

The Zoning Variance

The third major regulatory device is the zoning variance. The variance is an exception or exemption from strict application of a zoning ordinance when such application would result in special hardship to the property owner.[129] The variance is available by express authorization in zoning-enabling legislation,[130] and in some cases by implication from application of the "vested rights" theory.[131] The variance is viewed by some as necessary to defuse specific and limited situations that might give lie to constitutional challenges if the zoning ordinance were applied literally. As such, it is a legal safety valve.

There are two types of variances: the most familiar, the *area* variance; and the more rare, the *use* variance. The area variance grants relief from objective physical standards such as height, density, area, and setback restrictions. The use variance permits a use other than that permitted in the particular district. As such, it is a close cousin of the zoning amendment[132] and not available in all jurisdictions. The distinction between the area and use variance is usually obvious and is important because different issuance standards apply.[133]

Standards for Grant or Denial of a Variance

The power to grant or deny a variance is considered an "exceptional" power that can be "validly used only where a situation falls fully within the specified conditions."[134] Enabling legislation and zoning ordinances uniformly require a finding of "unnecessary hardship," a term used in the Standard State Zoning Act, although several states have added an alternative standard of "practical difficulties," coined initially by a 1920 amendment to the General City Law of New York, the first comprehensive zoning law.[135] Some ordinances also authorize a variance when the effect of zoning is "arbitrary."[136]

Many courts have struggled with application and refinement of these standards. Some courts consider the standard of "practical difficulties" too indefinite to be enforced and focus on what is considered the more restrictive "hardship" standard.[137] Other courts draw a distinction between use and area variances, granting a use variance only where there is unnecessary hardship, and an area variance when an owner can show practical difficulties.[138] The courts are not above missing the distinction between rezoning, which should be reserved for policy-making elected officials, and granting of variances by a nonelected body (the board of adjustment) in a quasi-judicial proceeding, based on a narrow definition of hardship.[139]

Unnecessary hardship is established when the record shows "(1) the land in question cannot yield a reasonable return if used only for a purpose allowed in the zone;[140] (2) that the plight of the owner is due to unique circumstances and not to the general conditions of the neighborhood, which may reflect the unreasonableness of zoning itself; and (3) that the uses to be authorized by the variance will not alter the essential character of the locality."[141]

When the hardship is self-imposed, as where property is purchased with knowledge that it does not comply with minimum lot requirements, the zoning board should deny the variance.[142] Reliance by a builder on an error by a city official who granted a permit for a building that violated the city's height restrictions was held to be an insufficient basis for a variance, with the court holding that reasonable diligence by the builder would have disclosed the actual height restriction.[143]

Dimensional, or *area*, variances have two sets of prerequisites, affirmative and negative, both of which must be established by the applicant "by a fair preponderance of the evidence." Affirmative prerequisites address the "physical peculiarit[ies] or exceptional situation or condition of the land," where the negative prerequisites require a showing that "no substantial detriment will be inflicted upon the public good and the intent and purpose of the zone plan and ordinance will not be substantially adversely affected."[144] Legislative modifications in New Jersey have been held to permit dimensional variances without a showing of hardship when "the characteristics of the land . . . present an opportunity for improved zoning and planning that will benefit the community."[145]

Area variances generally require less stringent standards than use variances. Courts are moving toward a balancing test in which the inquiry is whether strict application of the zoning ordinance will serve a valid public purpose that outweighs any injury to the landowner. In applying that test, a New York court required a zoning board to examine (1) the substantiality of the requested variance, (2) whether the variance would cause substantial change, and (3) whether alternatives for resolving the problem existed and whether justice was served by granting the variance.[146]

The Supreme Court of Missouri has approved use variances when the applicant establishes four elements: (1) there is unnecessary hardship in carrying out the strict letter of the ordinance; (2) the unique nature of the property makes relief necessary; (3) granting of the variance will not destroy the preservation of the plan; and (4) granting of the variance will result in "substantial justice for all."[147] Unnecessary hardship is the principal basis and may be proved by showing either deprivation of *any* permitted use or "unwarranted economic hardship" in achieving a permitting use.[148]

Some states have relaxed the unnecessary hardship test for use variances by substituting the statutory standard of "special reasons."[149] The New Jersey standard is further defined by two sets of elements: (1) statutory negative criteria that the variance will not be a substantial detriment to the public good and will not substantially impair the intent and purpose of the zoning plan and ordinance;[150] and (2) court-established affirmative criteria that the use variance will contribute to the general welfare or promote one or more of the purposes of zoning as defined by the statute, a test that proved relatively easy for a proposed institutional use to meet but considerably more difficult for a commercial use.[151]

As noted earlier, at some point the use variance resembles actual legislation to amend the zoning ordinance. Although presumably a higher burden of proof distinguishes use variances from rezoning cases, the result is essentially the same. The process by which the variance is achieved is probably lower in profile and the scope of judicial review less deferential than in the case of a rezoning. In one case, the court analyzed the uniqueness element of variance analysis in distinguishing it from the legislative process of rezoning.[152] As the affected parcel becomes smaller, the variance seems more appropriate to avoid a spot zoning result.[153] Conversely, as the number of parcels and overall amount of property affected by the change in permitted use becomes larger, rezoning is more compelling. "[W]here the hardship imposed on the applicant's land is shared by nearby land, relief should be addressed through legislative, rather than administrative means."[154] In reality, most rezonings are instigated by a single owner/developer and are concerned more with specifically tailoring a planned district to the proposed use and regulating that use than with expanding the permitted uses from those permitted by the existing zoning ordinance. In summary, the use variance may be most appropriate where hardship and uniqueness may be proved, but the local government's need to tailor zoning to the specific use, such as in a planned commercial district, is not present.

Finally, variances may be issued with conditions.[155] In one case, an owner wanted to build a 12-foot-high chainlink fence around a tennis court in an area where the zoning ordinance limited fence height to eight feet. The agency granted the variance, subject to the condition that the owner lower an existing 8-foot block wall to 42 inches. The board was aware that the owner was subject to a restrictive covenant requiring a block wall of at least five feet. The condition was upheld on appeal. The court ruled not only that the board had jurisdiction to impose conditions, but also that "restrictive covenants do not control a decision on the question of whether a variance should be granted."[156]

Ethical Issues

Local government is a complex, often amorphous, organization of full- and part-time staff, outside consultants such as planners, engineers, and lawyers, volunteer members of commissions, and politicians. These participants represent at least as many perspectives and agendas. This political complexity makes representing the municipality, or a private citizen before a municipality, like no other area of law practice. In assessing the actors' motives, exposure to public scrutiny, and susceptibility to the power of the media, the practice requires special sensitivity and finesse.

The land use lawyer's challenge is made greater by a specific set of ethical standards, in addition to the lawyer's own rules of professional conduct, that regulate ethical conduct of public officials.[157] The lawyer must be sensitive to proscriptions governing the conduct of, including contact with, such officials.

The issue that arises most frequently is conflict of interest.[158] Although the lawyer is, of course, governed at all times by his or her own rules against representing parties with adverse interests,[159] it is usually the conflict of interest of the public official that is at issue. Litigation focuses on the nature of the "interest"—statutes typically requiring an objective, economic interest such as a minimum ownership interest—and the directness of the connection. In many small municipalities, decision-making bodies are small in number, quorums are difficult, and most officials have some degree of prior contact, if not pecuniary relationship, with the applicant or the opposition. Indeed, a person is often elected as a result of prior active participation in an issue. Political campaigns and contributions are frequent areas of focus in this area, especially regarding large regional issues such as entertainment developments. In general, courts recognize this problem and view claims of conflicts of interest with deference to the official. "[P]ublic policy strongly encourges the giving and receiving of campaign contributions. Such actions are constitutionally protected and do not automatically create an appearance of unfairness."[160]

Once there is a conflict of interest, both voting and participation, without voting, may be proscribed. Participation is an especially broad concept and may include mere attendance at nonpublic work sessions or public meetings, even without speaking.

It is not feasible for the lawyer to investigate and rule out all such conflicts or potential conflicts. At a minimum, however, he or she should know the applicable statute and ordinances governing conflicts. The lawyer should then attempt, within reason, to learn the occupation of each member of the applicable commission or city council and inquire of the client as to any knowledge of, or relationship with, such officials. In cases where there is indication of possible conflict, the lawyer may obtain copies of disclosures required to be filed by elected officials. Such filings often are required to disclose companies in which the official has a "substantial interest."[161]

In most cases the official will identify the conflict and recuse himself or herself. If the official does not, however, the proceedings are exposed to invalidation by litigation or otherwise. The client will not be helped by the favorable vote of an official with a conflict of interest. Conversely, an unfairly biased official who successfully opposes an approval will expose the municipality to needless litigation.[162] In either event, a reviewing court is likely to view the conflict as invalidating the entire process, even where the offending vote did not figure in the final count.[163]

A conflict of interest may be more likely to be found in a quasi-judicial administrative proceeding than in a legislative proceeding such as a rezoning. One court has noted that "[i]n the legislative arena, there is no constitutional due process requirement of neutral decision makers. Instead, the check on the process is the ballot box."[164]

The participation of a member with a prohibited conflict of interest may be less likely to invalidate a proceeding, or even be viewed as a conflict in the first place, where his or her vote was not necessary to the outcome.[165]

A second common problem area is the revolving door. Many lawyers serve as city council members or as municipal counsel. The lawyers' Code of Professional Responsibility specifically prohibits a lawyer from representing private parties in connection with any matter in which he or she participated as a public official or an employee of a public body.[166]

A third area of frequent concern is the ex parte contact. The American Bar Associaton (ABA) Disciplinary Rule 7-104 provides that a lawyer may not

> [c]ommunicate or cause another to communicate on the subject of the representation with a party he knows to be represented by a lawyer in that matter unless he has the prior consent of the lawyer representing such other party or is authorized by law to do so.

This rule has been expressly stated not to apply to communications with government agencies because such communications are "authorized by law."[167] Typically, the lawyer will have direct contact with municipal officials long before any contact with the municipality's lawyer. This is an accepted mode of land use practice. The ex parte contact most often at issue refers to contacts with public officials outside of the public record. This type of contact is typically accepted in purely legislative matters but prohibited in administrative or adjudicative matters.[168] The distinction recognizes the political nature of rezonings and the importance of procedural safeguards in administrative and adjudicative hearings in which decisions are made on the basis of a record.

Other, less common areas of ethical concern in land use matters are the doctrines of "prejudgment," the relatively new problem of bad faith or appearance of fairness, and dual office holding.[169]

Municipal attorneys in private practice, especially those in large law firms with many clients whose firms also represent major cities, should be sensitive to the appearance of conflicts, even if the same do not invalidate the outcome.[170]

Finally, many land use lawyers are also lobbyists. Many public officials welcome direct contact by the land use advocate, but some may resist or even resent such contacts. It is helpful to contact city staff or the city's counsel regarding the wisdom—politically, if not ethically—of such approaches. In fact, some municipalities expressly prohibit or regulate such contacts and state sunshine acts may define regulated open meetings requiring notice and accessibility, to include such contacts.

Practitioner Perspectives

At the outset of a local land use matter, the attorney must counsel the client on the most advantageous vehicle for obtaining the client's building permit. As has been discussed, the zoning amendment, special-use permit, and variance are distinct but sometimes overlapping approval mechanisms. The advice of the zoning adminstrator about the appropriate vehicle, while presumptively acceptable, must be viewed critically. For example, the use variance resembles the zoning amendment, and application for a variance may permit the client to bypass an elected, legislative body and proceed directly through a board of adjustment to the local circuit court. Of course, in some circumstances, the board of adjustment does not act entirely independently of the elected officials, at least in the political sense. At any rate, the attorney must view the distinctions between the three processes skeptically and always with an eye toward whether it is necessary to make a record for ultimate judicial review or to avoid making a record or unnecessary assertions. As noted throughout this book, it is a rare development project that can accommodate the expense and delay of litigating with the authority; no attorney can competently represent his or her client, however, without assuming a judicial outcome.

Where judicial review will be limited to the municipal record, there are methods to walk the line between making a thorough, favorable record for litigation and offending the authority or risking creating new issues by overly lengthy, legalistic, or adversarial presentations. One such method is to submit written statements as exhibits without reading the statements in public. This approach permits an applicant to take aggressive approaches, even to the extent of citing specific legal authorities, without alienating swing votes. In all administrative matters, the applicant's attorney should verify or secure court reporting in advance of the applicable meetings, even including meetings at which no "public hearing," per se, is scheduled.

Successful representation in the land use regulatory process requires knowledge at several levels: (1) the basic principles of land use law, including litigation and civil procedure, (2) local rules and regulations, (3) general attitudes about land development in the community and specific positions on other controversial projects, and (4) physical details of the project at issue.[171] In addition to such knowledge, however, the practitioner and his or her client cannot proceed without credibility. In most, but not all cases, the practitioner must be willing and able to approach the staff, administrative body, elected legislative officials, and the public with respect and knowledge. The process is both legal and political. It is perhaps political first and legal/adversarial only second; many successful practitioners use the client's legal authority subtly and only as background leverage.

Most rezoning efforts benefit from a team approach. Certainly most applicants will not rely solely on an attorney to present the proposal. Composition of the team will vary, but members often include one or more of the client's business representative, legal counsel, a professional planner, an engineer or surveyor (depending on the jurisdictional requirements for certain functions), a traffic engineer, design specialists including architects and landscape designers, and increasingly more often now, an environmental engineer for impact studies. These roles often overlap, and many consulting firms offer these services.

It is not uncommon for a developer to have several professionals with whom he or she is comfortable. In that instance, practitioners need only be concerned with the quality of their work and their suitability for the jurisdiction. In other cases, practitioners may be asked to recommend consultants or to organize the development team. This recommendation can be appropriate, but it is not without risk. Not only will the practitioner have responsibility for legal work, but he or she will also be concerned with (and may be perceived as responsible for) the quality of the other professionals' work. In either case, the client should be asked to meet the consultants. The client, rather than the lawyer, should contract with the professionals chosen for the development team.

The nature of the political process varies widely from municipality to municipality, notwithstanding a common set of enabling statutes. Disagreements may reside at the higher level of policy determination about which people may legitimately disagree, for example, the extent to which growth in the jurisdiction should be encouraged or discouraged, and the form that land development should take; or, more commonly, debate may degenerate into unprincipled, ad hoc decision making. To participate effectively in the process, the practitioner must understand the political background of local land use decisions. Thus, knowing the players is an important part of evaluating a land use case.

Most land use applications proceed in the order of the land use staff, the planning body, and the legislative body.

Staff

Planning and zoning staff are usually professionals in a local planning department or representatives of other key agencies who have technical responsibility in land use matters such as public works, transportation, water, and sewer departments; however, the level of initiative, power, competence, and even integrity of these individuals is highly variable. To the extent that the agencies will provide either support or opposition to a proposal through a technical evaluation process or as advisors to the other players, it is essential that land use practitioners develop relationships with the staff, when possible, in an appropriate but positive way. Most, but not all, jurisdictions rely heavily on staff to distill project data and to screen for violations.

The practitioner should meet with staff prior to filing an application to solicit constructive comments or discuss legitimate concerns that may be addressed in the formal application or the presentation. When possible, the preliminary meetings should include the development team member, typically a project manager or engineer, who represents the discipline of the staff member. It is rarely effective for the applicant's attorney to meet with staff alone. In fact, early meetings are often best conducted without legal counsel, depending on the staff's attitude and the project's size.

Prior to the meeting, the client must consider how much flexibility it has with respect to the land use request. For example, if current regulations permit two houses per acre and the proposal calls for six houses per acre, the client might be asked whether a compromise of three, four, or five units per acre would still allow the client to complete the project with a reasonable profit.

If the jurisdiction or the area of law is new, a good way to get a sense for the staff's position and personality is to attend other public hearings in which the staff participates or to review previous reports that it may have filed in similar cases. It is also efficient to follow current and past agendas via the Internet.

The Planning Body

As noted in chapter 2, the planning board is most often a group of laypersons with some real estate, engineering, construction, or development experience but without formal planning training. Although the planning board may have final authority on some decisions, it is more often an advisory board to the legislative body charged with the ultimate zoning authority and is usually appointed by that body.

As with the staff, it is important to understand the dynamics of the planning board and the particular interests of individual members. Because planning board members usually come from different backgrounds and different geographic areas of the jurisdiction, each member may view certain aspects of a presentation differently. To the extent a planning board member advocates an agenda, it is important to understand that agenda and either embrace it or avoid it, as necessary.

The Elected Body

Like the planning board, the elected body, whether a city council, a board of county commissioners, or other governing body, is usually made up of laypersons without particular land use experience. Because zoning is just one of the many responsibilities of the local legislature, the political ramifications of zoning decisions may cause pure planning considerations to be outweighed by political realities.

It is also important to know the relationship between the planning and legislative body (e.g., whether a positive planning board recommendation on a rezoning matter is essential politically to a favorable decision from the legislative body). If so, practitioners must concentrate heavily on the hearings and deliberations of the planning board and not rely on overcoming a negative recommendation before the legislative body. If the practitioner is new to the process, the best education is to attend other hearings and to review previous case reports.

When development team members, including the principals and all or some of the technical support people, are new to a community, it is helpful to introduce team members to the staff, planning board, and legislative body by including slides, photographs, and brief biographical sketches in the presentations. This will humanize the process and give the decision-makers a sense of the abilities and experience of the people behind the land use proposal under consideration. The political nature of the process, including nominally administrative matters, makes it imperative that the most favorable and most accurate picture of the development team and proposal be presented.

The Presentation

When the client and attorney have decided to move forward with a case, the strategy of the presentation is important. The primary, often only, objective is to win approval at the local level; however, as noted previously, the first legal decision is whether the proceeding is legislative only, and not on the record for purposes of judicial review, or administrative, in which the record is more important. If the latter is the case, the path to approval is affected by the need to make a record. Even in the latter case, however, some clients, after being fully informed by counsel of the risks, will have no intention of pursuing judicial relief and may be somewhat more casual, but practical, about making a record.

The second analysis is evaluating the presence, motivation, and sophistication of opposition, in the form of a hostile city or, as has become common, a hostile and litigious neighborhood, even where city approval seems likely.

In a basic rezoning case, the legal issues generally are secondary to political and even the more objective, but equally ephemeral, land use planning issues. The legal issues are basic: What do the enabling legislation, the applicable ordinance, and case law require to be proved as a matter of law? Planning boards and legislative bodies often spend little time on legal theories. On the other hand, a successful administrative proceeding that cannot withstand a legal challenge by neighbors is of little value to a client. As discussed frequently throughout this treatise, this is the balance the practitioner must strike.

It is important not only for the body before which a presentation is made but also for the development team to understand what is essential legally and to determine who will address particular issues. Usually the attorney begins the presentation by introducing the speakers and stating the procedural posture of the application. Next, one member of the development team, often an engineer, states the basic physical characteristics of the project—location, acreage, and the like—following with a detailed explanation of a site plan, with overhead exhibits. It is often best to close with comments and a request for approval from a business person, preferably one who will remain on site when the project is operational, to move from consultants to the owner and personalize the project.

Following is one attorney's superficial outline that is typical:

Issue	*Participant*	*Exhibits*
1. Population change	Planner	Report
2. Adequacy of public facilities	Engineer	Staff Reports
3. Present and future transportation patterns	Traffic Engineer	Traffic Study Staff Reports
4. Compatibility with existing and proposed development for the area	Planner Real Estate Broker	
5. Relation to the Comprehensive Plan	Planner	Staff Reports
6. Fiscal impact on local government	Planner	
7. Suitability of property in question to the uses permitted under existing and proposed zoning classifications	Engineer	
8. Change in character of the neighborhood where property is located	Planner	Neighborhood map with changes (e.g., rezonings)
9. Mistake in existing zoning classification	Attorney	

The attorney must be prepared to clean up any presentation, restating, in conclusory terms if necessary, how the facts comply with the specific legal standards, and always striving first for local approval, but with an eye toward judicial review of the outcome, which is discussed next.

Notes

1. *See* pp. 196–97, 207, 210–11. *See, e.g.,* Cal. Gov't Code, §§ 65853, 65901 (West 1996); Conn. Gen. Stat. §§ 8-3 and 8-7 (1997); Ky. Rev. Stat. Ann. §§ 100.211, 100.237, and 100.241 (Michie 1997); Mass. Ann. Laws ch. 40A, § 14; Md. Code Ann. Art. 66B, §§ 4.05 and 4.07 (1997); Mo. Rev. Stat. §§ 89.060 and 89.080–090 (1996); N.J. Stat. Ann. §§ 40:55D-62, 40:55D-67, 40:55D-70 (West 1997); Pa. Stat. Ann. tit. 53, §§ 10601 and 10614 (West 1997); Va. Code Ann. §§ 15.1–491 (Michie 1997).

2. *See, e.g.,* Fla. Stat. Ann. § 163.3202(3) (West 1997). *See generally* pp. 141–42.

3. *See, e.g.,* Pa. Stat. Ann. tit. 53, § 10614 (West 1996); Zoning Ordinance, City of Webster Groves, Missouri, Ord. No. 5906 § 20 (1956).

4. *See, e.g.,* Pa. Stat. Ann. tit. 53, § 10614 (West 1996).

5. *See, e.g., id.*

6. *See, e.g.,* Pa. Stat. Ann. tit. 53, §§ 10617 and 10617.2 (West 1996); Zoning Ordinance, City of Webster Groves, Missouri, Ord. No. 5906, § 20 (1956).

7. Pa. Stat. Ann. tit. 53, § 10617 (West 1996). See chapter 6, p. 254, regarding standing principles.

8. *See, e.g.,* City of New York v. Bilynn Realty Corp., 499 N.Y.S.2d 1011 (Sup. Ct. 1986); Stell v. Jay Hales Dev. Co., 15 Cal. Rptr. 2d 220 (Cal. Ct. App. 1992); Davis v. J.C. Nichols Co., 714 S.W.2d 679 (Mo. App. 1986).

9. Parkview Assocs. v. City of New York, 519 N.E.2d 1372, *cert. denied,* 488 U.S. 801 (1988). *See also* Permanent Fin. Corp. v. Montgomery County, 518 A.2d 123 (Md. 1986) (requiring postconstruction reduction in size of building that had been constructed in accordance with building permit).

10. Finucan, *Skyscraper Compromise,* Planning, June 1991, at 33.

11. Day v. Ryan, 560 N.E.2d 77, 83 (Ind. Ct. App. 1990).

12. *Id.*

13. *See, e.g.,* Pa. Stat. Ann. tit. 53, § 10616.1 (West 1996).

14. Pa. Stat. Ann. tit. 53, § 10617 (West 1996).

15. Radach v. Gunderson, 695 P.2d 128, 131 (Wash. Ct. App. 1985). For a discussion of municipal tort liability in connection with negligence on the part of a zoning administrator, *see* C. Sands, M. Libonat & J. Martinez, Local Government Law, ch. 27 (1985 & Supp. 1991).

16. *See* chapter 6.

17. Quinn v. Town of Dodgeville, 364 N.W.2d 149, 155 (Wis. 1985); *see also* Bowman v. Greene County Comm'n, 732 S.W.2d 223 (Mo. Ct. App. 1987).

18. *See, e.g.,* MacLean v. Zoning Bd. of Adjustment of Borough of Crafton, 185 A.2d 533, 537 (Pa. 1962) (board of adjustment has no jurisdiction where request amounts to a rezoning under the guise of a variance), *applied in* West Torresdale Civic Ass'n v. Zoning Bd. of Adjustment of City of Philadelphia, 513 A.2d 515 (Pa. Commw. Ct. 1986), *aff'd by divided vote,* 576 A.2d 352 (Pa. 1988) (use of variance to release seven acres from residential use restrictions to permit commercial use was legislative act amounting to zoning amendment and thus beyond the power of the zoning board of adjustment); Rosedale-Skinker Improvement Ass'n v. Bd. of Adjustment of City of St. Louis, 425 S.W.2d 929 (Mo. 1968).

19. West Torresdale Civic Ass'n, 513 A.2d at 515.

20. *See, e.g.,* Saunders v. City of Jackson, 511 So. 2d 902, 906–07 (Miss. 1987) (denial of rezoning to anchor restricted commercial zone on site of former governor's home upheld as

legislative decision. "Where . . . there is substantial evidence supporting both sides of a rezoning application, it is hard to see how the ultimate decision could be anything but 'fairly debatable.' . . ."); Treme v. St. Louis County, 609 S.W.2d 706, 711–12 (Mo. Ct. App. 1980) (citing cases).

21. The leading case espousing this view is Fasano v. Bd. of County Comm'rs, 507 P.2d 23 (Or. 1973), *as modified by* Neuberger v. City of Portland, 603 P.2d 771 (Or. 1979). *See also* Bd. of County Comm'rs of Brevard County v. Snyder, 627 So. 2d 469 (Fla. 1993).

22. *See, e.g.,* Conn. Gen. Stat. § 8-2; Pleasant Valley Neighborhood Ass'n v. Planning & Zoning Comm'n, 543 A.2d 296 (Conn. 1988).

23. *See generally* pp. 25–35.

24. *See, e.g.,* Bell v. City of Elkhorn, 364 N.W.2d 144, 148 (Wis. 1985) (spot zoning is "the practice whereby a single lot or area is granted privileges which are not granted or extended to other land in the vicinity in the same use district"); Schubach v. Silver, 336 A.2d 328 (Pa. 1975).

25. *See* pp. 25–28.

26. *Bell,* 364 N.W.2d at 148.

27. *Schubach,* 336 A.2d at 336; *see also* Green v. County Council of Sussex County, 508 A.2d 882, 889 (Del. Ch. 1986), *aff'd,* 516 A.2d 480 (Del. 1986) (discriminatory zoning regulation that serves no rational public purpose is illegal spot zoning).

28. For commentary on the use of zoning, *see* E. Bassett, Zoning (1940); R. Babcock, The Zoning Game (1966); C. Weaver & R. Babcock, City Zoning: The Once and Future Frontier (1979); R. Babcock & C. Siemon, The Zoning Game Revisited (1985); Zoning and the American Dream: Promises Still to Keep (C. Haar & J. Kayden eds., 1989).

29. Boland v. City of Great Falls, 910 P.2d 890 (Mont. 1996).

30. Greater Yellowstone Coalition, Inc. v. Bd. of County Comm'rs of Gallatin County, 25 P.3d 168, 171 (Mont. 2001).

31. *Bell,* 364 N.W.2d at 148.

32. Standard State Zoning Enabling Act, § 5, n. 30 (U.S. Dep't of Commerce, rev. ed. 1926), *republished in* ALI, Model Land Development Code, Appendix A, TOD No. 1 (1968); *but see* Bjarnson v. County of Kitsap, 899 P.2d 1290 (Wash. Ct. App. 1995) (change in circumstances not required).

33. People's Counsel for Baltimore County v. Beachwood I Ltd. P'ship, 670 A.2d 484 (Md. App. 1995).

34. *See, e.g.,* Md. Code Ann. Art 66B, § 4.05 (1997); Mayor & Comm'rs of City of Jackson v. Wheatley Place, Inc., 468 So. 2d 81, 83 (Miss. 1985).

35. Boyce v. Sembly, 334 A.2d 137, 142–43 (Md. App. 1975).

36. *Id.*

37. *City of Jackson,* 468 So. 2d at 83 ("In the absence of agreements between all interested parties, an amendment to a zoning ordinance is not meant to be easy.").

38. Standard State Zone Enabling Act § 5, n. 31 (U.S. Dep't of Commerce, rev. ed. 1926), *republished in* ALI, Model Land Development Code, Appendix A, Tent. Draft No. 1 (1968).

39. *Bell,* 364 N.W.2d at 148.

40. *Schubach,* 336 A.2d at 336–37.

41. *Bell,* 364 N.W.2d at 148.

42. *Schubach,* 336 A.2d at 336–37.

43. *Fasano,* 507 P.2d at 26.

44. *See* n. 37.

45. *See, e.g.,* N.J. Stat. Ann. § 40:55D-63 (West 1997) (two-thirds vote required upon written protest by 20 percent of landowners included in proposed change or within 200 feet); *Bell,* 364 N.W.2d at 144 (ordinance requiring a three-fourths vote of city council to approve a rezoning when owners of 20 percent of land within 100 feet of parcel to be rezoned file protest).

46. *See, e.g.,* City of Eastlake v. Forest City Enter., Inc., 426 U.S. 668 (1976) (use of referendum with supermajority requirement (55 percent) for approval of zoning change does not violate the due process clause of the Fourteenth Amendment).

47. *See, e.g.,* Margolis v. District Court, 638 P.2d 297 (Colo. 1981) (rezoning is legislative for initiative/referendum purposes but quasi-judicial for purposes of determining standard for judicial review); Arnel Dev. Co. v. City of Costa Mesa, 620 P.2d 565 (Cal. 1980) (rezonings are legislative in character, regardless of the size of the tract). *See generally* Dukeminier & Krier, PROPERTY, 1170–72 (2d ed. 1988), discussing conflicting views concerning the *Fasano* rationale for characterizing zoning amendments as either legislative or adjudicative in nature.

48. N.J. STAT. ANN. § 40:55D-62 (West 1997).

49. McCarty v. City of Kansas City, 671 S.W.2d 790 (Mo. Ct. App. 1984). *See also* Vidal v. Lisanti Foods, 679 A.2d 206 (N.J. App. 1996) (holding that excessive granting of use variances may constitute exercise of the power to enact zoning amendments, a power reserved to the municipal legislative body).

50. *Id.* at 796 (quoting Millbrae Ass'n for Residential Survival v. City of Millbrae, 262 Cal. App. 2d 222, 69 Cal. Rptr. 251, 268 (1968) (change in development plan, as the equivalent of a zoning amendment, must be approved by three-fourths of city council because of landowner protests)).

51. *See generally* chapter 4.

52. *Bowman,* 732 S.W.2d at 226.

53. *See, e.g.,* N.J. STAT. ANN. § 40:55D-10.1 (West 1991) (informal, nonbinding review of concept plan at developer's request).

54. Use of preapplication conferences is discussed in greater detail on page 235.

55. *See, e.g.,* MO. REV. STAT. §§ 610.010–.030 (1996).

56. *See, e.g.,* MacLachlan v. McNary, 684 S.W.2d 534, 537 (Mo. Ct. App. 1984) (single-member body can be a governmental entity if member has decision-making powers).

57. *See, e.g.,* Sanders v. Benton, 579 P.2d 815, 819 (Okla. 1978); (citizens' advisory committee convened to make recommendations for location of community treatment center held not subject to open meetings law); Town of Palm Beach v. Gradison, 296 So. 2d 473, 476 (Fla. 1974) (citizens' planning committee held subject to open meetings law because town council had delegated governmental functions to it in the formulation of a recommended land use plan); McLarty v. Bd. of Regents of the Univ. System of Georgia, 200 S.E.2d 117 (Ga. 1973) (faculty-student advisory committee held not subject to open meetings law).

58. *See, e.g.,* Remington v. City of Boonville, 701 S.W.2d 804, 807 (Mo. Ct. App. 1985) (board of adjustment does not qualify for judicial body exemption from open meetings law, even when acting in quasi-judicial capacity); Town of Palm Beach v. Gradison, 296 So. 2d at 477 (citizens' planning commission held subject to open meetings law. "Rarely could there be any purpose to a nonpublic premeeting conference except to conduct some part of the decisional process behind closed doors"); Emmanuel Baptist Church v. North Cornwall Township, 364 A.2d 536, 541 (Pa. Commw. Ct. 1976) (zoning hearing board must comply with open meetings law in decisions regarding special-use permits.) See discussion in chapter 5, at n. 165.

59. See discussion of Vested Rights at chapter 4, n. 33.

60. *See, e.g.,* ST. LOUIS COUNTY, MISSOURI ZONING CODE § 1003.300.2 (1986).

61. *Id.*

62. *Id.* at § 1003.300.3(1).

63. Petition for a Change of Zoning form, St. Louis County, Missouri, November 5, 1979.

64. Petition for Special Procedure form, St. Louis County, Missouri, November 5, 1979.

65. *See, e.g.,* MD. CODE ANN. Art 66B, § 2.07 (1997); MO. REV. STAT. § 89.070 (1996); Murrell v. Wolff, 408 S.W.2d 842, 848 (Mo. 1966) (statutory requirement for referral to zoning commission relates only to original zoning ordinance and is not concerned with amendments).

66. Rev. Code of City of St. Louis, Missouri, tit. 26, § 26.92.020 (1986). *See, e.g.,* N.J. Stat. Ann. § 40:55D-64 (West 1997).

67. *See, e.g.,* N.J. Stat. Ann. § 40:55D-26 (West 1997); Rev. Code of City of St. Louis, Missouri, § 26.92.030 (1986).

68. *See, e.g.,* Rev. Code of City of St. Louis, Missouri, § 26.92.020 (1986) (Community Development Commission reports recommendations to petitioner, who may incorporate recommendations into a revised application). *See* p. 222.

69. Nollan v. California Coastal Comm'n, 483 U.S. 825 (1987).

70. *See, e.g.,* N.J. Stat. Ann. § 40:55D-26 (West 1997) (majority of full authorized membership rather than majority of quorum).

71. *See, e.g.,* Rhein v. City of Frontenac, 809 S.W.2d 107 (Mo. Ct. App. 1991).

72. *See, e.g.,* Cal. Gov't Code § 675854 (West 1996); N.J. Stat. Ann. § 40:55D-10 (West 1997); N.Y. Gen. City Law § 37 (McKinney 1997) (public hearing required before zoning amendment to conform to approved subdivision plat).

73. *See, e.g.,* Mo. Rev. Stat. § 89.050 (1996) (one hearing required); Pa. Stat. Ann. tit. 53, § 10609 (West 1997) (governing body required to holding hearing but planning agency hearing optional).

74. *See, e.g.,* St. Louis County, Missouri Code, § 1003.300.4 (1986).

75. *See, e.g.,* Cal. Gov't Code §§ 65090, 65091, and 65854.5; N.J. Stat. Ann. § 40:55D-12; Or. Rev. Stat. § 197.763.

76. *See, e.g.,* St. Louis County, Missouri Code, § 1003.300.7 (1986).

77. Dram Assocs. v. Planning and Zoning Comm'n of Town of Cromwell, 574 A.2d 1317, 1320 (Conn. App. Ct. 1990), *cert. denied,* 576 A.2d 544 (Conn. 1990).

78. Turner v. City of Atlanta, 357 S.E.2d 802 (Ga. 1987), *cert. denied,* 485 U.S. 934 (1988).

79. *See, e.g., Dram Associates,* 574 A.2d at 1320 (denial of opportunities to cross-examine witness is harmless error if testimony was not germane); Tate v. Miles, 503 A.2d 187, 191 (Del. 1986) (legislative hearings not required to be conducted as adversary proceedings).

80. Cal. Gov't Code §§ 65804 and 65854 (West 1996).

81. *See, e.g.,* N.J. Stat. Ann. § 40:55D-10 (West 1997).

82. *See, e.g.,* Md. Code Ann. Art. 66B, § 4.06 (1997); N.J. Stat. Ann. § 40:55D-10 (West 1997).

83. *See, e.g.,* N.J. Stat. Ann. § 40:55D-10 (West 1997).

84. *See, e.g.,* Revised Code of the City of St. Louis, § 26.92.010 (report submitted to petitioner, subsequently forwarded to the Board of Aldermen after introduction of rezoning ordinance).

85. Revised Code of City of St. Louis, Missouri § 26.92.020 (1986).

86. *See* pp. 224.

87. *See, e.g.,* Md. Code Ann. Art. 66B, §§ 4.04, 4.05 (1997); Mo. Rev. Stat. §§ 89.050, 89.060 (1996), N.J. Stat. Ann. §§ 40:55D-10, 40:55D-64 (West 1997); Pa. Stat. Ann. tit. 53, § 10609 (West 1997).

88. *See* p. 215.

89. Md. Code Ann. Art. 66B, § 4.05 (1997).

90. Parkridge v. Seattle, 573 P.2d 359, 365 (Wash. 1978).

91. Johnson v. City of Mount Vernon, 679 P.2d 405, 409 (Wash. 1984).

92. *Id.*

93. *Tate,* 503 A.2d at 191.

94. Cal. Gov't Code § 65009(b)(1) (West 1996).

95. *See, e.g.,* Hoffman v. City of Town & Country, 831 S.W.2d 223 (Mo. Ct. App. 1992).

96. *See* Clark v. City of Hermosa Beach, 56 Cal. Rptr. 2d 223 (Cal. Ct. App. 1996) (applicant denied due process when city refused to reopen public meeting to permit applicant to respond to concerns expressed by city council members after public portion of meeting closed).

97. *In re* Reynolds, 749 A.2d 1133, 1134 (Vt. 2000) (abstention of one planning commission member not counted with the majority under general state statute, contrary to common law).

98. *See* chapter 5 at n. 156.

99. *See, e.g.,* Mo. Rev. Stat., § 89.060 (1996). *See generally* Winslow v. Town of Holderness Planning Bd., 480 A.2d 114 (N.H. 1984); *Bell,* 364 N.W.2d at 144.

100. County of Fairfax v. Fleet Indus. Park Ltd. P'ship, 410 S.E.2d 669 (Va. 1991).

101. Temple Stephens Co. v. Westenhaver, 776 S.W.2d 438, 443–44 (Mo. Ct. App. 1989).

102. Christian Gospel Church, Inc., v. City and County of San Francisco, 896 F.2d 1221, 1226 (9th Cir. 1990), *cert. denied,* 498 U.S. 999 (1990) (protesting neighbors "were doing what citizens should be encouraged to do, taking an active role in the decisions of government").

103. *See* p. 222.

104. *Tate,* 503 A.2d at 191; *see also* Md. Ann. Code, Art. 66B, § 4.05 (1997) (legislative findings of fact required for specified items including population change, public facilities, transportation patterns, and recommendation of planning commission).

105. Cyclone Sand & Gravel v. Zoning Bd. of Adjustment, 351 N.W.2d 778 (Iowa 1984).

106. *See, e.g.,* Cal. Gov't Code § 65901 (West 1996); Md. Code Ann. Art. 66B, § 4.07 (1996); Pa. Stat. Ann. tit. 53, § 10909.1 (West 1997).

107. *See, e.g.,* N.J. Stat. Ann. § 40:55D-67 (West 1997).

108. State *ex rel.* McNary v. Hais, 670 S.W.2d 494 (Mo. 1984).

109. *Cyclone Sand & Gravel,* 351 N.W.2d at 781–82.

110. *Id.* at 781.

111. *See, e.g.,* Marquette Properties v. City of Wood Dale, 512 N.E.2d 371 (Ill. App. Ct.) (zoning ordinance required special-use permit for a planned unit development to be approved by an ordinance), *appeal denied,* 517 N.E.2d 1087 (1987).

112. Rev. Code of City of St. Louis, Missouri, § 26.80.010.3.

113. City of Chicago Zoning Ordinance, Art. 11.10-4.

114. *Id.* at 782; Blazier v. St. Clair County, 568 N.E.2d 508 (Ill. App. 1991) (denial of special-use permit upheld where one factor was creation of traffic problem).

115. Alachua County v. Eagle's Nest Farms, Inc., 473 So. 2d 257, 260 (Fla. Dist. Ct. App. 1985), *reh'g denied,* 486 So. 2d 595 (1986) (standards for private airstrip special-use permit upheld).

116. City of Cleburne v. Cleburne Living Center, 473 U.S. 432, 450 (1985).

117. State *ex rel.* Columbia Tower, Inc. v. Boone County, 829 S.W.2d 534 (Mo. Ct. App. 1992).

118. *Cyclone Sand & Gravel,* 351 N.W.2d at 778. One should consider, however, whether such unlawful delegation can occur in states where the legislative body also passes on the special-use permit.

119. *Cyclone Sand & Gravel,* 351 N.W.2d at 782.

120. *Id.* at 782.

121. Anthony v. Liberman, 175 N.Y.S.2d 743, 745 (Sup. Ct. 1958), *aff'd,* 183 N.Y.S.2d 996 (App. Div. 1959).

122. *See, e.g.,* 65 ILCS 5/11-13-1.1 (West 1997); *Marquette Properties,* 512 N.E.2d at 371.

123. *See, e.g.,* Md. Code Ann. Art. 66B, § 4.06 (1997).

124. Von Lusch v. Bd. of County Comm'rs, 302 A.2d 4 (Md. 1973).

125. *See, e.g., Cyclone Sand & Gravel,* 351 N.W.2d 778; *Blazier,* 568 N.E.2d at 511.

126. 65 ILCS 5/11-13-1.1 (West 1997), *construed in Marquette Properties,* 512 N.E.2d at 371.

127. *Marquette Properties, supra,* 512 N.E.2d at 371.

128. McDonald v. City of Ogdensburg Zoning Bd. of Appeals, 101 A.2d 900 (N.Y. 1984).

129. Matthew v. Smith, 707 S.W.2d 411, 413 (Mo. 1986) (citing City and Borough of Juneau v. Thibodeau, 595 P.2d 626, 633 (Alaska 1979) (board improperly granted variance

to property owner allowing property owner to rent two houses on one lot to different families, where unnecessary hardship not established in record)).

130. *See, e.g.,* MD. CODE ANN. Art. 66B, § 4.07(d)(3) (1997) (board of appeals has power to "authorize upon appeal in specific cases a variance from the terms of the ordinance"); Mo. REV. STAT. § 89.090 (1996) (variances authorized upon appeal where "practical difficulties or unnecessary hardship" exist).

131. See chapter 4, at pp. 151–53. *See, e.g.,* Miller v. City of Lake City, 789 S.W.2d 440 (Ark. 1990) (estoppel not found to permit duplex in single-family zone); Highland Park Cmty. Club of Pittsburgh v. Zoning Bd. of Adjustment of Pittsburgh, 506 A.2d 887 (Pa. 1986) (criteria for vested rights); Kolesar v. Zoning Hearing Bd., 543 A.2d 246 (Pa. Commw. Ct. 1988) (holder of vested right entitled to variance by estoppel); Appeal of Crawford, 531 A.2d 865 (Pa. Commw. Ct. 1987) (use of home for business for 20 years in violation of zoning ordinance insufficient basis for variance). *See generally* pp. 353–55.

132. *See* Vidal v. Lisanti Foods, 679 A.2d 206 (N.J. Ct. App. 1996) (holding that a board of adjustment may not grant use variances to such an extent that it usurps the power of the local legislative body to enact zoning amendments).

133. *See Matthew,* 707 S.W.2d at 413–14.

134. Devaney v. Bd. of Zoning Appeals of City of New Haven, 45 A.2d 828, 829 (Conn. 1946); Puritan Greenfield Improvement Ass'n v. Leo, 153 N.W.2d 162 (Mich. App. 1967).

135. *See Matthew,* 707 S.W.2d at 414–15 (discussing history of variance legislation).

136. *Devaney,* 45 A.2d at 829.

137. *See, e.g., id.*

138. *See, e.g., Matthew,* 707 S.W.2d at 413–14.

139. See discussion and n. 148. *See* Janssen v. Holland Charter Township Zoning Bd. of Appeals (Mich. App. 2002) (affirming use variance of 200-acre parcel based essentially on loss of market value).

140. This element is established only when the property cannot be used for any purpose permitted by the zoning ordinance. *Matthew,* 707 S.W.2d at 416–17 (citing Greenwalt v. Zoning Bd. of Adjustment of Davenport, 345 N.W.2d 537, 542–43 (Iowa 1984)); *see also* Busky v. Town of Hanover, 577 A.2d 406, 410 (N.H. 1990) (potential tripling in value of property by conversion from residential to commercial use insufficient basis for use variance).

141. *Matthew,* 707 S.W.2d at 416–17 (quoting Otto v. Steinhilder, 24 N.E.2d 851, 853 (N.Y. 1939)). For an example of a case in which a court ruled that a variance was properly granted, *see* Southland Addition Homeowner's Ass'n v. Bd. of Adjustment, City of Wichita Falls, 710 S.W.2d 194 (Tex. Ct. App. 1986) (variance properly granted where owner otherwise would be forced to cut down trees to build and where zoning ordinance required trees on commercial property). An example of a case in which a court ruled a variance was improperly granted is Battles v. Bd. of Adjustments and Appeals, City of Irving, 711 S.W.2d 297 (Tex. Ct. App. 1986), where a variance was improperly granted when the only hardship was the inability to construct an additional four units in the absence of the variance.

142. Sanchez v. Bd. of Zoning Adjustments of the City of New Orleans, 488 So. 2d 1277 (La. Ct. App. 1986).

143. Parkview Assocs. v. City of New York, 519 N.E.2d 1372 (N.Y. 1988).

144. Chirichello v. Zoning Bd. of Adjustment of Borough of Monmouth Beach, 397 A.2d 646, 650, 654 (N.J. 1979).

145. Kaufmann v. Planning Bd. of Warren, 542 A.2d 457 (N.J. 1988).

146. In the Matter of Townside Properties, Inc. v. Zoning Bd. of Appeals of Town of Huntington, 533 N.Y.S.2d 466 (App. Div. 1988).

147. *Matthew,* 707 S.W.2d at 415–16.

148. State *ex rel.* Tuck v. McDonald, 793 S.W.2d 616, 618 (Mo. Ct. App. 1990) (denial of variance for auto-repair shop use).

149. N.J. STAT. ANN. § 40:55D-70 (West 1997).

150. *Id.*

151. *See, e.g.,* Medici v. BPR Co., 526 A.2d 109, 113–18 (N.J. 1987) (reviewing reported cases and requiring enhanced proof and special findings to support use variance); Jayber, Inc., v. Municipal Council of the Township of West Orange, 569 A.2d 304 (N.J. Super. Ct. App. Div. 1990) (commercial use variance granted by zoning board of adjustment for private senior citizen congregate care housing facility upheld), *cert. denied,* 584 A.2d 214–15 (N.J. 1990).

152. Arndorfer v. Sauk County Bd. of Adjustment, 469 N.W.2d 831, 834 (Wis. 1991). *See also* Vidal v. Lisanti Foods, 679 A.2d 206 (N.J. Sup. Ct. App. Div. 1996) (holding that a board of adjustment may not grant use variances to such an extent that it usurps the power of the local legislative body to enact zoning amendments).

153. *See discussion* on pp. 197–200.

154. *Arndorfer,* 469 N.W.2d at 834.

155. Singleterry v. City of Albuquerque, 632 P.2d 345 (N.M. 1981).

156. *Id.* at 347.

157. *See, e.g.,* K.S.A. 75-4305 (1989); N.Y. GEN. MUN. LAW §§ 800 *et seq.;* N.J. STAT. ANN. 40 § 55D-23; C.G.S.A. § 1-79 *et seq.* (Conn. 1989); West F.S.A. § 112.311, *et seq.* (Fla. 1995); IC 36-7-4-223(b) (Indiana); CAL. GOV'T CODE § 87100 (West 1993).

158. As of the summer of 2001, "[i]ssues of alleged conflicts of interest continue[d] to dominate land-use litigation where ethics are concerned." Salkin, *Litigating Ethics Issues in Land Use: 2000 Trends and Decisions,* 33 URBAN LAWYER 687 (2001).

159. ABA MODEL CODE OF PROFESSIONAL RESPONSIBILITY, Disciplinary Rule 5-105.

160. Breakzone v. City of Torrance, 97 Cal. Rptr. 2d 467, 477 (2000).

161. *See* 5 ILL. COMP. STAT. ANN. ch. 420 § 4A-101(h) (1993).

162. *See, e.g.,* Clark v. City of Hermosa Beach, 56 Cal. Rptr. 2d 223 (Cal. Ct. App. 1996) (holding that developer was deprived of due process when one council member, whose own ocean view would be blocked by project, led the opposition to conditional-use permit).

163. *See* Aldom v. Roseland, 127 A.2d 190 (N.J. Super. Ct. 1956). *But see* Murach v. Planning & Zoning Comm'n, 491 A.2d 1058 (Conn. 1985).

164. Perry-Worth Concerned Citizens v. Bd. of Comm'rs of Boone County, 723 N.E.2d 457 (Ind. Ct. Ap. 2000). *In re* Tall Trees Construction Corp. v. Zoning Bd. of Appeals of Town of Huntington, 717 N.Y.S. 2d 369 (N.Y. Sup. Ct. 2000), in which the Court disapproved the participation (but not voting) of an official in a variance hearing pertaining to property adajacent to his own.

165. *See* Brooks v. Planning and Zoning Comm'n of Town of Haddam, 2000 WL 177195 (Conn. 2000).

166. ABA MODEL CODE OF PROFESSIONAL RESPONSIBILITY, Disciplinary Rule 9-101(B).

167. CAL. BUSINESS AND PROFESSIONS CODE, § 6076 (West 1962); Rule 4.2 Mo. Rules of Court, comment following.

168. *See* Tierney v. Duris, 536 P.2d 435 (Ore. Ct. App. 1975) (council member may have ex parte contact with rezoning applicant); *but see* Bjarnson v. County of Kitsap, 899 P.2d 1290 (Wash. Ct. App. 1995). For a helpful discussion of ethical issues in land use practice, *see* Salkin, *Ethics and the Land-Use Lawyer,* 5 LAND USE LAW & ZONING DIGEST 3 (May 1997); *See also* Chapter 6, n. 39 and pp. 270–71 for a discussion of ex parte contacts.

169. Salkin, *Supra,* at 695–96.

170. *See* A. Aiudi and Sons, LLC v. Plainville Planning and Zoning, 2002 WL 31082096 (2002), 72 Conn. App. 502 (2002); Florida Country Club, Inc. v. Carlton Fields, Wards, Emmanuel, South and Cutler, P.A., 98 F. Supp. 1356 (M.D. Fla. 2000).

171. *See* pp. 153–54. Some of the materials in this section were contributed by James A. Kenney III, Lexington Park, Maryland.

CHAPTER 6

Review of Land Use Decisions

Overview

Sources of power to review local land use decisions are state zoning-enabling statutes, common law principles, and state and federal statutes creating general judicial jurisdiction.[1] This chapter will discuss (1) the local level of review found in most states, known as the general "board of adjustment," and (2) the level of the state circuit courts. The circuit court level serves both as an appeal from the board of adjustment itself, in cases where the board of adjustment has initial appellate jurisdiction, and as an independent, direct level of appellate jurisdiction, notably in appeals of actions by the legislative body (whether acting in an administrative or legislative capacity), such as zoning amendments or conditional-use permits. Cities also may try to self-generate levels of review of land use decisions in addition to, or contradiction of, zoning-enabling legislation.[2]

The Board of Adjustment: Jurisdiction

State zoning-enabling statutes require the local zoning ordinance to provide an appeal from administrative decisions of the zoning enforcement officer. There are generally two stages of such appeal—administrative and judicial. The first level of review is before the administrative body, the board of adjustment. The second stage, appeal of the decision of the board of adjustment, is directly to the state court. Generally, an applicant must "exhaust his administrative remedies" by requesting and being denied relief from the board of adjustment before proceeding to judicial review in the state court.[3]

The board of adjustment is an administrative, nonelected panel, typically numbering three to five members, who are appointed by the local legislative body[4] or by the chief executive officer.[5]

Boards of adjustment have three essential functions: (1) to hear and decide appeals from administrative enforcement decisions of the zoning enforcement officer;[6] (2) to consider and decide applications for variances;[7] and (3) to administer special-use permit programs.[8] Boards of adjustment do not have legislative power but have substantial power in the enforcement and implementation of land use regulatory legislation.[9]

The importance of the appellate review function of the board of adjustment was underscored by the Supreme Court of Kentucky, when it held that the failure of a board to render a decision within a statutorily prescribed period (60 days from the evidentiary hearing) did not deprive the board of jurisdiction to decide the case.[10] Finding that the word *shall* in the statute prescribing the time limit for decision was "directory" rather than "mandatory," the court observed:

> The Board of Zoning Adjustment is an integral component of the process of adjudication of zoning disputes. The Board conducts a hearing replete with due process guarantees and renders findings of fact, conclusions of law, and a decision on the merits. Removal of the board from the process of adjudication would constitute elimination of the fact-finder and the parties would be without any record upon which to prosecute or defend an appeal. Indeed, it is doubtful that any appellate right would exist. . . . Divestiture of the Board's jurisdiction would, in every case, result in the affirmance of the building inspector's decision and would eviscerate the act. Surely, this was not the intent of the Legislature as such would violate the constitutional right of due process of law.[11]

As noted by the Kentucky court, if the board fails to perform its required duty to render a decision in a timely manner, the appellant may obtain a writ of mandamus to compel the board to take action.[12] In addition, state law may provide for criminal fines and/or removal of board members from office for failure to act.[13]

Standing to Appeal to the Board of Adjustment

Two classes of persons have standing to appeal to the board of adjustment: (1) persons "aggrieved" by a decision of the zoning enforcement officer and (2) other municipal officers or departments "affected" by such decisions.[14] To have standing as an aggrieved person or affected official, a person must establish that he or she has "a specific and legally cognizable interest" in the disputed matter and that he or she has been "directly and substantially affected" by the decision for which review is sought.[15] Persons "in close proximity" to property at issue qualify as aggrieved persons if they can show "legitimate" concerns, such as safety or "aesthetic impairment" of a neighborhood.[16] The interest alleged to be adversely affected may be an interest shared with other persons, but it must "exceed in degree the general interest in community good shared by all persons."[17] The term *aggrieved* is said to mean "something distinct from an adverse effect on some personal self-interest." Mere participation as a witness at a public hearing or other administrative proceeding does not confer aggrieved person status, but a person whose interest has been recognized by the decision-maker, who has appeared as a party to the proceedings, and who has asserted a position "on the merits as an interested person, rather than only as a source of information," can establish standing as an aggrieved person.[18] Under this standard, a private, nonprofit corporation was granted standing because one of its members was a landowner who had appeared at an administrative proceeding and submitted an uncontroverted affidavit of a "possible likelihood of damage" from a proposed expansion of a gravel extraction operation.[19]

Challenges to the jurisdiction of a board of adjustment based on lack of standing are waivable and therefore must be raised at the hearing before the board. Failure to do so at that point will deprive a reviewing court of jurisdiction to hear an appeal on the basis of lack of standing.[20]

The board's primary appellate jurisdiction is the correction of errors by the zoning enforcement official.[21] In carrying out that function, the board has a "duty to find and determine the facts"[22] and may not "pick and choose between similarly situated applicants" in requiring strict compliance with a particular ordinance.[23]

As noted previously, the board of adjustment has no legislative power. They, therefore, cannot enact, amend, or repeal a zoning ordinance, at least expressly. Board of adjustment orders, such as issuance of permits, in violation of existing zoning regulations are void and can be attacked directly or collaterally.[24] As will be seen, however, the line between legislative power and administrative power is not always clear, and the board has significant power to affect and effect land use policy.

Petition for Review by the Board of Adjustment

The administrative appeal process is initiated by filing a notice of appeal with the official whose decision is being appealed and with the board of adjustment.[25] The time limit for doing so may be set by the rules of the board of adjustment,[26] although enabling statutes often require that appeals be taken "within a reasonable time."[27] Some states require that appeals be taken within a specified period, such as 30 days after receipt of notice of the action that is being appealed.[28]

No particular format is required for the notice of appeal, except that it must state the grounds on which the appeal is based.[29] Upon receipt of the notice of appeal, the official whose decision is being appealed is required to "forthwith transmit" to the board all the papers that make up the official record on which the decision being appealed was based.[30] Some statutes specify that the official whose decision is being appealed becomes the "respondent" in any further proceedings.[31]

An important consequence of filing an appeal in most states is an automatic stay of all proceedings.[32] The automatic stay will not be imposed, however, if the official whose decision is being appealed files a certificate with the board stating facts that, in the official's judgment, demonstrate "imminent peril to life and property" if a stay were imposed.[33] If such a certificate is filed, a stay may be ordered only by issuance of a restraining order by the board or a court of record upon application, proper notice to the official whose decision is being appealed, and a showing of due cause for issuing a restraining order.[34]

Public Hearing Before the Board of Adjustment

Upon receipt of a notice of appeal, the board of adjustment must schedule a public hearing "at a reasonable time" with notice to the public as well as "due notice" to interested parties.[35] Some statutes give more specific instructions, such as Kentucky's requirement for "written notice to the appellant and the administrative official at least one (1) week prior to the hearing."[36] Most statutes permit "any party" to appear, either in person or by attorney or agent,[37] but some limit the specific right to appear and be heard to "interested" parties or "affected" parties.[38]

The purpose of the public hearing is to give interested parties an opportunity to present evidence for consideration by the board and to respond to evidence submitted by other parties. New evidence should not be accepted by the board in executive session meetings or other arrangements outside the confines of the public hearing unless all parties are present and have an opportunity to respond to the new material.[39] A corollary purpose of the public hearing is to require debate among opposing views. Thus it has been held that a decision based on an absentee vote by one board member was invalid for failure to permit debate by all members actually present at the same meeting.[40]

Open-meetings laws apply to boards of adjustment. Private discussions between a majority of the board and the board's lawyer prior to a public meeting "to seek legal advice about matters which are not litigation-related" have been held to violate the Indiana Open Door Law, for example.[41]

Timing and Basis for Board of Adjustment Decisions

Although most states do not require boards of adjustment to decide appeals within a specific time other than a "reasonable time,"[42] a few states have imposed time limits, such as 60 days after the public hearing, for board decisions.[43] When a statute imposing a time limit provides no sanctions for noncompliance or instructions respecting decisions that are delayed beyond the statutory deadline, courts have concluded that the legislature intended the time limit to be directory rather than mandatory.[44]

The appellate jurisdiction of the board of adjustment extends to three types of cases: (1) allegations that decisions made by public officials in enforcement of land use regulations are erroneous,[45] (2) matters referred to the board by ordinance for interpretation,[46] and (3) allegations that literal application of a particular land use regulation to a specific parcel of land will cause "practical difficulties or unnecessary hardship"[47] or will "deprive the applicant of reasonable capacity to make use of the land in a manner equivalent to the use permitted other landowners in the same zone."[48] Applicants in the third category are seeking variances, a topic discussed in detail in chapter 5.[49] In some jurisdictions Boards of Adjustment have jurisdiction to hear and decide requests for special-use permits, also discussed in chapter 5.[50]

In exercising appellate jurisdiction with respect to allegations of erroneous enforcement decisions, the board may reverse, affirm, or modify the decision being appealed[51] but must be careful not to cross the line between administrative interpretation and legislative policy-making by, in effect, amending the zoning ordinance.[52] Before making a decision, the board must hear and consider evidence, at least as to disputed matters. It must make its own factual findings and may not, for example, simply delegate its obligations by accepting the opinion of its lawyer.[53]

Decisions made by the board of adjustment under its interpretative authority generally are entitled to great deference and are actually controlling unless "unreasonable or irrational."[54]

Basis and Scope of Judicial Review of Zoning Decisions

Local zoning decisions usually are characterized as either administrative or legislative.[55] The distinction is important because the procedures for appealing a zoning decision to the state trial court, as well as the standards of review to be applied in that court, differ acutely.

If a zoning decision is characterized as legislative, the standard of judicial review is extremely deferential. A legislative zoning decision will be overturned only if it is not fairly debatable that it is arbitrary or unreasonable.[56] Courts traditionally have limited their review of legislative zoning decisions to determinations of whether there was "abuse of discretion, excess of power, or error of law."[57] Under the classic fairly debatable standard, courts refuse to second-guess or substitute their own judgment for the judgment of legislative bodies "if the validity of the legislative classification . . . be fairly debatable."[58]

An appellate court in Illinois summarized the deferential review standard:

> A rebuttable presumption exists that a zoning ordinance is valid and the challenging party must establish by clear and convincing evidence that the ordinance, as applied to their property, is arbitrary and unreasonable and bears no substantial relation to the public health, safety, or welfare. Where opinions may differ with regard to the reasonableness of the existing zoning classifications, the legislative judgment becomes exclusive. Of course, the mere existence of conflicting opinions on the record does not necessarily mean that the plaintiffs have failed to meet their burden of proof; rather, the court must determine from all the evidence whether the different opinions are reasonable and justifiable. Any conflicts in testimony are a matter for the trier of fact, and its determination will not be disturbed unless contrary to the manifest weight of the evidence; that is, unless it appears that the opposite conclusion is clearly evident.[59]

A large disparity in property value will not alone justify overturning a legislative decision to deny rezoning because virtually all residential zoning would be subject to attack.[60] In one case in which the facts weighed heavily in favor of overturning a denial of a rezoning request, however, the court held that the challenger need not prove that the property is totally unsuitable for any use as presently zoned; rather, "it is sufficient that a substantial decrease in value results from a classification bearing no substantial relation to the public welfare." [61]

The Supreme Court of Kansas has identified two sets of factors to be used in reviewing zoning decisions: (1) reasonableness factors for determining whether a zoning board acted reasonably with respect to requests for change and (2) scope-of-review factors for considering whether the first set of factors was properly used.

The Kansas reasonableness factors, which are suggestions for consideration rather than absolute requirements, are typical of standards governing judicial review of legislative decisions such as rezonings:

1. character of the neighborhood;
2. zoning uses of nearby properties;
3. suitability of the property for the uses to which it is restricted;
4. extent to which the change will detrimentally affect nearby property;
5. length of time the property has been vacant as zoned;
6. gain to the public health, safety, and welfare by the possible diminution in value of the plaintiff's property as compared to the hardship imposed on the plaintiff if his or her requests were denied;
7. recommendations of a permanent or professional planning staff;
8. conformance of the requested change to the city's master or comprehensive plan.[62]

Unlike the court's application of the reasonableness factors, application of the Kansas scope-of-review factors is not discretionary.

1. The local zoning authority, and not the court, has the right to prescribe, change, or refuse to change zoning.
2. The district court's power is limited to determining (a) the lawfulness of the action taken, and (b) the reasonableness of such action.
3. There is a presumption that the zoning authority acted reasonably.
4. The landowner has the burden of proving unreasonableness by a preponderance of the evidence.
5. A court may not substitute its judgment for that of the administrative body, and should not declare the action unreasonable unless clearly compelled to do so by the evidence.
6. Action is unreasonable when it is so arbitrary that it can be said it was taken without regard to the benefit or harm involved to the community at large, including all interested parties, and was so wide of the mark that its unreasonableness lies outside the realm of fair debate.
7. Whether action is reasonable or not is a question of law, to be determined upon the basis of the facts that were presented to the zoning authority.
8. An appellate court must make the same review of the zoning authority's action as did the district court.[63]

Illinois courts have identified similar factors to be considered in reviewing legislative zoning decisions:

1. existing uses and zoning of nearby property;
2. extent to which property values are diminished by the particular zoning restrictions;
3. extent to which the destruction of property value of the plaintiff promotes the health, safety, morals, or general welfare of the public;
4. relative gain to the public as opposed to the hardship imposed upon the individual property owner;
5. suitability of the subject for the zoned purposes;
6. length of time the property has been vacant as zoned, considered in the context of land development in the area;
7. care with which a community has undertaken to plan its land use development;
8. evidence, or lack of evidence, of community need for the use proposed by the plaintiff.

"No one factor," however, "is controlling."[64]

When the exercise or failure to exercise the legislative power to zone is challenged, courts have followed two approaches in judicial review, as noted by the Supreme Court of Washington:

> Against this background then, a distinction in the judicial role, procedure, and relief must be recognized between situations where zoning authorities have wholly omitted to exercise their power to modify or amend their ordinances to conform to changed conditions which clearly and patently render pertinent zoning regulations arbitrary and unreasonable, and situations where zoning authorities have in fact, either spontaneously or upon petition, held hearings and considered changed conditions in relation to their zoning ordinances and made a legislative determination that rezoning is either necessary or unnecessary.
>
> In the first situation, the court perforce must receive original evidence and, because the zoning authorities have not exercised their legislative powers, may, if the facts demand, declare outmoded regulations arbitrary, unreasonable, and void and may direct the zoning authorities to make appropriate revisions. If vested rights have not intervened, the court may also judicially declare when the regulations become void. The proceeding is original in nature and assumes the aspects of an action for declaratory relief.
>
> In the second situation, however, the court is reviewing legislative action taken by the proper zoning authorities. The review is appellate in nature and is ordinarily by way of *certiorari.* The court's attention, therefore, is limited to and focused upon the proceedings before the zoning authorities and whether such authorities, upon the basis of the circumstances and evidence before them, arbitrarily or capriciously exercised or refused to exercise their police and legislative powers which, in turn have resulted in

the imposition or continuation of clearly unreasonable and unrealistic zoning regulations. If, in keeping with the law governing such reviews, the
court so finds it may declare the action of the zoning authorities invalid,
the regulations resulting from such action void, and remand the matter to
the zoning authorities for appropriate action. In this situation, the invalidity
of the challenged regulations springs principally from the voided legislative
action of the zoning authorities rather than from preexisting events.[65]

Missouri courts have articulated the following standards for reviewing
the reasonableness of legislative zoning decisions:

> Since zoning and refusal to rezoning are legislative acts, . . . we review *de
> novo* any challenges to their validity. . . . Zoning ordinances are presumed
> to be valid. This presumption is rebuttable, and the challenger bears the
> burden of proving an ordinance's unreasonableness as applied to his
> property. . . .
>
> Any uncertainty about the reasonableness of a zoning regulation
> must be resolved in the government's favor: if the issue is at least fairly
> debatable, the reviewing court may not substitute its opinion for that of
> the zoning authority which enacted the challenged ordinance. . . . The
> analytical framework for reviewing zoning decisions is well settled:
> "First, the court reviews the property owner's evidence to determine
> whether the owner has rebutted the presumption that continuation of the
> present zoning was reasonable; and second, the court reviews the gov-
> ernment's evidence to determine whether such evidence makes the con-
> tinuance of the present zoning fairly debatable." [66]

In the case of administrative or quasi-judicial zoning decisions, the scope
of review is much less deferential. Review of administrative zoning decisions
is governed in most instances by state administrative procedure acts.[67] State
administrative procedure acts generally provide for filing a petition for review
of an administrative decision, the procedure and time limitations on such filings, necessary parties, the scope of judicial review, and the procedure for consideration of additional evidence upon judicial review.[68] State administrative
procedure acts will not govern review of legislative decisions such as rezonings, however.

In reviewing administrative zoning decisions such as those made by
boards of adjustment, courts are required to examine the decision in question
against at least two standards: (1) whether the decision was legal (i.e., whether
the decision-maker had legal authority to render the decision it made), and
(2) whether the decision "was supported by competent and substantial evidence upon the whole record" when viewed "in a light most favorable to the
findings of the board."[69] Substantial evidence has been defined as "such relevant evidence as a reasonable mind might accept as adequate to support a
conclusion."[70]

Although the court reviewing an administrative zoning decision has the
responsibility to determine whether the facts of the case support the decision

reached and may, in discharging this responsibility, hear additional evidence from the parties, there is general agreement that reviewing courts are "not free to decide the case anew."[71] For example, a New Jersey court has ruled that a trial judge may visit the site in dispute to get a better understanding of the evidence, but may not "go outside the record and base his ruling on facts gleaned from a personal inspection."[72] The standard has been also stated as requiring the complaining party to show that the board of adjustment's decision is illegal (i.e., an abuse of discretion).[73]

Typically there is a short limitations period, such as 30 days, for filing an action for judicial review of an administrative zoning decision. As already noted, other procedural requirements include service of process on the offending agency. Such requirements have been held to be jurisdictional when mandated by statute; thus failure to file a timely appeal or to notify an indispensable party can deprive the court of jurisdiction to hear the appeal.[74]

Some courts, however, have held that failure to give notice within the statutory time frame is not jurisdictional if notice is later given within a reasonable time because the parties already have been joined at the administrative proceeding stage.[75] Courts have construed time limits for appeals as beginning to run on the date of final passage of the zoning ordinance in question rather than the date of its first reading[76] and as being tolled by a pending petition for reconsideration before the administrative body whose decision is being appealed.[77]

Courts also have held that failure to join an indispensable party, such as a successful zoning board applicant, does not deprive a reviewing court of subject matter jurisdiction where there is no statutory requirement that the non-joined person be included in the appeal.[78] General requirements that named parties possess the capacity to sue or be sued have been held inapplicable to appeals from administrative decisions. Thus, in an appeal of a board of adjustment's decision, the failure to name individual members of the board where the board as a corporate body did not have the capacity to sue may not deprive the reviewing court of jurisdiction to hear the appeal.[79]

Of course, there must be a decision from which to appeal before such procedural requirements are triggered. Because statutes or ordinances establishing the procedural requirements usually include the requirement that the appeal specify the grounds on which it is based, it is not uncommon for a court to require that a decision of a local government entity acting in an administrative capacity "carry with it an opinion, memorandum or explanation of some kind."[80]

Not all local zoning actions are clearly legislative or administrative, and largely because of the different standards of review applicable to legislative versus administrative decisions, the question is often litigated.[81] Further, many large commercial projects invoke more than one form of decision or local authority. For example, the same project may require both a purely legislative rezoning as well as an administrative variance or conditional-use permit. In some jurisdictions, the same legislative body may act administratively with respect to some decisions, such as subdivision plat approval, and legislatively with respect to other decisions, such as rezoning the parcel at issue.[82] Finally, some local actions may be characterized as raising "purely legal" issues and invoking de novo, nondeferential review.[83]

In sum, the property owner must understand at the outset the essential nature of the municipal action he or she seeks.

Standing to Seek Judicial Review of Local Zoning Decisions

Statutes regulating the process for taking appeals from local land use decisions often create two classes of persons entitled to appeal: (1) "classically aggrieved" persons who meet the traditional test of standing discussed earlier with respect to boards of adjustment and (2) "statutorily aggrieved" persons, defined as persons who own land within a prescribed distance, such as 100 feet, from any portion of the land involved in a particular decision.[84] Statutory grants of standing, however, have not been considered to create constitutionally protected property interests in the appeal process. For example, the U.S. Court of Appeals for the Second Circuit has upheld the dismissal of a federal civil rights complaint challenging the failure to provide neighboring landowners with personal notice of otherwise appealable proceedings, such as the consideration of an application for approval of a subdivision plan.[85]

The traditional test of standing requires that some "special injury" be pleaded and proved. The complainant "must allege and show how he has been damaged or injured other than as a member of the general public."[86] General allegations of loss of full use of nearby public facilities,[87] adverse effect on property values,[88] competitive disadvantages occasioned by approval of a use variance one mile away,[89] or economic harm occasioned by allegedly inadequate environmental review of a proposed development project[90] have been held to be insufficient to confer standing. Ownership of a residential property separated by the subject property by three 50-foot-wide lots was held not to be ownership of property "adjacent to or surrounding" the subject property so as to confer standing.[91] An Illinois court has held, however, that the requisite injury may be met by proof that a rezoning will artificially drive up property values and cause rental increases against residential plaintiffs because of higher tax assessments in the neighborhood.[92]

Some state courts have decided standing questions by classifying cases into categories, however, liberalizing standing as the "public" nature of the claim increases. Thus standing to enforce valid zoning ordinances would require a showing of special damages different in kind from that suffered by the community as a whole, whereas standing to attack a zoning ordinance as void because of lack of notice or other defect may lie in any affected resident, citizen, or property owner.[93] "Strict rules of standing that might be appropriate in other contexts have no application where broad and long-term effects are involved."[94]

Liberal definitions of standing may not be applied both ways, however. City officials such as zoning inspectors and township trustees may not have standing to appeal adverse board-of-adjustment decisions in the absence of express statutory authority.[95] A zoning board, if acting in a quasi-judicial capacity, may have no standing to appeal from a court's reversal of the board's order.[96]

Organizations are often litigants in land use cases, adding complexity to the law of standing. It has become common for citizens affected by adverse zoning decisions to form not-for-profit corporations or other organizations to present a more coherent and effective representation in local zoning matters. The standing of such organizations in any given matter may not fit clearly within the judicial common law standing elements of "special injury" or "legally cognizable interest." In one particularly liberal case, the court held that a not-for-profit organization had standing to enforce the Fair Housing Act because it diverted time and money to investigate the alleged violation, which could have been put to better use elsewhere.[97] Moreover, the interest of such an organization cannot be based solely on the interests of its individual members.[98]

With the exception of organizational standing rules, federal standing rules generally are stricter than state rules. In the leading land use case *Warth v. Seldin*,[99] the Supreme Court denied standing to challenge the exclusionary effects of a suburban zoning ordinance to all but property owners. Federal courts have required complainants to allege injury that is (1) more than a generalized grievance, "distinct and palpable" and not "abstract" or "conjectural" or "hypothetical"; (2) fairly traceable to the defendant's allegedly unlawful conduct; and (3) likely to be redressed by the requested relief.[100]

The requirement of standing does not permit analysis of the plaintiff's motives. One court has approved, on the grounds of general taxpayer standing, the right of an economic competitor, against a claim of "rank commercialism," to sue to invalidate a land use approval. A waste disposal company was held to have standing to contest the grant of a competitor's permit as violative of the California Environmental Quality Act because the plaintiff was a taxpayer and owner of property with a "geographical nexus" to the permitted property.[101]

In both federal and state courts, standing is jurisdictional and thus can be raised at any time by the parties, as well as by the court on its own motion.[102] Thus, standing may be "lost," for example, where a proceeding is delayed and the applicant loses his purchase or option rights.[103] Standing requirements have been liberalized in many states as part of legislative policies "in favor of the enforcement of comprehensive plans by persons adversely affected by local action."[104]

Abstention

When review of administrative land use regulatory decisions is sought in federal court under the aegis of Section 1983 of the Civil Rights Act,[105] a federal court may decline review under the *Pullman* abstention doctrine,[106] even when the case otherwise may be properly before the court. The *Pullman* doctrine holds that federal courts should abstain from ruling if the following standards are met:

> 1) the complaint must touch a sensitive area of social policy into which the federal courts should not enter unless there is no alternative to adjudication; 2) a definitive ruling on the state issues by a state court could obviate the need for constitutional adjudication by the federal court; and 3) the proper resolution of the potentially determinative state law issue is uncertain.[107]

One federal appeals court invoked the *Pullman* doctrine in reversing a district court ruling on a developer's constitutional challenge to a slope-density formula imposed by the City of Los Angeles. The district court had ruled that the developer's application must be deemed approved under a California statute requiring reviewing agencies to render decisions on development project applications within one year after the application is received and accepted as complete by the agency. The Court of Appeals reasoned that "land use planning is a sensitive area of social policy" and concluded that state courts should be given the opportunity to construe the application of state statutes before federal courts decide the constitutional issues raised by the federal lawsuit.[108] Similarly, the Third Circuit has held that Pullman abstention was appropriate in a First Amendment case where there was a possibility that a state court would construe the local zoning ordinance to permit the operation of an adult bookstore.[109]

Under a second abstention doctrine, the *Burford* rule,[110] federal courts may be required to abstain from ruling in order to avoid interfering with a "complex state regulatory scheme concerning important matters of state policy for which impartial and fair administrative determinations subject to expeditious and adequate judicial review are afforded."[111] *Burford* abstention has been held proper by the U.S. Court of Appeals for the Fourth Circuit in zoning and subdivision approval cases in Maryland because the "procedures, programs, statutes, regulations, planning boards, and officials involved in the subdivision approval process qualify zoning . . . as being governed by a complex state regulatory scheme."[112]

A third abstention doctrine affecting land use controversies is the *Younger* doctrine.[113] Under the *Younger* doctrine, abstention is warranted "where federal jurisdiction has been invoked for the purpose of restraining state criminal proceedings, [with] exceptions for bad faith, harassment, or a patently invalid state statute."[114] *Younger* abstention is invoked most often in cases challenging local licensing ordinances regulating controversial activities such as adult entertainment in which criminal penalties may be assessed for violations. Courts have held that *Younger* abstention is proper when state criminal proceedings "were well underway," but improper when the challenged ordinance is similar to but not identical to the one under which the complainant was arrested.[115] A fourth species of abstention is based on the *Rooker/Feldman* doctrine, which holds that federal courts, excepting only the U.S. Supreme Court, have no authority to review a case that has been decided in a state court, at least where the federal and state issues are "inextricably intertwined."[116]

Because abstention is "the exception rather than the rule," abstention must be sought at the earliest practicable time. Failure to do so until after a case has been heard and appealed twice has been held to make abstention improper upon a subsequent review.[117]

Exhaustion of Administrative Remedies

Judicial review of local land use decisions most often is not available until the applicable administrative review procedures have been exhausted.[118] Rather than a jurisdictional requirement, the exhaustion doctrine generally is considered to be a judicial policy[119] that seeks to encourage correcting errors and settling disputes in the most expeditious manner by local agencies likely to have particularized knowledge and experience.[120] The Supreme Court of Washington has articulated the exhaustion doctrine as a three-part test, providing that courts should not intervene:

> (1) "when a claim is cognizable in the first instance by an agency alone"; (2) when the agency's authority "establishes clearly defined machinery for the submission, evaluation and resolution of complaints by aggrieved parties"; and (3) when the "relief sought . . . can be obtained by resort to an exclusive or adequate administrative remedy."[121]

Perhaps the most common situation in which courts can be expected to apply the exhaustion doctrine is the case of a landowner who challenges the application of a zoning ordinance to a particular piece of property without first seeking a rezoning or a variance.[122] In one case,[123] a county sought a court order declaring a city zoning ordinance unconstitutional as applied. The county bypassed the rezoning process and did not seek a variance, arguing that a landowner "should not have to go to the expense of preparing and going before an administrative body when the courts are available." In affirming the trial court's dismissal of the action, the appellate court declared that the county's argument "ignores the fact that much of the same expenses will be incurred in any route taken towards rezoning." In addition, while noting that prospective purchasers of the property in previous years had been denied rezoning requests, the court stated that it "cannot presume arbitrary or unreasonable action on the part of [the] City."[124]

Courts also have applied the doctrine in cases where neighboring landowners attempt to challenge decisions by administrative officials to permit particular uses of property without first complaining to the board of adjustment. For example, in *Burns v. Peavler*,[125] the court refused to permit a judicial challenge to a decision by a local zoning enforcement officer, which was later admitted to be erroneous because of the failure of the plaintiff to file a timely appeal to the board of adjustment as required by the planning and zoning statute. A strong dissent argued that the majority's decision to block a challenge to an admittedly erroneous decision because of the failure to follow administrative review procedure threatened the integrity of zoning statutes and ordinances prohibiting administrative officials from approving any building or use "which does not conform to the literal terms of the zoning regulations."[126]

Exceptions to the exhaustion doctrine apply when courts believe that the policy objectives of administrative efficiency and judicial economy are "outweighed by consideration of fairness or practicality."[127] The doctrine is not applied when resort to the administrative process would be futile,[128] such as in cases where land is rezoned as part of a comprehensive plan revision in a manner that has the effect of denying a pending application for rezoning.[129] The doctrine is not applied when local zoning ordinances provide for alternative methods of challenging zoning decisions, such as authorization to appeal decisions to a board of adjustment or instituting suit for an injunction to restrain violations of the ordinance.[130] Likewise, when multiple remedies are available from the same review board and one has been exhausted, courts have not required the others to be exhausted before accepting review of the decision on the first remedy sought.[131] Losing parties generally are not required to request rehearings before appealing to higher levels of review in the absence of statutory requirements to do so.[132]

A second exception is recognized when the constitutionality of a regulation in its entirety is being challenged[133] or the constitutionality of an agency's action in administering a regulation is raised as a defense to a suit seeking enforcement of the agency's decision.[134] Following the lead of the Supreme Court in *Village of Euclid v. Ambler Realty Co.*,[135] courts have reasoned that when the constitutionality of the entire regulatory scheme is challenged, the challenger should not be required "to pursue the machinery of the ordinance itself for his remedy."[136] The doctrine is based on the principle that "the administrative body does not have authority to determine the constitutionality of the law it administers; only the courts have that power."[137] When the challenge is to the ordinance "on its face," the challenger must identify "language in the ordinance which, without more, reasonably can be said to violate a specific constitutional guarantee."[138]

In cases where the constitutional challenge is raised as a defense to a suit seeking to enforce a land use regulation, most courts have held that requiring a landowner to first seek administrative relief before challenging a regulation as a defense to a complaint filed by the enforcing agency would be futile because the act of filing the complaint demonstrates clearly the position that the administrative agency is likely to take if such relief is sought.[139] In addition, courts have been willing to permit such challenges under the principle that a person should be able to raise "any defense which will exonerate the defendant from liability."[140] A few courts, however, have refused to allow defendants to raise constitutional challenges without first exhausting administrative remedies, reasoning either that it is not possible to determine whether a land use regulation is confiscatory without an application for relief being considered, at least when procedures for granting relief are contained in the ordinance[141] or that it is simply "incorrect procedure . . . to remodel the structure for a purpose prohibited by the ordinance and then, as a defense to an injunction suit, hit the city with the plea of an unfair ordinance."[142]

Other exceptions to the exhaustion doctrine have been recognized (1) to permit a state attorney general to exercise the broad enforcement powers of the chief legal officer of the state,[143] (2) to permit a property owner to challenge violations of land use regulations on adjoining or nearby property upon a showing that such violations have caused or will cause special damage to the property owner,[144] or (3) to provide judicial review for aggrieved persons who did not receive appropriate notice of administrative decisions, such as a negative declaration of environmental impact for a proposed development that was not made public until a hearing several months after the decision was made.[145] Occasionally an argument has been made that an exception to the exhaustion doctrine should be recognized for agency actions that are recommendations, such as reports of special masters, rather than final decisions, but courts generally have not been persuaded by the argument.[146]

In considering constitutional challenges to local land use regulatory decisions, federal courts commonly draw a distinction between the exhaustion-of-administrative-remedies doctrine and a related doctrine requiring an administrative action to be final before judicial review is available. In *Patsy v. Board of Regents*,[147] the Supreme Court held that state administrative remedies do not have to be exhausted before a suit is brought in federal court under 42 U.S.C. Section 1983.[148] The decision, however, has not enabled aggrieved property owners to bypass state administrative machinery entirely. In subsequent decisions the court has distinguished the exhaustion-of-remedies doctrine from the finality doctrine in holding that before an aggrieved property owner can get into federal court to challenge the constitutionality of a local land use decision, the property owner must establish that "the initial decision maker has arrived at a definitive position on the issue that inflicts an actual, concrete injury."[149] Application of this finality requirement has led to decisions that landowners may be required to apply for variances,[150] permits,[151] or approval of alternative uses of land[152] before being able to challenge in federal court the constitutionality of legislative disapproval of applications for permission to develop particular projects. In the words of the court, it is necessary to "know the nature and extent of permitted development before adjudicating the constitutionality of the regulations that purport to limit it."[153]

At least one lower court, however, has concluded that the finality doctrine does not require that an application for a variance be made in every case. The U.S. Court of Appeals for the Fifth Circuit did not require a complaining landowner to seek a variance from the board of adjustment when a local building inspector, following an interpretation of the zoning code he had received from the same board, imposed additional restrictions on the installation of equipment by nonfranchised cable TV operators. The court determined that the finality requirement was satisfied by the combination of the policy interpretation by the board and the execution of that interpretation by the building inspector.[154]

In a series of cases construing Supreme Court rulings on ripeness in the land use context, the U.S. Court of Appeals for the Ninth Circuit has held that the "futility" exception may be applied to the ripeness doctrine, but only when "at least one meaningful application" for a development project has been made and rejected, as well as a "meaningful application" for a variance.[155] Application for an amendment to a county general plan seeking the restoration of a less restrictive land use designation was held not to qualify as a meaningful application,[156] nor was an unsuccessful attempt to have an ordinance enacted with an express exemption from regulation for a particular apartment development.[157]

Ripeness may arise earlier than expected. Typical development projects require collateral approvals, and early approvals may become ripe and statutes of limitation may begin to run, even though numerous related approvals, such as site plan review, remain.[158]

Burden of Proof

The presumption of legislative validity normally attached to zoning decisions[159] requires persons who challenge zoning decisions on constitutional grounds to assume a difficult burden of proof.[160] Some states impose the beyond-a-reasonable-doubt standard,[161] whereas many others require proof by "clear and convincing evidence."[162]

The lawyer representing a landowner who is unsuccessful at the local level must determine the applicable burden of proof and carefully assess the quantum and quality of evidence available to discharge that burden. If the action is a legislative action such as a refusal to rezone, evidence of improper or purely political motive is helpful, but in most cases an expert opinion is necessary. The action must be nearly devoid of justification from the standpoints of land use and health, safety, and welfare. Evidence that there may be better ways of responding to a particular problem or that the landowner's property value will be reduced is rarely alone sufficient.

For example, the Supreme Court of Colorado dismissed evidence that enactment of a hillside erosion-prevention ordinance was not the best means available to address erosion and related problems associated with the development of residential housing on steep slopes because the question presented by the challenge to the validity of the ordinance was whether "the decision made is itself reasonably and rationally related to the problem being addressed," not whether it is the best approach.[163]

Although the presumption of validity imposes a heavy burden on challengers of legislative zoning decisions, it is not an absolute bar to success, and there are numerous cases in which the courts overturned purely legislative zoning decisions. Evidence that a parcel of land is economically unsuitable for the use permitted by a particular zoning classification has been held to rebut the presumption, particularly when the authority offers no evidence to refute the argument of economic unsuitability or to establish that the zoning being challenged offers a particular public benefit over and above that attributable to zoning in general.[164] Likewise, evidence that a legitimate business has been totally excluded by a zoning ordinance has been held to rebut the presumption.[165]

Extrinsic evidence may be used to overcome the presumption, such as evidence that the property in question was earmarked for open space in a master plan, other land also designated as open space has been acquired, and the practical effect of the challenged zoning decision was to prevent use other than as open space.[166]

In states that require local legislative bodies to state in writing the reasons for zoning decisions, the challenger's burden is to show "that the stated reasons are either without factual support in the record or are legally insufficient."[167]

The burden of proof can shift substantially when the challenged zoning decision is characterized as quasi-judicial or administrative rather than legislative. As discussed in the next two sections, several states draw a distinction between zoning decisions that promulgate general land use policies for a large area (legislative in character), from zoning decisions such as variances that resolve disputes regarding the appropriate use of a particular tract and zoning decisions that implement general land use policies through administration of special-use permit programs and anchoring floating zones (quasi-judicial or administrative in character). In the latter cases, the burden of proof shifts from the person challenging a decision to rezone or grant a variance or issue a special-use permit to the person seeking the change that is being challenged.[168] The courts will be less tolerant of subjective, political bases for decisions. Thus mere expressions of "concern" or opposition to a use proposed in an application for special-use permit will not satisfy the city's burden of proof in justifying denial of the permit.[169] For the challenged decision to be sustained, the person seeking the change must establish that the change is consistent with local comprehensive plans or mandatory state land use goals when such goals have been adopted.[170] In such cases, courts use the "traditional and non-deferential standard of strict judicial scrutiny . . . whereby a court makes a detailed examination of a statute, rule or order . . . for exact compliance with, or adherence to, a standard or norm."[171]

In administrative proceedings, cities often remain as casual in admitting evidence as in legislative matters. The risk of error on appeal by a nondeferential court, on the basis of an inadequate record, is thereby increased.[172]

Legislative versus Administrative Action

As already noted, important consequences flow from a judicial determination to characterize zoning decisions as legislative or administrative/quasi-judicial.[173] The U.S. Court of Appeals for the Fifth Circuit emphasized the point in *Shelton v. City of College Station*,[174] observing that legislative zoning decisions are reviewed to determine whether the facts on which the decision was based could not be reasonably conceived as true by the government decision-maker, while adjudicative regulatory decisions are reviewed to determine whether they are supported by adequate evidence in the record.

Administrative, or "contested case," local land use proceedings trigger trial-type procedural protections, including requirements of public notice, a taped or transcribed record, testimony under oath, and even discovery and cross-examination.[175]

The distinction between zoning decisions that are legislative in character (i.e., ones that declare public purposes and the means to carry out such purposes)[176] or actions "laying down general policies without regard to a specific piece of property,"[177] and ones that are administrative/adjudicatory in nature (i.e., applying the previously declared policy or standards to particular tracts of land or resolving disputes over the appropriate use for a particular parcel)[178] may be difficult to draw in specific cases. For example, the supreme courts of California and Oregon have disagreed on the proper characterization of a rezoning. In *Arnel Development Company v. City of Costa Mesa*,[179] the California court characterized the decision as legislative because of the process of reaching the decision (by the legislative body), whereas in *Fasano v. Board of County Commissioners*,[180] the Supreme Court of Oregon concluded that a rezoning to anchor a floating zone was administrative because it applied a previously declared policy to a special parcel of land.

Several courts have concluded that decisions not to rezone, or vetoes of amendments to zoning ordinances, are legislative because of their law-making, rather than law-interpretation or law-application, effect.[181] A minority of courts, following the reasoning of the Oregon court in *Fasano,* treat decisions regarding requests for rezonings as adjudicatory functions that must be supported by written findings of fact and conclusions of law.[182]

Of course, it should be noted that characterization of a zoning decision as administrative or adjudicatory rather than legislative does not give the reviewing court carte blanche to substitute its judgment for that of the regulatory body. In such cases, the court reviews the decision to determine whether it receives substantial support from the court's findings of fact. If so, the court may not overturn the decision, even if the findings of fact "leave the reasonableness of the board's action open to a fair difference of opinion."[183]

De Novo Judicial Review

The Standard State Zoning Enabling Act recognized that evidence in addition to that developed by a board of adjustment may be necessary "for the proper disposition" of appeals from board actions.[184] Although "certiorari provides limited review of fact findings of an inferior tribunal,"[185] most state zoning statutes have followed the lead of the zoning-enabling act and provide for additional evidence to be taken, and some statutes even require a de novo review.[186] The term *de novo review* in the context of zoning decisions is most often applied to declaratory judgment actions in which the court reviews legislative decisions such as rezonings and refusals to rezone. Such review is not based on the record before the legislative body and is not concerned with the record in any sense unless to establish improper notice or motive. The quantum or quality of evidence before the legislative body is not relevant, and such cases are typically decided on the basis of conflicting expert or other testimony presented to the court.[187]

The term *de novo review* is used in other contexts, however. It has a different meaning in the context of certiorari actions and zoning decisions that are not purely legislative, as noted by the Supreme Court of Iowa:

> The term "de novo" as used in either section does not bear its equitable connotation. It authorizes the taking of additional testimony, but only for the submission and consideration of those questions of illegality raised by the statutory petition for writ of certiorari. . . . The action of the trial court has the effect of a jury verdict and is appealable to us on assigned errors only. . . .
>
> In a certiorari proceeding in a zoning case the district court finds the facts anew on the record made in the certiorari proceeding. That record will include the return to the writ and any additional evidence which may have been offered by the parties. However, the district court is not free to decide the case anew. Illegality of the challenged board action is established by reason of the court's findings of fact if they do not provide substantial support for the board decision. If the district court's findings of

fact leave the reasonableness of the board's action open to a fair difference of opinion, the court may not substitute its decision for that of the board.[188]

In de novo review, testimony of decision-makers ordinarily may not be compelled to determine the evidence on which they relied or their reasons for voting in a particular way.[189]

Limitations Periods

Timing of judicial review of land use decisions is governed by various limitations periods or the doctrine of laches, depending on the nature of the underlying proceedings. Administrative matters, such as conditional-use permits, subdivision platting decisions, and board of adjustment decisions, typically are subject to specific, short-duration (30 days) limitations periods provided both in the state administrative review statutes or zoning-enabling statute and in the local ordinance, although local review periods that are longer than provided by statute should not be enforced. Local procedural ordinances generally face preemption questions when substantively different from enabling statutes.[190] Legislative matters, especially rezonings, are often considered equitable and governed by the nonspecific limitations of laches.[191]

Remedies

Although a court may not substitute its judgment for that of the local land use authority "as to the weight of the evidence on questions of fact,"[192] it can reverse or avoid the decision. Administrative review statutes commonly provide that land use decisions may be reversed or modified. For example, the Idaho Code authorizes courts to overturn land use decisions that are:

1. in violation of constitutional or statutory provisions;
2. in excess of the statutory authority of the agency;
3. made upon unlawful procedure;
4. affected by other error of law;
5. clearly erroneous in view of the reliable, probative, and substantial evidence on the whole record; or
6. arbitrary or capricious or characterized by abuse of discretion or clearly unwarranted exercise of discretion.[193]

Applying this statute, the Supreme Court of Idaho upheld a lower court's reversal of a rezoning decision because of the failure of the city commissioners to make written findings of fact to support the commissioners' conclusion that the rezoning in question was in accordance with the adopted plan. The court concluded that the commissioners' finding that the rezoning was in accordance "with the intent and policy" of the plan amounted merely to "a conclusion of law which if erroneous may be corrected by judicial review."[194] In remanding, the court stated that further proceedings could result in a valid rezoning as long as factual findings supported that conclusion.[195]

The Idaho court's decision reflects the traditional approach courts have taken to granting remedies when zoning decisions are overturned. The first and most common remedy is a declaration of invalidity of the particular decision being appealed.[196] As the Idaho court noted, however, this does not necessarily resolve the controversy because such a decision usually does not establish the appropriate range of permissible use for the land in question. The judicial order merely concludes that a particular decision with respect to permissible land uses was incorrect. Local legislative and administrative bodies have the responsibility for making the ultimate decisions regarding permissible land uses. Judicial remedies will prevent illegal decisions from being implemented but may not take regulatory power from the executive and legislative branches of local government.

Judicial decisions resolving zoning controversies, while usually focused on particular parcels of land, may have important effects extending beyond the interests of the parties to the dispute. Courts often will be faced with the question of what to do about the zoning of a parcel when the court has decided that the zoning designation in controversy is invalid. Courts have responded with a variety of remedies under their equitable powers to shape necessary relief, but the great majority agree that the separation-of-powers doctrine prevents the judiciary from usurping the legislative function of zoning.[197] Some courts have opted for an "unzoned approach," in which a judicial declaration of invalidity results in the land being declared unzoned until the zoning authority rezones the land in an appropriate manner.[198] The unzoned approach has been criticized as lacking predictability for neighboring property owners, a criticism also levied at the practice of designating a particular zoning classification, often one that is similar to or the same as zoning classifications nearby, as the one to be utilized after a declaration of invalidity and until the zoning authority rezones in an appropriate manner. The landowner is then permitted to make any use of the property permitted by the designated classification, a result that may give the person who lost the case more than he or she originally sought.[199]

The Supreme Court of Michigan, drawing on the experience of courts in Illinois,[200] Ohio,[201] and Virginia,[202] has adopted the Illinois "specific reasonable use" relief rule. Under this rule, a court that declares a zoning ordinance unconstitutional may also declare the plaintiff's proposed use of the land to be a reasonable, and thus permissible, use if the plaintiff meets the burden of establishing that the proposed use is reasonable and may issue an injunction prohibiting the regulatory body from interfering with that use. Under this rule, if the plaintiff meets his or her burden of showing reasonable use, the regulatory body may rezone, but only to a classification that is consistent with the plaintiff's proposed use.[203]

A variation of this remedy, called the *builder's remedy,* is often sought by a landowner who has successfully challenged the failure to rezone to allow his or her proposed use to be implemented. Builders' remedies may take the form of an order that the land be rezoned in a particular manner, that a permit be issued for a particular use, or that a comprehensive plan be modified to recognize a proposed use as consistent with the plan. Only in extreme circumstances, such as when a court is persuaded that a community is arbitrarily refusing to comply with a constitutional/judicial mandate to accept some affordable housing within its borders, will a court issue a builder's remedy.[204] Typically, however, a court may not order a zoning, but may only overturn it.

The New Jersey Supreme Court discussed in detail the use of builders' remedies in *Southern Burlington County NAACP v. Township of Mount Laurel (Mount Laurel II)*,[205] characterizing an order that an ordinance be amended as doing "very little different from ordering that a variance be granted" or from declaring an ordinance in violation of equal protection standards, the "effect of that often being not simply to allow a plaintiff to use his property in a manner not permitted by the ordinance, but to give the same right to an entire class."[206] The court approved the granting of builders' remedies when communities were found to be intentionally refusing to respond to the New Jersey constitutional mandate to avoid using the zoning power to exclude housing opportunities for persons of low and moderate income and to take affirmative steps to make a fair share of such housing opportunities available within their boundaries.

Damages generally are not available in ordinary zoning matters, but courts are increasingly willing to approve of damages awards when a zoning decision is held to be a "temporary taking,"[207] a violation of federal civil rights laws,[208] or in cases of "reprehensible" conduct and "flagrant misuse of government authority," such as revocation of valid permits without notice or good reason to stop construction of a condominium development in midcourse.[209]

Generally, injunctive relief is rarely available against the enforcement of a zoning ordinance or, conversely, the commencement of construction pursuant to a valid land use approval but is usually available in favor of the municipality to remedy violations of proscriptive provisions of the ordinance.[210]

Res Judicata

The doctrine of res judicata occasionally is applicable in zoning proceedings. Courts are reluctant to apply the doctrine to particular zoning controversies because of the continuing nature of the zoning process and the need for flexibility in administration of that process. The Supreme Court of Pennsylvania has articulated a four-part test that requires concurrence of all four elements in order for the doctrine to be applied:

1. identity of the thing sued upon;
2. identity of the cause of action;
3. identity of the parties; and
4. identity of the parties' capacity.[211]

Applying that test, the Commonwealth Court of Pennsylvania refused to bar a second application for a special-use permit in which the applicants expanded their theory from the theory that was rejected, and not appealed, in the first application for the permit.[212]

Governmental boards are bound by the doctrine equally with applicants. Thus a board may not unilaterally reopen proceedings to reverse itself regarding a zoning decision without a "substantial change in circumstances."[213]

Res judicata is especially relevent where an approval, such as legislative rezoning, is not subject to a clear statute of limitation and several parties, such as neighborhood opponents, may bring a series of legal attacks.[214]

Appellate Review

In general, the scope of review by an appellate court of a trial court's decision in a zoning matter is limited. In appeals from administrative agencies, such as zoning boards of adjustment, in which the trial court hears no new evidence, the scope of review of the appellate court is limited to a determination whether the land use regulatory agency whose decision is being appealed "committed a manifest abuse of discretion or an error of law."[215]

When the trial court receives additional evidence or when the proceeding contests the validity of a zoning decision made by a legislative body, such as an inverse condemnation suit, the trial court's resolution of conflicting evidence will not be overturned unless clearly erroneous,[216] nor will its determination of liability be reversed "if supported by competent, substantial evidence."[217]

The appellate court reviews the proceedings at which the challenged decision was made rather than the trial court proceedings.[218] Appellate courts have felt free to make an independent examination of the challenged proceedings and to "substitute [their] judgment for that of the trial court" on contested matters.[219]

As with all courts, appellate courts will resist giving advisory opinions.[220] When zoning disputes raise constitutional issues and the parties as well as the trial court treat the case as a matter in equity, reviewing courts may conduct a de novo review.[221]

Resolution of Zoning Disputes Through Arbitration or Mediation

Several jurisdictions are experimenting with various "early-warning" techniques to resolve zoning disputes before they escalate into major litigation, particularly in the context of disputes over whether a particular regulatory decision has "taken" property in a constitutional sense.[222] Examples of such techniques include the use of negotiation between landowners and landmark preservation boards to seek agreement on appropriate "controls and incentives" to preserve property receiving landmark designation while allowing the owner a reasonable return on investment[223] and the use of a two-step mediation/arbitration process to resolve disputes regarding appropriate rental increases under rent-control ordinances.[224] Pennsylvania, for example, has enacted legislation permitting mediation as a "wholly voluntary" supplement to zoning appeal procedures.[225]

The New Jersey Fair Housing Act,[226] enacted in response to the *Mount Laurel* cases,[227] establishes a mediation process for resolution of disputes regarding certain decisions of the Council on Affordable Housing, a state agency established to determine housing regions, estimate housing need, and establish criteria for determining municipal fair-share requirements under the *Mount*

Laurel principles. The Council is required to engage in mediation in the following situations:

1. when timely objections are filed to a municipality's proposed substantive certification that its fair share plan and housing element meet the requirements of the act; or
2. whenever exclusionary zoning litigation has been instituted against a municipality that has filed a fair share plan and housing element, or has filed a timely resolution of intent to participate in the fair-share determination process.[228]

In the latter case, the statute treats the mediation process as an administrative remedy that must be exhausted before a trial on the complaint may be obtained.[229] If objections cannot be resolved through the mediation process, the case is referred to an administrative law judge, who hears it in an expedited manner as a contested matter. The administrative law judge makes an initial decision and forwards that initial decision to the Council, which makes the final administrative decision on the matter. If the review and mediation process is not completed within six months of receipt of a request for mediation from a party who has instituted litigation, the party may be relieved of the obligation to exhaust administrative remedies upon motion to a court of competent jurisdiction.[230]

The Supreme Court of New Jersey upheld the constitutionality of the act in *Hills Development Company v. Bernards Township*.[231] With respect to using mediation prior to litigation when cities have filed fair-share plans, the court made the following observation:

> In any lawsuit attacking a municipality's ordinances that have received substantive certification as not in compliance with the Mount Laurel constitutional obligation, the plaintiff will be required to prove such noncompliance by clear and convincing evidence, and the Council shall be made a party to any such lawsuit. The difficulties facing any plaintiff attempting to meet such a burden of proof are best understood by noting the variety of methodologies that can be used legitimately to determine regional need and fair share as well as the many different ways in which a realistic opportunity to achieve that fair share may be provided. If the Council conscientiously performs its duties, including determining regional need and evaluating whether the proposed adjustments and ordinances provide the requisite fair share opportunity, a successful Mount Laurel lawsuit should be a rarity. There is therefore a broad range of municipal action that will withstand challenge, given this burden of proof.[232]

Mediation as an approach to resolution of zoning disputes has been suggested as part of a governmental "accommodation power" that can serve as a "middle ground" between use of eminent domain (taking with compensation) and police power regulation (no compensation). The accommodation power would be triggered whenever governmental control denied a landowner "reasonable beneficial use" or "adequate return," giving rise to options such as a variance, payment for the difference in value between the controlled value and the reasonable beneficial use value, or payment in nondollar values such as transfer of development rights. Mediation and the accommodation power may offer "a flexibility [to some forms of land use dispute] which can ease the conflict between the public and the private owner." Proponents of accommodation argue that it has potential in cases involving particular buildings, such as landmarks preservation, but doubt its ability to achieve much in disputes over environmental protection or resource preservation. They stress that the essential balancing process of "public benefit versus private detriment" cannot be reduced to "metric measure," but argue that the public can expect that "the process be open, that it be fair, that whenever possible it seek to accommodate."[233]

Practitioner Perspectives

In representing any client in a zoning matter, the lawyer should first determine the applicable local relief (e.g., legislative rezoning, administrative-board-of-adjustment variance or special-use permit, administrative subdivision approval by the legislative body) to determine the ultimate standard of judicial review applicable to the local action. The applicable relief is usually obvious, but counsel should always consider more favorable alternatives, especially with respect to ultimate judicial review. If, for example, judicial review would be highly deferential, such as applicable to legislative decisions, the better approach may be as a lobbyist/advocate rather than as trial counsel presenting evidence and making a record.

Second, counsel should thoroughly review the local ordinance for any procedural issues, including, most important, additional layers of review that are peculiar to the current jurisdiction and not necessarily contemplated or even authorized by the state enabling statutes. Some jurisdictions have much greater tolerance of, if not appetite for, redundant public hearings, although self-generation by the city of appellate review levels may be invalidated if contradictory to state enabling statutes.[234]

Local land use ordinances are notoriously inconsistent and redundant, both procedurally and substantively. Such ordinances are enacted incrementally over years of political administrations, and generally the poorer the city, the more ambiguous and irrational the ordinance. State enabling statutes do not make local ordinances in any way uniform, and local idiosyncracies are both a boon to and the bane of the land use lawyer.

In administrative land use matters and even in legislative matters in some jurisdictions, it is important both to make a record and to get a written decision based on a finding of facts.[235]

In an administrative hearing, the land use lawyer, like the trial lawyer, will make several conscious decisions about making a favorable record, beginning inquiries or making assertions that risk development of an unfavorable record, or simply permitting the record to remain inadequate. It is a rare case that benefits from an inadequate record, although a completely inadequate record, which does not even support meaningful judicial review, may give the lawyer a second bite of the apple upon remand. More often, as in cases where the vote is in doubt, or at least not assured, the lawyer does not want to (1) offend volunteer officials by "over-lawyering"; (2) encourage rebuttal by neighborhood opposition or city staff or legal counsel; (3) encourage improvement of the record by neighborhood opposition, which is often emotional but nonprobative or incompetent to a reviewing court; or (4) prolong proceedings and thereby increase risk.

Procedural items that must be a part of every record in administrative matters, and in some cases even in legislative matters, are as follows:

1. Notice: mailing or publication, as required;
2. Notice: receipt, as applicable;
3. Observance of all time periods for notice, usually minima;
4. Oath of witnesses;
5. Recording of testimony;
6. Marking and admission of exhibits;
7. Observance of Robert's Rules of Order, including requisite number and content of readings upon passage;
8. Adequate opportunity to be heard by opposition; and
9. Maintenance and proof of a purchase or option right, if not title to the subject property.

It is usually helpful to prepare a written statement for the record, even a conclusory one, because there are no rules of evidence or prohibitions on receipt of such items, as in the case of traditional trials.

To the extent that a client is relying on obtaining a favorable decision, it is important that the practitioner become involved in the decision process and seek the opportunity to help structure the decision and final opinion. Counsel should always ask to review proposed legislation or administrative findings prior to the hearing. In jurisdictions where it is appropriate to submit proposed findings or the practitioner has the opportunity to review and comment, counsel should do so, especially if the decision is in the client's favor and may have to be supported on appeal.

Zoning decisions may be made hastily and informally. The practitioner may, and usually does, meet local resistance from staff and officials who are volunteers and may not share the client's concern with the record and written proceedings. As in most zoning matters at the local level, counsel will have to walk a line between alienating such officials and protecting the client. Counsel should expect the officials to resist letting the applicant take the lead role in drafting findings or ordinances, especially when the municipality has active counsel of its own.

Despite counsel's best efforts, and although enabling legislation and ordinances enacted thereunder require findings of fact, local bodies often do not make good findings or accurately translate those findings into the ultimate decision. Those jurisdictions that utilize hearing examiners, particularly in the case of rezonings, are more likely to make better findings and have those findings relate to the ultimate conclusion than those jurisdictions where the board is responsible for the findings. Such decisions, even if not appealed, become the law applicable to a parcel and may run with the land, thus affecting the marketability of the property.

The presumptions, burden of proof, and judicial review limitations discussed in this chapter reinforce the need to win cases at the administrative or legislative level rather than relying on the courts. Reversals are unusual. In those jurisdictions where one is not likely to achieve a decision by the court other than a determination that the lower decision is to be upheld or reversed, judicial appeals are rarely a realistic alternative to the client whose project is behind schedule.

The land use lawyer for the applicant faces another set of issues not generally applicable in other adversarial proceedings—the multiplicity of opponents. Doctrines of res judicata, statutes of limitations, laches, multiple and perhaps inconsistent theories, and negotiating with unrepresented parties are hurdles when a project faces substantial neighborhood opposition.

Another consequence of the characterization of zoning decisions as legislative or administrative is the effect of that characterization on ex parte contacts (i.e., contacts with a decision-maker outside of the presence of the opposing party).[236] An experienced land use practitioner from Oregon made the following observations about such contacts in light of *Fasano v. Board of County Commissioners of Washington County*:[237]

> *Fasano* does regulate *ex parte* contacts—i.e., someone goes to the county courthouse for a private meeting with the county commissioner, urges that a certain fact is true or a certain policy interpretation is appropriate. The purpose of regulating *ex parte* contacts is not because *ex parte* contacts are wicked. The concern about *ex parte* contacts is that decision makers function best when they have the benefit of an adversarial proceeding in front of them.
>
> If parties with adverse interests compete in front of a tribunal, when one party says "X" is *not* true, it is likely the other party will say why he believes X *is* true. Similarly, if one party suggests something that is unreasonable in terms of policy interpretation, the other party is likely to say why. *Local officials, like judges, need this debate*. The evil in *ex parte* contacts is that the decision maker does not have the benefit of that kind of "checking" by the opposing party.
>
> Hence, policy dealing with *ex parte* contacts is not aimed primarily at invalidating local decisions tainted by *ex parte* contacts, but at requiring a disclosure of those contacts at the time of public hearing, on the record, in the form of a *statement of capacity to hear*. In that statement the local official should indicate the form of the contact, with whom it occurred, when, and most important, the substance of the contact. If the contact involves written materials, these should be forwarded to other parties immediately. By putting on the record the nature of the contact, the opposing side will have an opportunity to rebut the contentions made privately. This helps preserve the opportunity for the decision maker to have an adverse proceeding.

However, if there is no disclosure, and the *ex parte* contact is significant, reversal of the local decision is appropriate because impartiality has been denied.[238]

Finally, the practitioner should consider the use of consent decrees.[239]

Notes

1. For an example of general jurisdiction as a basis for judicial land use review power, see Bucktail, LLC v. County Council of Talbot County, 723 A.2d 440 (Md. App. 1999).

2. *See, e.g.,* American Tower Corporation v. Common Council of City of Beckley, 557 S.E.2d 752 (W. Va. 2002).

3. *See, e.g.,* KY. REV. STAT. ANN. § 100.347 (Michie 1997); Barner v. Bd. of Supervisors, 537 A.2d 922 (Pa. Commw. Ct. 1988); Butzgy v. Glastonbury, 523 A.2d 1258 (Conn. 1987); Charlotte v. Richmond, 609 A.2d 638 (Vt. 1992); Friends of Woodstock, Inc. v. Woodstock Planning Bd., 543 N.Y.S.2d 1007 (App. Div. 1989); *see also* pp. 256–59.

4. *See, e.g.,* MD. CODE ANN. Art. 66b, § 4.07 (1997).

5. *See, e.g.,* KY. REV. STAT. ANN. § 100.217 (Michie 1997).

6. *See, e.g.,* FLA. STAT. ANN. § 163.230 (West 1997); Hynes v. Pasco County, Fla., 801 F.2d 1269, 1270 (11th Cir. 1986) (construing FLA. STAT. ANN. § 163.230); TEX. LOCAL GOV'T CODE ANN. § 211.009(a)(1) (West 1995); Heritage Soc. of Washington County v. Neumann, 771 S.W.2d 563, 565 (Tex. Ct. App. 1989) (construing TEX. LOCAL GOV'T CODE ANN. § 211.009(a)(1) and upholding affirmance of building permit as within board of adjustment jurisdiction to hear and decide appeals).

7. *See, e.g.,* MO. REV. STAT. § 89.090.1.(3) (1996); White Castle Sys. v. Planning Bd. of City of Clifton, 583 A.2d 406 (N.J. Super. Ct. App. Div. 1990) (granting variances is within exclusive jurisdiction of board of adjustment), *cert. denied,* 598 A.2d 880 (N.J. 1991), *abrogated by* Coventry Square, Inc. v. Westwood Zoning Bd. of Adjustment, 650 A.2d 340 (N.J. 1994); *see generally* p. 229.

8. *See, e.g.,* MD. CODE ANN. Art. 66b, § 4.07(d)(2) (1997); Alachua County v. Eagle's Nest Farms, Inc., 473 So. 2d 257, 259–60 (Fla. Ct. App. 1985); *see generally* p. 225.

9. Sandy City v. Salt Lake County, 827 P.2d 212 (Utah 1992) (power to zone is legislative and cannot be delegated to board of adjustment); Holiday Homes, Inc. v. Butler County Bd. of Zoning Appeals, 520 N.E.2d 605 (Ohio Ct. App. 1987) (board has exclusive authority to grant conditional-use permits); *White Castle Systems,* 583 A.2d 406.

10. Ratliff v. Phillips, 746 S.W.2d 405 (Ky. 1988).

11. *Id.* at 406. *See also* Burwick v. Zoning Bd. of Appeals of Worcester, 306 N.E.2d 455, 459 (Mass. App. Ct. 1974) (expressing court's reluctance to penalize applicant for failures of the board over which the applicant had no control).

12. *Ratliff,* 746 S.W.2d at 406.

13. *See, e.g.,* KY. REV. STAT. ANN. §§ 100.99, 100.157 (Michie 1997).

14. *See, e.g.,* KY. REV. STAT. ANN. § 100.261 (Michie 1997); MD. CODE ANN. Art. 66B, § 4.07(e) (1997); MO. REV. STAT. § 89.100. (1996); N.Y. GEN. CITY LAW § 81 (McKinney 1997).

15. Palmer v. St. Louis County, 591 S.W.2d 39, 41 (Mo. Ct. App. 1979); *see also* Allen v. Burlington Bd. of Adjustment, 397 S.E.2d 657 (N.C. Ct. App. 1990); *see* pp. 254–55.

16. Wehrle v. Cassor, 708 S.W.2d 788, 791 (Mo. Ct. App. 1986); Wallace v. Bd. of County Comm'rs of Klamath County, 804 P.2d 1220 (Or. Ct. App. 1991) (adjacent property owners have standing).

17. FLA. STAT. ANN. § 163.3215(2) (West 1997).

18. Benton County v. Friends of Benton County, 653 P.2d 1249, 1255 (Or. 1982).

19. *Id.*

20. Frampton v. Zoning Bd. of Appeals for Town of Lloyd, 494 N.Y.S.2d 479, 481 (App. Div. 1985).

21. *See, e.g.,* Mo. Rev. Stat. § 89.090.1.(1) (1996); Nealy v. Cole, 442 S.W.2d 128 (Mo. Ct. App. 1969).

22. Mullen v. City of Kansas City, Mo., 557 S.W.2d 652, 654 (Mo. Ct. App. 1977).

23. Wolfner v. Bd. of Adjustment of City of Frontenac, 672 S.W.2d 147, 151 (Mo. Ct. App. 1984).

24. Davis v. J.C. Nichols Co., 768 S.W.2d 81, 83 (Mo. Ct. App. 1986), *appeal after remand,* 761 S.W.2d 735 (1988); *see also* Lower Merion Township v. Enokay, Inc., 233 A.2d 883 (Pa. 1967); Merritt v. Wilson County Bd. of Zoning Appeals, 656 S.W.2d 846, 854 (Tenn. Ct. App. 1983).

25. Ky. Rev. Stat. Ann. § 100.261 (Michie 1997); Md. Code Ann. Art. 66B, § 4.07 (1997); Mo. Rev. Stat. § 89.100 (1996); N.Y. Gen. City Law § 81 (McKinney 1997).

26. *See, e.g.,* Md. Code Ann. Art. 66B, § 4.07(e) (1997); Mo. Rev. Stat. § 89.100 (1996); N.Y. Gen. City Law § 81.2 (McKinney 1997).

27. *See, e.g., id.*

28. *See, e.g.,* Ky. Rev. Stat. Ann. § 100.261 (McKinney 1997); *see also* Iodice v. City of Newton, 491 N.E.2d 618 (Mass. 1986) (challenge dismissed for failure to adhere to 20-day time limit for appeal); Moyer v. Lehighton Borough Zoning Hearing Bd., 40 Pa. D. & C.3d 607 (1986) (board deprived of jurisdiction by failure to file appeal after 30 days from issuance of permit); Bosley v. Zoning Bd. of Appeals of City of New Haven, 622 A.2d 1020 (Conn. Ct. App. 1993) (statutory 30-day limit on time for appeal is applicable where board did not adopt rule specifying another time period).

29. *See, e.g.,* Ky. Rev. Stat. Ann. § 100.261 (Michie 1997); Md. Code Ann. Art. 66B, § 4.07(e) (1997); Mo. Rev. Stat. § 89.100 (1996); N.Y. Gen. City Law § 81.2 (McKinney 1997); *see also* Henze v. Wetzel, 754 S.W.2d 888 (Mo. Ct. App. 1988) (boards of adjustment not bound by technical rules of pleading).

30. *See, e.g., id.*

31. *See, e.g.,* Ky. Rev. Stat. Ann. § 100.261 (Michie 1997).

32. *See, e.g.,* Md. Code Ann. Art. 66B, § 4.07(f) (1997); Mo. Rev. Stat. § 89.100 (1996); N.Y. Gen. City Law § 81.3 (McKinney 1997).

33. *See, e.g., id.*

34. *See, e.g., id.; see also* Brandywine Park Condominium Council v. Members of Wilmington Zoning Bd. of Adjustment, 534 A.2d 286 (Del. Super. Ct. 1987) (due cause is shown by some probability of success on the merits, possibility of irreparable harm, and balancing of harm).

35. *See, e.g., id.*

36. Ky. Rev. Stat. Ann. § 100.263 (Michie 1997).

37. *See, e.g., id.;* N.Y. Gen. City Law § 81.4 (McKinney 1997).

38. Ky. Rev. Stat. Ann. § 100.263 (Michie 1997).

39. *See, e.g.,* Maitland v. Pelican Beach Props., Inc., 892 F.2d 245, 251 (3d Cir. 1989) (reversible error for board of land use appeals to allow ex parte information to be presented at executive session); Rodine v. Zoning Bd. of Adjustment, 434 N.W.2d 124 (Iowa Ct. App. 1988) (ex parte communications violate basic considerations of fairness). *See pp. 270–71 supra.*

40. S.I.S. Enterprises, Inc. v. Zoning Bd. of Appeals, 635 A.2d 835 (Conn. Ct. App. 1993).

41. Simon v. City of Auburn Bd. of Zoning Appeals, 519 N.E.2d 205, 211 (Ind. Ct. App. 1988); *see also* Wells v. Dallas County Bd. of Adjustment, 475 N.W.2d 680 (Iowa Ct. App. 1991) (open-meetings law applies to board of adjustment hearing on application for variance).

42. *See, e.g.,* Md. Code Ann. Art. 66B, § 4.07(g) (1997); Mo. Rev. Stat. § 89.100 (1996); N.Y. Gen. City Law § 81.4 (McKinney 1997).

43. *See, e.g.,* Conn. Gen. Stat. § 8-7d(a) (1997); Ky. Rev. Stat. Ann. § 100.263 (Michie 1997).

44. Donohue v. Zoning Bd. of Appeals, 235 A.2d 643 (Conn. 1967).

45. *See, e.g.,* KY. REV. STAT. ANN. § 100.257 (Michie 1997); MD. CODE ANN. Art. 66b, § 4.07(d)(1) (1997); MO. REV. STAT. § 89.090.1(1) (1996); N.Y. GEN. CITY LAW § 81.1 (McKinney 1997).

46. *See, e.g.,* MO. REV. STAT. § 89.090.1(2) (1996); N.Y. GEN. CITY LAW § 81.1.

47. MO. REV. STAT. § 89.090.1(3) (1996); *see also* N.Y. GEN. CITY LAW § 81.4 (McKinney 1997).

48. KY. REV. STAT. ANN. § 100.241 (Michie 1997).

49. *See supra* pp. 229–31.

50. *See generally supra* pp. 225–29.

51. *See, e.g.,* MD. CODE ANN. Art. 66B, § 4.07(h) (1997); MO. REV. STAT. § 89.090.2 (1996); N.Y. GEN. CITY LAW § 81.4 (McKinney 1997).

52. Lower Merion Township v. Enokay, Inc., 233 A.2d 883 (Pa. 1967); Father Ryan High School, Inc. v. City of Oak Hill, 774 S.W.2d 184, 189 (Tenn. Ct. App. 1988); Bowman v. Greene County Comm'n, 732 S.W.2d 223, 225 (Mo. Ct. App. 1987).

53. Rice v. Bd. of Adjustment of Village of Bel-Ridge, 804 S.W.2d 821, 824 (Mo. Ct. App. 1991) (denial of application for day-care center remanded for consideration whether day-care center constituted permissible "service facility serving neighborhood needs"); *but see* Spero v. Zoning Bd. of Appeals of Town of Guilford, 586 A.2d 590 (Conn. 1991) (relying partially on lawyer's advice does not constitute unlawful delegation of board's authority).

54. *See, e.g.,* Frampton v. Zoning Bd. of Appeals for Town of Lloyd, 494 N.Y.S.2d 479, 480 (App. Div. 1985) (upholding decision that general parking ban on tractor trailers was inapplicable to occasional social visits); Taxville Full Gospel Church v. West Manchester Township Zoning Bd., 38 Pa. D. & C.3d 554 (1982) (court will reverse zoning board's interpretation of local zoning ordinance only upon error of law or clear abuse of discretion); *but see* Holmes v. Bd. of Zoning Appeals of Jasper County, 634 N.E.2d 522 (Ind. Ct. App. 1994) (no deference given to zoning board's determination of pure questions of law).

55. *See* p. 261–62 (discussing the distinction between administrative and legislative actions).

56. Schad v. Borough of Mount Ephraim, 452 U.S. 61 (1981), *limitation of holding recognized by* Walker v. City of Kansas City, Mo., 911 F.2d 80 (8th Cir. 1990); Village of Euclid v. Ambler Realty Co., 272 U.S. 365 (1926); Sellon v. City of Manitou Springs, 745 P.2d 229 (Colo. 1987); Parranto Bros., Inc. v. City of New Brighton, 425 N.W.2d 585 (Minn. Ct. App. 1988) (citing State, by Rochester Ass'n of Neighborhoods v. City of Rochester, 268 N.W.2d 885, 888 (Minn. 1978)); Bowman v. Greene County, 732 S.W.2d 223, 224 (Mo. Ct. App. 1987) (quoting Kolb v. County Court of St. Charles County, 683 S.W.2d 318, 321 (Mo. Ct. App. 1983)).

57. Quinn v. Town of Dodgeville, 364 N.W.2d 149, 158 (Wis. 1985) (citing Buhler v. Racine County, 146 N.W.2d 403 (Wis. 1966)).

58. Village of Euclid v. Ambler Realty Co., 272 U.S. 365, 388 (1926).

59. Michalek v. Village of Midlothian, 452 N.E.2d 655, 663 (Ill. Ct. App. 1983).

60. *See* J.R. Green Properties, Inc. v. City of Bridgeton, 825 S.W.2d 684, 686 (Mo. Ct. App. 1992).

61. St. Lucas Ass'n v. City of Chicago, 571 N.E.2d 865, 873 (Ill. App. Ct. 1991).

62. Landau v. City Council of City of Overland Park, 767 P.2d 1290, 1294 (Kan. 1989) (citing Golden v. City of Overland Park, 584 P.2d 130 (Kan. 1978)), *holding modified,* Davis v. City of Leavenworth, 802 P.2d 494 (Kan. 1990).

63. Landau v. City Council of City of Overland Park, 767 P.2d 1290, 1295 (Kan. 1989) (quoting Dings v. Phillips, 701 P.2d 961 (Kan. 1985)), *holding modified,* Davis v. City of Leavenworth, 802 P.2d 494 (Kan. 1990).

64. New Lenox State Bank v. County of Will, 563 N.E.2d 505, 509 (Ill. Ct. App. 1990).

65. Bishop v. Town of Houghton, 420 P.2d 368, 372–73 (Wash. 1966).

66. White v. City of Brentwood, 799 S.W.2d 890, 892 (Mo. Ct. App. 1990) (quoting Elam v. City of St. Ann, 784 S.W.2d 330, 335 (Mo. Ct. App. 1990)).

67. *See, e.g.*, Mo. Rev. Stat. § 536.100, *et seq.* (1996); 55 ILCS 5/5-12012 (West 1997); *see also* Standard Oil Division of Amoco v. City of Florissant, 607 S.W.2d 854 (Mo. Ct. App. 1980).

68. *See, e.g.*, Mo. Rev. Stat. § 536.100, *et seq.* (1996); 55 ILCS 5/5-12012 (West 1997).

69. Tucker v. McDonald, 793 S.W.2d 616, 617 (Mo. Ct. App. 1990); *see also* Newman v. Zoning Bd. of Appeals of Yorktown, 503 N.Y.S.2d 601 (App. Div.) (decision of zoning board will be set aside only where record reveals decision was illegal, arbitrary, or an abuse of discretion), *appeal denied*, 501 N.E.2d 600 (N.Y. 1986); Schwartz v. Planning & Zoning Comm'n, 543 A.2d 1339 (Conn. 1988) (court's review is limited to determining whether administrative decision was unreasonable, arbitrary, or illegal).

70. Gatti v. Zoning Hearing Bd. of Salisbury Township, 543 A.2d 622, 625 (Pa. Commw. Ct. 1988).

71. Nolan v. Bd. of Adjustment of Iowa City, 350 N.W.2d 744, 746 (Iowa Ct. App. 1984); *see also* Love v. Bd. of County Comm'rs of Bingham County, 671 P.2d 471 (Idaho 1983) (Idaho statute prohibits reviewing court from substituting its judgment regarding the weight of the evidence on questions of fact), *appeal after remand*, 701 P.2d 1293 (Idaho 1985); Lazovitz v. Bd. of Adjustment, Berkeley Heights, 517 A.2d 486 (N.J. Super. Ct. App. Div. 1986); Frishman v. Schmidt, 466 N.Y.S.2d 452 (App. Div. 1983); Clinkscales v. City of Lake Oswego, 615 P.2d 1164, 1168 (Or. Ct. App. 1980) (in reviewing administrative decision of city council, court may not weigh the evidence even though it might reach a different conclusion).

72. Lazovitz v. Bd. of Adjustment, Berkeley Heights, 517 A.2d 486 (N.J. Super. Ct. App. Div. 1986).

73. Heritage Society of Washington County v. Neumann, 771 S.W.2d 563, 566 (Tex. Ct. App. 1989); *see also* Newman v. Zoning Bd. of Appeals of Yorktown, 503 N.Y.S.2d 601 (App. Div.), *appeal denied*, 501 N.E.2d 600 (N.Y. 1986); Schwartz v. Planning & Zoning Comm'n, 543 A.2d 1339 (Conn. 1988).

74. Humble Oil & Refining Co. v. Borough of East Lansdowne, 227 A.2d 664 (Pa. 1967); Reynolds v. Haws, 741 S.W.2d 582 (Tex. Ct. App. 1987) (ten days to file appeal); Burns v. Peavler, 714 S.W.2d 163 (Ky. Ct. App. 1986).

75. *See, e.g.*, Herd v. St. Charles County Comm'n, 764 S.W.2d 505, 506 (Mo. Ct. App. 1989) (quoting Cass County v. Dandurand, 759 S.W.2d 603, 606 (Mo. Ct. App. 1988)).

76. Leslie v. City of Henderson, 797 S.W.2d 718 (Ky. Ct. App. 1990).

77. Virgin Islands Conservation Soc'y, Inc. v. Virgin Islands Bd. of Land Use Appeals, 881 F.2d 28 (3d Cir. 1989).

78. *See, e.g.*, Fong v. Planning and Zoning Bd. of Appeals of Town of Greenwich, 563 A.2d 293, 297 (Conn. 1989).

79. *See, e.g.*, Drury Displays, Inc. v. Bd. of Adjustment of City of St. Louis, 781 S.W.2d 201, 202 (Mo. Ct. App. 1989).

80. Humble Oil & Ref. Co. v. Borough of East Lansdowne, 227 A.2d 664, 665 (Pa. 1967); *see also* Love v. Bd. of County Comm'rs of Bingham County, 671 P.2d 471 (Idaho 1983); Johnson v. City of Mount Vernon, 679 P.2d 405 (Wash. Ct. App. 1984).

81. *See* pp. 261–62.

82. *See* Schaefer v. Cleveland, 847 S.W.2d 867, 873 (Mo. Ct. App. 1993).

83. State of Minnesota, By Minnesota Park Lovers v. City of Minneapolis, 468 N.W.2d 566 (Minn. Ct. App. 1991) (holding that a city's decision that a conditional-use permit had expired was subject to de novo review as a question of law and not to the deferential standard of whether there was a reasonable basis for the city's decision).

84. *See, e.g.*, Conn. Gen. Stat. § 8-8(a) (1997); Fusco v. Connecticut, 815 F.2d 201, 204 n.3 (2d Cir.) (first group considered "classically aggrieved" and the second group considered "statutorily aggrieved"), *cert. denied*, 484 U.S. 849 (1987).

85. Fusco v. Connecticut, 815 F.2d at 204 n.3. (opportunity to appeal granted by statute to neighboring landowners is procedural in nature and does not create property interest enforceable by section 1983 action in federal court); *see also* South Hollywood Hills Citizens Ass'n for Pres. of Neighborhood Safety and the Env't v. King County, 677 P.2d 114, 118 (Wash. 1984) (notice by publication plus posting on affected property held sufficient notice to neighboring landowners).

86. Persons v. City of Fort Worth, 790 S.W.2d 865, 868–70 (Tex. Ct. App. 1990) (resident of neighborhood adjacent to city park lacked standing to oppose proposed expansion of city zoo in park where allegation of injury was limited to loss of some use of park); *see also* Pres. Alliance, Inc. v. Norfolk Southern Corp., 413 S.E.2d 519 (Ga. Ct. App. 1991) (plaintiff must suffer some special damage not common to similarly situated property owners); Barvenik v. Bd. of Aldermen of Newton, 597 N.E.2d 48 (Mass. 1992) (plaintiff must have special injury different from concerns of the rest of the community), *abrogated,* Marashlian v. Zoning Bd. of Appeals of Newburyport, 660 N.E.2d 369 (Mass. 1996).

87. Persons v. City of Fort Worth, 790 S.W.2d 865, 868–70 (Tex. Ct. App. 1990).

88. Dyer v. Zoning Bd. of Appeals of Arlington Heights, 534 N.E.2d 506, 510 (Ill. Ct. App. 1989).

89. Lauer v. City of Kenner, 536 So. 2d 767, 772 (La. Ct. App. 1988), *writ denied,* 538 So. 2d 594 (La. 1989).

90. Mobil Oil Corp. v. Syracuse Indus. Dev. Agency, 559 N.E.2d 641, 644 (N.Y. 1990).

91. Bangnall v. Town of Beverly Shores, 726 N.E.2d 782 (Ind. 2000).

92. Rodriguez v. Henderson, 578 N.E.2d 57 (Ill. Ct. App. 1991). The *Rodriguez* case illustrates the thinness of the line between standing issues and pleading issues as to whether the plaintiffs have stated a cause of action.

93. *See, e.g.,* Citizens Growth Mgmt. Coalition of West Palm Beach, Inc. v. City of West Palm Beach, Inc., 450 So. 2d 204, 206 (Fla. 1984), Burrtec Waste Indus., Inc. v. City of Colton, 119 Cal. Rptr. 2d 410 (Ct. App. 2002).

94. Burrtec Waste Indus., Inc. v. City of Colton, n. 93, *supra,* citing Bozung v. Local Agency Formation Comm., 529 P.2d 1017 (Cal. 1975).

95. *See, e.g.,* Kasper v. Coury, 555 N.E.2d 310, 312 (Ohio 1990); Speck v. Zoning Bd. of Appeals of City of Chicago, 433 N.E.2d 685 (Ill. 1982).

96. *In re* St. Tammany Parish Bd. of Adjustments, 676 So. 2d 119 (La. Ct. App. 1996) (holding that the board has no interest in preserving its own ruling).

97. Simovits v. Chanticleer Condominium Ass'n, 933 F. Supp. 1394 (N.D. Ill. 1996).

98. Citizens for Safe Waste Mgmt. v. St. Louis County, 810 S.W.2d 635, 639 (Mo. Ct. App. 1991) (stating "we decline to apply in zoning cases the liberalized federal rule of organizational standing").

99. 422 U.S. 490 (1975).

100. Love Church v. City of Evanston, 896 F.2d 1082, 1085 (7th Cir.), *cert. denied,* 498 U.S. 898 (1990) (mere possibility that church could have more easily acquired rental property absent special-permit requirement for churches did not confer standing to challenge permit requirement under First and Fourteenth Amendments); Baytree of Inverray Realty v. City of Lauderhill, 873 F.2d 1407 (11th Cir. 1989) (allegations of racially motivated actions influencing an adverse zoning decision sufficient to confer standing).

101. Burrtec Waste Indus. Inc. v. City of Colton, n. 93, *supra.*

102. Singal v. City of Bangor, 440 A.2d 1048, 1050 (Me. 1982).

103. *See, e.g.,* City of Madison v. Bryan, 763 S.2d 162 (Miss. 2000).

104. Southwest Ranches Homeowners Ass'n, Inc. v. Broward County, 502 So. 2d 931, 935 (Fla. Ct. App. 1987) (construing FLA. STAT. ANN. § 163.3215 (West 1997) to grant standing to citizens' groups to challenge decision regarding siting of sanitary landfill), *review denied,* 511 So. 2d 999 (Fla. 1987).

105. 42 U.S.C. § 1983 (1997). *See* pp. 102–04.

106. Railroad Comm'n v. Pullman Co., 312 U.S. 496 (1941).

107. Kollsman v. City of Los Angeles, 737 F.2d 830, 833 (9th Cir. 1984) (citing Richardson v. Koshiba, 693 F.2d 911, 915 (9th Cir. 1982)), *cert. denied*, 469 U.S. 1211 (1985).

108. *Id.* at 836–37.

109. Chez Sez III Corp. v. Township of Union, 945 F.2d 628 (3d Cir. 1991), *cert. denied*, 503 U.S. 493 (1992).

110. Burford v. Sun Oil Co., 319 U.S. 315 (1943).

111. Browning-Ferris, Inc. v. Baltimore County, 774 F.2d 77, 79 (4th Cir. 1985) (quoting Aluminum Co. v. Utilities Comm'n of North Carolina, 713 F.2d 1024 (4th Cir. 1983), *cert. denied*, 465 U.S. 1052 (1984)).

112. Meredith v. Talbot County, 828 F.2d 228, 232 (4th Cir. 1987) (refusal to permit subdivision and residential development of five lots inhabited by two endangered species).

113. Younger v. Harris, 401 U.S. 37 (1971).

114. Redner v. Citrus County, 919 F.2d 646, 649 (11th Cir. 1990), *reh'g denied*, 935 F.2d 1297 (1991), *cert. denied*, 502 U.S. 909 (1991).

115. *Id.*

116. *See* District of Columbia Ct. of Appeals v. Feldman, 460 U.S. 462 (1983); Anderson v. Charter Township of Ypsilanti, 266 F.3d 487, 492 (6th Cir. 2001).

117. Walnut Props., Inc. v. City of Whittier, 861 F.2d 1102, 1106 (9th Cir. 1988), *cert. denied*, 490 U.S. 1006 (1989).

118. South Hollywood Hills Citizens Ass'n v. King County, 677 P.2d 114 (Wash. 1984); Johnson's Island, Inc. v. Bd. of Township Trustees of Danbury Township, 431 N.E.2d 672 (Ohio 1982); Golden Gate Corp. v. Town of Narragansett, 359 A.2d 321 (R.I. 1976); St. Louis County v. City of Sunset Hills, 727 S.W.2d 412 (Mo. Ct. App. 1987); Burns v. Peavler, 714 S.W.2d 163, 166 (Ky. Ct. App. 1986); Harris Trust & Sav. Bank v. Duggan, 435 N.E.2d 130 (Ill. Ct. App. 1982), *aff'd on other grounds*, 449 N.E.2d 69 (Ill. 1983).

119. *See, e.g.,* Northwestern Univ. v. City of Evanston, 370 N.E.2d 1073 (Ill. Ct. App. 1977), *rev'd on other grounds*, 383 N.E.2d 964 (Ill. 1978); Fiore v. City of Highland Park, 221 N.E. 2d 323, 325 (Ill. Ct. App. 1966) (citing Westfield v. City of Chicago, 187 N.E.2d 208 (Ill. 1963)).

120. South Hollywood Hills Citizens Ass'n v. King County, 677 P.2d at 118; Fiore v. City of Highland Park, 221 N.E.2d at 325.

121. South Hollywood Hills Citizens Ass'n v. King County, 677 P.2d at 117–18 (quoting State v. Tacoma-Pierce County Multiple Listing Serv., 622 P.2d 1190 (Wash. 1980); Retail Store Employees Union, Local 1001 v. Washington Surveying & Rating Bureau, 558 P.2d 215 (Wash. 1976)).

122. *See, e.g.,* Ackerley Communications, Inc. v. City of Seattle, 602 P.2d 1177 (Wash. 1979), *cert. denied*, 449 U.S. 804 (1980); Bright v. City of Evanston, 139 N.E.2d 270, 274 (Ill. 1956) (citing cases); Winn v. City of Irving, 770 S.W.2d 10 (Tex. Ct. App. 1989); St. Louis County v. City of Sunset Hills, 727 S.W.2d 412 (Mo. Ct. App. 1987).

123. St. Louis County v. City of Sunset Hills, 727 S.W.2d 412 (Mo. Ct. App. 1987).

124. *Id.*

125. Burns v. Peavler, 714 S.W.2d 163 (Ky. Ct. App. 1986).

126. *Id.* at 167–68.

127. South Hollywood Hills Citizens Ass'n v. King County, 677 P.2d at 118.

128. *Id.*

129. Fiore v. City of Highland Park, 221 N.E.2d 323, 325 (Ill. Ct. App. 1966).

130. *See, e.g.,* City of Seymour v. Onyx Paving Co., 541 N.E.2d 951, 954 (Ind. Ct. App. 1989).

131. *See, e.g.,* Kuney v. Zoning Bd. of Appeals of the City of DeKalb, 516 N.E.2d 850, 852 (Ill. Ct. App. 1987).

132. *See, e.g.,* Portland Audubon Soc. v. Clackamas County, 712 P.2d 839, 842 (Or. Ct. App. 1986).

133. Harris Trust & Sav. Bank v. Duggan, 435 N.E.2d 130, 137 (Ill. Ct. App. 1982) (citing Northwestern Univ. v. City of Evanston, 383 N.E.2d 964 (Ill. 1978); Bare v. Gorton, 526 P.2d 379, 381 (Wash. 1974) (administrative body does not have the authority to determine the constitutionality of the law it administers)).

134. Johnson's Island, Inc. v. Bd. of Township Trustees of Danbury Township, 431 N.E.2d 672, 676–77 (Ohio 1982) (citing cases); Ackerley Communications, Inc. v. Seattle, 602 P.2d 1177 (Wash. 1979), *cert. denied,* 449 U.S. 804 (1980).

135. 272 U.S. 365, 386 (1926).

136. Bright v. City of Evanston, 139 N.E.2d 270, 274 (Ill. 1956).

137. Prisk v. City of Poulsbo, 732 P.2d 1013, 1017 (Wash. Ct. App. 1987); *see generally* K. DAVIS, ADMINISTRATIVE LAW TREATISE § 26.6 at 434 (2d ed. 1983).

138. Northwestern Univ. v. City of Evanston, 383 N.E.2d 964, 968 (Ill. 1978).

139. South Hollywood Hills Citizens Ass'n v. King County, 677 P.2d 114, 119 (Wash. 1984).

140. Johnson's Island, Inc. v. Bd. of Township Trustees of Danbury Township, 431 N.E.2d 672, 677 (Ohio 1982); County of Lake v. MacNeal, 181 N.E.2d 85, 90 (Ill. 1962).

141. People v. Calvar Corp., 36 N.E.2d 644, 645 (N.Y. 1941).

142. Provo City v. Claudin, 63 P.2d 570, 575 (Utah 1936).

143. Camp v. Mendocino County Bd. of Supervisors, 123 Cal. App. 3d 334, 176 Cal. Rptr. 620, 632 (1981).

144. Lee v. Osage Ridge Winery, 727 S.W.2d 218, 223 (Mo. Ct. App. 1987).

145. Gardner v. Pierce County Bd. of Comm'rs, 617 P.2d 743, 745 (Wash. Ct. App. 1980).

146. South Hollywood Hills Citizens Ass'n v. King County, 677 P.2d 114, 119 (Wash. 1984); *but see* Ace Delivery Serv., Inc. v. Boyd, 100 So. 2d 417 (Fla. 1958).

147. 457 U.S. 496 (1982); *see also* Grandison v. Smith, 779 F.2d 637, 642 (11th Cir.), *reh'g denied,* 786 F.2d 1119 (1986).

148. *See* pp. 102–04.

149. Williamson County Regional Planning Comm'n v. Hamilton Bank, 473 U.S. 172, 193 (1985); *see also* Pennell v. City of San Jose, 485 U.S. 1 (1988) (facial takings challenge to rent-control ordinance held premature); Coniston Corp. v. Village of Hoffman Estates, 844 F.2d 461, 463 (7th Cir. 1988) (federal suit seeking compensation for taking of property not ripe "until it is apparent that the state does not intend to pay compensation"); Norco Const., Inc. v. King County, 801 F.2d 1143, 1145 (9th Cir. 1986) (claim based on delay in making decision not matured until final decision is made).

150. Williamson County Regional Planning Comm'n v. Hamilton Bank, 473 U.S. 172, 188 (1985).

151. United States v. Riverside Bayview Homes, Inc., 474 U.S. 121, 127 (1985); United States v. Vogler, 859 F.2d 638, 642 (9th Cir. 1988), *cert. denied,* 488 U.S. 1006 (1989).

152. MacDonald, Sommer & Frates v. Yolo County, 477 U.S. 340, 352 (1986).

153. *Id.*

154. Video Intern. Prod., Inc. v. Warner-Amex Cable Communications, Inc., 858 F.2d 1075, 1087 (5th Cir. 1988), *cert. denied,* 490 U.S. 1047 (1989).

155. Kinzli v. City of Santa Cruz, 818 F.2d 1449, 1454–55, *modified,* 830 F.2d 968 (9th Cir. 1987), *cert. denied,* 484 U.S. 1043 (1988).

156. Lake Nacimiento Ranch Co. v. San Luis Obispo County, 841 F.2d 872 (9th Cir. 1987), *cert. denied,* 488 U.S. 827 (1988).

157. Shelter Creek Development Corp. v. City of Oxnard, 838 F.2d 375 (9th Cir.), *cert. denied,* 488 U.S. 851 (1988).

158. *See, e.g.,* Canal/Norcrest/Columbus Action Committee v. City of Boise, 39 P.3d 606 (Idaho 2001).

159. *See* pp. 249–54.

160. Pace Resources, Inc. v. Shrewsbury Township, 808 F.2d 1023, 1035 (3d Cir.), *cert. denied,* 482 U.S. 906 (1987); Sellon v. City of Manitou Springs, 745 P.2d 229, 232 (Colo. 1987); Quinn v. Town of Dodgeville, 364 N.W.2d 149, 154 (Wis. 1985); Harris Trust & Sav. Bank v. Duggan, 449 N.E.2d 69, 76 (Ill. 1983).

161. Sellon v. City of Manitou Springs, 745 P.2d 229, 232 (Colo. 1987); Quinn v. Town of Dodgeville, 364 N.W.2d 149, 154 (Wis. 1985).

162. Harris Trust & Sav. Bank v. Duggan, 449 N.E.2d 69, 76 (Ill. 1983); Home Bldg. Co. v. City of Kansas City, Mo., 666 S.W.2d 816, 819 (Mo. Ct. App. 1984) (citing 82 AM. JUR. 2d, *Zoning and Planning,* § 28 (1976)).

163. Sellon v. City of Manitou Springs, 745 P.2d 229, 233 (Colo. 1987).

164. Home Bldg. Co. v. City of Kansas City, Mo., 666 S.W.2d 816, 820 (Mo. Ct. App. 1984). *See also* Hoffman v. City of Town & Country, 831 S.W.2d 223 (Mo. Ct. App. 1992), and Rhein v. City of Frontenac, 809 S.W.2d 107 (Mo. 1991), in that the municipalities' respective refusals to rezone residential property to commercial property were held to be not fairly debatable and unreasonable in light of evidence of gross disparity in market value. The court in *Rhein* noted that the public interest that must be weighed in any rezoning inquiry was not determined solely by the interest of neighboring property owners, who nearly always oppose rezoning from residential to commercial use. *Rhein, id.* at 111.

165. Robertson County v. Browning-Ferris Indus. of Tennessee, Inc., 799 S.W.2d 662, 666 (Tenn. Ct. App. 1990); Moyer's Landfill, Inc. v. Zoning Hearing Bd. of Lower Providence Township, 450 A.2d 273 (Pa. Commw. Ct. 1982), *cert. denied,* 471 U.S. 1101 (1985).

166. Riggs v. Long Beach Township, 538 A.2d 808, 812–14 (N.J. 1988) (improper purpose for downzoning established by objective evidence).

167. Parranto Bros. v. City of New Brighton, 425 N.W.2d 585, 589 (Minn. Ct. App. 1988).

168. *See, e.g.,* Machado v. Musgrove, 519 So. 2d 629, 632 (Fla. Ct. App. 1987) (applying strict judicial scrutiny to question of whether zoning decision was inconsistent with comprehensive land use plan), *rev. denied,* 529 So. 2d 694 (1988).

169. Adelman Real Estate Co. v. Gabanic, 672 N.E.2d 1087 (Ohio Ct. App. 1996).

170. Neuberger v. City of Portland, 603 P.2d 771 (Or. 1979); *see also* Southwest Ranches Homeowners Ass'n v. County of Broward, 502 So. 2d 931, 936–37 (Fla. Ct. App. 1987) (construing statutory requirement for consistency with local comprehensive plan and subjecting decisions to approve uses more intensive than those proposed by the plan to stricter scrutiny than that provided by the fairly debatable rule).

171. Machado v. Musgrove, 519 So. 2d at 632.

172. *See, e.g.,* Heiss v. City of Casper Planning and Zoning Comm'n, 941 P.2d 27 (Wyo. 1997).

173. *See* pp. 249–54.

174. 780 F.2d 475, 479 (5th Cir. 1986), *cert. denied,* 477 U.S. 905; *see also* Conistony Corp. v. Village of Hoffman Estates, 844 F.2d 461, 468 (7th Cir. 1988) ("[L]egislatures can base their actions on considerations—such as the desire of a special interest group for redistributive legislation in its favor—that would be thought improper in judicial decision making"). *See* pp. 249–54.

175. *See, e.g.,* Fraubel v. Bd. of County Comm'rs of Teton County, 39 P.3d 420 (Wyo. 2002).

176. O'Loane v. O'Rourke, 42 Cal. Rptr. 283, 289 (1965) (adoption of a general plan is legislative in character and thus referendum on such adoption is available to the electorate).

177. Fasano v. Bd. of County Comm'rs, 507 P.2d 23, 26 (Or. 1973), *overruled on other grounds,* McGowan v. Lane County Local Gov't Boundary Comm'n, 795 P.2d 560 (Or. 1990).

178. O'Loane v. O'Rourke, 42 Cal. Rptr. 283, 289 (Dist. Ct. App. 1965); Fasano v. Bd. of County Comm'rs, 507 P.2d at 26; *see also* McCallen v. City of Memphis, 786 S.W.2d 633

(Tenn. 1990) (approval by city council of planned development held administrative rather than legislative); Alachua County v. Eagle's Nest Farms, Inc., 473 So. 2d 257, 260 (Fla. Ct. App. 1985) (denial or issuance of special-use permit is administrative act), *rev. denied*, 486 So. 2d 595 (1986 Fla.); Gay v. County Comm'rs of Bonneville County, 651 P.2d 560, 562 (Idaho Ct. App. 1982) (request for change in authorized land use for particular parcel is administrative in character).

179. 620 P.2d 565 (Cal. 1980), *transferred*, 178 Cal. Rptr. 723 (Cal. Ct. App. 1981).

180. 507 P.2d 23 (Or. 1973).

181. *See, e.g.*, Tate v. Miles, 503 A.2d 187, 191 (Del. Super. Ct. 1986) (although rezoning function is legislative, it resembles a judicial determination and thus record must be created or reasons given to facilitate possible, although limited, judicial review); Quinn v. Town of Dodgeville, 364 N.W.2d 149, 155 (Wis. 1985); Bowman v. Greene County Comm'n, 732 S.W.2d 223, 224 (Mo. Ct. App. 1987).

182. Cooper v. Bd. of County Comm'rs of Ada County, 614 P.2d 947 (Idaho 1980); Johnson v. City of Mount Vernon, 679 P.2d 405, 408 (Wash. 1984); *see also* Winslow v. Town of Holderness Planning Bd., 480 A.2d 114 (N.H. 1984) (decision regarding proposals to sub-divide property characterized as quasi-judicial, at least for purposes of determining whether due process requirement of impartial decision-maker was met).

183. Cyclone Sand & Gravel Co. v. Zoning Bd. of Adjustment of City of Ames, 351 N.W.2d 778, 783 (Iowa 1984); *see also* Richard J. Roddewig, *Recent Developments in Land Use, Planning and Zoning Law,* 22 Urb. Law. 719, 735 (1990) (arguing that "essential analogy" for "quasi-judicial" land use decisions is that of "contested case proceedings under adminis-trative procedure acts").

184. Standard State Zoning Enabling Act, § 7 (U.S. Dep't of Commerce, rev. ed. 1926), *published as* Appendix A, A Model Land Development Code (ALI TD No 1, 1968).

185. Weldon v. Zoning Bd. of City of Des Moines, 250 N.W.2d 396, 400 (Iowa 1977).

186. *See* Standard State Zoning Enabling Act (U.S. Dep't of Commerce, rev. ed. 1926), *published as* Appendix C, Model Land Development Code, p. 209.

187. *See* pp. 249–54; *contra,* Fasano v. Bd. of County Comm'rs, 507 P.2d 23 (Or. 1973); p. 261.

188. Weldon v. Zoning Bd. of City of Des Moines, 250 N.W.2d 396, 401 (Iowa 1977).

189. *See, e.g.*, Mayhew v. Town of Sunnyvale, 774 S.W.2d 284, 298 (Tex. Ct. App. 1989) (town councilman could not be compelled to testify in appeal of decision to deny applica-tion for planned development approval).

190. *See, e.g.*, Little v. City of Lawrenceville, 528 S.E.2d 515 (Ga. 2000).

191. *See* Bay St. Louis Community Ass'n v. Comm'n on Marine Res., 729 S.2d 796 (Miss. 1998) (30-day period governing appeals from administrative ruling under Coastal Wetlands Protection Act); City of Dalton v. Carroll, 515 S.E.2d 144 (Ga. 1999) (city not barred by laches in an enforcement case).

192. *See, e.g.*, Idaho Code § 67-5215(g); Love v. Bd. of County Comm'rs of Bingham, 671 P.2d 471, 472 (Idaho 1983).

193. Idaho Code § 67-5215(g).

194. Love v. Bd. of County Comm'rs of Bingham, 671 P.2d at 472.

195. *Id.* at 473, n. 2.

196. *See, e.g.*, Salameh v. County of Franklin, 767 S.W.2d 66, 68 (Mo. Ct. App. 1989) (judicial authority limited to declaring legislation void or invalid); Teed v. King County, 677 P.2d 179, 184–85 (Wash. Ct. App. 1985) (mandamus not available to compel rezoning).

197. *See, e.g.*, Schwartz v. City of Flint, 395 N.W.2d 678, 683 (Mich. 1986) (citing cases and authorities); Nopro Co. v. Town of Cherry Hills Village, 504 P.2d 344 (Colo. 1972); Pleas-ant Valley Neighborhood Ass'n v. Planning and Zoning Comm'n of South Windsor, 543 A.2d 296 (Conn. Ct. App. 1988); Home Bldg. Co. v. City of Kansas City, Mo., 666 S.W.2d 816 (Mo. Ct. App. 1984).

198. *See, e.g.,* City of Cherokee v. Tatro, 636 P.2d 337 (Okla. 1981); Atlanta v. McLennan, 226 S.E.2d 732 (Ga. 1976).

199. Schwartz v. City of Flint, 395 N.W.2d 678, 689 (Mich. 1986); *but see* Harris Trust & Sav. Bank v. Duggan, 435 N.E.2d 130 (Ill. Ct. App. 1982) (adoption of a "preamendment" classification ordered when amendatory zoning ordinance struck down as a "necessary consequence" of the declaration of invalidity, not judicial rezoning) (cited with approval in *Schwartz, id.* at 689 n.19).

200. Sinclair Pipe Line Co. v. Village of Richton Park, 167 N.E.2d 406 (Ill. 1960).

201. Union Oil Co. of California v. City of Worthington, 405 N.E.2d 277 (Ohio 1980).

202. Bd. of Supervisors of Fairfax County v. Allman, 211 S.E.2d 48 (Va. 1975), *cert. denied,* 423 U.S. 940 (1975).

203. Schwartz v. City of Flint, 395 N.W.2d at 692–93.

204. *See, e.g.,* Southern Burlington County NAACP v. Township of Mount Laurel, 456 A.2d 390, 452–59 (N.J. 1983) (*Mount Laurel II*) discussed on pp. 380–82; *see also* Britton v. Town of Chester, 595 A.2d 492, 497 (N.H. 1991). *Britton* applies the reasonableness standard for the builder's remedy, rather than the *Mount Laurel* test.

205. *Mount Laurel II,* 456 A.2d at 452–59 (N.J. 1983).

206. *Mount Laurel II,* 456 A.2d at 457.

207. *See generally* pp. 101–02.

208. *See* pp. 102–04.

209. Alger v. City of Mukilteo, 739 P.2d 1333 (Wash. 1987) (jury award of $1,369,400 for malicious revocation of building permits sustained).

210. *See* State *ex rel.* Helujon Ltd. v. Jefferson County, 964 S.W.2d 531 (Mo. App. 1998) (denial of injunction against casino development affirmed on other grounds); Sear v. Clayton County Bd. of Adjustment, 590 N.W.2d 512 (Iowa 1999) (injunction against city enforcement of ordinance without proper notice).

211. Schubach v. Silver, 336 A.2d 328, 332 (Pa. 1975); Harrington v. Zoning Hearing Bd. of East Vincent Township, 543 A.2d 226, 228 (Pa. Commw. Ct. 1988) (quoting *Schubach*).

212. Harrington v. Zoning Hearing Bd. of East Vincent Township, 543 A.2d 226 (Pa. Commw. Ct. 1988).

213. Holiday Inns, Inc. v. City of Jacksonville, 678 So. 2d 528 (Fla. Ct. App. 1996) (building code violation).

214. *See, generally,* Armeigh v. Baycliffs Corp., 690 N.E.2d 872 (Ohio 1998).

215. Gatti v. Zoning Hearing Bd. of Salisbury Township, 543 A.2d 622, 625 (Pa. Commw. Ct. 1988) (citing Valley View Civic Ass'n v. Zoning Bd. of Adjustment, 462 A.2d 637 (Pa. 1983)); *see also* Eubanks v. Bd. of Adjustment, 768 S.W.2d 624, 627 (Mo. Ct. App. 1989) (appellate court jurisdiction limited to review of the record of challenged proceedings).

216. Shapero v. Zoning Bd. of City of Stamford, 472 A.2d 345, 349 (Conn. 1984); Owensboro Metropolitan Bd. of Adjustments v. Midwest Outdoor Adver., Inc., 729 S.W.2d 446, 448 (Ky. Ct. App. 1987).

217. Department of Agric. and Consumer Serv. v. Mid-Florida Growers, Inc., 521 So. 2d 101, 104 (Fla. 1988), *cert. denied,* 488 U.S. 870 (1988); *see also* Nolan v. Bd. of Adjustment of Iowa City, 350 N.W.2d 744, 746 (Iowa 1984) (certiorari proceedings in zoning matters reviewed to determine whether court applied correct legal standards and whether its decision is supported by substantial evidence); First Nat'l Bank of Des Plaines v. County of Cook, 360 N.E.2d 1377, 1382 (Ill. Ct. App. 1977) (findings of trial court not disturbed unless manifestly against the weight of the evidence).

218. Rice v. Bd. of Adjustment, 804 S.W.2d 821, 822 (Mo. Ct. App. 1991); Heritage Soc'y of Washington County v. Neumann, 771 S.W.2d 563, 566 (Tex. Ct. App. 1989).

219. Call v. City of West Jordan, 727 P.2d 180, 182 (Utah 1986); Parranto Bros. v. City of New Brighton, 425 N.W.2d 585, 589 (Minn. Ct. App. 1988).

220. *See, e.g.,* 11126 Baltimore Blvd. v. Prince George's County, 924 F.2d 557 (4th Cir. 1991) (amendment to challenged ordinance deprived court of jurisdiction to review validity of ordinance before amendment as impermissible request for advisory opinion), *cert. denied,* 502 U.S. 819 (1991).

221. *See, e.g.,* Stone v. City of Wilton, 331 N.W.2d 398, 401 (Iowa 1983).

222. *See generally* Chapter 3 (discussing Supreme Court cases on the regulatory taking issue).

223. *See, e.g.,* SEATTLE, WASHINGTON CODE § 25.12.010 (1977); *see generally* P. Salsich, *Keystone Bituminous Coal, First English and Nollan: A Framework for Accommodation?,* 34 J. URB. & CONTEMP. L. 173, 191–200 (1988).

224. *See, e.g.,* SAN JOSE, CALIFORNIA MUNICIPAL CODE § 5702.3, *et seq.* (1979), *upheld in* Pennell v. City of San Jose, 485 U.S. 1 (1988).

225. PA. STAT. ANN. tit. 53, § 10908.1 (Purdon 1972 & Supp. 1991). The statute does not appear to require funding or the actual offer of mediation by the municipality.

226. N.J. STAT. ANN. §§ 52:27D-301–329 (West 1986).

227. Southern Burlington County NAACP v. Township of Mount Laurel, 336 A.2d 713 (N.J. 1975), *appeal dismissed and cert. denied,* 423 U.S. 808 (1975) (*Mount Laurel I*); Southern Burlington County NAACP v. Township of Mount Laurel, 456 A.2d 390 (N.J. 1983) (*Mount Laurel II*).

228. N.J. STAT. ANN. § 52:27D-315 (West 1991).

229. N.J. STAT. ANN. § 52:27D-316 (West 1991).

230. N.J. STAT. ANN. § 52:27D-319 (West 1991).

231. Southern Burlington County NAACP v. Township of Mount Laurel, 510 A.2d 621 (N.J. 1986) (*Mount Laurel III*).

232. Hills Dev. Co. v. Bernards Township in Sommerset County, 510 A.2d 621, 639 (N.J. 1986).

233. Berger, *The Accommodation Power in Land Use: A Reply to Professor Costonis,* 76 COLUM. L. REV. 799, 800–01, 817, 821–23 (1976) (commenting on Costonis, *"Fair" Compensation and the Accommodation Power: Antidotes for the Takings Impasse in Land Use Controversies,* 75 COLUM. L. REV. 1021 (1975)).

234. *See, e.g.,* American Tower Corporation v. Common Council of the City of Beckley, 557 S.E.2d 752 (W. Va. 2002).

235. Much of this section is contributed by James A. Kenney III, Lexington Park, Md.; *see also* discussion of ex parte contacts in chapter 5, "Ethical Isues," pp. 270–71.

236. *See* p. 233.

237. Fasano v. Bd. of County Comm'rs, 507 P.2d 23 (Or. 1973).

238. Richmond, MODELING YOUR CASE/SELECTING YOUR FORUM IN CONTESTING AND DEFENDING LAND USE RESTRICTIONS, Continuing Legal Education Satellite Network, Inc., New York (October 4, 1988).

239. For a discussion of the legal issues in interpreting and enforcing consent decrees, most notably in environmental and housing litigation, see Callis, *The Use of Consent Decrees in Settling Land Use and Environmental Disputes,* 21 STETSON L. REV. 871 (1992).

CHAPTER 7

Regulating Specific Uses

Overview

Zoning ordinances distinguish among more than simply the four classic categories of agricultural, commercial, industrial, and residential uses. Most ordinances also create subdistricts. Although commercial uses are the most notorious for consideration of specific requests for approvals, residential uses often receive more attention in the comprehensive zoning ordinance. A typical suburban zoning ordinance devotes half or more of its zoning district categories to residential subdistricts.[1]

In addition to creating perhaps 15 to 25 subdistricts, however, a well-conceived comprehensive zoning ordinance will anticipate and regulate specific problematic uses. This chapter examines the most closely regulated and often controversial subcategories of uses. The list is not comprehensive. The purpose of the chapter is rather to outline legal doctrine and practical considerations applicable to those uses that create the most litigation.

Segregation of Single-Family Housing

The classic, Euclidean-style comprehensive zoning ordinance segregated single-family housing from other uses simply by prohibiting in the single-family zone all but a few other low-density uses, such as farming, public parks, and reservoirs.[2] Over the years, additional uses compatible with single-family homes, such as churches, home occupations, libraries, playgrounds, police and fire stations, and schools, came to be accepted as permitted uses.

A greater variety of uses is now accepted in single-family neighborhoods, but the basic concept of segregating types of residential uses is as strong as ever and is perhaps the very definition of zoning.[3] Typically, residential subclassification proceeds from the lowest-density, large-tract detached homes to the highest-density, multifamily apartment housing, with each category prohibiting the next most dense use, but not necessarily vice versa. Because of the cumulative nature of the ordinance, a traditional feature of Euclidean zoning,[4] owners who could afford larger single-family lots could locate in all-residential districts, but owners or tenants of multiple-family dwellings were confined to the particular residential districts that permitted such uses.[5]

Although the literature is replete with criticism of this segregative propensity,[6] courts have been reluctant since *Euclid*[7] to disturb single-family district designations except when the designation is applied to a particular tract in a manner that effectively denies use of the property[8] or creates an irrational classification.[9]

Courts have been willing to uphold local legislative decisions to zone a community solely for single-family residential use when the community is relatively small and has been substantially developed as a residential bedroom community prior to the imposition of zoning, the zoning-enabling legislation does not prohibit single-zoned communities, and the single-zone decision will not unreasonably limit the use of individual tracts of land or constitute "exclusionary zoning."[10]

The very definition of *single-family dwelling* and, indeed, *family* has been litigated heavily and continues to be so, especially with respect to group homes and other nonnuclear living arrangements.[11] A *single-family dwelling* typically is defined as "a building designed for or occupied exclusively by one family."[12] Under this definition, the question arose as to whether a family may construct an addition containing a separate bedroom, a separate living room, a separate kitchen with its own entrance from the front of the building into a foyer, a full bathroom, a separate entrance from a new porch, and a new heating system with its own boiler, while keeping the same electric, gas, sewer, and water lines. The New Jersey Supreme Court said no, reasoning that the design of the building violated the zoning code because the separate kitchen, boiler, bathroom, heating system, and entrance enabled the addition to "function independently from the original residence." The fact that the addition was intended to provide living quarters for the widowed mother of one of the owners did not overcome the fact that the addition would enable the structure to support two families.[13]

In contrast, a New York court refused to focus on design alone. Applying a two-part test that evaluated the "design of the house" and the "nature of the occupancy," the court held that the addition of a separate kitchen to enable the mother and sister of the owner to reside in separate quarters did not convert a single-family residence into a two-family dwelling because only family members would be living in the building.[14]

Single-Family "Lifestyle"

In *Village of Belle Terre v. Boraas*,[15] the Supreme Court upheld an ordinance that limited the number of unrelated individuals who could live together in a single-family district. Although commentators have speculated that the origin of such regulations was a desire to keep boarding houses out of single-family areas,[16] after *Belle Terre,* so-called lifestyle regulations have been the focal point of an often bitter debate about whether regulation of the living patterns of individuals fundamentally is an appropriate use of the zoning power.

The zoning ordinance, or now more typically the state enabling statute, usually regulates living patterns through the definition of the term *family.*[17] The traditional definition, upheld in *Belle Terre,* defines family as a group of persons related by blood or marriage. This definition often includes a few unrelated persons, typically two or three, presumably to accommodate live-in help. The constitutionality of the traditional definition has been litigated in group home cases.[18]

Although the Supreme Court in *Belle Terre* deferred to state courts and the traditional definition of family established by local land use policy, the court has been willing to strike down the application when it becomes too intrusive, such as limiting the definition to nuclear families and prohibiting extended families such as grandparents and grandchildren from living together.[19] The court found the attempt to distinguish extended families from nuclear families to be a regulation "slicing deeply into the family itself" and unsupported by any legitimate governmental interests.[20]

State courts are divided on the enforceability, under state constitutional law principles, of the traditional definition of family. A decision by an appellate court in Missouri upholding the application of the traditional definition of family to an unmarried couple living together with their separate children is representative of those courts that are willing to defer to legislative decisions to limit the definition of family to biological or legal relationships.[21] The Missouri court found sufficient governmental interest in marriage and in "preserving the integrity of the biological or legal family" to sustain the application of the ordinance to an unmarried cohabiting couple.[22]

A sizable, and growing, number of courts have concluded that land use regulations applied to families must be broad enough to encompass various forms of nontraditional families. Rather than drawing distinctions among groups of persons who are living together on the basis of their biological or legal relationships, these courts use a "functional" definition of family that distinguishes persons who are living together as a "single housekeeping unit" from persons in transient situations who do not share housekeeping responsibilities.[23]

The Supreme Court of New Jersey, applying the functional test, affirmed a decision that ten unrelated college students living together in a house owned by relatives of one of the students constituted a family. The students were sophomores at the time of the purchase and planned to live together for their remaining three years of college. The students ate together, shared household chores, and paid expenses from a common fund. Each signed a four-month lease that was renewable if the house was in order at the end of the term. Although the court acknowledged that "[i]t is a matter of common experience that the costs of college and the variables characteristic of college life and student relationships do not readily lead to the formation of a household as stable and potentially durable as the one described in this record," the court agreed with the lower court's conclusion that the students' occupancy "show[ed] stability, permanency and [could] be described as the functional equivalent of a family."[24]

In holding that the male life partner of a deceased male tenant was not excluded from protection against eviction extended to resident family members upon death of a co-tenant/family member, the New York Court of Appeals applied the functional definition of family under a New York rent-control statute.

> [W]e conclude that the term family . . . should not be rigidly restricted to those people who have formalized their relationship by obtaining, for instance, a marriage certificate or an adoption order. The intended protection against sudden eviction should not rest on fictitious legal distinctions or genetic history, but instead should find its foundation in the reality of family life. In the context of eviction, a more realistic, and certainly equally valid, view of a family includes two adult lifetime partners whose relationship is long term and characterized by an emotional and financial commitment and interdependence.[25]

In *Charter Township of Delta v. Dinolfo*,[26] members of a religious group lived with families in their homes. Each home contained a husband, a wife, their children, and six unrelated individuals. The homes were in an area zoned single-family residential; the definition of family limited the number of unrelated individuals to two. The Michigan Supreme Court invalidated the ordinance on state constitutional grounds. Noting that a rational relationship must exist between valid legislative goals and the means used to achieve the goals, and that preservation of the residential nature of a neighborhood is a proper legislative goal, the court stated that it "must part company with the United States Supreme Court" in *Belle Terre* because use of the traditional definition of family to keep nontraditional groups of individuals out of residential neighborhoods was not related to the permissible legislative goal of preserving the residential character of those neighborhoods.[27]

> Plaintiff attempts to have us accept its assumption that different and undesirable behavior can be expected from a functional family. Yet, we have been given not a single argument in support of such an assumption. . . . Defendants, on the other hand, . . . present a compelling argument that the means are not rationally related to the ends sought.[28]

The Michigan court noted that courts that have invalidated restrictive definitions of family "have stressed that a line drawn near the limit of the traditional family is both over- and under-inclusive" because such ordinances "regulate . . . where no regulation is needed and fail . . . to regulate where regulation is most needed."[29] In a footnote, the Michigan court noted the following legislative attempts to preserve the family character of a neighborhood without unduly excluding nontraditional lifestyles:

> (1) an ordinance including within the definition of family "(a) collective number of individuals living together in one house under one head, whose relationship is of a permanent and distinct domestic character, and

cooking as a single housekeeping unit" and excluding various enumerated groups of individuals, such as societies and clubs, and those "whose
association is temporary and resort-seasonal in character or nature;"[30]

(2) an ordinance defining family to include "a collective body of persons doing their own cooking and living together upon the premises as a
separate housekeeping unit in a domestic relationship based upon birth,
marriage or other domestic bond as distinguished from a group occupying a boarding house, lodging house, club, fraternity or hotel."[31]

Some courts attempt to take a middle ground between the pro- and anti-
traditional family definition positions, refusing to permit use of the traditional
definition to exclude various types of group homes that feature surrogate parents or unrelated persons on the basis of their ages, but permitting regulation
of the number of unrelated persons who can live together in residential neighborhoods in order to prevent the use of single-family structures as boardinghouses.[32]

Provisions of the single-family residential portions of local zoning ordinances occasionally are drafted in such a way that courts are required to determine whether the intended regulation is of single-family *structures* or single-
family *uses*. In *City of Kenner v. Normal Life of Louisiana, Inc.*,[33] the Supreme
Court of Louisiana refused to construe an ordinance defining a single-family
dwelling as a disjunctive definition that permitted non–single-family uses of
dwellings designed for single families. The ordinance also contained a traditional definition of family. The court concluded that construing the definition
of single-family dwelling in the disjunctive, which a literal reading of the
words appeared to require, would render useless the definition of family in
the ordinance.[34]

Conversely, the Supreme Court of Missouri was more than willing to distinguish restrictions requiring single-family dwellings from restrictions
requiring single-family uses in construing a private restrictive covenant to
permit group homes for unrelated retarded individuals to operate in single-
family dwellings within the subdivision governed by the restrictive
covenants. The court's conclusion was influenced by the fact that, while the
restrictive covenant limited the property to residential uses, it did not qualify
the term "residential use" by adjectives such as "single-family," although it
applied such adjectives to the term "dwelling."[35]

In a Wisconsin case, the court applied both the concepts of single-family
dwelling and use to uphold a time-share arrangement for sharing a single-
family home by 13 separate owners.[36] The landowner's plot, which was in a
district zoned single-family residential, planned to construct a single-family
house that would be sold to 13 families under a time-share arrangement that
would permit each family to occupy the house for four weeks out of the year.
The owner's building permit was revoked, and the district court upheld the
revocation, reasoning that the owner's plan would violate the single-family
zoning restriction. The Wisconsin Court of Appeals reversed the decision.
Because the house would never be occupied by more than one family at a
time, the plan would not violate the zoning ordinance that prohibited use by

more than a single family, but did not require the same family to occupy the property for a specific period.[37]

State law and ordinance definitions of family may violate the Fair Housing Act Amendments of 1988[38] or constitute a regulatory taking. As to the latter, one court has held that a state zoning regulation authorizing the location of group homes in residential subdivisions constituted a taking within the Fifth Amendment, where the location of such homes would violate restrictive covenants, and the homeowners' beneficial interests in the restrictive covenants were "property" within the meaning of the Fifth Amendment.[39] The court declined to consider the effect of the Fair Housing Act Amendments of 1988 on the enforceability of the restrictive covenants, nor did it analyze whether application of the Fair Housing Act could constitute a taking in the same way as the Indiana statute.[40]

As noted earlier, the Fair Housing Act Amendments of 1988 expressly exempt local "restriction(s) regarding the maximum number of occupants permitted to occupy a dwelling."[41] In the 1995 case of *City of Edmunds v. Oxford House, Inc.,* the Supreme Court dealt squarely with the narrow issue of whether this provision immunized classical, Euclidean residential zoning restrictions concerning the definition of family.[42] The court answered no, drawing a clear line between land use restrictions and occupancy restrictions, the latter commonly found in building code ordinances rather than in zoning ordinances. Thus the local zoning authority may not use the occupancy loading exemption in the Fair Housing Act as immunity from scrutiny, under the act, for failure to make "reasonable accommodations" for the handicapped (or any other protected class) in land use policies. In *Edmunds,* the Supreme Court remanded for further consideration the issue of whether the city's refusal to permit in a single-family zoning district a group home of ten to twelve recovering alcoholics and drug addicts violated the Fair Housing Act as a failure to make a reasonable accommodation.[43] The latter issue should be the subject of substantial litigation.

As in the case of any zoning issue, the practitioner should check state law for enabling legislation dealing with group homes.[44]

Mobile Homes and Manufactured Housing

Mobile homes and various types of modular or manufactured housing are becoming increasingly important forms of affordable housing for persons and small families of low and moderate income.[45] Although mobile or manufactured homes are forms of single-family housing, they generally have been subjected to more stringent land use regulations than traditional, site-built housing because of their origin as "temporary" rather than "permanent" housing and the resultant "distinctions . . . [in] design, construction and general appearance." [46]

Advances in the technology of manufactured housing have led some jurisdictions to create separate categories of manufactured housing depending on whether the housing unit is constructed on a wheeled chassis and then attached to a pad with the wheels removed (manufactured homes) or whether the unit is assembled in a factory without a wheeled chassis and then transported to the site on which it is to be located (manufactured buildings).[47] Manufactured housing typically is subject to mobile-home regulations, whereas manufactured buildings tend to be regulated less stringently in the manner of site-built housing.[48]

Through various means, communities tend to confine mobile homes to mobile-home parks[49] or, in less restrictive schemes, to zoning districts where the distribution of mobile homes may be somewhat more haphazard. Regulatory devices include the special-use permit[50] and the floating planned unit development zone.[51] Mobile homes have been limited to one per parcel of land with the further restriction that they cannot be used as dwellings unless they are in a "trailer camp,"[52] and have been prohibited altogether unless in an "existing and recognized trailer court."[53] Mobile homes have been subjected to additional design restrictions to ensure compatibility with site-built homes when placed in the "best residential zoning classifications" in a community.[54]

Various reasons have been given for the more restrictive treatment of mobile homes. The Seventh Circuit, for example, noted that mobile homes are a "sufficiently distinct use of land to justify their separate classification for zoning purposes."[55] The Eleventh Circuit concluded that regulation of mobile homes was a valid use of police power because mobile homes may have an adverse effect on property values and are vulnerable to strong winds.[56] A Michigan appellate court has upheld regulation of mobile homes by imposing minimum width requirements on the basis that aesthetics is a legitimate end of police power.[57]

When mobile homes are permitted in residential districts other than separate mobile-home park districts, on-site placement regulations such as setback lines may not be substantially greater for mobile homes than similar regulations for site-built homes in the same district.[58]

Absolute prohibition of mobile homes and manufactured housing is invalid as unrelated to a legitimate governmental purpose.[59] Mobile homes and manufactured houses are not nuisances per se,[60] and they provide an important source of affordable housing for groups that tend to be excluded by overly restrictive single-family residential zoning.[61]

In recent years, states have provided express statutory protection for mobile-home owners and tenants by requiring local comprehensive plans to include specific provision for manufactured housing,[62] requiring an owner to provide six months' advance notice to mobile-home residents before accomplishing zoning changes that would terminate the use[63] and requiring submission of plans for relocation of ousted mobile-home residents upon application for zoning changes.[64] Tenant protection can also be provided by the municipality, and such a program has been upheld against a claim of taking.[65]

Age-Restrictive Zoning

Land use regulations designed to favor a group of persons based on their age (elderly) or disfavor them for the same reason (children) is a variation of lifestyle zoning. The combined inclusionary/exclusionary effects of such regulations can produce substantial local controversy.

The Comprehensive Amendments to the Federal Housing Act (Title VIII of the Civil Rights Act of 1968)[66] enacted in 1988[67] prohibit activities that have the effect or purpose of discrimination in housing based on "familial status" (i.e., denying housing to persons because of the presence of children younger than age 18 in a household that also includes a parent or other person having legal custody of the children).[68] The amendments expressly exempt "reasonable . . . restrictions regarding the maximum number of occupants" and "housing for older persons" (defined generally to include persons 55 years of age and older).[69] Local land use restrictions are subject to the amendments,[70] thereby invalidating zoning ordinances that, by purpose or effect, discriminate against families with minor children. Perhaps the most significant practical effect of the amendments is to allow lawyers' fees to the successful claimant.[71] The amendments have been upheld against the claim of a constitutional right to reside in adults-only communities.[72]

Notwithstanding the Fair Housing Act Amendments, age restrictions have long been subject to judicial scrutiny under state law. In *McMinn v. Town of Oyster Bay*,[73] the New York Court of Appeals struck down a local zoning ordinance definition of family that permitted two unrelated persons older than age 62 to live together in single-family residential districts, but denied the same privilege to younger persons as a violation of the due process and equal protection clauses of the state constitution. In addition to finding that the ordinance failed to include groups who met the "functional equivalent of a traditional family" test established in previous decisions involving lifestyle regulations,[74] the court concluded that the addition of an age restriction as a qualifier for such groups was "more restrictive . . . than is constitutionally permissible."[75]

The Supreme Court of New Jersey has upheld local land use restrictions favoring developments for elderly persons, such as separate mobile-home parks[76] and "senior citizen communities,"[77] but with the qualification that land use regulations favoring elderly housing should be permitted only after adoption of a comprehensive plan that evaluates the need for elderly housing and minimizes the exclusionary effects of such regulations.[78] The court has invalidated zoning ordinances that have exclusionary effects on families with minor children, such as requirements that the majority of units in a permitted apartment development have only one bedroom.[79]

The Supreme Court of California has struck down age-restrictive practices of private owners and condominium associations designed to exclude children under a state fair housing law, but has interpreted the statute to permit age discrimination, at the other end, for senior-citizen housing developments.[80]

One commentator has observed that communities attempting to accommodate the housing needs of both families with children and senior citizens, by prohibiting discrimination against children but permitting it in favor of senior citizens, are most likely to be successful if land use regulations "are supported by a careful consideration of the housing needs of the community; are part of a comprehensive scheme of planning and zoning; and are clearly calculated to result in housing that fits the needs of senior citizens." [81]

The special housing needs of elderly persons, such as for essential nutritional, physical, and social services in settings that permit them to live as privately and independently as possible, have been held to justify granting of a use variance to develop a congregate-care housing facility against the standard that use variances serve the general welfare and do not substantially impair applicable zoning policies.[82]

Accessory Uses

Zoning ordinances permit as "accessory" to permitted uses any use that is "secondary to" and "customarily incidental" to the principal use allowed by a zoning ordinance.[83] The accessory use typically must (1) support or serve the principal building or use; (2) be subordinate in area, extent, or purpose to the principal building or use; (3) contribute to the comfort, convenience, or necessity of occupants or activities of the principal building or use; and (4) be located on the same lot as well as in the same or less restrictive zoning district.[84]

Ordinances permitting accessory uses typically impose height, area, and distance regulations designed to emphasize the accessory nature of the use. A use that is determined to be accessory rather than part of the permitted use must comply with such regulations as long as they are reasonable.

A potentially popular application of the accessory-use concept would permit a portion of an existing single-family residence to be converted into housing for relatives of the owner-occupants of the primary single-family unit or permit the placement of a small, removable cottage in the rear of the lot to be used for the same purpose.[85] The interest that developed in these forms of housing in the 1980s was sparked by the convergence of two forces: substantial increases in the cost of traditional forms of housing and desires of elderly persons to maintain the independence and security generally found in single-family neighborhoods.[86] Because the introduction of accessory housing into a single-family residential community can raise concerns about the conversion of single-family homes into multiple dwellings (generally illegal under traditional zoning ordinances), advocates of such housing usually seek specific ordinance approval rather than attempting to qualify under traditional definitions of accessory use.[87]

A New York court concluded that a town may constitutionally limit granting permits for accessory apartments to owner-occupants as a reasonable means of maintaining the single-family character of the community while responding to the need for affordable rental units.[88]

Some states offer financial assistance to elderly homeowners seeking to add accessory housing units to their homes. For example, in 1986 the Connecticut Housing Finance Authority was granted the power to make loans to resident homeowners 62 years of age or older to enable them to convert a portion of their homes into rental units, "subject to applicable zoning regulations."[89]

Group Homes

Group homes are an important component of a variety of federal, state, and local social welfare programs providing services for children, nonviolent criminal offenders, persons with mental or physical handicaps, senior citizens, and victims of substance abuse or incurable diseases. Three characteristics distinguish group homes from traditional forms of housing: (1) the residents are unrelated to one another; (2) supervision is provided by live-in "surrogate parents" or by 24-hour professional staff working eight-hour shifts; and (3) support services such as counseling, education, and training are provided in addition to shelter.[90] Because of the rigidities built into the Euclidean zoning system,[91] operators of group homes often find themselves at odds with local zoning laws when they seek to locate their homes in single-family residential districts.

Ordinances authorizing group homes as either permitted uses or uses subject to a special-use permit requirement generally specifically define the group home. Like the definition of family, the definition of group home is controversial. For example, an Arizona ordinance defined the term *group home* as follows:

> A facility located in a residential area providing shelter and/or rehabilitation of up to eight (8) persons, regardless of age, referred by a government agency or duly licensed social service agency, who for various reasons cannot reside in their family home. Twenty-four-hour supervision is mandatory and professional supervision and consultation is available to residents of the home. The purpose of a group home is to provide services for persons who do not need the structure of an institution, but do need a transitional environment for future successful reentry into the community as an independent and productive person.[92]

Based on this definition, a proposal to provide elderly foster care for up to five elderly persons along with housing two permanent staff members of the nonprofit sponsor was denied as a proposal for a boarding or rooming house rather than a group home. The court characterized the group home definition in the ordinance as a halfway house providing transitional services, rather than a facility providing permanent lodging. In the court's view, the project contemplated more-or-less permanent lodging of frail elderly persons needing 24-hour care, whereas the ordinance definition contemplated facilities providing services for persons who "need a transitional environment for future successful reentry into the community." [93] Although local definitional determinations are not exempt from the Fair Housing Act as "occupancy restrictions,"[94] courts are not free to disregard state law definitions such as a statutory definition of "group home."[95]

Two types of local regulatory barriers are most common: (1) restrictive definitions of family, discussed earlier in this chapter in connection with lifestyle restrictions,[96] and (2) discriminatory special-use permit requirements.[97]

In addition to judicial determinations that group homes that function as families may not be excluded from single-family residential neighborhoods,[98] state legislatures have also attempted to resolve the locational conflicts by defining *single family* in zoning-enabling legislation to include residents of small-group homes.[99] States have done so by characterizing group homes as residential or single-family residential uses,[100] or by making group homes permissible uses in all zoning areas.[101]

Such statutes are usually designed to preempt restrictive local zoning ordinances, but courts do not always agree that preemption was the intended result. In *City of Kenner v. Normal Life of Louisiana, Inc.*,[102] the Louisiana Supreme Court affirmed the issuance of a permanent injunction prohibiting operation of a group home for the mentally retarded where a zoning ordinance restricted use of the property to "single-family residential" use. The ordinance definition of *single family* limited to four the number of unrelated individuals who could qualify as a family. The proposed group home would have housed six unrelated persons. The court reached its conclusion despite a 1983 law that stated in part, "[c]ommunity homes that provide for six or fewer mentally retarded individuals, with no more than two live-in staff, shall be considered a single-family having common interests, goals, and problems."[103] The court reasoned that this provision was not intended by the legislature to override local zoning ordinances and subdivision restrictions, partly because the statute stated specifically that "community homes may be operated by right in multiple-family residential districts," but contained no such statement with respect to single-family districts. The court distinguished *Tucker v. Special Children's Foundation*[104] and other earlier cases that had reached contrary results on the grounds that, in those cases, *single family* had not been restrictively defined in the applicable local ordinances.[105]

In addition to problems with the definition of *family*, group homes may face restrictive permit requirements. Such requirements will be upheld when they are rationally related to a permissible government goal, such as protecting the health and safety of the residents, but they will be invalidated if the requirements cannot be so linked. In the leading case of *City of Cleburne, Texas v. Cleburne Living Center*,[106] the Supreme Court struck down an ordinance requiring owners of group homes for the developmentally disabled to obtain annual special permits to operate in multifamily use districts but not requiring such permits for other uses, such as apartment buildings, boardinghouses, hospitals, and nursing homes.

Although the court held that mental retardation was not a quasi-suspect classification calling for a stricter standard of review and that cities could constitutionally treat certain classes of people such as the aged, disabled, and retarded differently from the general populace because of their special needs, the court concluded that a regulation supported by "mere negative attitudes, or fear, unsubstantiated by factors which are properly cognizable in a zoning proceeding" would not pass muster even under the more relaxed rational-basis standard. In the court's view, the regulation rested on an "irrational prejudice against the mentally retarded."[107]

Massachusetts, by exemption, in its enabling statute, protects group homes from regulations other than "reasonable regulations" concerning the bulk and height of structures, yard sizes, lot area, setbacks, and the like.[108] One ordinance limiting the footprint of group homes to 2,500 square feet was held invalid under the statute.[109]

Group homes received federal legislative support through the 1988 amendments to the Fair Housing Act,[110] when Congress added the handicapped to the list of protected groups. *Handicap* is defined to include "mental impairment which substantially limits one or more of such person's major life activities, . . . but . . . not . . . addiction to a controlled substance."[111] Unlawful discrimination includes "a refusal to make reasonable accommodations in rules, policies, practices, or services, when such accommodations may be necessary to afford such person equal opportunity to use and enjoy a dwelling."[112] Dwellings do not have to be made available, however, to handicapped persons "whose tenancy would constitute a direct threat to the health or safety of other individuals or . . . would result in substantial physical damage to the property of others."[113]

Because the Fair Housing Act applies to local land use restrictions,[114] the prohibitions against discrimination based on a handicap include exclusionary zoning practices against group homes serving handicapped persons. The act may also prohibit the refusal to grant a variance on the theory that a variance is a "reasonable accommodation" under the Act.[115] The Act has given rise to substantial litigation.

Extension of "the principle of equal housing opportunities to handicapped persons," one of the purposes of the 1988 Fair Housing Act Amendments,[116] raises questions about the validity of the common practice of limiting the concentration of group homes by imposing spacing regulations. A typical regulation may prohibit a group home from being located less than 1,000 feet, or one-quarter mile, from another group home.[117] One state's dispersal scheme has been invalidated on equal protection grounds.[118] An ordinance in St. Paul, Minnesota, however, imposing a 1,320-foot spacing requirement, survived a Fair Housing Act challenge in *Familystyle of St. Paul, Inc v. City of St. Paul*.[119] The court first held that the ordinance and a state statute authorizing spacing regulations were not preempted by the 1988 Fair Housing Act Amendments. The statute and ordinance were part of a regulatory scheme to implement a state policy of deinstitutionalization. The statute and ordinance regulated the facilities that housed handicapped persons but did not directly affect the residential choices individual persons may make. The court reasoned that because the Fair Housing Act was designed to protect the housing choices of individuals, it did not preempt state and local laws regulating the facilities housing such individuals.[120]

The court found no *intent* to discriminate in the state's policy of implementing deinstitutionalization by dispersing facilities for the mentally ill, but concluded that the dispersal policy had a disparate *impact* because the policy had the effect of limiting housing choices of handicapped persons. The court held, however, that the city had met its burden of showing that the dispersal policy fostered a "compelling governmental interest," that of "integrating the handicapped into the community."[121]

A statute that permits municipalities to treat group homes as conditional uses has also been struck down as violative of the Fair Housing Act.[122]

Handicapped persons are also protected against discrimination in land use by the Americans with Disabilities Act (ADA).[123] The ADA, generally effective on January 26, 1992, also prohibits discrimination in employment and public transportation.[124]

The operative land use provision of the ADA provides as follows:

No individual shall be discriminated against on the basis of disability in the full and equal enjoyment of the goods, services, facilities, privileges, advantages, or accommodations of any place of public accommodation by any person who owns, leases (or leases to), or operates a place of public accommodation.[125]

The ADA does not apply to residential uses.[126] A list of "places of public accommodation" is provided in the act and includes hotels, restaurants, office uses, retail uses, public uses such as zoos and amusement parks, and recreational uses.[127]

Notably, the public accommodation provisions of the act affect existing properties by prohibiting discrimination and defining *discrimination* to include "failure to make reasonable modifications in policies, practices, or procedures, when such modifications are necessary to afford such goods . . . to individuals with disabilities."[128] The ADA also prohibits failure to remove architectural barriers where such removal is "readily achievable," which is defined as "easily accomplishable and able to be carried out without much difficulty or expense."[129]

The ADA also affects new construction and alterations in both public accommodations and "commercial facilities."[130] This portion of the ADA defines discrimination to include "failure to design and construct facilities for first occupancy later than [January 26, 1993] that are readily accessible to and usable by individuals with disabilities."[131]

Enforcement remedies include those provided in the Civil Rights Act of 1964, injunctive relief, and enforcement by the Attorney General.[132]

Residential Treatment Centers

In addition to group homes,[133] other forms of housing that combine treatment with shelter have been subjected to close scrutiny. In *Transitions, Inc. v. Ashland Bd. of Zoning Adjustment*,[134] the conversion of a building to a halfway house for pre-released and paroled persons from state penal institutions in an area zoned for light industrial use was opposed by nearby property owners and residents. As a result of the protests, the local board of zoning adjustment revoked the owner's certificate of occupancy.[135] The circuit court upheld the revocation, finding that a halfway house was not a permitted use in the industrial zone. A Kentucky Court of Appeals reversed the revocation and ordered the permit to be reinstated. The court concluded that although halfway houses were not the type of use normally contemplated in industrial zones, the common use of the industrial zone designation as a "community's catch-all or 'anything goes' area . . . [for] aesthetically unattractive" uses, together with the fact that the ordinance contained a reference to residential uses in industrial zones being required to meet applicable area, yard, and height requirements, a list of prohibited uses in industrial areas that did not include halfway houses, and a statement that all uses not specifically prohibited in the industrial district are permitted, demonstrated persuasively that the original permit issued for the halfway house was not issued in violation of the zoning regulations.[136]

New York courts have upheld a decision to approve a drug abuse counseling center licensed by the state and staffed by licensed teachers, social workers, psychologists, psychiatrists, and "intensely trained paraprofessionals" as a permitted "professional office use" in a commercial and mixed-use district."[137] Such courts have also affirmed decisions to deny entry of drug rehabilitation halfway houses into single-family residential districts when there is "no clearly defined intent to preempt reasonable local regulation of the location and construction of these centers."[138]

An Ohio court concluded that an ordinance that prohibited "institutions primarily for the care of . . . alcoholics" in a hospital zone did not prohibit a hospital from building an alcoholic treatment center within its complex of six buildings, when the hospital taken as a whole was not "primarily" for the care of alcoholics.[139]

Ordinances limiting the number of persons who may occupy residential treatment centers and other forms of transitional housing have been upheld as reasonably related to the legitimate governmental purpose of regulating the density of activity in residential areas. For example, the Third Circuit held that a limit for transitional dwellings restricting the number of occupants to six persons plus a supervisory family or person was a reasonable density restriction.[140] The court declined to characterize the restriction as sex-based simply because a proposed transitional shelter for battered women allegedly was economically infeasible if the six-person limitation was enforced. The court rejected an argument that the failure to regulate the number of related persons who can live together meant that the regulation had a purpose other than density control by pointing out that the Supreme Court has ruled that such regulations would constitute impermissible intrusions into the "sanctity of the family." Applying the "deferential rational-basis standard" of review, the court concluded that the six-person limit for transitional housing in residential districts, as applied to the proposed battered women's shelter, was rationally related to the "legitimate government objective of controlling density in a residential neighborhood." The court also rejected a First Amendment freedom-of-association argument, holding that the six-person limit did nothing to prevent battered women from associating with one another. The court remanded for further consideration, however, an argument that the numerical limit impermissibly violated the 1988 Fair Housing Act Amendment provision adding "familial status" as a prohibited class of discrimination. The court concluded that the contention that counting children within the six-person limit operated to exclude women with children from transitional dwellings deserved greater consideration than the record before the court permitted.[141]

The tension between local loading and occupancy regulations and the Fair Housing Act Amendments of 1988 is a recurring theme in group home and treatment center litigation, and it has been held that the Act does not exempt local limits on occupancy by unrelated persons.[142] In one case,[143] a federal court declined *Pullman, Younger,* and *Burford* abstention[144] and ordered the modification of a state court order that prohibited nine recovering alcoholics from occupying a single-family home. The court specifically held that recovering alcoholics and addicts were intended to be included within the scope of the term *handicapped* as used in the Fair Housing Act amendments.[145] The court granted only temporary relief, however, pending outcome of a state court action to determine whether the initial order limiting occupancy to six residents was valid under state law.

Condominium Conversions

Conversion of apartments into condominiums has been a popular but controversial activity in several urban areas. Local governments have attempted to regulate condominium conversions in a variety of ways, most often through subdivision regulations, moratoria, or impact fees.[146] The Uniform Condominium Act, adopted by several states,[147] preempts local land use regulations of condominiums that are not imposed "upon a physically identical development under a different form of ownership."[148] The Supreme Court of Rhode Island went beyond the condominium statute's prohibition of discriminatory forms of regulation and concluded that a condominium is not a subdivision of land, but only a change in ownership; thus a proposed conversion of an existing, but valid nonconforming, parking use into a parking condominium was not subject to local subdivision regulations.[149]

A California court has upheld the imposition of relocation payments on an apartment owner who was converting apartments to condominiums.[150] After Los Angeles city officials gave tentative subdivision map approval[151] for a condominium conversion, the city passed an ordinance requiring landlords who were converting apartments into condominiums to pay up to $2,500 in relocation assistance to tenants who were being displaced. The court denied a challenge to the relocation ordinance by the developer who had received the tentative map approval, on the grounds that the ordinance did not impose additional conditions on the developer after his map had been approved. The ordinance did not affect the developer's ability to convert to condominiums. Rather, the ordinance imposed independent regulations applicable to all landlords. The court applied an analogy to impact fees charged to developers to alleviate costs for public facilities necessitated by land development, concluding that the relocation assistance payments were reasonable charges to "alleviate displacement and other adverse effects of . . . conversion" rather than unconstitutional special taxes.[152]

Approval of a tentative subdivision map for a condominium conversion under a San Francisco subdivision regulation ordinance that included condominium conversions within its jurisdiction was held not to have created such a vested right as to preclude enforcement of a subsequently adopted regulation requiring the units to be sold only to buyers who qualified as moderate-income families. The amendment was enacted as an emergency measure and granted the city a right-of-first-refusal at the original price, plus reasonable adjustments for improvements and cost-of-living increases. In concluding that the moderate-income limitation amendment was applicable to the conversion in question, the court found that the right obtained by the tentative map approval was the right to convert an apartment building into condominiums. This right was not affected by the intervening amendment, and there was no evidence that any interested party substantially changed its position as a result of the tentative map approval or any other government act prior to enactment of the moderate-income limitation regulation.[153]

Religious Uses

The constitutional law of regulation of religious uses has been codified, and may be largely preempted, by the enactment of the Religious Land Use and Institutionalized Persons Act of 2000 (RLUIPA).[154] RLUIPA was adopted in response to the Supreme Court's partial invalidation of the Religious Freedom Restoration Act of 1993, 107 Stat. 1488, 42 U.S.C. Sections 2000bb-2000bb-4 (RFRA), in *City of Bourne v. Flores*.[155] RFRA sought to "restore the strict scrutiny legal standard for governmental actions that substantially burdened religious exercise."[156] In *City of Bourne*, the Supreme Court held that Congress had exceeded its powers under Section 5 of the Fourteenth Amendment in enacting the RFRA.[157]

RLUIPA is intended to "remedy the well-documented discriminatory and abusive treatment suffered by religious individuals and organizations in the land use context."[158] The constitutionality of RLUIPA is discussed in chapter 3. RLUIPA has been upheld, however, against a township's claim that the Act *prefers* religion, in violation of the Establishment Clause, in *Freedom Baptist Church of Delaware County v. Township of Middletown*.[159] The town of Middletown had no zoning districts that permitted religious worship.[160]

RLUIPA was intended to "protect the free exercise of religion from unnecessary government interference."[161] The land use section of RLUIPA prohibits discrimination against religious assemblies and institutions, the total exclusion of religious assemblies from a jurisdiction, and unreasonable limits on religious assemblies and institutions.[162] The same section requires that land use regulations that substantially burden the exercise of religion be justified by a compelling governmental interest tracking the substantive language of its predecessor, RFRA.[163]

RLUIPA applies to the states, counties, municipalities, and any other governmental entities created under the authority of a state, including any branch, department, agency, instrumentality, or official of such governmental units, and any person acting under color of state law.[164] RLUIPA defines a land use regulation as a zoning or landmarking law, or the application of such a law, that limits or restricts a claimant's use or development of land (including a structure affixed to land), if the claimant has a property interest or an option to acquire such an interest in the regulated land.[165] A government agency implements a land use regulation only when it acts pursuant to a zoning or landmarking law that limits the manner in which land may be developed or used.[166]

In *Prater v. City of Burnside*, the Court found that the city did not act pursuant to a zoning or landmarking law when it chose to develop, rather than close, a dedicated roadway that was located between two lots owned by a church.[167] Because the city's decision regarding the fate of the roadway was not based on any zoning or landmarking law restricting the development or use of the church's property, RLUIPA was held inapplicable.[168]

RLUIPA defines "religious exercise" as any exercise of religion, whether or not compelled by, or central to, a system of religious belief.[169] "An individual's religious beliefs or practice need not be shared by other adherents of a larger faith to which the claimant also adheres."[170] Insincere religious claims are not religious exercise, and thus are not protected.[171] The use, building, or conversion of real property for the purpose of religious exercise is considered a religious exercise of the person or entity that uses or intends to use the property for that purpose.[172] It is only the use, building, or conversion for religious purposes that is protected and not other uses or portions of the same property.[173] For example, "if religious services are conducted once a week in a building otherwise devoted to secular commerce, the religious services may be protected but the secular commerce is not."[174]

In order to establish a prima facie case that RLUIPA has been violated, a claimant must present evidence that the government's denial of the zoning or rezoning application imposed a substantial burden on the religious exercise of the claimant.[175] Although RLUIPA does not define *substantial burden*, the legislative history evidences a Congressional intent that the standard under RFRA should apply.[176] The term *substantial burden* as used in RLUIPA should be interpreted by reference to Supreme Court jurisprudence.[177] "In order to show a free exercise violation using the 'substantial burden' test, the religious adherent has the obligation to prove that a governmental action burdens the adherent's practice of his or her religion . . . by preventing him or her from engaging in conduct or having a religious experience which the faith mandates."[178] This interference must be more than an inconvenience; the burden must be substantial and an interference with a tenet or belief that is central to religious doctrine.[179]

In *Murphy v. Zoning Commission of the Town of New Milford*,[180] a homeowner sought an injunction to bar enforcement of an order that he cease and desist from holding prayer meetings involving more than 25 persons in his home. Testimony by prayer group members that some prayer group participants stopped attending the prayer group sessions out of fear that they would be arrested by town officials was sufficient to provide evidence of a chilling effect on their right to associate, as well as their constitutional right to freedom of religion. "Foregoing or modifying the practice of one's religion because of governmental interference or fear of punishment by the government is precisely the type of 'substantial burden' Congress intended to trigger RLUIPA protections."[181] As such, the Court found that the zoning enforcement officer's order requiring the homeowner to ensure that the number of attendees at the prayer meetings never exceed 25 placed a substantial burden on the exercise of the homeowner's religion.[182]

RLUIPA does not "provide religious institutions with immunity from land use regulation, nor does it relieve religious institutions from applying for variances, special permits or exceptions, hardship approval, or other relief provisions in land use regulations, where available without discrimination or delay,"[183] nor does it impair the power of states and localities to enforce fire codes, building codes, and other measures to protect the health and safety of people using the land or buildings, such as children in childcare centers, schools, or camps run by religious organizations.[184]

Once a claimant has shown that the government's action has imposed or threatens to impose a substantial burden on the free exercise of their religious beliefs, the burden shifts to the government to show that there is a compelling state interest for imposing the burden and that the burden imposed is the least restrictive means of securing that interest.[185] Local governments have been held to have a compelling state interest in enforcing the town's zoning regulations and ensuring the safety and health of the town's residential neighborhoods.[186]

In addition to a compelling governmental interest, the government must show that the burden on religious exercise is the least restrictive means of furthering that compelling governmental interest.[187] The government must show that there are "no other alternative forms of regulation which would fulfill the state interest."[188]

RLUIPA also "preempts land use regulation that treats a religious assembly or institution on less than equal terms with a non-religious assembly or institution[189] and land use regulation that discriminates against any religious assembly or institution on the basis of religion or religious denomination."[190] The government "may not unreasonably exclude religious assemblies from a jurisdiction, or unreasonably limit religious assemblies, institutions, or structures within the jurisdiction."[191] Reasonableness is "determined in light of all the facts, including the actual availability of land and the economics of religious organizations."[192]

A person may assert a violation of RLUIPA as a claim or a defense in a judicial proceeding and award of appropriate relief against a governmental unit.[193] In the case of a violation by a state, RLUIPA must be enforced by suits against state officials or employees.[194] RLUIPA also expressly authorizes the United States to sue for injunctive or declaratory relief to enforce the statute.[195]

Where a zoning ordinance infringes on a constitutionally protected interest, such as freedom of religion, the ordinance must further a "substantial" government interest and must be "narrowly drawn" to lessen its impact on the protected activity.[196] But exclusion of churches from particular zoning districts such as residential or agricultural, however, "is not arbitrary per se."[197]

In reviewing the cases, the Supreme Court of Colorado noted that ordinances regulating the construction of church buildings tend to fall into one of three types: (1) express authorization of churches in particular districts, (2) express prohibition of churches in certain districts, and (3) authorization for churches in particular districts but only upon the granting of a special permit.[198] The constitutionality of the special-permit requirement of the so-called permissive type of regulation has been upheld by most courts.[199] The Colorado Court upheld an injunction to prevent a single-family residence from being used as a church in violation of a permissive ordinance against a claim that the ordinance imposing the special-permit requirement was unconstitutionally vague.[200]

In another case,[201] conditions to the issuance of a special-use permit that included building a fence were held not to be a violation of the Establishment of Religion Clause because the conditions had a purely secular purpose: the promotion of public health, safety, and welfare. Nor did the conditions violate the plaintiff's right to free speech because the conditions were not an attempt to regulate the content of the plaintiff's activities.

Zoning ordinances may regulate religious conduct as long as the regulation is reasonably related to a permissible state interest, such as protecting the public health, safety, or welfare, and the regulation does not regulate religious beliefs.[202] Such regulations must have both a secular purpose and a secular effect.[203] Applying that standard, an Illinois court held that imposition of an enrollment cap as a condition to granting a special-use permit for a parochial school in a residential neighborhood was not a violation of the free-exercise clause.[204]

Enforcement of a single-family residence district classification to prevent a minister from holding services in his home was upheld against a constitutional challenge. The court reasoned that "zoning for single-family dwellings promotes the public safety and welfare by minimizing congestion, encouraging stability and securing repose and solitude."[205] Churches may be attended by large crowds that create much noise, traffic, and litter. The zoning ordinance at issue was held to be reasonably related to the goals of single-family zoning because churches were permitted in other districts with larger lot sizes in which houses would not be crowded so closely together. The crowding was likely to magnify the adverse effects of a church in the community. Also, the ordinance did not totally prohibit religious worship in the township, did not regulate speech based on content, and did not regulate a specific belief.[206]

Constitutional issues implicated by regulation of religious uses intersect with other controversial uses, such as family definitions and day-care centers. Ordinances regulating the types of families permitted in single-family residential zones[207] have been invalidated when the effect was to exclude unrelated persons living together as a single housekeeping unit as religious households from single-family neighborhoods.[208] Denial of a special-use permit for a student center operated by a religious organization near a state university was invalidated as a violation of the free-exercise-of-religion clause, where nine special permits had been granted previously to religious organizations of different denominations.[209]

A New York court found that a Roman Catholic cemetery was a religious use within the meaning of a zoning ordinance permitting such uses, finding that the cemetery was a place of worship.[210] Operation of day-care centers and private nursing homes by religious communities as ancillary activities has been upheld on various grounds, including a finding that a day-care facility is an accessory use,[211] and that regulation of a privately operated nursing home for the benefit of religious community members who owned the facility would be an unwarranted infringement on the free exercise of religion.[212] Likewise, courts have refused to permit municipalities to block church-owned radio[213] and television[214] stations through the application of zoning regulations.

Not all ancillary activities are immune from regulation under the freedom-of-exercise principle, however. Zoning ordinances may exempt from regulation the use of land or structures for religious purposes, raising the definitional question of what is a religious purpose. Courts have not limited religious activity to prayer and worship, accepting within the definition such activities as religious education, day care, scouting, sporting activities, publications, public affairs programs, art and music programs, drug rehabilitation programs, and recreation programs.[215] A key factor is whether members of the religious institution are generally involved in the activity. Thus a pastoral counseling center proposed to be located on church-owned property by a nonprofit organization not affiliated with the church was held to resemble a mental-health clinic rather than a religious activity, despite "a layer of theological content" to the services offered by counselors who were ordained clergy or trained in theology.[216]

Application of landmark regulations to church buildings poses special problems because of the clash of values between the personal right of free exercise of religion and community interests in aesthetic and cultural preservation.[217] Applying the judicial standard of strict scrutiny, the Supreme Court of Washington struck down the application of the Seattle Landmarks Preservation Ordinance to church exteriors.[218] The court found that the requirement that church officials submit any plans for alteration of a church building exterior to the Landmarks Preservation Board, even when such plans may qualify for an ordinance exemption on the grounds that the changes are "necessitated by changes in the liturgy," created "unjustified governmental interference in religious matters." Finding no compelling governmental interest in the preservation of a church building's exterior, the court held that the community interest in landmarks preservation is "clearly outweighed by the constitutional protection of free exercise of religion and the public benefit associated with the practice of religious worship within the community."[219]

The Supreme Court vacated the Washington Supreme Court's decision,[220] however, citing its earlier holding that the free-exercise-of-religion clause was not violated by application of state drug laws to the religious use of a controlled substance. Stressing the general nature and validity of the drug law in question, the court stated that "[w]e have never held that an individual's religious beliefs excuse him from compliance with an otherwise valid law prohibiting conduct that the State is free to regulate."[221]

The Second Circuit upheld the application of New York City's Landmarks Law to prohibit St. Bartholomew's Church from replacing a church-owned building with an office tower. The court noted that the landmarks law was a "facially neutral regulation of general applicability,"[222] and concluded that Supreme Court free-exercise precedents were applicable. "The critical distinction is . . . between a neutral, generally applicable law that happens to bear on religiously motivated action, and a regulation that restricts certain conduct because it is religiously oriented." The fact that the denial of the church's plan to construct an office tower "drastically restricted the church's ability to raise revenues" did not render the decision invalid because "neutral regulations that diminish the income of a religious organization do not implicate the free exercise clause." Finally, the court held that the decision to deny permission to demolish the church-owned building was not a taking of property because the existing charitable and religious activities could be continued in the church's current facilities.[223]

The Supreme Judicial Court of Massachusetts reached the opposite conclusion, however, when faced with the application of a landmarks preservation regulation to the *interior* of a church building in Boston. Applying the free-exercise clause of the Massachusetts Constitution, the court held that the designation of the interior of a church as a landmark and the requirement that plans for the renovation of the interior be reviewed and approved by the Boston Landmarks Commission violated the free-exercise rights of the Jesuits who owned the church building. The court rejected the commission's argument that the design and placement of such items as the altar and organ were merely "secular question[s] of interior decoration," holding instead that the "configuration of the church interior is so freighted with religious meaning that it must be considered part and parcel of the Jesuits' religious worship."[224]

Governmental Facilities and Intergovernmental Conflicts

Application of local land use regulations to publicly owned buildings often creates conflicts between a "host" community seeking to regulate land use and an "encroaching" governmental entity (state, county, or city) attempting to avoid application of the regulation to a particular public facility.[225] A variety of trends, including urban redevelopment, proliferation of quasi-governmental political districts, deregulation and nontraditional land use by utilities, and regionalization have caused an increase in intergovernmental land use issues. Environmental regulation is also a fertile area for intergovernmental conflicts.[226] In resolving such conflicts, courts have applied a variety of tests, such as the governmental-proprietary test, the superior sovereign test,[227] the eminent domain test,[228] the statutory guidance (legislative intent) test, and the balancing-of-interests test.[229] In recent years courts have favored the statutory guidance/legislative intent test[230] or the balancing-of-interests test[231] as more likely to focus attention on the "public interests implicated in a particular land use dispute."[232]

The balancing-of-interests test requires the "encroaching" governmental unit to abide by the land use regulations of the "host" government unless a contrary legislative intent is expressed or a contrary result is dictated after consideration of factors such as "the nature and scope of the instrumentality seeking immunity, the kind of function or land use involved, the extent of the public interest to be served thereby, the effect local land use regulation would have upon the enterprise concerned and the impact upon legitimate local interests," as well as the "applicant's legislative authority, alternative locations for the facility in less restrictive zoning areas, . . . alternative methods of providing the needed improvement [and] intergovernmental participation in the project development process and an opportunity to be heard."[233]

The Supreme Court of Washington rejected all four tests in favor of a legislative intent test to conclude that a city was obligated to comply with a county's zoning code in locating a sewage-sludge and solid-waste disposal facility. The legislation in question did not provide detailed standards to guide cities in siting disposal facilities, nor did it purport to preempt the field of zoning regulations, the court noted. Because of the parallel delegation of zoning authority to counties and the legitimate interests that both governments have in resolving a siting dispute amicably, the court held that compliance with reasonable standards for obtaining a special-use permit, rather than immunity from or prohibition by zoning ordinances, was an effective way of settling such disputes "by a cooperative effort between interested parties who approach their differences with respect for the objectives of the other."[234]

In some cases, local zoning power may conflict with a state agency. In a Pennsylvania case, the court ruled that absent a specific legislative grant authorizing a state agency to override local zoning laws of a home-rule city, a state agency is subject to the jurisdiction of the local zoning board.[235] In California, on the other hand, state agencies are immune from local regulation unless immunity is expressly waived by statute.[236] In that state, case law has created the general immunity default, but statutes have substantially waived the immunity.[237] Thus a claim by a legislatively created conservancy that local zoning restrictions rendered its statutory mission illusory was rejected. Similarly, a Pennsylvania court held that a welcome center proposed by the State Department of General Services was not exempt from local zoning.[238]

Where a law authorizes a state agency to override local zoning laws, however, the state agency is exempted from having to comply with the zoning law.[239] A Missouri court has concluded that the state zoning-enabling statute authorizes regulation of private land uses only and is insufficient authority for a non–home-rule city to require a county agency carrying out a state policy in providing shelter for children under the supervision of the juvenile court, to comply with the city's zoning ordinances.[240]

Intergovernmental land use conflicts take a variety of forms, considering that the array of governmental and quasi-governmental entities includes not only federal, state, and local governmental bodies but also school, fire protection, water, sewer, arts and entertainment districts, and public utilities.[241]

Many intergovernmental conflicts are analyzed as preemption issues. Thus an ordinance regulating a railroad use may be invalid as preempted by the Interstate Commerce Commission (now Surface Transportation Board) authority.[242]

Occasionally a statute will specifically exempt "encroaching" local governments from "host" unit zoning regulations. In *Edelen v. Nelson County*,[243] residents attempted to block construction of a jail by the county. The residents argued that the allocable municipal zoning laws did not permit a jail. The Kentucky Court of Appeals held in favor of construction of the jail, reasoning that "a city or county is an instrumentality of state government, and as such, is immune from complying with zoning regulations" under a state statute granting zoning immunity.[244]

Billboards and Signs

Signs and billboards are among the most highly regulated, and litigated, of land uses. Billboards implicate visual blight and First Amendment rights.[245] Cities may not regulate the message, ideas, subject matter, or content of speech through billboards and signs.[246] Cities may, however, regulate the "time, place, and manner" in which billboards and signs are displayed, when such regulations advance a legitimate governmental interest, are "content neutral," and allow the information to be communicated in other manners.[247]

The test for regulation of commercial speech has four parts:

(1) The First Amendment protects commercial speech only if that speech concerns lawful activity and is not misleading. A restriction on otherwise protected commercial speech is valid only if it (2) seeks to implement a substantial governmental interest, (3) directly advances that interest, and (4) reaches no further than necessary to accomplish the given objective.[248]

The test requires that local governments articulate a reason for regulating commercial speech and demonstrate that the regulation goes no further than necessary to directly advance the stated reason. The "fit" between legislative ends and means need only be a "reasonable [one] whose scope [is] 'in proportion to the interest served.'"[249]

Failure to include a "statement of a substantial governmental interest" or to offer any extrinsic evidence of such interest may invalidate ordinances banning off-premise billboard advertising in areas zoned for commercial and industrial uses. General statements that zoning codes were adopted for the promotion of health, safety, morals, comfort, convenience, and the general welfare, or that signs contributed to obstruction of traffic and the creation of hazards to the health and welfare of the general public, were deemed to be insufficient to validate general prohibition of off-premises advertising signs.[250]

There are various forms of local regulation of billboards and signs. Some ordinances permit on-premise signs and restrict off-premises signs or ban them altogether.[251] Thus in *Georgia Outdoor Advertising v. City of Waynesville*,[252] a city's prohibition against virtually all off-premise advertising (billboards) was upheld because it furthered stated goals of aesthetics and safety, applied to all commercial signs, and allowed businesses to advertise on their own property.[253] Although an absolute ban of all signs may be invalidated as not "narrowly tailored" to protect a legitimate state interest,[254] an absolute prohibition of flashing signs has been upheld.[255]

In addition to time, place, and manner restrictions and height, area, and location restrictions, limitations on the content of on-premise signs has been upheld. A typical ordinance limits on-premise signs to "messages, commercial or non-commercial, related to activities conducted on the premises."[256] Like general zoning ordinances, sign ordinances are subject to nonconforming-use regulations and the concept of amortization, requiring the phase-out of nonconforming signs with a three- to six-year amortization period, for example.[257]

A sign regulation may implicate equal protection rights. In *North Olmsted Chamber of Commerce v. City of North Olmsted*,[258] an ordinance was invalidated on equal protection grounds where it favored signs of "public" or "semi-public" institutions.

Sign regulations have also been attacked, unsuccessfully as regulatory takings, such as in the case of amortization periods requiring removal of valuable billboards.[259]

For Sale signs are a frequent subject of sign litigation. The Seventh Circuit upheld a zoning ordinance that regulated the size, number, and placement of For Sale signs, based on the governmental interest of aesthetics, but struck down a $60 fee for the placement of such signs as not reasonably related to the costs of administering the ordinance.[260]

When linked to important governmental purposes, these methods of regulating billboards and signs have been upheld against First Amendment claims[261] or are invalid uses of police power (where, for example, the challenger argues that aesthetics is not a valid state objective).[262] Prohibitions against the posting of For Sale and Sold signs have been invalidated as impermissible content-based regulations.[263]

Removing visual blight has been accepted as a legitimate basis for an ordinance prohibiting the posting of signs on public property by supporters of political candidates, particularly when similar signs were permitted on private property.[264] A city may not totally suppress political speech, however. In *Matthews v. Town of Needham*,[265] a statute that barred political signs on residential property was held unconstitutional on the grounds that it effectively banned political speech.

Many ordinances limit political signs to prescribed periods before and after elections. A limitation of 17 days preceding an election has been struck down by one court.[266]

In *Gileo v. City of Ladue*, the Supreme Court invalidated an ordinance banning all signs within the city limits except those authorized for subdivision and residence identification, For Sale and For Rent signs, health inspection signs, and municipal signs when it was applied to prohibit a resident from placing a sign in her yard advocating peaceful negotiations rather than war in the Persian Gulf just prior to the outbreak of the Persian Gulf War.[267] The court held that an ordinance that completely bans all political speech but permits certain types of commercial speech is not content-neutral, nor were the exemptions to the ordinance content-neutral.[268]

In *Plain Dealer Publishing Company v. City of Lakewood*,[269] the Sixth Circuit held that a city may constitutionally ban newsracks from city streets where the regulation was content-neutral, served government purposes of aesthetics and traffic safety, and left open other means of distributing newspapers. The Supreme Court affirmed other parts of the *Plain Dealer* decision without addressing the constitutionality of this particular provision of the ordinance.[270]

Local sign regulation may also be preempted or restricted by state and federal statues.[271] The Seventh Circuit concluded that the Illinois Highway Advertising Control Act of 1971[272] permitted cities to regulate the height and design of highway signs, as well as ban signs, more than 600 feet from highways, but prohibited cities from regulating the size of a sign face within 600 feet of a highway or banning signs from industrial and commercial areas within 600 feet of highways.[273] Regulation of radio interference by a zoning ordinance has been held preempted by Section 253 of the Telecommunications Act of 1996.[274] An ordinance prohibiting signs advertising tobacco and alcohol products was upheld, however, against a claim of preemption by the Federal Cigarette Labeling and Advertising Act.[275]

Adult Entertainment

Regulation of adult theaters, like regulation of signs and religious uses, is limited by the First Amendment. Such regulation is constitutional only when it is not aimed at suppressing the content of speech, but rather at limiting the "secondary effects" of adult entertainment on the surrounding community.[276] Adult-use ordinances are reviewed under standards applicable to content-neutral time, place, and manner regulations, and generally will be upheld if the regulations are reasonable, serve a legitimate governmental purpose, and permit alternative avenues of communications.[277]

The leading case is *City of Renton v. Playtime Theaters, Inc.*,[278] which further defined the standards set forth in another important case, *Young v. American Mini Theaters*.[279] In *City of Renton*, plaintiffs challenged a statute that prohibited adult theaters from locating within 1,000 feet of a residential zone, church, park, or school. In upholding the statute, the court found that the statute was not an attempt to suppress adult entertainment entirely, but was merely an attempt to regulate the "time, place, and manner" of the adult entertainment.[280] Furthermore, the statute was valid because it was designed to preserve the quality of life, a substantial governmental interest, and did not make it impossible for the theaters to locate within the city limits, thus permitting alternative means of communication. However, when concentration/dispersal regulations have the effect of unreasonably limiting alternative economic locations for adult entertainment, the regulations may be held unconstitutional.[281] "Zoning ordinances that target the social ills associated with adult entertainment are constitutional if they are narrowly tailored to further a substantial government interest and allow for reasonable alternative avenues of communication."[282] Ordinances will be examined both on their face and "as applied."[283]

In *City of Erie v. Pap's A.M.*,[284] a divided Supreme Court held that bans on all nude dancing could be content-neutral, observing a distinction between supressing nude dancing and supressing "what . . . nude dancing communicates,"[285] stating that "being in a 'state of nudity' is not an inherently expressive condition,"[286] although nude dancing may be expressive conduct. In doing so, a plurality reached back to the relatively deferential four-part test governing the constitutionality of such ordinances, which it announced more than 30 years earlier in *U.S. v. O'Brien*,[287] "clarify[ing] that government restrictions on public nudity such as the ordinance at issue . . . should be evaluated under the framework set forth in *O'Brien* for content-neutral restrictions on symbolic speech."[288]

A city, in proving the presence of a governmental interest, may rely on the studies and experiences of other cities.[289] A city must show proof, however, that in regulating adult entertainment, it "was actually attempting to address the problem of urban blight."[290] The burden of proof imposed on municipalities is "to show that more than a rational relationship exists between the ordinance" and the governmental interest.[291] An ordinance restricting adult bookstores need not provide for waivers, in the nature of variances, or grandfathering to be constitutional.[292]

A combination of licensing and zoning requirements was upheld in part and invalidated in part in *FW/PBS, Inc. v. City of Dallas*.[293] Under a Dallas ordinance, adult businesses were required to be at least 1,000 feet from another sexually oriented business or a church, school, residential area, or park. In addition, a license was required to be obtained from the Chief of Police, for which applicants were required to permit inspection of their premises when open. The Supreme Court upheld the provisions of the ordinance regulating the location of sexually oriented businesses, including a determination that motels renting rooms for less than ten hours were sexually oriented businesses, but struck down the licensing provisions because they failed to specify a reasonable time for action on license applications and lacked a method for obtaining prompt judicial review.[294] In upholding the ordinance, the Fifth Circuit held that the ordinance regulated "only the secondary aspects of sexually oriented businesses." Thus the ordinance need only meet the reasonable time, place, and manner standard, rather than the more stringent standard applied to regulations of content.[295] The Supreme Court did not disturb that conclusion but disagreed with the lower court's approval of the licensing procedure because of the failure of the ordinance to establish a time limit within which necessary inspections must occur, holding that "[a] scheme that fails to set reasonable time limits on the decisionmaker creates the risk of indefinitely suppressing permissible speech."[296]

Similarly, an ordinance regulating adult uses must provide for prompt review by administrative or court appeal.[297]

Alcohol-serving uses are also subject to specific local regulation, usually through limitations on issuance of licenses, rather than zoning regulation. Licensing regulation raises constitutional issues similar to those applicable to zoning ordinances, however, including, for example, equal protection arising from ordinances requiring minimum separation of establishments.[298]

Notwithstanding the numerous Supreme Court pronouncements regarding adult uses, this area is among the most frequently litigated areas of land use regulation and remains somewhat fact-intensive.[299]

Commercial and Industrial Activities

In addition to the issues raised by the foregoing uses, generic commercial and industrial activities are often subjected to special regulations and are the classic foe of residential neighbors. Zoning-enabling statutes have been interpreted as not requiring municipalities to include commercial or industrial zones within the municipality when the municipality is small and has already been substantially developed as a residential community, and the resulting exclusion of commercial and industrial uses is reasonably related to the governmental interest in preserving the residential character of the community.[300]

Commercial and industrial zones also use regulatory devices employed in residential districts, such as special-use permits. It is not unusual for particular types of businesses, such as abortion clinics[301] or liquor stores,[302] to be required to obtain special permits or be subject to other regulations even in commercial or industrial districts, and the validity of such requirements will be tested under constitutional standards previously discussed.[303]

Regulations distinguishing personal use from commercial use and imposing stricter standards on commercial use, such as the operation of houseboats on a lake controlled by the federal government, have been upheld against equal protection and vagueness charges.[304]

Although the Euclidean concept of cumulative zoning permits residential uses in commercial and industrial zones,[305] noncumulative zoning ordinances in which residential uses are segregated from commercial and industrial uses have been upheld as reasonable exercises of police power.[306]

Transitional Uses

Transitions from one type of use to another, either because of change in character of an area or change in lifestyle of a landowner, may also create special regulatory problems. Local governments have dealt with transition issues through the flexible zoning techniques discussed in chapter 4 and the traditional devices for managing change discussed in chapter 5. One approach is the use of special zoning classifications that attempt to accommodate transition from residential to commercial use by permitting limited commercial use in residential structures as long as the exterior is not changed and unacceptable increases in traffic, noise, and activity do not result.

Administration of such an approach is not without difficulty, however. An example of the technique and the controversy that can arise is the litigation over the fate of the home of former Governor Ross R. Barnett in Jackson, Mississippi.[307] The home, a 7,000-square-foot, two-story colonial brick mansion built in 1964, fell into substantial disrepair after he entered a nursing home in 1983. The appraised value ($355,000), estimated cost of repairs ($55,000), and size of the home apparently discouraged buyers when the property was put up for sale.

Several years earlier the city of Jackson had adopted a floating zone, the "C–1A Restricted Commercial District." The ordinance permitted professional-office and limited-retail uses within a renovated residential structure as long as the residential character of the exterior was maintained. A prospective purchaser of the home attempted unsuccessfully to persuade the city to anchor the floating zone on the Barnett site. Despite expert testimony that the house suffered from "external obsolescence" and that the neighborhood had changed, as well as a petition in support of the rezoning signed by 90 persons in the general neighborhood, the Jackson City Council endorsed a recommendation to deny the petition because the petitioner "had failed to prove a community need for additional commercial property in the area or prove that a significant change in the land use character of the area had taken place."

The Mississippi Supreme Court upheld the decision as a legislative act that was fairly debatable. The court conceded, however, that the case presented a close question, one in which the city would have been justified in granting the rezoning as well as rejecting it. The court opined that the city may have made implementation of the transition-use concept too difficult by treating the application to anchor the floating zone merely as an extension of commercial use and suggested that the city consider the restricted commercial classification as a separate category. The court observed that the restricted commercial use for refurbished residences appeared to be "tailor-made" for the former governor's residence. "These types of large homes add value to any neighborhood, and builders and owners should not be discouraged from establishing stately homes because a zoning classification designed specifically to help preserve their structures turns out to be unavailable."[308]

Home Occupations

Advances in electronic technology coupled with substantial changes in traditional American lifestyles have caused an explosion in the number of Americans working at home. Euclidean zoning rigidity would prohibit such uses, but most communities allow home occupations, under varying degrees of regulation, either as permitted uses or as conditional uses requiring special permits. A typical ordinance authorizes home occupations as permitted uses in residential districts, subject to specific regulations including general prohibitions against signs, outside storage, changes in exterior appearance of the premises, sale of commodities or stock in trade, and employment of persons who are not residents of the home.[309] The definitions of home occupations vary, indicating a more or less restrictive approach.

Home occupations have been defined by the City of St. Louis as "accessory use[s] of a dwelling unit that constitute[s] either entirely or partly the livelihood of a person living in the dwelling unit."[310] In St. Louis County, home occupations have been defined as "domestic activit[ies] carried on by members of a family residing on the premises."[311] Both jurisdictions have specifically excluded certain occupations, but differ in the occupations on the excluded list. Beauty shops, barber shops, and music schools are on the county list of prohibited home occupations, while animal clinics, dancing schools, and doctor and dentist offices were on the city list. Architects, engineers, landscape architects, graphic artists, other designers, lawyers, insurance agents, brokers, "and members of similar professions" may "[p]ractice . . . their profession" in their homes in the city, subject to the general regulations for home occupations.[312] Occupations not enumerated as either permitted or prohibited uses may be allowed as conditional uses upon receipt of a special-use permit in the city, but no corresponding procedure has been included in the St. Louis County ordinance.[313]

Telecommunications

In the Telecommunications Act of 1996 (TCA),[314] Congress comprehensively deregulated the then-emerging American cellular telecommunications industry. Against the overall system of deregulation, however, in a section entitled "Preservation of Local Authority,"[315] Congress expressly preserved a degree of local power over cellular tower siting. The unambiguous objective of the TCA was to provide "a pro competitive, de-regulatory national policy framework designed to rapidly accelerate private sector deployment of advanced communications and information technologies and services to all Americans by opening all telecommunications markets to competition."[316]

It has been noted that "[the] statute fairly bristles with potential issues, from the proper allocation of the burden of proof through the available remedies for violation of the statute's requirements."[317] Some have been more critical.[318] Although there are at least ten meaningful elements of the statute,[319] five subsections are fundamental and have been construed in a significant number of reported decisions:

1. Unreasonable discrimination[320]
2. Effect of prohibiting wireless services[321]
3. Reasonably timely decision[322]
4. Decision in writing[323]
5. Supported by substantial evidence[324]

In enacting the substantial evidence standard, the statute borrows a well-known administrative law principle. It provides no express federal standard of review or burden of proof. "The TCA does not 'affect or encroach upon the substantive standards to be applied under established principles of state and local law.'"[325] There is thus an interplay between the TCA and existing federal and state law doctrines as to standard of review and burden of proof.[326] Although it has been held that the substantial evidence test governs TCA cases regardless of evidentiary burdens mandated by state law,[327] state zoning laws have been held to govern the weight of the same evidence.[328] It has also been held that the standard of review of a local authority's decision under the TCA is "'the same standard applied to federal administrative decisions.'"[329]

It is fair to characterize the standard of review under the TCA as similar to other administrative land use matters, that is "the traditional standard employed by courts for review of agency actions."[330] The court reviews the decision based on the entire record.[331] The distinction in the level of deference to local factual, versus legal, determinations remains, and decisions about legal conclusions, such as whether a denial has the effect of prohibiting wireless services, are reviewed *de novo*."[332]

Most TCA cases involve special- or conditional-use permits, the favored method of local regulation of cellular towers, and approximately 23 involve variances. Under state law principles, the type of local approval (conditional-use permit, variance, or rezoning) dictates the method and scope of review, including amount of deference, and the characterization of the underlying decision as "legislative," "administrative," or "quasi-judicial" therefore remains relevant.[333]

With respect to burden of proof, federal law trumps state law.[334] Upon denial of a cellular tower siting request, the municipality, not the provider, bears the burden of proof under the statute.[335] This shift of the traditional burden of proof has been justified by Congress's pro-provider intent in enacting the TCA.[336] In the context of the TCA, "substantial evidence" has been held to mean "such relevant evidence as a reasonable mind might accept as adequate to support a conclusion, requiring more than a mere scintilla, but less than a preponderance."[337]

The statute begins by providing that local jurisdictions "shall not unreasonably discriminate among providers of functionally equivalent services."[338] Thus there is such a thing as permissible "reasonable" discrimination.[339] Several courts have stressed that the provision does not prohibit discrimination *against* providers, only *among* providers.[340] In order to prove unreasonable discrimination, the provider must demonstrate both unequal treatment (relative to other providers) and that the unequal treatment was unfounded.[341] A mere denial of one application and grant of other applications, however, will not prove unfair discrimination, without evidence of "unreasonable" favoritism.[342]

The prohibition against discrimination among providers of "functionally equivalent services" does not protect wireless providers from discrimination in favor of traditional land-line providers.[343]

The unreasonable discrimination prohibition may overlap the other elements of the statute, in that discrimination will not be unreasonable if the subject cellular tower is "more intrusive" than existing cellular towers.[344] Discrimination may be easier to prove if there are competitors located in similarly zoned areas and the other statutory issues (discussed as follows) are neutral.[345] In summary, discrimination in the context of the TCA, like discrimination in other contexts, is a fact-intensive, case-by-case analysis.

Consistent with Congress's intent in promoting build-out of cellular infrastructure, the statute provides that local siting regulations "shall not prohibit or have the effect of prohibiting the provision of personal wireless services."[346] The statutory proscription has not, of course, been read literally. Otherwise, every denial would have "the effect of prohibiting" some measure of personal wireless services.[347] Thus the standard has been interpreted to lie somewhere between the extremes of absolute facial bans and absolute deference to provider discretion in placement of towers.

The "effect of prohibiting" provision has opened the door for providers to argue the issue of need or "significant gaps" in existing cellular coverage. Although need does not trump other factors and is only part of the overall calculus of TCA issues, the greater the evidence of need, the greater the likelihood that the court will overturn the denial.

To prevail on a prohibition claim, the provider first must show not only that a gap exists, but also that the gap is significant.[348] Given that virtually no municipality would purport to enact a facial ban on cellular towers, litigants and the courts have been sensitive to de facto bans. Limiting cellular towers to industrial zones, where the only industrial zone in the municipality is at an elevation that would prohibit any effective coverage, for example, may be effectively prohibitive. Obvious, but not necessarily absolute prohibitions, such as a prohibition against all cellular towers on mountaintops, have been held to violate the statute.[349] The "significant gap" standard requires municipalities not only to permit some cellular towers, but also to affirmatively consider whether cellular coverage is comprehensively available throughout the jurisdiction.[350] Second, the provider must show that the manner in which it proposes to fill a gap is not being served by another provider.[351]

It is virtually axiomatic in traditional land use matters that practically, if not legally, the municipality will want evidence that the provider has considered other sites. In TCA matters, consideration of alternatives is near the top of the list of issues. The cases have legitimated this concern by holding that the provider must show not only that there is a "significant gap," but also that it has attempted to acquire alternative locations that are less palatable.[352] This standard suggests that the provider submit evidence of an inventory of physically feasible sites and prove the legal unavailability of the sites, despite effort. The "significant gap" standard may also make evidence of the number of customers affected by the gap relevant.[353] Finally, case-by-case denials of permits at particular sites will not be construed as "effectively prohibiting" wireless services.[354]

Section 332(c)(7)(B)(ii) requires that the state or local government act on any requests for siting approval "within a reasonable period of time after the request is duly filed with such government or instrumentality, taking into account the nature and scope of such request." One state court has held that the provision does not require jurisdictions to give docket preference to wireless zoning requests.[355]

As noted, the essence of the statute is the requirement that cellular tower denials be supported by "substantial evidence."[356] This standard, although well-established in administrative law, has been characterized as "a legal term of art"[357] and is the subject of fully 54 percent, or approximately 57 of the 120 reported cases in the first five years of reported decisions.[358] "Substantial evidence" means "such relevant evidence as a reasonable mind might accept as adequate to support a conclusion."[359] Substantial evidence is "more than a mere scintilla, but less than a preponderance."[360] Substantial evidence is not a "large or considerable amount of evidence.'"[361]

As early as 1999, one court felt that there was "little agreement among the courts as to the meaning of substantial evidence [under the statute]."[362] The Conference Committee, in defining "substantial evidence," intended that the same standard apply as applied to federal administrative decisions.[363] In distilling the proliferation of substantial evidence cases since the enactment of the TCA, a few familiar categories of evidence have crystallized: (1) head count, (2) reasonable alternatives, (3) cost, (4) aesthetics, and (5) property values.

Head Count. The most ephemeral, subjective calculus that lies at the heart of most zoning issues is the extent to which purely political or democratic concerns are relevant and probative as against purely judicial or objective concerns. Typically, when the reviewing court is not impressed with the former, it will characterize the evidence as "conjecture," "generalized concerns," "conclusory," and the like. Such characterizations are legion in TCA cases.

It has been held expressly that decisions made by local governmental bodies are to be "given more deference where the decision is supported by the 'wide-spread opposition of a majority of the citizens . . . who voice their views.'"[364] Thus, under this view, "'[while] nothing is more common in zoning disputes than selfish opposition to zoning changes, . . . the Constitution does not forbid government to yield to such opposition.'"[365] Of course, citizen concerns, or downright opposition, should be reflected in a record in cellular tower requests.[366] One court, however, has taken judicial notice that "cellular towers are aesthetically unpleasing."[367] There is a tendency, however, to construe the statute as increasing the bar of competency to something more than purely political opposition.[368]

In the typical cellular tower proceeding, citizen opposition will make up in quantity what it lacks in quality. Thus several courts have rejected "generalized concerns," "conjecture," and "genuine, but unreasonable fears" as not constituting substantial evidence within the requirement of the statute.[369] In summary, if opposition is only political, the greater the number of opponents who articulate the opposition, the greater chance that such opposition will outweigh expert or other objective evidence. Even substantial democratic opposition, however, has not been held by itself to override more objective evidence with respect to the other, non–head-count standards, such as unavailability of reasonable alternatives, excessive cost of alternatives, placement in existing commercial zoning districts, and lack of diminution in property values.

Relevance of Reasonable Alternatives. Clearly, where topographic opportunities are limited, a court will be more likely to find that substantial evidence to deny a permit is lacking.[370] Stated another way, a complete absence of reasonable alternatives will "guarantee the rejection of every application" and violate the proscription against ordinances that have the "effect of prohibiting" personal wireless services.[371] At this point, any discussion within the "substantial evidence" test of reasonable alternatives overlaps with the proscription against ordinances that effectively prohibit personal wireless services.[372] In virtually all cases, the provider is benefited by testimony about efforts to locate reasonable alternatives, and whether or not the courts have specifically adopted such an element, local jurisdictions will do so.

Cost. Most jurisdictions will not hesitate to require the provider to spend more on a less offensive site, but only within limits.[373] "If wireless service providers are forced by local governments to incur such high expenses, the local government has accomplished through the back door what Congress has directly proscribed."[374]

Aesthetics. The weight of evidence of aesthetics in cellular tower placement is one of the most significant issues under the statute. Upon a first reading of the statute, aesthetics should be absolutely irrelevant, in that virtually no one would argue that even the best-designed cellular tower is aesthetically pleasing. Several courts have acknowledged the relevance, if not weight, of negative aesthetic evidence, but virtually no courts have affirmed a denial based on aesthetics alone.[375] Thus aesthetic considerations are relevant, provided they do not amount to a de facto prohibition of personal wireless services.[376]

Property Values. The familiar issue of effect on property values is no less relevant in TCA cases than in traditional zoning disputes, but "[the] evaluation of property value evidence under the TCA raises some difficult questions."[377] Bearing in mind that most federal courts have applied local and state laws governing the weight of evidence, the role of property value evidence may vary from state to state. Property value diminution alone, however, will not be held to justify denial of a permit. A lay opinion that a tower will affect property values "would result in all applications for such towers being rejected."[378] Expert testimony, on the one hand, that towers will have a "stigmatizing effect" may be given substantial weight.[379] Generally, expert testimony will trump constituent testimony with respect to property values.[380] Declining property value as a result of environmental concerns, however, may violate the statute's prohibition of environmental concerns as a basis for permit denial.[381] The denying authority will have the burden of supporting its decision where there is unrebutted provider expert testimony in the record.[382]

A surprising number of early cases construe, but do not hinge on, the requirement that any local denial of a cellular tower request be in writing and that the substantial evidence be "contained in a written record." The requirement that a decision be in writing and the requirement that a decision be "supported by substantial evidence contained in a written record" have been read separately.[383] Inasmuch as review of TCA decisions and other quasi-judicial administrative decisions is not de novo, but based on some measure of deference to an underlying record, the written decision is significant independently of the specific requirement.

Many jurisdictions intend to reduce the denial to writing, but are less concerned with explaining the basis for denial in the actual decision document. Generally, the requirement that a denial be in writing does not require written findings of fact and conclusions of law.[384]

No uniform set of guidelines governs the form of the written decision,[385] but there is some resistance to allowing the written record itself to satisfy the requirement of a "writing" reflecting the decision. This resistance is based in part on the TCA's distinction between a written denial and a written record.[386] Thus it is important that the municipality not rely on the written record to constitute the decision in writing. One court has held that the decision must include "a sufficient explanation of the reasons for the permit denial to allow a reviewing court to evaluate the evidence in a record supporting those reasons."[387]

The statute provides no specific remedies for violation of its substantive provisions. Generally, remedies issues in the TCA arena require urgency, and the TCA's express requirement that courts hear appeals "on an expedited basis"[388] has justified a liberal application of remedies. The following remedies have been expressly held to be available to address TCA violations: (1) summary judgment,[389] (2) mandamus,[390] (3) declaratory judgment,[391] (4) injunction,[392] and (5) Section 1983.[393]

Satellite dishes and cellular telecommunications towers are specifically regulated in most zoning ordinances. In one case, a 480-foot tower serving a college campus was upheld as an accessory use.[394] Historically, local zoning regulation of electric utility towers raised issues of police-power jurisdiction of municipalities over public utilities.[395] In at least one state, telecommunications providers have been held to be public utilities within the meaning of a statute exempting utilities from local zoning authority.[396]

Agricultural Uses

The continued growth of suburbs into agricultural areas and the general increase in land use sophistication of outlying counties have caused an increase in conflicts over agricultural uses. Although no special set of regulatory doctrines is applicable to such conflicts, conservation, growth management, nuisance law, and environmental preservation are significant recurring themes.

Many modern agricultural-use disputes involve hog farming or other animal husbandry issues. County ordinances limiting the number of "animal units" that may be housed on a given property have been upheld against a substantive due process claim that the ordinances do not reasonably measure waste output per unit of weight of the animal.[397] Many animal operations are subject to specific performance and setback standards, in addition to a limitation on the number of animal units.[398]

Many jurisdictions have created specific agricultural zoning districts, which regulate sensitive agricultural uses as conditional uses.[399]

Georgia has enacted a statute protecting agricultural uses from nuisance claims, including nuisance claims arising out of changes in conditions adjacent to the agricultural use.[400]

Practitioner Perspectives

The land uses described in this chapter are some of the most controversial. At the core of these controversies lie philosophical differences about the role of land use in modern life, reflecting in turn even more essential moral and religious beliefs. Perhaps none is more strongly held than the belief in entitlement to a safe and healthy quality of residential life. The lawyer representing a party in interest in such a conflict must appreciate the vigor and genuineness of such beliefs before he or she can be effective.

In practice, conflicts are site- or neighborhood-specific and pit current residents against a would-be developer. The developer by definition advances change and perhaps threatens the quality of life to those who by nature are suspicious of change. Planners have coined acronyms to describe the competing perspectives, including NIMBY ("Not in My Backyard") and LULU ("Locally Undesirable Land Use"),[401] and more recently, BANANA ("Build Absolutely Nothing Anywhere Near Anything"), CAVE ("Citizens Against Virtually Everything"), and NOPE ("Nowhere on Planet Earth"), to name a few. In some cases, emotions have run so high that developers have struck back at citizen opposition with civil lawsuits nicknamed SLAPPs ("Strategic Lawsuits Against Public Participation"). Although such suits generally have been unsuccessful,[402] critics argue that the time, expense, and stress of defending the suits keep other citizens from joining the debate.[403]

A prudent applicant will assess and usually accept neighborhood involvement, and in most cases will perform early reconnaissance through planning staff and local elected officials. Not all projects benefit from unlimited publicity and debate, however, and many will suffer from manipulation of the media by parties in opposition. The latter includes competing developers and persons such as lawyers, contractors, or politicians seeking personal economic leverage and gain. In large, controversial projects, it may be necessary to hire professional media consultants.

Some jurisdictions have institutionalized the concept of neighborhood ombudsperson or a form of alternate dispute resolution in an attempt to anticipate and diffuse unproductive debate. Proponents of the neighborhood involvement strategy believe that most of the concerns of fair-minded residents can be alleviated by early and accurate presentation of the facts of a proposal, before rumors start, and that many disputes can be resolved before emotions boil over.

Advocates of the quiet approach, on the other hand, believe that premature involvement of residents will only needlessly delay a development project, giving traditional and nontraditional opponents time to organize opposition for opposition's sake and undue extortive power. One concern is the difficulty in determining exactly what the fears and concerns may be in a given situation because of the traditional lack of organized citizen involvement in the land use process, thus confronting the developer with a "here today, gone tomorrow" type of organization presumably incapable of negotiating an agreement that will be honored. In projects involving large numbers of affected persons, it is never possible to determine absolutely whether spokespersons represent a cohesive group. Discussion and negotiation become unmanageable. The exposure to such a breakdown is increased in proportion to the public perception of the developer's wealth. The lawyer must enlist the help of the governing body in drawing a line in such a case.

Lawyers can play a crucial role in determining how developers and citizens respond to the citizen involvement question. In an Arizona case in which a developer proposed a group home for elderly persons, an appellate court made the following observations in affirming a denial of the conditional-use permit:

> The transcript of the hearing before the city council discloses that appellants had created a good deal of animosity in the neighborhood by their failure to talk with the neighbors prior to applying for the conditional use permit for [a previously sought] juvenile facility and prior to applying for the conditional use permit for the elderly group home. This led the neighbors and some members of the city council to be suspicious of the type of home proposed, and some members of the council and the neighborhood believed appellants were not truthful about the proposed use. Their suspicions were reinforced by appellants' refusal to disclose the background of any of the occupants of the proposed group home. It was evident that the neighbors and some members of the city council believed that the

home would be occupied by persons with some type of mental or behavioral disorder. The neighbors and some members of the council expressed the thought that they were not opposed to elderly programs but were opposed to group housing in single-family residences. A seeming substantiation of this fear was brought out by one member of the neighborhood who quoted from the Arizona Department of Health services site report which indicated that appellants were going to develop a new congregate living program in the [city] area where elderly, substance abuse, mental health, and other disabled clients would be sharing a living facility.[404]

Such fears and suspicions are not by definition ill-founded, but over time they have a way of igniting. The practitioner should not lightly accept delay in the approval process. It is ironic that in the Arizona case, what was proposed—a house for five elderly persons who needed 24-hour care because of their frail physical condition rather than any mental or behavioral disorder—had far less potential for disruption of a single-family environment than what was possible under the technical definition applied in the case: "shelter and/or rehabilitation of up to eight persons, regardless of age, . . . who for various reasons cannot reside in their family home."[405]

In large inner cities, practitioners can relate innumerable war stories of redevelopment projects defeated for the wrong reasons, leaving urban blight unremedied.

One of the obvious lessons of the Arizona case and others like it is that genuine sensitivity to environmental and social impact is essential in modern land use law practice. As pointed out in previous chapters, the lawyer must be careful always to make a record where possible and necessary and must exude firmness and resolution. In the end, however, effectiveness requires balance between firmness, on one hand, and sensitivity to competing interests, on the other. Such interests are both legal and political, unlike the typical lawsuit. In the local context, the lawyer is counselor, facilitator, and often mediator—in a very real sense a builder of community through the process of helping to accommodate the often conflicting values of privacy and growth.

Notes

1. ST. LOUIS COUNTY, MISSOURI CODE, §§ 1003.020, 1003.030 (1982). Subdistricts include single-family detached homes of various lot sizes, multifamily housing, and group homes.

2. Village of Euclid v. Ambler Realty Co., 272 U.S. 365, 380 (1926).

3. ST. LOUIS COUNTY, MISSOURI CODE, §§ 1003.107–.117 (1982).

4. *Village of Euclid*, 272 U.S. at 381.

5. ST. LOUIS COUNTY, MISSOURI CODE, §§ 1003.107–.125 (1982).

6. *See, e.g.*, Steinman, *The Effect of Land-Use Restrictions on the Establishment of Community Residences for the Disabled: A National Study*, 19 URB. LAW 1 (1987); Connor, *Zoning Discrimination Affecting Retarded Persons*, 29 WASH. U. J. URB. & CONTEMP. L. 67 (1985); Ziegler, *The Twilight of Single-Family Zoning*, 3 UCLA J. ENVT'L L. & POL'Y 161 (1983); Richards, *Zoning for Social Control*, 1982 DUKE L. J. 781; Sager, *Insular Majorities Unabated: Warth v. Seldin and City of Eastlake v. Forest City Enterprises, Inc.*, 91 HARV. L. REV. 1373 (1978); Sussna, *Residential Densities: A Patchwork Placebo*, 1 FORDHAM URB. L. J. 127 (1972).

7. *Village of Euclid,* 272 U.S. at 365 (no due process or equal protection violation in segregation of single-family uses from multiple-family uses).

8. *See, e.g.,* Arverne Bay Constr. Co. v. Thatcher, 15 N.E.2d 587 (N.Y. 1938) (single-family zoning designation in undeveloped area invalidated as "premature").

9. *See, e.g.,* City of Cleburne v. Cleburne Living Ctr., 473 U.S. 432 (1985) ("irrational prejudice" against group to be served is impermissible basis for classification requiring special permit for group homes for mentally retarded when other institutional uses were permitted as of right).

10. *See, e.g.,* McDermott v. Village of Calverton Park, 454 S.W.2d 577, 581–83 (Mo. 1970); Clarkson Valley Estates, Inc. v. Village of Clarkson Valley, 630 S.W.2d 151 (Mo. Ct. App. 1982). Exclusionary zoning is discussed on pp. 283–84 and 377–79.

11. *See* pp. 291–95. The definition of family is an integral part of any single-family land use zoning ordinance. *See* City of Edmunds v. Oxford House, Inc., 514 U.S. 725, 733 (1995).

12. *See, e.g.,* St. Louis County Zoning Ordinance, § 1003.020.3.(22); Northvale, N.J. Code, § 74-11 (1981), *construed in* Rowatti v. Gonchar, 500 A.2d 381, 384 (N.J. 1985). *See generally,* T. Burrows, *A Survey of Zoning Decisions* 13, Planning Advisory Service Report No. 421 (1989).

13. *Rowatti,* 500 A.2d at 386.

14. Stafford v. Inc. Village of Sands Point, 102 N.Y.S.2d 910 (Sup. Ct. 1951).

15. 416 U.S. 1 (1974) (six unrelated college students not a "single family").

16. D. Mandelker, Land Use Law 136 (2d ed. 1988).

17. The definition of family is an integral part of any single-family land use zoning ordinance. *See* City of Edmunds v. Oxford House, Inc., 514 U.S. 725, 733 (1995).

18. Whether a definition of "single-family" that excludes such a group home is constitutionally valid is explored on pp. 291–95.

19. Moore v. City of East Cleveland, 431 U.S. 494 (1977).

20. *Id.*

21. City of Ladue v. Horn, 720 S.W.2d 745, 751 (Mo. Ct. App. 1986), *citing with approval* Town of Durham v. White Enter., Inc., 348 A.2d 706 (N.H. 1975) (student renters not a family); Rademan v. City and County of Denver, 526 P.2d 1325 (Colo. 1974) (two married couples living as a "communal family" not a family); Prospect Gardens Convalescent Home, Inc. v. City of Norwalk, 347 A.2d 637 (Conn. 1975) (nursing-home employees living together not a family).

Whether to apply the traditional definition of family to land use regulations can become an emotional issue. In the spring of 1989, Denver, Colorado—one of the cities whose traditional definition of family ordinance had been upheld by state courts—abolished the ordinance by a 7–6 vote of the city council after lengthy and emotional debate. *Denver Kills a Law That Barred Unmarried Couples from a Home,* N.Y. Times, May 3, 1989, p. 24A.

22. *City of Ladue,* 720 S.W.2d at 752.

23. *See, e.g.,* Borough of Glassboro v. Vallorosi, 568 A.2d 888 (N.J. 1990); Braschi v. Stahl Assocs. Co., 543 N.E.2d 49 (N.Y. 1989); Charter Township of Delta v. Dinolfo, 351 N.W.2d 831 (Mich. 1984); City of Santa Barbara v. Adamson, 610 P.2d 436 (Cal. 1980); New Jersey v. Baker, 405 A.2d 368 (N.J. 1979); City of White Plains v. Ferraioli, 313 N.E.2d 756, 758 (N.Y. 1974) ("Zoning is intended to control types of housing and living and not the genetic or intimate family relations of human beings"); City of Des Plaines v. Trottner, 216 N.E.2d 116 (Ill. 1970).

24. *Borough of Glassboro,* 568 A.2d at 894–95.

25. *Braschi,* 543 N.E.2d at 53–54.

26. Charter Township of Delta v. Dinolfo, 351 N.W.2d 831 (Mich. 1984).

27. *Id.* at 351.

28. *Id.* at 841.

29. *Id.* at 841–42 (citing New Jersey v. Baker, 405 A.2d 368 (N.J. 1979) ("The fatal flaw in attempting to maintain a stable residential neighborhood through the use of criteria based upon biological or legal relationships is that such classifications operate to prohibit a plethora of uses which pose no threat to the accomplishment of the end sought to be achieved. Moreover, such a classification system legitimizes many uses which defeat that goal")).

30. *Id.* at 843–44 n. 8 (citing Kirsch Holding Co. v. Borough of Manasquan, 281 A.2d 513 (N.J. 1971)). The New Jersey Supreme Court held that this ordinance was sweepingly excessive and therefore invalid. *Kirsch,* 281 A.2d at 531.

31. *Dinolfo,* 351 N.W.2d at 843–44 n. 8 (citing Penobscot Area Hous. Dev. Corp. v. City of Brewer, 434 A.2d 14, 20 (Me. 1981)). The Maine Supreme Court found this ordinance valid. *Penobscot,* 434 A.2d at 20.

32. *See, e.g.,* the position of the New York courts in McMinn v. Town of Oyster Bay, 488 N.E.2d 1240 (N.Y. 1985) (age restrictions of unrelated persons invalidated); Group House of Port Washington, Inc. v. Bd. of Zoning and Appeals, 380 N.E.2d 207 (N.Y. 1978) (group homes for children who are the victims of unhappy homes may not be excluded); City of White Plains v. Ferraioli, 313 N.E.2d 756 (N.Y. 1974) (group homes for foster children may not be excluded); Baer v. Town of Brookhaven, 524 N.Y.S.2d 221 (App. Div. Dept.), *appeal denied,* 528 N.E.2d 515 (1988), *order aff'd,* 537 N.E.2d 619 (1989) (boardinghouses may be excluded, but definition of family must include surrogate families).

33. 483 So. 2d 903 (La. 1986).

34. Single-family dwelling was defined in the ordinance as "[a] building designed for or occupied exclusively by not more than one family." City of Kenner v. Normal Life of Louisiana, Inc., 483 So. 2d 903, 905 (La. 1986).

35. Blevins v. Barry-Lawrence County Ass'n for Retarded Citizens, 707 S.W.2d 407 (Mo. 1986).

36. State *ex rel.* Harding v. Door County Bd. of Adjustment, 371 N.W.2d 403 (Wis. Ct. App.), *rev. denied,* 375 N.W.2d 216 (1985).

37. *Id.* at 404.

38. 42 U.S.C. § 3601, *et seq.* (1997). *See* pp. 289–91 and 291–95.

39. Clem v. Christole, Inc., 548 N.E.2d 1180 (Ind. App. 1990), *opinion vacated on other grounds,* 582 N.E.2d 780 (Ind. 1991).

40. *Id.* at 1187. Whether the Fair Housing Act Amendments of 1988 would effectively overrule cases like *Clem v. Christole* may be open to question. *See also* pp. 289–91.

41. 42 U.S.C. § 3607(b) (1) (1997).

42. 514 U.S. 725 (1995).

43. *Id.* at 738. The parties stipulated that the residents were "handicapped" within the meaning of the Act. *Id.* at 729.

44. *See, e.g.,* WASH. REV. CODE § 35.63.220 (1994); MO. REV. STAT. § 89.020 (1996). *See* pp. 291–95.

45. *See, e.g.,* the National Mfr. Hous. Constr. and Safety Standards Act, 42 U.S.C. § 5401 *et seq.* (1997), authorizing the Department of Housing and Urban Development (HUD) to promulgate standards for the development and use of mobile or manufactured housing. HUD standards are published in 24 C.F.R. §§ 3280.1–.904 (1990).

46. *See, e.g.,* Clark v. Winnebago County, 817 F.2d 407, 409 (7th Cir. 1987) (distinction between mobile homes and site-built homes with respect to design, construction, and general appearance support legislative decision to establish separate mobile-home park district).

47. *See, e.g.,* FLA. STAT. ANN. § 553.36(11), *discussed in* Grant v. Seminole County, 817 F.2d 731, 733 (11th Cir. 1987).

48. *Grant,* 817 F.2d at 733.

49. *Clark,* 817 F.2d at 407 (unsuccessful challenge to validity of zoning ordinance that established mobile-home districts, prohibited use of mobile homes outside of the district, and established standards for the maintenance of mobile-home parks within the district); City of Brookside Village v. Comeau, 633 S.W.2d 790, 795 (Tex. 1982), *cert. denied,* 459 U.S. 1087 (1982) (upholding mobile-home park district regulation, but cautioning that "the assumption that all mobile homes are different from all site-built homes with respect to criteria cognizable under the police power can no longer be accepted"); Town of Stonewood v. Bell, 270 S.E.2d 787 (W.Va. 1980); *see also* OR. REV. STAT. §§ 197.475–.490 (declaring the policy of the state "to provide for mobile home parks within all urban growth boundaries to allow persons and families a choice of residential settings," and requiring cities and counties to establish "projection[s] of need for mobile home parks").

50. *Grant,* 817 F.2d at 731 (unsuccessful challenge to zoning ordinance that prohibited mobile homes outside of districts where that use was permitted); Horizon Concepts v. City of Balch Springs, 789 F.2d 1165 (5th Cir. 1986) (classification of mobile and modular homes as special uses upheld because of legitimate governmental interest in assuring that modular homes were not constructed faster than the necessary municipal services for residents of such homes could be provided); Gackler Land Co. v. Yankee Springs Township, 359 N.W.2d 226 (Mich. Ct. App. 1984), *aff'd* 398 N.W.2d 393 (1986) (all mobile homes located outside of mobile-home parks required to have special-use permits).

51. Fasano v. Bd. of County Comm'rs, 507 P.2d 23 (Or. 1973) (approving the concept but invalidating a specific decision to anchor floating zone because of inadequate showing that a change in land use would be in accordance with local comprehensive plan).

52. Town of Granby v. Landry, 170 N.E.2d 364, 366 (Mass. 1960) (law prohibiting more than one mobile home per lot is valid, although not part of comprehensive zoning ordinance and although town lacked comprehensive zoning plan).

53. Town of Stonewood v. Bell, 270 S.E.2d 787, 789 (W.Va. 1980) (regulation of the placement of mobile homes is a valid use of police power even where community did not first adopt a comprehensive plan).

54. *Gackler,* 359 N.W.2d at 228 (local government's authority to regulate placement of mobile homes not preempted by state regulation of safety and construction of mobile homes, and such local regulation is a valid use of police power).

55. *Clark,* 817 F.2d at 409.

56. *Grant,* 817 F.2d at 736; see *Comeau,* 633 S.W.2d at 794 ("Mobile home parks pose special health problems and are amendable to regulations designed to eliminate such hazards.")

57. *Gackler,* 359 N.W.2d at 230.

58. Town of Chesterfield v. Brooks, 489 A.2d 600 (N.H. 1985).

59. *See, e.g., Town of Stonewood,* 270 S.E.2d at 791–92 (reviewing cases).

60. Koston v. Town of Newburgh, 256 N.Y.S.2d 837 (N.Y. Sup. Ct. 1965).

61. *See, e.g.,* OR. REV. STAT. § 197.475 (state policy to provide for mobile-home parks "to allow persons and families a choice of residential settings"); Southern Burlington County NAACP v. Township of Mount Laurel, 456 A.2d 390, 450–51 (N.J. 1983) (*Mount Laurel II*) (overturning judicially sanctioned ban on mobile homes and requiring mobile-home zones to be created when necessary to meet fair-share housing requirements).

62. IDAHO CODE §§ 67-6508, 67-6509A (1995).

63. N.Y. REAL PROP. LAW § 233 (McKinney 1997).

64. MD. CODE ANN., Real Property, § 8A-1201 (1996).

65. Arcadia Dev. Corp. v. City of Bloomington, 552 N.W.2d 281 (Minn. App. 1996) (ordinance requiring mobile-home park owner to pay reasonable relocation costs to tenants upon closing of park).

66. 42 U.S.C. §§ 3601, 3631.

67. *Id.*

68. 42 U.S.C. § 3604 (1988).

69. 42 U.S.C. § 3607 (1988).

70. 42 U.S.C. §§ 3604(a), 3617; *See* City of Edmonds v. Washington, 115 S. Ct. 1776 (1996). Huntington Branch, NAACP v. Town of Huntington, 844 F.2d 926 (2d Cir. 1988), *cert. denied,* 109 S. Ct. 276 (1988) (refusal to amend zoning ordinance to permit multifamily housing outside of urban renewal held violative of Fair Housing Act); Metropolitan Hous. Dev. Corp. v. Village of Arlington Heights, 558 F.2d 1283 (7th Cir. 1977), *cert. denied,* 434 U.S. 1025 (1978) (local governments have statutory obligation to refrain from discriminatory zoning policies); *see generally* J. KUSHNER, FAIR HOUSING §§ 7.11, 8.18 (1983, 1988 Supp.).

71. 42 U.S.C. § 3613(a)(1)(A); Wesley Group Home Ministries v. City of Hallandale, 670 So. 2d 1046 (Fla. Ct. App. 1996).

72. Seniors Civil Liberties Ass'n v. Kemp, 761 F. Supp. 1528 (M.D. Fla. 1991), *aff'd,* 965 F.2d 1030 (11th Cir. 1992).

73. 488 N.E.2d 1240 (1985).

74. Group House of Port Washington, Inc. v. Bd. of Zoning & Appeals, 408 N.Y.S.2d 377 (1978); City of White Plains v. Ferraioli, 313 N.E.2d 756 (N.Y. 1974); *see generally* pp. 284–88.

75. McMinn v. Town of Oyster Bay, 488 N.E.2d 1240 (N.Y. 1985).

76. Taxpayer's Ass'n of Weymouth Township v. Weymouth Township, 364 A.2d 1016 (N.J. 1976), *appeal dismissed & cert. denied sub nom.,* Feldman v. Weymouth Township, 430 U.S. 977 (1977).

77. Shepard v. Woodland Township Comm. and Planning Bd., 364 A.2d 1005 (N.J. 1976).

78. *Weymouth Township,* 364 A.2d at 1040; *Shepard,* 364 A.2d at 1016; *see also* Southern Burlington County NAACP v. Township of Mount Laurel, 336 A.2d 713 (1975), *appeal dismissed & cert. denied,* 423 U.S. 808 (1975) (*Mount Laurel I*).

79. *Mount Laurel I,* 336 A.2d at 729; Molino v. Mayor and Council of Borough of Glassboro, 281 A.2d 401 (N.J. Super. Ct. Law. Div. 1971).

80. O'Connor v. Village Green Owner's Ass'n, 662 P.2d 427 (Cal. 1983) (condominium ban on children younger than age 19 invalidated); Marina Point, Ltd. v. Wolfson, 640 P.2d 115, 128 (Cal. 1982), *cert. denied,* 459 U.S. 858 (1982) (apartment ban on children invalidated as "differ[ing] fundamentally" from permissive age qualifications for housing for older persons).

81. Melious, *Striking a Compromise: Limiting the Exclusionary Impact of Age Discrimination in Housing,* 37 LAND USE L. & ZONING DIG. 3, 7 (Sept. 1985).

82. Jayber, Inc. v. Municipal Council of the Township of West Orange, 569 A.2d 304 (N.J. Super. Ct. App. Div.), *cert. denied,* 584 A.2d 214–15 (N.J. 1990). Variances are discussed on pp. 229–31.

83. Franchi v. Zoning Hearing Bd. of New Brighton, 543 A.2d 239, 240 (Pa. Commw. Ct. 1988) (use of duplex in residential district for an accounting office was a primary rather than accessory use); St. Charles County v. McPeak, 730 S.W.2d 611 (Mo. Ct. App. 1987) (landowners enjoined from repairing and storing trucks on property zoned residential); *see also* Singal v. City of Bangor, 440 A.2d 1048 (Me. 1982) (sale of gasoline not an accessory use to the operation of a grocery/superette in an area zoned for commercial use); Bd. of County Comm'rs of the County of Boulder v. Thompson, 493 P.2d 1358 (Colo. 1972) (storage of 60 automobiles, scrap metal, and other discarded materials not accessory use in district zoned for agricultural use); *see generally* Annotation, *Zoning: What Constitutes "Incidental" or "Accessory" Use of Business Property Zoned, and Primarily Used, for Business or Commercial Purposes,* 60 A.L.R. 4th 907 (1988); Annotation, *Residential Accessory Uses,* 54 A.L.R. 4th 1034 (1987).

84. *See, e.g.,* City of Richmond Heights v. Richmond Heights Presbyterian Church, 764 S.W.2d 647, 648 (Mo. 1989) (church-operated day-care center met ordinance definition of permitted accessory use in single-family residential district).

85. *See, e.g.,* P. Hare, *Accessory Apartments: Using Surplus Space in Single-Family Houses,* PLANNING ADVISORY SERVICE, Report No. 365, American Planning Association (1981). The PAS report applies the term "accessory apartment" to conversions of space within existing single-family homes, and distinguishes that form of housing from "shared housing" (use of some facilities in common, such as kitchens) and "echo housing—elder cottage housing opportunities" (separate, removable cottages). In this section, the term "accessory housing" will be used to include all three forms of housing.

86. *See generally,* M. GELLEN, ACCESSORY APARTMENTS IN SINGLE FAMILY HOUSING (Center for Urban Policy Research, Rutgers University, 1985).

87. Hare, *supra* n. 85, at 4–5, 9–23; *see also* P. HARE, CREATING AN ACCESSORY APARTMENT (1986).

88. Kasper v. Town of Brookhaven, 535 N.Y.S.2d 621 (N.Y. App. Div. 1988).

89. CONN. GEN. STAT. § 8-250 (37).

90. General Accounting Office, *An Analysis of Zoning and Other Problems Affecting the Establishment of Group Homes for the Mentally Disabled,* 1–2, 17–20 (1983); *see generally* Peter W. Salsich, *Group Homes, Shelters and Congregate Housing: Deinstitutionalization Policies and the NIMBY Syndrome,* 21 REAL PROP. PROB. & TRUST J. 413 (1986).

91. *See* pp. 283–88.

92. Zoning Ordinance of City of Casa Grande, AZ, *construed in* Behavioral Health Agency of Central Arizona (BHACA) v. City of Casa Grande, 708 P.2d 1317, 1320 (Ariz. Ct. App. 1985). The definition is also in play in state zoning-enabling statutes. *See, e.g.,* MO. REV. STAT. § 89.020 (1996).

93. *BHACA,* 708 P.2d at 1321.

94. City of Edmonds v. Oxford House, 514 U.S. 725 (1995). *See discussion* on pp. 284–88.

95. Taylor Home of Charlotte, Inc. v. City of Charlotte, 453 S.E.2d 170 (N.C. 1994).

96. *See* pp. 284–88.

97. *See* pp. 225–26; *See also* Cyclone Sand & Gravel Co. v. Zoning Bd. of Adjustment, 351 N.W.2d 778 (Iowa 1984); State *ex rel.* McNary v. Hais, 670 S.W.2d 494 (Mo. banc 1984).

98. Blevins v. Barry-Lawrence County Ass'n for Retarded Citizens, 707 S.W.2d 407 (Mo. 1986) (nonprofit group home functioning as family-style unit did not violate restrictive covenant providing for use for residential purposes only); Clark v. Manuel, 463 So. 2d 1276 (La. 1985) (nonprofit community home for mentally retarded persons is residential purpose and thus does not violate restrictive covenant limiting use to residential purposes); Costley v. Caromin House, Inc., 313 N.W.2d 21 (Minn. 1981) (for-profit group home operating as a single housekeeping unit did not violate zoning ordinance that permitted one- and two-family dwelling groups, nor did it violate restrictive covenant providing that only one dwelling and one garage be constructed per lot). *See also discussion* on pp. 284–88.

99. *See, e.g.,* N.Y. MENTAL HYG. LAW § 41.34(e) (McKinney); R.I. GEN. LAWS §§ 45-24-22, 45-24-23.

100. *See, e.g.,* DEL. CODE ANN. tit. 22 § 309(a); IOWA CODE ANN. § 358A.25.; MO. REV. STAT. § 89.020; VT. STAT. ANN. tit. 24, § 4409(d).

101. *See, e.g.,* MICH. STAT. ANN. § 5.2963(16a); W. VA. CODE § 27-17-2(a).

102. 483 So. 2d 903 (La. 1986).

103. *Id.* at 906–07 (La. 1986) (quoting LA. STAT. ANN. § 28:381(8)).

104. 449 So. 2d 45 (La. Ct. App. 1984) (group home permitted though building restrictions limited use of property to single-family residential use).

105. *City of Kenner, supra,* 483 So. 2d at 907.

106. 437 U.S. 432 (1985).

107. City of Cleburne v. Cleburne Living Ctr., 473 U.S. 432, 450 (1985).

108. MASS. GEN. LAWS, Ch. 40A, § 3.

109. Rogers v. Town of Norfolk, 734 N.E.2d 1143 (Mass. 2000).

110. Fair Housing Amendments Act of 1988, Pub. L. 100-430, Sept. 13, 1988, 102 Stat. 1619, amending 42 U.S.C. §§ 3601–31.; *see* chapter 3.

111. 42 U.S.C. § 3602(h).

112. 42 U.S.C. § 3604(f)(3)(B).

113. 42 U.S.C. § 3604(f)(9).

114. 42 U.S.C. §§ 3604(a), 3617; Huntington Branch NAACP v. Town of Huntington, 844 F.2d 926 (2d Cir. 1988), *aff'd per curiam,* 488 U.S. 15 (1988); Metropolitan Hous. Dev. Corp. v. Village of Arlington Heights, 558 F.2d 1283 (7th Cir. 1977); United States v. City of Black Jack, 508 F.2d 1179 (8th Cir. 1974), *cert. denied,* 422 U.S. 1042 (1975).

115. Judy B. v. Borough of Tioga, 889 F. Supp. 792 (M.D. Pa. 1995).

116. House Report, 1988 U.S. CODE CONG. & ADMIN. NEWS at 2174, *as quoted in* Familystyle of St. Paul, Inc. v. City of St. Paul, 728 F. Supp. 1396, 1399 (D. Minn. 1990), *aff'd,* 923 F.2d 91 (1991).

117. *See, e.g.,* MINN. STAT. ANN. § 245A.11, subd. 4 (prohibiting issuance of license to group home that would be located within 1,320 feet of existing group home unless municipality issues special-use permit), upheld in *Familystyle,* 728 F. Supp. at 1396.

118. Larkin v. State, 883 F. Supp. 172 (E.D. Mich. 1995), *aff'd,* 89 F.3d 285 (6th Cir. 1996).

119. 728 F. Supp. 1396 (D. Minn. 1990). *But see* Arc of New Jersey, Inc. v. State, 950 F. Supp. 637 (D.N.J. 1996).

120. In Gamble v. City of Escondido, 104 F.3d 300 (9th Cir. 1997), however, the court upheld denial of a conditional-use permit for a group home where evidence indicated that a significant portion of the home was used to provide health care. Another possible conflict between the Fair Housing Act Amendments and state laws pertains to state prohibitions against inquiring into handicapped status of prospective tenants. Such a law may be at odds with federal housing regulations that require a determination of eligibility for tenancy in subsidized housing for the disabled. Robards v. Cotton Mill Assocs., 677 A.2d 540 (Me. 1996).

121. *Familystyle,* 728 F. Supp. at 1403–05.

122. Arc of New Jersey, Inc. v. State, 950 F. Supp. 637 (D.N.J. 1996).

123. 42 U.S.C. § 12181, *et seq.*

124. *See* 42 U.S.C. § 12101, *et seq.* and 42 U.S.C. § 12131, *et seq.,* respectively.

125. 42 U.S.C. § 12182(a).

126. *See* 42 U.S.C. § 12181(2)(A).

127. 42 U.S.C. § 12181(7).

128. 42 U.S.C. § 12182(b)(2)(ii).

129. 42 U.S.C. §§ 12182(b)(2)(iv), 12181(9).

130. 42 U.S.C. § 12183.

131. *Id.*

132. 42 U.S.C. § 12188.

133. *See* pp. 291–95. On the difference between group homes and treatment centers, it has been held to be a violation of equal protection to treat treatment centers differently from group homes. Bannum v. City of Louisville, 958 F.2d 1354 (6th Cir. 1992).

134. Transitions v. Bd. of Zoning Adjustment of City of Ashland, 729 S.W.2d 459 (Ky. Ct. App. 1987) (property permitted to be used as halfway house where such use was not expressly prohibited in area zoned for light industrial use).

135. *Transitions,* 729 S.W.2d at 460.

136. *Transitions,* 729 S.W.2d at 460–61.

137. Taylor v. Foley, 505 N.Y.S.2d 166, 169 (N.Y. App. Div. 1986).

138. Ibero-American Action League, Inc v. Palma, 366 N.Y.S.2d 747, 748 (N.Y. App. Div. 1975) (*citing* People v. Renaissance Project, Inc., 324 N.E.2d 355 (1975)).

139. Bethesda Hospital and Deaconess Ass'n v. City of Montgomery, 501 N.E.2d 642 (Ohio Ct. App. 1985).

140. Doe v. City of Butler, 892 F.2d 315 (3d Cir. 1989).

141. *Id.* at 323–24.

142. City of Edmonds v. Oxford House, Inc., 514 U.S. 725 (1995), *discussed* on pp. 284–88.

143. Oxford House—Evergreen v. City of Plainfield, 769 F. Supp. 1329 (D.N.J. 1991).

144. *See* p. 255.

145. *Oxford House—Evergreen,* 769 F. Supp. at 1344. *See also* United States v. Southern Mgmt. Corp., 955 F.2d 914 (4th Cir. 1992).

146. *See generally* pp. 337–38 and 346–53.

147. Arizona, ARIZ. REV. STAT. ANN., §§ 33-1201–1270; Maine, ME. REV. STAT. ANN., tit. 33, §§ 1601-101–1604-118; Minnesota, MINN. STAT. ANN. §§ 515A.1-101–.4-117; Missouri, MO. STAT. ANN., §§ 448.1-101–448.4-120; New Mexico, N.M. STAT. ANN., §§ 47-7A-1–47-7D-20; North Carolina, N.C. GEN. STAT., §§ 47C-1-11–47C-4-120; Pennsylvania, 68 PA. CONS. STAT. ANN., §§ 3101–3414; Rhode Island, 1956 R.I. PUB. LAWS, §§ 34-36.1-1.01–4.20; Virginia, VA. CODE ANN., §§ 55-79.39; Washington, WASH. REV. CODE ANN., §§ 64.34.010–.950.

148. Uniform Condominium Act, § 106(b).

149. McConnell v. Wilson, 543 A.2d 249, 251 (R.I. 1988).

150. Briarwood Props. v. City of Los Angeles, 217 Cal. Rptr. 849 (1985).

151. *See* pp. 353–55.

152. Briarwood Props., 217 Cal. Rptr. at 855–56. *But see* Channing Props. v. City of Berkeley, 14 Cal. Rptr. 2d 32 (Cal. App. 1992). Impact fees are discussed on pages 346–53.

153. People v. Powers, 263 Cal. Rptr. 579 (1989), *review granted,* 786 P.2d 892 (1990), *modified,* 3 Cal. Rptr. 2d 34 (Cal. App. 1992). Vested rights are discussed on pp. 353–55.

154. 42 U.S.C. §§ 2000 cc. 5.

155. 521 U.S. 507 (1997)

156. 146 CONG. REC. E1234-05.

157. 521 U.S. at 536.

158. 146 CONG. REC. E1234-05 (daily ed. July 13, 2000) (statement of Sen. Canady).

159. 204 F. Supp. 857 (E.D. Pa. 2002).

160. *Id.* at 859. The Court had not ruled on the RLUIPA claim, as the decision was issued overruling the township's motion to dismiss.

161. 146 CONG. REC. E1563-01 (daily ed. Sept. 21, 2000) (statement of Sen. Canady).

162. 42 U.S.C. § 2000cc(b).

163. 42 U.S.C. § 2000cc(a),(b).

164. 42 U.S.C. § 2000cc-5(4).

165. 42 U.S.C. § 2000cc-5(5).

166. Prater v. City of Burnside, 289 F.3d 417, 432–34 (6th Cir. 2002).

167. *Id.*

168. *Id.* at 434.

169. 42 U.S.C. § 2000cc-5(7)(A).

170. 146 CONG. REC. E1563-01.

171. *Id.*

172. 42 U.S.C. § 2000cc-5(7)(B).

173. 146 CONG. REC. E1563-01.

174. *Id.*

175. San Jose Christian College v. City of Morgan Hill, No. C01-20857, 2002 WL 971779 at *2 (N.D. Cal. Mar. 5, 2002).

176. *Id.*

177. 146 Cong. Rec. S774-01 (daily ed. July 27, 2000) (joint statement of Sen. Hatch and Sen. Kennedy).

178. San Jose Christian College, 2002 WL 971779 at *2.

179. *Id.*

180. 148 F. Supp. 2d 173, 181 (D. Conn. 2001).

181. *Id.* at 189.

182. *Id.*

183. 146 Cong. Rec. S774-01.

184. 146 Cong. Rec. S10992-01 (daily ed. Oct. 25, 2000) (statement of Sen. Dewine and response of Sen. Kennedy).

185. 42 U.S.C. § 2000cc(a)(1); Murphy, 148 F. Supp. 2d at 190.

186. Murphy, 148 F. Supp. 2d at 190.

187. 42 U.S.C. § 2000cc(a)(1)(B).

188. Murphy, 148 F. Supp. 2d at 190, citing Sherbert v. Verner, 374 U.S. 398, 407 (1963).

189. 146 Cong. Rec. E1563-01. 42 U.S.C. § 2000 cc(b)(1).

190. *Id.* § 2000 cc (b)(2).

191. *Id.* § 2000 cc (b)(3).

192. *Id.*

193. 42 U.S.C. § 2000cc-2(a).

194. *Id.*

195. 42 U.S.C. § 2000cc-2(f).

196. Messiah Baptist Church v. County of Jefferson, 859 F.2d 820, 828 (10th Cir. 1988) (McKay, J., dissenting, citing Schad v. Borough of Mount Ephraim, 452 U.S. 61, 68 (1981) ("[W]hen a zoning law infringes upon a protected liberty, it must be narrowly drawn and must further a sufficiently substantial government interest")), *cert. denied*, 490 U.S. 1005 (1989); State v. Cameron, 445 A.2d 75 (N.J. Super. 1982) (zoning that prohibits religious worship in single-family zone is constitutionally valid where such worship is not excluded from entire township). *See generally* pp. 107–08.

197. Messiah Baptist Church, 859 F.2d at 823 (upholding denial of special-use permit to construct church on land zoned agricultural).

198. City of Colorado Springs v. Blanche, 761 P.2d 212, 216 (Colo. 1988) (quoting City of Englewood v. Apostolic Christian Church, 362 P.2d 172, 175–76 (1961) (McWilliams, J., concurring)).

199. *See, e.g.,* Christian Gospel Church, Inc. v. City and County of San Francisco, 896 F.2d 1221 (9th Cir.) (denial of special-use permit for church in residential neighborhood because of noise, traffic, and parking problems upheld as rationally related to permissible governmental interests and not imposing significant burden on current religious practices), *cert. denied*, 498 U.S. 999 (1990); *Blanche*, 761 P.2d at 216–17 (reviewing cases); *see also* Love Church v. City of Evanston, 896 F.2d 1082 (7th Cir.), *cert. denied*, 498 U.S. 898 (1990) (church lacked standing to challenge presumptively valid special-use permit requirement because of insufficient allegations of injury traceable to challenged regulation); *but see* Alpine Christian Fellowship v. County Comm'rs, 870 F. Supp. 991 (D. Colo. 1994) (holding requirement of special permit for religious school unconstitutional).

200. *Blanche*, 761 P.2d at 217–19.

201. First Assembly of God v. City of Alexandria, 739 F.2d 942 (4th Cir. 1984), *cert. denied*, 469 U.S. 1019 (1984).

202. *Messiah Baptist Church,* 859 F.2d at 824 (10th Cir. 1988). *See* pp. 107–08.

203. Grosz v. City of Miami Beach, 721 F.2d 729 (11th Cir. 1983), *cert. denied,* 469 U.S. 827 (1984).

204. Bethel Evangelical Lutheran Church v. Village of Morton, 559 N.E.2d 533 (Ill. Ct. App. 1990), *appeal denied,* 564 N.E.2d (1990).

205. State v. Cameron, 445 A.2d 75, 79 (N.J. Super. Ct. Law Div. 1982) (citing cases).

206. *Id.* at 80–82.

207. *See* discussion of lifestyle and group home regulation, chapter 7.

208. Charter Township of Delta v. Dinolfo, 351 N.W.2d 831 (Mich. 1984).

209. Islamic Ctr. of Mississippi v. City of Starkville, 840 F.2d 293 (5th Cir. 1988).

210. McGann v. Incorporated Village of Old Wesbury, 741 N.Y.S.2d 75 (N.Y. App. 2002).

211. City of Richmond Heights v. Richmond Heights Presbyterian Church, 764 S.W.2d 647 (Mo. 1989); *see generally* p. 291.

212. Cabinet for Human Res. Kentucky Health Facilities v. Provincial Convent of the Sacred Heart, 701 S.W.2d 137 (Ky. Ct. App. 1985), *appeal denied* (1986).

213. Burlington Assembly of God Church v. Zoning Bd. of Adjustment of Township of Florence, 570 A.2d 495 (N.J. Sup. Ct. Law Div. 1989) (refusal to grant variance to permit construction of radio antenna towers on church-owned building unconstitutionally infringed upon protected religious activity).

214. *Matter of Faith for Today,* 204 N.Y.S.2d 751 (N.Y. App. Div. 1960), *aff'd,* 174 N.E.2d 743 (1961).

215. Needham Pastoral Counseling Ctr., Inc. v. Bd. of Appeals of Needham, 557 N.E.2d 43, 47 (Mass. Ct. App.), *rev. denied,* 560 N.E.2d 121 (1990). The free-meals program has been added to the list of activities found to be part of the free exercise of religion. Western Presbyterian Church v. Bd. of Zoning Adjustment, 862 F. Supp. 538 (D.D.C. 1994).

216. *Needham Pastoral Counseling Ctr.,* 557 N.E.2d at 46.

217. *See* pp. 108–11.

218. First Covenant Church of Seattle v. City of Seattle, 787 P.2d 1352, 1360–61 (1990), *judgment vacated,* 499 U.S. 901 (1991).

219. *Id.*

220. City of Seattle v. First Covenant Church of Seattle, 499 U.S. 901 (1991).

221. Employment Div., Dep't of Human Res. of Oregon v. Smith, 494 U.S. 872, 878–79 (1990).

222. St. Bartholomew's Church v. New York City, 914 F.2d 348, 354 (2d Cir. 1990), *cert. denied,* 499 U.S. 905 (1991).

223. *Id.* at 356–57.

224. Society of Jesus of New England v. Boston Landmarks Comm'n, 564 N.E.2d 571, 573 (1990).

225. *See* Edelen v. Nelson County, 723 S.W.2d 887 (Ky. Ct. App. 1987).

226. *See* chapter 10.

227. *See, e.g.,* County Comm'rs of Bristol v. Conservation Comm'n of Dartmouth, 405 N.E.2d 637 (Mass. 1980).

228. *See, e.g.,* Witzel v. Village of Brainard, 302 N.W.2d 723 (1981).

229. City of Ames v. Story County, 392 N.W.2d 145, 147–49 (Iowa 1986) (reviewing cases).

230. Commonwealth Dep't of Gen. Serv. v. Ogontz Area Neighbors Ass'n, 483 A.2d 448 (Pa. 1984); Davidson County v. City of High Point, 354 S.E.2d 280 (N.C. Ct. App. 1987).

231. *In the Matter of the County of Monroe,* 533 N.Y.S.2d 702, 703 (Ct. App. 1988) (rejecting the governmental-proprietary test as having "outlived its usefulness"); *City of Ames,* 392 N.W.2d at 128; City of St. Louis v. City of Bridgeton, 705 S.W.2d 524 (Mo. 1986). Balancing of interests applied in City of Bridgeton v. City of St. Louis, 18 S.W.3d 107 (Mo. App. 2000).

232. *City of St. Louis,* 705 S.W.2d at 529.

233. *County of Monroe,* 530 N.E.2d at 204.

234. City of Everett v. Snohomish County, 772 P.2d 992, 998 (1989) (quoting Temple Terrace v. Hillsborough Ass'n for Retarded Citizens, Inc., 322 So. 2d 571, 579 (Fla. Dist. Ct. App.), *aff'd,* 332 So. 2d 610 (Fla. 1976)).

235. *Ogontz,* 483 A.2d at 448.

236. City of Malibu v. Santa Monica Mountains Conservancy, 119 Cal. Rptr. 2d 777, 780 (Cal. App. 2002).

237. *See, Id.,* citing Section 53091, CALIFORNIA GOV'T CODE.

238. Dept. of Gen. Serv. v. Bd. of Supervisors of Cumberland Township, 795 A.2d 440 (Pa. App. 2002).

239. London Grove Township v. South Eastern Chester County Refuse Auth., 517 A.2d 1002 (Pa. Commw. Ct. 1986) (refuse authority was an instrumentality of the state for purposes of law that exempted state instrumentalities from zoning ordinances of second-class townships).

240. City of Vinita Park v. Girls Sheltercare, Inc., 664 S.W.2d 256 (Mo. Ct. App. 1984).

241. *See, e.g.,* Sto-Rox School District v. Zoning Hearing Bd., 674 A.2d 352 (Pa. Ct. App. 1996) (holding no zoning authority to prohibit construction of school on property owned by school district).

242. Village of Ridgefield Park v. New York, Susquehanna & Western Railway Corp., 750 A.2d 57 (N.J. 2000) (ordinance preempted by ICC Termination Act of 1995, 49 U.S.C. § 10102. *But see* Florida East Coast Railway Co. v. City of Palm Beach, 110 F. Supp. 2d 1367 (S.D. Fla. 2000), holding ICC Termination Act did not preempt zoning ordinance that affected distribution of materials by railroad. *See also* discussion of preemption in chapter 10, at n. 43.

243. Edelen v. Nelson County, 723 S.W.2d 887 (Ky. Ct. App. 1987).

244. *Id.* at 889.

245. *See* pp. 107–08.

246. Linmark Assocs., Inc. v. Township of Willingboro, 431 U.S. 85 (1977) (ordinance prohibiting the posting of For Sale or Sold signs invalidated as impermissible content-based regulation of speech); National Adver. Co. v. City of Orange, 861 F.2d 246 (9th Cir. 1988) (ordinance banning both commercial and noncommercial off-site advertising subject to certain exceptions, but permitting both types of on-site advertising invalid as impermissible content-based regulation of noncommercial speech), *cert. denied sub nom.,* Town of Babylon v. National Adver. Co., 498 U.S. 852 (1990); Matthews v. Town of Needham, 764 F.2d 58, 59 (1st Cir. 1985) (citing Police Dep't of Chicago v. Mosley, 408 U.S. 92, 95 (1972)); *see also* Century 21—Mabel O. Pettus v. City of Jennings, 700 S.W.2d 809 (Mo. 1985) (state statute, Mo. REV. STAT. § 67.317, prohibiting municipalities from banning the post of For Sale signs on land upheld).

247. City Council of Los Angeles v. Taxpayers of Vincent, 466 U.S. 789 (1984) (ordinance prohibiting the posting of any signs on public property upheld); Metromedia v. City of San Diego, 453 U.S. 490, 516 (1981) (approving of regulations banning off-site commercial advertising signs while permitting on-site commercial advertising, but invalidating prohibition of all noncommercial advertising signs); Matthews v. Town of Needham, 764 F.2d 58 (1st Cir. 1985) (ordinance prohibiting political signs on private property while permitting posting of certain commercial signs invalidated).

248. National Adver. Co. v. Town of Babylon, 900 F.2d 551, 553 (2d Cir. 1990) (quoting Metromedia, Inc v. City of San Diego, 453 U.S. 490, 507 (1981) (plurality opinion)).

249. National Adver. Co. v. City and County of Denver, 912 F.2d 405, 409 (10th Cir. 1990) (quoting Bd. of Trustees of the State Univ. of New York v. Fox, 492 U.S. 469 (1989)).

250. National Adver. Co. v. Town of Babylon, 900 F.2d 551, 555 (2d Cir. 1990); *see also* Bell v. Township of Stafford, 541 A.2d 692, 700 (N.J. 1988) ("In view of Stafford's failure to justify the passage of such a broad and encompassing ordinance that substantially curtails freedom of speech and expression, we are constrained to declare it facially unconstitutional").

251. *See, e.g.,* City and County of Denver, 912 F.2d at 405 (ordinance banning all off-site commercial signs within 660 feet of a freeway but permitting on-site commercial signs under a certain size and noncommercial signs within the regulated area held facially valid); Major Media of the Southeast, Inc. v. City of Raleigh, 792 F.2d 1269 (4th Cir. 1986), *cert. denied,* 479 U.S. 1102 (1987).

"On-premise" signs are defined as signs that "direct attention to a business, profession, commodity, service, or entertainment conducted, sold, manufactured, or provided at a location on the premises where the sign is located or to which it is affixed." Major Media of the Southeast, Inc v. City of Raleigh, 792 F.2d 1269, 1270 (4th Cir. 1986). "Off-premises" signs are defined as those that "direct attention to a use, business, commodity, service, or activity not conducted, sold or offered where the sign is located." National Adver. Co. v. City of Rolling Meadows, 789 F.2d 571, 573 (7th Cir. 1986).

252. 833 F.2d 43 (4th Cir. 1987).

253. *See also* Naegele Outdoor Adver. v. City of Durham, 844 F.2d 172 (4th Cir. 1988) (ordinance prohibiting billboards within city upheld); Lindsay v. City of San Antonio, 821 F.2d 1103 (5th Cir. 1987) (ban on portable signs upheld), *cert. denied,* 484 U.S. 1010 (1988); Outdoor Systems, Inc. v. City of Mesa, 819 P.2d 44 (Ariz. banc 1991) (upholding absolute prohibition on all off-site signs and billboards under state zoning-enabling legislation).

254. Naturist Society, Inc. v. Fillyaw, 858 F. Supp. 1559 (S.D. Fla. 1995).

255. *See, e.g.,* Owensboro Metropolitan Bd. of Adjustment v. Midwest Outdoor Adver., 729 S.W.2d 446 (Ky. Ct. App. 1987).

256. Rzadkowolski v. Village of Lake Orion, 845 F.2d 653, 654 (6th Cir. 1988) (ordinance permitting on-site commercial and noncommercial messages in business districts, but effectively limiting to one the number of off-site billboards permitted throughout village because of size, distance, and zoning restrictions upheld as valid time, place, and manner regulation).

257. *See* pp. 172–74. *See, e.g.,* Major Media of the Southeast, Inc. v. City of Raleigh, 792 F.2d 1269 (4th Cir. 1986) (5.5-year amortization period); Northern Ohio Sign Contractors Ass'n v. City of Lakewood, 513 N.E.2d 324 (Ohio 1987); *but see* ARIZ. REV. STAT. ANN. § 9-462.02 (1996).

258. 86 F. Supp. 2d 755, 778–79 (N.D. Ohio 2000) ("It is beyond reason to think that the signs of public or semi-public entities are inherently safer or more aesthetically pleasing than signs of business entities."). *See also* Knoeffler v. Town of Mamakating, 87 F. Supp. 2d 332 (N.Y. 2000) holding exemption of "public convenience"–type signs violated First Amendment as content-based.

259. *See* Adams Outdoor Adver. v. City of East Lansing, 614 N.W.2d 634 (Mich. 2000).

260. South-Suburban Hous. Ctr. v. Greater South Suburban Bd. of Realtors, 935 F.2d 868 (7th Cir. 1991); *but see* Real Estate Bd. of Metropolitan St. Louis v. City of Jennings, 808 S.W.2d 7 (Mo. Ct. App. 1991), striking down a municipal ordinance limiting For Sale signs to a maximum of 6 inches by 13 inches as violative of state statute permitting signs of "reasonable dimensions").

261. For cases in which a sign ordinance was upheld against a constitutional challenge, *see* Georgia Outdoor Adver. v. City of Waynesville, 833 F.2d 43 (4th Cir. 1987) (billboard ordinance that permits only on-premise signs does not violate First Amendment); Don's Port Signs, Inc. v. City of Clearwater, 829 F.2d 1051 (11th Cir. 1987), *cert. denied,* 485 U.S. 981 (1988) (ordinance regulating size and use of portable advertising signs upheld);

Lindsay v. City of Antonio, 821 F.2d 1103 (5th Cir. 1987) (unsuccessful challenge to constitutionality of zoning ordinance that regulates portable signs); Major Media of the Southeast, Inc. v. City of Raleigh, 792 F.2d 1269 (4th Cir. 1986) (unsuccessful challenge to constitutionality of ordinance); Rzadkowolski v. Village of Lake Orion, 845 F.2d 653, 654 (6th Cir. 1988) (unsuccessful challenge to constitutionality of ordinance regulating off-premises signs); *but cf.* Matthews v. Town of Needham, 764 F.2d 58 (1st Cir. 1985) (town bylaw that prohibits political signs on residential property held unconstitutional on its face).

262. *See e.g.,* Temple Baptist Church, Inc. v. City of Albuquerque, 646 P.2d 565 (N.M. 1982).

263. Linmark Assocs. v. Township of Willingboro, 431 U.S. 85 (1977).

264. City Council of Los Angeles v. Taxpayers for Vincent, 466 U.S. 789 (1984).

265. 764 F.2d 58 (1st Cir. 1985).

266. City of Painesville Bldg. Dep't v. Dworken & Bernstein Co., L.P.A., 733 N.E.2d 1152 (Ohio 2000).

267. 512 U.S. 43 (1994).

268. 512 U.S. 43 (1994). *Id.* at 259.

269. 794 F.2d 1139 (6th Cir. 1986).

270. City of Lakewood v. Plain Dealer Publ'g Co., 486 U.S. 750 (1988).

271. Highway Beautification Act of 1965, 23 U.S.C. § 131; *see, e.g.,* State *ex rel.* Drury Displays v. City of Columbia, 907 S.W.2d 252 (Mo. Ct. App. 1995).

272. 605 ILCS 5/4-501 *et seq.*

273. National Adver. Co. v. City of Rolling Meadows, 789 F.2d 571 (7th Cir. 1986); *see also* Wheeler v. Comm'r of Highways, 822 F.2d 586 (6th Cir. 1987) (Kentucky Billboard Act and implementing regulations upheld as valid place and manner restrictions on outdoor advertising), *cert. denied,* 484 U.S. 1007 (1988).

274. Freeman v. Burlington Northern Broadcasters, Inc., 204 F.3d 311 (2d Cir. 2000).

275. Fed'n of Adver. Indus. Representatives, Inc. v. City of Chicago, 189 F.3d 633 (7th Cir. 1999). *See also* Skysign Int'l, Inc. v. City and County of Honolulu, 276 F.3d 1109 (9th Cir. 2000) (local sign ordinance covering signs in regulated airspace not preempted by FAA waivers).

276. City of Renton v. Playtime Theaters, Inc., 475 U.S. 41 (1986). See generally, chapter 3, *supra.*

277. *Id.*; FW/PBS, Inc v. City of Dallas, 837 F.2d 1298, 1301 (5th Cir. 1988), *aff'd in part, rev'd in part,* 493 U.S. 215 (1990); Matthews v. Town of Needham, 764 F.2d 58, 59 (1st Cir. 1985).

278. City of Renton v. Playtime Theaters, Inc., 475 U.S. 41 (1986).

279. 427 U.S. 50 (1976).

280. *City of Renton,* 475 U.S. at 46–47.

281. *See, e.g.,* Alexander v. City of Minneapolis, 713 F. Supp. 1296 (D. Minn. 1989), *reversed,* 928 F.2d 278 (8th Cir. 1991).

282. David Vincent, Inc. v. Broward County, Florida, 200 F.3d 1325, 1333 (11th Cir. 2000), quoting Renton at 50.

283. See *Id.*

284. 529 U.S. 277 (2000).

285. *Id.*

286. *Id.* at 289.

287. 591 U.S. 167 (1968).

288. 529 U.S. at 289.

289. *City of Renton,* 475 U.S. at 50; Pap's A.M. v. City of Erie, 674 A.2d 338 (Pa. Ct. App. 1996).

290. Christy v. City of Ann Arbor, 824 F.2d 489 (6th Cir. 1987), *cert. denied,* 484 U.S. 1059 (1988).

291. *Id.; see also* Walnut Props., Inc. v. City of Whittier, 861 F.2d 1102 (9th Cir. 1988) (distance regulation invalid when effect is to deny reasonable opportunity to operate adult business within city), *cert. denied*, 490 U.S. 1006 (1989); Ebel v. City of Corona, 767 F.2d 635 (9th Cir. 1985) (lack of alternate sites and 60-day amortization period for adult business invalidated as unreasonable).

292. David Vincent, Inc. v. Broward County, *supra*, at 1332.

293. 493 U.S. 215 (1990).

294. *FW/PBS*, 493 U.S. at 226–30, 236–37.

295. *FW/PBS*, 837 F.2d at 1302; *see also* SDJ, Inc. v. City of Houston, 837 F.2d 1268 (5th Cir. 1988) (licensing and zoning regulations for topless bars upheld), *cert. denied sub nom.,* M.E.F. Enterprises, Inc. v. City of Houston, 489 U.S. 1052 (1989).

296. *FW/PBS*, 493 U.S. at 226–27.

297. East Brooks Books, Inc. v. City of Memphis, 48 F.3d 220 (6th Cir.), *cert. denied*, 116 S. Ct. 277 (1995); Redner v. Dean, 29 F.3d 1495 (11th Cir.), *cert. denied*, 514 U.S. 1066 (1995).

298. *See, e.g.*, Consol. Gov't of Columbus v. Barwick, 549 S.E.2d 73 (Ga. 2001).

299. *See, e.g.*, Lim v. City of Long Beach, 217 F.3d 1050 (9th Cir. 2000), *cert. denied*, 121 S.C. 1189 2001.

300. Clarkson Valley Estates, Inc. v. Village of Clarkson Valley, 630 S.W.2d 151 (Mo. Ct. App. 1982).

301. Haskell v. Washington Township, 864 F.2d 1266 (6th Cir. 1988).

302. *See, e.g.*, Abilene Oil Distrib., Inc. v. City of Abilene, 712 S.W.2d 644 (Tex. Ct. App. 1986).

303. *See* pp. 90–94 (due process) and pp. 94–95 (equal protection).

304. Great American Houseboat Co. v. United States, 780 F.2d 741 (9th Cir. 1986).

305. Village of Euclid v. Ambler Realty Co., 272 U.S. 365, 380–81 (1926).

306. The leading case in this area, People *ex rel.* Skokie Town House Builders, Inc. v. Village of Morton Grove, 157 N.E.2d 33, 36 (1959), holds that "the only constitutional limitation upon a municipality's power to exclude future residences from commercial and industrial districts is that the exclusion bear a substantial relationship to the preservation of the public health, safety, morals, or general welfare."

307. Saunders v. City of Jackson, 511 So. 2d 902 (Miss. 1987).

308. *Saunders*, 511 So. 2d at 906–07. Because the practice of the Mississippi Supreme Court is to consider the question of "confiscatory" takings as "intertwined with [the Court's] review of whether [a] zoning decision is arbitrary, capricious or unreasonable, or whether it was fairly debatable," the Court dismissed a takings claim, finding nothing in Nollan v. California Coastal Comm'n, 483 U.S. 825 (1987) requiring a different result. *Id.* at 907, n. 3.

309. Rev. Code of City of St. Louis, § 26.80.060 (1986); Zoning Ord. of St. Louis County, § 1003.020 (43) (1986).

310. Rev. Code of City of St. Louis, § 26.08.240 (1986).

311. Zoning Ord. of St. Louis County, § 1003.020 (43) (1986).

312. Rev. Code of City of St. Louis, § 26.80.060 (1986); Zoning Code of St. Louis County, § 1003.020 (43) (1986).

313. Rev. Code of City of St. Louis, § 26.80.240.4 (1986).

314. 47 U.S.C. § 151, *et seq.* (2001) (Effective February 8, 1996) (hereinafter, "TCA"). Portions of these materials were taken from the article *Taking Stock of the First Five Years of Cellular Tower Siting Jurisprudence Under the Telecommunications Act of 1996*, 37 Real Property and Probate Journal 271, Summer 2002.

315. 47 U.S.C. § 332(c)(7) the relevant portions of which are quoted at note 319.

316. H.R. Conf. Rep. No. 104-458 (1996).

317. Cellular Tel. Co. v. Town of Oyster Bay, 166 F.3d 490, 494 (2d Cir. 1999).

318. *See,* AT&T Corp. v. Iowa Utilities Bd., 525 U.S. 366 (1999) ("It would be [a] gross understatement to say that the Telecommunications Act is not a model of clarity.").

319. 47 U.S.C. § 332(c)(7)(A)-(B).

> (7) Preservation of local zoning authority
>
> > (A) General authority
> >
> > Except as provided in this paragraph, nothing in this chapter shall limit or affect the authority of a State or local government or instrumentality thereof over decisions regarding the placement, construction, and modification of personal wireless service facilities.
> >
> > (B) Limitations
> >
> > > (i) The regulation of the placement, construction, and modification of personal wireless service facilities by any State or local government or instrumentality thereof—
> > >
> > > > (I) shall not unreasonably discriminate among providers of functionally equivalent services; and
> > > >
> > > > (II) shall not prohibit or have the effect of prohibiting the provision of personal wireless services.
> > >
> > > (ii) A State or local government or instrumentality thereof shall act on any request for authorization to place, construct, or modify personal wireless service facilities within a reasonable period of time after the request is duly filed with such government or instrumentality, taking into account the nature and scope of such request.
> > >
> > > (iii) Any decision by a State or local government or instrumentality thereof to deny a request to place, construct, or modify personal wireless service facilities shall be in writing and supported by substantial evidence contained in a written record.

320. 47 U.S.C. § 332(c)(7)(B)(i)(I).

321. 47 U.S.C. § 332(c)(7)(B)(i)(II).

322. 47 U.S.C. § 332(c)(7)(B)(ii).

323. 47 U.S.C. § 332(c)(7)(B)(iii).

324. *Id.*

325. Cellular Tel. Co. v. Town of Oyster Bay, 166 F.3d at 494, citing Cellular Tel. Co. v. Zoning Bd. of Adjustment, 24 F. Supp. 2d 359, 366 (D.N.J. 1998), *aff'd in part, rev'd in part,* 197 F.3d 64 (3d Cir. 1999).

326. *See,* 360° Communications v. Bd. of Supervisors, 211 F.3d 79, 83 (4th Cir. 2000) (applying Virginia rule that denial of conditional-use permit is legislative, not administrative act, but applying substantial evidence standard); Omnipoint Corp. v. Zoning Hearing Bd., 181 F.3d 403, 408–09 (3d Cir. 1999). *See also,* Omnipoint Communications Enters., L.P. v. Zoning Bd., 248 F.3d 101, 106 (3d Cir. 2001) ("[T]he first step for the court in a case in which the provider of wireless services is relying on state or local law is to identify the relevant issues under that law.").

327. Omnipoint Communications Enters., L.P. v. Zoning Bd., 248 F.3d 101, 106 (3d Cir. 2001). See also Sprint Spectrum, L.P. v. Willoth, 996 F. Supp. 253 (W.D.N.Y. 1998) (New York law requires provider to offer "compelling reasons" justifying its feasibility determination).

328. Cellular Tel. Co. v. Town of Oyster Bay, 166 F.3d at 494. *See, e.g.,* Seattle SMSA L.P. v. San Juan County, 88 F. Supp. 2d 1128, 1130 (W.D. Wash. 1997) (citing state enabling legislation).

329. Omnipoint Communications Enters., L.P. v. Zoning Hearing Bd., 248 F.3d 101 (3d Cir. 2001).

330. Telespectrum, Inc. v. Public Serv. Comm'n, 227 F.3d 414, 423 (6th Cir. 2000).

331. Cellular Tel. Co. v. Town of Oyster Bay, 166 F.3d at 494.

332. Town of Amherst v. Omnipoint Communications Enters., 173 F.3d 9 (1st Cir. 1999).

333. *Id.* (applying Virginia rule that denial of conditional-use permit is legislative, not administrative act, but applying substantial evidence standard); Omnipoint Corp. v. Zoning Hearing Bd., 181 F.3d 403, 408–09 (3d Cir. 1999).

334. Omnipoint Communications Enters., L.P. v. Zoning Hearing Bd., 72 F. Supp. 2d at 515.

335. Laurence Wolf Capital Mgmt. Trust v. City of Ferndale, 128 F. Supp. 2d 441, 446 (E.D. Mich. 2000).

336. *Id.*

337. *See* Section IV(D) *infra*; 360º Communications v. Bd. of Supervisors, 211 F.3d at 83.

338. 47 U.S.C. § 332(c)(7)(B)(i)(I).

339. APT Pittsburgh L.P. v. Lower Yoder Township, 111 F. Supp. 2d 664, 674 (W.D. Pa. 2000).

340. *See e.g.,* Sprint Spectrum L.P. v. Jefferson County, 968 F. Supp. 1457, 1467–68 (N.D. Ala. 1997).

341. Laurence Wolf Capital Mgmt. Trust v. City of Ferndale, 128 F. Supp. 2d 441, 449 (E.D. Mich. 2000).

342. *Id.*

343. Sprint Spectrum, L.P. v. Mills, 65 F. Supp. 2d 148, 157 (S.D.N.Y. 1999); H.R. CONF. REP. No. 104-458, 104th Cong. 2d Sess. 208 (1996); this kind of language resonates with the more free-form substantial evidence standard discussed in Section IV(D) *infra.*

344. APT Pittsburgh L.P. v. Lower Yoder Township, 111 F. Supp. 2d 664, 674 (W.D. Pa. 2000).

345. *See,* AT&T Wireless v. City Council, 155 F.3d 423, 428 (4th Cir. 1998).

346. 47 U.S.C. § 332(c)(7)(B)(i)(II).

347. Sprint Spectrum, L.P. v. Willoth, 176 F.3d 630, 639 (2d Cir. 1999).

348. Omnipoint Communications Enters., L.P. v. Newton Township, 219 F.3d 240, 244 (3d Cir. 2000); *cert. denied,* 531 U.S. 985 (2000).

349. *See, e.g.,* 360º Communications Co. v. Bd. of Supervisors, 50 F. Supp. 2d 551 (W.D. Va. 1999), *rev'd,* 211 F.3d 79 (4th Cir. 2000).

350. Omnipoint Communications MB Operations, LLC v. Town of Lincoln, 107 F. Supp. 2d 108, 117 (D. Mass. 2000).

351. Omnipoint Communications Enters., L.P. v. Newton Township, 219 F.3d 240, 244 (3d Cir. 2000); *cert. denied,* 531 U.S. 985 (2000).

352. Omnipoint Communications MB Operations, LLC v. Town of Lincoln, 107 F. Supp. 2d 108, 118 (D. Mass. 2000).

353. *Id.* at 119.

354. *See,* 360º Communications v. Bd. of Supervisors, 211 F.3d at 86.

355. American Tower, L.P. v. City of Grant, 621 N.W.2d 37 (Minn. 2001). *See also,* Sprint Spectrum, L.P. v. Zoning Hearing Bd., 43 F. Supp. 2d 534, 537 (E.D. Pa. 1999).

356. 47 U.S.C. § 332(c)(7)(B)(iii).

357. Omnipoint Communications Enters., L.P. v. Zoning Bd., 248 F.3d 101, 106 (3d Cir. 2001).

358. *See* n. 314, *supra, taking stock* [etc] at p. 279.

359. AT&T Wireless PCS, Inc. v. City Council, 155 F.3d 423, 430 (4th Cir. 1998).

360. 360º Communications Co. v. Bd. of Supervisors, 211 F.3d 79, 83 (4th Cir. 2000).

361. Pierce v. Underwood, 487 U.S. 552, 565 (1988) (quoting Consolidated Edison Co. v. NLRB, 305 U.S. 197, 229 (1938)).

362. Primeco Personal Communications, L.P. v. Village of Fox Lake, 35 F. Supp. 2d 643 (N.D. Ill. 1999).

363. *See* H.R. CONF. REP. No. 104-458, 104th Cong., 2d Sess. 208 (1996).

364. 360º Communications Co. v. Bd. of Supervisors, 50 F. Supp. 2d 551 (W.D. Va. 1999), citing AT&T Wireless PCS, Inc. v. City Council, 155 F.3d 423 (4th Cir. 1998).

365. *Id.*, citing Coniston Corp. v. Village of Hoffman Estates, 844 F.2d 461, 467 (7th Cir. 1988); *see also* AT&T Wireless PCS, Inc. v. City Council, 155 F.3d 423 (4th Cir. 1998), cited in Omnipoint v. Penn Forest Township, 42 F. Supp. 2d 493 (M.D. Pa. 1999), stating that the AT&T Wireless case suggests that public outrage standing alone can constitute substantial evidence to deny a zoning request.

366. 360º Communications v. Bd. of Supervisors, 211 F.3d 79. 83 (4th Cir. 2000).

367. *Id.*

368. *Id.*

369. AT&T Wireless Svcs., Inc. v. Orange County, 23 F. Supp. 2d 1355, 1362 ("the Board should give weight to community displeasure but cannot base its decision solely on this fact"); 360° Communications v. Bd. of Supervisors, 211 F.3d 79, 80–84 (4th Cir. 2000) ("virtually unanimous" citizen opposition relevant, where 13 citizens spoke in opposition); AT&T Wireless PCS, Inc. v. Winston-Salem Zoning Bd. of Adjustment, 172 F.3d 307, 315 (4th Cir. 1999) (150 local residents spoke in opposition); Cellular Tel. Co. v. Town of Oyster Bay, 166 F.3d 490, 495–96 (2d Cir. 1999) ("courts have split as to the weight to be afforded to constituent testimony on aesthetics, declining to adopt Fourth Circuit's more deferential head count standard, holding that 'volume and specificity' of citizen opposition do not reach the 'low threshold set by AT&T Wireless PCS, *supra*, 155 F.3d at 430.'"); Sprint Spectrum, L.P. v. Charter Township of West Bloomfield, 141 F. Supp. 2d, 799–800 (E.D. Mich. 2001); (holding that a "significant number of community residents" oppose the application); Wireless Serv. v. City of Moline, 29 F. Supp. 2d 915, 921–23 (C.D. Ill. 1998) (where "only four residents" express concern, versus 150 residents in the prior case); Nextel Communications, Inc. v. Manchester-By-The-Sea, 115 F. Supp. 2d 65, 67 (D. Mass. 2000) (aesthetic concerns of "a few" persons, especially when rebutted by experts or other administrative bodies, does not constitute substantial evidence).

370. *See e.g.,* 360º Communications v. Bd. of Supervisors, 211 F.3d at 83.

371. AT&T Wireless PCS, Inc. v. City Council, 155 F.3d at 423.

372. *See,* 360º Communications Co. v. Bd. of Supervisors, 50 F. Supp. 2d 551 at n. 19 (W.D. Va. 1999).

373. *Id.* at n. 20.

374. *Id.*

375. Omnipoint Corp. v. Zoning Hearing Bd., 20 F. Supp. 2d 875 (E.D. Pa. 1998) ("stating generalized concerns and conclusive statements within the record about the aesthetic and visual impacts on the neighborhood do not amount to substantial evidence") *aff'd,* 181 F.3d 403 (3d Cir. 1999); APT Minneapolis, Inc. v. City of Maplewood, 1998 WL 634224 (D. Minn. 1998); AT&T Wireless PCS, Inc. v. City Council, 155 F.3d at 428 (4th Cir. 1998).

376. Southwestern Bell Mobile Sys., Inc. v. Todd, 244 F.3d 51, 61 (1st Cir. 2001).

377. Cellular Tel. Co. v. Town of Oyster Bay, 166 F.3d at 496.

378. Sprint Spectrum L.P. v. Town of Farmington, 1997 WL 631104 (D. Conn. 1997).

379. *See,* Sprint Spectrum L.P. v. Willoth, 176 F.3d 630, 643 (2d Cir. 1999).

380. Cellular Tel. Co. v. Town of Oyster Bay, 166 F.3d at 496, *citing* Primeco Personal Communications, L.P. v. Village of Fox Lake, 26 F. Supp. 2d 1052, 1063 (N.D. Ill. 1998); Cellular Tel. Co. v. Rosenberg, 624 N.E.2d 990 (N.Y. 1993).

381. Sprint Spectrum L.P. v. Willoth, 176 F.3d 630, 643 (2d Cir. 1999); 47 U.S.C. § 332(c)(7)(B)(iv).

382. SBA Communications, Inc. v. Zoning Comm'n, 112 F. Supp. 2d 233, 240 (D. Conn. 2000).

383. AT&T Wireless, Inc. v. City Council, 155 F.3d 423, 429–30.

384. AT&T Wireless, Inc. v. City Council, 155 F.3d 423, 429–30 (decision reflected in condensed minutes and a letter with the word "denied" and the date of the decision held sufficient).

385. *See,* Southwestern Bell Mobile Sys., Inc. v. Todd, 244 F.3d 51, 59 (1st Cir. 2001).

386. *Id.* at 60.

387. *Id.*

388. 47 U.S.C. § 332 (c)(7)(b)(5).

389. *See* Cellular Tel. Co. v. Town of Oyster Bay, 166 F.3d at 490 (2d Cir. 1999).

390. Bell South Mobility v. Gwinett County, 944 F. Supp. 923, 929 (N.D. Ga. 1996).

391. *See, e.g.,* SBA Communications, Inc. v. Zoning Comm'n, 164 F. Supp. 2d 280 (D. Conn. 2001).

392. Omnipoint. Corp. v. Zoning Hearing Bd., 181 F.3d 403, 410 (3d Cir. 1999); *see* Cellular Tel. Co. v. Town of Oyster Bay, 166 F.3d 490, 497.

393. *See, e.g.,* Schiazza v. Zoning Hearing Bd., 168 F. Supp. 2d 361 (M.D. Pa. 2001); AT&T Wireless PCS Wireless, Inc. v. City of Atlanta, 210 F.3d 1322 (11th Cir. 2000); *But see* Omnipoint v. Pine Forest Township, 42 F. Supp. 2d 493 (M.D. Pa. 1999); Newton Township v. Zoning Hearing Bd., 1999 WL 387205 (E.D. Pa. 1999) (1983 claim impliedly foreclosed).

394. New York Botanical Garden v. Bd. of Standards and Appeals of the City of New York, 694 N.E.2d 424 (N.Y. App. 1998). *But see* Marchand v. Town of Hudson, 788 A.2d 250 (N.H. 2001) (100-foot ham radio antenna not an accessory use).

395. *See* pp. 154–56.

396. Campanelli v. AT&T Wireless Services, Inc., 706 N.E.2d 1267 (Ohio 1999).

397. Richardson v. Township of Brady, 218 F.3d 508 (6th Cir. 2000).

398. Altonberg v. Bd. of Supervisors of Pleasant Mount Township, 615 N.W.2d 874 (Minn. App. 2000); *in re* Conditional Use Permit, 613 N.W.2d 523 (S.D. 2000).

399. R.L. Hexum & Assocs., Inc. v. Rochester Township Bd. of Supervisors, 609 N.W.2d 271 (Minn. 2000).

400. 2002 Georgia New Laws, H.B. 1087.

401. *See, e.g.,* Brion, *An Essay on LULU, NIMBY, and the Problem of Distributive Justice,* 15 B. C. Envt'l Aff. L. Rev. 437 (1988).

402. *See, e.g.,* Christian Gospel Church, Inc. v. City and County of San Francisco, 896 F.2d 1221, 1226 (9th Cir. 1990) (no conspiracy to block First Amendment rights by protesting neighbors "doing what citizens should be encouraged to do, taking an active role in the decisions of government").

403. Bishop, *New Tool of Developers and Others Quells Private Opposition to Projects,* New York Times, April 26, 1991, p. B9.

404. Behavioral Health Agency of Central Arizona (BHACA) v. City of Casa Grande, 708 P.2d 1317, 1319 (Ariz. Ct. App. 1985).

405. *Id.* at 1320.

CHAPTER 8

Subdivision Regulations

Subdivision Regulation Distinguished from Zoning

State and local governments have regulated the division of land into smaller parcels from the early days of the country. During the laissez-faire period of the 19th century, land subdivision was regulated primarily to improve the land records system and to obtain accurate engineering data for development.[1]

As interest in land use regulation increased in the 20th century, subdivision regulations grew through stages into a parallel system of land use control aimed at ensuring that necessary public facilities, such as streets, roads, sewers, parks, and so on, would be in place for land development that was occurring.[2]

The growth-control movement of the late 1960s and early 1970s was implemented by expansion of the subdivision regulation technique to include controls designed to limit or manage the timing of land development. This in turn spawned the "adequate public facilities" standard of growth management, in which subdivision regulation statutes and ordinances were expanded to require an examination of the external effects of land development and a showing that public facilities would be able to handle expected increases in demand.[3]

Vocal resistance to continued use of the property tax to pay inflation-driven costs of sharp increases in demand for public services led many state and local governments to search for alternative sources of revenue during the 1980s. This led to the "fifth and most recent phase of subdivision regulation": the adoption of the exaction as a form of land use regulation.[4] Exactions come essentially in two forms: (1) required dedications of land or property interests in land; and (2) required payment of money through impact fees, in lieu fees, linkage fees, and the like. The purpose of exactions is to impose some or all of the public costs associated with a particular use of land on the persons who are putting the land to that particular use.[5]

Subdivision regulations complement zoning regulations, but differ from them in two ways: (1) subdivision regulations employ preset specifications and performance standards rather than territorial division as the basic frame-work for regulation; and (2) subdivision regulations focus more on the specific details of land development rather than on the types of uses being proposed. In jurisdictions where comprehensive plans are general guides to the promul-gation of zoning ordinances, an ordinance requirement that a proposed land subdivision "shall conform to the Comprehensive Plan" has been held to require only "general comport[ment] with the overall goals" of the plan and not specific compliance with the plan.[6] The subdivision regulatory process generally is implemented through a requirement that subdivision plats be filed and approved by local regulatory authorities before land may be subdi-vided and sold, or building permits issued.[7] The term *plat* is "a term of art in the planning profession . . . that [is] commonly understood . . . to [be] a sub-division map which has been prepared for approval by appropriate govern-mental authorities."[8]

Subdivision regulations apply to the division of land into parcels. The California statute defines *subdivision* as:

> the division, by any subdivider, of any unit or units of improved or unim-proved land, or any portion thereof, shown on the latest equalized county assessment roll as a unit or as contiguous units, for the purpose of sale, lease or financing, whether immediate or future except for leases of agri-cultural land for agricultural purposes.[9]

Applying a similar definition, the Supreme Court of Idaho held that the recording of a land survey is not a subdivision because "[a] record of survey is not intended to serve as evidence or notice that a landowner is seeking to partition into lots one of his tracts of land."[10] The Tennessee Court of Appeals rejected a landowner's attempt to evade subdivision regulation by arguing that his division of land did not require the construction of new streets or util-ities and was therefore not a subdivision within the definition in a state statute.[11] The Supreme Court of Rhode Island held that landowners who sub-divided their property into ten lots by deed without planning board approval and recorded the deeds were not entitled to rely on the fact that town officials erroneously recorded the deeds and then separately taxed the lots to support an argument of lawful subdivision.[12]

Because subdivision regulations focus on land development, they gener-ally are not applicable to condominium conversions and other changes in the ownership of land,[13] although some states, such as California, have specifi-cally extended subdivision regulations to condominiums.[14] Conversions that are accompanied by a change in land use, such as a shift from seasonal cot-tage or campground use to quasi-permanent multiple occupancy or conver-sion of a mobile-trailer park into a condominium, have been held subject to local subdivision regulations.[15] The Supreme Court of New Hampshire held that subdivision approval was required for a condominium declaration amendment that divided lands into separate lots (A and B) within a previ-ously approved expandable portion of the condominium.[16]

Enactment of Subdivision Regulations

As is the case with zoning regulations, authority to enact and enforce subdivision regulations is derived from the police power inherent in the state and delegated to local governments.[17] State enabling legislation may authorize several levels of subdivision regulation, generally in the following categories:

1) regulation of the contents and format of subdivision plats, as well as the procedure for submission and approval of plats[18]
2) regulation of the layout and quality of streets within subdivisions[19]
3) regulation of the location of utility lines and other public facilities to serve the subdivision, as well as requirements for construction of such facilities by subdivision developers and authorization to require developers to post bonds to secure construction of the required public facilities[20]
4) planning and design of sites, including regulation of lot sizes[21]
5) regulation of development to conserve natural resources such as air, energy, land, sunlight, water, and vegetation[22]
6) requirements that land, or its cash equivalent, be dedicated to public uses such as parks, playgrounds, schools, or trails[23]
7) authorization for the imposition of impact fees and other forms of exactions[24]

Local subdivision ordinances must comply with applicable provisions of enabling statutes. In *Kenai Peninsula Borough v. Kenai Peninsula Board of Realtors,* a local ordinance automatically approving any subdivision into lots of ten acres was invalidated because it conflicted with an Alaska statute requiring prior approval by local authorities of all subdivisions of tracts into two or more lots for the purpose of sale or building development.[25] The court viewed the local ordinance as an attempt to improperly create an exception to the state law.[26]

Subdivision regulations often require subdivision plats to conform to local master plans. Failure to do so is grounds for disapproval, even though the proposed use is permitted under local zoning regulations. For example, the Court of Appeals of Maryland affirmed the rejection of a preliminary subdivision plan proposing a density of 7.38 dwelling units per acre, well within the tolerance of the zoning classifications (8.0–11.9 units per acre) but considerably above the limits of a newly adopted master plan (2.7–3.5 dwelling units per acre).[27] In mandatory-planning states, such as California, subdivision maps (plats) must conform with valid general plans that have been enacted in accordance with the mandatory local planning laws. Failure to enact a valid general plan has led to injunctive relief, prohibiting local governments from giving approval to land subdivisions.[28]

The administrative structure of modern subdivision regulations was established in the 1920s. The Standard City Planning Enabling Act, published in 1928 by the Department of Commerce as a model act to complement the Standard State Zoning Enabling Act, identified subdivision regulation as a major component of comprehensive planning and delegated major responsibility for administering subdivision regulations to the local planning agency.[29] Drafters of the model act defended their recommendation as follows:

> [E]xcept in the case of major thoroughfares, most of the highways are located by . . . the subdividers of land. Obviously, the way the subdivider locates the streets and his lots determines, to as great an extent as any other factor, the adequacy and economy of the city's highway system, the density of population, the flow of traffic, the open spaces for light, air, health, and recreation. After the subdivider has sold his lots and people have built houses, it becomes almost inescapable that the public will accept, sooner or later, the streets and lots as laid out by the subdivider. Therefore, the subdivider has it in his power to dislocate or destroy the city plan, and the community must exercise this control at a time when the control can be made effective; namely, at the time of the subdividing or platting of the land.
>
> Provisions of this title provide an effective control in a way that will work no hardship on the legitimate subdivider but, on the contrary, will be a help to him. In the actual workings of such a system of control the planning commission and the subdivider usually cooperate to produce a result that will be beneficial to the community and subdivider alike. The statute will bring the subdivider and the commission into conference with each other, and the final result will usually be amicably reached. The commission will seldom have to impose its judgment over the hostile position of the subdivider, but these are the very cases in which the control is most essential.[30]
>
> The American Planning Association's (APA) *Growing Smart*[sm] project has prepared a model statute for subdivision control, drawn in part from the Standard City Planning Enabling Act and from the Kentucky, New Jersey, and Rhode Island statutes.[31] The model act mandates adoption of subdivision ordinances and describes minimum and optional provisions for such ordinances, including a broad definition of *subdivision* designed to include minor subdivisions and resubdivisions, although with abbreviated review.[32]

Administration of Subdivision Regulations

The administration of subdivision regulations is illustrated by the subdivision ordinance of St. Louis County. The ordinance establishes two basic subdivision processes: (1) the standard process requiring approval by the legislative body following a recommendation by the Department of Planning of the County[33] and (2) a streamlined process, called a "lot-split," for the division of an existing lot into not more than two parts. Lot-splits can be approved by the Department of Planning and do not have to be submitted to the County Council.[34] Other agencies that become involved at different stages of the approval process are the Metropolitan Sewer District, the County Department of Highways and Traffic, the County Department of Public Works, and the State Department of Natural Resources.[35]

Subdivision regulations must be administered in accordance with the standards imposed by enabling legislation and subdivision regulation ordinances, but negligent or unauthorized actions of land use officials in failing to follow applicable requirements for subdivision review and approval generally do not estop a municipality from enforcing valid regulations.[36]

Statutes regulating the platting or replatting of land may require that approval of a plat or replat be obtained from the planning commission before the plat can be recorded and building permits issued.[37] Although these statutes typically provide for enforcement by municipal officials, courts have been willing to grant standing to private individuals harmed by noncompliance, such as the purchaser of a subdivided parcel who was denied a building permit because of the failure of the seller to obtain an approved replat.[38]

As noted earlier, the focal point of subdivision regulation is the act of subdividing land. Counsel should be sensitive to the misconception that subdivision regulations permit control over land use. Enabling legislation authorizing local subdivision regulation has been held to be limited to developments that constitute a subdivision of land. The very definition of *subdivision* is often at issue. The Supreme Court of New Hampshire refused to permit a municipality to reject a building permit application for the construction of a covered swimming pool and other amenities on common ground in a condominium. Subdivision approval for the condominium development had been granted two years earlier, but the plans for the common area facilities had not been included in the subdivision plans previously submitted. Because no new subdivision of land was contemplated, the Court held that the municipal planning board had no authority under the municipality's subdivision regulations to regulate the construction of amenities, and thus a building permit could not be conditioned upon planning agency approval. The Court was not particularly troubled by the failure of the developer to include the amenities facility in its subdivision plans:

> Regardless of its motives, [the developer] cannot be penalized for failure to include its plans in the subdivision application. Although the planning board would have benefitted from knowing the details of [the] development plans at the outset, the planning board's subdivision regulations do not allow it to exercise the kind of control it would apparently like to have over [the] condominium development.[39]

The Court commented that the control sought by the municipality would have to be gained by the promulgation of site-plan review regulations, which the municipality had not done. Site-plan review regulations are discussed later in this chapter.[40]

The Application Process

As with zoning, subdivision regulation is a localized process. Generalizations about the process run the risk of oversimplification; however, examples can give a sense of what can be expected. St. Louis County, a Missouri home-rule county containing about 40 percent of the population in the St. Louis

metropolitan area, offers landowners in the unincorporated areas two procedures for subdividing land: (1) subdivision for land development and
(2) resubdivision of existing lots (lot-splits).

Subdivision for Land Development

The St. Louis County Subdivision Ordinance is typical of local application procedures. For approval of subdivisions in the county's unincorporated areas,
developers may first submit an optional sketch plan,[41] which should include
information such as the location of the tract in relation to its surroundings; the
names of the owners of adjoining property; the location of existing physical
features located within 150 feet, such as sinkholes, wet- and dry-weather
water courses, and floodplain areas; a rough sketch of the proposed site plan;
direction and distance to the nearest intersection; and a description of historic
buildings located in the tract. After review, the Department of Planning gives
its opinion of the plan's feasibility.

Next, the developer must submit a preliminary plat.[42] Information
required in the preliminary plat includes, but is not limited to, the items
listed for the sketch plan if one was not submitted, the proposed name of the
subdivision, the approximate area of the plat, contour data extending 150 feet
beyond the boundaries of the subdivision, the location of existing physical
features such as sewers, easements, and buildings that will remain after the
development, the location of existing and proposed streets, the approximate
area of proposed lots, an indication of building lines and setbacks, certification of the plat by the land surveyor or engineer who prepared the plat, and
comments by the officials of the fire district in which the land is located when
the development will have a single ingress and egress. If the proposed subdivision is for multifamily dwelling units or a development submitted under
flexible zoning procedures, the preliminary plat must include data on the size
of the tract, the maximum number of units allowed and proposed, the area
that will be covered by streets, parking ratios, and the distance between
structures.[43]

If the Department of Planning approves the preliminary plat, the developer must complete the final steps within two years.[44] First, improvement
plans detailing the construction and types of materials to be used must be submitted and approved. Improvement plans must include relevant information
identifying the developer and the registered professional engineer preparing
the plans, a key map showing the relationship of the area to be subdivided to
the tract, benchmark references, standards and specifications followed, grading and paving details, plans, profiles and details of streets, as well as sanitary
sewers, drainage channels, and the like. Improvement plans must be reviewed
by local sewer authorities as well as traffic and highway officials.[45]

Next, the final plat, which identifies all developed lots, including lots to
be developed in phases, and is intended to be recorded, is submitted to the
Department of Planning. Before the Department of Planning forwards the plat
to the County Council with its recommendation, the developer must submit
guarantees of the installation of water mains; a contract for street lighting
from the local utility company (which is optional and "to be accepted in lieu

of an increased value for escrow of actual construction costs"); verification of
the street names and addresses from the Department of Revenue; verification
of the location of fire hydrants from the Fire District; verification of tax payment; and verification of payment of highways inspection fees. The developer
also must pay subdivision processing fees and submit any special studies or
engineering calculations required, a trust indenture and warranty deed for
common land conveyance, verification of payment of connection fees to sewer
company, verification of proper placement of survey monuments from the
Department of Highways & Traffic, and a digitized version of the plat in a format compatible with the county's mapping software.[46]

After these steps are completed, the final plat is approved or disapproved
by the County Council.

Resubdividing Existing Lots (Lot-Splitting)

St. Louis County offers a simplified procedure for the subdivision of an existing lot into not more than two lots. The major difference in the lot-split procedure is that approval can be given by the Department of Planning without the
necessity of legislative action. Lot-splits are authorized for legal lots of record
under single ownership when the following criteria are met:

1. No additional improvements are required that would necessitate the
   posting of an escrow or bond, including concrete sidewalks, water
   mains, and landscaping within a street right-of-way dedication. Establishment of a right-of-way only shall not be construed as an improvement in this section.
2. No provisions for common land or recreational facilities are included
   in the proposal.
3. The use of the lot-split procedure does not adversely affect the subject
   parcel or any adjoining properties.
4. The proposed lot-split is not in conflict with any provisions of the zoning ordinance, of any special-procedure permit, or of this chapter.
5. No variances are required for this chapter.[47]

Lot-split applications are simplified, requiring two drawings of a certified
survey prepared by a registered land surveyor, containing legal descriptions
of both the original lot and each of the proposed lots; north arrow and graphic
scale; location of proposed and existing streets and adjoining property; location of all existing buildings; approval by local water and sewer authorities
shown on the tract drawings; name, address, and telephone number of the
owner of record; and a copy of the deed of record. The tract drawings must be
accompanied by a filing fee,[48] a certificate of nondelinquency of taxes, verification of adequacy of fire hydrants and water supply from the applicable fire
protection district, and verification of proper placement of survey monuments
or an escrow agreement or land subdivision bond to guarantee installation of
appropriate survey monuments.[49]

Approval of a lot-split application is nondiscretionary if the lot-split is
"found to be in compliance with the above requirements" of the subdivision
and zoning ordinances of St. Louis County.[50]

Resubdivisions can be controversial and can provoke challenges to simplified application procedures. The Supreme Court of Wyoming upheld an abbreviated resubdivision procedure, concluding that use of the abbreviated procedure did not conflict with state statutes and was not arbitrary or capricious. The court also held that neighbors did not have to consent to the resubdivision.[51] The Supreme Court of Vermont upheld denial of an application to subdivide a split lot (one that lies in more than one zoning district) because an ordinance required uses on a split lot to comply with district regulations for the district they are in, and the proposed subdivision would result in noncompliance on one of the lots.[52]

Approval of Subdivision Plats

Decisions regarding approval or disapproval of final subdivision plats are made by the local legislative body or planning commission, depending on the applicable state statute,[53] and must comply with statutory procedures.[54] In administering subdivision regulations, planning boards may be given discretion to waive certain requirements, such as road-grade requirements, cul-de-sac design requirements, street connection requirements, and sidewalk requirements, because of special circumstances. However, as the Supreme Judicial Court of Maine concluded, planning boards may not waive standards mandated by zoning ordinances, such as street widths, because such a waiver amounts to a variance and is governed by the statutory procedure for variances.[55] Subdivision decisions also are subject to the same constitutional limitations common to zoning decisions. Thus, in *Carlson v. Town of Beaux Arts Village*,[56] a town council's decision rejecting a subdivision application was overruled by a court that held the decision was arbitrary and capricious.[57] Although the owners had complied with all necessary zoning laws, their proposal to divide one lot into two parcels was denied by the town council because it would have created lots of a shape unlike any other in town. As the court stated, however, "[N]o ordinance . . . prohibits an irregularly shaped lot."[58]

Local officials must comply with the same rules requiring impartiality when administering subdivision regulations as when administrating zoning ordinances. In *Winslow v. Town of Holderness Planning Board*, the Supreme Court of New Hampshire upheld a lower court ruling invalidating a planning board's decision to waive lot size and frontage requirements of the town's subdivision regulations because a member of the planning board who voted in favor of the action had spoken in support of the landowner's application for waiver at a public hearing prior to his becoming a member of the planning board.[59] The Court concluded that the planning board played a quasi-judicial role when it administered the subdivision regulations by ruling on applications for waiver of particular regulations because its decision on an application for waiver "would have a disproportionately great impact on the [petitioner] and on owners of land abutting his, but comparatively little impact on other town residents" and in that respect resembled the judicial function of resolving disputes "between two or more parties with competing interests."[60] Judicial officials are held to a higher standard of impartiality than are non-judicial officials in order to safeguard the due process rights of the parties appearing before them. Planning board members administering subdivision regulations must meet the judicial test of impartiality, as must members of zoning boards of adjustment. When the test is not met even by only one member, any action taken by the board is voidable, the court concluded.[61]

When a landowner has complied with all of the requirements of applicable subdivision regulations, refusal of a county commission to approve the landowner's subdivision plan application has been held to be a violation of due process.[62] Likewise, statutory requirements that subdivision applications be approved, modified, or rejected within a certain number of days, with failure to act within the prescribed time limit considered as an approval, have been held mandatory. Under such rulings, landowners have been allowed to maintain mandamus actions for issuance of building permits when no action was taken on a site-plan application within the time specified in the statute.[63]

When state laws outline procedures that municipalities must follow in considering subdivision applications, ordinances that conflict with the statutory requirements have been invalidated. For example, the Alaska statute authorizing municipalities to impose subdivision regulations required that all subdivisions be submitted to the relevant platting authority for approval and permitted the platting authority to waive the approval requirement in individual cases when certain conditions were met. An ordinance that gave advance approval of all subdivisions of land into parcels of ten acres or more without the necessity of presenting a plat to the planning commission was invalidated because it dispensed with the requirement for individual consideration of waiver applications that the statute required.[64]

Conditions Attached to Subdivision Approval

Approval of subdivision plats is conditioned first on the successful completion of the application process, established in local subdivision regulations such as the St. Louis County example in the previous section, "The Application Process."

Additional conditions may be found in the applicable zoning ordinances. For example, in *Roeder v. Board of Adjustment of the City of Town and Country*, a local ordinance prohibited a subdivision of property into less than three acres unless the property fronted a street with a minimum 50-foot right-of-way.[65] Because the right-of-way was too small in this case, the subdivision application was denied. The owner's argument that a variance should be granted was rejected because the owner had failed to prove the requisite hardship.[66]

Subdivision plans often are approved on the condition that landowners satisfy additional requirements imposed by the governing authority. This is particularly true at the interim approval stage.[67] Conditions can range from a requirement that the city engineer certify that plans for road access are adequate[68] to the imposition, by deed restrictions, of architectural and landscaping controls,[69] as well as a variety of affirmative acts called *exactions*.[70] Conditions may be imposed as conditions precedent to final approval of a development plan[71] or as conditions subsequent to which failure to comply triggers repeal of the subdivision approval.[72]

Subdivision conditions must meet the same general standards of statutory authorization and constitutional validity as are imposed on other forms of land use regulation. Some states provide specific statutory authority for subdivision conditions,[73] but in most states communities must rely on implied powers from general subdivision regulation authorizations. Although courts have struck down specific ordinances imposing subdivision conditions as unauthorized,[74] the trend has been to find implied authorization for conditions from a broad reading of subdivision regulation–enabling legislation.[75]

Authorized conditions may only be imposed in accordance with the standards of the applicable authorization. For example, city officials may not impose water and sewer connection fees by administrative decision on developments whose final plats were approved prior to the effective date of the water and sewer fee ordinance,[76] nor may land dedication or in-lieu fees be imposed in violation of a subdivision regulation–enabling statute's requirement that a public hearing be held prior to the imposition of conditions at which the proposed land dedication or in-lieu fee condition is discussed.[77] However, negligent or unauthorized performance of functions required by subdivision-regulations ordinances, such as the failure to consider whether conditions to final approval of a subdivision plat had been met when final approval was given and the plat was recorded, generally will not estop a municipality from enforcing valid conditions.[78]

Constitutional questions associated with imposing conditions on subdivision approval are discussed in connection with the topic of exactions in the next section.

Exactions

During the 1980s, a variety of land use conditions called *exactions* gained widespread popularity. *Exactions* have been defined generally as "reasonable conditions for design, dedication, improvement and restrictive use of land"[79] and more specifically as "condition[s] of development permission that require . . . a public facility or improvement to be provided at the developer's expense."[80]

The term *exactions* covers a wide variety of land use conditions. In *New Jersey Builders Association v. Bernards Township,* the Supreme Court of New Jersey identified seven different kinds of exactions:[81]

1. requirements to dedicate land within a subdivision for public purposes
2. construction of public improvements within a subdivision, such as streets, sidewalks, and water and sewer lines[82]
3. construction of off-site improvements, such as roads or drainage systems[83]
4. requirements for park and recreation land dedication or in-lieu fee payments primarily, but not exclusively, for the benefit of residents of the new development[84]
5. impact fees, defined as "charges against new development for the purpose of raising money to defray costs of basic services local government provides to its citizens"[85]
6. fixed benefit assessments, a California innovation imposing the cost of a variety of public services on owners of undeveloped land[86]

7. linkage ordinances through which the right to develop property in certain ways, such as for commercial purposes, is conditioned upon receipt of a contribution of land or money to be applied toward land uses that have been established as priorities by the municipality, such as housing for low- and moderate-income persons[87]

Statutory Authorization/Control of Exactions

As the Supreme Court of New Jersey noted, exactions "reflect a policy choice that higher taxes for existing residents are less desirable than higher development costs for builders, and higher acquisition costs for new residents."[88] Expressing concern that "disproportionate or excessive use" of exactions could have undesirable effects on new development, particularly residential, the New Jersey Court read narrowly a state statue permitting municipalities to charge developers a pro-rata share of the cost of "reasonable and necessary" off-site street improvements and water, sewage, and drainage facilities.[89] The court concluded that the statute did not authorize a municipality to charge developers their share of the municipality's long-term road-improvement plan unless the municipality could demonstrate that the amount charged to the developer was based on a need arising "as a direct consequence of the particular subdivision or development under review."[90]

Similar conclusions that legislative authority to impose exactions should not be expanded beyond the purposes specifically authorized by such statutes have been reached by the Ninth Circuit when it struck down a development fee imposed by a redevelopment agency to reimburse a predecessor developer for the cost of an option deposit.[91] An appellate court in Washington reached the same conclusion when it held that a state environmental protection statute that authorized municipalities to condition subdivision approval upon the payment of impact fees to mitigate "specific environmental impacts"[92] did not permit the imposition of development fees of $200 per condominium unit to finance general park development and improvement because of the lack of "a reasonable relationship between the conditions or fees imposed and the environmental objectives."[93]

When municipalities stray too far afield from traditional land use regulation and attempt to use exactions as sources of public revenue, such as development fees to be used for general public facilities or housing for low-income families, courts have invalidated such exactions as unauthorized taxes.[94]

For example, municipalities in New Jersey that attempted to fund their *Mount Laurel* "fair share" affordable housing obligations[95] by imposing development fees to fund municipal rehabilitation of substandard housing or cash contributions to affordable housing trust funds as conditions for subdivision or site-plan approval on all new residential or nonresidential development were thwarted by an appellate court's conclusion that the mandatory fees were invalid taxes:

> A mandatory development fee applied indiscriminately as a price to build within the municipality has "no real and substantial relationship to the regulation of land," nor does it advance a purpose of zoning "in a manner permitted by the legislature," the court declared.[96]

Likewise, the Idaho Supreme Court invalidated a fee imposed on owners or occupants of property in the city of Pocatello to generate funds for repair of seriously deteriorated streets as a nonuniform tax imposed for a "nonregulatory" purpose.[97]

The Supreme Court of New Hampshire struck down a growth impact fee imposed on new construction within the city of Laconia. A fee of 69 cents per square foot of building area was imposed on new residential construction for a planned new school not yet under construction. Stressing the importance of a city following its own procedures, the court struck down the fee as a special assessment that was not enacted in accordance with the city's ordinance governing the levy of special assessments.[98]

These decisions have led to criticism about the inherent uncertainty of judicial policy setting through case-by-case adjudication and calls for legislative line drawing regarding the permissible reach of exactions. One commentator has argued for judicial deference to municipalities "because this is the result that is most likely to ensure that the legislature thereafter gives the matter its proper attention."[99]

Some states have responded to the call for legislative action by preempting local authority to impose developer fees and similar exactions except those "reasonably necessary as a direct result of the proposed development or plat."[100]

For example, Texas has enacted a comprehensive "impact fee" statute that establishes detailed regulations limiting the authority of local governments to impose impact fees on new developments "only to pay the costs of constructing capital improvements or facility expansions," with specific limitations placed on items that may qualify as costs "necessitated by and attributable to such new development."[101] Impact fees may be imposed only for capital improvements or facility expansions of water supply, treatment, drainage, and flood control; wastewater collection and treatment; and roadway facilities that are identified in a municipal capital-improvements plan. Impact fees may not be charged for repair, maintenance, or expansion of existing facilities to meet stricter regulatory standards or to provide better service to existing development;[102] nor may they be used to fund park needs, or on-site water, sewer, or traffic facilities that also are the subject of valid dedication or in-lieu fee programs.[103]

"Qualified professionals" must be used to prepare capital improvements plans and to calculate impact fees.[104] Impact fees imposed on individual development units are determined by first calculating the total number of projected service units, defined as "standardized measures of consumption, use generation, or discharge attributable to individual units of development,"[105] and then dividing that number into the projected total costs of the applicable capital improvements.[106]

Detailed procedures for adopting impact-fee ordinances are established, including requirements for appointment of an advisory committee that must include representatives of the real estate, development, or building industries, and conducting two separate public hearings, one to consider the "land use assumptions" that will be used to develop the capital-improvements plan and another to discuss the adoption of the capital-improvements plan that has been prepared and imposition of the impact fee.[107] Fees collected must be deposited in separate interest-bearing accounts and must be refunded upon application if existing facilities are available and service is denied, if the municipality has failed to commence construction within two years, or if service is not available within a reasonable period not to exceed five years from the date of payment of the fees.[108]

Land use assumptions and capital-improvements plans must be updated at least every three years, at which time a public hearing must be held to consider any modifications in the assumptions, plan, or impact fee.[109] Records of all public hearings must be made and maintained for public inspection for at least ten years after the hearing.[110] Municipalities may not impose moratoria on new development during the impact-fee imposition process.[111]

Persons who have exhausted all administrative appeals within the municipality and who are aggrieved by a final decision regarding impact fees may obtain a trial de novo of their complaint, but suits to contest an impact fee must be filed within 90 days from the date of adoption of the impact-fee ordinance, order, or resolution.[112]

The Texas statute has been praised as "a comprehensive piece of legislation . . . designed to create an ordered, predictable process for the consideration, adoption and assessment of impact fees . . . [and] intended to place careful controls upon the imposition and use of impact fees."[113]

Georgia enacted a similar statute in 1990, authorizing the use of impact fees, but only to cover the costs of new public facilities or services required because of new development.[114] The new law was reported to have been supported by developers as well as local governmental officials "in order to create a level on which all developers would be treated the same and to avoid the uncertainties that come with letting the courts gradually define the rules in a series of cases over a number of years."[115] Florida is in the forefront of managing growth through its "concurrency" legislation, which includes exactions.[116] At least 20 other states have adopted some form of legislation regulating local government use of exactions.[117]

Constitutional Issues Raised by Exactions

In addition to statutory authorization questions, exactions will be scrutinized under constitutional standards of due process, eminent domain, and equal protection. The *Nollan/Dolan* rule[118] requires conditions attached to development permits to meet a two-part test of (1) an "essential nexus" (relationship) between the permit condition and the public impact of the proposed development, and (2) a "rough proportionality" between the magnitude of the burden exacted by the condition and the likely effects of the proposed development.[119] The rough proportionality standard must be met by an "individualized determination" that the exaction is related "both in nature and extent" to the impact of the proposed development.[120] The *Nollan/Dolan* rule was formulated in two cases involving requirements that landowners dedicate permanent easements to the public as conditions for approval of development permits and imposes a heightened judicial scrutiny on such conditions.[121] In both cases, the Supreme Court invalidated the conditions because of failure by the government entities involved to establish the required relationship between the problems encountered and the conditions imposed.

The Ninth Circuit upheld Sacramento's Housing Trust Fund Ordinance, which requires as a condition of issuance of nonresidential building permits the payment of fees in an amount intended to make up the shortfall in financing for affordable housing for low-income persons.[122] Applying the *Nollan* tests, the court found a sufficient nexus in the record between the amount of the fees and the demand for low-income housing created by the subject nonresidential developments. The centerpiece of Sacramento's evidence was the report of its consulting firm on the need for low-income housing and the effect of nonresidential development on such need, together with the fact that the city reduced by one-half the consultant's final calculations regarding the amount of fees necessary to offset the costs of such development.[123] The court found ultimately that the fees did not constitute a taking under the Fifth Amendment. A strong dissent recounted the California history of fiscal woes and taxpayer revolts and accused the city of a "transparent attempt to force commercial developers to underwrite social policy."[124]

In *Ehrlich v. City of Culver City*,[125] the Supreme Court of California extended the reach of *Nollan/Dolan* to monetary exactions imposed on a single property owner as a condition to issuance of a development permit, but declined to apply the rule and its heightened scrutiny to a "generally applicable development fee or assessment." The court saw no logical difference between a requirement that a landowner convey a property interest or pay a monetary amount, when either is imposed on individuals under the government's monopoly power over development permits.[126] The court held that the city had met its burden of establishing a nexus between a rezoning and the imposition of a fee to mitigate the loss of land available for private recreational use but remanded the case because the city's evidence concerning the amount of the fee ($280,000) was insufficient under the rough proportionality standard.[127] The court, however, declined to apply the *Nollan/Dolan* rule to "generally applicable development fees or assessments."[128]

A concurring opinion stressed that "the taking of money is different, under the Fifth Amendment, from the taking of real or personal property." Monetary exactions such as taxes, special assessments, and user fees receive substantial judicial deference, and development fees that are "categorically applied to a general class—to all developments or to certain types of development" have and should continue to receive similar judicial deference, the concurrence stressed.[129]

Courts in Arizona,[130] Colorado,[131] Illinois,[132] Kansas,[133] and Maryland[134] have upheld impact fees established by the legislature affecting entire areas of a city, distinguishing them from the *Dolan*-type adjudicative decision to impose a fee affecting only an individual parcel.[135] The Supreme Court of Illinois upheld a statute authorizing urban counties and home-rule cities to impose transportation impact fees for the costs of local road improvements that are "specifically and uniquely attributable" to the new development because the statutory language incorporated the Illinois test, which is stricter than the *Dolan* test.[136] The Supreme Court of Kansas, in upholding a transportation impact fee ordinance enacted by a home-rule city, declined to apply *Dolan*, stating that no basis existed for the "critical leap which must be made from a fee to a taking of property."[137] The Court of Appeals of Maryland, in upholding a county-development impact tax pursuant to state enabling legislation, declined to apply *Dolan* because the impact tax was applied areawide rather than to a particular landowner, and the tax did not require landowners to deed portions of their property to the county.[138] The Supreme Court of Ohio, on the other hand, has concluded that the *Nollan/Dolan* "dual rational-nexus test" should be applied to impact fees as well as land dedications because it "balances both the interests of local governments and real estate developers without unnecessary restrictions."[139]

State courts have established three different exaction tests to determine whether an otherwise valid exaction becomes an unconstitutional taking.[140] The most demanding test is the "specifically and uniquely attributable" test developed by the Illinois courts, under which exactions are invalidated unless it can be shown that they are based on specific needs created by new development and that the benefits of the exaction will be enjoyed almost exclusively by residents of the development.[141] The least-restrictive test simply requires "very generalized statements" concerning the connections between a required dedication and a proposed development.[142] The third test is an intermediate one requiring a "reasonable relationship" between a required dedication and a proposed development.[143]

Although *Nollan* did not express a preference for any of the tests, state courts before and since *Nollan* have developed a preference for the "reasonable relationship" test. In the process, a discernible shift has been noted from a deferential application of the test to a "fairly rigorous analysis . . . [requiring] some real showing" that a proposed development will create a need and that the exaction imposed will respond to the need and also create "some degree of 'benefit' to the development."[144] The Supreme Court in *Dolan*[145] stated that the "reasonable relationship" test is closer to the constitutional norm than the other two, but nevertheless chose the term "rough proportionality" to avoid confusion with the rational-basis test of the Equal Protection Clause.[146]

The Court of Special Appeals of Maryland found a due process violation in the case of an exaction ordinance requiring subdivision developers to pay for on-site public improvements—such as extensions of streets and installation of curbs, gutters, and storm drains—and permitting developers to be reimbursed if the city later collected all or a portion of the costs from subsequent users.[147] The court indicated its sympathy with the plight of the first developer, who is required to bear the costs of public improvements that will benefit subsequent residents or other users of the facilities. The court suggested that a reimbursement requirement could bear a reasonable nexus to subdivision control but concluded that the ordinance in question failed for lack of adequate due process protection whether the scheme was classified as a special-benefit assessment or a subdivision exaction.[148]

The court indicated that a reimbursement scheme could meet due process standards, but only if the ordinance were narrowly drawn to identify the class of persons who might be subject to liability for subsequent assessment of costs, to indicate the circumstances under which the city would assess or collect from the class, to provide standards or criteria for determining the level of utilization of the facilities that would subject a person to assessment, and to establish a process for providing meaningful notice and hearing before proposed improvements are installed so that persons who might later be called on to pay for the improvements could have an opportunity to review the plans and challenge the manner or costs of the proposed improvements.[149]

The court also concluded that the person who first developed an area and was thus required to pay the costs of the public improvements associated with the development was not treated unfairly in an equal protection sense. Because any person who was the first to develop an area would be subject to the same requirement, equal protection laws were not violated by the application of the requirement to the developer in question unless the discrimination was invidious or unfair. Finding no suspect class or fundamental right at stake and identifying a rational relationship to a legitimate government interest in the reasonable nexus to subdivision control conceded by the developer who was seeking reimbursement, the court concluded that the developer's equal protection rights were not violated by imposition of the costs of public improvements necessary for completion of the subdivision.[150]

Florida has applied a "dual rational-nexus test." The local government must demonstrate (1) a reasonable connection, or rational nexus, between the need for additional facilities and the growth in population generated by the subdivision; and (2) a reasonable connection, or rational nexus, between the expenditures of the funds collected and the benefit accruing to the subdivision.[151] Under the second prong of the test, however, the court stayed enforcement of the impact fees until such time as substantially all of the municipalities within the subject county agreed to impose the fees, ensuring that the fees, collected by the county, will benefit all those who have paid them.[152] In applying the test, the standard is "growth of a particular subdivision," not countywide growth. Thus it was unconstitutional for a county to impose a public school impact fee on an age-restricted mobile-home park, the Supreme Court of Florida concluded.[153]

New Hampshire has enacted an impact-fee statute requiring that fees be reasonably related to the public burden caused by the development and that municipalities have improvement programs before imposing the fees.[154] In Utah, impact fees must be "reasonable."[155] In applying the reasonableness standard, the Supreme Court of Utah stated that "[t]he law does not make reasonableness turn on a formula, given the variety of factual circumstances in each case and the necessary elasticity of such words as 'reasonable' and 'equitable.'" Furthermore, fact gathering and analysis are "appropriate" staff tasks and not something that city council members must attend to personally.[156]

Constitutional challenges to linkage fees normally involve an argument that the linkage fee is not rationally related to the end to be achieved or, in some cases, that the end is not legitimate. For example, *Prisk v. City of*

Poulsbo[157] was a challenge to the constitutionality of park fees assessed against a developer of a condominium complex. The fees were invalidated. The city argued that a state statute requiring cities to ensure that provisions were made for open spaces, parks, and playgrounds[158] gave the city the authority to assess linkage fees. The court held that the statute did not allow cities to "require a developer to pay a park fee . . . as a condition to subdivision approval."[159] The city also argued that its fees were justified under the State Environmental Policy Act,[160] which gives a city the authority to impose fees to mitigate "specific adverse environmental impacts." The court ruled, however, that the city had not shown that the fees had a reasonable relationship to a valid environmental concern. "The need for parks is not an environmental concern simply because the city engineer calls it one."[161] Because the city had no statutory authority to impose the park fees on the developer, the fees were unauthorized taxes prohibited by the state constitution.[162] Similar utility connection fees, also challenged by the developer, were not unauthorized taxes because a state statute specifically authorized the city to impose the fees.[163]

Vested Rights Arising from Plan Approval

The popularity of various land use control techniques that require land development proposals to be subjected to a series of review steps or stages, such as preliminary and final plat approval and preliminary and final development plan review, has given new life to the vested-rights doctrine. The traditional purpose of the vested-rights doctrine in land use regulation settings has been to protect individuals who begin development in reliance on current zoning laws but fail to finish development before the laws are changed.[164]

Under the majority rule, vested rights arise when the developer substantially changes his or her position by "perform[ing] substantial work and incur[ring] substantial liabilities in good faith reliance upon a permit issued by the government."[165] Under this test, two actions must occur for vested rights to accrue: (1) granting of a permit to commence activities, and (2) actual construction rather than mere preparation to perform.[166] At some point, however, a developer may expend enough time and money short of actual construction to acquire a vested right in plan approval. In *Consaul v. City of San Diego,* the developer expended more than $60,000 over 22 months in engineering and consulting fees in procuring approval of a multifamily development plan, after which the city changed the zoning to single family.[167] The court also rejected the city's argument that issuance of a building permit was the only basis for application of the vested-rights doctrine.[168] If rights have been vested, authorized construction may not be prohibited by application of changes in zoning laws.[169] Most jurisdictions impose a duty of good faith to prevent a developer who knows of an impending land use regulation change from applying for a building permit a short time before the new law goes into effect.[170]

The good-faith rule, along with the requirement that a building permit actually be granted, was rejected by the Washington Supreme Court, reasoning that a bright-line rule in which rights vest automatically upon application is easier to administer.[171] The case concerned an owner who, with knowledge of an upcoming zoning change that would disrupt his plan for a multifamily development, spent $17,000 on improvements and applied for a building permit one day before downzoning of the property to single-family use became effective. The court ruled that the owner had a vested right to have his application processed under the zoning laws that were in effect on the date the application was filed. In reaching its decision, the court made the following observations concerning the "change in position" and "good faith reliance" elements of the majority rule:

> We prefer not to adopt a rule which forces the court to search through "the moves and countermoves of . . . parties . . . by way of passing ordinances and bringing actions for injunctions"—to which may be added the stalling or acceleration of administrative action in the issuance of permits—to find that date upon which the substantial change of position is made which finally vests the right. . . . The cost of submitting an application and the time limitation on commencing construction after a permit is issued are sufficient commitments to eliminate any need for the courts to inquire into the "good faith" of the applicant.[172]

The Washington rule has been codified[173] and applied to a preliminary plat application that included a planned unit development (PUD) proposal.[174]

In considering whether preliminary public steps prior to the building-permit stage can trigger vested rights, some courts have distinguished steps that are discretionary in nature from steps that are merely ministerial.[175] Under this approach, the final discretionary decision would confer vested rights. If, for example, tentative subdivision map approval is the final discretionary act and approval of a final subdivision map is ministerial, a developer would have a vested right to final map approval when tentative approval was granted and all valid conditions to the tentative approval were met.[176]

Where rights do vest, another issue is the precise nature of the rights. For example, in *Briarwood Properties v. City of Los Angeles,*[177] an owner was granted tentative map approval of a plan to convert apartment buildings into condominiums. A year later, Los Angeles passed an ordinance that required landlords to pay up to $2,500 in relocation costs to tenants who were displaced by condominium conversions. The owner argued that the ordinance should not apply to his property because tentative map approval had been granted. The court rejected the argument, noting that rights that vest are only those "specifically granted by the permit itself" and that there is no such thing as a "vested right to obtain a vested right."[178] Briarwood received and acted on its vested right to convert an apartment building to condominiums, but it did not receive a vested right to complete the conversion "free from application of . . . independent relocation assistance requirements . . . which in no way interfered with the conversion process," the court concluded.[179]

Statutory requirements that land use regulatory decisions be made within a certain length of time have been held not to grant vested rights to have an application for subdivision approved but only to have a decision rendered within the applicable time limit.[180]

Vested rights sometimes have been recognized on a theory of equitable estoppel, under which the good-faith reliance and substantial change in position that support the developer's vested-rights argument is "not solely on existing zoning laws or on good faith expectancy that his development will be permitted but on official assurances on which he has a right to rely that his project has met zoning, that necessary approvals will be forthcoming, and he may safely proceed with the project."[181] Under this standard, the "final discretionary action" on a specific project, such as a "special management area permit," may constitute the "official assurance" for zoning estoppel purposes,[182] but "detailed land use maps" enacted by a municipality to implement a general plan do not constitute agreements with developers that would supply the requisite "official assurance" for an estoppel theory of vested rights.[183] There are numerous cases in which municipal assurances of approval were held not to constitute a basis for granting a permit by estoppel.[184]

A vested right may be obtained and then lost by failure to act on the right. In *Lakeview Development Corporation v. City of South Lake Tahoe*,[185] the Ninth Circuit held that even if a developer obtained a vested right to complete construction, it waited too long to do so. The court held that the vested-rights claim was a "species of governmental estoppel."[186] Thus analyzed, the vested-rights/estoppel doctrine under state law may be distinguished from takings analysis under federal law, the former resting on "broader norms of equity," presumably applying a more generous analysis of fairness than the latter.[187]

Site-Plan Review

An important component of the subdivision regulation phase of land use control is site-plan review, normally carried out by the local planning body.[188] The general purpose of site-plan review is "to assure that on-site construction and improvements are properly carried out,"[189] completing a trilogy of land use regulations governing (1) type and intensity of use of land (zoning), (2) provision of necessary public facilities and services (subdivision regulation), and (3) relationship of structures to a specific parcel of land (site-plan review) in which the review process becomes progressively more detailed.[190] Building permits may be revoked if they are issued prior to site-plan review and approval. [191]

Originally sanctioned by judicial decisions construing general statutory language authorizing referral of land use control matters to planning boards before final action was taken,[192] specific site-plan review authority, and limitations on the exercise of that authority, have been incorporated into modern land use control statutes. The New Jersey statute is illustrative.[193]

New Jersey municipalities are authorized to require by ordinance that site plans be approved by resolution of the planning board, or the board of adjustment when a variance is being sought,[194] before permits may be issued for all developments except detached one- or two-dwelling-unit buildings.[195] A site plan is defined as:

> a development plan of one or more lots on which is shown (1) the existing and proposed conditions of the lot, including but not necessarily lim-

ited to topography, vegetation, drainage, flood plains, marshes and waterways, (2) the location of all existing and proposed buildings, drives, parking spaces, walkways, means of ingress and egress, drainage facilities, utility services, landscaping, structures and signs, lighting, screening devices, and (3) any other information that may be reasonably required in order to make an informed determination pursuant to an ordinance requiring review and approval of site plans by the planning board.[196]

Site-plan review ordinances under the New Jersey statute are required to include standards and requirements relating to preservation of existing natural resources on the site, safe and efficient traffic circulation, as well as parking and loading, location of structures, along with their landscaping and screening, exterior lighting needed for safety, and any requirements for street lighting, conservation of energy and use of renewable energy sources, and recycling of designated materials.[197] Other required provisions of site-plan review ordinances include procedures and standards for submission and processing of applications for development, as well as preliminary and final approval, requirements for conformity with applicable zoning ordinances, and performance in substantial accordance with applicable final development plans.[198] Optional provisions include a range of developer exactions,[199] "which are necessitated by a subdivision or land development,"[200] and standards "encouraging and promoting flexibility, and economy in layout and design" through PUD techniques.[201]

A uniform set of technical site-improvement standards was authorized in 1993[202] and promulgated in 1997[203] in order to reduce housing costs by reducing the "multiplicity of standards for subdivisions and site improvements."[204] The Supreme Court of New Jersey upheld the regulations against a facial challenge by the New Jersey Municipal League and 157 municipalities that the regulations impermissibly interfered with local zoning authority. In so doing, the court acknowledged that "the acts departs to some extent from the traditional 'home rule' aspect of zoning," but concluded that particular concerns "are best addressed in the forum of 'as-applied' challenges to particular regulations."[205]

The New Jersey statute establishes a two-step preliminary and final approval process, with site plans and supporting engineering documents to be submitted "in tentative form for discussion purposes" during the preliminary approval stage. Preliminary approval of small developments, ten acres and ten units or less, shall be granted or denied within 45 days of the submission of a completed application and within 95 days in the case of larger developments.[206] Failure to take action within the prescribed time period is deemed approval,[207] and failure to make timely disposition of site-plan applications has been identified as a violation of the *Mount Laurel* affordable housing requirements.[208] Preliminary approval gives the developer a three-year guarantee that the general terms and conditions on which the preliminary approval were granted will not be changed, except as may be required for public health and safety, and the right to submit an application for final approval within the three-year period, which may be extended for two additional years or, in the case of developments of 50 acres or more, a longer period deemed reasonable by the planning board.[209]

Final approval is required to be granted "if the detailed drawings, specifications and estimates of the application for final approval conform to the standards established by ordinance for final approval, the conditions of preliminary approval and, in the case of a major subdivision, the standards prescribed by the 'Map Filing Law,'" with action to grant or deny final approval required to be taken within 45 days after submission of a final application.[210] Final approval may be conditioned upon the receipt of appropriate performance and maintenance guarantees "assuring the installation and maintenance of on-tract improvements."[211]

Variances may be granted and simultaneous processing of subdivision applications and site plans may be authorized. When simultaneous processing is employed, the longest time period for action by the planning board applies.[212] Final approval gives the developer a two-year period, with extensions possible for particular situations, in which the zoning requirements applicable to the preliminary approval, along with other rights conferred by the preliminary approval, will not be changed.[213]

The site-plan review technique gives planning agencies "wide discretion to insure compliance with the objectives and requirements" of site-plan review ordinances, but it may not be used to prohibit an otherwise permitted use, such as a convenience store, because of the traffic volume the store might generate when the ordinance contained no standards for defining or measuring acceptable levels of traffic,[214] nor to deny approval to a fast-food restaurant site plan because of an existing off-site condition such as heavy traffic on adjoining roadways, unless the proposed means of ingress and egress to the site would create vehicular traffic problems.[215] Likewise, control of architectural design through site-plan review must be guided by specific standards that "adequately circumscribe the process of administrative decision," a standard not met by an ordinance criterion of "harmony with existing structures and terrain" when *harmony* is undefined in the ordinance.[216]

As noted earlier, site-plan review ordinances focus on spatial relationships on a particular parcel. As such, they are closer to building code ordinances than to zoning ordinances. Thus, in mandatory-planning states, adoption of a comprehensive plan is not a precondition to adoption of a site-plan review ordinance.[217] Site-plan review ordinances may be applicable to proposed improvements on already developed sites as well as to undeveloped land. When applicable to developed sites, such ordinances typically require the planning board to review the site plan in its entirety, not just plans for the particular improvement.[218] Approval of a site plan for the expandable portion of a condominium does not necessarily excuse a landowner from receiving subdivision approval before amending the condemnation declaration. The Supreme Court of New Hampshire concluded that an amendment to a condominium declaration creating separate lots (A and B) within the expandable land and effectively transferring ownership of land to the condominium association

> subdivided the expandable land to the extent it divided the land for the purpose of sale or conveyance of the condominium units. To the extent that this subdivision of the property for the condominium also created

expandable lands A and B as separate lots, however, it was done without planning board approval.[219]

When performing the site-plan review function, individual planning board members have been held to be entitled to absolute immunity from federal or state civil rights suits because of the quasi-judicial nature of their role in the site-plan review process, but such immunity is not granted to planning boards as governmental entities.[220] The discretion granted local planning boards under site-plan review statutes and ordinances has been held to prevent a landowner's expectation of success in obtaining site-plan approval "from rising to the level of certainty required to give rise to a property right" that would support a federal civil rights action for a taking of property arising from rejection of a site plan under an ordinance that was subsequently declared invalid in state court for granting too much discretion.[221] Persons challenging rejections of site plans must have a valid property interest in the land in question in order to have standing.[222] Planning boards are required to make written findings of fact to support administrative decisions, such as site plan approval or denial. Courts will not make independent judgments but rather will remand cases with inadequate findings to planning boards for further findings of fact to support the board's decision.[223]

Development Agreements

The complexity of modern land use regulation techniques and the resulting costs to developers in time and money have led several states to enact legislation authorizing municipalities to enter into agreements with developers limiting the effect that changes in land use laws will have on development projects. Such statutes are designed to give developers a measure of certainty regarding the rules governing their activities while avoiding the proscription against bargaining away the police power that traditionally has prevented cities from entering into contracts to exercise the zoning power in a particular way.[224] Florida authorizes local governments to enter into development agreements for up to ten years with "any person having a legal or equitable interest in real property."[225] At least two public hearings must be held prior to entering into, amending, or revoking a development agreement, one of which may be held by the local planning agency.[226] The statute specifies several items that must be included in a development agreement, including a description of public facilities to serve the development, the entity responsible for providing such facilities, the date any new facilities, if needed, will be constructed, and a schedule to ensure that necessary facilities are timed to the completion of the development.[227] Once a development agreement is executed, local land use laws and policies governing the development at the time of the agreement will remain in effect for the duration of the agreement. Subsequently adopted laws and policies may not be applied to the development unless a public hearing is held and the local government makes findings that the new laws or policies do not conflict with existing ones; are essential to public health, safety, or welfare; expressly state that they are to be applied to a development that is subject to a development agreement; and are specifically anticipated and provided for in the development agreement, unless substantial changes have occurred in conditions existing at the time of execution of the agreement or the agreement was based on substantially inaccurate information supplied by the developer.[228] Development agreements are to be recorded and run to successors in interest,[229] are to be reviewed at least annually, and can be revoked or modified for noncompliance.[230]

An alternative to the Florida approach is the New Jersey subdivision and site-plan review statute, which guarantees a developer who has received preliminary approval of subdivision or site plans a three-year period, which may be extended under certain circumstances, to obtain final approval and a two-year period after final approval, which also may be extended, during both of which periods the zoning requirements in effect at the time preliminary approval was granted and the rights conferred by reason of the preliminary approval will not be changed.[231]

The New Jersey Municipal Land Use Law, of which the subdivision and site-plan review law is a part, also encourages an informal review process between developer and planning board to permit discussion of concept plans for developments prior to the submission of an application for development. Neither party is bound by any concept plan or informal review, but the informal review is designed to expedite the land use regulation process and save time and money by permitting the parties to explore alternatives and discuss the feasibility of particular development concepts.[232]

When an agreement is made by a city official who lacks the authority to make the agreement, the agreement is void. Thus where a developer obtained a verbal promise by the mayor and the city council president to extend water and sewer service outside the city's boundaries, but where such a decision could be made only by the full city council, the developer had no enforceable agreement.[233]

Extraterritorial Regulation

Many states permit local governments to extend their land use regulation activities, including subdivision regulation and site-plan review, beyond their territorial boundaries.[234] The Supreme Court has upheld the use of extraterritorial police powers against due process and equal protection challenges brought by residents outside the municipality who claimed that their inability to vote for the officials who enacted the extraterritorial policies should render those policies invalid.[235] State courts have upheld extraterritorial exercise of subdivision regulation powers under state enabling legislation,[236] as well as imposition of impact fees.[237]

Conflicts in jurisdiction can arise between city and county land use control policies, particularly when an extraterritorial development is being proposed under unitary development procedures such as planned unit development/ cluster zoning.[238] Although state law may grant exclusive jurisdiction over zoning matters in unincorporated areas of a county to the county and exclusive jurisdiction over subdivision regulation within a limited contiguous

extraterritorial area to the adjoining city, PUDs involve the simultaneous application of both zoning and subdivision regulations to a tract of land as a unit.[239]
Concluding that "the touchstone of a city's power to impose subdivision controls
is not the division of a tract into two or more parcels but its development impact
upon existing facilities protecting the health and safety of the municipal residents," the Supreme Court of Illinois held that an undivided PUD tract of 50
acres is subject to adjacent municipal subdivision regulations. Under state legislation, extraterritorial subdivision regulation is authorized despite county
approval of the PUD plans, but only if the city subdivision regulation ordinance
defines subdivision to include PUDs (or the PUD is later subdivided into lots).[240]

Planning officials generally believe that extraterritorial jurisdiction can be
an effective technique for managing growth but note that it is most effective
when implemented cooperatively through intergovernmental agreements, in
which the interests of all affected communities can be addressed.[241]

Judicial Review of Subdivision Regulation Decisions

Administration of subdivision regulations by planning agencies is an administrative rather than a legislative function. Thus a planning commission does
not have discretion to deny approval of preliminary subdivision plats when
the proposals meet the minimum standards contained in the subdivision
ordinance, but does have discretion to decide whether the standards have
been met.[242]

Subdivision regulation decisions are reviewable for arbitrary and capricious actions,[243] defined as "willful and unreasoning action, without consideration and in disregard of facts and circumstances."[244] Applying that definition, a Washington court struck down a town council's decision to reject a
subdivision plan that met all existing land use regulatory requirements merely
because it would result in irregularly shaped lots as an arbitrary and capricious decision that would give the applicants "no basis for determining how
they could comply with the law."[245]

Subdivision regulation decisions are also reviewable to determine
whether the decision was made according to proper statutory procedures. For
example, in a case challenging a city ordinance that required subdividers to
pay a 7 percent impact fee, the ordinance was invalidated because the hearing
requirements were not met.[246]

Because of the similarity in the issues raised under subdivision regulation
ordinances, with issues arising in the administration of special-use permit and
variance techniques,[247] courts often apply the standards for exercise of discretion in special-permit and variance contexts to subdivision regulation and
site-plan review cases. Courts have deferred to reasons given by planning
commissions when "any one of several reasons submitted by the commission
for its action is reasonably supported by the record."[248]

Courts have refused to entertain complaints by neighboring residents
concerning traffic problems that may be caused by proposed developments
when the local planning agency has not yet ruled on a subdivision plat appli-

cation. The proper approach in such circumstances is to present objections to the planning commission when the subdivision plat application is considered.[249] Failure to do so at the time of preliminary plat approval can result in loss of opportunity to object to the final plat if the developer expends funds and begins construction "to meet the conditions in the preliminary plat approval."[250] Courts have refused to inquire into the motivation for a planning commission's denial of a subdivision plat absent a due process or equal protection violation allegation, but have held that a planning commission may be estopped from raising a specific deficiency if the commission did not mention the problem when it first made comments and suggestions to the developer about the plan under review.[251]

Practitioner Perspectives

Modern land use regulation has become a composite of zoning, subdivision regulation, and site-plan review, with each phase imposing more detailed analysis of the specifics of a land development project. Although zoning receives most of the publicity when controversies erupt, subdivision regulation is also contentious and often politicized as a result of the misconception that zoning is at issue.

The move toward more flexible use of police power by local officials is centered in modern subdivision regulations because conditions including exactions usually are added at this point. The flexibility built into the subdivision regulation structure leads inevitably to an increase in contact between developers and professional planning staffs.

As noted in chapter 2, practitioners are well advised to be sensitive to the concerns of the professional staff when applications for subdivision approval and site-plan approval are submitted. Clear articulation of the interests of the developer as well as the municipality become critical at this point. Because all developers understandably believe that their projects would be "good" for the community, there is a temptation to approach land use regulation, particularly at the subdivision regulation and site-plan review stages, as unreasonable attempts to block the "progress" that will come with the particular project under consideration. In reality, many situations that erupt into controversy at the subdivision and site-plan stages involve legitimate concerns that the communities have for seemingly mundane matters such as storm water runoff, inevitable increases in traffic, the impact of specific designs on surrounding neighborhoods, and so on. Counsel should be firm, however, in insisting that the objective standards of the subdivision ordinance be applied because many citizens and even regulatory officials tend to view subdivision approvals as forums for open debate on actual land use policy.

Successful practitioners often find themselves serving in a mediative capacity in which they are able to articulate the "interests of both sides" in such a way that modifications can be proposed and accepted to a particular project that will permit the project to go forward with its basic integrity intact, while responding to the legitimate concerns of the planning professionals and local legislators charged with responsibility of administrating an inherently political process in a fair manner.

Litigation in this setting can be counterproductive. It is expensive, time consuming, uncertain in outcome, and emotionally charged. Litigation is useful when fundamental constitutional rights are at stake, when arbitrary action is threatened, or when corruption is present. But when a land use dispute is basically a difference of opinion over the proper use of land, litigation rarely produces a satisfactory result.

Lemm Development Corporation v. Town of Bartlett,[252] discussed earlier in this chapter under "Administration of Subdivision Regulations," is a case on point. The litigation grew out of an argument over whether the town had authority under its subdivision regulation to review and approve or reject plans for a tennis/swimming pool facility planned for the common area of a previously approved condominium. No mention was made of the proposed facility when the subdivision plat for the condominium was approved. Jurisdiction over the facility plans was obtainable under site-plan review procedures, but the town had not adopted those regulations.

One of the town's main arguments was that the developer should have notified the town of its plans for the common area when the subdivision plat application was submitted. Because the developer had not included the facility on the subdivision plan, the city reasoned that it had the authority to review those plans when the facility was ready for construction. In holding that subdivision regulation authority did not extend to improvements on land that previously had been subdivided, the Supreme Court of New Hampshire brushed aside the town's argument about notice. The developer won the point, but the cost was high. The dispute lasted over two years. Delays of this magnitude can kill a project.

Is there a lesson to be learned from this case? Could the dispute have been avoided by better and earlier communication between the developer and the town planning officials? Practitioners for both sides have a role here. If the plans for the recreational facility had been drawn up by the time the subdivision application originally was submitted, what was gained by the failure to communicate those plans to the town? The town apparently believed the developer tried to mislead it. Resentment over a perceived slight could have influenced the Board of Selectmen when it denied the building permit. The developer won the point, but what about the next time the developer attempts to do business in that town? Will the developer be trusted? When so many decisions are discretionary under modern flexible land use regulations, will officials be willing to give the developer the benefit of the doubt, or will the regulators require the developer to dot all i's and cross all t's? Is a victory of this type really a Pyrrhic one?

From the town's perspective, was it necessary to engage in such a costly and protracted dispute? What was gained by refusing to issue the building permit without planning-board approval when the town had not implemented the site-plan review process that was the appropriate process for review? State enabling legislation for site-plan review existed at least since 1965, and the

New Hampshire Court had discussed a 1979 amendment requiring the adoption of site-plan regulations in a 1982 opinion.[253] Presumably the requirement for specific adoption of site-plan regulations was known to town officials. If they were interested in reviewing site plans such as the one in dispute, why had the town not adopted specific site-plan regulations?

These questions are raised to make the point that practitioners have an important responsibility to their clients and the public to anticipate possible controversies and strive to avoid them by emphasizing the importance of full disclosure of relevant information by the applicant and by being sensitive to the effect of delay caused by repeated reviews of project plans by municipal planning officials.

Notes

1. THE PRACTICE OF LOCAL GOVERNMENT PLANNING, 26–33, Frank S. So & Judith Getzels, eds. (2d ed., 1988); NATIONAL COMMISSION ON URBAN PROBLEMS, BUILDING THE AMERICAN CITY 201 (1968); R. Marlin Smith, *From Subdivision Improvement Requirements to Community Benefit Assessments and Linkage Payments: A Brief History of Land Development Exactions*, 50 LAW & CONTEMP. PROB. 5 (1987).

2. *See, e.g.,* Precision Sheet Metal Mfg. Co. v. Yates, 794 S.W.2d 545, 552 (Tex. App. 1990), *writ. denied* (1991) ("purpose of statute on plats is to require governmental approval to insure adequate provision has been made for streets, alleys, parks, and other facilities indispensable to the particular community affected").

3. F. So & J. Getzels, *supra*, n. 1, at 198–200.

4. *Id.*

5. *See generally* pp. 347–49. One commentator has referred to the growth of the use of exactions as "the hold-up state" of land use controls. Norman Williams, Jr., *And Now We Have Four Systems*, 12 VT. L. REV. 1, 7–10 (1987).

6. Urrutia v. Blaine County Bd. of Commr's, 134 Idaho 353, 358–59, 2 P.3d 738, 743–44 (2000) (denial of subdivision application for residential development that complied with agricultural-use zoning reversed because board focused solely on plan goal of preservation of agricultural lands).

7. *See, e.g.,* ALASKA STAT. § 40.15.010 (Michie 2000 & Supp 2001); CAL. GOV'T CODE §§ 66473.5, 66474 (West 2000); KY. REV. STAT. § 100.277 (Michie 1993); MD. CODE ANN. Art. 66B, § 5.05 (2001); MINN. STAT. ANN. § 462.358 (West 2001 & Supp. 2002); MO. REV. STAT. §§ 89.440, 89.450 (1998); TENN. CODE ANN. §§ 13-3-406, 13-3-410 (1998 & Supp. 2001), *construed in* Lake County v. Truett, 758 S.W.2d 529 (Tenn. Ct. App. 1988) (regional planning commissions).

"Ordinance 341 appears to be a typical subdivision ordinance prohibiting any person from creating a subdivision without complying with the regulations set forth in the ordinance." City of Coppell v. General Homes Corp., 763 S.W.2d 448, 456 (Tex. App. 1988), *cert. denied* (1989).

8. Sellon v. City of Manitou Springs, 745 P.2d 229, 234 (Colo. 1987) (failure to define terms "platted" and "unplatted" does not render hillside regulation ordinance void for vagueness).

9. CAL. GOV'T CODE § 66424 (West 1997 & Supp. 2002).

10. State v. Bilbao, 130 Idaho 500, 502, 943 P.2d 926, 928 (1997).

11. Loftin v. Langsdon, 813 S.W.2d 475 (Tenn. Ct. App. 1991).

12. Petrone v. Town of Foster, 769 A.2d 591, 594–95 (R.I. 2001).

13. *See, e.g.*, McConnell v. Wilson, 543 A.2d 249, 251 (R.I. 1988) (conversion of parking lot to parking condominium held a "mere change in the form of its ownership and not a subdivision of land"). *Cf.* Supervisor of Assessments of Baltimore County v. Chase Assocs., 306 Md. 568, 510 A.2d 568 (1986) (condominium conversion did not constitute a "subdivision" of property, and therefore did not trigger property tax reassessment).

14. Cal. Gov't Code § 66424 (West 1997 & Supp. 2002).

15. Planning Bd. v. Michaud, 444 A.2d 40 (Me. 1982) (conversion of seasonal-transient campground to quasi-permanent multiple occupancy); Town of Tuftonboro v. Lakeside Colony, Inc., 119 N.H. 445, 403 A.2d 410, 411 (1979) (conversion of a seasonal-cottage colony held a subdivision of real estate); People v. Grundy County Natl. Bank, 97 Ill. App. 3d 101, 52 Ill. Dec. 646, 422 N.E.2d 648 (1981) (conversion of a mobile-trailer park into condominiums).

16. Town of Windham v. Lawrence Sav. Bank, 776 A.2d 730, 734–35 (N.H. 2001).

17. *See, e.g.*, Alaska Stat. § 40.15.010 *et seq.* (Michie 2000 & Supp. 2001); Cal. Gov't Code § 66410 *et seq.* (West 1997 & Supp. 2002); Ky. Rev. Stat. § 100.273 *et seq.* (Michie 1993 & Supp. 2001); Md. Code Ann. Art. 66B, § 5.01 *et seq.* (2001); Minn. Stat. Ann. § 462.358 *et seq.* (West 2001); Mo. Rev. Stat. § 89.400 *et seq.* (1998); Tenn. Code Ann. § 13-3-403 (1998 & Supp. 2001), *construed in* Lake County v. Truett, 758 S.W.2d 529 (Tenn. Ct. App. 1988).

18. *See e.g.*, Ky. Rev. Stat. § 100.281(1) & (2). (Michie 1993 & Supp. 2001).

19. *See, e.g.*, Conn. Gen. Stat. § 8-26 (2001); Mo. Rev. Stat. § 89.410 (1998 & Supp. 2001).

20. *See, e.g.*, Md. Code Ann. Art. 66B, § 5.03 (1995 & Supp. 2001); Conn. Gen. Stat. § 8-26 2001; Town of Southington v. Commercial Union Ins. Co., 254 Conn. 348, 358–60, 757 A.2d 549, 556–57 (2000) (town has discretion to call bond upon default even if no lots have been conveyed).

21. *See, e.g.*, Minn. Stat. Ann. § 462.358 (West 2001).

22. *Id.*

23. *See, e.g.*, Ky. Rev. Stat. Ann. § 100.281(4) & (5) (Michie 1993 & Supp. 2001); Minn. Stat. Ann. § 462.358 (West 2001); Mo. Rev. Stat. § 89.410 (1998 & Supp. 2001).

24. *See generally* pp. 346–49.

25. 652 P.2d 471 (Alaska 1982).

26. *Id.* at 473.

27. Coffee v. Maryland-Nat'l. Capital Park & Planning Comm'n., 441 A.2d 1041, 1043–44 (Md. Ct. App. 1982), quoting Shoptaugh v. County Comm'rs, 37 Colo. App. 39, 41–42, 543 P.2d 524 (1975) ("subdivider must first meet the zoning regulations and then additionally must comply with the state and county subdivision regulations").

28. Camp v. Mendocino County Bd. of Supervisors, 123 Cal. App. 3d 334, 358–59, 176 Cal. Rptr. 620 (1981).

29. Standard City Planning Enabling Act, § 12 (Dept. of Commerce 1928), *reproduced as* ALI Model Land Development Code, app. B (Tentative Draft No. 1, 1988).

30. Standard City Planning Enabling Act, § 12 n. 62 (Dept. of Commerce 1928).

31. American Planning Association, Growing Smart^SM Legislative Guidebook: Model Statutes for Planning and the Management of Change 8–61 (Stuart Meck ed., 2002), citing Ky. Rev. Stats. §§ 100.273 to 100.292; N.J. Rev. Stat. Ch. 55D, Art. 6; R.I. Gen. Laws, tit. 45, ch. 23.

32. *Id.*

33. St. Louis County Subdivision Ord. § 1005.030 (adopted April 25, 1985).

34. *Id.* § 1005.110.

35. *See, e.g., id.* § 1005.0705.

36. *See, e.g.*, City of San Marcos v. R. W. McDonald Dev. Corp., 700 S.W.2d 674 (Tex. Ct. App. 1985), *reh'g denied.*

37. *See, e.g.*, Tex. Loc. Gov't Code Ann. § 212.009 (Vernon 1998 & Supp. 2002).

38. Precision Sheet Metal Mfg. Co. v. Yates, 794 S.W.2d 545 (Tex. Ct. App. 1990), *writ denied* (cause of action for equitable rescission stated).

39. Lemm Dev. Corp. v. Town of Bartlett, 580 A.2d 1082, 1084 (N.H. 1990) (subdivision regulations may not be used to regulate construction of amenities in common area of condominium prior to application for building permit).

40. *See* pp. 355–58.

41. St. Louis County Subdivision Ord. § 1005.050.1, available at http://www.co.st-louis.mo.us/plan/zoning/index.html.

42. *Id.* § 1005.060.1.

43. *Id.* § 1005.060.1(a).

44. *Id.* § 1005.060.4(d).

45. *Id.* § 1005.070.5(a).

46. *Id.* § 1005.090.9(a)–(l).

47. *Id.* § 1005.110.

48. The filing fee on the date of enactment of the ordinance was $50. St. Louis County Subdivision Ord., § 1005.370 (1985). In 2002, the filing fee was $300 for a preliminary plat and $50 for a lot-split.

49. *Id.* § 1005.110.3.(b) (1985).

50. *Id.* § 1005.110.3.(c) (1985).

51. Ahearn v. Town of Wheatland, 39 P.3d 409, 416–19 (Wyo. 2002).

52. Appeal of Windjammer Hospitality, 772 A.2d 536, 538–39 (Vt. 2001).

53. *See, e.g.* Mass. Ann. Laws ch. 41, § 81L (1993 & Supp. 2002) (planning board); Mo. Rev. Stat. § 89.020 (2001) (legislative body).

54. *See, e.g.* McElderry v. Planning Bd. of Nantucket, 431 Mass. 722, 726–27, 729 N.E.2d 1090, 1093–94 (2000) (affirmative vote of majority of planning board members required for approval).

55. York v. Town of Ogunquist, 769 A.2d 172, 176–78 (Me. 2001).

56. 41 Wash. App. 402, 704 P.2d 663 (1985), *rev. denied*, 104 Wash. 2d 1020 (1985).

57. *Id.* at 665 ("Arbitrary and capricious" was defined as "willful and unreasoning action, without consideration and in disregard of the facts and circumstances").

58. *Id.* at 666.

59. Winslow v. Town of Holderness Planning Bd., 125 N.H. 262, 268–69, 480 A.2d 114, 117 (1984).

60. *Id.* at 116.

61. *Id.* at 117.

62. Southern Co-op. Dev. Fund v. Driggers, 696 F.2d 1347 (11th Cir. 1983) (citing Broward County v. Narco Realty Co., 359 So. 2d 509 (Fla. Dist. Ct. App. 1978) as holding that under Florida law discretion of local officials to approve or disapprove subdivision applications "vanished" when petitioner had "done all the law required of him to entitle his plat to be recorded"). *See* State *ex rel.* Schaefer v. E.C. Cleveland, 847 S.W.2d 867, 873 (Mo. Ct. App. 1992) (held that the city planning and zoning commission and city council lacked the authority to deny a subdivision plat that complied with the subdivision ordinance).

63. Vartuli v. Sotire, 192 Conn. 353, 472 A.2d 336 (1984) (65 days for coastal site-plan review), *overruled by* Leo Fedus & Sons Constr. Co., Inc. v. Zoning Bd. of Appeals of Town and Borough of Colchester, 623 A.2d 1007 (Conn. 1993).

64. Kenai Peninsula Borough v. Kenai Peninsula Bd. of Realtors, 652 P.2d 471, 473 (Alaska 1982).

65. 726 S.W.2d 500, 502 (Mo. Ct. App. 1987).

66. *Id.* at 503.

67. *See* pp. 341–44.

68. *See, e.g.,* Sederquist v. City of Tiburon, 765 F.2d 756, 758 (9th Cir. 1985) (remanded for determination whether additional requirement that landowners obtain consent of neighbors for a master plan as a condition for approval of their subdivision application constituted illegal requirement for "joint action").

69. *See, e.g.,* Howard v. Village of Elm Grove, 80 Wis. 2d 33, 257 N.W.2d 850, 853 (1977) (rezoning of portions of a subdivision upheld as valid exercise of police power).

70. *See* pp. 346–49.

71. *See, e.g.,* City of San Marcos v. R. W. McDonald Dev. Corp., 700 S.W.2d 674, 676 (Tex. App. 1985) (compliance with hillside soil-erosion ordinance a condition precedent to final plat approval).

72. *See, e.g.,* Howard v. Village of Elm Grove, 80 Wis. 2d 33, 257 N.W.2d 850, 853 (1977) (failure to comply with requirements that all roads be completed within six months and that deed restrictions subjecting development to architectural and landscaping controls be imposed would activate automatic repealer of rezoning and plat approval).

73. *See, e.g.,* N.J. STAT. ANN. § 40:55D-42 (West 1991 & Supp. 2002) (authorizing municipalities to require developers to pay pro rata share of "reasonable and necessary" off-site improvements, *construed in* New Jersey Builders Ass'n v. Bernards Township, 108 N.J. 223, 528 A.2d 555 (1987)); TEX. LOC. GOV'T CODE ANN. § 395.011 (Vernon 1999 & Supp. 2002) (authorizing Texas municipalities to impose impact fees on new development); Associated Home Builders v. City of Walnut Creek, 4 Cal. 3d 633, 94 Cal. Rptr. 630, 484 P.2d 606 (1971) (construing statute authorizing mandatory land dedication or in-lieu fees as conditions to subdivision approval); Jenad, Inc. v. Village of Scarsdale, 18 N.Y.2d 78, 271 N.Y.S.2d 955, 218 N.E.2d 673 (1966) (statutory authority to require dedication of park land includes power to authorize in-lieu fee), *criticized by* Dolan v. City of Tigard, 512 U.S. 374, 389–90 (1994) (noting disapproval of lax standard of allowing "very generalized statements" to suffice about the connection between required dedication and proposed development).

See generally James E. Holloway and Donald C. Guy, *Land Dedication Conditions and Beyond the Essential Nexus: Determining "Reasonably Related" Impact of Real Estate Development Under the Takings Clause,* 27 TEX. TECH. L. REV. 73 (1996); A. Dan Tarlock, *Local Government Protection of Biodiversity: What Is Its Niche?,* 60 U. CHI. L. REV. 555, 598–602 (1993) (discussing biodiversity impact fees); Vicki Been, *"Exit" as a Constraint on Land Use Exactions: Rethinking the Unconstitutional Conditions Doctrine,* 91 COLUM. L. REV. 473 (1991); Wm. Terry Bray, David S. Caudill, & Jack E. Owen, Jr., *New Wave Land Use Regulation: The Impact of Impact Fees on Texas Lenders,* 19 ST. MARY'S L.J. 319 (1987); Donald L. Connors & Michael E. High, *The Expanding Circle of Exactions: From Dedication to Linkage,* 50 LAW & CONTEMP. PROBS. 69 (1987).

74. *See, e.g.,* City of Montgomery v. Crossroads Land Co., 355 So. 2d 363 (Ala. 1978), *discussed in* Bray, Caudill, & Owen, *New Wave Land Use Regulation: The Impact of Impact Fees on Texas Lenders,* 19 ST. MARY'S L.J. 319, 331 (1987) (parkland dedication or in-lieu fee).

75. *See, e.g.,* Call. v. City of West Jordan, 606 P.2d 217, 219–20 (Utah 1979) *(Call. I)* (ordinance imposing land dedication or in-lieu fee is "within the scope of authority and responsibility of the city government" when planning, zoning, and subdivision regulation enabling statutes "are viewed together"). *See also* Black v. City of Waukesha, 125 Wis. 2d 254, 371 N.W.2d 389, 390 (Ct. App. 1985) (citing Jordan v. Village of Menomonee Falls, 28 Wis. 2d 608, 615, 137 N.W.2d 442, 446 (1965), *appeal dismissed,* 385 U.S. 4 (1966) (subdivision regulation and zoning enabling statutes held to authorize land dedication and in-lieu fee conditions)); Savonick v. Township of Lawrence, 91 N.J. Super. 288, 219 A.2d 902, 906 (Law Div. 1966), *discussed in* John J. Delaney, Larry A. Gordon, & Kathryn J. Hess, *The Needs-Nexus Analysis: A Unified Test for Validating Subdivision Exactions, User Impact Fees and Linkage,* 50 LAW & CONTEMP. PROBS. 139, 146–47 (1987). *See generally* Bray, Caudill, & Owen, *New Wave Land Use Regulation: The Impact of Impact Fees on Texas Lenders,* 19 ST. MARY'S L.J. 319, 331–32 (1987).

76. City of Coppell v. General Homes Corp., 763 S.W.2d 448, 457 (Tex. App. 1988).

77. Call. v. City of West Jordan, 727 P.2d 180, 182–83 (Utah 1986) *(Call. III)*.

78. *See, e.g.,* City of San Marcos v. R. W. McDonald Dev. Corp., 700 S.W.2d 674, 677 (Tex. Ct. App. 1985), *reh'g denied. See generally* the discussion of vested rights on pp. 353–55.

79. Village Square No. 1, Inc. v. Crow-Frederick Retail Ltd. P'ship, 77 Md. App. 552, 551 A.2d 471, 475 (1989) (distinguishing special-benefit assessment).

80. Batch v. Town of Chapel Hill, 92 N.C. App. 601, 376 S.E.2d 22, 30 (1989) (quoting Ducker, *"Taking" Found for Beach Dedication Requirement,* 30 Loc. Gov't L. Bull. 2 (1987)).

81. 108 N.J. 223, 528 A.2d 555, 558–60 (1987).

82. *Id.* at 588 (citing Connors & High, *The Expanding Circle of Exactions: From Dedication to Linkage,* 50 Law & Contemp. Probs. 70 (1987)).

83. *Id.* at 558 (citing R. Marlin Smith, *From Subdivision Requirements to Community Benefit Assessments and Linkage Payments: A Brief History of Land Development Exactions,* 50 Law & Contemp. Probs. 5, 7–8 (1987)).

84. *Id.* at 558 (citing City of College Station v. Turtle Rock Corp., 680 S.W.2d 802 (Tex. 1984) (dedication of one acre per 133 houses, or payment in lieu, for neighborhood park purposes upheld)); Aunt Hack Ridge Estates v. Planning Comm'n, 160 Conn. 109, 273 A.2d 880 (1970) (dedication of 4 percent of subdivision but not less than 10,000 square feet for recreational use upheld); Jenad, Inc. v. Village of Scarsdale, 18 N.Y.2d 78, 218 N.E.2d 673, 271 N.Y.S.2d 955 (1966) (dedication of land, or payment of $250 per lot, for park purposes upheld); Jordan v. Village of Menomonee Falls, 28 Wis. 2d 608, 137 N.W.2d 442 (1965) (payment of $200 per lot, or dedication of land of equal value, for school, park, and recreational purposes upheld). *Contra* Pioneer Trust v. Village of Mt. Prospect, 22 Ill. 2d 375, 176 N.E.2d 799 (1961) (dedication of one acre per 60 housing units for public use invalid).

85. New Jersey Builders Ass'n v. Bernards Township, 108 N.J. 223, 528 A.2d 555, 558 (1987), quoting Currier, *Legal and Practical Problems Associated with Drafting Impact Fee Ordinances,* 1984 Inst. on Planning, Zoning and Eminent Domain 273–74, and citing Contractors & Builders Ass'n v. City of Dunedin, 329 So. 2d 314, 320 (Fla. 1976) (impact fee for water and sewer services justified if expansion is reasonably required and "use of the money collected is limited to meeting the cost of expansion"), *amended ordinance upheld,* City of Dunedin v. Contractors & Builders Ass'n, 358 So. 2d 846 (Fla.), *cert. denied,* 370 So. 2d 458 (Fla.), *cert. denied,* 444 U.S. 867 (1979); Hollywood, Inc. v. Broward County, 431 So. 2d 606 (Fla. Dist. Ct. App.), *rev. denied,* 440 So. 2d 352 (Fla. 1983) (land dedication or fee payment to assist county in developing park system upheld); Broward County v. Janis Dev. Corp., 311 So. 2d 371 (Fla. Dist. Ct. App. 1975) (impact fee for road-improvement purposes invalidated because of lack of standards governing expenditure of funds); Home Builders & Contractors Ass'n v. Bd. of County Commr's, 446 So. 2d 140, 143–44 (Fla. Dist. Ct. App. 1983), *rev. denied,* 451 So. 2d 848 (Fla.), *appeal dismissed,* 469 U.S. 976 (1984) (impact fee for road construction required by increased traffic from new developments, administered through creation of 40 zones and corresponding trust funds within the county and requirement that funds collected from development could be expended only within zone where development was located, upheld "as long as the fee does not exceed the cost of the improvements required by the new development and the improvements adequately benefit the development which is the source of the fee"). *See generally* James A. Kushner, *Property and Mysticism: The Legality of Exactions as a Condition for Public Development Approval in the Time of the Rehnquist Court,* 8 J. Land Use & Envtl. L. 53 (1992) (analyzes recent Supreme Court decisions).

86. New Jersey Builders Ass'n v Bernards Township, 108 N.J. 223, 528 A.2d 555, 558 (1987) (citing J. W. Jones Cos. v. City of San Diego, 157 Cal. App. 3d 745, 203 Cal. Rptr. 580 (1984)) ($27 million assessment on undeveloped parcels to cover half the cost of street and park improvements serving the area of the city assessed upheld).

87. *Id*. at 558 (citing Jerold S. Kayden & Robert Pollard, *Linkage Ordinances and Traditional Exactions Analysis: The Connection Between Office Development and Housing*, 50 LAW & CONTEMP. PROBS. 127 (1987)).

88. *Id*. at 560.

89. N.J. STAT. ANN. § 40:55D-42 (West 1991 & Supp. 2002).

90. New Jersey Builders Ass'n v. Bernards Township, 108 N.J. 223, 528 A.2d 555, 562 (1987). *See also* Berry v. Town of Danvers, 34 Mass. App. Ct. 507, 613 N.E.2d 108 (1993), where a Sewer Connection Permit Program (SCPP) increasing a $10 flat-rate connection fee to a $4 fee per gallon of sewage to be discharged daily for all landowners thereafter seeking to connect or increase usage was held an unlawful tax. Implemented to benefit the town's entire sewer system, the SCPP fees were not reasonably related to the system improvements necessitated by the connectors charged with the fees. In Lexington-Fayette Urban County Gov't v. F.W. Schneider, 849 S.W.2d 557 (Ky. Ct. App. 1992), a planning commission's conditioning of a zone change on construction of a bridge was held arbitrary and capricious by the Court of Appeals of Kentucky because the bridge did not constitute "additional public facilities made necessary by the development."

91. Price Dev. Co. v. Redev. Agency, 852 F.2d 1123 (9th Cir. 1988) (construing Cal. Subdivision Map Act, CAL. GOV'T CODE §§ 66410 to 66499.58 (West 1997)).

92. WASH. REV. CODE ANN. § 43.-21C.060 (West 1998 & Supp. 2002).

93. Prisk v. City of Poulsbo, 46 Wash. App. 793, 732 P.2d 1013, 1018–19 (1987), *rev. denied*, 108 Wash. 2d 1020 (1987) (citing Hillis Homes, Inc. v Snohomish County, 97 Wash. 2d. 804, 650 P.2d 193 (1982) (subdivision regulation statute does not give authority to require payment of fees in lieu of dedication of land as condition of subdivision approval)). *See also* City of Jonesboro v. Vuncannon, 837 S.W.2d 286 (Ark. 1992) (requirement of dedication of street right-of-way invalidated as not authorized by Arkansas statute, which only gave planning commission authority to implement a master street plan and which also expressly contemplated condemnation of roadways).

94. *See, e.g.*, Hillis Homes, Inc. v. Snohomish County, 97 Wash. 2d 804, 650 P.2d 193 (1982) (authority to impose land dedication for public facilities as condition to subdivision approval insufficient authority for imposition of taxes through developer fees), superseded by WASH. REV. CODE ANN. § 82.02.020 (as amended in 1982), rule stated in Ivy Club Investors v. City of Kennewick, 699 P.2d 782, 785–86 (Wash. App. 1985) (noting that § 82.02.020 overrules *Hillis* decision that governmental bodies have no express authority to impose a development fee or tax as a condition of subdivision approval). *But compare* San Telmo Assocs. v. City of Seattle, 735 P.2d 673 (Wash. 1987) (held unconstitutional an ordinance that required developer to construct low-income housing or contribute to fund for such housing as a tax on a limited number of property owners) with Southwick, Inc. v. City of Lacey, 795 P.2d 712 (Wash. Ct. App. 1990) (holding city council's imposition of site-specific conditions on proposed development were not unauthorized exaction of tax, fee, or charge).

95. *See* chapter 9.

96. Holmdel Builders Assn. v. Township of Holmdel, 232 N.J. Super. 182, 556 A.2d 1236, 1242 (App. Div. 1989), *aff'd in part, rev'd in part*, 121 N.J. 550, 582 A.2d 277 (1990).

97. Brewster v. City of Pocatello, 115 Idaho 502, 768 P.2d 765, 767 (1989).

98. Mooney v. City of Laconia, 133 N.H. 30, 573 A.2d 447 (1990).

99. John M. Payne, *From the Courts: Development Fee Developments*, 17 REAL EST. L.J. 71, 75 (1988).

100. WASH. REV. CODE ANN. § 82.02.020 (West 2000 & Supp. 2002).

101. TEX. LOC. GOV'T CODE § 395.001 *et seq.* (Vernon 1999 & Supp. 2002).

102. *Id*. § 2(c).

103. *Id*. §§ 1(2) & (4)(B).

104. *Id*. § 2(d)(1).

105. *Id.* § 1(10).

106. *Id.* § 2(2).

107. *Id.* § 3.

108. *Id.* §§ 4 & 5.

109. *Id.* § 6.

110. *Id.* § 8.

111. *Id.* § 8(f).

112. *Id.* § 9.

113. Bray, Caudill, & Owen, *New Wave Land Use Regulation: The Impact of Impact Fees on Texas Lenders,* 19 St. Mary's L.J. 319, 345 (1989). *See also* SB 361, 41st Leg., 1993 New Mexico Laws Ch. 122 (SB 361) New Mexico Housing-Development Fees Act (enacted April 1993) (authorizing New Mexico municipalities to impose impact fees under certain conditions). The impact-fee bill, drafted by the state homebuilders' association, was partly patterned after Texas law and was designed to facilitate historic preservation and to spawn revitalization efforts along New Mexico's segment of U.S. Route 66. The fees authorized to be assessed on new development may be used to fund public needs, such as improved transportation, water, and sewer upgrades and emergency services programs. *News of Planning Initiatives and APA Lobbying Efforts,* 59 Am. Plan. Ass'n 5 (May 1993).

114. Ga. Code Ann. § 36-71-1 *et seq.* (2000).

115. ACIR, *Georgia Becomes Seventh State to Legislate Development Impact Fees,* Intergovernmental Perspective 23 (Fall 1990).

116. *See* Thomas G. Pelham, *Adequate Public Facilities Requirements: Reflections on Florida's Concurrency System for Managing Growth,* 19 Fla. St. L. Rev. 973 (1992). *See* pp. 28–34.

117. *See, e.g.,* Ariz. Rev. Stat. § 9-463.05 (1996) (development fees); Cal. Gov't Code § 66000 *et seq.* (West 1997); Colo. Rev. Stat. Ann. § 29-1-801 *et seq.* (2001); Del. Code Ann. tit. 17, § 101 *et seq.* (1996); Ga. Code Ann. § 36-71-1 (2000); Haw. Rev. Stat. Ann. § 46-141 (Michie 2001); Idaho Code § 67-8201 (Michie 2001); 605 Ill. Comp. Stat. 5/1-101 *et seq.* (1993); Ind. Code Ann. § 36-7-4-1300 (Michie 1999); Me. Rev. Stat. tit. 30-A, § 4354 (West 1996); Md. Code Ann. Art. 25B, § 13D (2001) (development impact fees); Nev. Rev. Stat. Ch. 278B (2001); N.H. Rev. Stat. Ann. § 674.21 (1996); N.J. Stat. Ann. § 40:55D-42 (West 1991); N.M. Stat. Ann. § 5-8-1 (Michie 2001); Or. Rev. Stat. § 223.205–295 (2001); Pa. Stat. Ann. tit. 53, § 10502-A *et seq.* (West 1997); Tex. Loc. Gov't Code Ann. § 395.001 *et seq.* (Vernon 1999); Va. Code Ann. § 15.2-2317 to 2327 (Michie 1997); Vt. Stat. Ann. tit. 24, § 5200 *et seq.* (1992); Wash. Rev. Code Ann. § 82-02-090 (West 2000); W.Va. Code Ann. § 7-20-1 *et seq.* (Michie 2000); Wis. Stat. Ann. § 66.55 (West 1999).

These statutes are discussed in NAHB Research Center, Impact Fees and the Role of the State: Guidance for Drafting Legislation (1993). *See also* Martin L. Leitner & Susan P. Schoettle, *A Survey of State Impact Fee Enabling Legislation,* 25 Urb. Law. 491 (1993); Brian W. Blaesser & Christine M. Kentopp, *Impact Fees: The "Second Generation,"* 38 Wash. U. J. Urb. & Contemp. L. 55 (1990).

118. Nollan v. California Coastal Comm'n, 483 U.S. 825 (1987); Dolan v. City of Tigard, 512 U.S. 374 (1994). Both cases are discusssed in chapter 3 *supra.*

119. Ehrlich v. City of Culver City, 911 P.2d 429, 433 (Cal. 1996).

120. *Id.* at 442, quoting *Dolan,* 512 U.S. at 391.

121. *Nollan*—lateral access easement across beach area; *Dolan*—easement for bike trail across real property. *See also* Curtis v. Town of South Thomaston, 708 A.2d 657, 659–60 (Me. 1998) (applying *Nollan* and *Dolan* in upholding easement dedication requirement for fire pond).

122. Commercial Builders of N. California v. City of Sacramento, 941 F.2d. 872 (9th Cir. 1991).

123. *Id.* at 873–74.

124. *Id.* at 876.

125. 911 P.2d 429 (Cal. 1996).

126. *Id.* at 444.

127. *Id.* at 448–50.

128. *Id.* at 447, 450 (requirement to provide either art or a cash equivalent is a reasonable aesthetic regulation similar to building setbacks, parking and lighting conditions, landscaping requirements, and other design conditions).

129. *Id.* at 454–55.

130. Homebuilders Ass'n of Central Arizona v. City of Scottsdale, 930 P.2d 993 (Ariz. 1997).

131. Krupp v. Breckenridge Sanitation Dist., 19 P.3d 687, 698 (Colo 2001).

132. Northern Illinois Home Builders Ass'n v. County of DuPage, 165 Ill. 2d. 25, 208 Ill. Dec. 328, 649 N.E.2d 384 (1995).

133. McCarthy v. City of Leawood, 257 Kan. 566, 894 P.2d 836 (1995).

134. Waters v. Montgomery County, 650 A.2d 712 (Md. 1994).

135. *Dolan*, 512 U.S. at 391. *See* Robert H. Freilich & David W. Bushek, eds., Exactions, Impact Fees & Dedications: Shaping Land-Use Development and Funding Infrastructure in the Dolan Era (1995); Daniel J. Curtin & Adam V. Lingren, *Impact Fees after Dolan— Ehrlich v. City of Culver*, ABA State & Loc. L. News, vol. 19, no. 4, p. 3 (Summer 1996).

136. *Northern Illinois Home Builders*, 649 N.E.2d at 388–90.

137. *McCarthy*, 894 P.2d at 845.

138. *Waters*, 650 A.2d at 724.

139. Home Builders Ass'n v. City of Beavercreek, 729 N.E.2d 349, 356 (Ohio 2000).

140. Dolan v. City of Tigard, 512 U.S. 374, 389–91 (1994) (reviewing cases).

141. *Id.* at 389 (citing Pioneer Trust & Sav. Bank v. Mount Prospect, 22 Ill. 2d 375, 176 N.E.2d 799 (1961)).

142. *Id.* at 389 (citing Billings Props., Inc. v. Yellowstone County, 394 P.2d 182 (Mont. 1964); Jenad, Inc. v. Scarsdale, 218 N.E.2d 673 (N.Y. 1966), *criticized by* Dolan v. City of Tigard, 512 U.S. 374, 389–90 (1994) (noting disapproval of lax standard of allowing "very generalized statements" to suffice about the connection between required dedication and proposed development).

143. *Id.* at 390–91 (citing Simpson v. North Platte, 292 N.W.2d 297 (Neb. 1980); Jordan v. Menomonee Falls, 137 N.W.2d 442 (Wis. 1966); Collis v. Bloomington, 246 N.W.2d 19 (Minn. 1976); College Station v. Turtle Rock Corp., 680 S.W.2d 802 (Tex. 1984); Call v. West Jordan, 606 P.2d 217 (Utah 1979).

144. Fred P. Bosselman & Nancy G. Stroud, *Mandatory Tithes: The Legality of Land Development Linkage*, 9 Nova L.J. 381, 397–98 (1985). *See also* Thomas W. Ledman, *Local Governmental Environmental Mitigation Fees: Development Exactions, The Next Generation*, 45 Fla. L. Rev. 835 (1993).

145. 512 U.S. 374 (1994).

146. 512 U.S. at 391.

147. Village Square No. 1, Inc. v. Crow-Frederick Retail Ltd. P'ship, 77 Md. App. 552, 551 A.2d 471 (1989).

148. *Id.* at 475.

149. *Id.* at 476–77. *But cf.* Morris v. Prince George's County, 319 Md. 597, 573 A.2d 1346, 1349, n. 3 (1990) (criticizing the court's "rigid approach" in applying the plain meaning rule).

150. *Id.* at 477.

151. Contractors & Builders Assoc. of Pinellas County v. City of Dunedin, 329 So. 2d 314 (Fla. 1976), *on remand*, 330 So. 2d 744 (Fla. Dist. Ct. App. 1976) (applied to uphold impact fees in St. John's County, Fla. v. Northeast Florida Builders Ass'n., Inc., 583 So. 2d 635 (Fla. 1991)).

152. *St. John's County, Fla.*, 583 So. 2d at 638.

153. Volusia County v. Aberdeen at Ormond Beach, L.P., 760 So. 2d 126, 134–36 (Fla. 2000) (adults-only community does not increase the need for new schools).

154. N.H. Rev. Stat. Ann. § 674.21 (1996 & Supp. 2001). *See also* Ind. Code Ann. § 36-7-4-1321 (Burns 1997 & Supp. 2002).

155. Banberry Dev. Corp. v. South Jordan City, 631 P.2d 899, 904 (Utah 1981).

156. Homebuilders Ass'n of Utah v. City of Am. Fork, 973 P.2d 425, 430–31 (Utah 1999).

157. 732 P.2d 1013 (Wash. Ct. App.), *rev. denied,* 108 Wash. 2d 1020 (1987).

158. Wash. Rev. Code Ann. § 58.17.100 (West 1990 & Supp. 2002).

159. Prisk, 732 P.2d at 1018. *See also* R/L Assocs., Inc. v. City of Seattle, 113 Wash. 2d 402, 410, 780 P.2d 838 (1989) (construing statute prohibiting local government from imposing taxes, fees, or charges as conditions to building construction or land subdivision and concluding that a requirement to pay relocation assistance as a condition to receipt of a demolition license was invalid); Cobb v. Snohomish County, 64 Wash. App. 451, 829 P.2d 169 (1991), *rev. denied,* 119 Wash. 2d 1012, 833 P.2d 386 (1992) (statute permits voluntary agreements between developers and municipalities for payment of traffic impact fees as long as municipality can show that road improvements are "reasonably necessary" to mitigate direct impact of the development).

160. Wash. Rev. Code Ann. § 43.21C.060 (West 1998 & Supp. 2002).

161. *Prisk,* 732 P.2d at 1019.

162. *Id.* at 1018.

163. *Id. See also* Ford v. Georgetown County Water & Sewer Dist., 341 S.C. 10, 532 S.E.2d 873 (2000) (water and sewer connection fees and service charges were valid charges for services received and not unconstitutional taxes); Black v. City of Waukesha, 125 Wis. 2d 254, 371 N.W.2d 389 (Ct. App. 1985) (unsuccessful challenge to validity of school land and park land dedication fees as a condition of the securing of a building permit where state statute authorized such fees), citing Jordan v. Village of Monomonee Falls, 28 Wis. 2d 608, 615, 137 N.W.2d 442, 446 (1965), *appeal dismissed,* 385 U.S. 4 (1966).

164. *See, e.g.,* Burley Lagoon Improvement Ass'n v. Pierce County, 38 Wash. App. 534, 868 P.2d 503, 505 (1984) (citing Allenbach v. City of Tukwila, 101 Wash. 2d 193, 676 P.2d 473 (1984)).

165. Avco Cmty. Devs. Inc. v. South Coast Reg'l Comm'n, 17 Cal. 3d 785, 132 Cal. Rptr. 386, 553 P.2d 546, 550 (1976); Schubiner v. West Bloomfield Township, 133 Mich. App. 490, 351 N.W.2d 214, 219 (1984) (permit to commence operations is the sine qua non for obtaining "vested rights").

166. Schubiner v. West Bloomfeld Township, 133 Mich. App. 490, 351 N.W.2d 214, 219 (1984).

167. 6 Cal. App. 4th 1781, 8 Cal. Rptr. 2d 762, *rev. denied* (1992).

168. *Id.* at 1810. *See also, In re* Vermont Nat'l Bank, 597 A.2d 317 (Vt. 1991); Kasparek v. Johnson County Bd. of Health, 288 N.W.2d 511, 518–20 (Iowa 1980). For a contrary result, *see* Town of Stephens City v. Russell, 241 Va. 160, 165, 399 S.E.2d 814 (1991), holding that the developer acquired no vested right in existing zoning or a pending site plan, upholding the city's rezoning while the site plan was pending, where the developer had been issued no site-plan approval or building permit.

169. Avco Cmty. Devs., Inc. v. South Coast Reg'l Comm'n, 17 Cal. 3d 785, 553 P.2d 546, 550, 132 Cal. Rptr. 386 (1976); Burley Lagoon Improvement Ass'n v. Pierce County, 38 Wash. App. 534, 686 P.2d 503, 506 (1984).

170. Avco Cmty. Devs., *supra* n. 155. *See also* Winnaman v. Cambria Cmty. Servs. Dist., 208 Cal. App. 3d 49, 256 Cal. Rptr. 40, 44 (1989) (language of water and sewer connection fee ordinance prevented requisite good faith reliance necessary for accrual of vested rights).

171. Allenbach v. City of Tukwila, 101 Wash. 2d 193, 676 P.2d 473 (1984).

172. *Id.* at 475–76 (quoting Hull v. Hunt, 53 Wash. 2d 125, 331 P.2d 856 (1958) and State ex rel. Ogden v. Bellevue, 45 Wash. 2d 492, 275 P.2d 899 (1954)).

173. WASH. REV. CODE ANN. § 58.17.033 (West 1990 & Supp. 2002).

174. Ass'n of Rural Residents v. Kitsap County, 141 Wash. 2d 185, 193–95, 4 P.3d 115, 119–20 (2000) (preliminary plat and PUD proposal vested on the date of application).

175. *See, e.g.,* Youngblood v. Bd. of Supervisors, 22 Cal. 3d 644, 655–56, 150 Cal. Rptr. 242, 586 P.2d 556 (1978).

176. *See, e.g.,* Tosh v. California Coastal Comm'n, 99 Cal. App. 3d 388, 160 Cal. Rptr. 170, 173–74 (1979) (scenic easement condition to tentative subdivision approval not met prior to effective date of coastal regulations, preventing vested rights from accruing).

177. 171 Cal. App. 3d 1020, 217 Cal. Rptr. 849 (1985).

178. Briarwood Props. v. City of Los Angeles, 171 Cal. App. 3d 1020, 217 Cal. Rptr. 849, 854 (1985) (quoting Santa Monica Pines, Ltd. v. Rent Control Bd., 35 Cal. 3d 858, 201 Cal. Rptr. 593, 679 P.2d 27 (1984)).

179. Briarwood Props. v. City of Los Angeles, 171 Cal. App. 3d 1020, 217 Cal. Rptr. 849, 854 (1985). *But see* Channing Props. v. City of Berkeley, 14 Cal. Rptr. 2d 32 (Cal. App. 1992).

180. Carlson v. Town of Beaux Arts Village, 41 Wash. App. 402, 704 P.2d 663, 665 (1985) (citing Norco Const, Inc. v. King County, 97 Wash. 2d 680, 649 P.2d 103 (1982)).

181. County of Kauai v. Pacific Standard Life Ins. Co., 65 Haw. 318, 653 P.2d 766 (1982), *quoted in* Kaiser Dev. Co. v. City & County of Honolulu, 649 F. Supp. 926, 938 (D. Haw. 1986).

182. County of Kauai v. Pacific Standard Life Ins. Co., 65 Haw. 318, 327, 653 P.2d 766 (1982).

183. Kaiser Dev. Co. v. City & County of Honolulu, 649 F. Supp. 926, 937–38, 949 (D. Haw. 1986).

184. *See, e.g.,* Lehman v. City of Louisville, 967 F.2d 1474 (10th Cir. 1992), *related proceeding,* 857 P.2d 455 (Colo. Ct. App. 1992), *cert. denied,* 1993 Colo. LEXIS 710 (1993).

185. 915 F.2d 1290 (9th Cir. 1990), *cert. denied,* 501 U.S. 1251 (1991).

186. *Id.* at 1295.

187. *Id. See also* G.J.Z. Enters., Inc. v. City of Troy, 566 N.E.2d 876 (Ill. App. Ct. 1991) (upholding an injunction against enforcement of a city's stop-work order after the city learned that it had mistakenly issued the building permit, when 70 percent of a developer's apartment complex was complete).

188. *See, e.g.,* N.J. STAT. ANN. § 40:55D-37.

189. Lionel's Appliance Ctr., Inc. v. Citta, 156 N.J. Super. 257, 383 A.2d 773, 778 (Law Div. 1978).

190. *See, e.g.,* T.L.C. Dev., Inc. v. Planning & Zoning Comm'n, 215 Conn. 527, 577 A.2d 288, 289 (1990) (site-plan review authorized by statute "to aid in determining the conformity of a proposed building use or structure with specific provisions of [zoning] regulations").

191. Town of Johnston v. Pezza, 723 A.2d 278, 282 (R.I. 1999).

192. Kozesnik v. Montgomery Township, 24 N.J. 154, 131 A.2d 1 (1957).

193. N.J. STAT. ANN. §§ 40:55D-37 to –58 (West 1991 & Supp. 2002).

194. *Id.* § 40:55D-37.

195. *Id.*

196. *Id.* § 40:55D-7. For a history of a site-plan review in New Jersey, see Lionel's Appliance Ctr., Inc. v. Citta, 156 N.J. Super. 257, 383 A.2d 773, 776–79 (Law Div. 1978).

197. N.J. STAT. ANN. § 40:55D-41 (West 1991 & Supp. 2002).

198. *Id.* § 40:55D-38.

199. *See* pp. 346–49.

200. N.J. STAT. ANN. §§ 40:55D-39 (West 1991 & Supp. 2002).

201. *Id.* § 40:55D-39. *See generally* chapter 4.

202. N.J. Site Improvement Standards Act, L. 1993, c. 32, codified at N.J. STAT. ANN. §§ 40:55D-40.1 to 40.7 (West Supp. 2002).

203. N.J. ADMIN. CODE tit. 5, chaps. 21-4, 21-5, 21-6, 21-7; New Jersey State League of Municipalities v. Dep't of Comm. Affairs, 729 A.2d 21, 26 (N.J. 1999) ("Following two hearings and a period of public comment, the proposed [site improvement] standards, including the sidewalk requirement, were adopted and became effective on June 3, 1977").

204. N.J. STAT. ANN. § 40:55D-40.2(a) (West Supp. 2002).

205. New Jersey State League of Municipalities v. Dep't of Comm. Affairs, 158 N.J. 211, 226–27, 729 A.2d 21, 29–31 (1999).

206. N.J. STAT. ANN. § 40:55D-46.

207. *Id.* § 40:55D-46.c.

208. Morris County Fair Hous. Council v. Boonton Township, 220 N.J. Super. 388, 532 A.2d 280, 286–87 (Law Div. 1987). *See generally* chapters 3 and 9.

209. N.J. STAT. ANN. § 40:55D-49 (West 1991 & Supp. 2002).

210. *Id.* § 40:55D-50.

211. *Id.* § 40:55D-53.

212. *Id.* § 40:55D-51.

213. *Id.* § 40:55D-52.

214. PRB Enters. v. South Brunswick Planning Bd., 105 N.J. 1, 518 A.2d 1099, 1102 (1987). *But cf.* Friedman v. Planning and Zoning Comm'n of Town of Rocky Hill, 222 Conn. 262, 608 A.2d 1178 (1992) (special traffic consequences of a given site plan may be examined if permitted by applicable zoning regulations). In Southland Corp. v. Mayor & City Council of Laurel, 75 Md. App. 375, 541 A.2d 653 (1988), denial of a site plan on traffic access/congestion grounds had the effect of denying a permitted use.

215. Lionel's Appliance Ctr., Inc. v. Citta, 156 N.J. Super. 257, 383 A.2d 773, 779 (Law Div. 1978).

216. Morristown Road Assocs. v. Mayor & Common Council, 163 N.J. Super. 58, 394 A.2d 157, 163 (Law Div. 1978).

217. Bragdon v. Town of Vassalboro, 780 A.2d 299, 302 (Me. 2001).

218. *See, e.g.* Kurlanski v. Portland Yacht Club, 782 A.2d 783, 786 (Me. 2001) (boathouse permit application requires review of yacht club's entire site plan).

219. Town of Windham v. Lawrence Sav. Bank, 776 A.2d 730, 734 (N.H. 2001).

220. Bass v. Attardi, 868 F.2d 45, 50–51 (3d Cir. 1989); Anastasio v. Planning Bd., 209 N.J. Super. 499, 509 A.2d 1194 (App. Div.), *cert. denied*, 107 N.J. 46, 526 A.2d 136 (1986).

221. Dean Tarry Corp. v. Friedlander, 826 F.2d 210, 213 (2d Cir. 1987).

222. City of Madison v. Bryan, 763 So. 2d 162, 166 (Miss. 2000) (applicant did not have title or a valid option at time of challenge).

223. Chapel Road Assocs., L.L.C. v. Town of Wells, 787 A.2d 137, 140–41 (Me. 2001).

224. *See, e.g.*, U.S. Trust Co. v. New Jersey, 431 U.S. 1, 23 (1977); Kaiser Dev. Co. v. City & County of Honolulu, 649 F. Supp. 926 (D. Haw. 1986), *op. amended and superseded by* 913 F.2d 573 (9th Cir. 1990); Hartman v. Buckson, 467 A.2d 694 (Del. 1983); State *ex rel.* Zupancic v. Shimenz, 46 Wis. 2d 22, 174 N.W.2d 533 (1970) (distinguishing illegal contract zoning from enforceable restrictive covenants that act as motivation for otherwise valid rezoning actions).

For an excellent review of the legal questions raised by developer agreements, *see* Judith W. Wegner, *Moving Toward the Bargaining Table: Contract Zoning, Development Agreements, and the Theoretical Foundations of Government Land Use Deals*, 65 N.C. L. REV. 957 (1987). Several states have expressly authorized by statute the use of development agreements in the land use approval process. California was the first, followed by Arizona, Colorado, Florida, Hawaii, Idaho, Louisiana, Maryland, and Nevada. *See* Daniel J. Curtin & Scott A. Edelstein, *Development Agreements Practice in California & Other States*, 22 STETSON L. REV. 761, 766 (1993). *See also* David L. Callies & Julie A. Tappendorf, *Unconstitutional Land Development Conditions and the Development Agreement Solution: Bargaining for Public Facilities After Nollan and Dolan*, 51 CASE W. RES. L. REV. 663 (2001).

225. FLA. STAT. ANN. §§ 163.3223, 163.3229 (West 2000). *See also* David L. Callies & Julie A. Tappendorf, *Unconstitutional Land Development Conditions and the Development Agreement Solution: Bargaining for Public Facilities After Nollan and Dolan*, 51 CASE W. RES. L. REV. 663 (2001).

226. *Id.* § 163.3225.

227. *Id.* § 163.3227.

228. *Id.* § 163.3233.

229. *Id.* § 163.3239.

230. *Id.* § 163.3235.

231. N.J. STAT. ANN. §§ 40:55D-49, 40:55D-52 (West 1991 & Supp. 2002). Bleznak v. Evesham Township, 170 N.J. Super. 216, 406 A.2d 201 (Law Div. 1979) (nursery school could expand operations in accordance with preliminary and final site-plan approval even though rezoning one year after final site-plan approval made nursery school a nonconforming use). *See generally* pp. 355–58.

232. N.J. STAT. ANN. § 40:55D-10.1 (West 1991 & Supp. 2002).

233. Sproul v. City of Wooster, 840 F.2d 1267 (6th Cir. 1988). For a helpful outline of the legal issues raised by development agreements, *see* Delaney, *The Use and Abuse of Development Agreements,* AM. PLAN. ASS'N, PLANNING AND LAW, DIVISION NEWSL., Dec. 1990. *See also* Wegner, *Moving Toward the Bargaining Table: Contract Zoning, Development Agreements and the Theoretical Foundations of Government Land Use Deals,* 65 N.C. L. REV. 957 (1987).

234. In 1978, the Supreme Court noted that 35 states authorized local governments to exercise governmental powers beyond their boundaries. Holt Civic Club v. City of Tuscaloosa, 439 U.S. 60, 72 (1978) (citing Comment, *The Constitutionality of the Exercise of Extraterritorial Powers by Municipalities,* 45 U. CHI. L. REV. 151 (1977)).

235. Holt Civic Club v. City of Tuscaloosa, 439 U.S. 60, 69–70 (1978).

236. *See, e.g.,* Petterson v. City of Naperville, 9 Ill. 2d 233, 137 N.E.2d 371, 377 (1956) (1921 state law authorizing municipal planning and subdivision regulation gave "exclusive control in . . . areas within one and one-half miles outside the territorial limits of a municipality to municipalities which have an official plan in effect in such territory").

237. *See, e.g.,* Krughoff v. City of Naperville, 68 Ill. 2d 352, 369 N.E.2d 892, 896 (1977).

238. *See* chapter 4.

239. City of Urbana v. County of Champaign, 27 Ill. Dec. 777, 389 N.E.2d 1185, 1187 (1979) (citing Millbrae Assn. for Residential Survival v. City of Millbrae, 262 Cal. App. 2d 222, 242, 69 Cal. Rptr. 251, 266 (1968)).

240. City of Urbana v. County of Champaign, 76 Ill. 2d 63, 389 N.E.2d 1185, 1188 (1979).

241. *See, e.g.,* Manning, *Extraterritorial Strategies in Growth Management,* excerpted in the NEWSLETTER OF THE PLANNING & LAW DIVISION, AM. PLAN. ASS'N 3–6 (Jan. 1989). *See also* Ronald S. Cope, *Annexation Agreements – Boundary Agreements: Walking a Fine Line Into the Future – A Map of the Dangers to the Unwary Land Use Traveller,* 17 N. ILL. U. L. REV. 337 (1997).

242. Richardson v. City of Little Rock Planning Comm'n, 747 S.W.2d 116 (Ark. 1988) (marginal development potential of land insufficient basis for denial of subdivision plat that complies with standards of subdivision ordinance); Irwin v. Planning and Zoning Comm'n of Town of Litchfield, 244 Conn. 619, 628, 711 A.2d 675, 679 (1998).

243. Carlson v. Town of Beaux Arts Village, 41 Wash. App. 402, 704 P.2d 663, 665, *rev. denied,* 104 Wash. 2d 1020 (1985) (citing WASH. REV. CODE § 58.17.190 and State v. Rowe, 93 Wash. 2d 277, 609 P.2d 1348 (1980)).

244. Carlson v. Town of Beaux Arts Village, 41 Wash. App. 402, 704 P.2d 663, 665, *rev. denied*, 104 Wash. 2d 1020 (1985) (quoting State v. Rowe, 93 Wash. 2d 277, 284, 609 P.2d 1348 (1980)).

245. *Id*. at 665.

246. Call v. City of West Jordan, 727 P.2d 180, 183–84 (Utah 1986).

247. *See* chapter 5.

248. Friedman v. Planning and Zoning Commission of Town of Rocky Hill, 222 Conn. 262, 608 A.2d 1178 (1992).

249. *See, e.g.*, West Meade Homeowners Ass'n, Inc. v. W.P.M.C., Inc., 788 S.W.2d 365 (Tenn. Ct. App. 1989).

250. Stevenson v. Blaine County, 134 Idaho 756, 759–60, 9 P.3d 1222, 1225–26 (2000).

251. *See, e.g.*, Equicor Dev., Inc. v. Westfield-Washington Township Planning Comm'n, 758 N.E.2d 34, 39-40 (Ind. 2001).

252. 133 N.H. 618, 580 A.2d 1082 (1990).

253. Eddy Plaza Assocs. v. City of Concord, 445 A.2d 1106 (N.H. 1982).

CHAPTER 9

Overcoming Barriers to
Affordable Housing

The NIMBY Syndrome

Euclidean zoning,[1] characterized by the territorial division of land into zones and the segregation of uses within each zone, has from the beginning had an exclusionary bias.[2] One of the two main goals of the nation's first comprehensive zoning law, the New York City Building Zone Resolution of 1916, was to limit urban congestion.[3] The means chosen to accomplish this goal—segregation of land activities and the application of varying degrees of limitation on building height, size, and design[4]—reflected a community value judgment that different types of land activity were inherently incompatible and should be kept separate.

Early legal objections to the discrimination inherent in the zoning approach were overcome by the requirements that district boundary lines be drawn on the basis of objective standards, such as suitability of the land for particular uses, topography, existing patterns of development, and projected patterns of growth, and that all land within a particular zone be subject to the same set of regulations, thus producing a rational classification under the Equal Protection Clause.[5] The incompatibility of residential and industrial activity was considered to be obvious, thus separation of such activities made sense and the limitation on the use of private property that resulted was a reasonable exercise of police power.[6] Because all landowners within a given zone were permitted to make the same use of their property, no one was being treated unequally in the constitutional sense.[7]

As long as the public interest justifying zoning was perceived as concern over inanimate sources of harm—such as noise, pestilence, fire, and other common forms of urban displeasure—zoning was not seen as posing a threat to other cherished American freedoms, including the right to associate, move about freely, and seek housing of one's choice. The Supreme Court, however, in its landmark decision *Village of Euclid v. Ambler Realty Company*,[8] upholding the comprehensive zoning concept, presaged a future in which all sorts of "different" types of people would be excluded from suburban American with a bit of ill-considered dicta concerning apartment buildings, and by necessary implication their occupants:

> With particular reference to apartment houses, it is pointed out that the development of detached house sections is greatly retarded by the coming of apartment houses, which has sometimes resulted in destroying the entire section for private house purposes; that in such sections very often the apartment house is a mere parasite, constructed in order to take advantage of the open spaces and attractive surroundings created by the residential character of the district.[9]

Although it is unfair and a gross oversimplification to blame the Court for the housing problems of the poor, the disabled, and the elderly, the attitude reflected in that comment and the Court's relatively uncritical acceptance of the zoning concept[10] gave the stamp of approval to an approach to land use control that awarded preferential treatment to the freestanding, relatively large-lot, single-family housing developments that dominated suburbia for the next half century.[11]

When the exclusionary effects of Euclidean zoning on people became apparent in the late 1960s and early 1970s, many local conflicts concerning residential uses of land in the suburbs added a third interest group, people who wanted to live in the community, to the traditional antagonists, landowner/developers and neighbors.[12] Because of a laissez-faire attitude on the part of the federal courts[13] that was generally unsympathetic to the outsiders who wanted in, state courts became the battlegrounds for increasingly sophisticated zoning conflicts.

Since the mid-1960s, a substantial body of law has been developed, particularly in New Jersey,[14] New York,[15] and Pennsylvania,[16] that purports to outlaw egregious forms of exclusionary zoning. Unfortunately, because of the extraordinary difficulty of fashioning a remedy that would be politically acceptable and yet effective in responding to the needs of the excluded groups, little in the way of tangible change in housing patterns has taken place as a result of these cases.[17]

Running parallel to the attacks on exclusionary zoning, and affected substantially by exclusionary zoning attitudes, has been an effort to shift the focus of treatment for mentally retarded persons from large, impersonal state institutions to smaller facilities within such persons' home environs. The centerpiece of this effort is the group home, a cross between the modern single-family residence and the boardinghouse of the late 19th and early 20th centuries.[18]

In addition, other movements of recent years to provide housing for "service-dependent" populations that have been affected by prevailing attitudes of land use regulations include the growth of accessory apartments, elder cottage housing opportunity (ECHO) housing, congregate housing, nursing homes, and hospice centers as sources of housing for elderly persons;[19] the attempt to reduce recidivism by easing incarcerated individuals back into their home communities through halfway houses and to avoid incarceration for certain types of offenders by community sentencing alternatives;[20] residential treatment centers for alcoholics and drug addicts;[21] and the growth of shelters and transitional and permanent housing opportunities for homeless persons.[22]

Each of these activities has been characterized by often bitter local clashes between articulated public policies and local attitudes nurtured by the Euclidean approach to land use regulation in which single-family detached houses on relatively large lots are the favored—and in numerous residential neighborhoods the only—form of residential use. These attitudes are reflected both in local zoning ordinances and in private restrictive covenants.

In the bureaucratic lexicon of acronyms, the NIMBY syndrome often is manifested in these clashes. "I believe that (group homes, halfway houses, congregate facilities, shelters for the homeless, etc.) are good, but Not in My Back Yard."[23] To a certain extent, the fear of change manifested by the NIMBY syndrome may be traceable to the "parasite" mentality articulated by Justice Sutherland in his *Euclid* dicta.[24] Are the mentally retarded, homeless, elderly, disabled, and incarcerated today's "parasites," or are they our children, brothers and sisters, aunts and uncles, parents and grandparents?[25]

Exclusionary Zoning

The term *exclusionary zoning* is derived from the phenomenon of "fiscal zoning"—zoning to attract activities such as commercial and light industrial uses that would increase the tax base, rather than activities that would drain the tax base through increased pressure on public schools, local welfare agencies, public transit systems, and the like. Fiscal zoning generally has been discredited when used to keep out lower-income people.[26]

When zoning to improve fiscal ratables is combined with land use regulations that increase the required standard of housing quality beyond those necessary for health and safety and thereby "appear to interfere seriously with the availability of low- and moderate-cost housing where it is needed," a community is said to be engaged in exclusionary zoning.[27]

In a now-classic study published in 1971 of the zoning practices of four New Jersey counties on the outskirts of New York City, Williams and Norman identified six popular land use regulatory techniques that had particular impact on housing opportunities for low- and moderate-income persons:

> 1. *Minimum-Building-Size Requirements*—which are normally requirements for minimum floor space. Requirements for a larger house have the most obvious and direct influence on housing costs; for example, assuming average building costs of roughly $20 per square foot for tract housing (which may be optimistic), a requirement for a 1,200-square-foot house has practically the same effect as a requirement for houses costing about $24,000. The cost of the lot and of site development must of course be added, so that the actual figure would probably be around $30,000.[28]

[At 2002 prices in St. Louis, Missouri (approximately $75 per square foot), a 1,200-square-foot house would cost $90,000 to build before adding the cost of the land, site development, and builder's profits. —Eds.]

2. *The Exclusion of Multiple Dwellings–Single-Family Restrictions.* Among those architects and planners who have a special interest in housing costs, there has long been a widespread consensus that the most promising opportunity for good, inexpensive housing is to be found in some form of multiple dwellings. With the recent sharp rise in housing costs, this is probably even more true nowadays. Such housing may take a variety of different forms, and more may be available in the future— garden apartments, "town houses," and various developments in "modular housing," which may be coming as a result of the hoped-for industrialization of the building industry.

3. *Restrictions on the Number of Bedrooms.* When multiple dwellings are permitted, the number of bedrooms is often restricted, either by the zoning ordinance or by informal pressure. The most frequent provision requires that 80 percent of the dwelling units shall have only one bedroom, and permits up to 20 percent with two bedrooms—and none with more. The fiscal motivation for such restrictions is obvious. Equally clearly, multiple dwellings subject to such restrictions do not provide the type of housing needed by most families of normal size.

4. *Prohibition of Mobile Homes.* Such homes now provide the only new, inexpensive housing available in most areas, except for some public housing in the cities. They are efficient, readily available, and unnecessarily ugly.

5. *Frontage (i.e., Lot Width) Requirements.* The costs of site development, particularly for street paving and sewers, are fairly substantial, and so requirements for wide lots do affect the cost of housing noticeably. The impact of this factor depends of course on whether high standards for site development are imposed in subdivision control—and how high. Obviously, if curbs and storm sewers are also required, the cost will go up substantially. Still, it is lot width, probably even more than lot size, which tends to preserve that much-desired semi-rural atmosphere.

6. *Lot Size Requirements.* While this device has attracted most of the attention, its actual impact is questionable.[29]

In *Mount Laurel I,*[30] the Supreme Court of New Jersey held that a zoning ordinance that contravened the general welfare violated the state constitutional requirements of substantive due process and equal protection.[31] The court articulated the principle of "fair-share" housing and concluded that developing communities could not use their delegated police power to regulate land use in a manner that excluded housing for low-income persons. The constitutional obligation would be satisfied by "affirmatively affording a realistic opportunity" for the construction of a fair share of the present and prospective regional need for low- and moderate-income housing.[32] In *Mount Laurel II,*[33] the court returned to the original case after several intervening cases had fleshed out the law but failed to develop an effective remedy or means of administering the doctrine.[34] In an eloquent opinion designed to "put some steel into that doctrine"[35] and to emphasize that the *Mount Laurel* obligation is to provide a "realistic opportunity for housing, not litigation,"[36] the court reaffirmed the fair-share principle; concluded that it was applicable to all communities, whether developing or not, containing "growth areas" as shown on the concept maps of the New Jersey State Development Guide Plan; and held that municipalities' affirmative governmental obligation to provide a realistic opportunity for the construction of low- and moderate-income housing included the use of inclusionary devices, such as density bonuses and mandatory set-asides, as well as the elimination of unnecessary cost-producing land use requirements and restrictions.[37]

The *Mount Laurel* cases have contributed two main points to housing and land use control jurisprudence. First, there is a clear recognition that the concept of general welfare, on which zoning as well as all other exercises of police power ultimately rest, includes "proper provision for adequate housing of all categories of people."[38] *Mount Laurel I* contained extensive discussion of the importance of housing to individuals and the rationale for concluding that the term *general welfare* is broad enough in today's society to embrace notions of adequate housing.[39] In *Mount Laurel II*, the court restated the constitutional principle as follows:

> [T]he State controls the use of land, *all* of the land. In exercising that control it cannot favor rich over poor. It cannot legislatively set aside dilapidated housing in urban ghettos for the poor and decent housing elsewhere for everyone else. The government that controls this land represents everyone. While the State may not have the ability to eliminate poverty, it cannot use that condition as the basis for imposing further disadvantages. And the same applies to the municipality, to which this control over land has been constitutionally delegated.[40]

Second, *Mount Laurel I* also recognized that certain planning and regulatory decisions will have an impact beyond the boundaries of the particular decision-maker's sphere of direct control. When police power is delegated to local government, as in zoning, tax abatement, and eminent domain, the sphere of direct control and interest of the entity exercising the power is narrower than the sphere of control and interest of the delegating entity.[41] Justification for the ultimate use of police power, however, must relate to the general welfare of the people who are within the sphere of influence of the delegating agency. Thus, when the use of police power will have an impact beyond the boundaries of the entity exercising the power, "the welfare of the state's citizens beyond the borders of the particular municipality cannot be disregarded and must be recognized and served."[42]

Mount Laurel II acknowledges this point by reviewing the relationship of suburban exclusionary zoning to the continuing disintegration of cities and concluding that "[z]oning ordinances that either encourage this process or ratify its results are not promoting our general welfare, they are destroying it."[43]

Courts in several other states have expressed disapproval of exclusionary zoning, but generally have declined to adopt the mathematical approach to determining appropriate remedies of the *Mount Laurel* cases.[44] The Supreme Court of New Hampshire embraced the fair-share principle of *Mount Laurel* that requires all communities in a region to participate in efforts to accommodate affordable housing.[45] Because the court's rationale was based on the state zoning-enabling act, the decision has national significance.[46]

Reinvestment Displacement[47]

Displacement of persons as a result of governmental activity to promote redevelopment is an extremely complex issue affecting urban communities. It must be distinguished from normal turnover, which can be expected in any community because of the mobility of American society and the changing demands of the housing market.[48] During the past 50 years, reinvestment has occurred in two phases in most American cities. The first phase involves the acquisition by public authorities of abandoned or substandard but occupied buildings. This type of displacement is best illustrated by the urban renewal programs of the 1950s and 1960s.[49] The second phase involves situations where occupied buildings are acquired either by a private redevelopment entity or by persons moving into a particular neighborhood area as a result of reinvestment activities. In this phase, a question arises as to whether a sale is "voluntary" (i.e., whether the cost of complying with a redevelopment plan is so onerous that the occupier is forced to sell or move out).[50]

Displacement occurs in several situations. Clearance and redevelopment of residential areas for commercial and industrial purposes or for public facilities is the most visible example. This was the chief characteristic of the first phase of displacement. It is not nearly so prevalent today but does occur from time to time.

A major activity during a second-phase redevelopment effort is the substantial rehabilitation of residential structures. So-called gut rehabilitation, in which the shell of the building is retained but the interior is completely redone, normally cannot be accomplished while the building is occupied. Thus a type of "temporary" displacement takes place in which residents are removed for a period of time, anywhere from six months to two years, corresponding to the reconstruction.

The conversion of rental property to owner-occupied property can be a cause of displacement. In most situations where the conversion of an occupied building takes place, the current tenants are given some opportunity to purchase the units.[51] However, if the conversion results in substantial renovation of the units, the cost of acquisition and maintenance most likely will be considerably higher than the previous rental charges. If the tenants are persons of low or moderate income, it is unlikely that they will be able to purchase the units, and, consequently, those individuals will join the ranks of displaced persons.

A significant but still almost invisible type of displacement results from increased costs of occupation, such as higher rents, that follow substantial rehabilitation and the overall increase in property values that takes place as a neighborhood is upgraded.[52] Neighborhood and historic preservation efforts can result in substantially higher housing costs because of the often expensive attention to detail, such as brass kick-plates and colonial-style wood doors, required to preserve the character of the structure.[53] This situation is perhaps the most difficult to measure because it is almost indistinguishable from situations in which people voluntarily leave for any of the reasons that may be viewed as a normal part of the operation of the urban housing market.

The failure of subsidized housing projects can result in displacement of the occupants of those units, particularly if, in the process of foreclosure and resale, the subsidy is lost.[54] The result then becomes a substantially higher cost of occupancy, which has the effect of forcing the persons who were the beneficiaries of the subsidies of those units into the marketplace.

In most situations, a traditional view of public purpose tends to focus on the fact that the community at large will receive the benefit of a "better community" or will have "potentially harmful" situations removed from the community.[55] Some of the more insightful analyses recognize that the use of police power to remove harmful conditions or to prevent the spread of harmful conditions can result in displacement. As early as 1937, the New York Court of Appeals, in upholding application of a local housing code provision requiring alterations to existing structures as a reasonable exercise of police power, noted in passing that the result may be the closing of many tenement houses and the eviction of the tenants.[56] The court stated: "Argument may be made that before the Legislature causes the closing of tenement houses because they are unfit for habitation, provision should be made for better housing elsewhere for the evicted tenants."[57] But the court simply passed the argument to the legislature with the standard refrain that the problem is a matter for the legislature and not the court.[58]

Because the people who are displaced typically are disorganized, poor, depressed, and scattered, it has been extremely difficult, if not impossible, for them to articulate effectively either in court or in the legislature the enormity of the burden they are being asked to shoulder.

The *Mount Laurel* cases in New Jersey suggest an alternative approach to the question of responsibility for displacement in private redevelopment activities. Enough evidence has been gathered to establish that any decision by a local government to use the delegated police power to promote extensive reinvestment activities is going to affect the lives of those individuals in the target area, no matter how sensitive officials may be to meeting their specific needs.[59] If residents cannot afford the costs imposed on them by the reinvestment activity, the effect is likely to be a reduction or elimination of the shelter they have. If that effect is not addressed, the welfare of these residents, who are citizens of the delegating entity, is not recognized and served.[60] The exercise of police power in this particular instance, thus, would be questionable. In summarizing the rulings of *Mount Laurel I* and its progeny, the court in *Mount Laurel II* noted that every municipality had an obligation to its resident poor and that the "zoning power is no more abused by keeping out the region's poor than by forcing out the resident poor."[61]

The social costs of displacement are not confined to those who are displaced. Persons not displaced, both inside and outside the boundaries of the redevelopment area, may become caught up in the bitterness and frustrations engendered by public controversies over displacement. All taxpayers are affected by public expenditures for social welfare programs to repair the damage caused by displacement. The welfare of these individuals also goes unrecognized and unserved when predictable reinvestment displacement goes unattended.[62]

The essence of the *Mount Laurel* jurisprudence is that the effect of a local land use decision must be considered, particularly when the effect may be to retard housing opportunities of persons who otherwise may be expected to reside in that community. Reinvestment displacement raises the same question as exclusionary zoning, although the view is from a different angle. Displacement occurs in communities often because the community does not consider the impact that a particular exercise of police power may have on the people who are displaced.[63] Because the exercise of police power depends for its validity on the requirement that it promotes public health, safety, morals, or the general welfare, and because "proper provision for adequate housing of all categories of people is certainly an absolute essential in promotion of the general welfare,"[64] it follows that a community should be required to consider the impact of a decision to exercise police power on the long-term residents who may be disproportionately affected by that decision. Although in most private redevelopment activities the zoning power is not used, zoning is simply one manifestation of police power. Other uses of police power, such as code enforcement, the granting of tax abatement and eminent domain to private redevelopment corporations, the marshalling of resources, and the allocations of subsidies, may have the same effect of forcing out the resident poor.[65]

The Fair Housing Act

The Fair Housing Act prohibits zoning that discriminates on the basis of race, creed, color, family status, or national origin.[66] Although proof of discriminatory effect does not constitute a per se violation of the act,[67] a prima facie case of statutory violation can be established by a showing that the defendant's action "actually or predictably results in racial discrimination; in other words, that it has a discriminatory effect."[68] This discriminatory impact can exist in two forms: (1) as evidenced by harm to a particular minority, or (2) as evidenced by the way in which a community is harmed by segregation.[69] The plaintiff is not required to show discriminatory intent in order to establish a prima facie case.[70]

If the plaintiff establishes a prima facie case of discriminatory impact, the burden turns to the defendant, who can avoid liability by showing: (1) the action complained of served a legitimate government interest, and (2) no less discriminatory means existed to further that particular interest.[71] The burden to the plaintiff is balanced against the interests allegedly promoted by the defendant's actions. Two other factors are important to this inquiry. First, any evidence of discriminatory intent, although not a part of the plaintiff's prima facie case, will, if presented, weigh in the plaintiff's favor.[72] Second, if the plaintiff is planning to build the housing that is the subject of the suit—rather than suing to compel the government to build—the defendant's burden in justifying the questioned actions is greater.[73] If the defendant articulates "a legitimate, nondiscriminatory reason for its action, . . . the burden of production then shifts back to the plaintiff, who at all times has the burden of persuasion, to prove that the stated reason was pretextual."[74]

These rules were applied in *Huntington Branch, NAACP v. Town of Huntington*.[75] In this case, a zoning ordinance restricted multifamily housing projects to an urban-renewal area with a large minority population. When a builder presented a plan to build multifamily housing in a neighborhood that was 98 percent white, the town refused to amend its ordinance.[76] The U.S. District Court held that the town had not violated the Fair Housing Act.[77] On appeal, however, the Second Circuit reversed. First, the town's action of refusing to rezone had a discriminatory impact because it "perpetuated segregation" and imposed a greater burden on blacks than whites, where 24 percent of the town's black families needed subsidized housing, but only 7 percent of all Huntington families needed it.[78] Furthermore, the town could not justify its actions because the interests asserted (e.g., preventing traffic congestion) did not outweigh the burden of its actions on the plaintiffs.[79] Also, the town had not chosen the least discriminatory means of accomplishing its goal of encouraging restoration of the urban-renewal area. Although the town had argued that its zoning ordinance served this end by restricting new housing projects to the renewal area, which builders might otherwise avoid, the town could have accomplished this goal with tax incentives or abatements.[80]

In one ironic application of the Act, the Seventh Circuit upheld a not-for-profit corporation's affirmative marketing plan designed to attract white residents to a black section of Chicago.[81]

The familial status provisions of the Fair Housing Act Amendments of 1988 were upheld as applied to elderly residents in the case of *Seniors Civil Liberties Association v. Kemp*, rejecting the plaintiffs' argument that elderly residents had constitutional rights to reside in adults-only communities.[82] One court has held that recovering drug addicts are handicapped persons protected by the Act.[83]

The Fair Housing Act exempts zoning ordinances that reasonably restrict the maximum number of occupants in any particular dwelling.[84] In *City of Edmonds v. Oxford House, Inc.*,[85] the Supreme Court held that definitions of the term *family* in local zoning ordinances were not exempt from coverage of the Fair Housing Act under a statutory exemption for "any reasonable local, State, or Federal restrictions regarding the maximum number of occupants permitted to occupy a dwelling."[86] The decision had been watched closely by the supporters of special-needs housing, as well as local government officials and residents. Oxford House, a not-for-profit organization that provides permanent housing for adults recovering from alcoholism and drug addiction, opened a group home in the City of Edmonds, Washington, for 10 to 12 adults in a neighborhood zoned for single-family residents. Because more than five unrelated persons resided in the group home, the home did not qualify under the definition of *family* in the Edmonds zoning code. The city brought suit in federal court seeking a declaration that the Fair Housing Act does not prohibit the city from enforcing its family definition rule. Both sides agreed that occupants of the house were handicapped and therefore entitled to the protection of the Fair Housing Act, 42 U.S.C. Section 2604(f)(1)(A), if the occupancy rule exemption did not apply. The district court held that the definition of *family* was exempt from Fair Housing Act coverage. The Ninth Circuit reversed, holding that the occupancy rule exemption was inapplicable to definitions of *family* in local zoning codes.

In the majority opinion written by Justice Ginsburg, the Supreme Court read the statutory exemption narrowly to apply only to maximum occupancy restrictions designed to prevent overcrowding and not to all municipal land use restrictions. Justice Ginsburg concluded that family composition rules are an "essential component of single-family residential use restrictions." Maximum occupancy restrictions, on the other hand, ordinarily apply uniformly to all residents of all dwelling units. In noting that the distinction between land use regulations and maximum occupancy restrictions had been recognized by the Court in *Moore v. City of East Cleveland*,[87] Justice Ginsburg concluded that rules that "cap the total number of occupants in order to prevent overcrowding . . . fall within §3607(b)(1)'s absolute exemption from the FHA's governance; rules designed to preserve the family character of the neighborhood, fastening on the composition of households rather than on the total number of occupants living quarters can contain, do not."[88]

The Court stated that only the threshold question of statutory exemption was decided. Whether the application of the ordinance to the Oxford House Group Home violated the Fair Housing Act remained to be established.

The dissent argued that the majority failed to ask the right question and that by doing so failed to exhaust the category of restrictions exempted from the Fair Housing Act. To the dissent the "sole relevant question" is whether the zoning code imposes "any . . . restrictions regarding the maximum number of occupants permitted to occupy a dwelling."[89] The dissent argued that the code does not impose such restrictions and therefore is entitled to statutory exemption.

In *Oxford House v. City of St. Louis*,[90] the Eighth Circuit upheld a zoning ordinance that limited the number of residents in two group homes for recovering substance abusers to eight persons in each:

We conclude the eight-person rule is rational. Cities have a legitimate interest in decreasing congestion, traffic, and noise in residential areas, and ordinances restricting the number of unrelated people who may occupy a single family residence are reasonably related to these legitimate goals. The City does not need to assert a specific reason for choosing eight as the cut-off point, rather than ten or twelve. . . . We conclude the City's eight person restriction has a rational basis and thus is valid under the Fair Housing Act.[91]

Segregation of Multifamily Housing

Huntington Branch NAACP v. Town of Huntington[92] is a good example of the increasing willingness of federal courts to invalidate under the Fair Housing Act restrictive zoning ordinances that exclude multifamily housing from all or significant portions of a community. The *Huntington* zoning ordinances limited the development of multifamily housing projects to an urban-renewal area with a large black population. The town refused to revise its ordinances when a developer wanted to build a housing project in an area that was largely white. The Second Circuit held that the reasons given by town officials for refusing to rezone the subject property did not overcome the strong prima facie showing of discriminatory effect created by the "disproportionate harm to blacks and the segregative impact on the entire community resulting from the refusal to rezone."[93]

The court joined several other circuits in applying the disparate impact approach of Title VII cases to a Title VIII case in which a public entity is the defendant. Under disparate impact analysis, discriminatory effect, rather than intent, is the touchstone.[94] Once a prima facie case has been established, the burden shifts to the defendant municipality to "prove that its actions furthered, in theory and in practice, a legitimate, *bona fide* governmental interest and that no alternative would serve that interest with less discriminatory effect."[95]

In considering reasons for a refusal to rezone, the court noted that problems can usually be divided into "plan-specific" ones, which normally can be resolved in a less discriminatory manner, and "site-specific" ones, which cannot be justified by "*post hoc* rationalizations by administrative agencies."[96]

The use of referenda to block multifamily housing developments raises Fair Housing Act issues, as well as equal protection and substantive due process questions. For example, in *Buckeye Community Hope Foundation v. City of Cuyahoga Falls,* the Sixth Circuit Court of Appeals held that claims arose under the Fair Housing Act, and the Equal Protection and Due Process Clauses of the Constitution, when a city official refused to issue a building permit pending the outcome of a referendum opposing a multifamily apartment project, even though the city previously had approved the project's site plan.[97] On the Fair Housing Act question, the court held that the plaintiffs had stated both a discriminatory intent and a discriminatory effect claim. Genuine issues of material fact were raised, the court held, concerning whether the decision to stay the effect of the site plan approval by denying a building permit because of the pendency of a referendum "gave effect to the racial bias of its citizens."[98] In addition to meeting the three-factor *Arlington Heights* test for discriminatory effect—(1) How strong is the plaintiff's showing of discriminatory effect? (2) What is the defendants' interest in taking the action complained of? and (3) Does the plaintiff seek to compel affirmative action by the defendant or merely to restrain the defendant from interfering with efforts to provide housing?[99]—the plaintiffs also had to show "highly unusual circumstances" in order to prevail.[100] The court found such circumstances in that the city had "*never* used the powers of referendum to reject a site plan ordinance before this case . . . [and] the Ohio Supreme Court found that the defendants' use of the referendum to reject the plaintiffs' site plan violated the Ohio Constitution.[101]

On the other hand, the First Circuit was not persuaded that a municipality's recission of support for a proposed affordable housing project violated the Fair Housing Act.[102] Although the revocation was a "substantial departure from normal procedures" in that it followed an "unannounced reconsideration" of the development proposal, the court noted that procedural abnormalties "are only relevant within a larger scope."[103] Plaintiffs failed to produce sufficient evidence of discriminatory intent or discriminatory effect, the court concluded.[104]

Expansion of coverage of the Fair Housing Act to include discrimination because of the presence of minor children in the family[105] is likely to increase the pressure on local governments to ease restrictive zoning ordinances that exclude multiple-dwelling units from substantial portions of the residential areas in the community.[106]

Exclusion of multiple dwellings was one of the evils decried by the New Jersey Supreme Court in the *Mount Laurel* decisions striking down exclusionary zoning practices as arbitrary exercises of police power in violation of the state constitution and imposing affirmative responsibilities on New Jersey communities to do their fair share in providing realistic housing opportunities for persons of low and moderate income.[107] The legislature responded with enactment of the New Jersey Fair Housing Act,[108] which mandates local housing planning and authorizes the State Council on Affordable Housing to establish housing regions in the state, determine the housing needs of each region, and decide whether municipalities have met their housing obligations under the *Mount Laurel* fair-share scheme. The constitutionality of the act was upheld in 1986 by the Supreme Court of New Jersey in *Hills Development Company v. Bernards Township.*[109] Sixteen years later the New Jersey court returned to *Mount Laurel* issues in three cases. In upholding a decision to grant a builder's remedy authorizing the development of 300 multifamily units, the court reaffirmed that profit-motivated developers should be allowed to build housing sought by local markets (in this case, single-family homes), but that the town's ordinances had thwarted affordable housing development.[110]

Several other states have responded to the exclusionary zoning problem by requiring housing considerations to be included in the planning process that must accompany exercise of the zoning power.[111]

Mobile Homes and Manufactured Housing

Mobile homes and various types of modular or manufactured housing are becoming increasingly important forms of affordable housing for persons and small families of low and moderate income.[112] Although mobile or manufactured homes are forms of single-family housing, they generally have been subjected to more stringent land use regulations than traditional, site-built housing because of their origin as "temporary" rather than "permanent" housing and their resultant "distinctions . . . [in] design, construction and general appearance."[113]

Advances in the technology of manufactured housing have led some jurisdictions to create separate categories of manufactured housing depending on whether the housing unit is constructed on a wheeled chassis and then attached to a "pad" with the wheels removed (manufactured homes) or whether the unit is assembled in a factory without a wheeled chassis and then transported to the site on which it is to be located (manufactured buildings).[114] Factory-built "manufactured buildings" tend to be regulated in the manner of site-built housing, whereas wheeled-chassis "manufactured housing" usually is subjected to the more stringent mobile-home regulations.[115]

Although various means have been used to regulate mobile homes, communities tend to either confine mobile homes to mobile-home parks[116] or, in less restrictive schemes, to certain districts where the distribution of mobile homes may be somewhat more haphazard. For example, mobile homes have been regulated through the special-use permit device[117] or the floating-zone technique of a planned unit development (PUD).[118] Mobile homes have been limited to one per parcel of land, with the further restriction that they cannot be used as dwellings unless they are in a "trailer camp";[119] mobile homes may be prohibited altogether unless in an "existing and recognized trailer court";[120] or they may be subjected to additional design restrictions to ensure compatibility with site-built homes when being placed in the "best residential zoning classifications" in a community.[121]

Various reasons have been given for the more restrictive treatment of mobile homes. The Seventh Circuit, for example, noted that mobile homes are a "sufficiently distinct use of land to justify their separate classification for zoning purposes."[122] The Eleventh Circuit concluded that regulation of mobile homes was a valid use of police power because mobile homes may have an adverse effect on property values and are vulnerable to strong winds.[123] A Michigan appeals court has upheld regulation of mobile homes through imposition of minimum width requirements on the basis that aesthetics is considered a legitimate end of the police power.[124]

When mobile homes are permitted in residential districts other than separate mobile-home park districts, on-site placement regulations such as setback lines may not be substantially greater for mobile homes than similar regulations for site-built homes in the same district.[125]

Absolute prohibition of mobile homes and manufactured housing from a community can be expected to be invalidated as unrelated to a legitimate governmental purpose.[126] Mobile homes and manufactured houses are not nuisances per se,[127] and they provide an important source of affordable housing for groups that tend to be excluded by overly restrictive single-family residential zoning.[128] A Massachusetts statute granting first-refusal rights to owners of mobile homes when the land underlying the mobile-home community is being sold survived a constitutional challenge in *Greenfield Country Estates Tenants Association, Inc. v. Deep*.[129]

An Iowa statute prohibiting tax increment financing of public improvements within a development that excludes manufactured housing was held violated when a municipality approved a subdivision plat that included private restrictive covenants barring "modular or factory-built" houses in the subdivision. The Supreme Court of Iowa rejected the city's argument that the restrictive covenants were private contracts outside the reach of the statute.[130] On the other hand, the Supreme Court of Ohio invalidated a state law forbidding local governments from banning permanently sited manufactured homes from single-family districts. The court held that the statute was not a general law that took precedence over conflicting local laws because it applied to municipalities and not citizens generally. Also, newer subdivisions could *opt out* because of an exception allowing private covenants banning manufactured housing. The court concluded that the statute "strikes at the heart of municipal home rule."[131]

Group Homes

Group homes are an important component of a variety of federal, state, and local social welfare programs providing services for children, nonviolent criminal offenders, persons with mental or physical handicaps, senior citizens, and victims of substance abuse or incurable diseases. Three characteristics distinguish group homes from traditional forms of housing: (1) the residents are unrelated to one another; (2) supervision is provided by live-in surrogate parents or by 24-hour professional staff working eight-hour shifts; and (3) support services such as counseling, education, and training are provided in addition to shelter.[132] Because of the rigidities built into the Euclidean zoning system,[133] operators of group homes often find themselves at odds with local zoning laws when they seek to locate their homes in single-family residential districts.

Two types of barriers are commonly encountered: (1) restrictive definitions of family, discussed earlier in this chapter in connection with lifestyle restrictions,[134] and (2) discriminatory special-use permit requirements. In addition to judicial determinations that group homes that function as families may not be excluded from single-family residential neighborhoods,[135] states have attempted to resolve the locational conflicts by defining *single family* in zoning-enabling legislation to include residents of small group homes,[136] by characterizing group homes as residential or single-family residential uses,[137] or by making group homes permissible uses in all zoning areas.[138]

Such statutes usually are designed to preempt restrictive local zoning ordinances, but courts do not always agree that preemption was the intended result. In *City of Kenner v. Normal Life of LA, Inc.*,[139] the Louisiana Supreme Court affirmed the issuance of a permanent injunction prohibiting operation of a group home for the mentally retarded where a zoning ordinance restricted use of the property to "single-family residential" use. The ordinance definition of *single family* limited to four the number of unrelated individuals who could qualify as a family. The proposed group home would have housed six unrelated persons. The court reached its conclusion despite a 1983 law that stated in part, "Community homes that provide for six or fewer mentally retarded individuals, with no more than two live-in staff, shall be considered a single family having common interests, goals and problems."[140] The court reasoned that this provision was not intended by the legislature to override local zoning ordinances and subdivision restrictions, partly because the statute stated specifically that "community homes may be operated by right in multiple-family residential districts," but contained no such statement with respect to single-family districts. The court distinguished *Tucker v. Special Children's Foundation*[141] and other earlier cases that had reached contrary results on the grounds that in those cases, single family had not been restrictively defined in the applicable local ordinances.[142]

In addition to problems with the definition of family, group homes may face restrictive permit requirements. Such requirements will be upheld when they are rationally related to a permissible government goal, such as protecting the health and safety of the residents, but will be invalidated if the requirements cannot be so linked. In the leading case of *City of Cleburne v. Cleburne*

Living Center,[143] the Supreme Court struck down an ordinance requiring owners of group homes for the developmentally disabled to obtain annual special permits to operate in multifamily-use districts but not requiring such permits for other uses, such as apartment buildings, boardinghouses, hospitals, and nursing homes.

Although the Court held that mental retardation was not a quasi-suspect classification calling for a stricter standard of review and that cities could constitutionally treat certain classes of people—such as the aged, disabled, and retarded—differently from the general populace because of their special needs, the Court concluded that a regulation supported by "mere negative attitudes, or fear, unsubstantiated by factors which are properly cognizable in a zoning proceeding" would not pass muster even under the more relaxed rational-basis standard. In the Court's view, the regulation rested on an "irrational prejudice against the mentally retarded."[144]

Group homes have received federal legislative support through the Fair Housing Amendments Act of 1988 (FHAA).[145] A new category of prohibited housing discrimination, because of a handicap, was added. *Handicap* is defined to include "mental impairment which substantially limits one or more of such person's major life activities, . . . but . . . not . . . addiction to a controlled substance."[146] Unlawful discrimination includes "a refusal to make reasonable accommodations in rules, policies, practices, or services, when such accommodations may be necessary to afford such person equal opportunity to use and enjoy a dwelling,"[147] but dwellings do not have to be made available to handicapped persons "whose tenancy would constitute a direct threat to the health or safety of other individuals or . . . would result in substantial physical damage to the property of others."[148]

Because the Fair Housing Act applies to local land use restrictions,[149] the prohibitions against discrimination because of a handicap include exclusionary zoning practices against group homes serving handicapped persons.

In the first major test of the application of the 1988 Amendments to local zoning regulations, the Eighth Circuit upheld a state statute and a local ordinance imposing a dispersal requirement on group homes that required them to be at least one-quarter mile apart.[150] Applying the rational-basis standard of review,[151] the court held that the goals of nondiscrimination and deinstitutionalization are compatible and concluded that the dispersal requirement served the legitimate goal of ensuring that residential treatment facilities will be located "in the community" instead of in an institutional environment.[152]

Other courts, though, have rejected the "anti-clustering" basis for dispersal regulations, reasoning that spacing regulations permit communities to impose quotas on protected classes, thereby limiting their FHAA-protected right to live where they choose, in the residence they choose.[153] The burden of proof for reasonable accommodations claims is complicated by the multiple factors involved in the reasonable accommodations provisions: (1) "reasonable accommodations," (2) "necessary to afford," and (3) "equal opportunity to use and enjoy a building."[154] Most courts that have considered this issue have concluded that the plaintiff has the burden of establishing all three elements of the provision, particularly the "necessary" and "equal opportunity" prongs, after which the burden shifts to the defendant to show that the requested accommodations are unreasonable.[155]

Density Controls

In addition to height restrictions for buildings, municipalities can control the density of human activity by regulating the manner in which its population and buildings are distributed, through such devices as minimum lot sizes,[156] setback requirements,[157] and ratios of permissible usable space to lot or floor areas.[158]

Density controls have traditionally been regarded as valid uses of police power: "A quiet place where yards are wide, people few, and motor vehicles restricted are legitimate guidelines in land-use project addressed to family needs."[159] However, they must meet the standard of reasonableness as measured by the rational-basis test.[160] Applying that test, the Supreme Court of Connecticut invalidated a 1,300-square-foot minimum floor-area requirement for single-family homes.[161] In an exhaustive opinion, the Court concluded that a minimum floor-area requirement that was not linked to the number of persons occupying the regulated structure had no rational relationship to protection of public health, and that the challenged minimum floor-area requirement of 1,300 square feet did not have a rational relationship to the conservation of property values. The Court refused to accept the arguments that "more expensive single-family houses are more desirable and . . . more such houses generate more taxes from persons better able to pay more taxes with perhaps less demand upon municipal services."[162] No findings were made by the trial court that the proposed houses, which were designed for 1,026 square feet of floor space, would "decrease or destabilize" building values.[163] The Court stressed that possible beneficial effects are not the only items considered in evaluating the reasonableness of a regulation, but that possible harmful effects must also be considered. A minimum floor-area requirement that is higher than that required for health or safety reasons causes a substantial but unnecessary increase in the cost of houses and a corresponding decrease in affordability, the Court noted. In the case at bar, the difference in cost between the proposed 1,026-square-foot house and the required 1,300-square-foot house was estimated to be approximately $10,000, increasing the construction costs from $59,000 to approximately $70,000. This, plus the lack of evidence that the proposed modular houses would be "significantly undersized," cheap, or "aesthetically incompatible" with other houses in the neighborhood, as well as the lack of any link between the 1,300-square-foot floor-area requirement and public health concerns, led the Court to conclude that there was no rational basis for the requirement.[164]

In an important point with implications for local efforts to target the location of affordable housing, the Court dismissed as irrelevant the municipality's stress on significant efforts it had made in other districts to encourage more construction of affordable housing by reducing minimum floor-area requirements and permitting multiple-family dwellings. The Court noted that the Connecticut zoning-enabling act had been amended to require zoning regulations to "encourage the development of housing opportunities for all citizens of the municipality consistent with soil types, terrain, and infrastructure capacity."[165] Emphasizing the requirement that housing opportunities be encouraged for "*all* citizens," not just "in some zones for some citizens," the Court concluded that what was done in other districts was irrelevant to the challenged minimum floor-area requirement in the absence of any showing that the 1,300-square-foot requirement had any bearing on "soil types, terrain, and infrastructure capacity" of the districts in which the 1,300-square-foot minimum was in place.[166]

A dissenting opinion characterized the majority's finding of no rational relationship between floor-area requirements and conservation of property values as "an exercise in appellate factfinding upon a subject where . . . reasonable differences of opinion exist." Noting that the overall reduction in the cost of the proposed housing by elimination of the 1,300-square-foot requirement would be about 10 percent, from $109,000 to $99,000, the dissent doubted that such a reduction would have "any significant impact upon the affordability of housing." The "seriousness" of the problem of affordable housing should not be ignored, but a legislative rather than a judicial response is the only way an "adequate solution" can be found to "a social problem of this nature," the dissent concluded.[167]

Flexibility in the use of density controls is achieved by ordinances allowing cluster zoning or density zoning. Under such schemes, a developer who has a large tract of land to develop can vary the density within the tract, making some areas more dense than is allowed under the provisions of the zoning laws, provided that the overall density is within the limits imposed on the rest of the community.[168] Such density variation within a large tract is also a common feature of the planned unit development (PUD) concept.[169]

Where restrictions other than density controls prevent a developer from building on parts of a tract under development, the question sometimes arises whether this restricted land can be included in the overall density measurement of the entire tract. A New York court held that even though a developer could not build on 210 of his 450 acres because of the existence of a conservation easement, under a cluster zoning law the entire 450 acres could be counted in determining the number of units that could be constructed on the remaining 240 acres.[170]

Management of the overall growth of a community sometimes is attempted through the density-control technique of limiting the number of building permits that can be issued yearly. Courts tend to be suspicious of building-permit caps or quotas. In one case, the Supreme Court of New Hampshire invalidated an ordinance that limited the number of building permits that could be issued yearly to 3 percent of the total existing dwellings because of a lack of evidence linking the 3 percent limit to a legitimate growth-management concern. "Growth controls are intended to regulate and control the timing of development, not the prevention of development," the Court stated.[171]

Yet another technique sometimes advocated to control density is to impose a narrow definition of the family that can live in a single-family zone. The Supreme Court has upheld—over a strong dissent that failed to see how a definition of family affected density of use—an ordinance that defined *family* to mean "one or more persons related by blood, adoption, or marriage, or not more than two related persons."[172]

Where a plan meets the density requirements of the master plan, it cannot be rejected without good reasons. Courts have reversed denials of development plans where local regulatory bodies failed to provide factual findings and reasons for denial adequate to give development guidance in reapplying and to provide courts a basis for judicial review.[173]

If density requirements in adopted master plans conflict with density requirements in zoning ordinances, and local subdivision ordinances require subdivision plans to meet the density requirements of the master plan, courts have enforced the subdivision ordinance requirement of consistency with the master plan, even though the subdivision plan meets the density requirements of the zoning ordinance.[174]

Inclusionary Zoning

As early as 1961, the principles of flexible zoning described in chapter 4[175] began being used for what the Court of Appeals of New York has termed "uneconomic but necessary uses."[176] Rather than using zoning negatively to exclude activities, certain forms of flexible zoning began to be used positively to encourage the inclusion of desirable items such as open space, amenities, and public areas for artistic and cultural activities. In the 1970s and 1980s, communities began to add affordable housing to the list of activities supported by inclusionary zoning.

Two techniques have most commonly been utilized: (1) the set-aside program, in which an allocation is made of a specified percentage of units in a large residential development as below-market price (BMP) units[177] or moderately priced dwelling units (MPDUs);[178] and (2) the density bonus program, in which awards are made of increases in allowable densities when BMP or MPDU housing is included in large residential developments.[179]

Set-asides

Set-aside programs may be either voluntary or mandatory, although studies have found that developers generally have been reluctant to participate in voluntary set-aside programs, leading advocates to press for mandatory programs.[180] Mandatory set-aside programs typically require a relatively small percentage, usually ranging from 5 to 25 percent, of developments in certain zones or in certain configurations, such as PUDs, to be comprised of low- or moderate-cost housing.[181] They are typically imposed as conditions to rezoning or site-plan approval[182] and are subject to the *Lucas*[183] and *Nollan/Dolan*[184] takings tests discussed in chapter 3.

Density Bonuses

Density bonus programs are voluntary programs that offer developers an increase in the permitted density of residential projects either by a sliding scale that increases the permitted density as the number of low- or moderate-cost units increases, or by a fixed amount for participation in an affordable housing program.[185] For example, a 1990 amendment to the Virginia zoning-enabling statute authorizes cities and counties of certain populations to enact density bonus programs for projects of 50 or more units in which densities may be increased by 20 percent of the applicable density range for single-family housing, detached or attached, and 10 percent for multiple-family housing, in return for allocations of at least 12.5 percent of the total number of units to affordable single-family housing and at least 12.25 percent to affordable multiple-family housing.[186]

Set-aside and density bonus programs may be operated separately from each other and may be voluntary or mandatory, but most observers believe their potential is most likely to be realized when they are combined in a mandatory set-aside program that grants density bonuses as a form of "compensation" to participating developers.[187] Mandatory set-asides must overcome several problems, including constitutional questions, political objections, retention of affordability of set-aside units over time, and the possibility of developer evasion of set-aside requirements by building conventional units first and then not completing the project.

The basic constitutional questions are the familiar ones of taking, substantive due process, and equal protection. In *Mount Laurel II*, the Supreme Court of New Jersey confronted the substantive due process question, posed in the guise of an attack on inclusionary zoning techniques as "impermissible socio-economic use[s] of the zoning power, . . . not substantially related to the use of land."[188] The court upheld the use of density bonuses and mandatory set-asides for construction of affordable housing when a showing is made that the *Mount Laurel* obligation to provide "a realistic opportunity for the construction of [a] fair share of the lower income housing allocation" cannot be satisfied "simply by removal of restrictive barriers."[189] Citing its earlier decision rejecting due process and equal protection challenges to a zoning ordinance that permitted mobile homes in a zone restricted to elderly persons or families,[190] the Court declared that:

> [T]he . . . special need of lower income families for housing, and its impact on the general welfare, could justify a district limited to such use and certainly one of lesser restriction that requires only that multi-family housing within a district *include* such use (the equivalent of a mandatory set-aside).[191]

The Court attacked the socioeconomic argument against inclusionary zoning head-on, saying it was "nonsense" to single out inclusionary zoning because "practically any significant kind of zoning now used has a substantial socio-economic impact and, in some cases, a socio-economic motivation."[192] On the question of authority to engage in inclusionary zoning, the Court stated that prohibiting affirmative devices "seems unfair" in view of the long-standing approval of large-lot, single-family residence districts, which the court noted was "keyed, in effect," to income levels. Although zoning ordinances must by statute be designed to focus on the appropriate use of land,[193] this does not mean that zoning ordinances must be limited to considerations of the "physical use" of land, the Court declared:

> All of the physical uses are simply a means to [the ends of zoning]. . . . We know of no governmental purpose relating to zoning that is served by

requiring a municipality to ingeniously design detailed land use regulations, purporting to be 'directly tied to the physical use of the property,' but actually aimed at accommodating lower income families, while not allowing it directly to require developers to construct lower income units.[194]

The Court did not directly respond to the taking challenge against inclusionary zoning, but it appeared to reject it in an important footnote, the premise of which is supported by Supreme Court takings jurisprudence:

> The *explicit* requirement of lower income units in a zoning provision may be necessary if the municipality's social goals are to prevail over neutral market forces. Zoning does not require that land be used for maximum profitability, and on occasion the goals of zoning may require something less.[195]

As might be expected, the *Mount Laurel* approach advocating mandatory set-asides as part of an affirmative effort to provide affordable housing can cause intense political problems. Aside from the serious question of the proper role of the judiciary in resolving social problems,[196] opposition may be expected from neighboring residents to proposals to increase allowable density through density bonuses[197] and from developers fearing loss of profit potential if mandatory set-asides are implemented.

New Jersey's experience in the late 1980s, the first five years after *Mount Laurel II*,[198] points up two profit-related problems with mandatory set-asides: (1) the difficulty in producing a profitable multifamily development when a percentage of the rents must be set at a below-market rate, and (2) the clear preference of developers for ownership units, single-family or condominium, over apartments. Without substantial federal or state housing subsidies, set-aside programs are not likely to produce housing for the low-income persons of society, although they have been shown to be effective in producing affordable housing for moderate-income families.[199]

A study of inclusionary housing programs in California found that at least 64 local jurisdictions in California had implemented such programs. Approximately 25,000 affordable units had been produced or were in the pipeline by November 1994. In addition, more than $24 million had been collected in fees that developers were permitted to pay in lieu of actually constructing affordable units. Inclusionary requirements ranged from 5 to 66 percent of the units in a particular development, with the most popular percentage being 10 percent. Required terms of affordability ranged from ten years to perpetuity. Two-thirds of the programs were mandatory, and mandatory programs had produced the most very low and low-income affordable units compared to units produced under voluntary programs.[200]

Zoning Override ("Anti-Snob") Legislation

Some states have responded legislatively to affordable housing issues by modifying the local zoning procedures for reviewing affordable housing development applications. These modifications may include changes in the zoning appeals procedures and standards of review.

Massachusetts

One of the first states to respond legislatively to the exclusionary zoning phenomenon was Massachusetts, when it enacted its celebrated "anti-snob" law in 1969.[201] Rather than mandate affordable housing set-asides or authorize density bonuses, the anti-snob law established a housing appeals committee in the state Department of Community Affairs with authority to override local zoning decisions blocking low- or moderate-income housing developments, defined as housing subsidized by any federal or state housing production program.[202]

Under the Massachusetts statute, public agencies and private organizations proposing to build low- and moderate-income housing may bypass local regulatory agencies by submitting a single application to the local zoning board of appeals,[203] which is responsible for coordinating an analysis of the application by interested regulatory agencies, conducting a public hearing, and making a decision regarding the application. Comprehensive permits or approvals may be issued by the board of appeals, which must act within 40 days after termination of the public hearing.[204]

If the application is denied or approved with conditions that make the project "uneconomic," the developer may appeal to the state housing appeals committee, with the issues being whether the decision is "reasonable and consistent with local needs."[205] The statute provides that requirements or regulations are "consistent with local needs" if they are imposed after a comprehensive hearing in one of the following two situations:

> 1) more than 10 percent of the housing units, or at least 1.5 percent of the total land area zoned for residential, commercial, or industrial use in the municipality is low or moderate-income housing; or 2) the proposal would result in low or moderate-income housing construction starts on more than three tenths of one percent of the land area, or ten acres, whichever is larger, in a calendar year.[206]

If the state housing appeals committee concludes that the local zoning decision is not consistent with local needs, it vacates the decision and orders a comprehensive permit or approval to be issued, provided that the proposed housing would not violate safety standards contained in federal or state building and site-plan requirements.[207]

Housing advocates report that the state housing appeals committee has been aggressive in enforcing the spirit as well as the text of the law. As of January 1, 1989, more than 35,000 units of affordable housing had been proposed and 17,000 units built since enactment of the statute.[208] Mediation services offered by the Massachusetts Mediation Service, a state agency, have been instrumental in resolving about 25 percent of cases appealed to the state housing appeals committee.[209]

Connecticut

Twenty years after the Massachusetts statute was enacted, Connecticut followed suit with a similar zoning override procedure, the Connecticut Affordable Housing Appeals Act ("Appeals Act"), although the override power was delegated to the judiciary rather than to a state administrative agency.[210] Developers of affordable housing may appeal adverse land use regulatory decisions to the superior court of Hartford-New Britain. Affordable housing is defined as assisted housing or housing in which at least 20 percent of the dwelling units will be conveyed by deeds containing covenants or restrictions limiting sale prices or rents to levels enabling persons and families with median income or less to pay no more than 30 percent of their annual income for housing.[211]

Upon appeal, the burden shifts to the local agency to prove, based on the evidence in the record, that:

> (1) the decision from which such appeal is taken and the reasons cited for such decision are supported by sufficient evidence in the record; (2) the decision is necessary to protect substantial public interests in health, safety, or other matters which the commission may legally consider; (3) such public interests clearly outweigh the need for affordable housing; and (4) such public interests cannot be protected by reasonable changes to the affordable housing development.[212]

If the burden is not met, the court is directed to "revise, modify, remand, or reverse" the decision consistent with the evidence presented.[213] Communities are exempt from the affordable housing override provisions if at least 10 percent of the existing housing units are affordable or they have received a certificate of affordable housing project completion from the Connecticut commissioner of finance, which carries with it a one-year exemption.[214]

The Appeals Act has been controversial. Municipalities have objected that the statute abrogates their home-rule authority. Planners have feared that builders could blackmail communities into accepting development proposals despite planning objections by threatening to file an affordable housing proposal if the first proposal were rejected.[215] Amendments in 2000 increased the percentage of required affordable housing units to 30 percent and the required length of affordability to 40 years.[216] Developers seeking affordable housing approval must file two new documents: an Affordability Plan and a Conceptual Site Plan. The Affordability Plan must include "draft zoning regulations, conditions of approvals, deeds, restrictive covenants or lease provisions that will govern affordable dwelling units."[217] Connecticut Law Professor Terry Tondro, a co-chair of the Blue Ribbon Commission on Housing that proposed the Appeals Act, gives mixed reviews to the first ten years of experience with the Act. On the one hand, local planning and zoning bodies now must state the reasons for their decisions regarding affordable housing proposals. On the other hand, the Connecticut Supreme Court has accepted the use of "unsupported assertions" as reasons and has limited the area of need determinations to the municipality in which the site in question is located.[218] In addition, the 2000 amendments have, in Tondro's opinion, "increased the complexity of the reviews required for affordable housing projects, so that instead of simplifying these applications we have burdened them even more than before."[219]

California

California has enacted a series of provisions designed to improve the procedural posture of affordable housing development proposals, including limitations to adverse design criteria, requiring specific public health or safety reasons for disapproving or reducing densities of housing developments that are consistent with local zoning and general plans, and imposing the burden of proof on local government when a developer or other person appeals a permit denial or density reduction.[220]

Many California cities and towns have enacted inclusionary housing programs, and the movement has been spreading across the country.[221] Such ordinances tend to be controversial because developers and landowners may perceive them to be uncompensated transfers of property. Most courts that have confronted inclusionary housing ordinances have upheld them, although a Colorado ski community's ordinance was held violative of the state's anti–rent-control ordinance.[222] A California court upheld a 10 percent mandatory set-aside requirement after refusing to apply the *Nollan/Dolan* heightened scrutiny. The Home Builders Association of Northern California (plaintiffs) argued unsuccessfully that there was no "essential nexus" or "rough proportionality" between the impact of property development and the required set-aside.[223]

In addition, a California statute establishes a state pilot project in conjunction with an inter-regional partnership (IRP) in the San Francisco Bay area to provide incentives "to improve the balance of jobs and housing." Incentives include tax credit priority, return of property taxes, pooling of redevelopment funds, and tax-increment financing. Eligible projects are affordable housing developments "in areas with job surpluses" and "job generating projects in areas with housing surpluses."[224]

Planning for Affordable Housing

As noted in chapter 2, several states require municipalities to engage in comprehensive planning or specify the subjects that must be included in local comprehensive plans. Housing is a major element that must be covered under these planning statutes.

As an example of the specific detail required by the California statute, the housing element must include a seven-point assessment of housing needs and inventory of relevant resources and constraints. Analyses must be made of population and employment trends, household characteristics, and inventory of available land; potential government constraints on development of housing for all income levels, such as land use controls, site improvement requirements, fees, and exactions; nongovernmental constraints, such as availability of financing, price of land, and cost of construction; special housing needs of groups such as handicapped, elderly, large families, farmworkers, families with female heads of households, and persons needing emergency shelter; and opportunities for energy conservation. In addition, a statement of community housing goals, qualified objectives and policies, and a five-year schedule of proposed actions to be taken by the local government to implement housing policies and achieve housing goals and objectives must be included.[225]

As an example of the detail Florida requires in the mandatory elements of a local comprehensive plan, the housing element must consist of standards, plans, and principles to be followed in:

a. The provision of housing for all current residents and anticipated future residents of the jurisdiction.
b. The elimination of substandard dwelling conditions.
c. The structural and aesthetic improvement of existing housing.
d. The provision of adequate sites for future housing, including housing for low-income and moderate-income families, mobile homes, and group home facilities and foster care facilities, with supporting infrastructure and public facilities.
e. Provision for relocation housing and identification of historically significant and other housing for purposes of conservation, rehabilitation, or replacement.
f. The formulation of housing implementation programs.
g. The creation or preservation of affordable housing to minimize the need for additional local services and avoid the concentration of affordable housing units only in specific areas of the jurisdiction.[226]

Planning for affordable housing received a boost from Congress with the enactment of the National Affordable Housing Act of 1990.[227] Under the Act, an important component of a new housing block grant (HBG) as well as continuation of community development block grant (CDBG) funding is the requirement that recipient jurisdictions prepare and submit to HUD a five-year comprehensive housing affordability strategy (CHAS), which must be updated annually.[228]

The Act lists 15 items that must be included in a CHAS.[229] HUD has combined the CHAS and the CDBG-required community development plan into one Consolidated Plan that serves as the planning document for a variety of federal housing and community development grant programs, and has organized those items into the following five components: (1) *needs assessment*, both current and projected for five years; (2) *market and inventory conditions*, including population trends and information on assisted- and public-housing stock; (3) *strategies*, including priorities for a five-year period; (4) *resources*, both needed and anticipated from the private and public sectors, and coordination of such resources; and (5) *implementation plans and goals*, including the number of persons and families expected to be provided with affordable housing over the five-year period.[230] Coordination between state and local governments in preparation of their respective strategies is urged, but units of general local government are not required to obtain approval of their strategies from their state government.[231] The Act requires HUD to approve housing strategies within 60 days of receipt, unless HUD finds that the strategy is "inconsistent with the purposes of this Act," or that the information required to be submitted "has not been provided in a substantially complete manner."[232]

Recipient communities are required to explain in their housing strategies whether the cost of housing or incentives to provide affordable housing are affected by local property tax, zoning, land use control, and related public policies, along with strategies to "remove or ameliorate [their] negative effects," but adoption of such policies may not be a basis for HUD disapproval of a Consolidated Plan.[233]

Practitioner Perspectives

Conversations with representatives of nonprofit housing organizations, along with perusal of the current literature on the topic, have identified three broad areas in which lawyers can assist affordable housing efforts:[234]

1. Offer legal services on a pro bono or reduced-fee basis to nonprofit housing organizations.
2. Encourage real estate developer clients to renew efforts to produce affordable housing through joint ventures with nonprofit housing organizations and public/private partnerships with interested local governments.
3. Participate in community-based efforts to reduce local opposition to apartments or other forms of multifamily housing in single-family residential neighborhoods.

Legal Services to Nonprofit Housing Organizations

Topics of Legal Services. Most of the organizations in need of legal assistance are local, neighborhood-based nonprofit organizations that wish to provide housing in their communities, either by themselves or in concert with more experienced, profit-motivated enterprises. Some of the topics for which legal assistance may be needed include:

1. Establishing the basic structure of the organization—drafting articles of incorporations and bylaws, seeking tax-exempt status, etc.
2. Providing tax information and advice, including but not limited to annual filings; some sophisticated issues regarding compliance with federal and state tax laws can arise from nonprofits' participation in the business of housing.
3. Representing nonprofits at real estate closings and in formal or informal negotiations with other development participants.
4. Interpreting federal, state, or city regulations for a given housing program, including allowable use of funds, financing requirements, tenant selection criteria, reporting, and other administrative requirements.
5. Complying with fair housing laws, particularly the Fair Housing Amendments Act of 1988; fair housing laws place important restrictions on landlords' flexibility with respect to the selection and treatment of tenants. Nonprofits become landlords when they get into the housing business, a fact that often proves troubling to them. The consistent tenant selection standards required by the Fair Housing Act may cause trouble for nonprofits that house people based on ad hoc assessments of need. Fair housing issues may arise more often in areas with mixed incomes, which also are areas that cities are likely to promote when the new-housing block-grant program becomes operational.

6. Establishing fair and reasonable property management practices and procedures, and representing nonprofits when necessary in implementing the management system through grievance procedures, court proceedings, etc.

Levels of legal experience. There are at least two levels of legal experience required for effective assistance to nonprofits. The organizational, recurring compliance, and property management assistance can be provided quite well, for the most part, by younger members of the bar—law firm associates with one to five years of experience. Interpretation of program regulations can also usually be handled by this group.

More sophisticated questions involving tax laws, federal and state investment regulations, and corporation and partnership laws may require the help of experienced real estate practitioners who are knowledgeable about development and financing issues. Providing housing for low-income persons is a business, even though nonprofit organizations may be involved. The same basic questions concerning tax consequences, potential liability, appropriate legal entities, and acquisition and disposition of property that are raised in commercial developments are raised in low-income housing developments. This level of assistance may be best provided by lawyers who have had substantial experience in real estate development of one type or another.

Encouraging Developer Involvement in Affordable Housing Initiatives

Federal and state housing programs are complex pieces of legislation that require patience and understanding, as well as willing participants, for their success. Real estate lawyers can provide a valuable service to developer clients and to local communities by learning the details of the programs and encouraging participation in them.

Reducing Local Opposition to Nontraditional Housing

The search for affordable housing for both low- and moderate-income families often leads to forms of housing that do not comply with local land use regulations designed to promote single-family, detached housing on relatively large lots. Accessory housing, group homes, townhouses, and apartment clusters are some examples. Opposition to such forms of housing may often be caused by a fear of the unknown—a concern that the introduction of nontraditional forms of housing into a single-family residential neighborhood will somehow cause harm to the neighborhood.

Analysts have identified two basic strategies that nontraditional housing providers use to communicate with prospective neighbors: (1) a collaborative, high-profile approach in which direct contact is made with representatives of the community in advance of commencement of operations; and (2) an autonomous, low-profile approach in which the interests of potential housing consumers are emphasized and advance contact or "permission" to enter a neighborhood is not sought.[235] The 1988 Amendments to the Fair Housing Act,[236] along with enactment of the Americans with Disabilities Act[237] and the

Cranston-Gonzalez National Affordable Housing Act,[238] are believed to have established a legal basis for a "rights-based" strategy of "aggressive autonomy" characterized by "independent siting actions on the part of facility operators and advocates."[239]

Lawyers can work to defuse these fears through analysis of particular proposals, discussion with affected residents, and mediation of disputes between proponents and prospective neighbors. The June 1990 issue of the *Arbitration Journal* contains an excellent analysis of the potential for use of mediation as a technique for resolving site-specific public policy disputes, such as often flare up when apartments or other forms of multifamily housing are proposed as affordable housing.[240]

The HUD Advisory Commission on Regulatory Barriers to Affordable Housing submitted its recommendations in 1991. Areas of concern to the Commission include zoning ordinances, subdivision controls, building codes, impact fees, permit requirements, environmental regulations, and rent controls. Because most of these issues are locally implemented, major efforts at change will have to be locally based. Knowledgeable real estate lawyers can examine the impact that current practices have on housing for low- and moderate-income families in their communities and help craft modifications to local regulations that remove artificial barriers to affordable housing without jeopardizing the legitimate interests of affected communities.

Examples of Pro Bono Representation

It is probably neither possible nor wise to attempt to specify precisely what lawyers might expect to do as pro bono counsel, but some examples of recent activities may help develop a sense of the range of possibilities.

In Nashville, a lawyer attended an American Bar Association (ABA) satellite seminar in December 1989. One person present at the seminar was a law school classmate who had worked for Legal Services Agency for the last 15 years. The two of them compared notes concerning housing, with the legal services lawyer saying, "I know a dozen theories on which I can sue a slumlord, but I don't know how to help someone create a new housing project." The real estate lawyer responded that, while he had learned a lot about real estate law in the last 15 years, he did not know what he could do to help house the homeless people that he drove by every day on his way to work. That conversation resulted in a referral to the real estate lawyer of the director of a nonprofit community service organization who had identified a motel that offered the potential for renovation as a single-room-occupancy (SRO) facility. Over the next several months, the lawyer negotiated a contract for purchase of the property, which was contingent upon receipt of 100 Section 8 certificates from HUD, the availability of bank financing, and zoning changes. Nine months later the zoning approval had been granted and everything was in place to satisfy a loan commitment from a consortium of local banks to enable the nonprofit organization to acquire and renovate the facility.

A law firm in Chicago has served as pro bono counsel for a neighborhood redevelopment organization that was incorporated in 1979 by members of a church that had been located in the community since the turn of the 20th century. Over the ensuing decade the organization grew to the point that it employed 400 people and had an annual budget of more than $4.5 million. During that time it has created more than 400 housing units with a total investment of $17 million in the community. The organization also provides health and family services, senior services, and an employment center, along with cultural and educational activities. The law firm adopted the organization and serves as its general counsel. A variety of legal services are provided by partners and associates of the law firm.

Several lawyers in St. Louis joined forces with accountants, architects, bankers, social workers, and other professionals to provide pro bono representation to nonprofit groups involved in the preservation and development of affordable housing, as well as groups establishing homeless shelters. The committee offers supportive training and informational publications to volunteer attorneys and nonprofit developers regarding such information as selection of the appropriate entity, financing alternatives, transactional issues, introducing professionals to the mentality of nonprofit corporations, and ways in which corporate clients can contribute through use of tax incentives and other federal programs.

These examples suggest three different ways that interested lawyers can become involved in low-income housing efforts: (1) by direct personal contact with individuals in legal services organizations and nonprofit groups who have specific projects that need real estate legal services; (2) by law firm involvement as pro bono counsel for nonprofit organizations, with the contacts coming initially from members of the firm who belong to churches and other institutions that sponsor neighborhood development programs; and (3) by contacting local bar associations, legal services organizations, and law schools and joining local affordable-housing programs.

Sources of Information and Contacts

The ABA Commission on Homelessness and Poverty has identified different programs sponsored by bar associations, legal services, and/or law schools that offer various types of pro bono legal services to people who need assistance in obtaining housing. The U.S. Conference of Mayors has identified more than 100 housing programs under a listing it calls "Partnerships for Affordable Housing" that are sponsored or assisted in some way by cities.

Other sources of information concerning local housing organizations include the Enterprise Foundation, which publishes a directory of approximately 100 nonprofit organizations with which it works in 30 cities, and the National Low Income Housing Coalition (NLIHC), 1012 Fourteenth Street NW, Suite 1500, Washington, D.C. 20005; (202) 662-1530. The NLIHC works with nonprofits throughout the country.

The problem of affordable housing and its more visible symptom, homelessness, is an issue of growing concern throughout the country. Lawyers with real estate practice skills can perform invaluable public services in helping fledgling local housing efforts reach fruition.

Land use practitioners report that the land use process is changing. Many communities are running out of developable land, with the result that much of the future land use activity is expected to redevelop already developed areas rather than to expand into undeveloped areas. More attention must be paid to the impact such activity will have on people in the path of redevelopment. In such areas, affordable housing issues are likely to come into sharp focus. Lawyers with experience in real estate development can give something of inestimable value back to their communities by joining local efforts to remove barriers to affordable housing.

Notes

1. The term *Euclidean zoning* refers to a particular type of land use control, characterized by a cookie-cutter pattern of rigid, rectangular districts, which was upheld by the Supreme Court in Village of Euclid v. Ambler Realty Co., 272 U.S. 365 (1926). *See* Robert Kratovil, *Zoning: A New Look,* 11 CREIGHTON L. REV. 433, 434 n. 6 (1977).

2. An earlier version of pp. 377–79 appeared in Peter W. Salsich, Jr., *Group Homes, Shelters and Congregate Housing, Deinstitutionalization and the NIMBY Syndrome,* 21 REAL PROP., PROB. & TR. J. 413–17 (1986). Reprinted with permission.

3. David Alan Richards, *Downtown Growth Control Through Development Rights Transfer,* 21 REAL PROP., PROB & TR. J. 435 (Fall 1986). The other goal was the encouragement of "intensive development of tax-generating property." *Id.*

In *Euclid,* Justice Sutherland noted that the "crux" of modern zoning legislation was "the creation and maintenance of residential districts from which business and trade of every sort, including hotels and apartment houses, are excluded." 272 U.S. at 390.

4. *See, e.g.,* DANIEL R. MANDELKER, ET AL., PLANNING AND CONTROL OF LAND DEVELOPMENT 197 (5th ed., 2001); SEYMOUR I. TOLL, ZONED AMERICA 78–187 (1969); JOSEPH D. McGOLDRICK, SEYMOUR GRAUBARD, & RAYMOND J. HOROWITZ, BUILDING REGULATION IN NEW YORK CITY 93 (1944); E. BASSETT, ZONING, 9 (1940).

5. *See* Euclid v. Ambler, 272 U.S. at 365 (1926).

6. *Id.* at 389–90.

7. *Id.*

8. 272 U.S. 365 (1926).

9. *Id.* at 394.

10. "If the validity of the legislative classification for zoning purpose be fairly debatable, the legislative judgment must be allowed to control." *Id.* at 388.

11. The ordinance construed in *Euclid* was an example of the "hierarchy of uses" concept of zoning. The most restrictive zone was the U–1 zone, which permitted only single-family residences, agricultural uses, and related activities. 272 U.S. at 381. In all other zones, the uses were cumulative, meaning that uses permitted in a more-restricted zone also were permitted in a less-restricted zone. *See generally* D. Mandelker, *supra* n. 4, at 70–75.

12. The literature is replete with commentary on the exclusionary zoning phenomenon, most of it critical. *See, e.g.,* ANTHONY DOWNS, OPENING UP THE SUBURBS, 317–49 (1973); RICHARD P. FISHMAN, HOUSING FOR ALL UNDER LAW, 54–55 (ABA Advisory Commission on Housing and Urban Growth, 1978); ADVISORY COMMISSION ON REGULATORY BARRIERS TO AFFORDABLE HOUSING, "NOT IN MY BACKYARD:" REMOVING BARRIERS TO AFFORDABLE HOUSING (U.S. Dept. of HUD, 1991).

13. Warth v. Seldin, 422 U.S. 490 (1975) (nonresidents lack standing to challenge allegedly exclusionary zoning ordinances in federal court); *see generally* D. Mandelker, *supra* n. 4, at 360–63.

14. *In re* Egg Harbor Assoc. (Bayshore Centre), 94 N.J. 358, 464 A.2d 1115 (1983) (*Mount Laurel I*); Southern Burlington County NAACP v. Township of Mount Laurel, 92 N.J. 158, 456 A.2d 390 (1983); Oakwood at Madison, Inc. v. Township of Madison, 72 N.J. 481, 371 A.2d 1192 (1977); Southern Burlington County NAACP v. Township of Mount Laurel, 67 N.J. 151, 336 A.2d 713 (1975), *appeal dismissed and cert. denied,* 423 U.S. 808 (1975) (*Mount Laurel II*).

15. Blitz v. Town of New Castle, 463 N.Y.S.2d 832 (App. Div. 1983); Robert E. Kurzius, Inc. v. Inc. Village of Upper Brookville, 414 N.E.2d 680 (N.Y. 1980), *cert. denied,* 450 U.S. 1042 (1981); Berenson v. Town of New Castle, 341 N.E.2d 236 (N.Y. 1975).

16. *In re* appeal of Elocin, Inc. 461 A.2d 771 (Pa. 1983); Surrick v. Zoning Board, 382 A.2d 105 (Pa. 1977); Township of Willistown v. Chesterdale Farms, Inc., 341 A.2d 466 (Pa. 1975); Appeal of Girsh, 263 A.2d 395 (Pa. 1970); National Land & Inv. Co. v. Easttown Township Bd. of Adjustment, 215 A.2d 597 (Pa. 1965).

17. Chief Judge Wilentz expressed the frustration of the New Jersey Supreme Court over the lack of progress in ten years of litigation under *Mount Laurel I*:

> After all this time, ten years after the trial court's initial order invalidating its zoning ordinance, Mount Laurel remains affected with a blatantly exclusionary ordinance. . . . We have learned from experience, however that unless a strong judicial hand is used, *Mount Laurel* will not result in housing, but in paper, process, witness, trials and appeals.

Southern Burlington County NAACP v. Township of Mount Laurel (*Mount Laurel II*), 456 A.2d 390, 410 (1983).

18. The history and philosophy of this movement has been summarized as follows:

> *Historical Background*
> Following World War II, community day programs and outpatient clinics were developed for people who otherwise would have been placed in institutions. These programs and clinics demonstrated that most people could receive more appropriate care in the community than they could in an institution.
>
> With the development of community alternatives came the philosophy of "normalization." This philosophy maintains that people should remain in as normal an environment as possible.
>
> As a reflection of this social philosophy, judicial decisions were made which required government to treat institutionalized people so as to facilitate their return to society as soon as possible. Further, case law was developing which indicated that if confinement is necessary, it must take place in the least restrictive setting possible.
>
> A growing body of scientific evidence demonstrated that most people can be helped to overcome developmental, emotional, and intellectual deficits if given the appropriate opportunities to do so.
>
> *Philosophical Background*
> The policies of deinstitutionalization and diversion are based on the premise that less restrictive residential settings afford greater opportunity for individualized activities and freedom of choice for residents. Significant evidence demonstrates that institutional care can produce side effects which are often more debilitating than the disorder. Isolation, lack of motivation, dependency, and loss of basic social skills have all been seen as the result of institutional placement.
>
> Community-based programs work closely with existing community resources and usually have an informal administrative structure. In addition, community-based programs offer services that facilitate family interaction, given greater

access to employment opportunities, and increase chances for moving into more independent living or home care.

Implicit in the social policy of developing community-based residential facilities are the assumptions that:

1. The individual's ability to cope with the environment will be increased as his or her ability to control the environment is increased;
2. Coping with the environment becomes more effective as increasingly complex behaviors are mastered or regained.
3. Successful coping with the environment is a function of the degree to which the individual assimilates or reassimilates cultural standards.

Florida Department of Health and Rehabilitative Services, *Guidelines for Zoning and Special Community Housing* 5–6 (1983).

19. *See, e.g.,* Edward H. Ziegler, *The Twilight of Single-Family Zoning,* 3 UCLA J. ENVTL. L. & POL'Y 161, 195–201 (1983).

20. *See, e.g.,* The Missouri Community Sentencing Act of 1983, MO. REV. STAT. § 217.777 (1996). *See also* MO. REV. STAT. § 559.120 (1999) (allowing probation and requiring participation in a program pursuant to § 217.777, RSMo, when, among other exceptions, "traditional institutional confinement . . . is not necessary for protection of the public").

21. The New Jersey Superior Court, Appellate Division, drew a sharp distinction between residential facilities for recovering addicts and group homes for developmentally disabled persons in Open Door Alcoholism Program v. Bd. of Adjustment, 491 A.2d 17 (N.J. Super. Ct. App. Div. 1985).

22. For a discussion of some of the causes of displacement, *see* Peter W. Salsich, Jr. *Displacement and Urban Reinvestment: A Mount Laurel Perspective,* 53 U. CINN. L. REV. 333, 335–43 (1984).

23. A 1980 study in Jacksonville, Florida, of attitudes regarding group homes found such evidence of the NIMBY phenomenon that it was titled, "But Not in My Neighborhood." *Guidelines for Zoning and Special Community Housing, supra* n. 18, at 11. *See also* Robert L. Schonfeld, *Not In My Neighborhood,* 13 FORD. J. URB L. 281 (1985).

24. *See* text accompanying n. 9, *supra.*

25. In advocating support from local residents for a proposed group home in St. Louis County, John Twiehaus, Superintendent of the St. Louis Developmental Disabilities Treatment Center, commented: "It's by the grace of God that we make it through life without having this. They could as easily be our own sons and daughters." ST. LOUIS POST-DISPATCH, November 4, 1984, p. C3.

26. *See, e.g.,* Beck v. Raymond, 118 N.H. 793, 801, 394 A.2d 847 (1978). However, courts have approved the use of zoning to increase tax ratables to improve the economic balance of the community as long as such fiscal zoning was reasonably linked to a "legitimate comprehensive plan for the zoning of the entire municipality." Gruber v. Mayor and Township Comm. of Raritan Township, 39 N.J. 1, 9–11, 186 A.2d 489, 493 (1962).

27. Norman Williams, Jr. & Norman, *Exclusionary Land Use Controls: The Case of North-Eastern New Jersey,* 22 SYRACUSE L. REV. 475, 478 (1971). *See generally* MICHAEL N. DANIELSON, THE POLITICS OF EXCLUSION (1976); LEONARD S. RUBINOWITZ, LOW-INCOME HOUSING: SUBURBAN STRATEGIES (1974); Eric J. Branfman, et al., *Measuring the Invisible Wall: Land Use Controls and the Residential Patterns of the Poor,* 82 YALE L. J. 483 (1973); Lawrence G. Sager, *Tight Little Islands: Exclusionary Zoning, Equal Protection and the Indigent,* 21 STANFORD L. REV. 767 (1969). An amicus curiae brief of the American Planning Association argued that:

Exclusionary zoning is particularly pernicious because lower income individuals are unable to find affordable housing near suburban places of work, necessitating lengthy commuting trips. As these areas typically have limited, if any, mass transit, the journey to work must be by automobile, creating additional economic hardship for lower income individuals.

Brief of American Planning Association, RICHARD F. BABCOCK & FRED P. BOSSELMAN, EXCLUSIONARY ZONING: LAND USE REGULATION AND HOUSING IN THE 1970S, 114–15 (1973).

28. *See, e.g.,* Country Club Estates, L.L.C. v. Town of Lorna Linda, 281 F.3d 723, 724 (8th Cir. 2002) (increase in minimum square footage from 1,640 to 1,800 for single-family, single-story buildings in designated areas not facially unreasonable; as-applied challenge not ripe because of failure to exhaust administrative remedies). Using the $75 per-square-foot construction cost average for the St. Louis area noted in the text, an 1,800-square-foot house will cost $135,000 to build, not counting land, site preparation costs, and developer profit.

29. Williams and Norman, *Exclusionary Land Use Controls: The Case of North-Eastern New Jersey,* 22 SYRACUSE L. REV. 475, 481, 484 (1971).

30. Southern Burlington County NAACP v. Township of Mount Laurel, 67 N.J. 151, 336 A.2d 713 (1975).

31. N.J. CONST. Art. I, § 1. Although the court focused on state constitutional due process and equal protection issues, the main thrust of the case centered on use of the police power. 67 N.J. at 174–80, 336 A.2d at 725–28. A concurring judge would have reached the same result by interpretation of the terms "general welfare in the zoning enabling statute." 67 N.J. at 193, 336 A.2d at 735 (Mountain, J., concurring).

32. *Id.* at 187–88, 336 A.2d at 731–32.

33. Southern Burlington County NAACP v. Township of Mount Laurel, 92 N.J. 158, 456 A.2d 390 (1983).

34. *See, e.g.,* Home Builders League v. Township of Berlin, 81 N.J. 127, 405 A.2d 381 (1979); Pascack Ass'n, Ltd. v. Washington Township, 74 N.J. 470, 379 A.2d 6 (1977); Fobe Assoc. v. Demarest, 74 N.J. 519, 379 A.2d 31 (1977); Oakwood at Madison, Inc. v. Township of Madison, 72 N.J. 481, 471 A.2d 1192 (1977).

35. *Mount Laurel II,* 92 N.J. at 200, 456 A.2d at 410.

36. 92 N.J. at 352, 456 A.2d at 490.

37. 92 N.J. at 258–74, 456 A.2d at 441–50.

38. *Mount Laurel I,* 67 N.J. at 179, 336 A.2d at 727.

39. *Id.*

40. *Mount Laurel II,* 92 N.J. at 209, 456 A.2d at 415.

41. For discussion of the problems of externalities and spheres of control, *see* TILLO E. KUHN, PUBLIC ENTERPRISE ECONOMICS AND TRANSPORT PROBLEMS 8 (1962); DANIEL R. MANDELKER ET AL., PLANNING AND CONTROL OF LAND DEVELOPMENT 130–34 (1979); Allison Dunham, *A Legal and Economic Basis for City Planning,* 58 COLUM. L. REV. 650 (1958).

42. *Mount Laurel I,* 67 N.J. at 177, 336 A.2d at 726.

43. *Mount Laurel II,* 92 N.J. at 211 n. 5, 456 A.2d at 416, n. 5.

44. *See, e.g.,* Britton v. Town of Chester, 134 N.H. 434, 595 A.2d 492, 497–98 (1991) ("builder's remedy is appropriate, but remedy is available only if the developer's proposal is "reasonable, i.e., providing a realistic opportunity for the construction of low- and moderate-income housing and consistent with sound zoning concepts and environmental concerns"). In addition to the *Mount Laurel* cases in New Jersey, cases reviewed by the APA in its brief for *Britton* include Associated Home Builders, Inc. v. City of Livermore, 18 Cal. 3d 582, 557 P.2d 473, 135 Cal. Rptr. 41 (1976); Sturges v. Town of Chilmark, 380 Mass. 246, 402 N.E.2d 1346 (1980); Smookler v. Wheatfield Township, 394 Mich. 574, 232 N.W.2d 616 (1975); Suffolk Hous. Serv. v. Town of Brookhaven, 70 N.Y.2d 122, 511 N.E.2d 67, 517 N.Y.S.2d 924 (1987); Surrick v. Zoning Hearing Bd., 476 Pa. 182, 382 A.2d 105 (1977).

45. Britton v. Town of Chester, 595 A.2d at 496.

46. *Id. Cf.* C. Hayes, *Suburbanities Housing 'Shield' Is Found Illegal,* WALL STREET JOUR-
NAL, August 2, 1991, p. B1.

47. An earlier version of pp. 382–84 appeared in Salsich, *Displacement and Urban Reinvestment: A Mount Laurel Perspective,* 53 U. CINN. L. REV. 333, 339–43, 363–68 (1984).
Reprinted with permission.

48. Government intervention in the housing market traditionally has consisted of
fine-tuning the natural process of filtering. This concept assumes that government policies
can help all housing consumers best by bolstering new production. Adding new units to
the supply of housing, even if they are high-cost, will aid low-income families because better units gradually will open up to them.

For the filter process to function properly, a normal rate of vacancy is needed. Unless
a certain percentage of dwellings remains temporarily vacant, the necessary rate of residential mobility cannot occur. Thus there is a certain optimum level of housing vacancies
that is desired and necessary to the functioning of the filtering process. The concept of
turnover is simply a change in occupancy. Relating vacancy rate to turnover allows a certain predictability in meeting the needs of a particular group with a known housing stock
at a given vacancy rate. WALLACE SMITH, HOUSING: THE SOCIAL AND ECONOMIC ELEMENTS
145–46 (1970). For an analysis of the filtering pattern in terms of household and housing
characteristics, *see* WALLACE SMITH, FILTERING AND NEIGHBORHOOD CHANGE (1964).

Federal housing policy historically has favored new construction on the assumption
that all subsequent occupants have successively lower incomes. By constructing high-cost
new housing, the lower-income housing needs will be served. Sands, *Housing Turnover:
Assessing Its Relevance to Public Policy,* 42 J. AM. INST. PLANNERS 419, 422–24 (1976); *see also*
WILLIAM G. GRIGSBY, HOUSING MARKETS AND PUBLIC POLICY (1963).

Anthony Downs provides an insightful analysis of how the filtering image has combined with housing and building codes to create and foster exclusionary land practices where
"thousands of the poorest households . . . concentrate in urban centers." Anthony Downs, *The
Successes and Failures of Federal Housing Policy,* 34 PUB. INTEREST 124, 125–27 (1974).

Critics of the filtering concept strike at the lack of true accessibility for all consumers,
especially minorities and large families, and the fact that a disproportionately large share
of the national housing policy has benefited those above the poverty level through the tax
code and housing subsidies. *See* ARTHUR P. SOLOMON, HOUSING THE URBAN POOR 196
(1977). For a policy analysis revealing the major actors in the setting of national housing
policy, *see* HAROLD WOLMAN, POLITICS OF FEDERAL HOUSING (1971).

49. *See* 42 U.S.C. §§ 1450–60 (1976). Under the urban-renewal program, "[r]edevelop-
ment was in essence a bulldozing technique. It tended to throw the baby out with the bath-
water; valuable, usable buildings were destroyed along with the slums. . . . [S]ome communities used redevelopment for 'Negro removal.' " LAWRENCE FRIEDMAN, GOVERNMENT
AND SLUM HOUSING: A CENTURY OF FRUSTRATION 161, 167 (1968) (footnote omitted).

50. One of the major stumbling blocks to an effective analysis of displacement is the
question of whether a particular move is voluntary or involuntary. *See, e.g.,* HUD, DIS-
PLACEMENT REPORT 8 (1979).

The federal Uniform Relocation Act does not require that a move be involuntary for
an eligible person to receive relocation benefits. 42 U.S.C. §§ 4601 *et seq.* (2002).

51. By 2002, the Uniform Condominium Act (UCA) had been enacted in 13 states:
ALA. CODE §§ 35-8A-101 *et seq.* (2002); ARIZ. REV. STAT. ANN. §§ 33-1201 *et seq.* (West
2000); ME. REV. STAT. ANN. tit. 33, §§ 1601-101 to 1604-118 (West 2001); MINN. STAT. ANN.
§§ 515A.1-101 to 515A.4-117 (West 2002); MO. REV. STAT. §§ 448.1-101 to 448.4-120 (2000);
N.C. GEN. STAT. §§ 47C-1-101 *et seq.* (2000); N.M. STAT. ANN. § 47-7A-1 to 47D-20 (Michie
2000); PA. CONS. STAT. ANN. §§ 3101–3413 (West 1994); R.I. GEN. LAWS § 34-36.1-1.01 (1995);
TEX. PROP. CODE ANN. (Property) § 82.001 (Vernon 1995); VA. CODE ANN. § 55-79.39 (Michie

2002); WASH. REV. CODE ANN. §§ 64.34.010 *et seq.* (West 1994). In addition, five states had adopted the Uniform Common Interest Ownership Act (UCIOA), including: ALASKA STAT. § 34.08.010 *et seq.* (Michie 2001); COLO. REV. STAT. ANN. § 38-33.3-101 to 38-33.3-319 (West 2000); CONN. GEN. STAT. ANN. § 47-200 (West 1995); MINN. STAT. ANN. §§ 515 B.1-101 to 515B.4-118; W. VA. CODE §§ 36B-1-101 *et seq.* (2001). The uniform acts require tenants to be given 120 days' notice of a proposed conversion, 60 days to purchase their units, and 180 days to match the price of another purchaser if the tenant has not purchased the unit during the 60-day period. U.C.A. § 4-112 (1980).

Legislation aimed at controlling the rate of condominium conversions raises several constitutional issues regarding the taking of property. *See, e.g.,* Victoria A. Judson, *Defining Property Rights: Constitutionality of Protecting Tenants from Condominium Conversion,* 18 HARV. C.R.-C.L. L. REV. 179 (1983).

52. Preliminary reports from an effort by the city of San Diego to track movement of tenants from apartments after property rehabilitation indicated that the average rent went up 26 percent following rehabilitation and that within two years almost 60 percent of the tenants had left. GAO, RENTAL REHABILITATION WITH LIMITED FEDERAL INVOLVEMENT: WHO IS DOING IT? AT WHAT COST? WHO BENEFITS?, 22–23 (1983) (GAO/RCED-83-148) [hereinafter cited as RENTAL REHABILITATION].

53. According to the GAO study, a New Britain, Connecticut, rehab project spent $6,800 to replace all bathroom fixtures and kitchen and pantry floor coverings, even though code standards required considerably less for compliance. The investor-owner had requested the general improvements as part of the rehabilitation, and the city had incorporated it into the project. Rents increased 36 percent. RENTAL REHABILITATION, *supra* n. 51 at 20–22.

Historic district zoning may impose affirmative duties on property owners that may increase housing costs beyond the owner's ability to pay. *See* Judy G. Meffert, *Affirmative Maintenance Provisions in Historic Preservation: A Taking of Property?,* 34 S.C. L. REV. 713, 716–17 (1981). The article cited several cases in which these provisions were seen as a "reasonable use" of the local government's regulatory power of private property. *Id.* at 726–29. *See, e.g.,* Maher v. City of New Orleans, 516 F.2d 1051 (5th Cir.), *cert. denied,* 426 U.S. 905 (1975); Figarsky v. Historic Dist. Comm'n, 171 Conn. 198, 368 A.2d 163 (1976).

54. In United States v. St. Paul Missionary Pub. Hous., Inc., 575 F. Supp. 867 (N.D. Ohio 1983), the court held that HUD may foreclose on a Section 8 housing complex for elderly and low-income families despite the owner's claim that HUD's failure to pay subsidies caused the default. *See also* Alexander v. HUD, 441 U.S. 39 (1979); Fed. Prop. Mgmt. Corp. v. Harris, 603 F.2d 1226 (6th Cir. 1979); Richard T. LeGates & Chester Hartman, *Displacement,* 15 CLEARINGHOUSE REV. 207, 215 (1981) at 215 (characterizing this problem as a growing one, along with the threat of displacement, "as the first generation of public housing projects terminate their original forty-year annual federal contributions contracts").

55. The Fifth Amendment requires that no property be taken for "public use without just compensation." U.S. CONST., amend. V. The law of eminent domain, then, is limited constitutionally by the definition of public use. Judicial interpretation initially limited governmental taking to property that would be put to actual use by the public—hence comes the public-use test. *See* Philip Nichols, Jr., *The Meaning of Public Use in the Law of Eminent Domain,* 20 B.U. L. REV. 615 (1940), *see also* Neil H. Lebowitz, *Poletown Neighborhood Council v. City of Detroit: Economic Instability, Relativism and the Eminent Domain Public Use Limitation,* 24 WASH. U. J. URB. & CONTEMP. LAW 215, 221 (1983).

In 1954, the Supreme Court in *Berman v. Parker* addressed the constitutionality of a public taking for private use in the condemnation of an area for subsequent private redevelopment, 348 U.S. 26, 28 (1954). The blighted area contained viable commercial properties. Thus the redevelopment project was designed not to rid the area of the evils of slum housing but, as the petitioner contended, to create a "better balanced, more attractive community." *Id.* at 31. The court addressed the question of public use as a police power action:

> The definition is essentially the product of legislative determinations addressed to the purposes of government. . . . Subject to specific constitutional limitations, when the legislature has spoken, the public interest has been declared in terms well-nigh conclusive. In such cases the legislature, not the judiciary, is the main guardian of the public needs. . . . This principle admits of no exception merely because the power of eminent domain is involved.

Id. at 32 (citations omitted). The Court consequentially expanded the traditional public-use test to a public-purpose test and tied the judiciary's hands: "The role of the judiciary in determining whether that power [of eminent domain] is being exercised for a public purpose is an extremely narrow one." *Id.* (citations omitted). Thus the Supreme Court allowed the public taking of private property for later use by a private agency, testing the public-use constitutional question against a more liberal public-purpose standard. *See* Henry W. McGee, Jr., *Urban Renewal in the Crucible of Judicial Review*, 56 Va. L. Rev. 826 (1970). The public-purpose concept in eminent domain recently has been expanded to include a private corporation's promise of economic benefit. In financially troubled Detroit, a 465-acre residential area was declared blighted for the employment promise that a GM plant offered on that location. Poletown Neighborhood Council v. City of Detroit, 410 Mich. 616, 304 N.W.2d 455 (1981); *see* Neil H. Lebowitz, *Poletown Neighborhood Council v. City of Detroit: Economic Instability, Relativism and the Eminent Domain Public Use Limitation*, 24 Wash. U. J. Urb. & Contemp. L. 215 (1983); *see also* Hawaii Hous. Auth. v. Midkiff, 467 U.S. 229, 240 (1984) (finding public-use requirement "coterminous with the scope of a sovereign's police powers"); Laura Mansnerus, *Public Use, Private Use and Judicial Review in Eminent Domain*, 58 N.Y.U. L. Rev. 409, 424–44, 444–55 (1983) (arguing that legislative decision making at local level is entitled to less deference by judiciary than at higher levels because there is less public participation; advising that such local decision making fits less comfortably into doctrine of separation of powers; concluding that courts should weigh constitutionality of enabling legislation in blight redevelopment actions with stricter scrutiny than presently used; arguing court should use a means test against public-purpose requirement to each factual determination).

For an opinion offering a conceptual framework in support of present judicial interpretations of takings and the public use requirements vis-à-vis regulations for the public welfare, *see* John A. Humbach, *A Unifying Theory for Just Compensation Cases: Takings, Regulations & Public Use*, 34 Rutgers L. Rev. 243 (1982).

The privatization of the urban redevelopment process through the statutory encouragement of private urban redevelopment has added a significant dimension to the displacement issue. *See* Mo. Rev. Stat. §§ 353.010–.180 (1978). In some instances these corporations are awarded the power of eminent domain without many of the constitutional or legal constraints to which government agencies would be subject. Under *Young v. Harris*, for example, a private urban redevelopment corporation with eminent domain powers was not required to provide relocation benefits under the URA as a state agency. *See* 599 F.2d 870, 877 (8th Cir.), *cert. denied*, 444 U.S. 993 (1979).

Regulation of land use based on aesthetics has been accepted as a valid exercise of police power and entitled to the proper legislative presumption. Courts sometimes use a means-end test to see if the intended good measures up to the harm caused. *See* Samuel Bufford, *Beyond the Eye of the Beholder: A New Majority of Jurisdictions Authorize Aesthetic Regulation*, 48 U.M.K.C. L. Rev. 125 (1980); Marc David Bishop, State v. Jones; *Aesthetic Regulation—From Junkyards to Residences?* 61 N.C. L. Rev. 942 (1983); Louis B. Meyer, III, *Zoning –*

Stronger Than Dirt: Aesthetics-Based Municipal Regulation May Be A Proper Exercise of the Police Power – State v. Jones, 18 Wake Forest L. Rev. 1167 (1982).

56. Adamec v. Post, 273 N.Y. 250, 7 N.E.2d 120 (1937).

57. *Id.* at 125.

58. *Id.*

59. *See e.g.,* Salsich, *Displacement and Urban Reinvestment: A Mount Laurel Perspective,* 53 U. Cin. L. Rev. 335, 335–40 (1984), discussing studies of displacement.

60. *Mount Laurel I,* 336 A.2d at 726.

61. *Mount Laurel II,* 456 A.2d at 418.

62. *Mount Laurel II,* 456 A.2d at 416, n. 5.

63. Evidence reviewed by HUD makes a persuasive case that displacement is a predictable byproduct of urban reinvestment, although the amount of displacement that occurs as a result of a particular activity remains questionable. HUD, Residential Displacement—An Update 22–37 (1981).

64. *Mount Laurel I,* 336 A.2d at 727.

65. *See supra* notes 47–58 and accompanying text.

66. 42 U.S.C §§ 3601–31 (2000).

67. Burrell v. City of Kankakee, 815 F.2d 1127, 1131 (7th Cir. 1987).

68. Huntington Branch, NAACP v. Town of Huntington, 844 F.2d 926, 934 (2d Cir. 1988), *reh'g affirmed,* 488 U.S. 1023 (1989) (quoting United States v. City of Black Jack, 508 F.2d 1179, 1184–85 (8th Cir. 1974), *cert. denied,* 422 U.S. 1042 (1975)).

69. *Id.* at 937.

70. *Id.* at 934 (citing United States v. Yonkers Board of Educ., 837 F.2d 1181, 1217 (2d Cir. 1987)); Robinson v. 12 Lofts Realty, Inc., 610 F.2d 1032, 1036 (2d Cir. 1979); Resident Advisory Bd. v. Rizzo, 564 F.2d 126, 146–48 (3d Cir. 1977), *cert. denied,* 435 U.S. 908 (1978).

71. 844 F.2d at 936 (citing Resident Advisory Board v. Rizzo, 564 F.2d 126 (3d Cir. 1977), *cert. denied,* 435 U.S. 908 (1978)).

72. *Id.* at 936.

73. *Id.*

74. Avalonbay Communities, Inc. v. Town of Orange, 256 Conn. 557, 597, 775 A.2d 284, 310 (2001) (applying McDonnell Douglas Corp. v. Green, 411 U.S. 792, 802 (1973) and distinguishing LeBlanc-Sternberg v. Fletcher, 67 F.3d 412 (2d Cir. 1995), *cert. denied sub. nom.* Airmont v. LeBlanc-Sternberg, 518 U.S. 1017 (1996) (plaintiffs failed to establish that the presence of families with children was motivating factor underlying defendants' decision to place plaintiffs' land within proposed industrial park, thereby blocking plaintiffs' planned affordable housing development).

75. *Huntington Branch,* n. 68 *supra.*

76. *Id.* at 928.

77. Huntington Branch, NAACP v. Town of Huntington, 668 F. Supp. 762 (E.D.N.Y. 1983), *rev'd,* 844 F.2d 926 (2d Cir. 1988).

78. *Huntington Branch,* 844 F.2d at 937–38.

79. *Id.* at 940.

80. *Id.* at 939.

81. South Suburban Hous. Ctr. v. Greater South Suburban Bd. of Realtors, 935 F.2d 868 (7th Cir. 1991).

82. 781 F. Supp. 1528 (M.D. Fla. 1991).

83. United States v. Southern Mgmt. Corp., 955 F.2d 914 (4th Cir. 1992). For discussion on the effect of the Fair Housing Act Amendments of 1988 on specific uses such as senior housing, group homes, and residential treatment centers, see chapter 7.

84. 42 U.S.C. §§ 3604, 3607 (2000).

85. 514 U.S. 725 (1995). An earlier version of this discussion appeared in PROBATE AND PROPERTY, July/August 1995 at p. 14. Reprinted with permission of the American Bar Association.

86. 42 U.S.C. § 3607(b)(1) (2000).

87. 431 U.S. 494 (1977).

88. 514 U.S. at 735.

89. 514 U.S. at 748.

90. 77 F.3d 249 (8th Cir. 1996).

91. *Id.* at 252.

92. 844 F.2d 926 (2d Cir.), *aff'd,* 488 U.S. 15 (1988).

93. *Id.* at 938–42.

94. *Id.* at 934–36, noting that the four-factors test of *Arlington Heights II* (Metropolitan Hous. Dev. Corp. v. Village of Arlington Heights, 558 F.2d 1283, 1287–90 (7th Cir. 1977), *cert. denied,* 434 U.S. 1025 (1978)), which includes a requirement of some evidence of discriminatory intent, is properly applicable to a final determination on the merits and would place too onerous a burden on plaintiffs at the prima facie case stage.

95. Huntington Branch NAACP v. Town of Huntington, 844 F.2d 926, 937 (2d Cir.), *aff'd,* 488 U.S. 15 (1988) (emphasis added).

96. *Id.* at 939–40.

97. 263 F.3d 627 (6th Cir. 2001), *cert. granted* 122 S. Ct. 2618 (6/24/02).

98. *Id.* at 640.

99. *Id.,* citing Metro. Housing Dev. Corp. v. Village of Arlington Heights, 558 F.2d 1283, 1290 (7th Cir. 1977).

100. *Id.,* citing Arthur v. City of Toledo, 782 F.2d 565, 575 (6th Cir., 1986).

101. *Id.,* citing Buckeye Cmty. Hope Found., v. City of Cuyahoga Falls, 82 Ohio St. 3d 539, 697 N.E.2d 181, 186 (1998).

102. Macone v. Town of Wakefield, 277 F.3d 1 (1st Cir. 2002).

103. *Id.,* at 7, citing Village of Arlington Heights v. Metro. Hous. Dev. Corp., 429 U.S. 252, 267 (1977).

104. *Id.,* at 7–8 (distinguishing United States v. City of Black Jack, 508 F.2d 1179, 1184–86 (8th Cir. 1975) (extensive information regarding racial segregation); Kennedy Park Homes Ass'n v. City of Lackawanna, 436 F.2d 108, 113 (2d Cir. 1970) (evidence of blatant segregation).

105. Fair Housing Amendments Act of 1988, 100 Pub. L. 430, Sept. 13, 1988, 102 Stat. 1619 (amending 42 U.S.C. §§ 3602, 3604(a)).

106. Age-restrictive zoning is discussed in chapter 7, *infra.*

107. Southern Burlington County NAACP v. Township of Mount Laurel, 67 N.J. 151, 336 A.2d 713, *appeal dismissed and cert. denied,* 423 U.S. 808 (1975) (*Mount Laurel I*); Southern Burlington County NAACP v. Township of Mount Laurel, 92 N.J. 158, 456 A.2d 390 (1983) (*Mount Laurel II*).

108. N.J. STAT. ANN. § 52:27D-301 *et. seq.* (West 2002).

109. 103 N.J. 1, 510 A.2d 621 (1986).

110. Toll Brothers, Inc. v. Township of West Windsor, 803 A.2d 53, 85 (N.J. 2002). *See also* Fair Share Hous. Ctr., Inc. v. Township of Cherry Hill, 802 A.2d 512 (N.J. 2002) (township could not exclude a large parcel of vacant land as a site for affordable housing by imposing a development fee on the property owner); Bi-County Dev. of Clinton v. Borough of High Bridge, 805 A.2d 433 (N.J. 2002) (developer who makes payments in lieu of actually constructing affordable housing is not entitled to benefit from the *Mount Laurel II* obligation on municipalities to remove unnecessary requirements, which are barriers to the construction of affordable housing).

111. *See generally* pp. 396–99, *infra.*

112. *See, e.g.,* the National Manufactured Housing Construction and Safety Standards Act, 42 U.S.C § 5401 *et seq.,* authorizing the Department of Housing and Urban Development (HUD) to promulgate standards for the development and use of mobile or manufactured housing. HUD standards are published in 24 CFR §§ 3280–3382 (2002).

113. *See, e.g.,* Clark v. County of Winnebago, 817 F.2d 407, 409 (7th Cir. 1987) (distinction between mobile homes and site-built homes with respect to design, construction, and general appearance support legislative decision to establish separate mobile-home park district). Motor homes and house trailers are sometimes lumped in with mobile homes and manufactured houses; however, they are considerd recreational vehicles rather than dwelling units and are not covered by land use regulations of mobile homes and manufactured houses unless specifically included in the local regulation. See, *e.g.,* Farrior v. Zoning Bd. of Appeals, 70 Conn. App. 86, 796 A.2d 1262, 1267–68 (2002) (citing cases).

114. *See, e.g.,* FLA. STAT. ANN. § 553.36(11), *discussed in* Grant v. Seminole County, 817 F.2d 731, 733 (11th Cir. 1987).

115. Grant v. County of Seminole, 817 F.2d 731 (11th Cir. 1987).

116. Clark v. County of Winnebago, 817 F.2d 407 (7th Cir. 1987) (unsuccessful challenge to validity of zoning ordinance that established mobile-home districts, prohibited use of mobile homes outside of the district, and established standards for the maintenance of mobile-home parks within the district); City of Brookside Village v. Comeau, 633 S.W.2d 790, 795 (Tex. 1982) (upholding mobile-home park district regulation, but cautioning that "the assumption that all mobile homes are different from all site-built homes with respect to criteria cognizable under the police power can no longer be accepted"); Town of Stonewood v. Bell, 165 W. Va. 653, 270 S.E.2d 787 (1980).

117. Grant v. County of Seminole, 817 F.2d 731 (11th Cir. 1987) (unsuccessful challenge to zoning ordinance that prohibited mobile homes outside of districts where that use was permitted); Horizon Concepts v. City of Balch Springs, 789 F.2d 1165 (5th Cir. 1986) (classification of mobile and modular homes as special uses upheld because of legitimate governmental interest in assuring that modular homes were not constructed faster than the necessary municipal services for residents of such homes could be provided); Gackler Land Co., Inc. v. Yankee Springs Township, 138 Mich. App. 1, 359 N.W.2d 226 (Mich. Ct. App. 1984) (all mobile homes located outside of mobile-home parks required to have special-use permits). *See generally,* chapter 5.

118. Fasano v. Bd. of County Comm'rs of Washington County, 264 Or. 574, 507 P.2d 23 (1973) (approving the concept but invalidating a specific decision to anchor floating zone because of inadequate showing that a change in land use would be in accordance with local comprehensive plan). *See generally,* chapter 4.

119. Town of Granby v. Landry, 341 Mass. 443, 170 N.E.2d 364, 366 (1960) (law prohibiting more than one mobile home per lot is valid, although not part of comprehensive zoning ordinance and although town lacked comprehensive zoning plan).

120. Town of Stonewood v. Bell, 165 W.V. 653, 270 S.E.2d 787, 789 (1980) (Regulation of the placement of mobile homes is a valid use of police power, even where community did not first adopt a comprehensive plan.).

121. Gackler Land Co., Inc. v. Yankee Springs Township, 138 Mich. App. 1, 359 N.W.2d 226, 228 (1984) (local government's authority to regulate placement of mobile homes not preempted by state regulation of safety and construction of mobile homes, and such local regulation is a valid use of police power). *But see* Mich. Mfr. Hous. Ass'n v. Robinson, 73 F. Supp. 2d 823, 826–27, 28 (W.D. Mich. 1999) criticizing *Gackler* on preemption issue, which would seem to allow local governments to regulate land use through the guise of a safety provision.

122. *Clark,* 817 F.2d at 409.

123. *Grant*, 817 F.2d at 736. *See also* City of Brookside Village v. Comeau, 633 S.W.2d 790, 794 (Tex. 1982) ("Mobile home parks pose special health problems and are amendable to regulations designed to eliminate such hazards.").

124. *Gackler*, 359 N.W.2d at 230.

125. Town of Chesterfield v. Brooks, 126 N.H. 64, 489 A.2d 600 (1985).

126. *See, e.g.*, Town of Stonewood v. Bell, 165 W. Va. 653, 270 S.E.2d 787, 791–92 (1980) (reviewing cases).

127. Koston v. Town of Newburgh, 256 N.Y.S.2d 837 (N.Y. Sup. Ct. 1965).

128. Southern Burlington County NAACP v. Township of Mount Laurel, 92 N.J. 158, 456 A.2d 390 (1983) (overturning judicially sanctioned ban on mobile homes and requiring mobile-home zones to be created when necessary to meet fair-share housing requirements).

129. Knudson v. City of Decorah, 622 N.W. 2d 42, 54 (Iowa 2000).

130. City of Canton v. State, 766 N.E.2d 963, 970 (Ohio 2002).

131. 666 N.E.2d 988 (Mass. 1996).

132. GENERAL ACCOUNTING OFFICE, AN ANALYSIS OF ZONING AND OTHER PROBLEMS AFFECTING THE ESTABLISHMENT OF GROUP HOMES FOR THE MENTALLY DISABLED, 1–2, 17–20 (1983). *See generally* Salsich, *Group Homes, Shelters and Congregate Housing: Deinstitutionalization Policies and the NIMBY Syndrome*, 21 REAL PROP., PROB. AND TR. J. 413 (1986).

133. *See* pp. 283–88, *supra*.

134. *See* pp. 284–88, *supra*.

135. *See* pp. 284–88, *supra*.

136. *See, e.g.*, N.Y. MENTAL HYG. LAW § 41.34 (McKinney 2000).

137. *See, e.g.*, DEL. CODE ANN. tit. 22, § 309(a) (2002); IOWA CODE ANN. § 335.25.3 (2002); MO. REV. STAT. § 89.020; VT. STAT. ANN. tit. 24, § 4409(d) (2001).

138. *See, e.g.*, MICH. COMP. LAWS ANN. § 125.286a (West 1997); W. VA. CODE § 27-17-2(a) (2001).

139. City of Kenner v. Normal Life of Louisiana, Inc., 483 So. 2d 903 (La. 1986).

140. *Id. quoting* LA. STAT. ANN. § 28:381(8) (West 2002).

141. Tucker v. Special Children's Found., 449 So. 2d 45 (La. Ct. App.) *cert. denied*, 450 So. 2d 959 (La. 1984) (group home permitted though building restrictions limited use of property to single-family residential use).

142. *City of Kenner*, 483 So. 2d at 907.

143. City of Cleburne v. Cleburne Living Ctr., 473 U.S. 432 (1985).

144. *Id.* at 450.

145. Fair Housing Amendments Act of 1988, Pub. L. 100–430, 102 Stat. 1619, *amending* 42 U.S.C. § 3604 *et seq.*

146. 42 U.S.C. § 3602(h) (West 1995).

147. 42 U.S.C. § 3604(f)(3)(B) (West 1995).

148. 42 U.S.C. § 3604(f)(9) (West 1995).

149. 42 U.S.C. §§ 3604(a), 3617 (West 1995); Huntington Branch NAACP v. Town of Huntington, 844 F.2d 926 (2d Cir. 1988), *aff'd.*, 488 U.S. 15; Metropolitan Hous. Dev. Corp. v. Village of Arlington Heights, 558 F.2d 1283 (7th Cir. 1977), *cert. denied*, 434 U.S. 1025 (1978); United States v. City of Black Jack, 508 F.2d 1179 (8th Cir. 1974), *cert. denied*, 422 U.S. 1042 (1975).

150. Familystyle of St. Paul, Inc. v. City of St. Paul, 923 F.2d 91 (8th Cir. 1991).

151. City of Cleburne v. Cleburne Living Ctr., 473 U.S. 432, 446 (1985).

152. Familystyle of St. Paul, Inc. v. City of St. Paul, 923 F.2d 91, 94 (8th Cir. 1991).

153. *See, e.g.*, Larkin v. State of Michigan Dep't of Social Servs., 89 F.3d 285, 290 (6th Cir. 1996); Bangerter v. Orem City Corp., 46 F.3d 1491, 1503 (10th Cir. 1995); 161 F. Supp. 2d 819, 838 (N.D. Ill. 2001); Oconomowoc Residential Programs, Inc. v. City of Greenfield, 23 F. Supp. 2d 941, 954 (E.D. Wis. 1998); Children's Alliance v. City of Bellevue, 950 F. Supp. 1491, 1499 (W.D. Wash. 1997) ("Courts should be wary of justification purporting to help

members of the protected class; the court should assess whether the benefits of the requirement 'clearly' outweigh the burdens.").

154. 42 U.S.C. § 3604(f)(3)(B).

155. Lapid-Laurel v. Zoning Bd. of Adjustment of Township of Scotch Plains, 284 F.3d 442, 456–59 (3d Cir. 2002), following Groner v. Golden Gate Gardens Apartments, 250 F.3d 1039, 1045 (6th Cir. 2001); Bryant Woods Inn, Inc. v. Howard County, 124 F.3d 597, 603–04 (4th Cir. 1997); Elderhaven, Inc. v. City of Lubbock, 98 F.3d 175, 178 (5th Cir. 1996).

156. *See, e.g.,* Friends of the Shawangunks, Inc. v. Knowlton, 64 N.Y.2d 387, 476 N.E.2d 988 (1985) (one-acre minimum lot size required for residential unit); Negin v. Bd. of Bldg. & Zoning Appeals, 69 Ohio St. 2d 492, 433 N.E.2d 165 (1982) (ordinance establishing minimum lot size for home construction invalidated as applied to particular lot).

157. Gorieb v. Fox, 274 U.S. 603, 608 (1927) (upholding building line setback requirement from street).

158. *See, e.g.,* Builders Serv. Corp. v. Planning & Zoning Comm'n of Town of East Hampton, 208 Conn. 267, 545 A.2d 530, 536 (1988) (statutory authority to regulate size of buildings includes authority to establish minimum floor-area requirements).

159. Village of Belle Terre v. Boraas, 416 U.S. 1, 9 (1974).

160. *See, e.g.,* Builders Serv. Corp. v. Planning & Zoning Comm'n of Town of East Hampton, 208 Conn. 267, 545 A.2d 530, 539 (1988) (rejecting argument that Supreme Court in Nollan v. California Coastal Comm'n, 483 U.S. 825 (1987) established a stricter standard of review for land use regulation cases).

161. Builders Service Corp. v. Planning & Zoning Comm'n of Town of East Hampton, 208 Conn. 267, 545 A.2d 530 (1988).

162. *Id.* at 543.

163. *Id.* at 544.

164. *Id.*

165. CONN. GEN. STAT. § 8-2(a) (2001).

166. *Builders Service Corp., supra* n. 161, at 548–50.

167. *Id.* at 551–53.

168. *See, e.g.,* N.Y. TOWN LAW § 281; Friends of the Shawangunks, Inc. v. Knowlton, 64 N.Y. 2d 387, 476 N.E.2d 988, 992 (1985) (cluster zoning involves "trade-off of increased density on the developed portion of the land in return for preserving undeveloped the remainder of the land"). Cluster zoning is discussed in chapter 4.

169. *See, e.g.,* Lutz v. City of Longview, 83 Wash. 2d 566, 520 P.2d 1374, 1376 (1974) ("PUD achieves flexibility by permitting specific modifications of the customary zoning standards as applied to a particular parcel"); Johnson v. City of Mount Vernon, 37 Wash. App. 214, 679 P.2d 405, 408–09 (1984) (PUD request is akin to a rezone and denial must be accompanied by written findings including reasons for denial). Cheney v. Village of New Hope, 241 A.2d 81 (Pa. 1968) is an important early case on this point. *See generally* chapter 4.

170. Friends of the Shawangunks, Inc. v. Knowlton, 64 N.Y.2d 387, 476 N.E.2d 988 (1985).

171. Stoney-Brook Development v. Town of Fremont, 474 A.2d 561, 564 (N.H. 1984) (growth-rate limit chosen because it was growth rate of year of enactment held arbitrary as "taken out of a hat"). *See generally* chapter 4.

172. Village of Belle Terre v. Boraas, 416 U.S. 1, 2 (1974). *See generally* chapter 7.

173. Kenart & Assoc. v. Skagit County, 37 Wash. App. 295, 680 P.2d 439, *rev. denied,* 101 Wash. 2d 1021 (1984).

174. Coffey v. Maryland-National Capital Park & Planning Comm'n, 441 A.2d 1041 (Md. 1982). *See generally* chapter 8.

175. *See* chapter 4.

176. Asian Americans for Equality v. Koch, 72 N.Y.2d 121, 527 N.E.2d 265, 269 (1988).

177. Gregory M. Fox & Barbara R. Davis, *Density Bonus Zoning to Provide Low and Moderate Cost Housing,* 3 HASTINGS CONST. L. Q. 1015, 1027 (1977).

178. Thomas Kleven, *Inclusionary Ordinances—Policy and Legal Issues in Requiring Private Developers to Build Low Cost Housing,* 21 UCLA L. REV. 1432, 1442 (1974).

179. *See generally* Fox & Davis, *Density Bonus Zoning to Provide Low and Moderate Cost Housing,* 3 HASTINGS CONST. L. Q. 1015 (1977); Kleven, *Inclusionary Ordinances—Policy and Legal Issues in Requiring Private Developers to Build Low Cost Housing,* 21 UCLA L. REV. 1432 (1974).

180. *See, e.g.,* Southern Burlington County NAACP v. Township of Mount Laurel, 92 N.J. 158, 265–68, 456 A.2d 390, 445–46 (1983).

181. A feasibility study for a proposed mandatory set-aside program in Princeton Township, New Jersey, concluded that mandatory set-asides could be structured to enable developers to obtain adequate profits, particularly if no more than 34 percent of the units were required to be reserved for lower-income people. Divided between low income (14 percent at most) and moderate income, the mandatory set-aside was allowed to be phased in over three five-year increments, and necessary upzoning to higher densities was done only after developers purchased property so that they could capture significant increases in land value. N.J. DEPARTMENT OF COMMUNITY AFFAIRS, THE PRINCETON HOUSING PROPOSAL: A STRATEGY TO ACHIEVE BALANCED HOUSING WITHOUT GOVERNMENT SUBSIDY 445, n. 28, at 13–26 (1977), *discussed in* Southern Burlington Township NAACP v. Township of Mount Laurel, 92 N.J. 158, 266, 456 A.2d 390, 446, n. 29 (1983).

182. *See, e.g.,* VA. CODE ANN. § 15.2-2001 (1997), authorizing "reasonable conditions," and §§ 15.2-2304 and 2305, authorizing affordable housing ordinances. *See generally* chapter 8.

183. Lucas v. South Carolina Coastal Council, 505 U.S. 1003 (1992).

184. Nollan v. California Coastal Comm'n, 483 U.S. 825 (1987); Dolan v. City of Tigard, 512 U.S. 374 (1994).

185. Southern Burlington County NAACP v. Township of Mount Laurel, 92 N.J. 158, 456 A.2d 390, 445 (1983) (*Mount Laurel II*), *citing* Gregory Mellon Fox & Barbara Rosenfeld Davis, *Density Bonus Zoning to Provide Low and Moderate Cost Housing,* 3 HASTINGS CONST. L. Q. 1015, 1060–62 (1976).

186. VA. CODE ANN. § 15.2-2305A (1997), *noted in* Theodore Taub, *The Future of Affordable Housing,* 22 URB. LAW. 659, 666 (1990).

187. *See, e.g.,* Southern Burlington County NAACP v. Township of Mount Laurel, 92 N.J. 158, 456 A.2d 390, 445–50 (1983) (*Mount Laurel II*).

188. *Id.* at 448–450.

189. *Id.* at 443–48.

190. Taxpayers Ass'n of Weymouth Township v. Weymouth Township, 80 N.J. 6, 364 A.2d 1016 (1976).

191. Southern Burlington County NAACP v. Township of Mount Laurel, 92 N.J. 158, 456 A.2d 390, 448 (1983) (*Mount Laurel II*).

192. *Id.* at 449.

193. N.J. STAT. ANN. § 40:55D-62 (a) (West 2002).

194. Southern Burlington County NAACP v. Township of Mount Laurel, 92 N.J. 158, 456 A.2d 390, 449–50 (1983) (*Mount Laurel II*).

195. *Id.* at 450, n. 34. *See generally* chapter 3.

196. In addition to the lengthy *Mount Laurel* litigation, New Jersey courts have wrestled with the judicial-legislature role question in a series of cases involving public-school financing. Robinson v. Cahill, 67 N.J. 333, 339 A.2d 193 (1975), *cert. denied,* Klein v. Robinson 423 U.S. 913 (1975). For an excellent analysis of the constitutional and political issues

raised when courts become actively involved in seeking to resolve basic zoning problems through judicial remedies, *see* John M. Payne, *Delegation Doctrine in the Reform of Local Government Law: The Case of Exclusionary Zoning,* 29 RUTGERS L. REV. 803 (1976). For additional discussion of the *Mount Laurel* doctrine, see Peter H. Schuck, *Judging Remedies: Judicial Approaches to Housing Segregation,* 37 HARV. C.R. – C.L.L. REV. 289, 309–19 (2002); Richard G. Lorenz, *Good Fences Make Bad Neighbors,* 33 URB. LAW 45 (2001); John M. Payne, *Fairly Sharing Affordable Housing Obligations: The Mount Laurel Matrix,* 22 W. NEW ENG. L. REV. 365 (2001) (part of a symposium on Massachusetts' Comprehensive Permit Law, discussed at notes 201–09, *infra,* and accompanying text); Naomi Bailin Wish & Stephen Eisdorfer, *The Impact of Mount Laurel Initiatives: An Analysis of the Characteristics of Applicants and Occupants,* 27 SETON HALL L. REV. 1268 (1997).

197. For example, the city of Black Jack, Missouri, was the target of lengthy litigation during the 1970s because of its efforts to block a federally subsidized apartment project. The city was incorporated after a public controversy arose following announcement of preliminary approval by HUD of a subsidized apartment project in then-unincorporated St. Louis County. As its first act after incorporation, the city enacted a zoning ordinance in which the project site was zoned for single-family residential use, thereby blocking the project. In the last stages of the litigation, after the city had been found to have violated the Fair Housing Act by its actions in denying zoning approval for the proposed project, the Eighth Circuit directed the district court to fashion a remedy that would require the city to take affirmative steps to provide low-cost housing. The court suggested that the parties meet and attempt to prepare a mutually satisfactory plan. In making its suggestion, the court commented favorably on the use of mandatory set-asides, but expressed concern that increased densities resulting from density bonuses or waiver of density restrictions would increase the difficulty in maintaining the project and might become self-defeating. Park View Heights Corp. v. City of Black Jack, 605 F.2d 1033, 1039, n. 6 (8th Cir. 1979). The case finally was settled after almost ten years of litigation when Black Jack formally welcomed an alternative subsidized project on another site that was proposed by a different developer. The Black Jack zoning code later was revised to authorize a "density development" procedure allowing density clusters as long as overall density is not increased, but not making any provision for increasing density through density bonuses.

198. Southern Burlington County NAACP v. Township of Mount Laurel, 92 N.J. 158, 456 A.2d 390 (1983) (*Mount Laurel II*).

199. For a detailed analysis concluding that the *Mount Laurel* approach can produce affordable housing but that more than judicially mandated set-asides is required for a complete housing policy, *see* Martha Lamar, et al., *Mount Laurel At Work: Affordable Housing in New Jersey,* 1983–88, 41 RUTGERS L. REV. 1197 (1989).

200. SHOSHANA ZATZ, CREATING AFFORDABLE COMMUNITIES: INCLUSIONARY HOUSING PROGRAMS IN CALIFORNIA 1–2 (California Coalition for Rural Housing Project 1994). *But see* Benjamin Field, *Why Our Fair Share Housing Laws Fail,* 34 SANTA CLARA L. REV. 35 (1993) (finding substantial noncompliance in Bay Area localities with statutory requirements for housing planning, and advocating an administrative enforcement mechanism as a replacement for the existing judicial enforcement mechanism).

201. MASS. GEN. LAWS ANN. ch. 40B, §§ 20–23 (West 1994). For reviews of the operation of the Massachusetts statute, *see* Lauren J. Resnick, *Mediating Affordable Housing Disputes in Massachusetts: Optimal Intervention Points,* ARB. J., June 1990, vol. 45, no. 2 at 15; Taub, *The Future of Affordable Housing,* 22 URB. LAW. 659, 664 (1990).

202. MASS. GEN. LAWS ANN. ch. 40B, § 20 (West 1994).

203. *See* chapter 6.

204. MASS. GEN. LAWS ANN. ch. 40B, § 21.

205. *Id.,* § 23.

206. *Id.*, § 20. *See* Bd. of Appeals v. Hous. Appeals Comm. in Dep't of Cmty. Affairs, 363 Mass. 339, 294 N.E.2d 393 (1973) (upholding statute against illegal spot zoning, violation of home rule, and vagueness challenges).

207. MASS. GEN. LAWS ANN. ch. 40B, § 23.

208. Resnick, *Mediating Affordable Housing Disputes in Massachusetts: Optimal Intervention Points,* ARB. J., June 1990, vol. 45, no. 2 at 15, 20.

209. *Id.* at 20.

210. CONN. GEN. STAT. ANN. § 8-30g.

211. *Id.* at § 8-30 g(a)(1).

212. *Id.* at § 8-30 g(c).

213. *Id.*

214. *Id.* at § 8-30g(g).

215. Terry J. Tondro, *Connecticut's Affordable Housing Appeals Statute: After Ten Years of Hope, Why Only Middling Results?* 23 W. NEW ENG. L. REV. 115, 128 (2001).

216. *Id.*, at 152, discussing Act effective Oct. 1, 2000, Pub. Act No. 00-206, 2000 Conn. Acts 962, 963 (Reg. Ses.) (amending § 8-30g(1) by adding new definitions).

217. *Id.*, at 153, discussing 2000 Conn. Acts at 963, adding new section 8-30g(b)(1)(E).

218. Tondro, n. 214 *supra*, at 138–152, discussing Christian Activities Council, Congregational v. Town Council (Glastonbury), 735 A.2d 231 (Conn. 1999).

219. *Id.*, at 164.

220. CAL. GOV'T CODE § 65913.2(a) (West 1997); CAL. GOV'T CODE §§ 65589.5(d)–(f) (West Supp. 1997); CAL. EVID. CODE § 669.5 (West 1997); CAL. GOV'T CODE § 65589.6 (West 1997). Katherine E. Stone & Philip A. Seymour, *California Land-Use Planning Law: State Preemption and Local Control,* in STATE & REGIONAL COMPREHENSIVE PLANNING 203 (Peter C. Buchsbaum & Larry J. Smith eds., 1993).

221. Daniel J. Curtin, Jr., Cecily T. Talbert, and Nadia L. Costa, *Inclusionary Housing Ordinance Survives Constitutional Challenge in Post-Nollan-Dolan Era: Homebuilders Association of Northern California v. City of Napa,* LAND USE LAW & ZON. DIG., vol. 54, no. 8 (Aug. 2002) at p. 3, notes 1 & 2, citing Nadia I. El Mallakh, *Does the Costa-Hawkins Act Prohibit Local Inclusionary Zoning Programs?* 89 CALIF. L. REV. 1847, 1861–62 (2001) (at least 108 cities and 15 counties) and Laura M. Padilla, *Reflections on Inclusionary Housing and a Renewed Look at Its Vitality,* 23 HOFSTRA L. REV. 539 (1995). Curtin et al. also cite a website with information about the inclusionary housing movement nationally, www.inhousing.org/USA%2OInclusionary/USA%2OInclusion.htm.

222. Curtin, n. 221 at 3, n. 4, citing Town of Telluride v. Lot Thirty-Four Venture, L.L.C., 3 P.3d 30 (Col. 2000) (mandatory set-aside for 40 percent of employees in new development and establishing a base rental rate).

223. Homebuilders Ass'n of Northern California v. City of Napa, 90 Cal. App. 4th 188, *cert. denied,* 122 S. Ct. 1356 (2002), discussed in Curtin et al. at 5–6, as well as in Note, 115 HARV. L. REV. 2058 (2002), and Comment, 36 U.S.F.L. REV.

224. CAL. GOV'T CODE § 65891.1 *et seq.* (West 2002).

225. CAL. GOV'T CODE § 65583 (1997).

226. FLA. STAT. ANN. §163.3177(6)(f)1(a)–(g). (West 1995).

227. Cranston-Gonzalez National Affordable Housing Act, Pub. L. 101-625, 104 Stat. 4079 (42 U.S.C. §12701 *et seq.* (1990)).

228. *Id.*

229. Section 105, Cranston-Gonzalez National Affordable Housing Act, Pub. L. 101-625, 104 Stat. 4079, 42 U.S.C. 12705 (1995).

230. 24 C.F.R. §§ 91.1 *et seq.* and 91.200 *et seq.* (2002); *HUD Organizes CHAS Requirements in Five Components, Preliminary Notice Shows,* 18 HOUSING & DEV. REP. 827 (Feb. 4, 1991).

231. Cranston-Gonzalez National Affordable Housing Act, 42 U.S.C. 12705(d).

232. *Id.* at § 105(c), Cranston-Gonzalez National Affordable Housing Act, 42 U.S.C. 12705(c).

233. *Id.* at § 105(b)(4) & (c)(1), 42 U.S.C. § 12705(b)(4) & (c)(1).

234. An earlier version of pp. 401–05 was included in the program materials, *Ethics and Professionalism for Real Property and Probate and Trust Practitioners in the 1990's,* ABA Section of Real Property, Probate and Trust Law, Spring 1991 CLE and Committee Meeting, Orlando, FL. Used with permission.

235. MICHAEL DEAR, GAINING COMMUNITY ACCEPTANCE 35–38 (Robert Wood Johnson Foundation, 1991) (stressing the importance of careful analysis before a particular strategy is chosen).

236. 42 U.S.C. § 3601 *et seq.* (1995).

237. 42 U.S.C. § 12101 *et seq.* (1995). *See* 42 U.S.C. §12212 (1995), encouraging use of alternative methods of dispute resolution "[w]here appropriate and to the extent authorized by law."

238. 42 U.S.C. § 12701 *et seq.* (1995).

239. MICHAEL DEAR, GAINING COMMUNITY ACCEPTANCE 39, 48–49 (Robert Wood Jackson Foundation, 1991).

240. Resnick, *Mediating Affordable Housing Disputes in Massachusetts: Optimal Intervention Points,* 45 ARB. J. 15 (1990).

CHAPTER 10

Environmental Land Use Regulation

Federal Environmental Protection Legislation

Modern environmental regulation began with the enactment of the National Environmental Policy Act of 1969[1] and the Clean Air Act of 1970,[2] followed by the Federal Water Pollution Control Act Amendments of 1972,[3] the Noise Control Act of 1972,[4] the Coastal Zone Management Act of 1972,[5] the Federal Water Pollution Control Act Amendments of 1972, later renamed the Clean Water Act,[6] the Endangered Species Act of 1973,[7] the Hazardous Materials Transportation Act of 1974,[8] the Resource Conservation and Recovery Act of 1976,[9] the Toxic Substances Control Act of 1982,[10] and the Comprehensive Environmental Response, Compensation, and Liability Act of 1980 (CERCLA, or "Superfund").[11] In general, the federal statutes imposed a "program of cooperative federalism," in which the applicable federal agency establishes standards for environmental protection and the states develop plans and regulations to ensure that the federal standards are met.[12] This scheme relies on the use of permits as a regulatory device[13] and grants private citizens enforcement rights through civil actions court.[14]

The federalization of environmental land use regulation was set back in one context in *Solid Waste Agency of Northern Cook County v. U.S. Army Corps of Engineers*,[15] in which the Court invalidated an attempt by the U.S. Army Corps of Engineers to expand the definition of *navigable waters* under the Clean Water Act to include entirely intrastate bodies of water if such areas served as habitat for migratory birds.

Another feature of federal environmental protection policy, and one that has been adopted by states as well, is the "environmental impact statement," which requires regulators to consider, in advance, the environmental effects of land use and development. Under the National Environmental Policy Act, federal agencies considering a "major federal action significantly affecting the quality of the human environment" are required to prepare an environmental impact statement to identify significant environmental consequences of the proposed action and consider ways to minimize adverse effects.[16]

Environmental impacts have been described as "scattered bits of a broken chain, some segments of which have numerous links, while others have only one or two. Each segment stands alone, but each link within each segment does not."[17] Applying that metaphor, the Ninth Circuit upheld a decision by the Army Corps of Engineers to consider only the impact of a proposed golf course on a meadow containing pockets of wetlands, and not the impact of the entire multimillion-dollar ski resort of which the golf course was a part, on uplands regulated by state and county environmental laws. The court concluded that the golf course in the meadow and the uplands ski resort were "separate segment[s] of chain . . . [rather than] two links of a single chain."[18]

Federal environmental regulation of land use raises issues of federalism when it conflicts with state interests and environmental jurisdiction. In an interesting three-way jurisdictional dispute, the federal Environmental Protection Agency (EPA) was held to have jurisdiction to grant an Indian tribe jurisdiction to regulate, under the Clean Water Act, a lake entirely within the boundaries of its reservation, as against a state's claim that it had jurisdiction and that, as owner of the lake bed itself, the federally appointed tribal jurisdiction was precluded.[19]

State Environmental Protection Legislation

Federal environmental statutes often authorize, and in fact encourage, states to assume responsibility for environmental regulation. When states do so in a fashion that meets federal standards, issuance of federal permits are suspended in areas covered by an approved state program.[20]

Many states, particularly the most populous and industrialized, and those with ecologically fragile areas such as coastlines and wetlands, have responded to environmental concerns with sophisticated state regulatory programs that have significant impact on local land use control programs. Examples include air pollution control,[21] agricultural and forestland preservation,[22] comprehensive coastal and shoreland regulation,[23] environmental protection,[24] hazardous-waste disposal,[25] solid-waste disposal,[26] water pollution control,[27] wetlands protection,[28] stormwater control,[29] and even motor-vehicle–related concerns arising from hauling of nonhazardous materials.[30]

As is the case with federal environmental protection legislation, the main emphases of state environmental protection legislation are on establishing standards of environmental quality and implementing those standards through a permitting system that must be integrated into local land use regulation programs. Details of federal and state regulation systems and their relationship to local land use regulation programs are discussed in the sections of this chapter dealing with specific substantive areas of regulation, such as coastal areas and wetlands.

The Public Trust Doctrine

One important common law doctrine relative to environmental regulation and land use control, particularly with respect to coastal areas and shorelands, is the Public Trust Doctrine.[31] The doctrine traces its origins to the Roman concept of "natural laws":

> Things common to mankind by the law of nature are the air, running water, the sea, and consequently the shores of the sea; no man therefore is prohibited from approaching any part of the seashore, whilst he abstains from damaging farms, monuments, edifices, etc. which are not in common as the sea is.[32]

The Public Trust Doctrine came to the United States as part of the English common-law tradition that "the king held title to all the lands below the high water mark which were affected by the ebb and flow of the tides."[33] Because such lands were thought to be incapable of private occupation and were thus more appropriate for public uses, the king's right to use and transfer such lands was held "in trust for the benefit of the public."[34]

The Supreme Court has reaffirmed the principle that states entering the union acquired title to "all lands under waters subject to the ebb and flow of the tides" and that states, as sovereigns, hold such lands "in trust for the public."[35]

Of prime interest to environmentalists and landowners is the question of whether the Public Trust Doctrine, expressed as a public easement on privately owned lands, should be confined to the public uses in existence at the time of the acceptance of the doctrine or whether it can be extended to modern public recreational uses, such as swimming, beach strolling, and sunbathing. The Supreme Judicial Court of Maine opted for the narrow view when it invalidated the Maine Public Trust in Intertidal Land Act, which extended the public trust concept to include a public easement for general recreation, as an unconstitutional taking of private property for a public use without just compensation.[36] The court concluded that the Public Trust Doctrine must be confined to the common-law public easement for "fishing, fowling, and navigation and related uses." Private landowners held the property subject to the public easement, but state laws expanding the easement to general recreational uses would constitute a taking of the power to exclude, for which compensation is required, the Court concluded.[37]

Whether construed narrowly or more broadly, the Public Trust Doctrine has important implications for land use control. Regulations imposed by the government trustee on behalf of the public do not face the *First English*[38] compensation issue because no property interest is taken by such regulations as long as they do not impose greater restrictions than required to protect the public trust. The Public Trust Doctrine may be eroded, however, by the Supreme Court's decision in *Lucas v. South Carolina Coastal Council*,[39] where the Court declined even to discuss—much less apply—the doctrine in a case involving a head-on conflict between state regulation of coastal areas and private property rights.[40] In addition, the definition of the public "trustee" may be construed narrowly to prohibit delegation by the state to local authorities.[41]

Relationship of Environmental Regulation and Land Use Control

Federal and state environmental protection laws have a significant effect on local land use control programs. Federal environmental laws, in particular, have made the federal government an active participant in land use regulation.

Environmental-permitting regulations control land use directly, in a fashion similar to traditional local zoning regulation. There are, however, fundamental differences between "environmental" land use regulation (oceans only) and traditional zoning (local) land use regulation. The Supreme Court articulated the difference as follows:

> Land use planning in essence chooses particular uses for the land; environmental regulation, at its core, does not mandate particular uses of the land but requires only that, however the land is used, damage to the environment is kept within prescribed limits.[42]

Both environmental protection and land use regulation powers are derived from the police power of the state to protect public health, safety, and welfare. When these powers are exercised both by federal and state government, or state and local authorities, conflicts can arise. Courts generally will approach such conflicts by determining first whether the opposing regulations can coexist. Federal preemption is typically the issue.

The Second Circuit, for example, held that the zoning regulations of a town in Connecticut were not preempted by the federal Resource Conservation Recovery Act (RCRA)[43] or by prior approvals issued by federal and state environmental agencies. At issue was the question of whether a chemical company had to obtain local permits before "capping" a 4.25-acre, 40-foot-high pile of chemical waste on its property. In affirming a district court's injunction against implementing the capping plan, the Second Circuit noted that RCRA expressly declined to preempt more stringent local site selection regulations, and that federal and state officials had indicated their concurrence with the lack of intent to preempt construction of that statute by stating publicly that a new plan would have to be submitted if the Connecticut courts agreed that the current plan would violate local zoning regulations.[44]

The Tenth Circuit, on the other hand, held that a Denver zoning ordinance prohibiting the maintenance of hazardous waste in areas zoned for industrial use was preempted by CERCLA.[45] The problem involved an EPA decision that the best way to clean up several sites that had been contaminated by radioactive waste was to store the waste at a particular site. The court found an actual conflict between the Denver zoning ordinance and the EPA remedial order and concluded that a limited express preemption provision in the statute did not preclude a finding of implied preemption of local zoning laws that "could override CERCLA remedies."[46]

State preemption of local regulation is also an issue. State preemption will be analyzed on the traditional grounds of legislative intent, consistency, comprehensiveness of state regulations, and frustration of purpose by local regulation.[47]

One way to determine whether coexistence is possible is to emphasize the differences in regulatory concepts noted by the Supreme Court in *Granite Rock*.[48] Thus the Commonwealth Court of Pennsylvania has concluded that while the Pennsylvania Solid Waste Management Act preempts local laws "which would preclude or prohibit the establishment of a hazardous-waste treatment or disposal facility,"[49] the Act does not prohibit the enactment of "appropriate" zoning ordinances.[50] A buffer zone around a proposed hazardous-waste disposal facility was held to be an appropriate local land use regulation, "as long as it does not impose stricter engineering or geological standards than those provided by state regulations,"[51] but a requirement for a half-mile setback between a waste site and a cemetery that was enacted without compliance with the requirements for planning consideration and procedural safeguards of the state zoning-enabling act was held to be an illegal attempt to impose stricter local standards on landfill sites.[52]

Conversely, a Florida appellate court has concluded that issuance of state air-pollution permits must be based "solely on compliance with applicable pollution control standards and rules," and may not be denied because of "alleged non-compliance with local zoning ordinances, land-use restrictions or long-range development plans."[53]

Environmental regulations can add years of delay and millions of dollars to large land development projects. For example, Vermont's Act 250[54] requires all commercial and public developments, as well as residential projects of ten units or more, to be reviewed by regional planning agencies that must consider ten environmental and planning criteria, including water use, sewage disposal, and soil erosion.[55] Ironically, while developers generally bemoan such extensive regulation, bankers in Vermont were reported to believe that the tough environmental reviews may have saved Vermont's banks from the worst effects of the 1990–1991 recession by discouraging poorly capitalized developers from proceeding with development projects.[56]

As the sophistication of environmental regulation and land use control programs increases, identifying the relevant differences and similarities between the two becomes an important aspect of dispute resolution in complex matters.[57]

Administration of Environmental Land Use Controls

The key land use elements of the environmental regulation process are analysis of the impact of such uses on the environment and minimization of such impacts through a permitting system usually administered by federal or state agencies but sometimes delegated to local officials.

Environmental protection legislation is based on a policy of disclosure and evaluation of environmental effects, rather than rigid imposition of substantive environmental protection standards. The Supreme Court has concluded that it is "well- settled" that the National Environmental Policy Act of 1969 (NEPA),[58] which established national environmental policy and upon which state environmental policy statutes are based, "does not mandate particular results, but simply prescribes the necessary process . . . [which includes] a set of 'action-forcing' procedures that require that agencies take a 'hard look' at environmental consequences. . . . If the adverse environmental effects of the proposed action are adequately identified and evaluated, the agency is not constrained by NEPA from deciding that other values outweigh the environmental costs."[59]

The typical environmental review process is illustrated by the California Environmental Quality Act (CEQA)[60] and the CEQA Guidelines implementing the Act that are promulgated by the State Resources Agency.[61] Local agencies are required to follow a three-level environmental review process:

1. No further agency evaluation required: projects within categories exempt from administrative regulation, such as construction of a family home or transfers to preserve open space and projects which are certain not to have significant environmental effects; [62]
2. Initial threshold study required: projects that carry the "possibility" of significant environmental effect; [63]
3. Results of initial threshold study:
    (a) Environmental Impact Report (EIR) required: When "substantial evidence" exists that "any aspect of the project, either individually or cumulatively, may cause a significant effect on the environment."[64] An existing EIR may be used if one has been prepared "which adequately analyzes the project at hand,"[65] including an environmental impact statement prepared for the same project under the National Environmental Policy Act[66] or the Tahoe Regional Planning Compact.[67]
    (b) Negative Declaration: May be issued when the initial threshold study demonstrates that the proposed project "will not have a significant effect" on the environment.[68] A negative declaration is "a written statement briefly describing the reasons that a proposed project will not have a significant effect on the environment and does not require the preparation of an environmental impact report."[69]

The Connecticut Environmental Policy Act requires a public "scoping meeting" upon petition by 25 persons within ten days of notice to provide for public comment on required actions under the environmental impact statement.[70]

The phrase *significant environmental effects* has been defined as "a substantial, or potentially substantial, adverse change in any of the physical conditions within the area affected by the activity including land, air, water, mineral, flora, fauna, ambient noise, and objects of historical or aesthetic significance."[71] Government agencies must consider the cumulative effects, including prior actions of the agency over an extended period of time, of an action in preparing an environmental impact statement.[72]

The environmental impact statement is not required to address purely social or economic effects of a proposed development. Thus, in *Vega v. County of Los Angeles*,[73] the California Court of Appeals declined to require an analysis, under CEQA, of the balance or imbalance of jobs and affordable housing resulting from a long-term, 22,000-unit housing development.

A "fair argument" test has been articulated that requires an EIR to be prepared whenever "it can be fairly argued on the basis of substantial evidence that a project can have a significant environmental impact."[74] But that test does not change the burden placed on the challenging party "to demonstrate that the agency failed to consider facts that, if true, would show that the permitted project could have a substantial effect on the environment."[75]

Determination that an EIR is required, or that one is not required through issuance of a written "Negative Declaration," must take place before approval or disapproval of a project.[76] Negative declarations do not have to "contemplate every imagined possibility" as long as an "objective, good-faith effort . . . [to] produc[e] . . . information sufficient to permit a reasonable choice of alternatives . . ." is made.[77]

An EIR must identify the "significant environmental effects," indicate those effects that can be avoided or mitigated, describe possible mitigation measures, and "suggest and evaluate alternatives to the proposed action."[78] The mitigation discussion requirement, which is common to statutes based on NEPA, has been construed by the Supreme Court as a procedural requirement "to ensure that environmental consequences have been fairly evaluated . . . and [not] a substantive requirement that a complete mitigation plan be actually formulated and adopted" as part of the preparation of an environmental impact report or statement.[79]

Environmental impact legislation adopts a comprehensive process of "extensive research and information gathering, consultation with other state and local agencies and with persons or organizations directly concerned, public review and comment, evaluation and response to comments, and detailed findings."[80] The full process can take years, as a federal court noted in commenting that the Army Corps of Engineers held what amounted to a "seven-month public hearing" as part of its deliberations leading to the conclusion that an environmental impact statement was not necessary for a proposed domed football stadium to be constructed on wetlands in St. Louis County, Missouri.[81]

A reviewing court will not substitute its judgment for the conclusions of a challenged environmental impact statement (EIS), but it will endeavor to "ensure that, in the light of the circumstances of a particular case, the [reviewing] agency has given due consideration to pertinent environmental factors." The test is whether the agency has given a "hard look" at the environmental impact of a particular activity and whether it has made a "reasoned elaboration" of the basis for its determination.[82]

Although EIR statutes are "essentially procedural act[s] designed to insure that . . . responsible . . . agencies make fully informed and well-considered environmental decisions,"[83] such statutes have been held to "confer substantive authority" on cities, acting through local officials, to deny building permits on the basis of "adverse environmental impacts disclosed by an EIS."[84]

The Environmental Permit Process

In addition to the environmental impact review process discussed previously,[85] environmental regulation is accomplished generally through a detailed permitting process covering several media. Perhaps the most important environmental permit statute affecting land use is the Federal Clean Water Act.[86] The Clean Water Act establishes several different permitting systems. An exception to the Act's general prohibition of the discharge of pollutants into navigable waters is the National Pollution Discharge Elimination System (NPDES), under which the EPA may issue permits allowing discharge of effluent into navigable waters or into publicly owned treatment works under special conditions specified in the permits.[87] The Act also establishes a permit system to regulate the placement of fill materials into navigable waters at "specified disposal sites."[88] Both programs permit states to take over the regulatory process by establishing appropriate state permitting programs.[89]

The permitting process may be quite technical, with considerable detail, even minutiae, required as early as in the permit application. For example, air-discharge permits may require 30 days of chemical sampling at the top of a stack and often require computer modeling of the dispersion of particulates, sulfur oxides, and the like. Water-discharge permits require nearly as much time and expense.[90]

The New Jersey Freshwater Wetlands Protection Act[91] illustrates the use of environmental permits and their impact on local land use control practices. The legislative purpose of the act is to establish a "systematic review" of activities in freshwater wetlands areas that will provide "predictability in the protection of freshwater wetlands." In order to accomplish the goal of preserving the "purity and integrity" of freshwater wetlands from "random, unnecessary, or undesirable alteration or disturbance," the State assumes the freshwater wetlands permit jurisdiction previously exercised by the Army Corps of Engineers under the Clean Water Act.[92]

The statute regulates removal of soil, sand, gravel, or aggregate material; drainage or disturbance of the water level or water table; dumping, discharging, or filling with any materials; driving of pilings; placing of obstructions; and tree cutting of plant life "which would alter the character of a freshwater wetland."[93] Basic farming and ranching activities, as well as harvesting of forest products under an approved forest management plan, are exempt from freshwater wetlands regulation, except for the discharge of dredged or fill materials into a freshwater wetland in order to "bring . . . an area of freshwater wetlands into a use to which it was not previously subject" if such activity would impair the flow or circulation patterns of the waters or reduce their reach.[94]

The New Jersey statute subjects regulated activities to a multistage process that includes an optional request for a letter of interpretation to establish that the site of a proposed activity is within a freshwater wetland or transition area,[95] a mandatory freshwater wetlands permit to conduct a regulated activity within a freshwater wetland,[96] and a mandatory transition-area waiver to conduct a prohibited activity, such as excavation, dumping, erection of structures, placing of pavements, or destruction of plant life, within a transition area.[97]

The permit system is administered by a state agency,[98] which is required to consolidate the processing of "wetlands-related aspects" of other regulatory programs, such as sewer extension approvals, in order to develop "a timely and coordinated permit process" that is consistent with the Federal Clean Water Act.[99]

Prior to action on a request for a permit or a hearing, comments must be sought from the EPA. Notice of an application for a permit must be published in the bulletin of the state agency, but a public hearing is not required "unless there is a significant degree of public interest in the application," which would be evidenced by submission of written requests for a hearing within 20 days of publication of the notice. Decisions on completed applications must be made within 90 days of receipt of comments from the EPA or 180 days of submittal of the completed application, whichever is later.[100] Comments must also be sought and considered from state, regional, and local environmental commissions and planning boards affected by the application, as well as the general public.[101]

Permits may be issued only if the agency finds that the proposed activity either is "water-dependent . . . and has no practicable alternative" to involving freshwater wetlands, or is "nonwater-dependent" but has rebutted a presumption that there is a practicable alternative to involving freshwater wetlands, and in either case meets the following standards: (1) will result in only "minimum feasible alteration or impairment" of the aquatic ecosystem, (2) will not jeopardize endangered species, nor cause or contribute to water pollution, (3) will not impair marine sanctuaries, (4) will not cause or contribute to "a significant degradation" of ground or surface waters, and (5) is "in the public interest, is necessary to realize the benefits derived from the activity, and is otherwise lawful."[102]

The New Jersey statute lists seven factors to be considered in determining whether a proposed regulated activity is in the public interest, including (1) the "public interest in preservation of natural resources and the interest of the property owners in reasonable economic development," (2) the relative extent of public and private need for the activity, (3) practicability of using reasonable alternative locations, (4) extent and permanence of beneficial or detrimental effects, (5) quality of the wetland affected, (6) public and private economic value of the proposed activity, and (7) the ecological value of the wetland, as well as the probable impact on health and fish and wildlife.[103]

The New Jersey statute also establishes a Wetlands Mitigation Bank and a Wetlands Mitigation Commission to provide funds for mitigation projects, including land acquisition for restoration of degraded freshwater wetlands, and to preserve freshwater wetlands and transition areas "of critical importance in protecting freshwater wetlands."[104] The act authorizes the issuance of temporary emergency permits,[105] as well as general permits and the adoption of nationwide permits approved by the Army Corps of Engineers under certain circumstances.[106]

Upon request by the owner, local tax assessors are required to take into account denial of an application for a permit when valuing, assessing, or taxing the property.[107] Appeals are through an administrative hearing and review by the state department head in accordance with the New Jersey Administrative Procedure Act.[108] Civil and criminal penalties are provided for violation of the act.[109]

The mere fact that a permit is required before a particular use of private property can be undertaken, or that a permit has been denied, does not constitute a "taking" of property in violation of the U.S. Constitution.[110] A taking can occur, however, if permit denial or conditions attached to permit approval fail either the "legitimacy test" of reasonable means to a legitimate goal or the "economic impact test" of allowing some reasonable economic use of the property.[111] In recognition of this point, the New Jersey Freshwater Wetlands Act authorizes landowners affected by permit decisions to seek a court determination of whether the applicable permit decision constitutes a taking of property without just compensation. If a court concludes that a taking has occurred, the department is given three statutory options: (1) compensate the property owner for the "full amount of the lost value," (2) condemn the property under state eminent domain laws,[112] or (3) modify the permit action or inaction "so as to minimize the detrimental effect to the value of the property."[113]

Permit Programs for Wetlands and Other Environmentally Sensitive Areas

Wetlands, found throughout the United States, develop anywhere there is a surface depression on the land or an abundance of groundwater. The development of areas that are designated as wetlands is regulated at both the federal and state levels. At the federal level, the Army Corps of Engineers and the EPA operate a permit program. These two agencies derive their authority from Section 404 of the Clean Water Act,[114] which prohibits the placement of fill materials in U.S. waters unless authorization is granted by the Army Corps of Engineers. The Corps construed the term *waters* to include "freshwater wetlands," which are defined as

> those areas that are inundated or saturated by surface or ground water at a frequency or duration sufficient to support, and that under normal circumstances do support, a prevalence of vegetation typically adapted for life in saturated soil conditions. Wetlands generally include swamps, marshes, bogs, and similar areas and have hydrophytic vegetation, hydric soils, and "wetlands" hydrology.[115]

The Supreme Court upheld the Corps' assertion of jurisdiction over wetlands and provided judicial support for the Clean Water Act permit system in *United States v. Riverside Bayview Homes*.[116] Landowners unsuccessfully challenged the permit system as an unconstitutional taking of property. The Court held that "[o]nly when a permit is denied and the effect of the denial is to prevent 'economically viable' use of the land in question can it be said that a taking had occurred."[117]

Wetlands jurisdictional determinations by the Corps District Engineer are final because there is no provision in the Clean Water Act or Corps regulations for an administrative appeal, unlike in the case of denial of NPDES permits. Appeal of wetlands determination is by suit in federal district court.

In *Hoffman Homes, Inc. v. EPA*,[118] the scope of the EPA's jurisdiction over wetlands was given some definition before the ruling was subsequently vacated to allow settlement negotiations. The court held that the EPA had no regulatory authority over an intrastate wetland solely on the ground that migratory birds could benefit from use of the wetland, citing the Clean Water Act and the Commerce Clause. The case is a helpful analysis of the distinction between the Army Corps of Engineers' jurisdiction over navigable waters and the EPA's jurisdiction under the Clean Water Act.

The vacated decision in *Hoffman* was vindicated, however, and a trend toward expansion of Army Corps' jurisdiction over so-called 404 permits stalled, by the Supreme Court holding in *Solid Waste Agency of Northern Cook County (SWANCC) v. U.S. Army Corps of Engineers*.[119] In *SWANCC*, the court held that the Army Corps had no authority to enact a rule including an intrastate body of water within the defintion of *navigable waters* on the basis that the body of water served as a habitat for migratory birds. The court expressly declined to extend *Bayview Homes*.[120] The Corps and the EPA, after the SWANCC decision, issued a joint memorandum of understanding affirming that both federal agencies will continue to exercise broad jurisdiction and continue to interpret *navigable* to include all waters that are navigable in fact and including the highest reaches of their tributaries.[121]

As noted, Section 404 prohibits the discharge of dredged or filled material into the "waters of the United States" without a permit issued by the Army Corps of Engineers.[122] For several years, the Corps took the position that Section 404 applied to discharges but not to extractions of materials. The Corps' interpretation was challenged in *North Carolina Wildlife Federation v. Tulloch*.[123] To settle the litigation, the Corps agreed to promulgate regulations that clarify that mechanized land clearing, ditching, channelization, and other excavation activities do involve the discharge of dredge or fill materials when performed in navigable waters.[124] Activities involving only cutting or removing vegetation above the ground (such as mowing, rotary cutting, and chainsawing), where the activity neither substantially disturbs the root system nor involves mechanized pushing, dragging, or other similar activities that redeposit excavated soil, do not need a Section 404 permit.[125]

In *American Mining Congress v. United States Corps of Engineers*,[126] however, the District Court for the District of Columbia invalidated the *Tulloch* Rule, holding that the Corps exceeded its authority in promulgating a rule that incidental fallback was a discharge. The court defined *incidental fallback* as returning dredged material to virtually the same spot from which it came. In an effort to prevent the large-scale destruction of wetlands that the EPA and the Corps alleged would take place following rescission of the *Tulloch* Rule, both federal agencies appear to be more aggressive in implementing existing authority.

Regulatory jurisdiction over wetlands increasingly has been delegated to states and municipalities.[127] By the mid-1990s, more than 20 states had enacted wetlands protection laws, presumably partly in response to the perceived inefficiency and delay in wetlands permitting at the federal level. Maryland legislation provides that "a person may not dredge or fill on State wetlands without a license."[128] The Board of Public Works grants or denies licenses and is assisted in its determination by the Secretary of Natural Resources.

Under New York's Freshwater Wetlands Act, the state Environmental Conservation Department must map wetland sites of more than 12 acres. In order to develop designated lands, a permit is required. The department may deny a permit if it determines that development would damage the wetlands.[129]

New York has also enacted the Tidal Wetlands Act,[130] which was the subject of a taking claim in *De St. Aubin v. Flacke*.[131] The Court of Appeals of New York noted that because the regulations imposed by this act are stringent, the legislature "has provided property owners with a unique remedy against an unconstitutional taking within the context of the regulatory scheme itself."[132] The court summarized:

> [I]f a permit is denied or the permit offered is more limited in scope than that sought, the owner may seek judicial review of the administrative denial in a two-step proceeding. If the court finds that the permit denial is supported by substantial evidence, then a second determination is made in the same proceeding to determine whether the restriction constitutes an unconstitutional taking requiring compensation. The taking determination is made on the basis of a full evidentiary hearing and if the landowner prevails the Commissioner is directed, at his option, to either grant the requested permit or institute condemnation proceedings.[133]

In this case, the state refused a permit to develop wetlands; however, certain development was permitted in uplands areas. These uplands were subject to single-family town zoning regulations; the state restrictions required a 20,000-square-foot minimum lot. Given the relatively large minimum-lot size, the developer wanted to place two-family duplexes or condominiums on each of these lots. This was not possible, however, under the single-family town zoning regulations. Thus the developer argued that he had been denied all reasonable use of his property.

The key question was whether the town would be likely to either rezone or grant the developer a variance permitting the multifamily residences he wanted to build. In the lower courts, the developer prevailed on his taking claim. The result, however, was overturned on appeal. The lower court had required the defendant, the state Commissioner of Environmental Conservation, to prove that a rezoning that would permit development was reasonably likely, rather than properly putting the burden on the developer to prove that all use was precluded because of the unlikelihood of this rezone. "This allocation of the burden of proof constituted error and it cannot be found harmless," the court held.[134]

Sometimes wetlands and other environmentally sensitive areas are protected by state legislation that links state and local environmental regulations to the zoning process. For example, a local floodplain zoning ordinance in Wisconsin provided:

> No developments shall be allowed which, acting alone or in combination with existing or future similar uses, cause an increase equal to or greater than 0.1 foot in height of the regional flood on any main stem, tributaries to the main stem of any stream, drainage ditches, or any other drainage facilities.[135]

In a suit brought by the state against a developer for violation of the ordinance, the court held that statutory requirements that local flood-plain ordinances be upgraded to include the most current data required the trial court to permit the state to introduce evidence from a state hydraulic analysis, even though the city had come to a different conclusion regarding the proper location of boundary lines between floodways and floodplains.[136]

Protecting Coastal Areas Through Permit Programs

The Federal Coastal Zone Management Act,[137] in furtherance of national policy to protect the coastline of the United States, encourages states to accept responsibility for regulation of coastal development through implementation of a development permit process.[138]

An example of state legislation designed to preserve coastal areas is the Maryland Chesapeake Bay Critical Area Protection Program.[139] The legislation created the Chesapeake Bay Critical Area Commission, which consists of 26 voting members appointed by the governor. The commission assists local jurisdictions in the Chesapeake Bay area in drafting a program to help preserve protected areas.

The protected areas include not only the Chesapeake Bay but also all state and private wetlands.[140] These areas, however, are subject to exclusions by local jurisdictions. Such exclusions include urban areas developed to the extent that the environmental program "would not substantially improve protection of tidal water quality or conservation of fish, wildlife, or plant habitats,"[141] and urban areas separated from open water by a buffer zone of wetlands.[142] Exclusions by local jurisdictions must be approved by the commission.[143]

If a local jurisdiction does not develop a protection program, the commission assumes this responsibility.[144] In either case the program is made up of the following elements: a map of the critical area; a zoning map for the area; if necessary, new or amended subdivision regulations, a comprehensive plan, zoning ordinances, enforcement laws, and grandfather clauses; standards for development approval; provisions limiting development of the critical area; buffer areas along shorelines; minimum setbacks along shorelines; designation of shorelines acceptable for public activities, such as parks and scenic drives; designation of shorelines acceptable for ports; provisions for the harvesting of timber; and regulation of pollutants, but not in areas where the topography prevents runoff.[145]

The legislation also establishes guidelines for intrafamily transfers[146] and creates the Chesapeake Bay Trust, which is designed to "promote public awareness and participation in the restoration and protection of the water quality and aquatic and land resources of the Chesapeake Bay."[147]

A Delaware law similar to the Maryland legislation withstood a challenge based on the dormant commerce clause.[148] The Delaware Coastal Zone Act (CZA) bans bulk-product transfer facilities in Delaware's coastal zone. The plaintiff planned to load coal into deep-draft supercolliers in Big Stone Anchorage in Delaware Bay. Because this service would allow coal exporters to sail from the East Coast fully loaded—something otherwise impossible because of shallow bays—the plaintiff's plan would have allegedly reduced shipping costs and made U.S. coal more competitive in world markets.

The CZA, however, prohibited the use in the Delaware coastal zone. The plaintiff challenged the constitutionality of the statute, arguing that it was a violation of the dormant commerce clause.[149] The court rejected this argument, reasoning that the burden the act imposes "is a nondiscriminatory burden that must be shouldered by any coal transporter, regardless of state affiliation."[150]

Although Delaware won the case, one of its defenses to the plaintiff's challenge was rejected. Because a state law does not violate the commerce clause if Congress has consented to the law, Delaware argued that the Federal Coastal Zone Management Act (CZMA), which provides funding for state laws designed to protect coastal zones, established that "Congress clearly demonstrated that it intended to remove from Commerce Clause scrutiny state coastal-zone management programs approved under the Act."[151] This argument was rejected because the CZMA states that it is not intended to diminish federal jurisdiction. Thus it is unlikely that Congress intended to "transfer Commerce Clause authority from Congress to the states," the court concluded.[152]

Vested Rights and Supplemental Environmental Reviews

Vested-rights rules applicable to local land use regulations[153] also have been applied to the environmental regulations. A Washington appellate court, construing the environmental review policies of the State Environmental Policy Act,[154] and local environmental policy ordinances as "zoning and building ordinances" for purposes of the vested-rights doctrine, struck down a decision of the Seattle City Council to limit the allowable height of a proposed apartment complex tower to eight stories when the zoning envelope[155] in effect at the time the application for approval was submitted allowed buildings in excess of 16 stories.[156]

New land use policies for multifamily buildings that would restrict the height to 60 feet had been approved after the application was filed. Under Washington law, vested rights are determined as of the date of the submission of a permit application.[157] Although previous Washington cases had not addressed the issue of whether the vested-rights doctrine should apply to environmental regulation decisions, the court held that the doctrine was "equally appropriate" for environmental policy ordinances because, "in the urban setting, [environmental policy] ordinances address the same issues that are addressed by zoning ordinances, such as building heights, setbacks, open space, and density of housing."[158]

Because the environmental review process may consist of several time-consuming stages[159] and land development proposals are rarely static, supplemental environmental review and environmental impact statements are frequently attacked by development opponents. The Supreme Court has concluded that, while the NEPA does not specifically address the issue of supplemental review, the "action-forcing" purpose of the Act may at times require the preparation of "post-decision" supplemental environmental impact statements:[160]

It would be incongruous with . . . [the] approach to environmental protection [of focusing on environmental effects rather than mandating particular substantive environmental results], and with the Act's manifest concern with preventing uninformed action, for the blinders to adverse environmental effects, once unequivocally removed, to be restored prior to the completion of agency action simply because the relevant proposal has received initial approval.[161]

"Changed economic circumstances", including, for example, a reduction in revenue from an activity, may require supplementation of an environmental impact statement.[162]

Because of the procedural nature of NEPA, the Court noted that there might be a time in the life of a project when NEPA should no longer be applicable "because the agency would no longer have a meaningful opportunity to weigh the benefits of the project versus the detrimental effects on the environment," but that point is not necessarily reached at the beginning or even at substantial completion of construction.[163]

The standard that governs an agency's decision whether to prepare a supplemental EIS is the "rule of reason," the application of which "turns on the value of . . . new information to the still pending decisionmaking process." Judicial review of an agency's decision is based on the "arbitrary and capricious" standard of the Administrative Procedure Act (APA) rather than the stricter "in accordance with law" or "without observance of procedure required by law" standards of the APA.[164]

The vested-rights doctrine governs the standards under which an application for permission to engage in a particular activity is to be judged.[165] A decision that a supplemental EIS should be prepared, or even that an activity should be halted,[166] because of "significant new information" is not a change in the standards governing a regulatory decision-making process, but rather a decision to continue to apply the existing regulatory standards on the basis of the new information.[167] Vested rights became a problem in the Washington case because the decision of the Seattle City Council to reduce the permitted height of the apartment tower was based on policies and standards that had not been formally adopted at the time the permit application was submitted, rather than on the application of existing standards to new information.[168]

Responsibility for Environmental Compliance

A common theme of federal and state environmental law is that liability for the cost of cleanup and other responses to environmental damage is placed on landowners as well as actual polluters.[169] This "liability chases title" policy imposes strict liability on current as well as previous owners of contaminated land regardless of whether they actually engaged in, or even knew about, the environmentally damaging activity.[170]

Statutes typically authorize the imposition of government liens on contaminated property to recover cleanup costs. These liens, as do other government liens, take priority over nongovernmental liens.[171] Response actions undertaken to remove hazardous wastes or otherwise clean up contaminated property can be extremely expensive. In one celebrated case in which a bank that took title to contaminated property through foreclosure was held responsible for the cleanup costs, the government's bill was almost twice the amount of the defaulted mortgage note.[172]

Environmental Audits

A staple of environmental compliance and transactional practice is the environmental audit, used initially to attempt to establish an innocent-purchaser defense available under CERCLA and similar state statutes,[173] but now designed to establish a "realistic accounting and allocation of transaction liabilities and costs."[174]

Environmental audits usually are conducted in two phases: Phase I, which includes a site visit, inspection of records and interviews of knowledgeable parties, and Phase II, in which air, soil, and water samples are tested. Phase I audits are relatively inexpensive, ranging from several hundred to a few thousand dollars, but Phase II audits can cost much more,[175] involving sample testing and delay.

Questions concerning the environmental audit, including cost and who pays, selection of an auditing firm, confidentiality of inspections and data obtained, and entities who can rely on the audit report, should be covered in the real estate purchase and sale agreements. A panel of the Utah State Bar Real Property Section recommended that the following provisions regarding environmental audits be included in commercial real estate contracts:

> (1) indemnities (often the consultant wants indemnities from the entity requesting the audit); (2) releases and limits on liability; (3) insurance; (4) standard of care; (5) scope of work; (6) cost; (7) timing; (8) confidentiality and reporting to enforcement agencies; (9) access to past and present employees; (10) site access.[176]

Disclosure Requirements

A major consequence of the strict liability scheme of environmental legislation is the importance being placed on disclosure of environmental problems by sellers. Buyers are demanding representations or disclosure, even if limited to the actual knowledge of a designated representative of the seller, both to assess the risks associated with the purchase of property and to lay the groundwork for assertion of the innocent-landowner defense if environmental problems surface later.[177] The innocent-landowner defense requires purchasers to undertake "all appropriate inquiry into the previous ownership and uses of the property consistent with good commercial or customary practice."[178]

States have enacted environmental disclosure statutes, typically called Responsible Property Transfer Acts, which require sellers of land subjected to uses likely to have produced environmental contamination to provide environmental data to sellers prior to closing.[179] The statutory disclosure requirements are quite detailed, as the Indiana disclosure questionnaire reproduced in Appendix A to this chapter indicates. Disclosure documents must follow a prescribed format and are required to be recorded.[180]

Regulation of Contaminated Property

Because environmental problems arising from land use usually involve socially useful activities such as farming, manufacturing, and energy production, environmental laws typically require that consideration be given to the costs of cleanup or pollution avoidance and the social or economic value of the pollution source, as well as the extent of harm caused by the activity, in fashioning an appropriate remedy for violation of environmental laws.[181] In addition to enforcement actions, which can lead to substantial fines and even jail terms for violation of environmental laws,[182] statutes often provide alternatives to strict compliance through land use regulatory techniques.[183]

For example, the Illinois Environmental Pollution Act authorizes the Illinois Pollution Control Board to grant variances,[184] site-specific regulations,[185] and adjusted standards.[186] Variances, pejoratively called "official licenses to pollute in violation of established regulations,"[187] may be granted for temporary periods to enable study and implementation of new technology or a different method of operation designed to eventually achieve compliance with state standards.[188] As with traditional zoning variances,[189] pollution control variance decisions are designed to prevent arbitrary and unreasonable hardship and are quasi-adjudicatory in nature, although the state Pollution Control Board can impose emission limits as variance conditions, a decision that is quasi-legislative in nature.[190]

Site-specific regulations amount to permanent reductions in environmental standards that may be granted upon a showing that compliance with general statewide regulations is "technically infeasible or economically unreasonable" or both.[191] Site-specific regulations are final rules and thus must be adopted in accordance with the notice and public comment provisions of the Illinois Administrative Procedure Act.[192] The quasi-legislative nature and permanency of site-specific regulations resembles the zoning amendment.[193]

An alternative approach is the "adjusted standard," which is designed to create a permanent, site-specific standard in a streamlined fashion for cases in which a showing is made that the petitioner has "significantly different" circumstances from those considered when general standards were adopted, no new adverse health or environmental effects will result from the proposed adjusted standard, and the adjusted standard is "consistent" with applicable federal regulations.[194] The statutory requirement that the state board grant adjusted standards when the three factors have been met makes the adjusted standard technique appear similar to the special-use permit.[195]

Other Environmental Issues Affecting Land Use Determinations

Preserving Agricultural Lands

For environmental and other reasons, states have become increasingly interested in preserving agricultural lands. One way of preserving agricultural lands is through zoning regulations. For example, an area can be zoned agricultural exclusively, prohibiting further residential and commercial development.[196] Sometimes a system of transferred development rights (TDRs) accompanies downzoning to preserve agricultural lands.[197]

The Michigan Farmland and Open Space Preservation Act[198] provides a tax-credit incentive. The Act authorizes owners of qualified farmland or open space to enter into development agreements or development easements with local governments and the state Department of Natural Resources. Agreements may extend for a term, not less than ten years, and provide the landowner with a credit on his or her Michigan income tax by the amount the property taxes on the land exceed 7 percent of the household income of the property owner.[199] Land eligible for the development rights tax program includes single-ownership farms of three types: (1) 40 acres or more devoted primarily to agricultural use; (2) 5 to 39 acres devoted primarily to agricultural use, which have produced a gross annual income of $200 per acre of cleared and tillable land; and (3) specialty farms as designated by the state Department of Agriculture with gross annual incomes from agricultural use of $2,000 or more, as well as land designated as historic open space, riverfront open space, or shoreland open space.[200]

Applications for development rights agreements or easements are submitted to the applicable local government. If approved by the local legislative body, they are forwarded to the Department of Natural Resources, which also must approve them. Development rights easements also must be approved by the state legislature. Applications rejected at the local level may be appealed to the department, which has authority to override the local decision.[201]

Once approved and executed, development rights agreements and easements run with the land. New owners can qualify for tax credits, but only if they execute a declaration that they will observe all provisions of the agreement or easement and accept all responsibilities of the agreement or easement.[202] Development agreements or easements may be terminated upon application and approval by the local legislative body or the state department on appeal, but only for one of three reasons: (1) the agreement or easement causes continuing economic inviability, defined as continued uneconomic operation rather than merely foregoing the opportunity to obtain higher returns; (2) surrounding conditions or significant natural physical changes in the land are generally irreversible and permanently affect the land; or (3) in the case of an agreement, physical obstacles to agricultural operations exist or essential agricultural practices cannot be carried out; in the case of an easement, the affected property "no longer bears significant importance to the public interest."[203]

Rural landowners may also be exempted by agricultural land preservation laws from imposition of special assessment for sewers, water, and lights; however, the Michigan Court of Appeals held that such laws do not exempt rural landowners from zoning ordinances requiring owners to use the public sewer system.[204]

Hazardous-Waste Disposal

In a case construing the right of the EPA to enter property for cleanup where the owner did not consent to entry, the Second Circuit voided a search warrant issued by a magistrate for entry onto the owner's property. The warrant was issued pursuant to Sections 104(a), 104(b), and 104(e) of CERCLA.[205] These sections give the president the authority, through the EPA, to arrange for the cleanup of hazardous-waste sites; however, the court, reading the statute strictly, held that the statute gave the EPA no express right of entry.

> In our view, the sections relied upon by the EPA do not give it the author- ity to do that which it seeks to do and which the magistrate and the dis- trict judge permitted. The statute is not as ambiguous as it is lacking. We cannot, out of a zeal to rid our environment of its hazards, rewrite the statute for the EPA.[206]

Subsequent amendments to Section 104 resolved the uncertainty in favor of granting the EPA a right of entry.[207] In addition, the EPA has successfully used Section 106 of CERCLA to gain access in cases of imminent hazard where immediate removal of hazardous substances was in order.[208]

Siting of Hazardous-Waste Disposal Facilities

Construing Iowa statutes, the Iowa Supreme Court held that a landfill operated by an electric utility was exempt from county zoning legislation even though the landfill was not on the same site as the generating plant. The landowners who brought suit contended that the exemption applied only to utilities located on a single site. The Iowa Code defines a *facility* as "any electric power generating plant or a combination of plants at a single site with a total capac- ity of one hundred megawatts of electricity or more."[209] The landowners argued that the phrase "at a single site" modified the entire clause. The court, however, disagreed, holding that the power plant did not have to be on a sin- gle site if it had a total capacity of 100 megawatts of electricity or more.[210]

Brownfields

Industrial sites now abandoned or idled because of environmental contami- nation are commonly referred to as *brownfields*. Federal and state regulations of these sites has had the unintended effect of hampering the transfer and redevelopment of brownfields because of the high costs and risks associated with these areas.[211] States across the country are looking at various initiatives to remedy the situation. Illinois is one such state that has enacted laws to reclaim these areas by limiting liability, developing reasonable cleanup crite- ria, and allocating money to cover the cleanup costs from "orphan shares."[212] One of the key features of Illinois' law is that it allows flexibility in the level of remediation required at any given site based on background levels of con- tamination in the area[213] versus the previous standard requiring remediation to the point where children could play without significant risk of harm. Fur- thermore, the law authorizes the issuance of a "no further remediation" letter on the site that is recorded with the recorder of deeds and "provides prima facie evidence that the site, when used according to the terms of the letter, no longer poses a threat to human health and the environment."[214] Section 58.9 of the law estimates joint and several liability for costs incurred by state and local governments. Federal environmental law, however, is still applicable.

Other brownfield legislation includes transferable tax credits in the amount of approved cleanup costs.[215] Although specific brownfield legislation does not exist at the federal level, Congress has considered several amendments to address these issues. In the meantime, federal requirements and liabilities may limit the effectiveness of the Illinois initiatives on joint and several liability for brownfield cleanup.[216] Although the full impact of Illinois' law is not yet known, it appears to strike a much-needed balance between environmental and economic concerns.

Judicial Review

Judicial review of federal, state, or local environmental regulatory decisions may be sought for several reasons, including due process claims based on failure to give notice and an opportunity to participate in an environmental review process, and abuse of discretion claims under federal or state administrative procedure statutes or specific environmental regulation statutes.[217]

In determining the extent of judicial review of a particular environmental policy decision, the lawyer must pay close attention to the language of the applicable statute. Some statutes, such as CERCLA,[218] provide that judicial review of particular kinds of decisions, usually of a remedial nature, must be delayed until the challenged regulatory action has been completed.[219] Statutes may also provide a particular form of review, or severely limit judicial review, thus rebutting the "presumption that individuals can bring suit to challenge agency actions that cause legally cognizable injury" under the Federal Administrative Procedure Act or its state counterparts.[220]

When judicial review is limited to whether an agency decision was "arbitrary or capricious," the Supreme Court has held that the reviewing court's inquiry must be "searching and careful" but based on the narrow standards of whether the decision was based "on a consideration of the relevant factors" and whether there has been a "clear error in judgment":

> When specialists express conflicting views, an agency must have discretion to rely on the reasonable opinions of its own qualified experts even if, as an original matter, a court might find contrary views more persuasive.[221]

Statutes commonly provide that when an agency decision is attacked that has been the subject of a public hearing at which evidence was required to be taken and the agency had discretion to make factual determinations, the reviewing court "[may] not exercise . . . independent judgment on the evidence" but may determine only whether the decision in controversy "is supported by substantial evidence in the light of the whole record."[222]

When injunctive relief is sought, such as a preliminary injunction to block construction of a highway through a state park because of an alleged failure to comply with federal and state environmental laws, the decision of whether to grant the relief sought "is committed to the sound discretion of the trial court . . . and will not be disturbed on appeal unless the record shows an abuse of that discretion, regardless of whether the appellate court would, in the first instance, have decided the matter differently."[223]

Applicable rules of standing must of course be met by persons seeking judicial review of environmental regulation decisions.[224] The Supreme Court has held that property owners subject to regulations under the Endangered Species Act[225] have standing to challenge enforcement actions under the Act. Although the landowners' interests were economic rather than environmental, they were sufficient to meet the expanded standing contemplated by the citizen-suit provision of the statute.[226]

Courts sometimes apply abstention doctrines to environmental litigation. In *Meredith v. Talbot County,*[227] the Fourth Circuit abstained, under both the *Pullman*[228] and *Burford*[229] abstention doctrines, from deciding a challenge to a five-acre set-aside requirement on which permit approval was conditioned. A developer's permit was approved after he agreed to set aside five acres for the protection of two endangered species that were found in the area being developed. Subsequently, the developer challenged the conditions to permit approval, alleging an unconstitutional taking had occurred or, in the alternative, asking for injunctive relief that would permit development of the property.

Talbot County officials who imposed the conditions had acted pursuant to the Chesapeake Bay Critical Area Protection Program.[230] Because the court considered this a "complex state regulatory scheme," it abstained from deciding the developer's challenge based on the *Burford* doctrine. This doctrine enables "federal courts to avoid needless conflict with the administration by a state of its own affairs."[231]

In abstaining, the court also acted pursuant to the *Pullman* doctrine, which states that abstention is appropriate if "the case may be disposed of by a decision on questions of unsettled state law."[232] Here the relevant portion of the state law had not yet been interpreted by state courts. Moreover, if the state courts granted the developers injunctive relief, the "federal constitutional questions raised in the complaint would disappear," the court concluded.[233]

Citizen Suits to Enforce Environmental Policies

An important aspect of environmental regulation legislation is the inclusion in many statutes, particularly at the federal level, of provisions authorizing private citizens to participate in the enforcement process through the prosecution of "citizen suits." Most of the environmental statutes authorizing citizen suits against alleged violators of environmental regulations limit jurisdiction of private enforcement activities to cases in which prospective relief to stop some violation is sought, although some statutes have been amended to broaden private enforcement jurisdiction to past as well as present violations.[234] Such statutes also generally require that prior notice of intent to file citizen suits be given to appropriate regulatory officials so that they will have an opportunity to enforce the statute.[235]

Statutes limiting citizen-suit jurisdiction to present or future violations are premised on the notion that the citizen suit is designed to "supplement rather than supplant" governmental enforcement, and that permitting citizen suits for "wholly past violations" would undermine this supplementary role.[236] Such statutes have been construed, though, to confer citizen-suit jurisdiction on federal district courts when "citizen-plaintiffs make a good-faith allegation of continuous or intermittent violation" of environmental law, without requiring proof of the allegations at the time jurisdiction attaches.[237]

Environmental legislation authorizing citizen suits has been held to confer federal jurisdiction to hear such suits against a state in its regulatory capacity for failure to promulgate or implement environmental regulations required by a federal statute on the theory that "[p]ermitting citizens to sue states to make sure they enact the regulatory schemes to which they have committed themselves furthers [the] Congressional goal [of ensuring state compliance with Federal statutes]."[238]

Citizen suits brought under legislation authorizing such suits for present or future violations have been held to be properly dismissed when a consent decree is entered in an EPA action filed after the citizen suit.[239] Landowners also may take advantage of citizen-suit provisions authorizing "any person" to file suit, such as contained in the Endangered Species Act,[240] to challenge agency actions applicable to their property.[241]

Private property owners may take advantage of citizen-suit provisions to secure cleanup of neighboring property that is causing contamination by runoff.[242] One important incentive for citizen suits is the possible awarding of attorneys' fees to the "prevailing party."[243]

Environmental Justice

With federal, state, and local regulations come concerns over environmental racism, an issue brought to government attention with a 1994 Executive Order.[244] Federal agencies must now include in their missions strategies to achieve environmental justice by identifying and addressing the adverse health or environmental effects of programs and policies on minority and low-income populations.[245] The national movement traces its beginnings to a 1982 decision to site a hazardous-waste facility in Warren County, North Carolina, a predominantly African-American community.[246] Public outcry led to an investigation by the U.S. General Accounting Office, which found that three of the four major hazardous-waste sites in the region were located in predominantly minority communities.[247] Even though it was unsuccessful, the protest did spark further study of the problem.

In 1987, the United Church of Christ Commission for Racial Justice released a study that found a significant correlation between race and the location of hazardous- waste sites.[248] This study and others like it have drawn much criticism. One such criticism is that the study did not consider the racial makeup of the community when the facility was originally sited, but only considered the current racial characteristics of the surrounding communities.[249] Others have argued that natural market forces result in the siting of locally undesirable land uses (LULUs) in minority and low-income neighborhoods.[250] Generally, the cost of land and labor is lower in such communities, making it more economically feasible for hazardous-waste companies to locate their facilities in such areas. Furthermore, the presence of such facilities would cause wealthier residents to leave the area, thereby increasing the low-income population.[251] This market force theory has its own critics.

Some legal scholars argue that the siting of LULUs does not create low-income, minority communities, but that LULUs are usually placed in already-existing minority communities.[252] In addition, all forms of racism contribute to existing environmental injustice. For example, redlining by banks and insurers has prevented redevelopment capital from flowing into minority communities, resulting in declining property values and increasing the availability of vacant land.[253] The combination of vacant land and low property values creates the incentive to locate heavy industrial uses in these areas. Once these uses have a stronghold in the area, current zoning laws will then perpetuate the problem because similar facilities will now be the best fit for the area, thereby increasing the concentration of hazardous sites in low-income, minority communities. If communities, however, consider environmental justice issues during the local planning process, the concentration of LULUs in minority neighborhoods can be addressed. Several states have already begun the process.

States are enacting equitable distribution or fair-share provisions to deal with the siting of LULUs. Arkansas creates a rebuttal presumption against locating solid-waste disposal sites within 12 miles of each other.[254] In Kentucky, siting decisions must consider the economic and social impacts of the facility on the community.[255] In Minnesota, authorities can license only one hazardous-waste site in each county.[256] Although legislation at the state level is progressing, Congress has yet to pass appropriate legislation. Several bills addressing environmental justice have been introduced, but none have passed.[257] While Congress continues to debate the issue, the Supreme Court has created a hurdle of its own in redressing environmental racism.

In 1977, the Supreme Court ruled that a race-neutral law with a disparate impact violates the Equal Protection Clause only if proof of a discriminatory intent exists.[258] So far, plaintiffs have been unable to meet this heavy burden.[259] Some commentators suggest, however, that Title VI of the Civil Rights Act of 1964 may provide some relief.[260] Title VI prohibits discrimination in federally funded programs and requires proof only of discriminatory impact, not intent.[261] To counter the plaintiff's proof of a discriminatory impact, the defendant must provide "evidence of legitimate, nondiscriminatory reason for its action."[262] Although federal law may provide some avenues in which to pursue environmental justice claims, actions brought in state courts have met with more success.

In New York, a court found that a proposal to build a new parking garage in the Lower East Side of Manhattan violated the New York City Charter.[263] The charter requires siting decisions to consider the social and economic impacts of such facilities on the surrounding areas. Furthermore, the decision must consider whether the distribution of the burden and benefits of the facility in light of the need for the service and its cost is fair.[264] In California, a court required the government to provide the environmental impact statement, notice of meetings, and other relevant documents in Spanish, in a case dealing with the siting of an incinerator in a Latino neighborhood.[265] Private enforcement provisions of some statutes may provide another means to pursue environmental justice claims.

Citizen-suit provisions in some statutes allow individuals to act as private attorney generals to enforce those laws and provide some relief.[266] Environmental laws like the Clean Air Act,[267] the Clean Water Act,[268] and CERCLA[269] have such provisions; however, substantive and procedural limitations of these laws may prevent the effective use of such suits by low-income and minority communities.[270]

In addition to private suits, local grassroots efforts have made headway. For example, a local African-American community group, Citizens Against Nuclear Trash (CANT), fought to prevent the Nuclear Regulatory Commission from siting a plutonium enrichment facility in their Louisiana community.[271] In Chicago, the People for Community Recovery (PCR) trains neighborhood residents in lead abatement and safety techniques.[272] Efforts such as these help provide citizens with the means to fight environmental discrimination. Cooperation among citizen groups, industry, developers, and government is essential to balance environmental and economic concerns and provide incentives for clean, safe development.[273]

Use of Negotiation and Mediation to Resolve Environmental Land Use Disputes

Nonadversarial methods of conflict resolution, such as negotiation and mediation, have shown promise as a means of resolving environmental disputes.[274] Interest in "consensual dispute settlement" is said to be influenced by three factors: "the cost of environmental conflict, dissatisfaction with traditional approaches to dispute resolution, and the success of some preliminary efforts using consensual methods."[275]

In a study evaluating the results of the first decade of use of nonadversarial techniques to resolve environmental disputes (1975–1984), the Conservation Foundation reported that environmental mediation had grown from a handful of cases to involvement in more than 160 disputes, with "the primary issues involved in these cases . . . divided into six broad categories: land use, natural resource management and use of public lands, water resources, energy, air quality, and toxins."[276] Most of the cases involved site-specific disputes, although disputes over general policy were also mediated. Land use disputes accounted for more than half of the cases.[277]

Two forms of nonadversarial dispute resolution have predominated in the environmental field—negotiation and mediation. Negotiation is "a method for consensual dispute settlement in which only the principal parties participate . . . [and seek] a voluntary settlement themselves without the assistance of an intermediary."[278]

Mediation is "a voluntary process in which those involved in a dispute jointly explore and reconcile their differences" with the assistance of a "neutral facilitator" (mediator) who "has no authority to impose a settlement . . .

[but whose] strength lies in the ability to assist the parties in resolving their own differences."[279]

Supporters of mediation as a means of resolving environmental disputes cite standard criticisms of litigation, such as cost, time, formality, and rigidity,[280] as well as the positive virtues of mediation as offering "a constructive means of striking a balance between developers and environmental groups" and a means that "allows . . . the parties to focus on what is truly at issue."[281]

In support of the last point, practitioners have stressed the "procedure-oriented" nature of much of the environmental legislation:

> [T]he ultimate issue is almost always what happens on the ground— whether and how the dam gets built, the highway is constructed, or the mine developed. However, when the dispute winds up in court, it is almost always fought on other issues—whether alternatives were honestly evaluated, whether enough hearings were held, or whether adequate data were presented—rather than the substantive questions which are the "real" issues for both developers and environmentalists. . . .
>
> Mediation may be a way of getting results on the ground and of approaching directly the substantive issues which are the center of everyone's concern. . . . A commitment to protect wildlife or water quality, going beyond any applicable legal requirements, may be much more valuable [to environmentalists] than an order requiring an agency to hold more hearings or rewrite an environmental impact statement. From the developer's point of view, agreeing to mitigation measures may allow development to proceed more quickly, more efficiently, and at less expense than litigation.[282]

Commentators have noted that mediation is not a panacea for resolving environmental disputes, particularly because of special difficulties often present in environmental disputes, including the possibility of "truly irreversible effects such as habitat destruction or species extinction," the "indeterminate nature, boundaries, and costs" of environmental disputes, questions concerning the "public interest"—what it is and who serves it—and problems with implementation of "novel" or "informal" environmental agreements.[283]

In response to the special difficulties associated with environmental disputes, the early experiences of environmental mediators, and "public participation efforts" associated with urban planning, commentators from the planning profession have offered "a conflict resolution strategy . . . especially tailored to the unique demands of environmental disputes" that incorporates the following nine steps:

1. Identifying the parties that have a stake in the outcome of a dispute
2. Ensuring that groups or interests that have a stake in the outcome are appropriately represented
3. Narrowing the agenda and confronting fundamentally different values and assumptions
4. Generating a sufficient number of alternatives or options

5. Agreeing on the boundaries and time horizon for analysis
6. Weighing, scaling, and amalgamating judgments about costs and benefits
7. Determining fair compensation and possible compensatory actions
8. Implementing the bargains that are made
9. Holding the parties to their commitments

The authors of the nine-step strategy comment that it is presented in a sequential, "idealized" fashion and note that in practice, the steps may have to be juggled in order to maintain the necessary flexibility of the process.[284]

Political scientists have cautioned that environmental mediation is fraught with political tensions, generally fueled by suspicions of power-imbalance and the possibility of being "co-opted." A "healthy suspicion" of mediation has been advocated in some quarters, particularly when "the offer to mediate comes from [the] opponents [of environmentalists]." Rather than "waste time avoiding or condemning mediation," environmentalists have been encouraged to "turn to the more difficult task of . . . promoting greater societal appreciation of the importance of environmental values and the costs of continuous development."[285]

Practitioner Perspectives

Since the early 1980s, environmental law has become a distinct and substantial area of law practice. Federal and state administrative regulations continue to become more comprehensive and complex. The scope of, and liability imposed by, the statutes and regulations referred to in this chapter now support an entire industry of engineers, inspectors, laboratories, citizen groups, government regulators, and lawyers. Most large law firms and corporate legal departments have full-time environmental lawyers who do not practice real estate or zoning law per se. This chapter provides only an outline of the major issues in environmental land use regulation.

The primary arena of traditional, nonenvironmental land use regulation is city hall. The primary arenas of environmental land use regulation are the state and federal regulating agencies. As noted in this chapter, the fundamental difference in the two areas of practice is the *use* orientation of local zoning regulation versus the *damage,* or *liability,* orientation of environmental law. Local land use regulation remains more occupied with planning and assessing the prospective effects of land uses relative to each other than with assessing or avoiding liability for physical damage to the environment.

The two areas of land use regulation intersect when owners argue for relief from traditional zoning regulation on the basis of federal preemption. Another point of convergence arises out of federal floodplain designations pursuant to floodplain maps published by the Federal Emergency Management Agency (FEMA). Such floodplain designations are often applied locally as a zoning "overlay" district, triggering a layer of specific land use restrictions on development within the floodplain. These regulations sharply limit development and marketability of floodplain real estate and ripple through to land use planning both within and adjacent to floodplain areas. Finally, local zoning officials often expressly condition approvals or environmental permits from upstream agencies, most commonly the U.S. Army Corps of Engineers under Section 404 permitting. Local zoning requirements often affect such federal permitting, or vice versa, when federal mitigation or protection requirements affect a site plan or local stormwater requirements. In such cases, it is important to identify federal issues early, and in any event before finalizing local approvals.

Environmental lawyers are not entirely occupied with damage assessment and avoidance but are also called on to assist purchasers and their lenders in evaluating the potential effects of known or possible contaminants. In the typical transaction, known or suspected conditions are not completely liquidated or otherwise quantifiable but are considered in light of the totality of the business transaction. Such conditions are almost always resolved by negotiation.

The most successful environmental land use lawyers thus are not technicians who apply rigid scientific standards to land use operational issues or liability disputes. Rather, these lawyers make informed judgments about risks and benefits, nearly always in consultation with trained engineers, and certainly in light of the business or regulatory perspective of the client. Thus, while there certainly are established lists of contaminants and regulatory "action" levels for concentration of the same in the ground, air, building materials, or groundwater, much of the environmental practitioner's work involves the margins. In addition, the engineer's determination of the actual levels of such materials in the environment is not always precise or infallible. In all events, the environmental lawyer must establish a working rapport with qualified and trusted environmental engineers. In the end, however, environmental land use practice, like traditional areas of practice, is often more art than science.

Notes

1. 42 U.S.C. § 4321 *et seq.* (1994).
2. 42 U.S.C. § 7401 *et seq.* (1994).
3. 33 U.S.C. § 1281 *et seq.* (1994).
4. 42 U.S.C. § 4901 *et seq.* (1994).
5. 16 U.S.C. § 1451 *et seq.* (1994).
6. 33 U.S.C. § 1251 *et seq.* (1994).
7. 16 U.S.C. § 1531 *et seq.* (1994).
8. 49 U.S.C. § 5101 *et seq.* (1994).
9. 42 U.S.C. § 6901 *et seq.* (1994).
10. 15 U.S.C. § 2601 *et seq.* (1994).
11. 42 U.S.C. § 9601 *et seq.*
12. American Lung Ass'n v. Kean, 871 F.2d 319, 322 (3d Cir. 1989) (federal courts have jurisdiction to hear citizens' suits against state agencies to compel promulgation and implementation of ground-level ozone emission regulations under Clean Air Act); Shanty Town Assocs. P'ship v. EPA, 843 F.2d 782, 791–92 (4th Cir. 1988) (while states have primary responsibility for control on nonpoint source pollution under the Clean Water Act, states do so as "agents for the implementation of federal water pollution control policy").
13. *See* pp. 427–30.
14. *See* pp. 441–42.

15. 531 U.S. 159 (2001).

16. Shanty Town Assocs. P'ship v. EPA, 843 F.2d 782, 786 (4th Cir. 1988) (citing 42 U.S.C. § 4332 (2)(c)).

17. Sylvester v. U.S. Army Corps of Eng'rs, 871 F.2d 817, 822 (9th Cir. 1989).

18. *Id.* at 823.

19. Wisconsin v. Envtl. Prot. Agency, 266 F.3d 741 (7th Cir. 2001).

20. *See, e.g.,* Clean Water Act, 33 U.S.C. §§ 1342(b) and 1342(c)(1) (1988).

21. *See, e.g.,* ARIZ. REV. STAT. ANN. § 459-402 *et seq.* (West Supp. 1990); CAL. PUB. RES. CODE § 21080.5(j) (West Supp. 1991); FLA. STAT. ANN. § 403.087 *et seq.* (West Supp. 1991) (air quality); IND. CODE ANN. § 13-1-1-1 *et seq.* (Burns 1989 & Supp. 1991); LA. REV. STAT. ANN. § 30.2011 *et seq.* (West 1989 & Supp. 1991); MD. ENVTL. CODE ANN. § 2-104 (Michie 1987); N.Y. ENVTL. CONSERV. LAW § 8-0109 (McKinney 1984 & Supp. 1991); TENN. CODE ANN. § 53-3408 *et seq.* (Michie 1987 & Supp. 1990) (Air Quality Control Act).

22. *See, e.g.,* ILL. STAT. ANN. ch. 5, § 1001 *et seq.* (Smith-Hurd Supp. 1991) (Agricultural Areas Conservation and Protection Act); MD. AGRIC. CODE § 8-501 *et seq.* (Michie 1985 & Supp. 1990) (Maryland Soil Conservation District Law); MICH. STAT. ANN. § 26.1287 *et seq.* (Callaghan 1982 & Supp. 1991) (Farmland and Open Space Preservation Act); N.C. GEN. STAT. § 106-65.43 (1988) (Biological Organism Act); N.J. STAT. ANN. § 13:8A-1 *et seq.* (West 1979) (Green Acres Land Acquisition Act) and § 13:18A-1 *et seq.* (Michie 1985 & Supp. 1990) (Pinelands Protection Act).

23. *See, e.g.,* CAL. PUB. RES. CODE § 30000 *et seq.* (West 1986 & Supp. 1991) (Coastal Act); CONN. GEN. STAT. §§ 22a-90 to -112 (West 1985 & Supp. 1991) (Coastal Management Act); DEL. CODE ANN. tit. 7, § 7000 *et seq.* (1983 & Supp. 1990) (Coastal Zone Act); FLA. STAT. ANN. § 380.19 *et seq.* (West 1988 & Supp. 1991) (Coastal Management Act); MD. NAT. RES. CODE ANN. §§ 8-1801 to -1910 (Michie 1990 & Supp. 1991) (Chesapeake Bay Critical Area Protection Program); MICH. STAT. ANN. § 13.1831 *et seq.* (Callaghan 1987) (Shorelands Protection and Management Act); N.J. STAT. ANN. § 13:19-1 *et seq.* (West 1979 & Supp. 1991) (Coastal Area Facility Review Act); WIS. STAT. ANN. § 144.26 *et seq.* (West 1989 & Supp. 1991) (Shoreland Regulation).

24. *See, e.g.,* CAL. PUB. RES. CODE § 21000 *et seq.* (West 1986 & Supp. 1991); IND. CODE ANN. § 13-1-10-1 *et seq.* (Burns 1990); MINN. STAT. ANN. § 116d.01 *et seq.* (West 1987 & Supp. 1991); N.J. STAT. ANN. § 13:1D-1 *et seq.* (West 1979 & Supp. 1991); OR. REV. STAT. § 468.005 *et seq.* (1989); N.Y. ENVTL. CONSERV. LAW § 8-0101 *et seq.* (McKinney 1984 & Supp. 1991). The relationship of State Environmental Policy Acts (SEPAs) to local land use planning and regulations is discussed in Daniel Mandelker, *Melding State Environmental Policy Acts with Land Use Planning and Regulations,* 49 LAND USE LAW, no. 3 (March 1997) at p. 3.

25. *See, e.g.,* MONT. CODE ANN. § 75-10-401 *et seq.* (1989) (Hazardous Waste and Underground Storage Tank Act); N.J. STAT. ANN. § 13:1E-49 *et seq.* (West Supp. 1991) (Major Hazardous Waste Facilities Citing Act) and § 13:1K-6 *et seq.* (West Supp. 1991) (Environmental Cleanup Responsibility Act); OR. REV. STAT. § 466.005 *et seq.* (1989) (Hazardous Waste and Hazardous Materials); PA. STAT. ANN. tit. 35, § 60:18.101 *et seq.* (Purdon Supp. 1991) (Solid Waste Management Act); WASH. REV. CODE ANN. § 70.105.007 (West Supp. 1991) (Hazardous Waste Management).

26. *See, e.g.,* MO. REV. STAT. § 260.200 (Vernon 1990 & Supp. 1991); N.J. STAT. ANN. § 13:1-5.1 *et seq.* (West Supp. 1991) (Solid Waste Management Act); PA. STAT. ANN. tit. 35, § 6018.101 *et seq.* (West Supp. 1991) (Solid Waste Management Act); TENN. CODE ANN. § 68-31-101 *et seq.* (Michie 1987 & Supp. 1990) (Solid Waste Disposal Act).

Missouri's statute was signed into law by Governor Ashcroft in September 1990 and is one of the nation's toughest solid-waste disposal laws. It includes recycling provisions, some of which became effective in 1991 (e.g., refrigerators and tires).

27. *See, e.g.,* FLA. STAT. ANN. § 376.011 *et seq.* (West 1988 & Supp. 1991) (Pollutant Spill Prevention and Control Act); TENN. CODE ANN. § 70-324 *et seq.* (Michie 1987 & Supp. 1990) (Water Quality Control Act); N.J. STAT. ANN. § 58:10A-1 (West 1982 & Supp. 1991) (Water Pollution Control Act).

28. *See, e.g.,* ALASKA STAT. § 46.40.010-.210 (1990); CAL. PUB. RES. CODE §§ 30000–30900 (West 1986 & Supp. 1991) (Coast Acts); CONN. GEN. STAT. §§ 22a-36 to -45 (West 1985 & Supp. 1991) (Inland Wetlands and Watercourse Act); FLA. STAT. ANN. §§ 161.011–.58 (West 1990) (Beach and Shore Preservation Act); HAW. REV. STAT. §§ 205A-1 to -49 (1985 & Supp. 1987) (Coastal Zone Management Law); LA. REV. STAT. ANN. §§ 49:213.1–.22 (West 1987 & Supp. 1991) (State and Local Resources Management Act); MD. NAT. RES. CODE Ann. §§ 9-101 to -502 (Michie 1990) (Wetlands Law); MICH. STAT. ANN. § 13.1831 *et seq.* (Callaghan 1987) (Shorelands Protection and Management Act); S.C. CODE ANN. §§ 48-39-10 to -220 (Law Co-op 1987 & Supp. 1990) (Coastal Zone Management Act). *See also* Sedgley & Watson, *Land Use Regulation by the Virginia Marine Resources Commission: The Virginia Wetlands Act and Coastal Primary Sand Dune Protection Act,* 7 VA. J. NAT. RES. L. 381 (1988).

29. *See* Kahana Sunset Owners Ass'n v. County of Maui, 947 P.2d 378 (Hawaii 1997) (requiring environmental assessment under state law for drainage system to serve proposed 300-residence development).

30. *See* Omya, Inc. v. Town of Middlebury, 758 A.2d 777 (Vt. 2000) (affirming denial by state environmental board of permit amendment to permit more truck trips through town).

31. *See generally* Butler, *The Commons Concept: An Historical Concept with Modern Relevance,* 23 WM. & MARY L. REV. 835 (1982); Comment, *The Public Trust Doctrine in Maine's Submerged Lands: Public Rights, State Obligation and the Role of the Courts,* 37 ME. L. REV. 105 (1985). The doctrine also applies to inland water bodies, however. See Community Nat'l Bank v. Vermont, 782 A.2d 1195 (Vt. 2001).

32. Bell v. Town of Wells, 557 A.2d 168, 181 n. 2 (Me. 1989) (Wathen, J., dissenting, quoting Inst. 2.1.1).

33. *Id.* at 181 (Wathen, J., dissenting, citing Shively v. Bowlby, 152 U.S. 1, 11 (1894); Blundell v. Catterall, 106 Eng. Rep. 1190, 1193 (1821)).

34. *Id.* at 181 (Wathen, J., dissenting, citing Shively v. Bowlby, 152 U.S. 1, 11–13 (1894)).

35. *Id.* at 181 (Wathen, J., dissenting, citing Phillips Petroleum Co. v. Mississippi, 484 U.S. 469 (1988)).

36. *Id.* at 177.

37. *Id.* at 177–78, *quoting* Nollan v. California Coastal Comm'n, 483 U.S. 825, 832 (1987). The Supreme Court of Wisconsin, on the other hand, took a relatively expansive view of the state's rights and responsibilities as public trustee in *Just v. Marinette County,* 201 N.W.2d 761 (Wis. 1972), finding that the state actually had an "active public trust duty" to promote, as well as protect and preserve, navigable waters for fishing, recreation, and scenic beauty. *Id.* at 768. In a subsequent case, however, the court found that an expansive state role in protection of coastal areas could be achieved through harm/benefit analysis, and the Public Trust Doctrine was not necessary to achieve such result. Marshall & Ilsley Bank v. Town of Somers, 414 N.W.2d 824 (Wis. 1987). *See generally* Joseph Sax, *Property Rights and the Economy of Nature: Understanding* Lucas v. South Carolina Coastal Council, 45 STANFORD L. REV. 1433 (1993), for an argument that *Lucas* overruled Just v. Marinette County. *See also* Marine One, Inc. v. Manatee County, 898 F.2d 1490 (11th Cir. 1990) (applying Florida's version of the public trust doctrine to turn back a takings challenge to the denial of marine-construction permits).

38. First English Evangelical Lutheran Church v. County of Los Angeles, 482 U.S. 304 (1987). *See* chapter 3.

39. 505 U.S. 1003 (1992).

40. *See* chapter 3.

41. *See* Fafard v. Conservation Comm'n of Barnstable, 733 N.E.2d 66, 70 (Mass. 2000).

42. California Coastal Comm'n v. Granite Rock Co., 480 U.S. 572 (1989) (Coastal Zone Management Act does not automatically preempt all state regulation of activities on federal lands).

43. 42 U.S.C. § 6901 *et seq.* (1988).

44. North Haven Planning & Zoning Comm'n v. Upjohn Co., 921 F.2d 27 (2d Cir. 1990). *See* Upjohn Co. v. North Haven Planning & Zoning Comm'n, 616 A.2d 786 (Conn. 1992), where the Supreme Court of Connecticut corroborated the holding of the Second Circuit, reasserting that neither EPA approval of a company's plan to cap and monitor a sludge pile of hazardous waste may preempt a local zoning commission's denial of an application for such action.

45. 42 U.S.C. § 9601.

46. United States v. City and County of Denver, 100 F.3d 1509, 1513 (10th Cir. 1996), *citing* Freightlines Corp. v. Myrick, 115 (1995).

47. *See* Fafard v. Conservation Comm'n of Barnstable, 733 N.E.2d 66, 71 (Mass. 2000).

48. California Coastal Comm'n v. Granite Rock Co., 480 U.S. 572 (1989).

49. PA. STAT. ANN. tit. 35, § 6018.101 *et seq.* (Purdon 1972 & Supp. 1991).

50. Longenecker v. Pine Grove Landfill, Inc., 543 A.2d 215, 216 (Pa. Commw. Ct. 1988).

51. *Id.*

52. *Id.*

53. Council of Lower Keys v. Charley Toppino & Sons, 429 So. 2d 67, 68 (Fla. Dist. Ct. App. 1983). *See also* Village of Westwood v. Bd. of Adjustment of Municipality of Creve Coeur, 811 S.W.2d 437 (Mo. Ct. App. 1991) (applying preemption to uphold city's deferral to county-level review of proposed hospital incinerator).

54. VT. STAT. ANN. tit. 10, § 6001 (1975 & Supp. 1990).

55. *Id. See also* Southview Assocs. v. Bongartz, 980 F.2d 84 (2d Cir. 1992), *cert. denied*, 113 U.S. 1586 (1993), where the Second Circuit affirmed the Vermont Environmental Board's denial of Southview's permit application for the development of vacation homes, holding that a seasonal occupation of the land by an estimated 20 deer left numerous alternative uses of the property. Furthermore, Southview's submission and denial of one proposal was held not indicative of whether subsequent proposals, potentially yielding economic benefit, would likewise be denied by the board.

When Southview Associates purchased the 88-acre parcel of land in Vermont, it erroneously believed that its proposed development was in accordance with Act 250, a law created to ensure that development does not threaten or detrimentally impact the state's environmental resources; however, because a rarefied winter habitat for white-tailed deer existed on the property, the Vermont Environmental Board found that Southview's proposal did threaten an environment uniquely suited for the deer.

56. Feder, *Vermont Development Laws May Have Saved Its Banks*, N.Y. TIMES, March 4, 1991, p. C1.

57. *See, e.g.*, De St. Aubin v. Flacke, 496 N.E.2d 879, 883, (N.Y. 1986) ("The core of the problem is that development of the property is regulated by two separate branches of government [State-tidal wetlands and Town-zoning]"). *See generally* p. 444.

58. 42 U.S.C. § 4321 *et seq.*

59. Robertson v. Methow Valley Citizens Council, 490 U.S. 332 (1989).

60. CAL. PUB. RES. CODE § 21000 *et seq.* (West 1986 & Supp. 1991).

61. CAL. ADMIN. CODE tit. 14, § 15000 *et seq.*, "which are binding on all public agencies." Long Beach Sav. & Loan Ass'n v. Long Beach Redev. Agency, 188 Cal. App. 3d 249, 232 Cal. Rptr. 772, 776 n.7 (Ct. App. 1986).

62. *Long Beach Sav. & Loan Ass'n,* 232 Cal. Rptr. at 776.

63. *Id.* at 776 (citing No Oil, Inc. v. City of Los Angeles, 529 P.2d 66 (Cal. 1974)).

64. CAL. PUB. RES. CODE §§ 21100, 21151 (West 1986 & Supp. 1991). *No Oil, Inc.,* 529 P.2d at 69; *Long Beach Sav. & Loan Ass'n,* 232 Cal. Rptr. at 776.

65. *Long Beach Sav. & Loan Ass'n,* 232 Cal. Rptr. at 776.

66. 42 U.S.C. § 4321 *et seq.*

67. CAL. GOV'T CODE § 66801 *et seq.* (West 1983 & Supp. 1991); CAL. PUB. RES. CODE § 21083.5(a) (West 1986 & Supp. 1991).

68. CAL. ADMIN. CODE, tit. 14, § 15083; *No Oil, Inc.,* 529 P.2d at 69 (1974); *Long Beach Sav. & Loan Ass'n,* 232 Cal. Rptr. at 776 (1986) (citing COUNCIL ON ENVIRONMENTAL QUALITY, GUIDELINES ON PREPARATION OF ENVIRONMENTAL IMPACT STATEMENTS § 1500.5, 38 Fed. Reg. 20552 (1973); Hanly v. Mitchell, 460 F.2d 640 (2d Cir. 1972); Hanly v. Kleindienst, 471 F.2d 823 (2d Cir. 1972); Envtl. Defense Fund, Inc. v. Ruckelshaus, 439 F.2d 584, 598 (D.C. Cir. 1971)).

69. CAL. PUB. RES. CODE § 21064 (West 1986 & Supp. 1991); *Long Beach Sav. & Loan Ass'n,* 232 Cal. Rptr. at 777 (1986).

70. Connecticut 2002 Laws, H.B. 5708, Public Act. 02-121.

71. CAL. ADMIN. CODE tit. 14, § 15382. *Long Beach Sav. & Loan Ass'n,* 232 Cal. Rptr. at 776, n. 8.

72. Hall v. Norton, 266 F.3d 969, 977 (9th Cir. 2001).

73. 2002 WL 66359 (Cal. App. 2002).

74. *Long Beach Sav. & Loan Ass'n,* 232 Cal. Rptr. at 781 (citing No Oil, Inc. v. City of Los Angeles, 529 P.2d 66 (Cal. 1974).

75. Missouri Coalition for Env't v. U.S. Corps of Engr's, 866 F.2d 1025, 1033 (8th Cir.), *cert. denied,* 493 U.S. 820 (1989) (burden not met to show need for environmental impact survey for proposed domed football stadium in wetlands area).

76. *No Oil, Inc.,* 529 P. 2d at 73–74.

77. *Long Beach Sav. & Loan Ass'n,* 232 Cal. Rptr. at 780–81 (citing cases).

78. CAL. ADMIN. CODE tit. 14, § 15126; *Long Beach Sav. & Loan Ass'n,* 232 Cal. Rptr. at 777.

79. Robertson v. Methow Valley Citizens Council, 490 U.S. 332, 352 (1989).

80. Long Beach Sav. & Loan Ass'n v. Long Beach Redev. Agency, 188 Cal. App. 3d 249, 232 Cal. Rptr. 772 (1986) (citing Cal. Pub. Res. Code §§ 21080.3, 21080.4, 21153, 21082.1)).

81. Missouri Coalition for Envt. v. U.S. Corps of Engr's, 678 F. Supp. 790, 796–97 (E.D. Mo. 1988), *aff'd,* 866 F.2d 1025, 1033 (8th Cir. 1989).

82. Akpan v. Koch, 75 N.Y.2d 561, 554 N.E.2d 53, 57–58, 555 N.Y.S.2d 16, (1990) (upholding conclusion that proposed urban redevelopment project will not cause significant secondary displacement).

83. Missouri Coalition for Envt. v. U.S. Corps of Engr's, 866 F.2d 1025, 1032 (8th Cir. 1989), *cert. denied,* 493 U.S. 820 (1989).

84. Polygon Corp. v. City of Seattle, 578 P.2d 1309, 1312–13 (Wash. 1978).

85. *See* pp. 421–22.

86. 33 U.S.C. § 1251 *et seq.* (1988).

87. 33 U.S.C. §§ 1311(a) and 1342.

88. *Id.* § 1344.

89. *Id.* §§ 1342(c) and 1344(c).

90. *Id.* § 1342.

91. N.J. STAT. ANN. § 13:9B-1 *et seq.* (West Supp. 1991).

92. *Id.* § 13:9B-2; 33 U.S.C. § 1344.

93. N.J. STAT. ANN. § 13:9B-3 (West Supp. 1991).

94. *Id.* § 13:9B-4.

95. *Id.* § 13:9B-8.

96. *Id.* §§ 13:9B-9 to -13.

97. *Id.* §§ 13:9B-16 to -18. A *transition area* is defined as "an area of land adjacent to a freshwater wetland which minimizes adverse impacts on the wetland or serves as an integral component of the wetlands ecosystem." *Id.* § 13:9B-3.

98. N.J. Department of Environmental Protection, N.J. STAT. ANN. § 13:9B-3 (West Supp. 1991).

99. N.J. STAT. ANN. § 13:9B-5 (West Supp. 1991).

100. *Id.* § 13:9B-5.

101. *Id.* § 13:9B-9(b).

102. *Id.* § 13:9B-9(b)(1)–(9).

103. *Id.* § 13:9B-11.

104. *Id.* §§ 13:9B-14 and -15.

105. *Id.* § 13:9B-24.

106. *Id.* § 13:9B-23.

107. *Id.* § 13:9B-19.

108. N.J. STAT. ANN. §§ 13:9B-20; 52:14B-1 *et seq.*

109. *Id.* § 13:9B-21.

110. United States v. Riverside Bayview Homes, Inc., 474 U.S. 121 (1985); *see also* Natural Res. Comm'n of Indiana v. Amax Coal Co., 638 N.E.2d 418 (Ind. 1994) (conditioning a permit to use groundwater so as to prevent harm to property not within the permit area was not a taking).

111. Nollan v. California Coastal Comm'n, 483 U.S. 825 (1987). Freilich & Chinn, *Fine-tuning the Taking Equation: Applying It to Development Exactions*, 40 LAND USE L. & ZONING DIG. pt. I (Feb. 1988). *See generally* chapter 3.

112. N.J. STAT. ANN. § 20:3-1 *et seq.* (West Supp. 1991).

113. *Id.* § 13:9B-22.

114. 33 U.S.C. § 1344 (1988); United States v. Riverside Bayview Homes, Inc., 474 U.S. 121 (1985).

115. 33 C.F.R. § 328.3(b), 40 C.F.R. § 230.3; FEDERAL MANUAL FOR IDENTIFYING AND DELINEATING JURISDICTIONAL WETLANDS (1987), adopted by EPA and Corps agreement. 58 Fed. Reg. 4995 (Jan. 19, 1993); 33 C.F.R. § 323.2(c)(1978).

116. United States v. Riverside Bayview Homes, Inc., 474 U.S. 121 (1985).

117. *Id.* at 126.

118. 961 F.2d 1310 (7th Cir.), *vacated & reh'g granted*, 975 F.2d 1554 (7th Cir. 1992).

119. 531 U.S. 159 (2001).

120. *Id.* at 171–72.

121. *See* GARY S. GUZY & ROBERT M. ANDERSEN, MEMORANDUM: SUPREME COURT RULING CONCERNING CWA JURISDICTION OVER ISOLATED WATERS (EPA, Jan. 19, 2001), available at http://www.epa.gov/owow/wetlands/swanccnav.html.

122. 33 U.S.C. § 1362(7). *See also* 33 C.F.R. pt. 323.

123. No. C90-713-5-BO (E.D.N.C. 1992).

124. Clean Water Act Regulatory Programs, 58 Fed. Reg. 45,008 (Aug. 25, 1993); 33 C.F.R. pt. 323; 40 C.F.R. 232.2.

125. *Id.*

126. 951 F. Supp. 267 (D.D.C. 1997), *reh'g denied*, 962 F. Supp. 2d (D.D.C. 1997).

127. *See* Fulton, *The Wetlands Morass*, 57 PLAN No. 8, at 12 (Aug. 1991).

128. MD. NAT. RES. CODE ANN. § 9-202 (Michie 1990 & Supp. 1991).

129. *See generally* N.Y. ENVTL. CONSERV. § 24-0301 (McKinney 1986 & Supp. 1991); Spears v. Berle, 48 N.Y.2d 254, 397 N.E.2d 1304, 422 N.Y.S. 2d 636 (1979).

130. N.Y. Envtl. Conserv. § 25-0101 *et seq.* (McKinney 1986 & Supp. 1991).

131. 496 N.E.2d 879 (N.Y. 1986).

132. *Id.* at 881.

133. *Id.* at 881; N.Y. Envtl. Conserv. § 25-404 (McKinney 1986 & Supp. 1991).

134. 496 N.E.2d at 887.

135. La Crosse City Ords., § 15.03(B)(1); State v. City of La Crosse, 354 N.W.2d 738, 739 (Wis. 1984).

136. State v. City of La Crosse, 354 N.W.2d at 741.

137. 16 U.S.C. § 1451 *et seq.* (1988).

138. *Id.* § 1452(1), *discussed in* LaVallee Northside Civic Ass'n v. Virgin Islands Bd. Coastal Zone Mgmt. Comm'n, 866 F.2d 616, 619–20 (3d Cir. 1989) (permit issuance is the event that marks the beginning time allowed for taking an administrative appeal, which must be done before judicial review will be granted under Virgin Islands Coastal Zone Management Act).

139. Md. Nat. Res. Code Ann. § 8-1801 *et seq.* (Michie 1990 & Supp. 1991). *See* Meredith v. Talbot County, 828 F.2d 228 (4th Cir. 1987) (complex state regulatory scheme of Chesapeake Bay Critical Area Protection Program justifies application of abstention doctrines to dispute over subdivision and residential development).

140. Md. Nat. Res. Code Ann. § 8-1807(a) (Michie 1990 & Supp. 1991).

141. *Id.* § 8-1807(b)(1).

142. *Id.* § 8-1807(b)(2).

143. *Id.* § 8-1807(3).

144. *Id.* § 8-1809.

145. *Id.* § 8-1808(c).

146. *Id.* § 8-1808.2.

147. *Id.* § 8-1901.

148. Del. Code Ann. tit. 7, § 7003 (Michie 1987 & Supp. 1990); Norfolk Southern Corp. v. Oberly, 822 F.2d 388 (3d Cir. 1987).

149. See chapter 3.

150. *Id.* at 407.

151. *Id.* at 394.

152. *Id.*

153. See chapter 4, p. 151.

154. Wash. Rev. Code § 43.21C.010 *et seq.*

155. *See* p. 177.

156. Victoria Tower P'ship v. Seattle, 49 Wash. App. 755, 745 P.2d 1328 (1987).

157. *See* chapter 8.

158. Victoria Tower P'ship v. Seattle, 745 P.2d 1328, 1331 (Wash. Ct. App. 1987).

159. *See, e.g.,* Robertson v. Methow Valley Citizens Council, 490 U.S. 332 (1989), *discussing* 16 U.S.C. §§ 528, 1600 *et seq.*; 36 C.F.R. § 251.54(f) (three-stage permit process for ski areas in national forests, including two separate environmental analyses).

160. Marsh v. Oregon Natural Res. Council, 490 U.S. 360, 369–70 (1989).

161. *Id.* at 371.

162. *See* Friends of the Wild Swan v. Dep't of Natural Res., 6 P.3d 972, 978 (Mont. 2000).

163. Id. at 371–72 (quoting TVA v. Hill, 437 U.S. 153, 188 n. 34 (1978)).

164. *Id. But see* Hall v. Norton, 266 F.3d 969, 977 (9th Cir. 2001) (applying abuse of discretion standard).

165. *See* chapter 4, p. 151; ch. 8 p. 353.

166. *See, e.g.,* Envtl. Defense Fund v. Tennessee Valley Authority, 468 F.2d 1164, 1174–81 (6th Cir. 1972), *cited with approval,* Marsh v. Oregon Natural Res. Council, 490 U.S. 360 (1989).

167. Marsh v. Oregon Natural Res. Council, 490 U.S. 360 (1989).

168. Victoria Tower P'ship v. Seattle, 745 P.2d 1328, 1331–32 (Wash. Ct. App. 1987).

169. *See, e.g.,* 42 U.S.C. § 9607; 15 U.S.C. §2615 (1988).

170. *See, e.g.,* S. Rep. No. 848, 96th Cong., 2d Sess. 34 (1980) (CERCLA), *reprinted in* ILL CERCLA Legislative History at 308, 340–41 (1982); J.V. Peters & Co. v. Envtl. Prot. Agency, 767 F.2d 263, 266 (6th Cir. 1985); New York v. Shore Realty Corp., 759 F.2d 1032, 1042 (2d Cir. 1985); United States v. Maryland Bank & Trust Co., 632 F. Supp. 573 (D. Md. 1986).

171. *See, e.g.,* N.J. REV. STAT. § 58:10-23, 11, 13(f) (West 1991).

172. United States v. Maryland Bank & Trust Co., 632 F. Supp. 573 (D. Md. 1986).

173. *See, e.g.,* 42 U.S.C. § 9601 (35)(A) (1988); 415 ILCS 5/22.2(j) (Smith-Hurd 1996).

174. Rohrmann & Hoffman, *Environmental Audits: Assessing Environmental Liability in Real Estate Transactions,* 77 ILL. BAR J. 690, 693 (Sept. 1989).

175. Spendlove (ed.), *Buying or Selling a Business: A Multidisciplinary Approach,* 3 UTAH BAR J. No. 5, at 8, 14 (May 1990).

176. *Id.*

177. 42 U.S.C. § 9601 (35)(A) (1988) and Annotations 14 and 15.

178. *Id.* § 9601(35)(B); Rohrmann & Hoffman, *Environmental Audits: Assessing Environmental Liability in Real Estate Transactions,* 77 ILL. BAR J. 690, 692 (Sept. 1989).

179. *See, e.g.,* CONN STAT. ANN. tit. 22a, § 134a *et seq.* (West 1985 & Supp. 1991); IND. STAT. ANN. § 13-7-22.5-1 *et seq.*; N.J. STAT. ANN. § 13:1K-6. Rohrmann & Hoffman, *Environmental Audits: Assessing Environmental Liability in Real Estate Transactions,* 77 ILL. BAR J. 690, 691 (Sept. 1989).

180. *See, e.g.,* IND. STAT. ANN. §§ 13-7-22.5-15 and 13-7-22.5-16 (Burns, 1990).

181. *See, e.g.,* 415 ILCS 5/33(c) *discussed in* Maher & Rosenwinkel, *A Guide Through Illinois' Environmental Regulatory Maze,* 78 ILL. BAR J. 18, 19 (Jan. 1990).

182. *See* State *ex rel.* Miller v. DeCoster, 608 N.W.2d 785 (Iowa 2000), Commonwealth Edison v. United States, 271 F.3d 1327 (Fed. Cir. 2001).

183. Maher & Rosenwinkel, *supra* n. 181, at 20–23.

184. 415 ILCS 5/35(a) (Smith-Hurd 1996).

185. *Id.* at 5/27(a).

186. *Id.* at 5/28.1(a).

187. Maher & Rosenwinkel, *supra* n. 181, at 20.

188. 415 ILCS 5/36(b) (Smith-Hurd 1996); City of Mendota v. Pollution Control Bd., 514 N.E.2d 218, 222–23 (Ill. App. Ct. 1987), *noted in* Maher & Rosenwinkel, *supra* n. 181, at 20.

189. *See* chapter 5.

190. Willowbrook Dev. Corp. v. Illinois Pollution Control Bd., 92 Ill. App. 3d 1074, 416 N.E. 2d 385 (1981); Monsanto Co. v. Pollution Control Bd., 67 Ill. 2d 276, 367 N.E.2d 684, 689–90 (1977), *discussed in* Maher & Rosenwinkel, *supra* n. 181, at 22.

191. 415 ILCS 5/27(a) (Smith-Hurd 1996); Central Illinois Pub. Serv. Co. v. Pollution Control Bd., 511 N.E.2d 269, 272 (Ill. App. Ct. 1987), *noted in* Maher & Rosenwinkel, *supra* n. 181, at 22.

192. 415 ILCS 5/26; 5 ILCS 100/5-40(b) (Smith-Hurd 1996).

193. *See* chapter 5.

194. 415 ILCS 5/28.1(c) (Smith-Hurd 1996), *discussed in* Maher & Rosenwinkel, *supra* n. 181, at 23.

195. *See* chapter 5.

196. *See, e.g.,* Furey v. City of Sacramento, 780 F.2d 1448 (9th Cir. 1986). *See also* chapter 7.

197. *See, e.g.,* West Montgomery County Citizens Ass'n v. Maryland-National Capital Park & Planning Comm'n, 522 A.2d 1328 (Md. 1987).

198. MICH. STAT. ANN. § 26.1287 *et seq.* (Callaghan 1987).

199. *Id.* § 26.1287(10).

200. *Id.* § 26.1287(2).

201. *Id.* § 26.1287(5).

202. *Id.* § 26.1287(11).

203. Mich. Comp. Law §§ 554.741–.745 (West 1991).

204. Village of Peck v. Hoist, 396 N.W.2d 536 (Mich. Ct. App. 1986).

205. 42 U.S.C. § 9601 *et seq.*

206. Outboard Marine Corp. v. Thomas, 773 F.2d 883, 890 (7th Cir. 1985).

207. 42 U.S.C. § 9604(e)(3)(4).

208. *See, e.g.,* BF Goodrich Co. v. Martha, 697 F. Supp. 89 (D. Conn. 1988).

209. Iowa Code § 476A.1(1) (West 1976 & Supp. 1991).

210. Reid v. Iowa State Commerce Comm'n, 357 N.W.2d 588 (Iowa 1984).

211. Michael J. Fleck, *The Illinois Brownfields Law: Environmental Protection Meets Economic Productivity,* 84 Ill. Bar J. 400 (1996). For a discussion of an analysis of liability and Superfund issues at a brownfields site, *see* Bruce Diamond, *Opportunities in Brownfields,* 56 Mortgage Banking 89 (1996).

212. Fleck, *supra* n. 211, at 401. Orphan shares are those cleanup costs that cannot be allocated to responsible parties. *Id.*

213. 415 ILCS 5/58.5.

214. Fleck, *supra* n. 211, at 403.

215. *See, e.g.,* § 447.700 *et seq.,* Vernons Mo. Stat.

216. *Id.* at 403–04.

217. *See, e.g.,* Marsh v. Oregon Natural Res. Council, 490 U.S. 360 (1989) (decision that supplemental environmental impact statement was unnecessary upheld as not arbitrary or capricious); Quince Orchard Valley Citizens Ass'n v. Hodel, 872 F.2d 75 (4th Cir. 1989) (plaintiff's delay in pursuing action justified district court's denial of preliminary injunction against construction of four-lane highway through state park); Alabama v. Envtl. Prot. Agency, 871 F.2d 1548 (11th Cir. 1989) (Alabama citizens lacked standing to challenge toxic waste cleanup plan in Texas that involved shipments of toxic waste to Alabama); Long Beach Sav. & Loan Ass'n v. Long Beach Redev. Agency, 188 Cal. App. 3d 249, 232 Cal. Rptr. 772 (1986) (decision to prepare a negative declaration rather than a supplemental environmental impact report supported by substantial evidence in the record as a whole).

218. 42 U.S.C. § 9601 *et seq.* (1988).

219. Alabama v. Envtl. Prot. Agency, 871 F.2d 1548, 1557 (11th Cir.), *cert. denied,* 493 U.S. 991 (1989).

220. *Id.* at 1559.

221. Marsh v. Oregon Natural Res. Council, 490 U.S. 360, 378 (1989).

222. *See, e.g.,* Long Beach Sav. & Loan Ass'n v. Long Beach Redev. Agency, 188 Cal. App. 3d 249, 232 Cal. Rptr. 772, 777, n. 10, 782 (1986) ("record as a whole" test applied to uphold decision to issue a negative declaration rather than a supplemental environmental impact review under California Environmental Quality Act).

223. Quince Orchard Valley Citizens Ass'n v. Hodel, 872 F.2d 75, 78 (4th Cir. 1989) (denial of preliminary injunction affirmed).

224. *See, e.g.,* Alabama v. Envtl. Prot. Agency, 871 F.2d 1548, 1554–56 (11th Cir. 1989) (constitutional due process claims of challengers to decision to permit toxic wastes to be shipped into Alabama from Texas dismissed because of failure to allege "personal injury fairly traceable to the defendant's allegedly unlawful conduct and likely to be redressed by the requested relief" (quoting Allen v. Wright, 468 U.S. 737, 751 (1984)), Shanty Town Assocs. P'ship v. Envtl. Prot. Agency, 843 F.2d 782, 788 (4th Cir. 1988) (interest in obtaining sewer service sufficient to confer standing on developer to contest restrictive conditions attached to grant of federal funds to municipality for construction of sewer collection system).

225. 16 U.S.C. § 1531 *et seq.* (1994).

226. Bennett v. Spear, 117 S. Ct. 1154, 1160–69 (1997).

227. 828 F.2d 228 (4th Cir. 1987).

228. Railroad Comm'n v. Pullman Co., 312 U.S. 496 (1941).

229. Burford v. Sun Oil Co., 319 U.S. 315 (1943).

230. Md. Nat. Res. Code Ann. § 8-1813(a)(2) (Michie 1990 & Supp. 1991).

231. Meredith v. Talbot County, 828 F.2d 228, 231 (4th Cir. 1987).

232. *Id.* at 232.

233. *Id.* at 232.

234. *See, e.g.,* Gwaltney of Smithfield v. Chesapeake Bay Found., Inc., 484 U.S. 49, 58 (1987) (comparing the Clean Water Act, 33 U.S.C. § 1365(a); Clean Air Act, 42 U.S.C. § 7604; Resource Conservation and Recovery Act of 1976, 42 U.S.C. § 6972; Toxic Substances Control Act, 15 U.S.C. § 2619 (prospective relief only), with 1984 amendments to Solid Waste Disposal Act, 42 U.S.C. § 6972(a)(1)(B) (1988) (citizen suits authorized against past or present violators)).

235. *See, e.g.,* 42 U.S.C. § 6972(b).

236. Gwaltney of Smithfield v. Chesapeake Bay Found., Inc., 484 U.S. 49, 60–62 (1987) (quoting legislative history, "'[t]he Committee intends the great volume of enforcement actions [to] be brought by the State,' and that citizen suits are proper only 'if the Federal, State, and local government agencies fail to exercise their enforcement responsibility.'" S. Rep. No. 414, 92d Cong., 1st Sess. 64 (1971), *reprinted in* 2 A Legislative History of the Water Pollution Control Act Amendments of 1972, at 1482 (1973)).

237. Gwaltney of Smithfield v. Chesapeake Bay Found., Inc., 484 U.S. 49, 56 (1987).

238. *See, e.g.,* American Lung Ass'n v. Kean, 871 F.2d 319, 325 (3d Cir. 1989).

239. Envtl. Prot. Agency v. City of Green Forest, 921 F.2d 1394, 1403 (8th Cir. 1990).

240. 16 U.S.C. § 1540(g) (1994).

241. Bennett v. Spear, 117 S. Ct. 1154, 1162–66 (1997).

242. *See* §§ 106 and 107 of CERCLA, 42 U.S.C. §§ 9606 & 9607 (1994).

243. *See* Idaho Conservation League, Inc. v. Russell, 946 F.2d 717 (9th Cir. 1991) (denying lawyers' fees to prevailing party where plaintiffs did not prevail against the Envtl. Prot. Agency, the party from whom they sought fees).

244. Exec. Order No. 12,898, 59 Fed. Reg. 7629 (1994).

245. *Id.* § 1-101.

246. Eileen Gauna, *Federal Environmental Citizen Provisions: Obstacles and Incentives on the Road to Environmental Justice,* 22 Ecology L.Q. 1, 9 (1995).

247. *Id.,* citing U.S. Gen. Accounting Office, GAO/RCED-83-168, Siting of Hazardous Waste Landfills and Their Correlation with Racial and Economic Status of Surrounding Communities 1 (1983). *See also* Paul Mohai, *The Demographics of Dumping Revisited: Examining the Impact of Alternate Methodologies in Environmental Justice Research,* 14 Va. Envtl. L.J. 615 (1995); Vickie Been, *Locally Undesirable Land Uses in Minority Neighborhoods: Disproportionate Siting or Market Dynamics?* 103 Yale L.J. 1383 (1994).

248. *Id.,* citing United Church of Christ Commission for Racial Justice, Toxic Wastes and Race in the United States (1987). *See also* Mohai, *supra* n. 226 at 616.

249. Thomas Lambert, et al., *A Critique of "Environmental Justice,"* NLCPI White Paper 6 (Jan. 1996).

250. Seth D. Jaffe, *Market Perspectives: The Market's Response to Environmental Inequity: We Have the Solution: What's the Problem?,* 14 Va. Envtl. L.J. 655, 658 (1995).

251. *Id.* at 658–59.

252. Charles P. Lord, *Community Initiatives: Environmental Justice Law and the Challenges Facing Urban Communities,* 14 Va. Envtl. L.J. 721, 727 (1995).

253. *Id.* at 728.

254. ARK. CODE ANN. § 806-1501 (Michie 1993).

255. KY. REV. STAT. ANN. § 224.46-830(2) (Baldwin 1992).

256. MINN. STAT. § 115A.21(1) (1993).

257. *See* Environmental Justice Act of 1992, H.R. 5326, 102d Cong., 2d Sess. (1992); Environmental Justice Act of 1992, H.R. 2105, 103d Cong., 1st Sess. (1993); Environmental Justice Act of 1993, S. 1161, 103d Cong., 1st Sess. (1993); Environmental Equal Rights Act of 1993, H.R. 1924, 103d Cong., 1st Sess. (1993).

258. Village of Arlington Heights v. Metropolitan Dev. Hous. Corp., 429 U.S. 252 (1977).

259. Adam D. Schwartz, *The Law of Environmental Justice: A Research Pathfinder*, 25 ENVTL. L. REP. 10543 (Oct. 1995).

260. *See* James H. Colopy, *The Road Less Traveled: Pursing Environmental Justice through Title VI of the Civil Rights Act of 1964*, 13 STANFORD ENVTL. L.J. 125 (1994); Donna Gareis-Smith, *Environmental Racism: The Failure of Equal Protection to Provide a Judicial Remedy and the Potential of Title VI of the 1964 Civil Rights Act*, 13 TEMP. ENVTL. L. & TECH. J. 57, 72–78 (1994).

261. Neil A. F. Popovic, *Pursing Environmental Justice with International Human Rights and State Constitutions*, 15 STANFORD. ENVTL. L.J. 338, 346 (1996).

262. NAACP v. Medical Center, Inc., 657 F.2d 1322, 1333 (3d Cir. 1981).

263. Silver v. Dinkins, 601 N.Y.S.2d 366 (N.Y. Sup. Ct. 1993), *aff'd*, 602 N.Y.S.2d 540 (N.Y. App. Div. 1993).

264. NEW YORK CITY CHARTER § 203(a) (1995).

265. El Pueblo Para el Aire y Agua Limpio v. County of Kings, 22 ELR 20357 (Cal. Super. Ct., Dec. 30, 1991).

266. See discussion at n. 213, *supra*. Gauna, *supra* n. 246, at 40–76.

267. 42 U.S.C. § 7604 (1988 & Supp. V 1993).

268. 33 U.S.C. § 1365 (1988).

269. 42 U.S.C. § 9659 (1988).

270. Gauna, *supra* n. 246, at 43–44.

271. Deeohn Ferris, *Community Initiatives: New Public Policy Tools in the Grassroots Movement: The Washington Office on Environmental Justice*, 14 VA. ENVTL. L.J. 711, 716 (1995).

272. *Id.* at 717.

273. For a further discussion of environmental justices concerns, *see* ENVIRONMENTAL JUSTICE (B. Bryant, ed., 1995) and Emily J. Vaias, *The Environmental Justice Movement: Discriminatory Intent on NIMBYism and LULUs at Work?*, AM. PLAN. ASS'N PLAN. & L., Summer 1994, at 3–4. *See generally* AMERICAN PLANNING ASSOCIATION, PLANNING AND COMMUNITY EQUITY (1994).

274. *See, e.g.*, G. Bingham, *Resolving Environmental Disputes: A Decade of Experience*, THE CONSERVATION FOUNDATION (1986); Watson & Danielson, *Environmental Mediation*, 15 NAT. RESOURCES LAW 687 (1982); Susskind & Weinstein, *Towards a Theory of Environmental Dispute Resolution*, 9 ENVTL. AFFS. 311 (1980).

275. Susskind & Weinstein, *Towards A Theory of Environmental Dispute Resolution*, 9 ENVTL. AFFS. 311, 314 (1980).

276. Bingham, *Resolving Environmental Disputes: A Decade of Experience*, THE CONSERVATION FOUNDATION 30 (1986).

277. *Id.* at 30–32.

278. Susskind & Weinstein, *Towards a Theory of Environmental Dispute Resolution*, 9 ENVTL. AFFS. 311, 314 (1980).

279. *Id.* at 314 (quoting a definition by Gerald W. Cormick, Director of the Office of Environmental Mediation, Institute for Environmental Studies, University of Washington

in O'Connor, *Environmental Mediation: The State-of-the-Art* 2 (EIA Rev. No. 2, Oct. 1978) (published by the Laboratory of Architecture and Planning, MIT)).

280. *See, e.g.,* Susskind & Weinstein, *Towards a Theory of Environmental Dispute Resolution,* 9 ENVTL. AFFS. 311, 314–21 (1980).

281. Watson & Danielson, *Environmental Mediation,* 15 NATL. RES. L. 687, 689 (1983).

282. *Id.* at 687, 689–90.

283. Susskind & Weinstein, *Towards a Theory of Environmental Dispute Resolution,* 9 ENVTL. AFFRS. 311, 323–36 (1980).

284. *Id.* at 336–46.

285. Amy, *The Politics of Environmental Mediation,* 11 ECOLOGY L.Q. 1, 19 (1983).

APPENDIX 10-A

Indiana Responsible
Property Transfer Law

13-7-22.5-15. Form of disclosure document.—A disclosure document delivered by a transferor of property under this chapter must follow this form:

A WARNING TO THE PARTIES TO A TRANSFER OF PROPERTY: It is highly unlikely that the single act of reading this document would be found to constitute "all appropriate inquiry into the previous ownership and uses of the property" so as to protect you against liability under the "innocent purchaser" provision of the federal Comprehensive Environmental Response, Compensation and Liability Act, 42 U.S.C. 9601(35)(B). You are strongly encouraged not only to read this document carefully but also to take all other actions necessary to the exercise of due diligence in your inquiry into the previous ownership and uses of the property.

ENVIRONMENTAL DISCLOSURE DOCUMENT
FOR TRANSFER OF REAL PROPERTY

The following information is
provided under IC 13-7-22.5,
the Responsible Property Transfer Law.

For Use By County
Recorder's Office
County

Date
Doc. No.
Vol.
Page
Rec'd by:

I. PROPERTY IDENTIFICATION
    A. Address of property: _____

                                               Street

_____
        City or Town   Township
    Tax Parcel Identification No. (Key Number): _____

B. Legal Description:
    Section _____ Township_____ Range _____
    Enter or attach complete legal description in this area:

LIABILITY DISCLOSURE

Transferors and transferees of real property are advised that their ownership or other control of such property may render them liable for environmental cleanup costs whether or not they caused or]contributed to the presence of environmental problems in association with the property.

C. Property Characteristics:
    Lot Size _____ Acreage _____

    Check all types of improvement and uses that pertain to the property:
    _____ Apartment building (6 units or less)
    _____ Commercial apartment (over 6 units)
    _____ Store, office, commercial building
    _____ Industrial building
    _____ Farm, with buildings
    _____ Other (specify)

II. NATURE OF TRANSFER

			Yes	No
A.	(1)	Is this a transfer by deed or other instrument of conveyance of fee title to property?	____	____
	(2)	Is this a transfer by assignment of over 25% of beneficial interest of a land trust?	____	____
	(3)	A lease exceeding a term of 40 years?	____	____
	(4)	A collateral assignment of beneficial interest?	____	____
	(5)	An installment contract for the sale of property?	____	____
	(6)	A mortgage or trust deed?	____	____
	(7)	A lease of any duration that includes an option to purchase?	____	____
B.	(1)	Identify Transferor:		

Name and Current Address of Transferor

                                                                        Trust No.

Name and Address of Trustee if this is a transfer of beneficial interest of a land trust

---

(2) Identify person who has completed this form on behalf of the Transferor and who has knowledge of the information contained in this form:

Name, Position (if any),   Telephone No.
and address

C.   Identify Transferee:

_____

Name and Current Address of Transferee

III. ENVIRONMENTAL INFORMATION
   A.   Regulatory Information During Current Ownership
        1. Has the transferor ever conducted operations on the property which involved the generation, manufacture, processing, transportation, treatment, storage, or handling of a "hazardous substance," as defined by IC 13-7-8.7-1? This question does not apply to consumer goods stored or handled by a retailer in the same form and approximate amount, concentration, and manner as they are sold to consumers, unless the retailer has engaged in any commercial mixing (other than paint mixing or tinting of consumer-sized containers), finishing, refinishing, servicing, or cleaning operations on the property.

                                                        Yes _____
                                                        No _____

        2. Has the transferor ever conducted operations on the property which involved the processing, storage, or handling of petroleum, other than that which was associated directly with the transferor's vehicle usage?

                                                        Yes _____
                                                        No _____

        3. Has the transferor ever conducted operations on the property which involved the generation, transportation, storage, treatment, or disposal of "hazardous waste," as defined in IC 13-7-1?

                                                        Yes _____
                                                        No _____

        4. Are there any of the following specific units (operating or closed) at the property that are used or were used by the transferor to manage hazardous wastes, hazardous substances, or petroleum?

	Yes	No
Landfill	____	____
Surface Impoundment	____	____
Land Application	____	____
Waste Pile	____	____
Incinerator	____	____
Storage Tank (Above Ground)	____	____
Storage Tank (Underground)	____	____
Container Storage Area	____	____
Injection Wells	____	____
Wastewater Treatment Units	____	____
Septic Tanks	____	____
Transfer Stations	____	____
Waste Recycling Operations	____	____
Waste Treatment Detoxification	____	____
Other Land Disposal Area	____	____

If there are "YES" answers to any of the above items and the transfer of property that requires the filing of this document is other than a mortgage or trust deed or a collateral assignment of beneficial interest in a land trust, you must attach to the copies of this document that you file with the county recorder and the department of environmental management a site plan that identifies the location of each unit.

5. Has the transferor ever held any of the following in regard to this real property?

    (A)   Permits for discharges of wastewater   Yes _____
           to waters of Indiana.   No _____

    (B)   Permits for emissions   Yes _____
           to the atmosphere.   No _____

    (C)   Permits for any waste storage, waste   Yes _____
           treatment, or waste disposal operation.   No _____

6. Has the transferor ever discharged any   Yes _____
wastewater (other than sewage) to a publicly   No _____
owned treatment works?

7. Has the transferor been required to take any of   Yes _____
the following actions relative to this property?   No _____

    (A)   Filed an emergency and hazardous chemical   Yes _____
           inventory form pursuant to the federal   No _____
           Emergency Planning and Community Right-
           to-Know Act of 1986 (42 U.S.C. 11022).

    (B)   Filed a toxic chemical release form   Yes _____
           pursuant to the federal Emergency   No _____
           Planning and Community Right-to-Know
           Act of 1986 (42 U.S.C. 11023).

8. Has the transferor or any facility on the   Yes _____
property or the property been the subject of any   No _____
of the following state or federal governmental
actions?

    (A)   Written notification regarding known,   Yes _____
           suspected, or alleged contamination on or   No _____
           emanating from the property.

    (B)   Filing an environmental enforcement case   Yes _____
           with a court or the solid waste   No _____
           management board for which a final
           order or consent decree was entered.

    (C)   If the answer to question (B) was then   Yes _____
           indicate whether or not the final order or   No _____
           decree is still in effect for this property.

9. Environmental Releases During Transferor's Ownership.

    (A)   Has any situation occurred at this site   Yes _____
           that resulted in a reportable "release" of   No _____
           any hazardous substances or petroleum
           as required under state or federal laws?

    (B)   Have any hazardous substances or   Yes _____
           petroleum that were released come into   No _____
           direct contact with the ground at this site?

If the answer to question (A) or (B) is Yes, have any of the following actions or events been associated with a release on the property?

_____ Use of a cleanup contractor to remove or treat materials including soils, pavement, or other surficial materials?

_____ Assignment of in-house maintenance staff to remove or treat materials including soils, pavement, or other surficial materials?

_____ Sampling and analysis of soils?

_____ Temporary or more long term monitoring of groundwater at or near the site?

_____ Impaired usage of an onsite or nearby water well because of offensive characteristics of the water?

_____ Coping with fumes from subsurface storm drains or inside basements?

_____ Signs of substances leaching out of the ground along the base of slopes or at other low points on or immediately adjacent to the site?

(C) Is there an environmental defect (as defined in IC 13-7-22.5-1.5) on the property that is not reported under question (A) or (B)?

Yes _____
No _____

If the answer is Yes, describe the environmental defect:

_____
_____
_____
_____

10. Is the facility currently operating under a variance granted by the commissioner of the Indiana department of environmental management?

Yes _____
No _____

11. Has the transferor ever conducted an activity on the site without obtaining a permit from the U.S. Environmental Protection Agency, the commissioner of the department of environmental management, or another administrative agency or authority with responsibility for the protection of the environment, when such a permit was required by law?

Yes _____
No _____

If the answer is Yes, describe the activity:

_____
_____
_____
_____

12. Is there any explanation needed for clarification of any of the above answers or responses?

_____
_____
_____
_____

B. Site Information Under Other Ownership or Operation
   1. Provide the following information about the previous owner or about any entity or person to whom the transferor leased the property or with whom the transferor contracted for the management of the property:
   Name: _____

   _____

   Type of Business
   or property usage _____

   _____

   2. If the transferor has knowledge, indicate whether the following existed under prior ownerships, leaseholds granted by the transferor, other contracts for management or use of the property:

	Yes	No
Landfill	_____	_____
Surface Impoundment	_____	_____
Land Application	_____	_____
Waste Pile	_____	_____
Incinerator	_____	_____
Storage Tank (Above Ground)	_____	_____
Storage Tank (Underground)	_____	_____
Container Storage Area	_____	_____
Injection Wells	_____	_____
Wastewater Treatment Units	_____	_____
Septic Tanks	_____	_____
Transfer Stations	_____	_____
Waste Recycling Operations	_____	_____
Waste Treatment Detoxification	_____	_____
Other Land Disposal Area	_____	_____

IV. CERTIFICATION
   A. Based on my inquiry of those persons directly responsible for gathering the information, I certify that the information submitted is, to the best of my knowledge and belief, true and accurate.

   _____
   TRANSFEROR (or on behalf of Transferor)
   B. This form was delivered to me with all elements completed on
   _____ 19 _____

   _____
   TRANSFEREE (or on behalf of Transferee)
[P.L.166-1989, §1; P.L.19-1990, §33.]

TABLE OF CASES

INDEX

Salsich, *Life After the Takings Trilogy—A Hierarchy of Property Interests?*, 19 Stetson L Rev 799–811 (1990). Reprinted by permission from Stetson Law Review.

Salsich, *Neighborhood Collaborative Planning*, Growing Smart Working Papers, Vol. 2, American Planning Association (November 1996)

Salsich & Eastman, *Supreme Court Decides in Favor of Group Homes*, Probate & Property, July/August 1995, p. 14. Reprinted by permission from the American Bar Association.

Schwab & Brower, *Sustainable Development: Implementation at the Local Level*, Land Use Law & Zoning Digest 3–7 (April 1997).

Spendlove ed, Morris, Johns, Maxfield, Cerruti, & Fowler, *Buying or Selling a Business: A Multi-Disciplinary Approach*, 3 Utah BJ No 5, at 8, 14 (May 1990). Reprinted by permission of the Utah Bar Journal.

Toll, S. *Zoned American*, 123–40 (1969). Reprinted by permission of Seymour I. Toll.

Tryniecki, *Cellular Tower Siting Jurisprudence Under the Telecommunications Act of 1996 – The First Five Years*, 37 Real Prop, Prob & Tr J 272 (Summer 2002). Reprinted by permission from the American Bar Association.

Sullivan & Kressel, *Twenty Years After—Renewed Significance of the Comprehensive Plan Requirement*, 9 Urb L Ann 33, 41 (1975).

Susskind & Weinstein, *Towards a Theory of Environmental Dispute Resolution*, 9 Envtl Aff L Rev 311–14, 336–46 (1980–81). Reprinted with permission of Boston College Environmental Affairs Law Review.

Watson & Danielson, *Environmental Mediation*, 15 Nat Resources Law 687, 689–90 (1983). American Bar Association of Natural Resources Law. Reprinted with permission.

Williams & Norman, *Exclusionary Land Use Controls: The Case of North-Eastern New Jersey*, 22 Syracuse L Rev 481, 484. Reprinted by permission from Syracuse Law Review.